National Information Infrastructure Initiatives

National Information Infrastructure Initiatives

Vision and Policy Design

edited by Brian Kahin and Ernest J. Wilson III

A Publication of the Harvard Information Infrastructure Project in Collaboration with the Global Information Infrastructure Commission

The MIT Press, Cambridge, Massachusetts, and London, England

RECEIVED

OCT 0 2 2012

This book was printed and bound in the United States of America.

Library of Congress Cataloging-in-Publication Data

National information infrastructure initiatives: vision and policy design /
edited by Brian Kahin and Ernest J. Wilson III.
    p.   cm.—(A Publication of the Information Infrastructure Project)
    Includes bibliographical references and index.
    ISBN 0-262-11219-1 (hc.: alk. paper).—ISBN 0-262-61125-2 (pb.: alk. paper)
    1. Information superhighway—Government policy—United States. 2. Information networks—Government policy—United States. 3. Telecommunications policy—United States. I. Kahin, Brian. II. Wilson, Ernest J., III. III. Series.
HE7572.U6N383   1996
004.6'74—dc20   96-19114
                                     CIP

Contents

Contents

Contents

Preface

Over the past two decades, national governments have recognized that fundamental changes were under way in telecommunications and computers. Commissions have been formed. Reports have been issued. Often, however, the focus and interest have dissipated. Sometimes reforms were initiated, but progress has been slow.

The acceleration of industry convergence and the information revolution in the 1990s has challenged governments anew. With different rationales and different strategies, countries have made greater efforts to address these changes in a concerted and coherent manner. Beginning with Singapore's vision of an "intelligent island" in 1992, and spurred the following year by U.S. Vice President Al Gore's vision of a "National Information Infrastructure," many countries launched initiatives that reflected their economy, political environment, and other national circumstances. These efforts reached critical mass in 1994, which inspired recognition of a Global Information Infrastructure and plans for a G-7 Conference on the Global Information Society in February 1995.

These recent initiatives are distinguished by two interrelated characteristics: an extraordinarily *broad scope* that can encompass not only telecommunications but also computers, content, and a myriad of applications that could transform much of our lives; and an unprecedented engagement with the private sector, which is expected to provide resources for and help design the advanced information infrastructure. The NII will be driven largely by consumer and business demands, and it is the private sector that is expected to respond to those demands. The broad scope means that policy makers confront a wider than expected variety of stakeholders and interests, many of which are blurred and convergent. This demands intense and continuing reassessment of competition policy and public-sector/private-sector relationships across a spectrum of policy domains.

These national initiatives have typically involved:

• *Formulating a vision.* This may include a shorthand concept, such as "information superhighway" or "information society," that gives the public an easy way to conjure and reference the changes.

• *Marshaling appropriate policies or policy frameworks.* This may mean recasting or redirecting existing policies to account for changes in technology. In a fully developed information infrastructure initiative, policies are addressed as an interrelated whole.

• *Strategies for implementation.* This means the specific programs or activities that advance or carry out the policies. These may encompass new regulatory frameworks, tax incentives, privatization, promotional rhetoric, procurement programs, and research funding. Strategies often require continued policy development because of the volatile nature of technologies and emerging markets, as well as the difficulty of foreseeing the impact on different sectors of the economy.

We see in this book a wide variety of approaches, some very directed and formal, some reactive and ad hoc. Following the scope of the most complete frameworks, we asked authors to look at communications, computing, and content in the country of their expertise and to help the reader understand how the national policy design and strategy are defined along these three historically distinct dimensions. While telecommunications liberalization in pursuit of the "information superhighway" is often the most visible item on the policy agenda, technology policy, public-sector and public-interest applications, and information law and policy also play important roles. The mix naturally depends on national circumstance and the vision of national leaders.

The experience of the last few years is only the beginning. The impact, social and political as well as economic, will be felt in fits and starts over a long period of time. The diffuse benefits and the sheer unpredictability make it difficult to sustain a single initiative in the name of information infrastructure or expectations of an "information society."

The form and degree of engagement between policy makers and the private sector differ from industry to industry, but converging industries necessarily find themselves concerned with the issues of their neighbors. While the greatest policy changes have been taking place in telecommunications, where the public-sector role has been most prominent, the greatest changes in technology and the market are driven by the computer industry. As boundaries blur, new territories and new businesses emerge in the interstices, typically with policy interests that need time to develop and find expression. Policy makers struggle to define fair competition and balance old principles in unmarked terrain, conscious that the landscape may shift—undoubtedly will shift—again tomorrow.

These difficulties are compounded by the growing internationalization of information infrastructure. The communications and content are especially complex because of the strongly held social values embodied in national policies. While telecommunications facilities are subject to controls by national governments as a matter of practice and practicality, content is less and less bound to physical place as the Internet and underlying infrastructure develop. A companion volume, *Borders in Cyberspace*, edited by Brian Kahin and Charles Nesson, demonstrates how national information policies are challenged by a globalized infrastructure in which individuals are increasingly empowered and active.

This volume, by contrast, focuses on efforts to define a broad but coherent set of national policies to advance the development of information infrastructure. The motivation for most initiatives has been innovation, economic growth, and competitive advantage. There is concern about diminished employment in telephone services, but information infrastructure is seen as generating a wealth of positive externalities and as an economic driver across all sectors of the economy.

The chapters that follow represent a first effort to analyze these initiatives with the distance that time brings. In general, the authors were not directly involved in the formulation of the initiatives or subsequent policy development; but they are experts who have watched closely. Their views are their own. The Global Information Infrastructure Commission and the Harvard Information Infrastructure Project are pleased to offer these independent perspectives as a contribution to dialogue and debate.

Brian Kahin and Ernest J. Wilson III

Acknowledgments

Information infrastructure has had a strong transnational, indeed global, dimension ever since sailing ships began to carry letter mail on the high seas. But in today's increasingly integrated global economy, nations rich and poor are looking to their own information infrastructures as a key part of their development strategies. In this effort private-sector firms play a leadership role, not only because the stakes are high for many of them, but because this dimension of infrastructure, unlike transportation, has emerged from private innovations built on public or private telecommunications services. In this process governments have nevertheless played important and sometimes critical roles, not less in the United States than in nations which have yet to privatize the telecommunications sector.

Thus it was particularly appropriate that this book, and the workshop in which many of the issues were discussed, received support and participation by a number of U.S.-based firms as well as from the Global Information Infrastructure Commission. The Commission, in which I am pleased to participate, comprises representatives of some 38 international enterprises around the world, along with other experts and authorities. Advanced Network and Services, EDS, Nynex and Motorola provided essential financial support as well as significant participation in this GII project. In addition, the support of AT&T, Bellcore, Hughes and IBM made it possible for the Information Infrastructure Project at Harvard's John F. Kennedy School of Government to host the project through its Center for Business and Government (CBG) and the Science, Technology and Public Policy Program of the Center for Science and International Affairs (CSIA).

We are particularly grateful to John White, director of the CBG at the time the project was initiated, who left for government service before the project was completed. His shoes have been amply filled by Professor Roger Porter, the current CBG director, who continues this collaboration.

A number of the contributions from other nations in this volume—notably Singapore, Korea, Japan and France—received support, at least in part, from the Center for Research on Information Technology and Organizations at the University of California at Irvine. Finally, we are especially appreciative of the contribution Tim Leshan made not only to the preparation of this volume but to the organization and conduct of the workshop that led to it.

As in any international project of this kind there are many other institutions and individuals who have provided support for the individual country efforts; they cannot all be thanked here, but their contributions are deeply appreciated none the less.

Thinking rationally about policy development and execution in a field as new, dynamic and important as information infrastructure can be a difficult enterprise. The participants in this project have collectively made, we believe, a significant step in this direction; their efforts are particularly appreciated.

Lewis Branscomb
Aetna Professor in Public Policy and Corporate Management, Emeritus

Introduction: The What, Why, Where, and How of National Information Initiatives

Ernest J. Wilson III

The comparative study of public policy design and implementation has a long and honorable tradition within the social sciences. While one can trace the modern lineage of comparative policy analysis back to Max Weber, more recent authors include Dye (1972), Rose (1973) and Lindberg (1977). The topics they study span the gamut from social policy to defense, energy and the environment, health care and science policy. As we approach the study of how different countries design and implement their national information infrastructures, we can draw on an established tradition of social science scholarship.

In the development of any body of knowledge, there are always shifting emphases and changing foci. A close reading of policy studies reveals a kind of "product cycle" within each of the substantive policy areas, especially for the newer, more technologically driven subjects like energy, the environment and, more recently, information and communications policies. There appear to be at least four phases to the product cycle.[1] Each new wave centrally informs the public debate, before a new set of issues comes to the fore in the next phase. They differ by their arguments, their audience and their principal authors.

In phase one, the technical phase, a once quiescent technical issue handled in the middle ranks of public bureaucracies is propelled into public view and onto the action agenda of senior policymakers. For example, the 1973 energy crisis and environmental shocks like Love Canal or Three Mile Island politicized technical issues and precipitated greater policy attention to these issues (Wilson 1987).

Typically, the works that dominate this phase are authored by engineers, scientists or economists whose purpose most often is to explain the most advanced, cutting-edge features of the new technological issue to other like-minded experts. The policy problem is defined in technical terms, needing a technical solution. Some argue that more and better technology assessment is central to enhancing the efficiencies of government policies and private investment strategies. Autio and Hameri (1995) concentrate on the dynamics and the structure of technological systems in general. In the burgeoning literature on the information revolution, even a casual reading reveals this technical trend. A powerful technical orientation is not entirely surprising given the central role of technological change in the information revolution, including new technologies for digitalization, compression and growing computer power.

In the second phase, social theorists take up the issue. This new group of analysts has slightly different purposes and audiences. Social theorists and journalists grab the idea of the technology and find within in it answers to a whole raft of societal problems. Their purposes are more ambitious than phase-one writers, and they seek a broader audience of non-specialists. Their writings are often utopian, apocalyptic, hyperbolic, asserting that technique X will advance democracy, improve the quality of life, guarantee the survivability of the planet, transform international relations (Lovins 1981). The primary focus of their curiosity is how the new technology will reshape society (Toffler 1990). Information guru George Gilder proclaims that the new information technologies "will blow apart all the monopolies, hierarchies, pyramids, and power grids of established industrial society."[2]

In phase three, other non-technological dimensions are brought into the picture by a wider group of social scientists. One finds more careful attention to institutional, political and distributional issues. Analysts recognize that diffusion rates for the new technology will be shaped by existing institutional incentives (OTA 1995, pp. 43–44). They see that technical changes create losers as well as winners, and begin to analyze the potentially dark side for poor people or poor countries. The title of Burstein and Kline's new work captures this two-sided perspective: *Road Warriors: Dreams and Nightmares Along the Information Highway* (1995). The information haves and have-nots are put on the agenda nationally and internationally (Curtis 1988 and Lanvin 1995). Also, alternative or complementary strategies become visible for different firms in the same industry (e.g., Bell Atlantic vs. AMERITECH, or the Apple strategy vs. the IBM strategy). As the scope of analysis widens, observers recognize that different countries, like different firms, can approach the same policy issues in very different ways.

In phase four, the discussion is opened still further and more university-based scholars take up the issue, as much to test traditional concepts and hypotheses from their respective disciplines, as to explicate the intricacies of the topic at hand. This represents the normalization of social science analysis. These successive waves do not replace one another, but over time add to the richness of the available literature. The process is additive. Still, a distinctive gap remains between the technical approach of phase one and the social science approach of phase four, a topic to which I return below.

The comparative study of the information revolution is now sliding from the second into the third phase. My reading of the literature in economics, political science, sociology and business suggests that most of the work today is still rather focused on technical issues, such as standards for interconnection, touting the technical advantage of the Internet or describing the growth of wireless technologies (OTA 1995). Only recently are analysts bringing distributional and institutional elements to the fore. With few exceptions (Evans 1995) we have yet to see the wave of scholarly social science studies that invariably follows the work of industry, think tank or government analysts.

Given this perspective, I wish to advance the debate modestly and perhaps sharpen the discussion by posing a series of research and conceptual questions that draw lessons from the differing experiences of national and global information infrastructure initiatives. This chapter is meant to be useful to academic, business and other analysts anxious to enhance public and private sector performance. While we concentrate on the debate within the United

States, there are parallel concerns in other countries. Kumon suggests, for example, that the debates over technology in Japan are also just beginning to move across professional boundaries and to engage non-technical concerns (Kumon 1995).

What Are We Comparing?

Let us agree for the moment that we are comparing and trying to explain the emergence of something frequently cited and variously defined—a national information infrastructure (NII). This is an inchoate, multidimensional phenomenon, a turbulent and controversial mix of public policy, corporate strategies, hardware and software that shapes the way consumers and citizens use information and communications. The U.S. government General Accounting Office defines it as "A popular term for the emerging global broadband digital meta-network" (GAO 1995, p. 72). For Drake, from a strictly network perspective, the NII is "an extremely heterogeneous collection of local and regional information infrastructures and long-haul networks ... [whose] component parts will be developed at different rates and organized in different ways" (Drake 1995a, p. 4). Finding this definition insufficient, he reformulates it to "the computerized networks, intelligent terminals, and accompanying applications and services people use to access, create, disseminate, and utilize *digital* information" (Drake 1995a, p. 5, emphasis added). Most observers would agree that a sensible definition of an NII would include some combination of the following elements.

Technical Systems

Technical systems are at the heart of the NII, which can be described in highly technical terms, and usually is (Solomon 1995). The Internet, landlines, satellites or telecommunications systems linking local, national and international users are often the principal subjects of cross-border comparisons. Here one concentrates on the design, distribution and uses of the hardware and the software systems that comprise the national "networks of networks" (OECD 1995). Looking comparatively, are there significant cross-national differences in the architecture and interconnection of the various constituent technical subsystems? For example, technical systems can be more or less open, more or less integrated, and each country has different penetration rates for different technologies, often using different standards. An alternative technical formulation is to define different levels or layers of information systems—from transport, to local networks, to applications and management (GAO 1995, p. 12). A big split in the literature occurs between those who emphasize telecommunications as the core of the NII's technical system, and those who give pride of place to the Internet and other digitized, multimedia technologies (Kahin 1994).

Sectors

Others start their analyses of the NII with the structure and dynamics of economic sectors of the economy (Willenius & Stern 1994). Market structure and industrial organization are central to this approach. Peter Cowhey and others argue that the key to understanding the differences between the NII in the United States and the NIIs in Europe, for example, is their different market structures. Uniquely among its competitors, the U.S. market for the supply of information technology (IT) goods and services is characterized by a very wide range in the size of firms and variability of market niches. The NII in the United States has firms across virtually every information market, from small start-ups in everything from software to long distance services, to medium-sized companies, as well as huge Fortune 100 corporations. By contrast, European supplier markets possess telecommunications and large firms (many state-owned), but lack the wealth of small, newer firms that add depth, innovation, commercial diversity and distinctive political dynamics to the U.S. political economy (Cowhey 1990,1995). Europe's more protectionist, top-down approach to the NII reflects these differing market realities. Therefore, to compare NIIs through a sectoral approach, one begins with the structure of domestic markets (and, for political economists, the interest groups and backers that form around those distinct markets and firms). One examines cross-nationally the relative size of the sectors, changing market shares, and degrees of vertical and horizontal integration of each of the relevant industries that together constitute the information/communications sector (computers, software, systems integration, telecommunications, etc.). This sectoral approach to the NII quickly leads one to consider the critical, if very difficult, issue of convergence. Convergence is the merging of distinct IT industries and the creation of new ones made possible by digitalization (Institute for Information Studies 1994). Arguably, convergence is the single most critical dynamic shaping the NII and the Global Information Infrastructure (GII) today, driven by the interaction of new technologies, fluid corporate restructuring and emerging and intersecting markets. The resultant new "digitized" industrial structure has enormous implications for corporate strategies, and for the design and implementation of regulatory policy. This is an essential area requiring much more national and comparative work.

Government Policy

Governments play a huge role in the construction and management of NIIs. At a minimum, the comparative study of NIIs must study the actions of governments (Rose 1973). There are at least two subsets of relevant government policy actions one could compare and contrast:

1. *Generic policy issues:* How does the information/telecommunications sector handle the most basic policy issues that confront all governments and all sectors? These include determining the relative balance between monopoly and competition; between public and private control; and between foreign and domestic ownership. These policy questions, which are addressed by comparativists like Peter Hall and Andrew Shonfield (1969) are major issues in all sectors, including IT.

2. *Industry-specific policy issues:* Each industry, from health care to transportation, is characterized by specific issues particular to it. For the IT industry, these include intellectual property rights, interconnectivity, universal service, open markets and others (OTA 1995). Traditional IT issues are also reshaped and redefined by new issues such as the growing trade in information services (Aronson and Cowhey 1988). Perhaps the greatest crosscutting challenge in

analyzing the GII, which practitioners and policy analysts recognize, is to understand the dramatic reduction in government's direct ownership and control of the IT industry, and today's more liberalized environment in which the authority of the private sector has dramatically grown.

Institutional Structures

Another way to define the NII is as a set of interlocking institutions that together guide or constrain the behavior of consumers, suppliers, public officials and citizens. Much of the work in the comparative policy field concentrates on the organizations and institutions responsible for designing and implementing particular policies (March and Olsen 1989). Mintzberg (1983), for example, insists on the importance of both the internal structures and the immediate organizational environment of large policy organizations. Hahm and Plein (1995) analyze the role of the institution of the presidency in technological development in Korea. Saumon and Puiseux (1977) use organigrams and flowcharts to capture the essence of French energy policy from an institutional perspective.

In his work on national energy policies, Lindberg compares several national cases and points to the great difficulty that governments have experienced in coordinating the contradictory roles thrust upon them in the course of the evolution of the energy problem (Lindberg 1977, p. 335). National policymaking, in his view, is characterized by "fragmented and incoherent policy making" within the government, and contention with competing groups and a powerful "industrial technocracy" beyond it. Institutional analyses are starting to appear in the NII literature as well. Geller echoes Lindberg's findings in his "Reforming the U.S. Telecommunications Policymaking Process," where he characterizes the U.S. system as continuing the "defects of a generation ago—the antiquated law, the fragmented policy process, the absence of FCC commissioners with deep experience in telecommunications," but the costs of fragmentation are much greater than ever before in the face of convergence and globalization (Geller 1995, p. 116).

A recent comparative volume on telecommunications in transition compares a range of institutional issues including the role of the Organization for Economic Cooperation and Development

(OECD), the General Agreement on Trade and Tariffs (GATT) and legal initiatives of the European Union (EU) (Steinfield, Bauer and Caby 1994). The strong version of this argument is that the NII is not just a technical system, but is best understood as an interlocking system of institutions whose rules and incentives shape the technical, commercial and civic actions of information consumers and producers. This "institutions first" position can be counterpoised to the "technology first" position described above.

Sub-national Groups and Individuals

The intentions, interests and behaviors of self-interested groups and individuals in markets and political settings are important determinants of policy outcomes and also may be the focus of comparative NII studies (Dye 1972). Self-interested maneuvering can occur in every kind of national and international policy arena, as groups and individuals jockey for position and relative advantage. The press has documented the extraordinary multiparty lobbying and almost unprecedented expenditure of money that swirled around the passage of the 1996 telecommunications legislation in the United States.

In the information arena, Dowmunt and his collaborators pinpoint grassroots efforts by local community groups to create their own video records and gain access to national and urban communication systems (Dowmunt 1993). Ronfeldt's path-breaking work combining information revolution trends with sophisticated political and institutional analysis of non-governmental organizations (NGOs) is also noteworthy (Ronfeldt 1993). Drake concentrates on more conventional lobbying by NGOs to influence national telecommunications policies (Drake 1995b).

Culture, Communications and Media

There is a distinct intellectual tradition of research and writing that defines communications and information issues more from the perspective of content, freedom of expression and culture. With a very different research agenda derived from broadcasting and media concerns, publications like the *Journal of Communication,*

Critical Studies in Mass Communication, European Journal of Communication and others take up these content-related policies. These concerns are sometimes expressed in the U.S. debate over the NII, but arguably have played second fiddle in the press and policy discussions to the more economic and telecommunications-related themes of pricing, regulatory reforms, competition and other market- and technology-oriented issues. While these two streams of analysis have tended to be quite separate, with digitalization and growing technological convergence we will see more and more "boundary conflicts" between them. "Government media policies can no longer be exclusively guided by cultural values, and telecommunications should also pursue objectives outside the technological and economic field" (Cuilenburg and Slaa 1993). Future definitions of national information infrastructures in the United States and the United Kingdom will almost certainly encompass more concerns about content, audience and culture. Already, intellectual property rights, v-chips and French cultural requirements intersect both domains and are among the most politically charged controversies in the field.

Smart analysts recognize that all these elements are important and should be carefully weighed and balanced in any serious study of the NII. However, in their definitions of national information infrastructures, most authors stress one factor over the others. The challenge is to appreciate what is gained and lost in employing or rejecting different elements of a definition.

An unavoidable question naturally arises: shouldn't one be highly skeptical of a strictly *national* approach to explaining information and communications developments, given today's global markets and cross-border transactions? Since technology, globalization of production and international competition have rendered national borders superfluous, then the study of information infrastructures should be strictly global and not narrowly national.

The current debate over the global information infrastructure, and the references at meetings of the Group of Seven leading industrialized countries (G-7) and other international gatherings to the information haves and have-nots, occurs against the background of an already established body of work. Much of it concentrates on the interactions among nations within the international community, especially on the information disadvantages of poor countries and the relative advantages of the rich (Frederick 1993). Gonzalez-Manet (1992), a Cuban writer, takes a left cut on international information equity, reminiscent of the debates over the "New International Information Order" in the 1970s. Hamelink's (1994) work gives a detailed historical review of the evolution of institutions, arguments and policy decisions in the field of international information and communications relations between the North and South.

However transnational the issues may be, national politicians and policymakers first calculate their consequences at the national level. The issue of winners and losers for governments and their political leaders will be calculated mainly at the national level. Most telecommunications firms serve national markets. Regulatory structures are put in place mainly to structure domestic markets, not foreign ones, for the benefit of local suppliers and consumers.

The most interesting and important questions for business today are institutional and political, posed and answered at the national level. This argument does not deny the importance of global factors; rather, it insists that an essential starting point for understanding even the global information infrastructure is the national political economy. This approach recognizes that important telecommunications rules and regulations will be written in international and regional fora like the International Telecommunications Union (ITU), the World Trade Organization (WTO) and the European Union (EU), but insists that the outcomes will express preferences negotiated by national governments.

Why Are National Information Infrastructures Different?

Whether comparing technical systems, market structures or group behaviors, we want to account for cross-system similarities and differences among them. Why do some NIIs quickly incorporate the newest information technologies (e.g., Finland has one of the highest rates of cellular phone penetration in the world), while others lag behind? Why are some countries innovators in telemedicine, but not in distance education? Why has post, telephone and telegraph (PTT) privatization proceeded further in Chile than in Brazil? Taking NII structure and performance as the dependent variable to be explained, what independent variables have caused these differences to appear in different countries? Here the challenge is twofold—to identify those cross-national differences, and then to speculate about their origins.

The comparativist can generate any number of hypotheses to explain variation among NIIs. For example, can we explain Finland's high cellular phone penetration rate in terms of enlightened government regulatory policy or the structure of the domestic supplier industry where Nokia, the world class competitor, is based? Why do two countries at the same level of development have very different NIIs? Dependent variables could include varying degrees of political centralization vs. decentralization; differences in gross domestic product per capita; corporatist vs. non-corporatist forms of interest mediation; market structure; or differing national research and development strategies.

Why Are We Comparing?

Martin Staniland (1985) and others identify at least two purposes of analysis and explanation. On the one hand, scholars are mainly interested in explaining the complexity and depth of a topic (George 1993). Their purpose is general understanding for its own sake. Sophisticated scholars seek to test hypotheses derived from general models against the facts of the case at hand. They seek alternative explanations to account for the same facts, and their conclusions are often indeterminate.

On the other hand, corporate strategists and policy analysts are action-oriented. They seek guides to better action, not just better understanding. They seek information that allows them to shape public policy or corporate strategy in order to advance the purposes of their home unit—to expand market share, increase earnings, shape citizen behavior, etc. Knowledge is instrumental. These differences are as evident in the field of information and communication as in others.[3]

For example, one can contrast Stephen Krasner's abstract, scholarly and model-driven treatment of the International Telecommunications Union and other telecommunications organizations with the more applied evaluations of Rutkowski, the ITU and the World Bank (Krasner 1991, Rutkowski 1995, Tyler 1993, World Bank 1995). National-level studies can be extremely useful for State Department desk officers, Commerce Department officials at overseas posts or newly appointed country representatives from IT companies.

How Are We Comparing?

Each discipline has its own way of describing the world. It makes a huge difference to dispassionate understanding and to partisan action if the analyst begins with the underlying assumptions of methodological individualism of neoclassical economics, or instead with the group-oriented pluralist political analysis of Robert Dahl (1961). Does the paradigm assume perfect information and a rational selection of goals and strategies by self-interested individuals? Does it assume a neutral, nonpartisan state? Or does the paradigm begin with the standard operating procedures, entrenched institutional interests and muddling through, or "satisficing" behavior of organizational analyses? (Allison 1971). No single approach is ideal; they all have their blind spots in understanding topics like the information revolution and comparing their incidence cross-nationally. These differences can translate into public policy (Keyfitz 1995).

Regrettably, at this moment in the study of the information revolution we lack even minimal agreement on what constitutes an inclusive, high-quality NII study. There is little discussion of the methodological issues I identify here—what, why and how. In essence, the debate is not yet fully engaged either within disciplines or across them.

What Is Actually Available To Compare?

It would be ideal if we had rich empirical descriptions and detailed materials on the NIIs of all countries, but we do not. There appear to be very few country studies which integrate the many elements of NIIs into a single work. More common are national or regional studies that review a single element of the NII, such as broadcasting, the print media or telephony.[4]

Instead, one is obliged to work with incomplete information. Data-based studies by international agencies like the superb tables of the ITU, and the commercial equivalents by companies like DataQuest, provide discrete facts—telephones per capita, spending on computer R&D, etc.—but these are rarely integrated into a whole picture of a country's NII.

Another source for further comparative work comprises the official studies and reports by national governments, reports by international organizations and analyses by independent scholars and researchers.

More and more governments are preparing their own national reports describing and characterizing their own information/communications situation. The two principal U.S. government documents are *US NII: An Agenda for Action* (1994) and *GII: Agenda for Cooperation* (1995). National studies also exist for Denmark, Canada, France, Singapore and Japan (OECD 1995).

International organizations have also been quite active. One well known for its cross-national policy work is the OECD. In a document dated June 13–14, 1995, the OECD reports on current or proposed actions for the NIIs of 12 leading member states and tries to identify similarities and differences among them (OECD 1995).

The OECD document is organized around a set of initial definitions and the identification of common economic, social and cultural objectives of national IT policies. It finds that, despite some differences in the definitions, underlying terms such as "information infrastructure," "information highway," and "information society" present

a concept based broadly on broadband communication technologies which, through the process of digitalization of communication infrastructures, the convergence of these technologies with broadcasting technologies, and recent developments allow rapid transmission of large quantities of information at low cost. Broadband can carry integrated data, video, text and voice traffic. (OECD 1995, p. 5).

The national reports typically go beyond pure technology to discuss "the potential impact these technological innovations have on modern society and the potential economic and social benefits [they] provide. In this sense the term information infrastructures refers to the ability of new technologies to transform the way we work, play, learn and live." Indeed, the report emphasizes the continuing diversification and sophistication of the demand side of the equation. It points out that "Existing social and economic structures at the macro, meso and micro levels are gradually changing" (OECD 1995, p. 5).

The OECD report is a consensus document of shared or leading themes among 12 countries, discussing ten key issues found in most national reports on the subject. It highlights areas of agreement or disagreement on each issue. Although it is a useful compendium of national initiatives and intentions, methodological concerns are not much evident here; there is little effort to pick and choose and establish mutually agreed upon approaches to constructing national baselines for comparison. The report does find common understandings about the meaning of IT (broadly defined to include digitalization, convergence, etc.); however, it does not suggest causal relations among the factors. At best, it is a kind of policy catalogue; it is not a research agenda or strategy.[5]

Other international organizations are also involved in the effort to collect and evaluate new information and communications data. The World Bank is shifting toward an innovative framework for analyzing NIIs through "knowledge assessments" and "national information strategy systems." These tend to be more methodologically explicit and well developed than those of the OECD, reflecting perhaps the applied and programmatic purposes of the Bank (Talero and Gaudette 1995). While there are general analytic Bank reports on IT use in Asia or Latin America, there are not yet many publicly available country studies of the sector. One hopes that the Bank's new INFODEV project will produce country studies that will be available to researchers beyond the organization.

Independent scholars and analysts have also done solid comparative work, as is evident in *Telecommunications Policy* and other sector journals. Drake (1995a) is another example. These works address methodological and substantive issues, tend to be more critical of government actions and more clearly identify winners and losers than do official reports. Still, phase four has not yet arrived—it is telling that there are very few studies of international telecommunications and information in the leading policy and political science journals. With the exception of Cowhey (1990), Evans

(1995), and Krasner (1991), few leading scholars have done serious academic work on the subject. By far, most of the work is in more applied professional journals like *Telecommunications Policy*.

So What?

The devastating "so what?" question is as important as the others which have proceeded it. Why should anyone care about comparative political economy analyses of national approaches to the information revolution?

The analytic approach I suggest here responds to both scholarly and practical concerns. A private sector group, the Global Information Infrastructure Commission, asked its 30 commissioners, all of whom are CEOs or very senior officers in the private sector and in governments, to identify the most critical issues that directly concerned them and their company. Invariably they identified institutional and political impediments to building the GII as their primary concern. The CEOs are seeking ways to advance political and strategic agreement among themselves and between their firms and governments on key matters like setting standards, market access, and pro-investment regulations and laws. Their concerns are not to find the one best technology or the single most efficient computer software package. There is no denying that these technology and product development challenges are very important to companies; if they do not continually improve their products in today's extremely competitive markets, then they will be out of business. Still, analysts can only describe and seek to manage operations in this dynamic environment if they possess a sure-footed understanding of key public and private actors and their strategic interests, as well as the changing rules of the game, other actors' preferred outcomes, and who is likely to win and lose from various resolutions of the critical issues. In other words, the CEOs are concerned about issues of political economy.

For private corporate actors, therefore, the response to the "so what?" question about the value of national case studies must be nuanced since the opportunity cost of studying any one issue over another is greater than in the university. Corporate analysts will compare and contrast NIIs when doing so is relevant for core business activities like sales, investment, market openings, competition, sourcing and government relations. For them, national studies may be especially useful in newly emerging markets (e.g., Vietnam, South Africa) where national information is more scarce. The work of consulting firms like the British company, Analysys, are especially important in this respect.

Government officials also need case studies. While no two countries will ever have identical NIIs or identical policies, lessons can be learned on such issues as how to sequence communications reform decisions, or the possible benefits and costs of alternative institutional and regulatory arrangements (such as separating posts from telecommunications or using price caps). At a minimum, decision makers, especially relatively inexperienced ones in developing countries, can be made aware of the particularly crosscutting nature of information issues (Wilson 1995).

For scholars, the answer to "so what?" is more straightforward: like mountain climbers, they reply, "Because it is there." The payoff for traditional scholars comes in contributing to theory building. Still, the issues raised by the information revolution are important from the perspective of many academic disciplines, from economics to international relations, to the sociology of work and industrial relations. And, as indicated, there is a long tradition of university and think tank-based interest in the study of policy domains.

Let us take one example of a major substantive issue usefully addressed through comparative national studies, with benefits for both scholars and practitioners. The search for "best practices" is now a growth industry from China to Chile. Companies and government agencies are feverishly seeking information on new successes in areas ranging from technical applications to regulatory reforms to technology diffusion. They want to find what works. They seek successes in one country to apply in their own. This is a useful exercise. However, there is a real danger that companies or governments will use "quick and dirty" superficial comparisons to latch onto an initiative or technology that appears to work in one national setting, and automatically apply it to another setting, hoping it will work there too. By concentrating on the application or government action isolated from its unique local context, the analyst misses the institutional, technological, political and even cultural features of the environment that made possible the initiative's success. Also, further analysis may reveal that an apparent success in one delimited domain may generate substantial and unacceptable costs in another. These nuances and insights can be captured through comparative national studies.

What Should We Do Now?

At this stage of our analysis of national information infrastructures, the greatest benefit for intellectual and applied purposes will come from posing tough institutional, political and distributional questions about national information systems in a variety of countries, rather than reproducing specialized technical studies for narrow audiences. In terms of my opening argument, we need to turn to phase-three issues.

An excellent example of an effective political economy approach to phase-three issues is the Office of Technology Assessment's 1990 report, *Critical Connections* (OTA,1990). That study linked the existing communications regime, interactions between technology and society, the opportunities and constraints the new technologies created, the response of "key stakeholders and decision making processes" and the outcomes of those decisions about new technologies (OTA 1990, pp. 34–35). The OTA defined information and communications in terms that could also define the core of the NII:

a) norms, values, goals and roles that sustain and maintain communication within a given realm;

b) communication infrastructure that supports and facilitates communication processes; and

c) decision making processes and the rules and regulations that govern how the communication regime is managed and regulated. (OTA 1990, p. 35).

(Appliances and consumers can be added to this formulation to make it more complete.)

To compare NIIs more successfully, we need more and better information. Ironically, there is a dearth of good national information on the information revolution. Ideally, we need all kinds of information and data simultaneously and quickly. But in the real world of constrained resources and opportunity costs, some things are more important than others. I believe the following should be the comparativist's top priorities.

• *Case studies* of NIIs in a variety of countries, large and small, developed and underdeveloped. Where possible, case studies should consistently compare two or more comparable units—countries, policies, markets and so forth. At a minimum, we badly need rigorous single cases. These cases should go beyond telecommunications to include descriptions of what Talero calls "strategic information systems" that encompass not just technology, but "people, work processes, incentives, data, transactions, constraints and outcomes. Therefore variables such as policies, institutions, business processes, organizational arrangements, existing rents, power structures and even social organization are indispensable aspects of successful [strategic information] systems development" (Talero 1994, p. 19).

• *Hypotheses* that are explicit and used to guide empirical research, and that can help answer critical questions.

• A *political economy* approach that concentrates on institutional players seeking to redefine dominant rules and norms as the information and communications revolution unfolds; an approach that identifies patterns of winners and losers that emerge domestically and internationally (Mansell 1993, Mosco and Wasko 1988). Analysts need to concentrate on the rules of the game as they are contested in national and international fora as digitalization, convergence, and falling costs undercut old commercial and social patterns and create new ones.

• Substantively, identify and analyze the central dynamic of the *expanding authority and power of the private sector* in IT.

There are, of course, other issues that can usefully be analyzed to help move the study of this important transformation toward phase four, toward a more "normal science" approach to information and telecommunications policies and national information infrastructures. But these four constitute a good start.

Notes

1. There are a variety of ways to think about different phases or shifting emphases. Emmanuel Mesthene (1986), head of a Harvard technology project in the 1960s, identified three schools dealing with the introduction of new technologies, which might be summarized as: technology is really good; technology is really bad; technology is no big deal. A related theme is how some issues get defined as problems or opportunities, and are then placed on the policy agenda. Rochefort and Cobb (1994) recently identified six factors that shape whether and how an issue like information and communications gets on the public agenda, including the issue's severity, incidence, novelty and proximity. The tremendous growth of attention to the information revolution, with cover stories in news magazines and as the subject of best-selling books, suggests this is happening. Rochefort and Cobb remind us that problem definition is not always neutral; it is "at once to explain, to describe, to recommend, and above all, to persuade" (1994).

2. The Gilder quotation continues: "It will undermine all totalitarian regimes. Police states cannot endure under the advance of the computer because it increases the power of the people far faster than the powers of surveillance. All hierarchies will tend to become 'heterarchies'—systems in which each individual rules his own domain. In contrast to a hierarchy ruled from the top, a heterarchy is a society of equals under the law." (Drake 1995a, p. 10).

3. Examples of national and regional studies include Michalis' (1994) piece on Greece, the *Journal of Communication*'s 1994 back-to-back five-article collections on media in China (Vol. 44, No. 3) and on Latin American media (Vol. 44, No. 4). While most of the work is on NII policy in the developed world, one can cite the national study of Kenya by Akwule (1995) and the regional focus of Bourgault (1995). The Third World as a whole is analyzed in the Lerner and Schramm classic of 1966, and Geoffrey Reeves' more recent *Communications and the 'Third World'* (1993). But systematic comparisons of two or more NIIs or institutions are rare in the literature.

4. Corporate research and development in information and telecommunications are the subject of consultant reports, organizational studies and conferences. IIR Ltd. in conjunction with several information and telecommunications companies sponsored the First Annual Symposium on Research and Development in Telecommunications, in which topics relevant to national information infrastructures included EU policies for supporting research, "Examining the Development of Emerging Markets as a Source of R&D Excellence," and "Making Effective Use of the Opportunities for Collaborative Research with Academic Institutions."

5. Somewhat more helpful was the OECD workshop on "The Economics of the Information Society," Toronto, June 28–29, 1995. The latest OECD document, a synthesis report, advances the debate even further (OECD 1995).

References

Akwule, Raymond. "Telecommunications in Kenya: Development and Political Issues," *Telecommunications Policy* (September–October 1992), pp. 603–611.

Allison, Graham T. *Essence of Decision: Explaining the Cuban Missile Crisis.* New York: Harper Collins, 1971.

Aronson, Jonathan David and Peter Cowhey. *When Countries Talk: International Trade in Telecommunications Services.* Cambridge, MA: Ballinger, 1988.

Autio, Erkko and Ari-Pekka Hameri, "The Structure and Dynamics of Technological Systems: A Conceptual Model," *Technology in Society* Vol. 17, No. 4 (1995), pp. 365–384.

Bourgault, Louise M. *Mass Media in Sub-Saharan Africa.* Bloomington, Indiana: University of Indiana Press, 1995.

Burstein, Daniel and David Kline. *Road Warriors: Dreams and Nightmares Along the Information Highway.* New York: Dutton, 1995.

Cowhey, Peter F. "Building the Global Information Highway: Toll Booths, Construction Contracts, and Rules of the Road," in William J. Drake, ed. *The New Information Infrastructure: Strategies for U.S. Policy,* New York: Twentieth Century Fund Press, 1995, pp. 175–204.

Cowhey, Peter F. "The International Telecommunications Regime: The Political Roots of Regimes for High Technology," *International Organization* Vol. 44, No. 2, (Spring 1990), pp. 169–200.

Cuilenburg, Jan van and Paul Slaa. "From Media Policy Towards a National Communications Policy: Broadening the Scope," *European Journal of Communication,* Vol. 8, (1993), pp. 149–176.

Curtis, Terry. "The Information Society: A Computer-Generated Caste System?" in Vincent Mosco and Janet Wasko, eds. *The Political Economy of Information.* Madison, Wisconsin: University of Wisconsin Press, 1988, pp. 95–107.

Dahl, Robert A. *Who Governs? Democracy and Power in an American City.* New Haven, CT: Yale University Press, 1961.

Dowmunt, Tony, ed. *Channels of Resistance: Global Television and Local Empowerment.* London: British Film Institute, 1993.

Drake, William J., ed. *The New Information Infrastructure: Strategies for U.S. Policy.* New York: Twentieth Century Press, 1995a.

Drake, William J. "The National Information Infrastructure Debate: Issues, Interests, and the Congressional Process," in William J. Drake, ed. *The New Information Infrastructure: Strategies for U.S. Policy.* New York: Twentieth Century Press, 1995b, pp. 305–344.

Dye, Thomas. *Understanding Public Policy.* Englewood Cliffs, NJ: Prentice-Hall, 1972.

Evans, Peter B. *Embedded Autonomy: States and Industrial Transformation.* Princeton, NJ: Princeton University Press.

Feigenbaum, Harvey. "French Policy toward its Movie Industry," typescript, George Washington University, 1995.

Frederick, Howard. *Global Communication and International Relations.* Belmont, CA: Wadsworth Publishing, 1993.

Geller, Henry. "Reforming the U.S. Telecommunications Policymaking Process" in William J. Drake, ed. *The New Information Infrastructure: Strategies for U.S. Policy.* New York: Twentieth Century Press, 1995, pp. 115–136.

General Accounting Office. *Information Superhighway: An Overview of Technology Challenges.* Washington, DC: January 1995.

George, Alexander L. *Bridging the Gap: Theory and Practice in Foreign Policy.* Washington, DC: U.S. Institute of Peace Press, 1993.

Gonzalez-Manet, Enrique. *Informatics and Society: The New Challenges.* Norwood, NJ: Ablex Publishing Company, 1992.

Hahm, Sung Deuk and L. Christopher Plein. "Institutions and Technological Development in Korea." *Comparative Politics,* Vol. 28, No. 1 (October 1995), pp. 55–76.

Hamelink, Cees J. *The Politics of World Communication: A Human Rights Perspective.* London: Sage, 1994.

Heidenheimer, Arnold, Hugh Heclo and Carolyn Teich Adams. *Comparative Public Policy: The Politics of Social Choice in Europe and America.* New York: St. Martins Press, 1975.

Institute for Information Studies. *Crossroads on the Information Highway: Convergence and Diversity in Communications Technologies.* The Aspen Institute and Northern Telecoms, 1994.

Kahin, Brian. "Networks, Standards, and Intellectual Property: The Fabric of Information Infrastructure" in *20/20 Vision: The Development of a National Information Infrastructure.* Washington, DC: U.S. Department of Commerce, March 1994, pp. 109–124.

Keyfitz, Nathan. "Inter-disciplinary Contradictions and the Influence of Science on Policy," *Policy Sciences,* Vol. 28 (1995), pp. 21–38

Krasner, Stephen. "Global Communications and National Power: Life on the Pareto Frontier." *World Politics* Vol. 43, No. 3 (1991), pp. 336–366.

Kumon, Shumpei. "Can Japan Succeed in Chigoyo-Ka (Enterprise Formation)? *Technological Forecasting and Social Change,* Vol. 49, no. 2 (1995) pp. 147–164.

Lanvin, Bruno. "Why the Global Village Cannot Afford Information Slums", in Drake, *The New Information Infrastructure,* pp. 205–222.

Lerner, Daniel and Wilbur Schramm. *Communications and Development in Developing Countries.* Honolulu: East-West Center, 1966.

Lindberg, Leon N., ed. *The Energy Syndrome: Comparing National Responses to the Energy Crisis.* London: Oxford University Press, 1977.

Lovins, Amory B. *Energy Policies for Resilience and National Security: Final Report to the Council on Environmental Quality,* Executive Office of the President, Washington, D.C. San Francisco, CA: Friends of the Earth, 1981.

Mansell, Robin. *The New Telecommunications: A Political Economy of Network Evolution.* London: Sage, 1993.

March, James G. and Johan Olsen, *Rediscovering Institutions: The Organizational Basis of Politics.* New York: Free Press, 1989.

Mesthene, Emmanuel G. "Technology: The Opiate of the Intellectuals" in Albert H. Teich, ed. *Technology and the Future.* New York: St. Martins Press, 1986, pp.72–95.

Michalis, Maria. "Whither Greek Telecommunications Policy? Politics, the State and Telecommunications Policy in Greece," *European Journal of Communication.* Vol. 9, No. 4 (December 1994), pp. 441–460.

Mintzberg, Henry. *Power in and Around Organizations.* Englewood Cliffs, NJ: Prentice-Hall, 1983.

Mosco, Vincent and Janet Wasko. *The Political Economy of Information.* Madison, WI: University of Wisconsin Press, 1988.

Office of Technology Assessment. *Global Communications: Opportunities for Trade and Aid.* Washington, DC: 1995

Office of Technology Assessment. *Critical Connections: Communication for the Future.* Washington, DC: 1990.

OECD. "National Policy Frameworks for Information Infrastructures," Working Party on Telecommunications and Information Services Policies, Directorate for Science, Technology and Industry, Committee for Information, Computer and Communications Policy. Paris: OECD, 1995.

OECD. *Telecommunication Network-Based Services: Implications for Telecommunication Policy.* ICCP/87.5 Paris: OECD, 1988.

Quester, George H. *The International Politics of Television.* Lexington, MA: Lexington Books, 1990.

Reeves, Geoffrey. *Communications and the 'Third World.* 'London: Routledge, 1993.

Rochefort, David A. and Roger W. Cobb, eds. *The Politics of Problem Definition: Shaping the Policy Agenda.* Lawrence, KS: University Press of Kansas, 1994.

Ronfeldt, David. "Institutions, Markets and Networks: A Framework About the Evolution of Societies." Santa Monica, California: Rand, December 1993

Ronfeldt, David, and Cathryne Thorup. "North America in the Era of Citizen Networks: State, Society and Security." RAND Paper P-7945, September, 1995.

Rose, Richard. "Comparing Public Policy: An Overview," *European Journal of Political Research,* Vol. 1 (March 1973), pp. 67–96.

Rutkowski, Anthony M. "Multilateral Cooperation in Telecommunications: Implications of the Great Transformation" in William J. Drake, ed. *The New*

Information Infrastructure: Strategies for U.S. Policy. New York: The Twentieth Century Fund Press, 1995.

Saumon, Dominique and Louis Puiseux. "Actors and Decisions in French Energy Policy," in Leon N. Lindberg *The Energy Syndrome: Comparing National Responses to the Energy Crisis.* Lexington, MA: Lexington Books, 1977, pp. 119–172.

Shonfield, Andrew. *Modern Capitalism: The Changing Balance of Public and Private Power.* London: Oxford University Press, 1969.

Smith, Anthony. *The Politics of Information: Problems of Policy in Modern Media.* London: Macmillan Press, 1978.

Solomon, R. J. "Telecommunications for the Twenty-first Century" in W.J. Drake, ed. *The New Information Infrastructure: Strategies for U.S. Policy.* New York: The Twentieth Century Fund Press, 1995, pp.93–114

Staniland, Martin. *What Is Political Economy?* New Haven: Yale University Press, 1985.

Steinfield, Charles, Johannes M. Bauer and Laurence Caby, eds. *Telecommunications in Transition: Policies, Services and Technologies in the European Community.* London: Sage, 1994.

Talero, Eduardo. "A Demand-Driven Approach to National Informatics Policy," *13th World Computer Congress 94,* Volume 3. K. Duncan and K. Krueger, eds. Elsevier Science B.V. (North-Holland)

Talero, Eduardo and P. Gaudette. "Harnessing Information for Development: World Bank Group Vision and Strategy," Washington, DC: World Bank, July 1995.

Toffler, Alvin. *Powershift: Knowledge, Wealth, and Violence at the Edge of the 21st Century.* New York: Bantam Books, 1990.

Tyler, Michael. *The Changing Role of Government in an Era of Telecom Deregulation.* ITU Regulatory Colloquium No.2, Geneva: International Telecommunications Union, 1993.

U.S. Government. *Global Information Infrastructure: Agenda for Cooperation.* Washington, DC: February 1995.

U.S. Government. *National Information Infrastructure: Agenda for Action.* Washington, DC: 1994.

Willenius, Bjorn and Peter A. Stern. *Implementing Reforms in the Telecommunications Sector.* Washington, DC: The World Bank, 1994.

Wilson, Ernest J. III. "Africa and the Global Information Infrastructure," *Africa Communications* (May/June 1995), pp. 40–43.

Wilson, Ernest J. III. "The Petro-Political Cycle," in Richard L. Ender and John Choon Kim, eds. *Energy Resources Development: Politics and Policies.* New York: Quorum Books, 1987, pp.1–20.

Wilson, Ernest J. III. "World Politics and International Energy Policy," *International Organization,* Vol. 41, No.1 (1987), pp.125–150.

Implementing the NII Vision: Singapore's Experience and Future Challenges

Poh-Kam Wong

Introduction

Over the last three decades, Singapore has achieved one of the most rapid rates of economic growth among developing countries and newly industrializing economies (NIEs). Since the early 1980s, the Singapore government has also been among the most aggressive in promoting the diffusion and adoption of information technology (IT). The level of informatization of the Singaporean economy in the mid-1990s probably ranks among the highest among NIEs (see Table 1). It is therefore of no surprise that, in the early 1990s, the Singapore government was one of the first in the world to articulate a vision of developing a broadband national information infrastructure (NII) as a means of achieving its national socioeconomic goal (National Computer Board 1992).

In actually implementing the vision, however, Singapore faces not only complex policy and institutional reform issues common to other countries seeking to promote NII development (e.g., competition policy, universal access policy, funding mechanisms, convergence of telecommunications and media regulatory domains), but also challenges specific to its status as a small, newly industrializing economy. Without a substantial home market of its own, located far from the lead user markets (particularly the United States), and lacking large domestically based corporations with advanced technologies, deep pockets and global clout, Singapore has few comparative advantages to influence the global directions of NII-related

Table 1 Informatization Indicators for Singapore

Consumer Electronics (1995)

% of households owning:

at least one TV	100%
two or more TVs	43%
VCR	86%
two or more VCRs	15%
laser disc player	16%

Newspapers (1994)

Total newspaper circulation/pop.	35.1%

IT (1994)

% of households:

having a PC at home	30%
having a modem connection	10%
subscribing to Teleview	4–5%
having an Internet account	5–6%
% of companies with 10+ employees using computers	90%
Average number of PCs/terminals per 100 employees	36
% of companies using computer linked to LAN	58%

Telecommunications (1994)

Number of subscribers/100 population:

telephone lines (DEL)	44.7
pagers	26.8
mobile phones	7.6

Sources: Consumer Electronics: Survey Research Singapore; Newspapers: Singapore Facts & Pictures 1995; IT: National Computer Board; Telecommunications: Singapore Telecom

technological developments or mass-market trends. Whatever NII systems Singapore adopts must be able to plug into the global networks of NIIs emerging in the advanced industrialized countries. A key challenge facing NIEs like Singapore thus is timing. By moving early while global NII developments are still emerging, Singapore can hope to gain competitive advantages over other NIEs or even advanced industrialized countries, but in the process runs a high risk of betting on the wrong technologies or focusing on the wrong markets. By waiting until the dominant features of the new NII industry are already clear, however, Singapore will lose whatever lead it may hope to gain over other NIEs, let alone its chance to leapfrog over more advanced countries.

With small domestic markets and few technological resources of their own, small NIEs like Singapore cannot build an NII using their own technological sources, and cannot hope to recover the cost of building an NII based purely on current domestic demand. Hence, unlike the advanced industrialized countries, Singapore faces the challenge of leveraging the advanced technological resources and regional market reach of global firms from the advanced countries to help build an NII that will be made more commercially viable by serving the larger regional demand of global firms. In this regard, the policy framework and investment regulatory environment must be sufficiently open and attractive to encourage foreign technology suppliers and lead users to transfer their technologies as well as to bring regional market business to Singapore.

Finally, the distinctive "communitarian" ideology of the Singaporean political leadership (Chua 1995) creates a unique set of policy concerns unlike those of Western social democracies. Singapore's political leadership has consistently espoused the need to promote social and community values through exercising control over what it believes to be undesirable information. This communitarian ideology prescribes restriction of individual freedom of expression in the public domain, and, by extension, control over freedom of the press. Consequently, the development of an NII poses the interesting question of how the promise of information abundance is to be reconciled with the communitarian ideology.

The aim of this chapter is to provide an independent analysis of Singapore's NII initiatives thus far and to highlight the outstanding policy challenges in the future. The first section briefly analyzes the context in which the IT2000 initiative was formulated in 1991, particularly the development status of Singapore's information technology, telecommunications and media industries and their regulatory environments until the early 1990s. The second section describes the specific NII goals and strategic thrusts originally propounded in the IT2000 vision, and reviews the policy and institutional frameworks initially proposed for their implementation. The third section provides an independent assessment of the evolution of the implementation framework and highlights some of the major policy decisions, institutional reforms and development projects initiated thus far. The fourth section provides a summary assessment of the implementation process, while the fifth section identifies unresolved issues and key policy challenges in the future. The sixth section provides some concluding observations on Singapore's NII development experience and prospects for the future.

Antecedents to the NII Initiative: Background on Singapore's Evolving IT Industry and Policy

Establishment of the National Computer Board

Singapore first started to pay attention to the potential of exploiting IT to improve economic performance in the early 1980s. In 1981, it was one of the first countries in the world to establish a public agency, the National Computer Board (NCB), to promote computerization and IT industry development in a coordinated manner. One of the earliest tasks of the NCB was to initiate an ambitious program of computerizing government services. This Civil Service Computerization Program (CSCP) in effect made the government sector the lead user of computer technology in the country. The fact that the NCB was established under the Ministry of Finance gave it the clout needed to plan and implement computerization projects for the entire public sector.

Another early task of the NCB was to coordinate computer education and training to ensure that the output of computer manpower from the various training institutions would meet industry needs. A third task of the NCB was to help promote the development of an export-oriented software industry. This was done primarily by coordinating with the Economic Development Board (EDB) to encourage leading global IT vendors to use Singapore as their regional marketing, technical support and software development hub in Asia.

National IT Plan (NITP)

Under the initiative of the NCB, a National IT Plan (NITP) was formulated in mid-1985 to map out a strategy to promote IT development in Singapore. The plan identified seven building blocks:

• *IT Manpower:* to develop a corps of IT professionals with the right blend of skills for extensive and innovative exploitation of IT;

• *IT Culture:* to cultivate popular understanding and appreciation of IT in order to facilitate its application;

• *Information Communication Infrastructure:* to build an efficient information communication infrastructure and promote its creative and widespread use;

• *IT Applications:* to promote widespread and effective IT applications in every sector of the economy in order to improve productivity and create competitive advantages;

• *IT Industry:* to foster the growth and technological sophistication of the IT industry in order to support the extensive and innovative application of IT and the export of competitive IT products and services;

• *Climate for Creativity and Entrepreneurship:* to raise indigenous IT development and marketing capabilities to the level of international competitiveness; and

• *Coordination and Collaboration:* to make the most of limited resources through coordination of public and private sector organizations involved in IT development.

The plan considerably broadened the scope of government involvement in IT promotion and policy. As the agency entrusted to spearhead the implementation of the plan, the NCB expanded its activities and influence significantly over the next few years. IT applications in the public sector accelerated: between 1985 and 1990, the number of mainframe/minicomputers installed in government departments jumped from 35 to 107, and the number of applications systems developed increased from 72 to 293, while annual government computer spending increased from S$14 million to S$200 million. Some of the public sector IT applications have received international recognition; TRADENET is the best-known example.

Several new institutions were established by the NCB to pursue its widened role. For example, the Information Technology Institute (ITI) was formed in 1986 to undertake applied research and development. The Information Communication Institute of Singapore (ICIS) was set up in 1989 in collaboration with AT&T Bell Labs to provide postgraduate telecommunications software training, and the Japan-Singapore Artificial Intelligence Center (JSAIC) was established in 1990 to promote artificial intelligence technologies. New promotional programs include technical and financial assistance for small enterprises (Small Enterprise Computerization Program), subsidies for IT training of office workers (IT POWER Program), and grants for advanced IT manpower training (CITREP Scheme). Annual events such as the National IT Award, National IT Week and an IT software competition were also launched to promote IT awareness among the populace.

IT Diffusion and Industry Development

Spurred on by the various pro-IT policies and programs of the NCB and other government agencies, IT usage expanded rapidly in Singapore throughout the 1980s (see Table 2). By the mid-1990s, over 90 percent of organizations employing 10 persons or more had computerized. At the same time, the production and export of IT hardware and software grew significantly into a major industry in Singapore, albeit one mainly dominated by foreign IT companies. As Table 3 shows, direct export of computer systems and IT services to end-users had increased more than sixfold to S$2.2 billion in 1994 from just S$358 million in 1990. These figures do not include the export of computer peripherals like hard disk drives and printers. Although not as dramatic, domestic IT spending also registered strong growth from S$1.5 billion in 1990 to S$2.8 billion in 1994. Of the total sales of S$5 billion recorded by the IT industry in 1994, about 72 percent were derived from hardware, 12 percent from software and 16 percent from IT services (National Computer Board 1995b).

Table 2 Computer Penetration in Enterprises Employing 10 Persons or More, Singapore, 1982–1994

	% Establishments Using Computers	Average # of Employees per PC/Workstation/ Terminals	% Establishments with Local Area Networks
1982	13	N/A	N/A
1985	35	N/A	N/A
1987	59	N/A	N/A
1989	68	5.0	N/A
1992	84	3.8	39
1994	90	2.8	58

Source: NCB IT Usage Survey, various years

Table 3 Growth of Singapore's IT Industry, 1982–1994

	IT Sales in S$ million		
	Domestic IT Sales	Export IT Sales	Total IT Sales
1982	208.5	50.5	259.0
1983	303.4	64.3	367.7
1984	382.9	64.3	473.8
1985	435.4	90.9	560.7
1986	505.8	125.3	649.2
1987	613.7	143.5	789.1
1988	827.8	175.4	1065.3
1989	1126.0	237.5	1483.5
1990	1490.5	357.5	2147.8
1991	1804.0	657.2	2644.2
1992	1877.2	840.2	3019.1
1993	2092.3	1625.3	3717.6
1994	2793.4	2214.8	5008.2
Average annual growth, 1982–1994	24.1	37.0	28.0

Source: NCB Annual IT Industry Survey, various years.
Note: Sales refer to all IT-related sales (hardware, software and IT services) to end-users by IT vendors only. The figures therefore differ from production output figures of IT-hardware-manufacturing establishments by EDB, and also from export statistics of IT products by TDB. All figures are in current prices.

Telecommunications and Media Industry Development up to
the Early 1990s

Telecommunications has always been recognized as a strategic
infrastructure supporting Singapore's role as a regional manufacturing, trade and financial services hub. Although the public
telecom operator, Singapore Telecom (STel), has a monopoly in
virtually all areas of telecommunications except terminal equipment, it has proven remarkably dynamic and efficient, in contrast
to public telecommunications operators (PTOs) in many other
countries (Kulwant 1994; Wong 1993). The World Competitiveness Report has consistently ranked Singapore among the best in
terms of telecommunications infrastructure.

In the case of the media industry, the government has maintained tight control over newspaper publishing and broadcasting
since political independence (Kuo 1993). Practically all local
dailies are published by one company (Singapore Press Holdings
[SPH]) closely linked to the government, while the state-owned
Singapore Broadcasting Corporation (SBC) had a monopoly over
terrestrial broadcasting (three TV channels and radio stations)
prior to its corporatization in 1994. Until the early 1990s, no public
cable TV was permitted, while satellite broadcast receiving dishes
continue to be banned to this day. The government on the whole
maintains a very strict policy against pornography, and exerts tight
censorship control over movies and imported videos. While foreign news publications circulate freely in Singapore, they are
subject to the government's right-of-reply policy. Senior political
leaders also have not hesitated to resort to the court of law to act
against the press when it publishes things they consider libelous.

A New NII Vision for the 1990s

In the early 1990s, a transition began in Singapore's political
leadership. In November 1990, the premiership was transferred
from Mr. Lee Kuan Yew to Mr. Goh Chok Tong. The new prime
minister's vision for Singapore was put forth shortly thereafter in a
document called *The Next Lap* which likened economic development to a marathon race in which Singapore had done well in the

first lap as an NIE. In the next lap of the race, the document envisioned Singapore joining the ranks of developed nations by the end of the century, and challenged Singaporeans to prepare for the tougher competition in the "top league" of nations. Information, knowledge and technology were identified as the most important factors for success in the next lap (Government of Singapore 1991).

IT2000 Vision Plan

Right after the release of *The Next Lap,* the NCB initiated an "IT2000" study in January 1991 to examine how IT can create new national competitive advantages and enhance the quality of life in Singapore by the year 2000. The study involved extensive consultation with industry leaders, academics and senior government officials, who were grouped into working committees covering eleven major economic sectors: Construction and Real Estate; Education and Training; Financial Services; Government Services; Healthcare; IT Industry; Manufacturing; Media, Publishing and Information Services; Retail, Wholesale, and Distribution; Tourism and Leisure Services; and Transportation.

The result of the study was the drafting of an IT2000 vision plan. The plan was subsequently approved by the Cabinet, and in March 1992 it was released to the public as *The IT2000 Report: Vision of an Intelligent Island.* This was one and a half years before the Clinton-Gore Administration announced the National Information Infrastructure Initiative in the United States (Information Infrastructure Task Force 1993), and more than two years before the release of the Bangemann Report to the European Union (Bangemann Group 1994) and the MITI Report in Japan (Ministry of International Trade and Industry 1994).

The IT2000 Report envisions that, within 15 years, Singapore will be

among the first countries in the world with an advanced nation-wide information infrastructure. It will interconnect computers in virtually every home, office, school, and factory. The computer will [by then] evolve into an information appliance, combining the functions of the telephone, computer, TV and more. It will provide a wide range of communication modes and access to services. Text, sound, pictures, videos, documents, designs and other forms of media can be transferred and shared through this broadband information infrastructure made up of optical fibers reaching to all homes and offices, and a pervasive wireless network working in tandem . . . (p. x)

The report further identifies five strategic thrusts for Singapore to leverage this nationwide information infrastructure (National Computer Board 1992, pp. 19–36):

• *Developing a Global Hub.* Singapore has prospered in the past by plugging into global business networks as an efficient regional business hub. The key strategic role of an NII is thus to further enhance and sustain Singapore as a highly efficient center for goods, services, capital, information and people. Through the NII, Singapore aims to become a global business, services and transportation hub.

• *Boosting the Economic Engine.* The second strategic role of the NII is to boost productivity in existing industries as well as to create whole new businesses for the economy. The NII will be used to enable Singapore to move toward high value-added manufacturing with coordinating links to lower-cost manufacturing centers in the region. The NII will also constitute an important infrastructure to promote Singapore as an intelligent commerce and distribution center. Other perceived economic spinoffs include re-engineering the construction industry and enhancing the tourism sector.

• *Enhancing the Potentials of Individuals.* Recognizing that skills, creativity and knowledge will become even more critical in determining success in international competition in the next lap, the third strategic thrust is to exploit the multimedia capability of the NII and the availability of more powerful and affordable information devices to enhance the learning capability of individuals. Potential areas of exploitation include extensive use of multimedia technologies in schools and tertiary institutions; interactive distance education; enhancing indigenous media industries and cultural institutions through the creation of an electronic media marketplace; facilitating access to international and local databases; and providing extra help for the disadvantaged.

• *Linking Communities Locally and Globally.* The fourth strategic thrust is to use the NII to help Singaporeans to extend and strengthen their personal ties locally and globally through the creation of electronic communities. Potential projects include the establishment of a community telecomputing network to help create more involved and cohesive communities, and the development of a "Singapore International Net" to improve access to Singaporeans overseas and to promote Singapore to foreigners.

• *Improving the Quality of Life.* The fifth strategic thrust is to enrich the lives of Singaporeans by exploiting the NII to increase their discretionary time and to create more leisure options. Potential areas of application include reducing the need to travel for business or government transactions through the availability of one-stop, non-stop government and business services on the NII; teleshopping; cashless transactions; telecommuting; easy commuting via electronic road-pricing and an intelligent transport system; better healthcare; and intelligent buildings.

At the heart of the new IT2000 plan is a "3C" view of IT: computation, conduit and content. Whereas computation was the focus of the previous National IT Plan, in the 1990s and beyond IT will be increasingly driven by the development of more advanced, ubiquitous information networks and the digitalization of content.

To turn the vision into reality, therefore, the IT2000 plan proposes two major paradigm shifts: the need to develop an integrated and advanced national information infrastructure, and the need to promote content digitalization and the development of multimedia content industries.

Recognizing that the broader 3C components of the NII are under the purview of several government agencies as well as the need to involve both private and public sectors, the plan proposes a multi-agency implementation framework involving the following key organizations (Figure 1):

• An NII Group (NIIG) within the NCB to develop a master plan and spearhead the implementation of the NII;

• Singapore Telecom and the Singapore Broadcasting Corporation to continuously improve their network infrastructures;

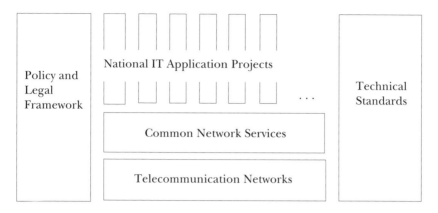

Figure 1 National Information Infrastructure: A New Strategic Framework.
Source: NCB (1992).

• A Project Specification Team under the NCB in partnership with organizations in the private and public sectors to conduct feasibility studies and develop systems specifications and funding mechanisms for national IT application projects; and

• A high-level committee to oversee and guide the highly coordinated multi-agency effort needed to implement the NII.

Implementing the Vision

Overall Implementation Framework

In endorsing *The IT2000 Report*, the government affirmed the broad vision it proposes, and entrusted the NCB to develop a master plan and spearhead the implementation of the NII. For this purpose, the NCB was provided with funding to establish the NIIG and Project Specification Team. However, as *The IT2000 Report* does not formulated any specific projects, the government only agreed to fund the implementation of approved NII projects on a case-by-case basis.

Thus, although the plan was officially adopted by the government and subsequently received wide domestic and international media attention, it did not actually carry with it a significant budget to implement any NII projects. Indeed, the document was seen as more of a broad strategic vision statement than a concrete plan proposing specific projects. Although several major project ideas were raised as part of the plan formulation process and mentioned in the report, none were concrete enough to be fundable. The strategic intent of the plan was to seek national consensus on a shared vision and to establish a broad framework to mobilize and coordinate the many different government agencies that have to be involved in implementing actual projects.

In line with a recommendation of the plan, the existing Committee on National Computerization (CNC), which had oversight over the NITP, was reconstituted into a high-level steering committee called the National IT Committee (NITC) to provide the needed policy coordination across ministries to oversee and guide the implementation of the plan. Headed by a senior minister of state for defense, and with the deputy prime minister as advisor, the committee elevated the status of, and enlarged the representation of key stakeholders in, the previous CNC. In addition to the vice-chancellors of the two local universities, the committee members now comprise the permanent secretaries of five ministries (Ministry of Information and the Arts, Ministry of Finance, Ministry of Trade and Industry, Ministry of Communications, and Ministry of Labor), the chairmen/chief executives of four statutory boards (NCB, EDB, Tourism Promotion Board, and the National Science and Technology Board [NSTB]), with the chairman of Singapore Telecom being the lone private-industry representative.

The NCB's Evolving Role

Although the NCB was given the leading role in developing and promoting implementation of the plan, it soon found this new responsibility to be much more complex and difficult than its previous tasks. Indeed, serving as the chief architect of the national information infrastructure, as in the initial vision, turned out to be NCB's most difficult task for two reasons.

First, the NII as proposed in the IT2000 plan was only an abstract idea without concrete specifications of the network technologies and applications involved. No other country, including the more advanced industrial countries, has developed a broadband NII yet, and most of the applications envisioned in the IT2000 plan have not yet been deployed on a commercial scale anywhere. Developing a master plan would thus require the NCB to be at the frontier of telecommunications technologies. Moreover, the NCB would need to plan for applications requirements in the abstract since no actual applications are ready for deployment.

Second, the NCB has no direct jurisdiction over the development of the physical network facilities under Singapore Telecom and the Singapore Broadcasting Corporation. At the time the IT2000 plan was announced, the government was still undecided on a number of major policy issues regarding telecommunications and broadcasting which would significantly influence the future course of development of the underlying networks upon which the NII was to be built.

During 1992–1994, the NCB established a new NII Division to house both the NIIG and the Project Specification Team to work on the overall architecture as well as specific project proposals. It soon became clear, however, that the original idea of formulating a comprehensive master plan, including detailed architectural specifications, was too ambitious a task in the face of dynamic technological and market changes and evolving telecommunications and media policy changes subject to broader political considerations. The ambitious goal of formulating a master plan was gradually reduced to focusing on the specifications and design of generic "middleware," or common utility services with multiple applications. At the same time, the scope of work on project specifications was also increasingly redirected to applications that are deployable on existing networks and involve a shorter time horizon, rather than emphasizing immediate broadband usage.

In mid-1994, the NCB began a series of demonstrations of middleware prototypes and potential applications to organizations including the Telecommunications Authority of Singapore (TAS), the Ministry of Communications, Singapore Telecom, the Ministry of Information and the Arts (MITA), the IT industry, and academic and research institutions. These prototype demonstrations, as well as a number of progress reports on the NCB's NII specifications efforts (Yap 1994), received mixed reactions in the IT community. Some industry experts and academic researchers stated that the prototypes were still far from being implementable because scalability and technology platform issues had not been resolved. The potential applications that were demonstrated apparently also failed to attract substantial funding commitments from the NITC or from private industries. An attempt to seek NSTB funding for research and development grants for NCB-proposed, NII-related, applications-development projects was also unsuccessful.

It was not until 1995, when a significant restructuring of the NCB itself took place, that a significant source of funding for NII-related development was established. As part of the implementation of the Strategic Economic Plan (SEP) formulated in the early 1990s by MTI, a S$2 billion industry cluster development fund (CDF) was established by the government in 1993 to fund new industry development and industry revitalization investment programs. The fund was meant primarily for EDB to fund industry restructuring programs and to co-invest in new high-tech industries with multinational corporations and local companies. In September 1995, it was announced that a sum of S$200 million from this fund would be allocated for an IT Industry Cluster Development Fund (ITCDF) to fund IT2000-related projects.

The new funding mechanism coincided with a major re-engineering of the NCB's mission and organization in the middle of 1995. As a result of the restructuring of the NCB, its new responsibilities have been defined as follows:

- Deploying IT2000 flagship projects;
- Promoting IT culture;
- Nurturing emerging IT industries;
- Overseeing IT manpower development; and
- Evolving an information infrastructure.

The attendant organizational changes introduced to enable the NCB to carry out its new mission have been described as "the biggest restructuring in NCB's 14-year history" by the new chairman, Mr. Lim Swee Say. In particular, the earlier emphasis on NII planning and architectural specifications was reduced in scope with the dissolution of the NII Division. It was also decided that the part of the NCB responsible for developing and implementing applications systems for various government departments under the Civil Service Computerization Program would be privatized. Instead, the NCB would serve as the Chief Information Officer for the government, providing strategic planning advice rather than doing the actual implementation. The NCB's direct involvement in applications development would instead be focused on major IT2000-related applications, with emphasis given to applications with nearer-term deployment prospects. Moreover, splitting up the original NII Division into eight new industry applications clusters within the NCB organizational structure put new emphasis on partnerships with the relevant private industry or government agencies. The eight clusters include: Construction, Digital Library, Education, Healthcare, Manufacturing & Distribution, New Media & Internet, Public Services, and Tourism & Leisure. An Information Infrastructure Group remains mainly to monitor global NII developments, as well as to focus on continuing the development of prototype network "middleware" that runs on the Internet for eventual commercial deployment.

The original mission of promoting IT culture and manpower development was retained in the re-engineered NCB, but the areas of emphasis have shifted. The existing Division of Industry Promotion was reorganized as the Industry and Technology Division to give it a stronger mandate to nurture new, emerging IT industries such as multimedia content development, networking technologies and Internet-related information services. IT manpower development initiatives were also geared toward training to fill anticipated gaps in the new IT skills required, as well as to accelerate retraining of existing IT professionals to prevent their obsolescence in the new networked economy. The priority target group for IT culture promotion has now shifted to school children.

Thus, while the original IT2000 plan envisages a central coordinating and leadership role for the NCB to champion its development, in actual fact, subsequent developments indicate that a number of other major stakeholders—in particular the Ministry of Communications and the Ministry of Information and the Arts— have come to play increasingly important roles, which are analyzed below.

Telecommunications Competition Policy and Network Development Strategies in the 1990s

As in many other countries throughout the world, Singapore experienced a period of tremendous telecommunications development in the first half of the 1990s. Four major structural changes occurred or were set in motion during these years.

First and foremost was the privatization of Singapore Telecom, the national post and telecommunications organization, in 1993. Although preparation for liberalization of competition was an important consideration in the privatization decision, another major factor was facilitating the internationalization of STel to exploit growing regional and global business opportunities. The privatization of STel was also politically important as it was the first of a series of major privatization exercises. Symbolically, Singaporean citizens were allotted shares at a heavy discount to market valuation to demonstrate that ordinary citizens could share the wealth created by well-run government enterprises.

Second, a major policy shift in favor of liberalization of competition was introduced, opening an increasing range of telecommunications services to competition. Table 4 summarizes some of the key liberalization decisions made by the Telecommunications Authority of Singapore in recent years. Although the pace of liberalization may be slower than in other countries like Malaysia or Hong Kong, the changes introduced so far have nonetheless been very significant from the historical perspective of telecommunications development in Singapore. In the course of three years, several new and powerful players have emerged in the telecommunications industry where only one existed before. The new entrants include some of the largest conglomerates in Singapore which have significant government investment (known locally as "government-linked companies," or GLCs), including the Singapore Technology Group, the Sembawang Group, the Keppel Group and Singapore Press Holdings (SPH).

Third, a policy decision was made to accelerate the island-wide deployment of fiber optics. Even before its privatization, STel had announced plans to wire up all buildings and homes on the island with fiber optics by the year 2005. As one of the conditions for its privatization, STel had apparently been committed to continue the

Table 4   Schedule of Telecommunications Services Liberalization in Singapore

Telecommunications Sector	Current Status of Liberalization
Local fixed-line telephony	STel will maintain its monopoly until 2007, but by April 2002, other operators may be licensed to provide fixed telecommunications services, provided these are ancillary to their principal services.
International calls	STel will maintain its monopoly until 2006.
Mobile telephony and paging	STel's current monopoly will expire on April 1, 1997; a second license for mobile phones and three additional licenses for paging have been approved.
Public trunk radio network operation	A second license will be issued by January 1, 1996.
VSAT	Household use remains prohibited, but since early 1995 companies are allowed to operate their own VSATs for intra-corporate use and closed user networks. Reception of TV broadcast signals remains prohibited.
Satellite uplink/downlink	Prior to 1994, only STel and SBC (now TCS) were licensed; since then, Singapore Technologies Teleport has been licensed to provide services to other broadcasters (but not telecom services), while foreign broadcasters have also been licensed to transmit their own signals (ESPN, Disney).
Differential global positioning system (DGPS)	Two licenses were issued by the end of 1994, others to be approved if necessary.
Multimedia broadband switching network	SCV is currently licensed to deliver video signals to the home. STel has been given a license to conduct VOD trials over its telecom network. A third licensed operator may be allowed in three to five years' time.
Value-added networks (VANs)	VAN operators are currently allowed to offer their services only to their own subscribers. In the near future, they will be allowed to connect to one another through leased circuits.
Internet access provision	Two other operators have been licensed in addition to STel.

Sources: Compiled from various press reports

fiber-to-the-curb laying program after privatization. This task was made easier by the fact that Singapore's building codes already required all high-rise buildings to be equipped with a main distribution frame (MDF) room to house telecommunications equipment serving building occupants. By December 1994, all MDF rooms in the central business district had been linked by fiber optics, while 75 percent of all public housing units were linked. By August 1995, it is estimated that some 158,000 km of fiber optics had been laid, covering 80 percent of all high-rise buildings in Singapore (Koh 1995).

Last but not least, a major policy decision had been made in 1994 that in effect would encourage the convergence of telecommunications and broadcasting. In an interview published on September 1, 1994, the Information and the Arts Minister stated for the first time that the government's long-term intention is for Singapore homes to be plugged into the interactive multimedia world via two separate lines: one to be provided by the telephone company and the other to be provided by the cable TV company.

To move in that strategic direction, in 1993 the government decided to promote cable TV by setting up Singapore Cable Vision (SCV). SCV began a program to wire up all homes in Singapore in 1995 by laying coaxial cables to individual housing units, while relying on STel's fiber-optic network as the backbone. This policy ensures that there will be at least one conduit to each home; i.e., the government was committed to providing broadband universal access before the year 2000. However, the option is also open for STel to lay a second conduit to the home if it makes business sense. Thus, the "last mile" will in effect be served by a dual-conduit policy. Although SCV is currently only allowed to carry video signals over its coaxial network, there are strong hints that in the future SCV may be allowed to carry telecommunications signals as well. According to a recent statement by the Minister of Communications, this could come as early as 2002 or even sooner, even though STel's original monopoly license extends to 2007. Meanwhile, STel was licensed by the Telecommunications Authority of Singapore in 1995 to conduct a video-on-demand (VOD) trial; should the trial be successful, there is a strong possibility that STel will be given a full license to provide interactive video services to the home. This could come as early as 1997 (Koh 1995). Hong Kong Telecom's announcement of a plan for a full commercial launch of VOD in 1996 has given added incentive for STel to be allowed to go into VOD as well. The stage has thus been set for the convergence of telecommunications and broadcast media.

In addition to promoting universal access via broadband fixed wireline, TAS has been actively encouraging the deployment of wireless technologies by introducing greater competition. Even before liberalization, Singapore had achieved the highest pager penetration in the world, and one of the highest levels of mobile phone penetration in Asia. Three new paging service licenses and a second cellular phone license have since been issued; the latter is committed to deploying personal communication system (PCS) based on new code division multiple access (CDMA) technology. Singapore is also one of the first countries in the world to begin implementing electronic road-pricing (ERP) using wireless technologies, and one of the first in Asia to promote wireless tracking services using geographic-positioning-system (GPS) technology.

Corporatization of the National Broadcasting Authority

To prepare for the impending technological convergence, the government also made major policy decisions affecting the broadcast media industry. In October 1994, the national broadcasting corporation—Singapore Broadcasting Corporation—was corporatized and replaced by a new holding company called Singapore International Media (SIM). The old SBC functions were broken up, and became four separate subsidiaries of SIM. Two of the subsidiaries—Television Corporation of Singapore (TCS) and TV Twelve—were each given two public broadcast channels, and the latter was tasked with providing public interest programs that are not necessarily commercially viable. The third subsidiary, Radio Corporation of Singapore (RCS), took over all of SBC's existing radio stations, while the fourth subsidiary, SIM Communications, was established to move into cable TV and multimedia.

Cable TV

As mentioned earlier, the government announced a policy to promote public cable television for the first time in 1993, reversing an earlier stand that prohibited cable TV from competing with free-to-air broadcast TV. This was shortly before the corporatization of the Singapore Broadcasting Corporation was implemented. A company called Singapore Cable Vision was established initially as a joint venture between SBC and Singapore International Media, offering three subscription TV channels via free-to-air broadcast. In July 1994, a new four-member consortium comprising SIM, two other local government-linked companies (Singapore Technologies and Singapore Press Holdings) and U.S.-based Continental Cablevision Inc. (CCV) was formed to invest in a S$500 million program to provide cable TV access to all Singapore homes by 1998. SCV signed an agreement to connect its "to-the-home" coaxial cables with STel's fiber-optic networks to the curb. A 30-channel service started operating in a regional town center (Tampines) in June 1995. As of November 1995, it was reported that 36,000 homes were already cabled, with actual cable subscription reaching 4,300 (the original three-channel service has meanwhile attracted about 30,000 subscribers).

Although SCV is currently licensed to provide cable TV services only, the dual-conduit policy announced earlier has given it the option to seek a license to provide interactive multimedia services to the home via PC or TV in the future. Meanwhile, direct satellite broadcast reception dishes continue to be banned for general households in Singapore, although use by business corporations for data communication has been liberalized.

One strategic intention underlying the decision to accelerate cable TV deployment is to preempt the demand for access to satellite broadcasts. The government evidently believes that it can exert greater control over programming piped through cable TV channels than programming sent via satellite broadcast.

Online Information Services and the Internet

Singapore was one of the first Asian countries to adopt videotext technology. In the mid-1980s, STel (then a public telecommunications operator) was asked to deploy videotext services on a national scale. The result was the development of Teleview, which initially was meant to be accessed through TV in the home, but subsequently was redirected to be linked up through PCs. Although

Teleview boasted of having state-of-the-art videotext technology at the time of its public launch in 1989, the text-based interface and proprietary nature of information-presentation software became significant liabilities when the Internet began to take off in the early 1990s, particularly when the World Wide Web (WWW) made graphic user interface (GUI) the de facto norm for online information service users. A number of other implementation decisions, including the centralized server architecture and limited server channel capacity (resulting in long response time), coupled with inappropriate pricing policies, further limited the appeal of Teleview, with subscription plateauing at less than 20,000 (three percent of households). Although a 1994 promotional strategy to boost subscription rates by including a 14.4 kbps modem at a subsidized price did raise the total subscription base to over 30,000 (about five percent of households), subsequent growth has been flat, and many subscribers are very-low-frequency users.

Singapore was also one of the first countries in Asia to adopt the Internet. The National University of Singapore was among the first in Asia to introduce WAIS and Gopher servers in 1992, and the World Wide Web in 1993. Although Internet service became available nationwide in 1993 (under the name of Technet) with funding from the National Science and Technology Board, it was initially confined only to the research community, including all tertiary educational institutions, public research institutes and private companies engaging in R&D activities. While there has been a substantial increase in research and innovative experimentation on the Internet among this select "elite" community, widespread penetration of the Internet into general businesses and households was delayed until late 1994, when the government finally decided to promote the Internet more broadly. The initial government hesitation was due primarily to concern about widespread access to pornographic materials, although some overseas commentators have ascribed an intent to perpetuate strict censorship over information in general.

As is characteristic of the Singapore government, actions shifted once a clear policy decision was made. While STel was initially the sole licensed public Internet server (Singnet), the government privatized Technet in 1995 through a public tender bidding exercise. The bid was won by a consortium of subsidiaries of several government-linked corporations, Sembawang Corp (via Sembawang Media), Singapore Technologies (via ST Computer Systems) and SIM, and the service was renamed Pacific Net. A third access license offered for public tender was won by another consortium of GLCs (Singapore Press Holdings and ST Telecommunications), even though a consortium led by a major foreign telecom player (AT&T) submitted the highest bid. Prices have been falling steeply as competition increases.

Besides increasing the number of servers, the government also announced policies to promote the diffusion of the Internet to secondary and primary schools. A pilot project called Accelerating the Use of IT in Primary Schools (AITP) was launched in 1995 by the NCB and the Ministry of Education to test the use of multimedia courseware and the Internet in primary schools, with eventual deployment in all primary schools targeted for 1997. In 1994, Internet access began to be encouraged in secondary schools.

While the status of Teleview remains uncertain at this stage due to the explosion of interest in the Internet, another player has recently entered the public online information services scene: Singapore Network Services (SNS). SNS was originally formed to commercialize TradeNet and other electronic data interchange (EDI) services in Singapore. Its main shareholders are the Trade Development Board, STel, the Civil Aviation Authority of Singapore (CAAS) and the Port Authority of Singapore (PSA), which were all intimately involved in promoting the use of TradeNet to facilitate external trade and transport transactions. The successful widespread diffusion of TradeNet has won SNS international recognition (including its inclusion in ComputerWorld's 1995 list of the top 100 IT users in the world). SNS has since introduced a wide array of EDI network services in Singapore (e.g., LawNet for the legal community, MediNet for the healthcare industry, ProfNet for public procurement, RetailNet for retailers), and can boast of more than 13,000 business customers. SNS has also recently started to internationalize by exporting its network management expertise and/or co-investing in EDI network services in Canada, Mauritius, China, the Philippines and Malaysia.

Despite regional expansion, SNS clearly felt threatened by the mushrooming of the Internet as a universal network platform. In late 1995, SNS decided to enter the public online information service business by licensing the Livewire technology developed by the NCB. SNS also seeks to enter the Internet content publishing and packaging businesses, joining entrepreneurial startups as well as publishing giants like SPH.

To complete the picture on public online information services, the NCB has been working for some time on a project to develop a nationwide public information kiosk system (Singatouch) that would enable members of the public to conduct a variety of transactions and information retrieval tasks at conveniently located information kiosks. These transactions include reservation and purchase of tickets for events (e.g., movies, concerts, sports events) and tourist resorts, banking transactions, an online tourist guide, an electronic bus guide and government transactions. Commercial introduction of the project is planned for 1996, with NETS (the company currently involved in providing online financial transaction services for bank ATMs and retail electronic fund transfer at point-of-sale [EFTPOS]) likely to be a major partner. Promotion of smartcard technology is also being actively pursued.

Strategic Response by the Media Industry

The "3C" convergence's effect on Singapore's media industry extends not only to broadcasters, but also to major print media publishers. Foremost among these is SPH, Singapore's giant newspaper publisher. SPH was formed in 1984 through a merger of Singapore's major newspaper groups, and it currently publishes all the major dailies in the three main languages (English, Chinese and Malay). As a major content owner, SPH made early moves into videotext (via Teleview) and audiotext services, in addition to online database services (Newslink). SPH similarly embraced the Internet revolution quite early. Not only does it publish WWW versions of all its major dailies and periodicals, but it also was among the first to offer online financial information services. Moreover, as a major stakeholder in one of the consortiums holding an Internet access provider license, SPH is well placed to leverage its strong position in content as a potential differentiation tool. The fact that SPH has been allowed into Internet services as well as other telecommunications and broadcasting services (SPH is an equity partner in SCV as well as in a cellular and paging consortium) clearly indicates that the government has adopted a flexible policy toward cross-media ownership.

New NII Applications

As mentioned earlier, the NCB has refocused its efforts toward accelerating the development and subsequent deployment of several new NII applications. Some of these efforts have reached the threshold stage of deployment. For example, as pointed out earlier, by late 1995, a prototype middleware that runs on the Internet called Livewire was licensed to SNS to form the basis of its new thrust into online information services. Another imminent deployment is the public information kiosk system. Other flagship projects currently under active development include:

• *Construction and Real Estate Network (CORENET):* The objective of CORENET is to use IT to re-engineer business processes in the construction industry so as to achieve a quantum leap in turn-around time, productivity and quality. The proposed network is envisaged to provide a wide range of system services, including: plan checking, concurrent design, electronic submission, information services, an automatic quantities takeoff system, electronic inspection and an integrated project management system.

• *Student-Teacher Workbench (STW):* The aim of STW is to enhance teaching and learning in secondary schools by giving teachers and students access to a rich depository of multimedia courseware and content. The project was initiated as a joint program with the Ministry of Education, with the first pilot phase involving six secondary schools. Ten industry partners have so far committed S$5 million in equipment and manpower resources to participate in the pilot project. These partners include PC hardware and systems companies (Creative Technology, Aztech Systems and IPC), software development companies (Primefield and Ednovation), courseware development companies (Time Publishing, ST Computer, Jostens Learning Corporation and Educational Trend) and a tertiary educational institution (Ngee Ann Polytechnic).

• *Digital Museums and Libraries:* This undertaking stems from the recommendations of the report of a national review committee on the future development of Singapore's public library system. Called *Library 2000: Investing in a Learning Nation,* the committee's report highlighted the need to transform the traditional public library system into a network of multimedia information services. The development of digital contents formed a key element of this transformation strategy. Initial projects include involving the National Science and Technology Board to develop a science and technology InfoNet to link eight tertiary and specialized libraries to provide information electronically to Singapore's R&D and scientific communities, as well as developing a virtual museum for the National Museum.

• *Electronic Road-Pricing System:* Singapore was one of the first countries in the world to introduce road-pricing to control traffic congestion in the early 1980s. In the early 1990s, a plan for an electronic road-pricing system that would automatically detect and charge road usage fares on vehicles entering selected roads via wireless communications technology was announced. After two rounds of testing, a tender was awarded in 1995 for the construction of an electronic road-pricing system to replace the existing manual road-pricing system. The new system will require the attachment of a prepaid cashcard on all vehicles entering selected roads, where usage fares will be deducted automatically by the system. Full deployment of the system is expected in 1997.

Development of a Broadband Network Testbed

Quite early in the planning phase for NII implementation, the NCB recognized the need to establish a broadband network testbed that can be used for experimental testing, research and trial deployment of potential NII applications prior to their commercial launching. The NCB formulated a "collabrium" concept to involve potential NII application developers and users from both the private and public sectors to share the cost of developing and running a common testbed network that provides sufficient functionality and scalability features. However, initially the proposal did not attract a sufficient commitment of funds from interested parties because of its ambitious scope and uncertainties in the technological platform in the face of rapid technological change. It was not until early 1995 that funding from the NSTB was secured to get the broadband testbed off the ground. Called the National High Speed Testbed, the network is based on ATM, which has become the de facto switching technology for broadband testbeds around the world. The testbed currently has nine approved participating organizations: the NCB, three public IT R&D institutes (ITI, ISS and the National Supercomputing Research Center), three tertiary institutions, STel, a leading local IT firm (IPC) and a developer of intelligent buildings (Orchard Park Suites). The NCB serves as the host for the Project Management Office. Meanwhile, STel has started to conduct broadband integrated services digital network (ISDN) trials on its own.

Promotion of Singapore as a Regional Telecommunications and Broadcasting Hub

One of the strategic thrusts of the NII is to enhance Singapore as a regional business hub. Even while the physical infrastructure is still being built by STel and SCV, the government has begun aggressively wooing global multinational corporations to use Singapore as a regional telecommunications and broadcasting hub through a combination of investment incentives, liberalization policies and the promise of sustained superiority in infrastructure compared to other countries in the Asian Pacific region. By the end of 1993, Singapore had succeeded in attracting a significant number of value-added service providers like Reuters, Telerate and SITA to use Singapore as their regional hub. More recently, a regional broadcasting hub role is emerging, with several major broadcasters, publishers and other content providers including HBO, the Discovery Channel, Time-Life Asia, Walt Disney, MTV, ESPN and ABN setting up content production and distribution operations in Singapore to service Asia.

The development of these regional hub operations is important not only because it creates new high-value-added jobs, but also because it provides the commercial demand and applications expertise that will eventually drive the deployment of broadband network services in the future.

Summary Assessment of the NII Implementation Process

With the benefit of hindsight, one can see that the NCB initially underestimated the technological complexity of the IT2000 vision, and at the same time overestimated the potential market demand for broadband network services. The core capabilities that the NCB has established over the years through its civil service computerization projects have been based primarily on computer technologies and applications, whereas the task of designing and building a broadband NII requires new core competencies in telecommunications technologies and applications.

Beyond telecommunications, the NCB also needed to contend with a number of other major stakeholders in the new information economy. These include broadcasting and other publishing media under the Ministry of Information and the Arts (in relation to content); education and training under the Ministries of Education and Labor (also in relation to content); trade, financial services and new information services industries under the Ministry of Trade & Industry (in relation to electronic commerce and investment promotion); and the Ministry of Law (in relation to intellectual property rights laws related to new forms of information goods and network transactions). Unlike the earlier case of NITP implementation, in which most of the policy issues related to the NCB's computerization promotion efforts were relatively non-controversial and involved little overlap with the jurisdiction of other ministries, the changes proposed in the IT2000 vision call for potentially significant policy changes by these ministries and thus require extensive policy coordination. Although there has been a genuine "buy-in" to the IT2000 vision by all the ministries concerned, and a high-level policy coordinating mechanism exists in the NITC, the process of working out policy coordination at the level of project implementation can be protracted. Although the NCB has set up an NII Policy Research Group to analyze policy issues and propose policy options to facilitate the implementation of the IT2000 vision, it is in practice limited by its lack of expertise in many of the policy areas that it has to grapple with, and the need to consult and involve other government agencies calls for the development of new policy coordination skills.

Policies related to the media industries are invariably among the most politically sensitive in most countries. In Singapore, the political leadership's commitment to the communitarian ideology makes information policy formulation and implementation even more complex. Thus, although the widespread diffusion of the Internet would have been seen as desirable from the perspective of promoting IT culture, electronic commerce and new information services industries, it was not until the Minister of Information and the Arts announced a clear policy decision to encourage Internet use that the NCB could aggressively champion Internet-related developments. Similarly, the participation of the Ministry of Education provided the impetus to accelerate the development of the student-teacher workbench project. Finally, competition policies in the telecom market were developed by the TAS under the Ministry of Communications, while the policy decision on whether there should be one or two carrier networks for broadband information transmission was probably made at the highest political level.

Another major complicating factor is the rapid pace of technological change and market development. While the IT2000 vision clearly anticipated the global shift toward network applications and digitized contents, the pace of change and the specific forms that it has taken nonetheless caught government planners and even industry leaders in the advanced industrialized countries by surprise. For example, the surge in popularity of the World Wide Web and the emerging paradigm of "the network is the computer" clearly were not anticipated three years ago. At the same time, the highly touted high-definition TV (HDTV) revolution in the late 1980s became an embarrassment to its Japanese promoters by the mid-1990s, while the promise of a mass market for video-on-demand has ebbed with surprising speed as the sobering results of a number of ongoing trials are emerging in the United States.

Technological platforms and integration strategies have become even more fluid than they were three years ago when the IT2000 plan first contemplated the idea of a broadband integrated information network. Mobile communications and digital satellite transmissions are emerging as potentially viable alternative means of providing local multimedia access even while cable TV battles with fiber optics and ADSL-rejuvenated copper wires for the "last mile." In terms of switching technologies, while ATM has made significant progress, widespread deployment remains elusive in the near term. Narrow ISDN, which was written off in the early 1990s as obsolete, may yet be revived as Internet (and perhaps personal video-conferencing) demand for higher bandwidth continues to surge. Finally, the fear of monopoly dominance by Microsoft operating systems is being replaced by new optimism about the emergence of platform-independent network programming technologies like Java.

In the face of such massive technological and business market fluidity, no clear indications have emerged as to which applications and technology platforms will drive broadband services. Instead, the rise of the Internet has given greater urgency to developing applications that can be deployed on top of existing infrastructures and the Transmission Control Protocol/Internet Protocol (TCP/IP) protocols. Thus, paradoxically, the pervasive network and computing envisioned by IT2000 have come sooner than antici-pated, but the expected deployment on broadband networks has receded further into the future.

These turns of events clearly suggest that a reprioritization of the IT2000 implementation strategy is needed. In particular, while the dual-conduit policy will ensure universal access to broadband services by the year 2000, the actual deployment of specific broad-band network services cannot be technology-driven, but must await the development of sufficient market demand. Moreover, market demand for broadband services is unlikely to emerge full-blown; instead, it is more likely to be stimulated by, and to evolve from, applications deployed earlier. In investing in nationwide cable TV, the government has provided one major application that will help pay for the cost of one access conduit to all homes, while STel's VOD trial portends another potential application that will contrib-ute toward funding a second conduit. However, the deployment of these applications will take some time, and their commercial viability is not assured. In the meantime, rather than waiting for other demands to emerge, a more pragmatic strategy would be to hasten the development of other applications that can be commer-cially deployed on existing infrastructures in the near term to stimulate future demand for broadband services. This reorientation is urgently needed to take advantage of the explosive growth of the Internet. Finally, by stressing near-term deployment viability and the presence of immediate customers (whether private or public), this "bootstrap" approach would help recover the eventual cost of building the broadband network infrastructure.

It is to the NCB's credit that it grasped the new realities quickly and concentrated its implementation efforts on specific applications-oriented developments deployable in the near term without a fully functional broadband network. The significant re-engineering of the NCB's organizational structure and mission reflects this new reality, and indicates the readiness of the political leadership to make significant organizational changes in key institutions in order to deal with new challenges.

Given the paradigm shift toward networks and content already identified in the IT2000 vision plan, it is inevitable that the Ministry of Communications and the Ministry of Information and the Arts must play larger roles in the implementation of the plan. Despite initial doubts by foreign observers, both ministries have moved with surprising speed toward putting in place the framework and structure for NII deployment. In particular, the dual-conduit policy and commitment to fiber deployment will ensure that Singapore will have universal access (and most likely, user choice of the "last mile" conduit) by the year 2000. While it is a moot point whether the NII vision has helped galvanize the necessary government policy decisions, the policy framework in place at the end of 1995 is clearly much more coherent than that of its predecessor.

Future Prospects and Challenges

The IT2000 plan started as a broad vision with few details. It attracted wide media attention, and to a certain extent may have raised expectations beyond what is realistically achievable in the short run. In the initial years of trying to implement the vision, policymakers had to grapple with rapid technological change and the complexity of policy coordination, which was further complicated by the absence of clear policies on telecommunications and broadcasting. In the four years since the plan was introduced, however, major new policy decisions have been made in several critical areas, and a coherent policy framework is beginning to emerge. At the same time, the NCB has narrowed and more sharply focused its implementation role. Although technological and industry dynamics remain fluid and dependent on developments in advanced countries, there is now a more concrete sense of strategic directions and visible progress. Nevertheless, future NII development in Singapore will face a number of new and important challenges.

First and foremost, the Singapore government clearly needs to attract more companies, both domestic and foreign, to invest in new NII-related innovations and applications in the near future. The lead that Singapore now has over most other Asian countries in terms of physical infrastructure development will not translate into superior competitive advantages unless a continuous stream of new, leading-edge applications is deployed to exploit the more advanced infrastructures. Establishing or creating market demand for new applications and services will be the key factor, not technology. In this regard, the small size of Singapore's domestic market is clearly a disadvantage that needs to be offset by skillful exploitation of its dense urban configuration as a lead-user market for other Asian cities and regions. By mastering the learning curve faster than its neighbors, Singapore can gain a temporary window of competitive advantage, as well as leverage its early experience to quickly export know-how to other parts of the region. In the latter endeavor, however, Singapore will need to compete against more advanced countries even further along the learning curve by focusing on applications, knowledge and content that have uniquely Asian or regional characteristics.

Another major challenge facing Singapore is how to promote the growth of indigenous start-up companies to ride the wave of the new emerging NII-related industries. So far, most of the major players in the business are either multinational corporations using Singapore as a regional hub, or large local conglomerates, primarily the government-linked companies. The recent success of Singaporean firms in the soundcard industry—Creative and Aztech—offers an example of what the Singapore government would clearly like to see replicated in other emerging NII-related markets. Although recently there have been some promising spinoffs from government research institutes and universities (e.g., the first Internet publishing and packaging firm, Silkroutes, was formed by ex-NCB staff), the challenge facing the government is how to nurture and promote more vibrant local multimedia and other NII-related services despite two major obstacles—the absolute scale disadvantage and distance from lead-user markets, particularly the United States. One emerging approach is the formation of collaborative R&D consortia that pool the resources of small local firms and government R&D institutes. The recent formation of the NSTB-funded Digital Media Consortium (DMC), which involves three public R&D institutes (ISS, ITI and IME) and three local IT companies (Creative, Aztech and IPC) working with the Massachusetts Institute of Technology's Media Lab is a good example of this kind of development.

Third, while a clear policy framework for encouraging competition, providing universal access and user choices in "the last mile" has been established, many contentious policy issues are likely to surface in the future. Debates over the extent of editorial control that the Singapore Broadcasting Authority can exercise over program content on SCV's cable TV or STel's potential VOD services are likely to emerge when these services are widely deployed. STel's monopoly on the fixed telecommunications backbone and SPH's monopoly on local press content may diminish over time via the Internet and other NII-related developments, but if they do not, then debate over the need to accelerate the liberalization of fixed telecommunications, or over cross-media ownership and control, will no doubt arise. An immediate concern, for example, is whether the current high tariff rates on narrow ISDN are justified, or whether TAS should ask STel to reduce them substantially to promote the spread of Internet use (and possibly personal video-conferencing use in the future).

Last but not least, it will be interesting to see how far the Singapore government will succeed in reconciling its unique brand of communitarian ideology with the challenge of information abundance posed by NII developments. Singapore's political leaders have consistently argued that a communitarian political system can coexist with free-market capitalism; indeed, they argue that the former provides a better institutional framework than does the

Western social democratic system for fostering rapid economic growth in the developing world. Singapore's economic success so far has provided its political leaders with a proven track record to back their claim. Despite major clashes with the Western press, Singapore has continued to attract investments by multi-national corporations throughout the first half of the 1990s. More recently, Singapore's success in developing itself into a regional broadcasting hub, despite the continuation of its strong stance toward the media (the "right-of-reply" rule; the strict ban on pornography and satellite receiving dishes), has once again confounded certain foreign critics who predicted Singapore's early demise in the Information Age. Minister of Information and the Arts George Yeo has asserted that, although technical advances will make controlling information increasingly difficult, Singapore's government will not give up trying to deter what it considers "information pollution." However, recent policy developments suggest that the emphasis may be shifting toward taking a proactive role to create more "wholesome" alternatives rather than stopping unwholesome ones. Greater emphasis will also be placed on parental responsibility in providing guidance and supervision over information access by children within the family, and local community responsibility in exercising control over the distribution of undesirable information.

Conclusion

From a grand but vague vision, Singapore's IT2000 vision plan is slowly but surely taking shape and moving in promising directions, despite some initial uncertainties caused by rapid technological change, market fluidity and impending telecommunications and broadcasting policy reforms. Although the NCB's more focused approach now emerging represents a scaled-down vision, it has benefited from greater coherence and clarity in the policy framework for telecommunications and broadcasting. Indeed, the implementation framework that has emerged over the last few years actually represents a return to a development strategy that has enabled Singapore to excel in exploiting IT in the past. In essence, this strategy has two major thrusts:

• An applications-driven orientation, focusing on combining Singapore's strengths and capabilities in some existing niche area where it already excels with the exploitation of new technology to achieve even greater excellence. Rather than seeking to be a technological leader in mass markets where many large, global players are jostling for position, Singapore is content to be a fast follower in these markets, while concentrating its main energies on becoming a lead user in selected applications where it is strong (e.g., sea and air transport/logistics, urban planning and development, public transport, government information services, multicultural media contents). The government will continue to play an important role as many of the potential application areas will involve government agencies working in collaboration with private firms or industry groups.

• An external-market, technology-driven orientation, focusing on attracting world-class multinational corporations and talents to use Singapore as a regional hub, thereby ensuring that leading-edge business users will drive the country's future infrastructure deployment and, in turn, transfer advanced technologies and lead-customer knowledge to local firms.

This two-pronged strategy does not preclude Singapore from investing substantial public R&D efforts to attack niche technology markets that may be relatively neglected by the big players, or where technological shifts have created new opportunities for small players. Indeed, key NII-related technologies are likely to be given higher priority in future national technology plans, and R&D investment by local IT firms will increase substantially over the next few years. Nonetheless, this thrust toward indigenous innovation will continue to complement the larger two-pronged strategy for some time to come.

Future NII development on a global scale will continue to be driven by significant technological and market fluidity. What we understand as NII today has evolved beyond recognition since it was first conceived just five years ago, and by the year 2000 our understanding of what constitutes NII will no doubt be very different from today. Such uncertainties notwithstanding, the policy framework and implementation strategy that have been put in place by the Singapore government over the last few years provide sufficient ground for cautious optimism that many of the original goals of the IT2000 vision will indeed be realized, although perhaps not by the end of the year 2000 and not necessarily in the form originally envisaged. It is also likely that many of the IT applications inspired by this IT2000 vision will be seen, in retrospect, as crucial to sustaining the competitiveness and productivity of Singapore's economy at the dawn of the next millennium. If this happens, the IT2000 vision will have truly served its purpose.

References

Ang, B. H. and B. Nadrarajan. 1995. "Censorship and the Internet: Singaporean perspective." *On the Internet.* November/December 1995. pp.28–33.

Bangemann Group. 1994. E*urope and the global information society: Recommendations to the European Council.* Brussels, Belgium.

Chua, B. H. 1995. *Communitarian ideology and democracy in Singapore.* London: Routledge.

"ISDN returns to home port." *Computerworld.* (Singapore Edition). March 3–9, 1995.

Economic Development Board. 1995. *Economic Development Board yearbook 1994/ 95.* Singapore: EDB.

Government of Singapore. 1991. *The next lap.* Singapore: Times Edition.

Information Infrastructure Task Force (IITF). 1993. *The national information infrastructure: Agenda for action.* National Telecommunications and Information Administration, Washington, D.C. September 15.

IMD. 1995. *World competitiveness report 1995.* Davos, Switzerland.

"$200 million fund will speed up IT2000 projects." *IT Focus.* September 1995.

Kahin, B., ed. 1992. *Building information infrastructures.* New York: McGraw-Hill.

Koh, P. K. 1995. Video-on-demand: A market-technology analysis." Singapore: Advanced Study Project, School of Postgraduate Management Studies, National University of Singapore.

Kulwant Singh. 1994. Corporate strategy in the intelligent island: The case of Singapore Telecom." *Industrial and Corporate Change.*

Kuo, Eddie C. Y. 1993. "Communications scene of Singapore." In *Asian communications handbook,* A. Goonasekera and D. Holaday, eds. Singapore: Asian Media Information Center (AMIC).

Ministry of Information and the Arts. 1994. *Library 2000: Investing in a learning nation.* Singapore: Singapore National Printers.

Ministry of International Trade and Industry. 1994. *Program for advanced information infrastructure: Summary report.* Tokyo: MITI.

Ministry of Trade & Industry. 1991. *Towards a developed nation: The strategic economic plan.* Singapore: MTI.

National Computer Board. 1992. *IT2000: Vision for an intelligent island.* Singapore: NCB.

National Computer Board. 1995a. *National Computer Board yearbook.* Singapore: NCB.

National Computer Board. 1995b. *Singapore IT industry survey 1995.* Singapore: NCB.

National Computer Board. 1995c. IT2000 action plan: From vision to reality. Published on WWW site: http://www.ncb.gov.sg.

National Computer Board. 1994. *Singapore IT usage survey 1994.* Singapore: NCB.

National Science & Technology Board. 1991. *National technology plan.* Singapore: NSTB.

Singapore Telecom. 1995. *Annual report 1994/5.* Singapore: STel.

Telecommunications Authority of Singapore. 1994. *Annual report 1993/4.* Singapore: TAS.

Wong, P. K. 1993. "Economic growth and information-telecommunications infrastructures in Singapore." Paper presented at the International Conference on Economic Growth and Information-Telecommunications Infrastructures in Asia, Tokyo. March 18–19, 1993.

Wong, P. K. 1994. "Singapore's technology strategy." In *The emerging technological trajectory of the Pacific Rim,* D. F. Simon ed. New York: M. E. Sharpe.

Wong, P. K. 1995. "Small, newly industrializing economies facing technology globalization: A Singaporean perspective." In *Management of technology and regional development in a global environment,* L. A. Lefebvre and E. Lefebvre eds. London: Paul Chapman.

Wong, S. H. 1992. "Exploiting information technology: A case study of Singapore." *World Development* 20, No.12, pp.1817–1828.

Yap, M. 1994. "Singapore NII: Beyond the information highway." *Information technology* 6, No.1, pp.11–19.

Back to the Future: Japan's NII Plans

Joel West, Jason Dedrick, and Kenneth L. Kraemer

In 1993, Japan began debating plans for a nationwide digital communications network (often referred to as a national information infrastructure (NII) or "information superhighway"[1]). Because such an infrastructure is potentially the largest public works project since the construction of the *shinkansen* (bullet trains) of the 1960s, the debate was entered by the leading industrial companies, corporate think tanks, academia and several government ministries.

Despite the inherently new opportunities and challenges of such a network, the "visions" and other elements of the debate fell back on old intellectual concepts of a Japanese information society. The plans reverted to familiar top-down policies that favor producers over consumers, with actual implementation hamstrung by established patterns of bureaucratic infighting. Allied with government bureaucrats were Japan's large electronics firms, which remain focused on hardware production and, at the same time, continue to crowd out smaller, more innovative firms that develop software and information content.

Some concerned Japanese advocated more radical policy changes, notably centered on telecommunications deregulation. But these changes seem unlikely in the near term due to structural impediments in the national political system.

This overview summarizes the policymaking processes at work in the recent Japanese NII debate. Because much of the debate is an explicit reaction to U.S. NII plans, it also highlights a few of the similarities and differences between those plans, as well as those issues universal to most countries planning to build an NII.

Background: Economic and Political Institutions

The postwar Japanese "miracle" was one of rapid economic and technological development, although the economic benefits accrued more to large industrial firms than individual consumers.[2] These firms worked closely with the national ministries, including, in the case of computer and electronics technologies, participation in government-sponsored R&D projects.

National Ministries

The formal structure of the current Japanese government is set by the Constitution of 1947, which was imposed by the U.S. Occupation. Although politics exist at the prefectural and municipal levels, essentially all significant regulatory and spending authority is concentrated at the national level; the prefectures lack the authority of Canadian provinces or German *Länder*, let alone an American state. The national political authority is vested in the two-chamber Diet, headed by the Prime Minister, and from 1956 to 1993 was ruled by a single party, the Liberal Democratic Party (LDP). Despite this political continuity, career bureaucratic officials held considerable power and influence, particularly during the period 1950–1973.[3]

For NII policy-making, the two most significant government ministries are the Ministry of International Trade and Industry (MITI) and the Ministry of Posts and Telecommunications (MPT).[4] MITI traces its background to the prewar Ministry of Commerce and Industry and the wartime Ministry of Munitions, but is best known as the architect of the growth of export-oriented heavy industries and electronics in the three decades following the war (Johnson 1982). The ministry holds central technology incubation and other policy-making functions, both directly and through the AIST (Agency of Industrial Science and Technology).

MPT at one time had the configuration of a traditional government PTT, but in 1953 the Nippon Telegraph and Telephone (NTT) Company was spun off as a government corporation, leaving MPT with postal functions—including the key national postal savings system—and telecommunications and broadcasting regulatory responsibilities.[5] Unlike other some other Japanese ministries, MPT does not take a clientelist view on behalf of NTT, but instead has been attempting to re-assert its authority through proposals of an AT&T-style divestiture (Vogel 1996).

For most other firms, however, the ministries have strongly identified with the interests of their associated firms (and vice versa), ties that are strengthened by the retirement of ministry bureaucrats in their mid-1950's into senior executive, board member and "advisor" positions with leading Japanese firms; this process is known as *amakudari,* or "descent from heaven" (Johnson 1974).

Industrial Structure and Development of the Electronics Industry

As part of its postwar economic development, fledgeling electronics firms were supported in the 1950's and 1960's with now-familiar tools of infant industry protection, both by discouraging foreign competition through tariffs and investment restrictions, subsidies and export promotion (Johnson 1982; Okimoto 1989; Mason 1992).

In the 1960's and 1970's, such industry promotion efforts focused on the production of mainframe computers by these same electronics firms. Both MITI and NTT promoted leading electronics firms by funding joint public-private R&D projects. When MITI gave subsidies of ¥70 billion for its New Series Project—joint R&D at Japanese firms to develop mainframe computers to catch up with IBM's 370 series—NTT funded its four *den-den*[6] (NEC,Fujitsu, Hitachi, Oki) companies to produce computers that would be used in its telephone switching systems (Anchordoguy 1989). MITI's funding also helped establish the Japanese semiconductor industry, spending ¥200 billion on the VLSI project targeting mainframe semiconductors that helped Japanese firms develop Dynamic Random-Access Memories (DRAM's).

This R&D funding was concentrated in the overlapping oligopolies of the Japanese computer and telecommunications industries that some scholars argue act as *de facto* cartels. As shown in Table 1, these leading computer and telecommunications firms also overlap the prominent Japanese consumer electronics producers, with most having pre-war origins.

These firms have, in turn, been part of larger organizations of inter-connected firms that dominate Japanese industry. These industrial groupings are normally classified into two types (1) horizontally diversified cross-shareholdings known as *kigyô shudan*, and (2) vertically integrated production and distribution systems known as *keiretsu*. (Kikkawa 1995). The better known are the horizontal industrial groupings formed, in part, to prevent hostile takeovers, which—though lacking the centralized authority of the prewar *zaibatsu* holding companies—have established preferential capital and buyer relationships that enable coordinated action and risk sharing (Fruin 1992; Gerlach 1992). Many of the leading electronics firms play an active role in their group's governance through participation in the presidents' council that coordinates intra-group cooperation (Miyashita and Russell 1994). A few large firms lack strong group ties, but many head their own vertical *keiretsu*. There also exist a tier of smaller electronics firms—including Alps, Casio, Kyocera, Kenwood, Pioneer, TEC—which act as suppliers to the large firms or sell a narrower range of end-user products.

Motivations: The Origins of Japan's NII Plans

Plans for an NII are based on the prediction that developed nations will shift from an industrial society, in which tangible objects are manufactured, to an information-based society, in which knowledge is gathered and sold. In Japan, Masuda predicted that a combination of computer and communications technology would bring "the increasing emancipation of man from labor for subsistence" (1980, p. 62). More recently, the Telecommunications Council (*denshi tsûshin shingikai*, an advisory group to the Ministry of Posts and Telecommunications) said the NII could address Japan's problems of an aging population and over-dependence on Tokyo, and shift Japan to an "intellectually creative society" (Tele-

Table 1 Top Japanese Electronics Companies, Fiscal Year 1994

Company	Year Founded	Ind. Group	New Series	Den-den	R&D%	Sales (¥ bill.)	CE	PC	SC
Matsushita Electric	1935	Sumitomo†			8.5%	4,441	2	6	
Hitachi	1920	DKB, Fuyo, Sanwa	•	•	10.2%	3,742	6	4	3
Toshiba	1904	Mitsui	•		8.3%	3,325	3	3	2
NEC	1899	Sumitomo	•	•	9.6%	3,007	1		1
Mitsubishi Electric	1921	Mitsubishi	•		6.6%	2,488	5	5	5
Fujitsu	1935	DKB	•	•	12.2%	2,260		2	4
Sony	1946	Mitsui†			12.7%	1,882	1	8	
Sharp	1935	Sanwa			8.9%	1,262	8	7	
Sanyo Electric	1950	Sumitomo†			7.7%	1,065			
Fuji Electric	1923	Fuyo			5.5%	561			
Victor Co. of Japan	1927	Sumitomo†			6.7%	541	4		
Oki Electric	1949	Fuyo	•	•	6.2%	536			

† Not a member of the presidents' council for the industrial group.

CE, PC, SC: Ranking among Japanese firms for consumer elecronics, personal computers, and semiconductors, based upon total sales (domestic sales for PC's). Semiconductor sales for calendar 1994.

Note: The Japanese government fiscal year extends from April 1 to March 31, and is used by the government, listed corporations and trade associations for reporting most financial results and other statistics.

Sources: Toyo Keizai (1995), Miyashita & Russell (1994), Dodwell (1988), Yano Keizai (1995), Dataquest (1996), Anchordoguy (1989).

communications Council 1994a). Not coincidentally, the creation of an information society would create new economic opportunities in software, services, entertainment and information content, all of which are presently areas of weakness in the Japanese economy.

Of course, anywhere NII plans are being discussed—whether the United States, Japan, Singapore, Korea or Europe—there is an implicit or explicit subtheme of technological competitiveness in computer and communications industries. In Japan, this subtheme is an especially powerful motivator in the 1990s, as Japan's electronics giants have suffered through a decline in revenues and a collapse in profitability. An additional powerful force behind the recent surge of interest in the NII in Japan has been fear of falling behind the United States in an important economic arena—a concern which became acute with the Clinton administration's 1993 announcement of its NII strategy. Finally, the emergence of the NII issue in Japan has coincided with the quest for a new mission on the part of key economic ministries, particularly the Ministry of

International Trade and Industry (MITI) and the Ministry of Posts and Telecommunications (MPT).

These four issues—creating an information economy, bolstering the electronics industry, reacting to the U.S. challenge, and redefining bureaucratic missions—are the key factors motivating Japan's drive to develop an NII strategy. The following discussion looks more closely at each of these issues.

Jôhô-Ka: Creating the Information Society

The phrase *jôhô-ka*—usually translated by the quasi-English word "informatization" and denoting change to an information-oriented society—has been a slogan of Japanese government policy for more than two decades, even though the actual effect of the slogan has been minimal. It is generally associated with two threads— the abstract concept of Japan as an information society, and a shift in government industrial policy away from heavy industries in the late 1960s and early 1970s.

In the early 1960s, the phrase "information industry" was popularized by Tadao Umesao, while *jôhô-ka* is credited to Yujiro Hayashi of the Economic Planning Agency in 1967.[7] In 1971, a report of the Industrial Structure Council advocated a transformation of the Japanese economy from traditional heavy industries to "knowledge intensive" ones (Morris-Suzuki 1988, p. 27). The "oil shock" of 1973–74 made salient home the country's vulnerability as a resource-poor industrial nation, and Johnson places MITI's first detailed vision of a "knowledge-intensive industrial structure" at November 1974 (1982, p. 301).

Hiromatsu and Ohira (1991) argue that though this first "information society boom" had little impact in Japan, it was exported to Europe, from which it inspired a similar boom in North America and started a second boom in Japan in the late 1970s and early 1980s. Certainly from the 1980s onward, the shift to an information society was repeatedly cited as a national goal, as in Prime Minister Nakasone's speech opening the Diet in February 1984, and became the subject of various books, articles and television programs (Morris-Suzuki 1988, p. 28).

Since the initial conception of information technologies, the Japanese government has spawned many research and demonstration projects in software and related technologies, including the Fifth Generation Computing Project, Pattern Information Processing System, Sigma (Anchordoguy 1989; Fransman 1990) and the more recent Real World Computing project. But despite the desirability to shift from producing tangible ("hard") to intangible ("soft") goods, Japan has not become a major worldwide supplier of software and other intangible information technology products.

Thus far, Japan's role in the global computer industry has remained primarily in electronic components and peripherals, with a limited role in complete computer systems and a negligible role in software; by one calculation, the size of the information industry increased only from 3.1% to 4.0% of gross domestic product (GDP) in the period 1975–1985 (Hiromatsu and Ohira 1991). Public policy debates on information technology are still dominated by considerations of manufacturing and selling hardware—perhaps because the major electronics *keiretsu* still have far more political influence than smaller software-only firms.

Catching up with the United States

Although elements of what is now considered NII have been discussed in Japan for many years, the rhetoric in the period 1993–1995 seems driven by a "catch up" mentality—the view that Japan is behind in both plans for an information infrastructure, and key technologies such as networking and software.[8]

Such a mentality became one of the periodic fads of the Japanese popular press. A visit to a Tokyo bookstore during this period would turn up several magazines and dozens of popular books devoted exclusively to multimedia, NII and the coming revolution in the information industries. Many examined technological issues, while others examined U.S. policies or explicitly paint an imminent economic rivalry with the United States. Representative is the book cited by Glen Fukushima (1995) entitled *Jôhô Superhighway no Kyôi: Nihon Jôhô Sangyô Kaimetsu no Kiki* ("The Threat of the Superhighway: The Crisis of the Annihilation of the Japanese Information Industry").

In the words of Teruyasu Murakami, a prominent Japanese multimedia expert at the Nomura Research Institute:

Last year [1993], we had a new social infrastructure boom. The argument suddenly erupted around March. The point was [made] that in the Japanese budgeting system, only hardware investments such as construction of bridges or highways or airports are the subject of construction bonds. [It was argued] that bonds should be able to fund software development, including communication development.[9]

This argument was made by [those in] politics and industries from mid-1992. Throughout the year 1992 there wasn't any enthusiasm [for it], but in February–March of 1993, suddenly this argument came to the surface in mass communications, TV, newspapers....

Gore's superhighway idea triggered the whole argument about a national information infrastructure in Japan . . . It's a sort of artificial social phenomenon, not driven by Japanese society's national indigenous needs (Interview, August 29, 1994).

Murakami said Japanese politicians and businessmen were very concerned about U.S. NII plans, because policy recommendations from the President's Commission on Industrial Competitiveness (President's Commission 1985) in the U.S. had, in his words, "dramatically changed" U.S. science and technology policy toward Japan. The May 1993 report of a similarly named industry group (Council on Competitiveness 1993a) raised concerns that this pattern would be repeated, although the latter report received little notice in the U.S. (West 1996).

Similarly, Japanese policymakers intently studying the United States government can recite Vice-President Gore's "Five Points" for any future U.S. NII: (1) encourage private investment; (2) promote competition; (3) quick regulatory response; (4) network access for all information providers; and (5) universal service. These points have gone generally unnoticed in the U.S. popular media or in the high-tech community, and given the complexity of the U.S. policymaking process, were likely to face major revisions even before the 1994 elections brought Republican control of the Congress.

There are three possible explanations for such a Japanese fixation on United States' policy proposals far beyond their actual importance in U.S. policy:

• *Confusion of the External Perspective.* The United States is unusually diverse in both its social composition and the range of opinions that enter the public discourse. It is difficult for an outsider to distinguish between the president's nominal and actual power, the actual influence of industry, or between legislative proposals that are seminal and those that are "dead on arrival."

• *Greater Perceptivity from an External Perspective.* Japan's industry has been credited with taking a longer view than that in the United States, while its press is considered more international in focus. The Japanese may be recognizing merit in U.S. ideas that go unremarked here: so when Kumon (1994) cited Gore's five points, he could be anticipating that they would play a role in policy outside the United States—as happened when they were later proposed as a global goal for the February 1995 meeting on the global information infrastructure held by the Group of Seven (G-7) industrialized countries. (NTIA 1994).

• *External Threat as an Internal Weapon.* It is also possible that the competitive threat of U.S. plans is being used in Japan as a consensus-building tool. It is well understood within Japan that government and industry do better when competing with an external economic rival, because it provides the external pressure necessary to speed up the decision-making process and force things to a conclusion. A crisis of competitiveness—real or imagined—has moved the Japanese closer to an information revolution in the last two years than anything in the preceding twenty.

Samuels (1994) notes that such Japanese desires to catch up to Western technology have driven national policy for the past 150 years, while West (1996) argues that since the 1980's, such "competitiveness" concerns have provided a positive feedback loop between technology policies of Japan and the United States.

A few (mainly in the United States) have suggested that Japan lacks the creativity or other elements necessary for technological leadership, and thus needs to have a model to emulate. According to John Stern, then Vice-President for Asian Affairs of the American Electronics Association, "The Japanese catch up better than they lead. . . .This is a nation that got rich following the taillights of America" (Interview, September 1, 1994).[10] But despite the "catch-up" rhetoric, there is little sense among Japan's business and government leaders that the country is irretrievably behind. They face a number of problem areas in their NII plans, but, according to telecommunications executive Teiichi Aruga, "If these issues are resolved, playing rapid catch-up is Japan's forte." One of these issues, Aruga notes (1994), is the emphasis in existing NII tests and discussions on producer rather than, user motivations.

Since that time, Japanese strengths and American weaknesses have been more openly voiced. For example, a Kobe University professor (Seki 1995) published a lengthy (if often inaccurate) critique, entitled "Piecemeal nature putting potholes in the U.S. info highway," criticizing competition between cable TV and regional telephone companies in the United States and questioning the value of PC-savvy executives. Such outward criticism may be intended to rebuild Japanese self-confidence after excesses of catch-up rhetoric, or it may be intended to focus Japanese energies on building within the country, rather than constantly watching outside.

Producer Motivations: Reviving Japan's Electronics Industry

Much of the debate about the Japanese NII has been framed around the potential revenues and jobs it would generate for many of Japan's electronics industries by incubating a domestic market base for future exports. Such a concept is not new, of course, but instead has been the underlying rationale for Japanese high-tech industrial policy throughout the past 35 years.

What was new during the 1993–1994 period was the unaccustomed difficulties faced by various Japanese industries, which were pinched since the bursting of the "bubble economy" led to recession and an end to four decades of almost uninterrupted economic growth. Adding to weak domestic demand, exports of Japanese-made goods were threatened by continuing *endaka*, or the strong yen. This meant that large Japanese electronics firms were cutting back production in the home islands, moving manufacturing to China and Southeast Asia and searching desperately for new products to manufacture in Japan to sustain both the health of their companies and, by providing jobs, their standing in Japanese political debates.

It is no coincidence that the "catch up" panic came in 1993, in the middle of a 10% two-year decline in Japan's industrial production

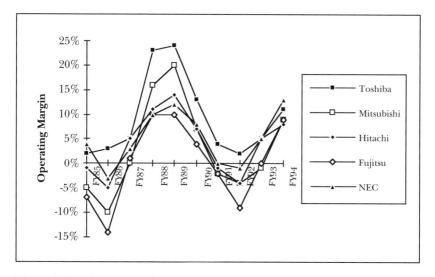

Figure 1 Profits of Japan's Top Five Electronics Companies. Source: Nomura Research Institute.

and a slump in the profits of major electronics firms (Figure 1). Advocates of NII investment have used job creation as a justification: take the oft-cited report by the MPT's Telecommunications Council, which includes a table that explicitly equates NII with jobs (Telecommunications Council 1994c, p. 14; emphasis in the original):

Multimedia Markets (annual revenues in 2010)

New markets related to the fiber-optic network	¥56 trillion
Existing multimedia markets	¥67 trillion
Total	**¥123 trillion**

Jobs created through the construction of the fiber-optic network
Approximately **2.43 million**

As Stern (1994) noted, however, this employment figure would constitute a greater percentage of the labor force than the present-day auto and consumer electronics industries—combined.

Such an emphasis on domestic job creation is consistent with Japan's postwar economic policies, but sustaining this attitude into the 1990s could potentially cause two sources of trade friction. For advanced electronics products, Japanese industries are at par with

U.S. rivals in several key technologies: Anderson (1995) notes that NTT considers Japanese industry ahead of the U.S. in several hardware technologies such as Asynchronous Transfer Mode (ATM) telecommunications switches, but lagging in other areas such as software. The implication that all the jobs created by Japan's NII will be Japanese suggests a continuing policy of favoring Japanese products over imports—which would, in turn, would create new sources of potential trade friction with the United States.

At the low end, both Japan and the United States are at an economic disadvantage compared to low-cost producers in the rest of East Asia, so it is natural to assume that (absent explicit governmental policy) many of the jobs involved in manufacturing mass-market consumer electronics products will be created in other East Asian nations, and not in Japan. As the wealthiest country in East Asia, Japan's potential for political leadership in the region lies in using that wealth to promote regional economic growth. Some Asian specialists believe to continue economic growth in the region, Japan must act as a consumer market for manufactured exports from other Asian countries, the way the United States has for decades. Such a step would also improve the quality of life of Japanese consumers. But the tone of the NII debate shows that any shift from a producer-driven economy to a consumer-driven economy has yet to begin.

The Vision: An Information/Communications-Based Economy

Japan's vision of the NII was continuously evolving during the period 1993–1994, with different versions coming from various players such as MPT, NTT and MITI. The most influential government document in starting the debate was MPT's 1994 document "Reforms Toward the Intellectually Creative Society of the 21st Century." NTT's NII vision is spelled out in the 1994 publication "NTT's Basic Concept and Current Activities for the Coming Multimedia Age." In addition the Management Coordination Agency of the Prime Minister's office has published a plan for government computerization (MCA 1994), and think tanks such as the Nomura Research Institute have developed their own visions of Japan's NII (see Murakami 1993).

The term *jôhô tsûshin* ("information/communications") is the focal point of both MPT's and NTT's NII visions. MPT (Telecommunications Council 1994b) speaks of a transition from the existing socioeconomic system to a different system founded on a new paradigm. That new paradigm is defined as an "intellectually creative society based on info-communications." Likewise, NTT (1994) argues that "the information communications industry contributes to the enrichment of people's lives and the activation of industry activities." Each of the visions emphasizes the role of the NII in promoting future economic growth and enriching the lives of citizens.

While the notions of realizing a comfortable lifestyle and promoting mutual understanding are emphasized in MPT's vision, those goals have been reiterated in various government visions for two decades. Why then has NII suddenly taken on such urgency in the past few years? Al Gore might be a proximate cause, but a more fundamental issue is revealed in the MPT report.

The international competitive environment is changing in step with the progress of yen appreciation and the growth of the newly industrializing countries, and Japan is increasingly shifting its production facilities overseas, especially in the manufacturing industries where competitiveness has been declining.... (T)he shift of production overseas is continuing at a fast pace, giving rise to fears of a hollowing-out of industry. For this reason, too, it is imperative that Japan switch to a new highly productive framework for industry and employment, a framework centered on areas with high intellectual added value (Telecommunications Council 1994b, p. 2).

As this paragraph illustrates, NII in Japan is primarily a response to the declining competitiveness of Japanese industry. Building the NII would respond to the challenges of *endaka* and hollowing-out in two critical ways. First, it would create new economic activities to replace activities that will inevitably continue to move offshore in response to *endaka*. The new activities would include production of intellectual property, such as software, information content, entertainment and information services. They would also include production of new multimedia and telecommunications equipment in which Japan could leverage its existing strengths in hardware technology to create a competitive advantage.

Second, the creation of an advanced national information infrastructure would help make existing industries more productive and competitive through the application of network technologies within and among corporations. A specific concern expressed in Japan is that the U.S. NII will give American companies a competitive advantage, and it is clearly expected that Japanese companies need access to a comparable infrastructure to compete.

The elements of Japan's NII visions focused on creating an information/communications-based economy, and the benefits expected to spring from such an effort. They include: producing new multimedia products and services; installing a nationwide broadband, fiber-optic telecommunications infrastructure; creating hardware products that can be manufactured domestically; developing software capabilities; and improving productivity of the economy through application of information and communications technologies.

Multimedia

Multimedia—the anticipated convergence of audio, video and computing technologies—has been the great anticipated growth market for Japan's electronics companies for many years. They have developed both new products, such as Sony's handheld Data Discman and Fujitsu's home PC series FM Towns, and promoted existing products such as CD-ROMs and even *karaoke* as part of an anticipated "multimedia revolution."

While touting multimedia as a potentially huge industry, the Telecommunications Council report remains vague on its definition of multimedia. New multimedia markets are defined as those "newly created by program distribution, production of terminal devices, network operations and others related to the development of the fiber-optic network." Existing markets expected to expand by 67 trillion yen include "video equipment, telecommunications equipment, computers and video software." In effect, the report is including the entire electronics and telecommunications industry under the term "multimedia." There is no estimate of the growth of those industries in the absence of a universal fiber-optic network, hence no true estimation of the additional value to be produced by building such a network, just the assertion that building the network will create 123 trillion yen in economic activity and more than 2 million new jobs.

Regardless of how vaguely the term "multimedia" is defined (and those hyping multimedia in the United States and elsewhere are not much more precise), it is clear that the NII vision in Japan is based on the belief that multimedia will be a tremendous driver of economic growth in coming years. Multimedia is expected to revive the stagnant consumer electronics industry by linking it to computing and telecommunications and giving Japan's electronics companies a new edge over their Asian competitors. It is also expected to enable Japan to make inroads in the entertainment and software industries, where Japanese companies have been unable to challenge the dominance of Hollywood, Silicon Valley and Redmond.

Broadband, Fiber-Optic Communications Infrastructure

The link from multimedia to an information infrastructure is straightforward. Only multimedia content—home movies (video on demand), interactive video games, interactive education, business videoconferencing, and so on—requires the bandwidth to justify a nationwide digital telecommunications network supplanting the existing telephone network. Such a network is the cornerstone of the plans of Japan (and other nations) for an "information society" in which information is conveyed digitally between citizens, business and government, rather than via mail, fax, telephone or television.

Japan's NII plans stated that this multimedia system will be delivered via a fiber-optic network. In the United States, corresponding plans called for a hybrid of fiber optics, coaxial cable, enhanced copper wire and wireless. Coaxial cable TV lines serve the vast majority of U.S. homes and have the capacity to provide high-bandwidth transmission. In Japan, expensive, tightly regulated cable TV has not caught on, available to only 22% of all TV households and subscribed to by a mere 5% (Yamazaki 1994). So Japan's initial NII visions called for building a pure fiber-optic network.

In 1994, NTT announced plans to wire every Japanese household with fiber optics by 2015. But then MPT announced a target date of 2010, so NTT changed its projections to 2010 as well. Today, many officials and observers privately say fiber-to-the-home will not happen by 2010, both because of cost and because there is no clear demand on the part of users for such high-speed service to the home.[11] However, there is still a clear emphasis on building the infrastructure as a means of stimulating demand, rather than waiting for demand to drive investment in the infrastructure.

New Hardware Opportunities

The NII is seen as a means to stimulate domestic demand for computer hardware, consumer electronics and communications equipment. Some of the major categories of hardware include PCs and peripherals, set-top boxes, semiconductors, high-definition TV (HDTV), handheld personal digital assistants (PDAs), video servers, fiber-optic cable and digital switching equipment. Some of this demand, particularly for telecommunications equipment, will come from the actual construction of the NII. Demand for products such as computers, HDTV, video servers, PDAs and various consumer devices would be driven by the availability of multimedia content over the NII.

In addition, the creation of domestic markets for such products is expected to support exports. Japan's large, sophisticated domestic market for consumer electronics is credited with supporting exports of TVs, VCRs, video games, Walkman radios and numerous other devices. By contrast, Japan's slow adoption of PCs is one reason for the lack of export success in that industry. By stimulating domestic demand for multimedia hardware, it is hoped that new products will be developed for export and profits from the domestic market will support an export drive. Such a strategy is based on the earlier successes of Japan's automobile and consumer electronics industries, but also reflects the pattern followed by the U.S. PC industry. This aspect of the NII is not discussed as directly in the various NII visions, but given the strong concern over *endaka* and hollowing-out, there is no doubt as to the perceived need to develop new export opportunities for Japan's manufacturers.

Developing Software and Services Capabilities

Software and services are the fastest growing segments of the information technology industry worldwide and still offer better profit opportunities than most of the brutally competitive hardware industry. Japan has tried for decades to catch up in software, through a number of government R&D programs as well as corporate efforts, but if anything, has continued to fall further behind the U.S. industry.

Japan's software industry lags far behind that of the United States in almost every key dimension. In applications software, eight of the ten largest firms are American, while only one is Japanese. For systems software, seven are U.S. firms and none are Japanese (Office of Industries, U.S. International Trade Commission 1995). Japanese software companies have almost no presence outside their domestic market. They continue to focus on custom programming, while the global market is shifting rapidly to packaged applications. Most importantly, virtually every key software architecture is controlled by U.S. companies.[12] The only important exception is video game software, which runs on architectures controlled by Nintendo and Sega. Even the Japanese domestic market for packaged software is dominated by U.S. applications, and IBM's DOS-V and Microsoft Windows are unifying the formerly fragmented PC applications market.[13] The Japanese market is still relatively small for information services, such as systems integration, outsourcing, online services and network services. Japanese companies have failed to compete outside the domestic market for such services, and are beginning to face foreign competition in their home market.

The other essential "soft" component of a multimedia future is content. Such an imperative motivated the purchase of Hollywood properties (MCA, Columbia Pictures, Columbia Records) by Japanese electronics companies, since Japanese-produced entertainment exports are largely confined to video games, karaoke and animation. The anticipated synergies between "hard" and "soft" goods have not been realized, and one of the major acquisitions, MCA, has since been sold by Matsushita to a Canadian owner. Meanwhile, Japanese firms such as Sony have experimented with

U.S.-based new media subsidiaries and joint ventures, but, in the end, the predominant share of the world's entertainment content still comes from the United States

The NII offers new opportunities for Japan in software and services. Multimedia and interactive markets are still in their infancy, and new kinds of content and entertainment are sure to be developed. As new markets develop, it is believed that opportunities will be created for Japanese companies to develop their capabilities in software, services and content and challenge the present U.S. dominance in those areas. Even if U.S. firms set the standards, such standards provide a well-defined target that will play to Japan's forte: manufacturing high-quality complex products that conform to those standards (West 1995).

NII as a Productivity Tool for Government and Industry

One possible role for the NII is as a tool for increasing productivity in government and industry. For the post-"bubble" industries, economists and other analysts have pointed to the poor productivity of Japan's white collar work force (compared to other industrialized nations) as one of the problems that needs to be addressed to aid in economic recovery (Yamakoshi 1995). Greater use of information technologies, such as PCs, e-mail and groupware are among the technological fixes that have been proposed to increase such productivity.

Government information systems have also lagged behind those of other leading industrial powers. Murakami (1993) argues that the Japanese bureaucrats have computerized each ministry separately, rather than coordinating and integrating work between ministries. He proposed an interministerial network based on a system of common document interchange formats that would also be connected to local governments and private users. Such a system could be expected to reduce and rationalize administrative tasks, reduce the use of paper (and thus office space), improve information sharing between various levels of government, and improve decision-making. Also, by computerizing this information, the government's information could be more readily accessible as an information asset for all of Japanese society.

NII Plans and Initiatives

Japan's bureaucratic elites, particularly at MITI, have been credited with engineering the postwar economic miracle that turned Japan into a manufacturing powerhouse and the world's second largest economy. However, the 1990s found MITI a victim of its own success: Japan's manufacturers no longer needed MITI's protection and increasingly ignored its guidance, while few of the later technology development projects (e.g., Sigma, Fifth Generation Computing Systems Project) had produced any commercially successful technologies.

So it is not surprising that MITI was ready to jump at an opportunity such as the NII, which promises to remake Japan's industrial structure. But NII is largely a telecommunications issue, and as such falls within the purview of the previously second-tier MPT. MPT sees the NII as an opportunity to further expand its influence and achieve the status of an economic pilot agency, comparable to the Ministry of Finance (MOF) and MITI.

The jockeying for influence was not limited to MITI and MPT. The NII is seen by many in the bureaucracy as an opportunity to expand their influence and create a new, attractive mission for their ministry or agency. This creates bureaucratic rivalries that have slowed the development of a coherent NII strategy, manifested by various competing ministerial plans. Participants in NII conferences are treated to a parade of representatives from Japanese ministries, always including MITI and MPT but often featuring the Science and Technology Agency and other groups; even the national broadcaster NHK offered its own vision (Latzer 1995). Each speaker presents a "Vision of a Multimedia Society" that differs more in who is presenting it in than in the details of how the vision would be implemented.

MPT

Like other national ministries, MPT develops its policies with the help of various permanent and *ad hoc* advisory groups known as *shingikai,* which consist largely of business and academic leaders. Such groups examine ministerial proposals and develop plans that reflect the desires of the constituencies represented on the panel, and that will also be supported by those constituencies once their report is released (Fukunga 1995).

So the influential Telecommunications Council (1994a) report in May 1994 came from a 21-member panel that included the chairman of both Hitachi and Nikkei (Japan's leading financial publisher), as well as four professors and a vice president of *Rengô*, the leading labor union; its communications policy committee was headed by the chairman of Daiwa Bank's affiliated research institute. The origins of the report, its distribution,[14] and its content all contributed to it being the most often quoted of the competing "visions" developed at this time.

The report emphasizes Japan's economic challenges for the 21st century, and argues that information communications can both facilitate the nation's decentralization and help develop Japan's creativity. The latter goal would be obtained through the informatization of education, medical care and government services, achieved through development of application databases and applications.

The two most-often quoted figures from the report are the aforementioned estimated annual size of multimedia-related markets (¥123 trillion) and the new jobs created (2.43 million). Less often quoted are the estimated implementation costs that range from ¥33 to ¥53 trillion, plus ¥42 trillion for underground wiring.

The fiber-optic network would be rolled out in three five year phases culminating in 2010. The first phase would emphasize the center city of prefectural capitals, the second would include all cities with a population of at least 100,000, and the final phase would extend to cover 100% of the nation. The first phase would also connect schools, hospital libraries and other public institutions, with the development of public applications. Since such application development is essential to take advantage of the hardware infrastructure, the MPT vision argues that the public sector must lead the development and trial deployment of such applications so that they can be put to practical use by the year 2000.

The report recommends interest-free loans and tax incentives to fund private development of the fiber-optic network. Local governments should also encourage replacing overhead cables with underground ones, as well as facilitating right-of-way for both underground and above-ground lines.[15] To implement the necessary services, regulatory reforms should encourage the expected convergence of broadcasting and telecommunications, while considering a fiber-optic version of universal service.

Finally, the report anticipates the development of systems and standards as the basis for the Japanese NII, arguing for new standards from Japanese trade associations as well as cooperation on international networks with the International Telecommunications Union (ITU).

MITI

MITI's (1994) proposal for an "advanced information infrastructure" has similar goals to the MPT report. Noting the limited use of information technologies by public agencies, it emphasizes five priority areas: education, research, medical/social services, government administration and libraries. It outlines specific plans in each of these areas for linking government agencies, private homes and creating online databases to support these goals.

As with the MPT report, it notes the need for new standards for the information infrastructure, and also measures to facilitate the use of copyrighted material in new multimedia software. Such software is a major priority of the MITI report, which advocates the creation of various multimedia information centers (for creating content) and various programs and reforms to improve the software development capabilities of Japanese industries.

MITI is focusing on applications for the NII, not on creating the communications infrastructure itself, which is clearly MPT's turf. MITI sought the support of other ministries for its NII plan by including them as partners who would receive funding for their own NII applications. MITI's role was to be catalyst, coordinator and project manager. This was an attempt to carve out its own niche and enlist other parts of the government bureaucracy in support of its plan (Interviews with MITI officials, October 1995).

NTT

The quasi-private Nippon Telegraph and Telephone is active in the NII debate in Japan, and its views are taken very seriously for two reasons. First, even if it should lose its national monopoly on local service, NTT will be the central player in the implementation of a Japanese NII. Second, NTT has a large telecom R&D budget: for fiscal 1993, this amounted to ¥288 billion as compared to ¥35 billion for MPT (MPT data). NTT's R&D and procurement have historically played major roles in the competitiveness of Japanese industry, not only in telecommunications, but also in computers and semiconductors (Anchordoguy 1989, pp. 39–42, 138–140).

Continuing such research is a major part of NTT's own vision, which would include digital packet-switching, high-speed transmission, low-priced optics, image encoding and voice/character recognition and translation technologies (NTT 1994).

The NTT plan outlines the various services the firm intends to offer, but at the same time advocates government assistance as essential for the development of the information infrastructure. As with the other reports, it lists software and content as areas where Japan lags the United States, using comparisons between the two countries such as the number of online databases and even dubious comparisons such as the number of universities offering degrees in TV/motion picture production.

The Reality: NII in the Japanese Context

Government vs. Private Roles

Despite the perceived importance of such networks, the up-front costs are such that few consumer-oriented system will be self-supporting in the foreseeable future. As Egan (1991) explains:

Broadband telecommunication poses a very difficult "chicken and egg" problem for society…First there are the "high-tech" supply-side economists, who claim that we should immediately adopt and deploy new digital fiber-optic and radio technologies, based on the assumption that consumers will find new applications for them. Then there are demand-side economists, who claim that until there is a demand driver, we should not spend money on new technology for fear that we may create an expensive solution for which there is no corresponding problem (p. ix).

But under Egan's bifurcation, few examples of pure demand-side approaches can be found among early adopters of NII technology:

the current approach in many technologically advanced nations (including Japan, Singapore and the United States) is supply-side. For our purposes, a more useful distinction may be drawn over the center of policy leadership, corresponding to Zysman's (1983) distinction between government (state) and business leadership of industrial development.

How large a government role is appropriate (or necessary) in developing an NII? As the "info highway" metaphor suggests, an NII fits the classical definition of a public good—something whose benefit is spread throughout society. This would imply a government-dominant model of encouraging telecommunications development. Dutton et al. (1987) note that an assumption that "telecommunications are a public utility rather than a private commodity" (p. 22) is common to "wired cities" plans dating back to the 1960s. To emphasize the importance of the public nature of telecommunications, U.S. Vice President Gore (1993) cited the Titanic disaster as an example where the profit-making nature of radio communications caused messages to go unreceived which could have prevented the collision or speeded up rescue operations.

On the other hand, every developed or developing nation has one or more telecommunications companies, with heavy investment in wiring, right-of-way, switching facilities and staff. These companies must either play a key role in a digital communications network or eventually go out of business, obviously an option few telecom executives are considering. Similarly, many countries have cable television companies delivering broadcast (one-to-many) video service that would also be supplanted by interactive (two-way) video carried on an NII.

Such communications service companies see both an opportunity and a threat in plans for an NII. Most are working hard to earn a role in the government's plans. At the same time, many companies are also working to preempt government leadership, by launching pilot projects to demonstrate that an NII can be built without state intervention.

One key issue is the risk (for either government or industry) in building a national system before the technology and its uses are well-defined. As a U.S. industry group noted, "it is impossible to predict accurately the future path of the market for technology" (Council on Competitiveness 1993b, p. iv).

Even government-led systems assume a role for private funding, since few governments have the billions of dollars required to wire geographically remote locations door-to-door. In these cases, government funding may be limited to seed projects, with regulatory powers used to direct private funding through incentives (increased rate of return) or coercion (mandated universal service). Of course, where the telecom or cable companies are completely or partially nationalized, the distinction between government and industry leadership becomes one of national budgeting and intra-governmental power struggles, as can be seen in Japan.

At this point, it seems that the Japanese government has decided to concentrate on the twin roles of regulator and promoter, while allowing the private sector to build the infrastructure and develop commercial products. This division of labor is not so different from that in the United States, although the form it takes is different. The Japanese ministries play a larger role as both regulator (MPT) and promoter (MPT, MITI and others), while the U.S. system is more diffuse, with important roles played by Congress, the bureaucracy, the courts, and state and local governments.

Supply-driven vs. Demand-driven

The consumer has been noticeably absent from the NII debate in Japan. The assumption seems to be "if we build it, they (the consumers) will come," and the talk is almost exclusively of the economic benefits accruing to the producers, the influence gained by Japanese ministries and so on, rather than of any demonstrable consumer demand. This is far from the standard view of the "marketing concept" which focuses on customer needs (for a comprehensive review, see Kohli and Jaworski 1990).

Of course, nominal consumer desires are postulated, with video-on-demand and long-distance medical imaging being the ubiquitous examples. But these are prototypical needs, placeholders used to advance the discussion of the technology until a real reason can be found. Market tests—both in the 1980s and more recently—have been failures (Kageki 1994), but plans are proceeding ahead anyway, despite a notable lack of consumer enthusiasm (Sato 1994).

This problem is not unique to the Japanese debate. In the United States, Iacono and Kling (1995) argue that "technological utopianism" has been used to sell the NII concept, and Kling adds that the same Information Infrastructure Task Force reports closely studied by the Japanese were seriously flawed:

They were superficial in particular points, particularly in failing to examine why some of these experiments had not expanded and why some of them were not widely adopted. It was simply assumed that new information technologies would be the catalyst for expansion (Interview, May 24, 1995).[16]

Instead of consumer uses, King and Kraemer (1995) predict near-term market demand will center on businesses even though public rhetoric has centered on servicing individual consumers. Moreover, they argue that firms will be merely taking away each others markets rather than creating new markets.

Such an approach is symptomatic of technology-driven rather than market-driven thinking. The sharing of chest X-rays with specialists 200 kilometers away could be done by extending existing high-speed trunk lines to a few hundred hospitals, without the expense of building the information superhighway to the front door of more than 60 million households and firms.[17] And postulating an interest in video-on-demand ignores the ready availability of an established, much lower-tech alternative: the corner video store. (The presumed advantages of video-on-demand over the corner video store include availability but not price: forecasts all assume consumers will pay significantly more for the marginal convenience.) Such an absence of market-driven thinking does not bode well for the huge unanswered question of the NII: the cost of wiring each of those 60 million sites by the target date of 2010.

Beyond the technological impacts, a few Japanese have also considered the potential social impact of an NII. Kumon, the executive director of the Tokyo-based Center for Global Communications, predicted that in addition to spawning a "third industrial revolution" (a phrase he attributes to George Gilder), the developing information infrastructure will also spawn a social revolution, creating a new class of network-aware citizens, or "netizens":[18]

Just as during the 17th, 18th, and 19th centuries bourgeois citizens wanted to take part in their societies, [netizens] will demand something different from mass democracy in the 20th century. They will demand a freedom of informational activities—just as the original bourgeoisie demanded freedom of business activities as against the chartered monopolies of their time. . . .

The netizens want to have much greater freedom in terms of sending out information and having access to information. . . . Today, broadcasting is monopolized, chartered to a chosen few of society. Netizens are demanding that anyone should have access (Interview, August 30, 1994).

Meanwhile, Sawa (1994) of Kyoto University argues that "the multimedia-oriented information society will succeed only when individualism is respected" and predicted failure for MPT plans unless education and other social reforms are made.

While precursors to today's NII have been discussed since *jôhô-ka* came into fashion in the early 1970s, such social revolutions do not appear to be among the stated goals of big business and the bureaucracy, which have been leading the NII debate. And few participating in the NII debate (including Kumon) expect the outcome of NII will be the transformation of Japan into a "consumer economy," as is so often postulated by American economists.

Bureaucratic Rivalry

Given the central role of the Japanese bureaucracy in the nation's economic miracle over the past 50 years, it is not surprising that business and the media eagerly await each new glimpse into the plans of the unelected officialdom. But despite its spectacular successes with Japan's auto and electronics industries, and efforts to assert leadership (see MITI 1994), MITI seems consigned to play a consultative—if not subordinate—role in developing Japan's digital communications industries.

MITI's problem is, in fact, summed up by two words, "digital" and "communications." Regulation of industries in digital technology (i.e., computers) is under MITI's authority—except when they involve communications, which are governed by MPT. As Murakami put it "In the past, industrial policy was masterminded by MITI. Now you have to think about the Ministry of Post and Telecommunications" (Interview, August 29, 1994). MITI's emphasis on developing "multimedia software" (software being a traditional MITI purview) is one way to assure a continuing role in the debate.

In addition to MITI and MPT, other ministries and agencies have offered their "visions" of an information society, each competing for support from public and private opinion leaders.[19] Similarly, various ministries have demonstration projects for the city of the future: MITI calls them "new media communities," whereas MPT sponsors "teletopias," and the Ministry of Agriculture has its own "greentopias".[20]

Various ministries also sponsor competing private or quasi-private nationwide fiber-optic communications networks. As noted earlier, MPT has mixed relations with the one-time government agency NTT. Among the three new common carriers (NCC's) that are NTT's long-distance competitors, MPT favors DDI (Daini Denden Inc., or "second phone company"), co-founded by a former NTT executive,[21] the Ministry of Construction favors Teleway, whose lines are buried alongside of the ministry's national highways, and the Ministry of Transportation has backed Japan Telecom, a spin-off of Japan Railways, which built its fiber-optic lines along JR tracks—much as Sprint used the track of the Southern Pacific Railroad in the United States Meanwhile, MITI favors various regional carriers tied to MITI-regulated electric power companies, such as Tokyo Electric Power (TEPCO) affiliate TTNet.[22] Even the Ministry of Health got into the picture with a three-year pilot project to lay fiber-optic cables through water pipes ("Optical-Fiber Study" 1995).

Such diffusion of interests has its price. As several authors (see for example Watanabe 1994; Yamanashi 1995) have noted, many Japanese feel that these turf wars jeopardize the nation's multimedia future. Nonetheless, the jockeying for influence—primarily the rivalry between MITI and MPT—permeates the NII debate. The recent clash between these two ministries has reopened the "VAN wars" of the early 1980s, in which they fought for jurisdiction over Value-Added-Networks that provide online information and digital communication services, the forerunner of today's content providers and commercial Internet service providers.

In 1981, MPT proposed tough regulations for the new VAN providers, which, Johnson (1989) argues, was successfully opposed by MITI on grounds that it regulated both computer-based communications and also international trade. In 1982, regulation of many small and medium-sized VANs was liberalized, but MPT's revised 1983 proposal sought to tightly regulate large service providers, banning foreign ownership of both telecommunications systems owners (such as long-distance carriers) and those VAN companies that provided international service. Aided by the *Keidanren*, Japan's most powerful business association, MPT won Diet approval in 1984 for digital telecom regulation—but with less control over foreign entrants—and the net result was a liberalization of the VANs to permit competition for NTT (Yamada 1992). However, several scholars (Johnson 1989; Vogel 1996) argue that it also led to a net increase in the regulatory power of MPT.

As in the earlier turf battle, MPT is again holding the high cards. In the final analysis, it is hard to see how a national information infrastructure that replaces analog voice circuits to each home with digital data circuits could be considered anything but a telecommunications, and thus MPT, affair. If it wins major control, MPT will guide both the nature of the network itself, as well as the specifications for the equipment to be manufactured for use in homes, offices and switching stations throughout the nation. For this reason, reports from MPT and its allies, such as the Telecommunications Council, offer the clearest glimpse into the future of Japan's NII.

Despite liberalization, MPT's continuing bias toward regulation will continue to impede the diffusion of network services. For example, as a legacy of the 1981–1984 VAN wars, MPT requires a Special Type II license for those VAN resellers who provide international service, but an easier Type II license for domestic-only VANs. This meant that, according to NTT figures, only about 70% of the Internet sites in Japan in May 1994 were licensed for international e-mail (Goto 1994); since one e-mail addressing system is used worldwide, the distinction is primarily a regulatory one rather than a technical one. A VAN provider can apply for a domestic license and provide international service (as happened in 1993), but that firm risks losing access to all circuits from an MPT-regulated carrier if MPT discovers the subterfuge. By contrast, no state or federal permits are required to provide worldwide e-mail services in the United States, and by mid-1993, service providers began to sprout up weekly.

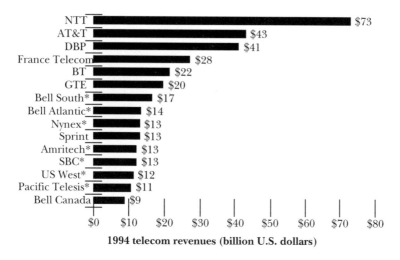

Figure 2 Telecommunications Carriers in Japan, the United States, Germany, France, the United Kingdom and Canada. Asterisks indicate Regional Bell Operating Companies ("Baby Bells"). Source: MPT (1995).

NTT's Central Role and Disputed Future

NTT is the world's largest telecommunications company (Figure 2) and is central to any Japanese plans for an NII: as noted earlier, all early NII plans assumed would NTT will be building the information infrastructure to the consumer's door. NTT was a government corporation until 1985, when it lost its monopoly on long-distance service, was officially spun off as a "private" company and MPT acquired responsibility for regulating it. Even after stock sales from 1986 to 1989, the Ministry of Finance still holds about two-thirds of the shares of NTT; with ongoing MPT influence, NTT has become at best a quasi-private corporation.

After this 1985 "privatization," the question of encouraging further competition for NTT—by breaking it up *à la* AT&T's 1982 spin-off of the "Baby Bells"—was postponed. Complete privatization has also been on hold since the collapse of the post-"bubble" stock market, because MOF has not wanted to sell shares in the face of declining prices. The NTT privatization law scheduled a first review of NTT's status for 1990, when MPT hoped it could win support for breakup; those hopes went unrealized (Vogel 1996). However,

Table 2 NTT's Share of Domestic Telecommunications Segments

Market	Share (%)	Revenues (¥ billion)
Telephone service	93.3	4,865
Leased circuits	82.8	574
Cellular phone†	60.7	873
Paging†	61.8	273

† Service by NTT DoCoMo affiliate.
All revenues for fiscal year ending March 31, 1994.
Source: MPT (1995).

with the prospect of an expanded information infrastructure, and the ongoing market power of NTT to crowd out smaller rivals, MPT and the NCCs renewed their push to break up NTT; the first salvo in the new battle came with an MPT (1995) report documenting NTT's market concentration (Table 2).

This battle over NTT's future has been waged in the court of public opinion, gaining strength in 1995. MPT argued that breaking up NTT would create a dynamic telecommunications market, with competition leading to lower prices and new services. NTT responded that competition is now international, and that it should be allowed to stay intact to compete in international markets. NTT also argued that a breakup would damage network coherence. Finally, NTT argued that its R&D labs are a national resource that should be preserved, noting decreased R&D spending after the 1982 breakup of AT&T.

NTT made two preemptive strikes against divestiture in late 1995. First, it announced that it would increase potential competition by allowing rivals in local service to connect to its switched network. It also announced that it would eliminate 50,000 of its 200,000 workers to reduce its operating costs, in return for keeping the company intact. At the time, the NTT president said, "We present this restructuring on the assumption that the breakup will not go forward" (Timmermans 1995). One industry analyst argued that NTT's pricing structure for interconnection made the offer for network access "a fake," intended to win political points rather than create true competition. Potential local competitors are mostly small carriers, cable TV companies and other utility companies that have their own fiber-optic networks within cities. None have the capital or technology to compete nationwide with NTT in local service.

NTT's plan to cut labor costs will be difficult to implement, given the political clout of NTT's *Zendentsu* union. The average salary at NTT is estimated at between 8 million and 10 million yen (US$80,000–100,000) per year, and NTT has a higher worker/customer ratio than its international competitors. *Zendentsu* has not agreed to job or salary cuts, and past efforts to spin off units such as NTT's Software Center were successfully thwarted by the union.[23]

At the same time, each side's true motivations have been questioned. NTT supporters have charged that MPT's break up efforts are mainly an attempt to create more regulatory jobs and *amakudari* retirement slots for MPT bureaucrats. Meanwhile, a former NTT executive conceded that the real purpose of NTT's 1995 announcements was to widen the debate from NTT breakup to a complete rewrite of telecommunications policy—giving NTT more opportunity to stall the effort in the Diet.

The battle lines were drawn (Table 3) and the Diet is, in fact, where the issue is likely to be resolved. The February 1996 report by MPT's advisory council delivered the predictable recommendation that NTT be split into three firms: a national long-distance company, and local telephone companies for eastern and western Japan (Choy 1996). The equally predictable opposition by NTT and its allies prevented MPT from adopting the plan (as it originally hoped) before fiscal 1995 ended in March 1996.

The near-term prospects for a breakup are slim, due to severe political instability. The weak three-party coalition led by prime minister Ryûtarô Hashimoto includes the Socialist Party, which opposed the breakup because *Zendentsu* is a major source of grassroots political organization and campaign funds. Meanwhile, all parties are focused on the next election, due by June 1997, which will realign electoral power between urban and rural constituencies and is also likely to lead to major changes in the relative strengths of these parties.

An election that produces a single-party Cabinet—controlled either by the LDP or the *Shinshintô* opposition party—could conceivably result in more decisive action taken on NTT's future. But

Table 3 Alliances Competing over NTT's Future

Pro-breakup: MPT, NCCs, cable television companies, other potential competitors

Anti-breakup: NTT, NTT's *den-den* equipment suppliers, *Zendentsu* union

Uncertain: Political leaders, MITI, Ministry of Finance

the LDP has many reasons to oppose a breakup, which Hashimoto personally opposed in 1990. One reason is the vocal public opposition coming from the NTT-aligned *den-den* electronics firms like NEC that have been major LDP contributors (Choy 1996). And as Keio University's Margarethe Estevez noted, "Even LDP members—unless they have a strong incentive in favoring the breakup—would rather not touch this issue. It's better not to make enemies" (Interview, May 14, 1996). NTT's future would certainly be dragged out if it means a rewrite of the Telecommunications Basic Law, which would require resolving the demarcation between long-distance service, domestic and international service, Type I and Type II service, and broadcast and cable TV.

A key factor in the eventual success of any breakup campaign will be the positions taken by MITI and MOF, both of which had strongly opposed breakup in 1990 but did not openly advocate those positions in the 1996 debate. For MOF, the key issue is maximizing the value of the government's shares in NTT. The value of each share has dropped by two-thirds since the company was first privatized in 1987 (Figure 3), although in mid-1996 the government's 65.5 percent share was still worth ¥8 trillion (about U.S. $80 billion).

In the past it was assumed that MOF would oppose a breakup on the assumption that it would decrease NTT's share prices. However, in 1995, the Nomura Research Institute produced a report stating that NTT would actually be worth more in parts than as a whole, as the smaller units could pursue profitable alliances to enter new markets and cut costs. Morgan Stanley came to a similar conclusion (Interview with Tadao Saito, October 23, 1995). This perspective has been encouraged by the increase in AT&T's share prices after its second, self-imposed breakup in 1996.

Absent strong leadership from the Diet or intervention by MOF, the question of NTT's future is likely to drag out. The short-term prospects are for increased competition through reduced telecommunications regulations and liberalization of the terms enjoyed by NTT's competitors.[24] Anticipating a delay in the NTT breakup, MPT proposed a series of liberalizations in January 1996, including deregulation of wireless communications rates and decreased regulation of Type II carriers (Choy 1996). It did not include one change sought by NTT, a deregulation of Type II (value-added) services. By opening its local lines to competitors, NTT hopes to compete in value-added services free of MPT's regulation—risking its monopoly profits in local service to pursue future growth markets in value-added services.

Both MPT and NTT expect that NTT will eventually compete directly with KDD.[25] Since the spin-off of both companies from MPT in 1953, both have been restricted to their respective domestic and international markets; even their corresponding competitors are restricted to these same markets. The MPT advisory report called for KDD to be allowed to enter the Japanese domestic market, while NTT has long sought the ability to expand into international markets—which MPT would only agree to (if ever) as the last step in any series of reforms.

Meanwhile, MPT's short-term reforms call for loosening restrictions on foreign shareholdings of NTT and KDD stock (currently less than two percent each, vs. 14 percent for DDI). This would allow the firms to join one of the global telecommunications alliances being formed around cross-investments between foreign partners.

But such marginal tinkerings do not address the inflexibility of the current regulatory regime, which maintains artificial market barriers between different categories of service and hamstrings NTT and its competitors alike. Nor are the near-term changes likely to markedly increase the efficiency of NTT or decrease the high cost of telecommunications. Both the continuation of such problems and the uncertainty surrounding NTT's future are major obstacles to the development of Japan's NII, either by NTT or its competitors.

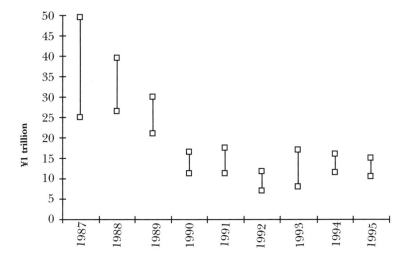

Figure 3 Total Market Capitalization of NTT. Source: *Japan Company Handbook.*

An Artificial Schedule without Financing

The minimum cost for extending fiber-optic lines to every business and individual neighborhood is put at ¥33 trillion; with associated switching systems, extending a line to every home and undergrounding the entire system, the total could be as high as ¥95 trillion (Telecommunications Council 1994c, p. 5). Most of this cost will have to be advanced ahead of actual revenues, because the development model is not based on pay-as-you-go market-driven development, and because of an ambitious deadline of 2010; not coincidentally, 2010 is five years ahead of the Clinton administration's target date for the United States

To prime the pump, MPT in January 1995 announced an FY 1995 ¥32.3 billion loan program for building fiber-optic networks, with the money offered to NTT, other Type I carriers, and cable TV operators. Of that, ¥30 billion will be loaned through the Japan Development Bank, and ¥2.3 billion will come from the MPT general account; an unspecified additional amount will be provided by local governments from existing regional development loan programs. Further financing proposal were expected from MPT, the Ministry of Finance and the Ministry of Home Affairs ("MPT Establishes" 1995).

MPT and MITI both launched spending sprees to develop NII projects. Each budgeted close to US$1 billion for in FY 1995 for a variety of projects, including video-on-demand, education, telemedicine and local government networks. MPT's projects focus more on communications infrastructure, while MITI concentrates on applications development. The two ministries are operating independently rather than cooperating, as each competes to encompass NII and multimedia under its jurisdiction. In addition, NTT is running its own testbed projects as it implements its own NII vision.

But where will the other trillions come from? One possibility is raising rates for existing NTT subscribers, another is government financing: both face potentially crippling political and practical obstacles. NTT customers already pay more for their services than consumers in many industrialized countries, so the impracticality of raising rates was clearly acknowledged by NTT President Masashi Kojima when he said "Financing is the real challenge. Here, the 'if we build it they will come' model may no longer work. Most customers are satisfied with conventional telephony; they don't want advanced services to be funded by their telephone bill" (Aizu 1994, p. 164).

Much of the pressure for financing stems from the artificial schedule. Given that the financing mechanism (and basic consumer demand) is completely unresolved, the dates announced for completion of the NII reflect more the pride, power ambitions, and national competitiveness of the sponsors than realistic projections of Japan's information future. As an example, at a June 1994 conference in Tokyo, the NTT representative anticipated completion of the national network by 2015, but the MPT representative used the deadline of 2010 contained in its report (Telecommunications Council 1994a); thus, subsequent NTT presentations used the 2010 date. While Japan's "catching up" mentality is second to none, until the details become more concrete, such announced dates must be considered goals rather than predictions.

Also unknown are the long-term impacts of the January 1995 Hanshin Earthquake, which killed 5,502, destroyed nearly 200,000 homes and caused an estimated ¥6 trillion in damage (Nikkei 1996a). In addition to rebuilding costs projected to cost national and local budgets more than ¥10 trillion, the painful vulnerability of Japan's urban areas to inevitable quakes has rekindled talk of decentralization, which would be greatly aided by an NII—as demonstrated by temporary telecommuting during Kobe's reconstruction. At the same time, the Internet showed a small fraction of its potential, with real-time eyewitness reports, photographs and casualty lists posted online at Kobe University and elsewhere for readers throughout Japan and the world.

Limited User Experience

Japan faces even more serious problems than the United States in gaining end-user acceptance for the NII: Japanese homes and businesses have relatively limited experience with public networks in particular (e.g., the Internet) and computers in general. In 1994, Japan ranked only 17th worldwide in per capita computer installations (Stern 1994), although it moved up in the rankings after annual PC sales increased by 130% between 1993 and 1995 (IDC 1996). Even though visionaries in Japanese industry, government and academia may be able to look beyond their immediate experience, such limited experience will make both accurate market research and demonstration projects far more difficult to implement.

According to MPT (Telecommunications Council 1994b, p. 31), in 1994 Japan had a third the rate of PC penetration and one-sixth the rate of Local Area Network connectivity of the United States; similar measures of Japan's perceived disadvantage were circulated by a MITI-affiliated non-governmental organization (See Table 4). A major reason for this was the long delay in developing usable computer representations of the complex Japanese language, in terms of both the input and display of more than 6,000 characters in common use (Choy 1989; Snellen 1991; Cottrell 1994).

Mechanical or electromechanical solutions made typewriters prohibitively expensive, so the lack of a solution prior to the refinement of personal word processors in the 1980s means that relatively few men over the age of 30 have the keyboard skills necessary to type Japanese for e-mail messages, while the huge popularity of faxes has made the adoption of e-mail more difficult (Negroponte 1994). Many Japanese are concerned because elec-

Table 4 Positions of the United States and Japan on PC and Telecommunications Measures

	United States	Japan
PCs shipped (1994)	18.6 million	3.0 million
PCs per 100 employees (1994)	55.1	14.7
Computer use by managers (1994)	64%	8%
Systems on Internet (Jan. 1995)	3.2 million	97 thousand
Charge for leased lines (1994))	¥0.4 million	¥2.7 million
CATV households (1993)	61.5%	4.7%

Source: JIPDEC (1995), p. 10.

tronic mail was rarely used ("Industry leaders" 1994), even in the most beneficial applications such as submitting documents for typesetting (Noguchi 1994); again, this shows signs of changing in the wake of the exploding popularity of PCs and the Internet. In the long run, the availability of graphical user interfaces and the development of voice and character recognition software are likely to minimize the difficulties imposed by the Japanese language.

While the United States may have an advantage in starting its infrastructure, early in this century Veblen (1915) pointed out that such advantages may not only be temporary, but that first-moving countries may actually be at a disadvantage by going first and letting others learn from their mistakes.[26] Though Veblen was talking about English railroads rather than U.S. information highways, Florida and Keeney (1990) specifically argue that the United States has a habit of breakthrough innovation while failing to commercialize those innovations, and that Japan in particular benefits from more consistent product development follow-through in a wide range of industries.

In the meantime, one approach is for Japanese firms to place significant marketing and R&D resources in a market which has a more experienced user base—i.e., the United States. Such an approach has already begun, with the three largest *den-den* firms selling ATM telecommunications switches to U.S. NII demonstration projects and telephone companies, and plans to establish ATM manufacturing plants in the United States because they "want to get closer to their large customers" (Valigra 1994).

Competing Paradigms: Interactive TV or the Internet?

The original Japanese visions of NII were based on the notion of a single unified network serving as a pipeline for providing information and entertainment in a mostly one-way direction. The technology of choice is broadband ISDN linking content providers to households, who will choose from a menu of content choices determined by the providers. This notion is now being challenged by the rapid expansion of the Internet in Japan. The Internet was slow to catch on in Japan, in part because of the high cost of telecommunications, MPT's licensing power over Internet access providers, and government efforts to enforce Open Systems Interconnection (OSI) standards while the world was embracing TCP/IP.

Another reason was the interest by many players in an Interactive TV model, an updated version of MITI's and MPT's earlier teletext experiments (West 1996). Kumon distinguishes between the Internet model of NII, which is user controlled and allows users to send as well as receive information, and the interactive TV model which is controlled by industry and allows limited interactivity (Interview, October 24, 1995). He argues that most major players in Japan's NII debate, including MPT and the NCCs had paid almost no attention to the Internet and have no understanding of its significance. They are more interested in how to weaken NTT rather than consider the more fundamental issues of what the nature of NII should be.

Kumon argues that NTT's July 1995 announcement of an Open Computer Network (now due to be rolled out in 1997) was generally ignored by the media, but is a significant decision, as it means that B-ISDN will be almost discarded and replaced by separate networks for telephony and computers.[27] The notion is that the computer network will be based on economically self-supporting demand, rather than universal service, meaning that businesses in particular will have access to the high-speed digital communications that they need without having to wait for, or subsidize, universal service.

Whatever the debate between Interactive TV and the Internet among those crafting telecommunications policy, among businesses and consumers the issue was quickly settled. In 1995 "Internet" replaced "multimedia" as the catchword in Japan. One reason was on the content side: businesses were immediately able to use the Internet to advertise and put information online, rather than waiting for new infrastructure to be developed. The large firms quickly staked out their turf in this new virtual market. The leading financial publisher, Nikkei, published a Japanese Internet yellow pages in book form (Nikkei 1996b), an online directory of Japanese companies, a weekly table of new URL listings and took a 10% defensive stake in a new online service joint venture with American Online and the Mitsui trading company. Apparently unconcerned about short-term revenues, the five national newspapers (including Nikkei's flagship *Nihon Keizai Shimbun)* and even local newspapers have been publishing free online editions since 1995 that put some of their U.S. counterparts to shame.

Both the availability and business promotion of Internet content, in turn, fueled both a consumer Internet mania and also an estimated 65% one-year increase in PC sales (IDC Japan 1996). Internet service providers continued to sprout up while providers such as Niftyserve (like their U.S. counterparts) added Internet services: total Internet users in Japan exceeded 2 million in 1995. While Internet e-mail addresses—other than the occasional Niftyserve address—were rare for employees of large Japanese firms in 1994, by March 1996 e-mail addresses had become commonplace as 40% of large firms had internal e-mail systems ("Over 40%" 1996).

But there are reasons to suspect that the diffusion of Internet computing in Japan is a kilometer wide and a centimeter deep. The use of URL's in ads parallels the long-standing use of English in advertising and packaging to give products a more "international" feel. The average Japanese may recognize individuals words, but extended usages are clearly intended more for effect than content.[28] This is best understood as part of the long-standing *kokusai-ka* (internationalization) fad that has left Japan still very inward-looking.[29]

So while Interactive TV proponents continued to plan for the future, the Internet seized the contemporary Japanese imagination and seems unlikely to let go. This paralleled the shift in the U.S.

during the same period, in which visions of fortunes to be made making "set-top boxes" for interactive TV slipped away as 1995's trials showed the same disappointing results as earlier teletext experiments. The idea that key applications would be primarily one-way services (such as video-on-demand) has been replaced by network services such as the Internet. The rapid development of technologies such as web browsers like Netscape and Sun's Java technology suggests the Internet model is winning in the United States. If Japan makes the wrong choice, it could invest billions in an NII model that actually reinforces its position as an information backwater rather than tapping into the global information revolution.

Conclusions

The development of Japan's plans for a future information infrastructure hearken back to its past patterns of successful postwar economic development, involving many of the same actors involved in the creation and growth of the domestic consumer electronics, computer and semiconductor industries.

Some of these patterns relate to early part of the postwar period,[30] with its emphasis on following and catching up to technologies developed in the United States and the use of government-funded R&D projects to develop new technologies. Others correspond to the economically and technologically mature Japan of the more recent past, such as the disputes between government ministries vying for policy leadership.

Unfortunately, some the problems of the past remain unsolved. Despite many successes, not all of the past government "visions" were on target: the 1994 vision of fiber to the home by the year 2010 is no more realistic than the many failed teletext demonstration projects of the 1980's. Despite multi-billion yen government support for improved software development dating back at least to 1976 (Okimoto 1989:80), well-founded concerns remain for the ability of Japanese firms to produce world-class software. Consortia of the major Japanese electronics firms (e.g. Pollack 1995) continue to be formed to address the problem, even as Japan's only net exporters of software remain the innovative small- and medium-sized game software makers that must compete with these large firms for scarce engineering talent (JEIDA 1995).

Also unaddressed are fundamental problems in telecommunications services. The "informatization" of Japan increased dramatically in 1995, when PC sales increased by two-thirds and businesses raced to provide content on the World Wide Web. But the most serious obstacle to Internet usage remains: the high cost of telecommunications faced by individuals, firms and Internet service providers. Just as consumers did not adopt PC's until prices dropped below ¥200,000 ($2,000) in response to increased competition, without drastically improved efficiency or competition for NTT, users will see little more than the pattern of modest price reductions over the past 20 years, stiffling usage indefinitely. Such telecommunications reform seems unlikely in the near term due to fierce domestic opposition and weak political leadership.

Meanwhile, as Callon (1996: 2) notes, the environment for the development of Japan's high-technology industries has changed in three ways. A "catch up" strategy following the global leader doesn't work for a nation that itself has become a technological leader, and skills required for leading rather than following are very different.[31] Second, government ministries face a relative loss of power compared to Japanese firms that have grown up to be rich and powerful global competitors. Finally, many of the industry promotion tools used when Japan was a developing country are no longer applicable now that Japan has the highest per capita income of the G-7 nations and maintains persistent surpluses with leading trading partners.

At the same time, currency appreciation and other pressures are moving the manufacturing base of Japanese firms to elsewhere in Asia, increasing the pressures to develop new competencies in software and multimedia content. Despite such pressures, the large Japanese electronics firms are focusing on near-term hardware opportunities, both in low-risk areas such as ATM switches and more speculative areas such as Internet-oriented PDAs (Ohta 1996; Funk 1996).

Even if Japan cannot fulfill its ambitions to be *the* world leader in digital telecommunications, the outcome of current NII strategies is likely to be completion of a high-quality digital infrastructure. If, as elsewhere, fiber optics are too expensive, then the network may be completed using a combination of accelerated copper wiring, coaxial cable, wireless or satellite technologies. But the end result is given—some form of digital communications infrastructure will exist in Japan—even if the technology, use, financing, ownership and schedule are not.

Failing to understand such use runs the risk that the network will be grossly underutilized: Japan's widely available but little-used ISDN infrastructure offers a cautionary precedent.[32] Within a definition of an NII as computers, conduit and content (Kahin, this volume), Japan's problem will be the pricing of the conduit, i.e., the telecommunications services that transmit content to the computers. Computers are not a problem: Japanese firms have proven themselves more than capable of producing affordable, high-quality electronics hardware, and the recent surge in domestic PC shipments suggest that their PC successes may soon match earlier ones in consumer electronics, components and large computers. The country can certainly afford to widely adopt such PC's, which can then be used to access the wide range of content (both domestic and imported) available in the Japanese media. But as long as the telecommunications sector remains a tightly regulated near-monopoly, telecommunications services will remain expensive: this increases the cost and decreases the amount of content available to Japanese consumers, while limiting the target audience available to fledgling domestic content and software producers.

Thus Japan is *en route* to building an information highway without really understanding where that highway leads to in the end. Despite three decades of discussing a shift to an information society, many of the accompanying social and economic changes remain unexamined and unimplemented. Some changes have begun with the end of the bubble economy, but in predicting Japan's information future, it would be a mistake to ignore the tremendous structural inertia that continues the policies and attitudes of the past.

Notes

1. In English, the term "information superhighway" has been most popular, as used by Gore (1991), but is often shortened to "info highway;" its equivalent in Japanese (*jôhô haiue*) has also been used. The term "national information

infrastructure" seems to have first been used in Singapore, as in (NCB 1992); the Japanese equivalent is *jôhô infura*, which is now preferred, at least in policymaking circles. Other variants on the NII theme include "Asian information infrastructure," "global information infrastructure" (GII), etc.

2. As a leading Japanese political reformer wrote: "Japan raised itself from the ashes of war to become an economic superpower boasting one of the world's highest incomes. Nonetheless, the people living in this supposed economic giant do not feel as though they are living rich lives." (Ozawa 1994: 153).

3. I will not deal here with the issue of the relative power of political and bureaucratic officials, which is the most controversial issue in any discussion of Japanese policy.

4. It is beyond the scope of this chapter to summarize Japan's postwar industrial policy and the central role played by government ministries, even if limited to just high technology industries. The standard discussion of the role of MITI is given by Johnson (1982), while the interpretation of Okimoto (1989) emphasizes the role of private firms; Johnson, et al., (1989) offers views of Japan's developmental policies in several industries. The best account of the incubation of Japan's mainframe computer industry is given by Anchordoguy (1989), while it, along with Fransman (1990) and Flamm (1987, pp. 125-153), outline Japan's computer industrial policy. Other relevant discussions would include Japanese incubation of the semi-conductor industry (Anchordoguy 1989, pp. 138-147; Mason 1992, pp. 174-187; and Okimoto *et al.* 1984, pp. 95-115). See Callon (1995), however, for a skeptical view of more recent technology policy efforts.

5. Although the official English title is "Ministry of Posts and Telecommunications", the ministry is still known in Japanese by its original title, *yûseishô*, which means "Government Postal Ministry."

6. The term *den den* comes from NTT's nickname. Nippon Telegraph and Telephone is a translation of *nippon denshin denwa*, which was abbreviated *den den kosha* during the period (1953-1985) NTT was a government corporation.

7. Ito (1991), referring to Umesao (1963), Hayashi (1969).

8. This is consistent with Calder's conception of Japan's postwar economic policy as that of a "Reactive State": see (Calder 1988). For a more detailed discussion of catch-up rhetoric in Japan's NII plans and links to Japan's postwar technological development, see West (1996).

9. It should be noted that construction bonds do not count against the national government's requirement to balance the budget, i.e., they can be used to pay for deficit spending (Lincoln 1988, p. 74), thus overcoming one potential objection from the powerful Ministry of Finance.

10. The view that Japanese are not innovative is not universally shared, even among Americans. The work of two Hitotsubashi University professors (Nonaka and Takeuchi 1995) became a successful business book in the U.S. by purporting to offer the secrets of Japanese innovation.

11. Of course, if enhanced copper wiring technologies such as ADSL (Asynchronous Digital Subscriber Line) are successful, this would solve the problems faced by both Japan and the U.S. regarding increased bandwidth at a reasonable cost. It would also obviate the need for Japan to build fiber-to-the-home and also its disadvantage due to low cable penetration.

12. This includes DOS-Windows (Microsoft), Macintosh (Apple), UNIX (various versions from IBM, Hewlett-Packard, Sun and DEC), Netware (Novell) and IBM's mainframe operating system.

13. For more detailed analysis of the troubles of the Japanese software industry, see Cottrell (1994), Baba, et al. (1995), Nakahara (1993), and Dedrick and Kraemer (1995).

14. The report was printed in both Japanese and English, as well as in a widely-distributed ten-page summary. The rapid availability of the English summary contributed to its heavy use outside Japan, as did its publication (in both languages) on the World Wide Web once MPT established a web site later in 1994.

15. The net effect of such right-of-way policies would assist the development of rivals to NTT's network, since NTT already has a national right-of-way network.

16. West (1996) argues that such utopianism could also be seen in plans for picturephones, personal digital assistants, wired cities and telecommuting.

17. The Telecommunications Council Report (1994c: 27) projects 54 million households and 7 businesses in the year 2010.

18. The "netizen" term has already been expropriated in the United States by *Wired* magazine for its series on the 1996 campaign.

19. For a generalized typology of bureaucratic rivalry in the Japanese government, see Campbell (1984).

20. So, for example, the MPT vision makes a priority of wiring "teletopia cities" by 2000, but no mention is made of MITI's "new media communities" (Telecommunications Council 1994a, p. 49).

21. Unlike Teleway and Japan Telecom, DDI lacked a development partner to provide a ready-made right-of-way for fiber-optic cables, so DDI is more dependent than NTT and the other NCC's on microwave relay transmissions—which proved to be an advantage in the January 1995 Hanshin earthquake (Kageki 1995).

22. In May 1996, three of these companies announced plans to link their regional networks to form, in effect, a fourth NCC rival to NTT's long-distance service, although the initial emphasis would be on providing leased-lines to business customers.

23. Despite such opposition, NTT Data and NTT DoCoMo were successfully spun off.

24. For a discussion of the contradictions between deregulation and liberalization, see Vogel (1996).

25. *Kokusai Denshin Denwa,* or International Telegraph and Telephone.

26. Golder and Tellis (1993) make the same point about "first-mover" companies that pioneer new types of products.

27. NTT's decision to offer OCN is probably influenced by the fact that its existing narrow-band ISDN network is underused and is a big money loser. But the decision was not without its controversy, as something akin to a religious war was waged within NTT's ranks between rival camps favoring the interactive TV and Internet models (Interview with Izumi Aizu, Glocom, October 23, 1995).

28. Few Japanese know enough English to read the the 35-word quality explanation on the best-selling can of beer; other English usages strike native speakers as bizarre, such as the cream-substitute powder named "Creap".

29. To make the link even more explicit, in May 1996 the Ministry of Foreign Affairs offered subway posters promoting its home pages, which provided Japanese citizens with information about other countries in the "World Jump" section.

30. The dividing point could be taken as the end of the "era of high-speed growth" (1973 when Japan faced its initial "oil shock"), although the major turning point in U.S.-Japan relations marked by the so-called "Nixon shocks" (1973) might also be used.

31. So after trailing the United States and Europe in first-generation cellular wireless telecommunications, MPT and Japanese producers sought to gain an advantage in export markets by rushing the completion of the lower-cost next-generation technology, called PHS (personal handyphone system) in Japan. Some early indications (e.g., Takezaki 1996) suggest these efforts were premature, although Funk (1996) argues the cost advantages of PHS will enable it to gain market share against cellular once coverage is extended to a larger area.

32. The superhighway metaphor is useful here. Some countries have built sparkling new expressways to relieve traffic congestion on established highways, then charged high tolls to drive on the new highways. As a result, the new highways are relatively untravelled with hardly a motel or restaurant to be seen.

References

Aizu, Izumi. 1994. Not Problems, Opportunities. *Wired* (December), pp. 163–165, 209–212.

Anchordoguy, Marie. 1989. *Computers Inc.: Japan's challenge to IBM.* Cambridge, MA: Harvard University Press.

Anderson, Stephen J. 1995. From Crisis to Information Society in Japan. Paper at the Japan Studies Association of Canada conference, University of Victoria.

Aruga, Teiichi. 1994. Japan's Current Status: The Formation of a Next-Generation Social System. Paper at the symposium on The Future of Japan's National Information Infrastructure, Stanford University.

Baba, Yasunori; Takai, Shinji; Mizuta, Yuji. 1995. The Japanese Software Industry: The "Hub Structure" Approach. *Research Policy* (May), pp. 473–486.

Calder, Kent. 1988. Japanese Foreign Economic Policy Formation: Explaining the Reactive State. *World Politics* (July), pp. 517–541.

Callon, Scott. 1995. *Divided Sun : MITI and the breakdown of Japanese high-tech industrial policy, 1975–1993.* Stanford, CA : Stanford University Press.

Campbell, John Creighton. 1984. Policy Conflict and Its Resolution within the Governmental System. In Ellis Krauss, Thomas Rohlen, Patricia Steinhoff, (Eds.), *Conflict in Japan* (Honolulu: University of Hawaii Press).

Choy, Jon. 1989. The Changing U.S.-Japan Microcomputer Market. *JEI Report* (July 28), 29A: 1–11.

Choy, Jon. 1996. NTT May Avoid Breakup But Not Stiffer Competition, *JEI Report*, 8B, March 1.

Cottrell, Tom. 1994. Fragmented standards and the development of Japan's microcomputer software industry. *Research Policy* (March), pp. 143–174.

Council on Competitiveness. 1993a. *Vision for a 21st Century Information Infrastructure.* Washington, DC: Council on Competitiveness. May.

Council on Competitiveness. 1993b. *Competition Policy: Unlocking the National Information Infrastructure.* Washington, DC: Council on Competitiveness. December.

Dataquest. 1996. Worldwide Semiconductor Market Grew 40% in 1995 (press release), San Jose, CA: Dataquest.

Dedrick, Jason and Kenneth L. Kraemer. 1995. Behind the Curve: Japan's PC Industry. *Global Business* (December). In Japanese.

Dodwell. 1988. *The Structure of the Japanese Electronics Industry.* Tokyo: Dodwell Marketing Consultants.

Dutton, William H., Jay G. Blumler and Kenneth L. Kraemer. 1987. Continuity and Change in the Conception of the Wired City. In Dutton, Blumler and Kraemer (Eds.), *Wired Cities: Shaping the Future of Communications* (Boston: G.K. Hall).

Egan, Bruce L. 1991. *Information Superhighways: The Economics of Advanced public Communication Networks.* Boston: Artech House.

Flamm, Kenneth. 1987. *Targeting the Computer: Government Support and International Competition.* Washington, DC: Brookings Institution.

Florida, Richard and Martin Kenney. 1990. *The Breakthrough Illusion: Corporate America's Failure to Move from Innovation to Mass Production.* New York: Basic Books.

Fransman, Martin. 1990. *The Market and Beyond: Cooperation and Competition in Information Technology Development in the Japanese System.* Cambridge: Cambridge University Press.

Fruin, W. Mark. 1992. *The Japanese Enterprise System: Competitive Strategies and Cooperative Structures.* New York: Oxford University Press.

Fukunga, Hiroshi. 1995. Policy Puppet Show: How Councils of Inquiry "Debate" Key Issues. *Tokyo Business Today* (October), pp. 18–21.

Fukushima, Glen. 1995. Multimedia Wars? *Tokyo Business Today* (January), p. 52.

Funk, Jeffrey. 1996. Japan's Personal HandyPhone System (PHS) Achieves a Dramatic Turnaround. Tokyo: Asian Technology Information Program, Report 96.043.

Gerlach, Michael. 1992. *Alliance Capitalism: The Social Organization of Japanese Business.* Berkeley: University of California Press.

Golder, Peter N. and Gerard J. Tellis. 1993. Pioneer Advantage: Marketing Logic or Marketing Legend? *Journal of Marketing Research,* 30, 2 (May), pp. 158–170.

Gore, Albert, Jr. 1991. Information superhighways: The next information revolution. *Futurist,* Vol. 25, No. 1, pp. 21–23.

Gore, Albert, Jr. 1993. Remarks at the National Press Club, December 21.

Goto Shigeki. 1994. The Future of Japan's National Information Infrastructure. Paper at The Future of Japan's National Information Infrastructure Symposium, Stanford University, U.S.-Japan Technology Management Center.

Hayashi, Yujiro. 1969. *Jôhôka shakai: Hado na shakai kara sofuto na shakai e* [*Informatizing society: From a hard society to a soft society*]. Tokyo: Kodansha.

Hiromatsu, Takeshi and Gosei Ohira. 1991. *Information Technology and Japanese Economy: An Empirical Analysis on the Size of Information Economy.* Tokyo: University of Tokyo, Komaba Department of Social and International Relations, Working Paper No. 19.

Iacono, Suzanne and Rob Kling. 1995. Computerization Movements and Tales of Technological Utopianism. In Rob Kling (Ed.), *Computerization and Controversy: Value Conflicts and Social Choices* (New York: Academic Press).

IDC Japan. 1996. IDC Japan Forecasts Japanese Market to Surpass 10 Million Units by 1997. Tokyo: IDC Japan Ltd., February 6.

Industry Leaders Getting E-mail Message. 1994. *Nikkei Weekly* (September 26), p. 13.

Ito, Youichi. 1991. Birth of Jôhô Shakai and Jôhôka Concepts in Japan and Their Diffusion Outside Japan. *Keio Communication Review,* 13: 3–12.

JEIDA. 1995. *Sofutouea Yushutsunyû Tôkei Chôsa 1994 nen Jisseki.* Tokyo: Japan Electronic Industries Development Association.

JIPDEC. 1995. *Informatization White Paper.* Tokyo: Japan Information Processing Development Center.

Johnson, Chalmers, Laura D'Andrea Tyson and John Zysman (Eds.). 1989. *Politics and Productivity: The Real Story of Why Japan Works.* Cambridge, MA: Ballinger.

Johnson, Chalmers. 1982. *MITI and the Japanese Miracle.* Stanford: Stanford University Press.

Johnson, Chalmers. 1989. MITI, MPT and the Telecom Wars. In Chalmers Johnson, Laura D'Andrea Tyson and John Zysman (Eds.), *Politics and Productivity: the Real Story of Why Japan Work*. (Cambridge, MA: Ballinger).

Johnson, Chalmers. 1974. The Reemployment of Retired Government Bureaucrats in Japanese Big Business, *Asian Survey*, 14, 11, reprinted in Chalmers Johnson, *Japan: Who Governs?* (New York: Norton, 1995).

Kageki, Norri. 1994. Market Test Shows Multimedia Not Ready for Prime Time. *Nikkei Weekly* (October 3), pp. 1, 8.

Kageki, Norri. 1995a. Telephone Lifelines Bounce Back. *Nikkei Weekly* (January 23), p. 8.

Kikkawa, Takeo. 1995. *Kigyo Shudan:* The Formation and Functions of Enterprise Groups, *Business History*, 37 (2): 44–53.

King, John L. and Kenneth L. Kraemer. 1995. Information Infrastructure, National Policy, and Global Competitiveness. *Informatization Infrastructure and Policy*, 4, pp. 5–28.

Kohli, Ajay and Bernard Jaworski. 1990. Market Orientation: The Construct, Research Propositions, and Managerial Implications. *Journal of Marketing* 54 (April), pp. 1–18.

Kumon, Shumpei. 1994. The GII Initiative: Its Significance and the Challenges for Japan. Paper at the Symposium on Multimedia Communications and the High-Speed, Intelligent, Distributed, Cooperative Computing Environment of the Year 2010, Tokyo, September 13.

Latzer, Michael. 1995. Japanese Inforrmation Infrastructure Initiatives: A Politico-economic Approach. *Telecommunications Policy*, 19, 17 (Oct.), pp. 515–529.

Lincoln, Edward J. 1988. *Japan Facing Economic Maturity*. Washington, DC: Brookings.

Mason, Mark. 1992. *American Multinationals and Japan: The Political Economy of Japanese Capital Controls, 1899–1980*. Cambridge, MA: Harvard University Press.

Masuda, Yoneji. 1980. *The Information Society as Post-Industrial Society*. Tokyo: Institute for the Information Society.

MCA. 1994. *Denshi seifu no jitsugen wo mokushi shite* [Aiming at the implementation of electronic government]. Tokyo: Management Coordination Agency, Office of the Prime Minister, October.

MITI. 1994. *Program for Advanced Information Infrastructure*. Summary Report. Tokyo: Ministry of International Trade and Industry, May.

Miyashita, Kenichi and David Russell. 1994. *Keiretsu: Inside the Hidden Japanese Conglomerates*. New York: McGraw-Hill.

Morris-Suzuki, Tessa. 1988. *Beyond Computopia: Information, Automation and Democracy in Japan*. London: Kegan Paul.

MPT. 1995. Review of the Future Status of NTT. Tokyo: Ministry of Posts and Telecommunications.

MPT Establishes Special Loans for the Development of the Subscriber Optical Fiber Network. 1995. *MPT News* (January 23). Tokyo: Ministry of Posts and Telecommunications.

Murakami, Teruyasu. 1993. Proposal for Japan: A New Deal in Information Technology Infrastructure. *NRI Quarterl,* (Autumn), pp. 68–87.

Nakahara, Tetsushi. 1993. The Industrial Organization and Information Structure of the Software Industry: A U.S.-Japan Comparison. Stanford University, Center for Economic Policy Research, policy paper no. 346.

NCB. 1992. *A Vision of Intelligent Island: the IT2000 Report.* Singapore: National Computer Board.

Negroponte, Nicholas. 1994. The Fax of Life: Playing a Bit Part. *Wired* (April).

Nikkei. 1996a. *Japan Economic Almanac 1996.* Tokyo: Nihon Keizai Shimbun.

Nikkei. 1996b. *Nikkei Intaanetto Ierôpeiji 96.* Tokyo: Nihon Keizai Shimbun.

Noguchi, Yukio. 1994. Multimedia? We Don't Even Have E-mail Yet! *Tokyo Business Today* (November), p. 9.

Nonaka, Ikujiro and Hirotaka Takeuchi. 1995. *The Knowledge-Creating Company: How Japanese Companies Create the Dynamics of Innovation.* New York: Oxford University Press.

NTIA. 1994. U.S. Goals and Objectives for the G7 GII Conference. Washington, DC: National Telecommunications and Information Administration, September 14.

NTT. 1994. How Is Information Communications Changing? NTT's Basic Concept for the Coming Multimedia Age. Conference presentation, Japan-U.S. Information Infrastructure Symposium, Tokyo, June 13.

Ohta, Tamio. 1996. Interview: Tosaka Kaoru, NEC Torishimariyaku Shihainin, *Nikkei Pasokon* (January 19), pp. 148–151.

Okimoto, Daniel. 1989. *Between MITI and the Market: Japanese Industrial Policy for High Technology.* Stanford, CA: Stanford University Press.

Okimoto, Daniel, Takuo Sugano, and Franklin B. Weinstein (Eds.). 1984. *Competitive Edge: The Semiconductor Industry in the U.S. and Japan.* Stanford, CA: Stanford University Press.

Optical-Fiber Study Looks at Water Pipes. 1995. *Nikkei Weekly* (February 27), p. 2.

Over 40% of Japanese Firms Endorse Homepages: Nikkei. 1996. *Nikkei Weekly* (April 11).

Ozawa, Ichirô. 1994. *Blueprint for a New Japan,* translated by Louisa Rubinfien. Tokyo: Kodansha.

Pollack, Andrew. 1995. Japan Pushing Information Software, *New York Times* (January 16), p. C3.

President's Commission on Industrial Competitiveness. 1985. *Global Competition: The New Reality* (Vols. I–II). Washington, DC: U.S. Government Printing Office.

Samuels, Richard. 1994. *"Rich Nation, Strong Army": National Security and the Technological Transformation of Japan*. Ithaca, NY: Cornell University Press.

Sato, Kyoko. 1994. Multimedia Future Still a Pipe Dream to Many. *Japan Times Weekly International Edition* (August 22–28), p.13.

Sawa, Takamitsu. 1994. Japan May Nix Multimedia. *Japan Times* (August 29), p. 18.

Seki, Hideo. 1995. Piecemeal Nature Putting Potholes into U.S. Info Highway. *Nikkei Weekly* (January 2), p. 7.

Siwek, Stephen and Kent Mikkelsen. 1996. A 20th Century Business Success Story: U.S. Software Industry Trends, 1987–1994. Washington D.C.: Business Software Alliance.

Snellen, Ignace Th.M. 1991. Informatization in Japanese Public Administration. *Informatization and the Public Sector*, pp. 247–267.

Stern, John. 1994. Government and Regulatory Perspectives. Paper at The Future of Japan's National Information Infrastructure Symposium, Stanford University, U.S.-Japan Technology Management Center.

Takezaki, Noriko. 1996. Japan's Personal Handyphone System: Down for the Count? *Computing Japan* (April): 24–27.

Telecommunications Council. 1994a. *21 seiki no chiteki shakai e no kaikaku ni mukete* [*Reforms toward the intellectual society of the 21st century*]. Tokyo: Ministry of Posts and Telecommunications, May.

Telecommunications Council. 1994b. *Reforms toward the Intellectually Creative Society of the 21st Century*. Tokyo: Ministry of Posts and Telecommunications, May.

Telecommunications Council. 1994c. *Reforms toward the Intellectually Creative Society of the 21st Century*. English translation of Report Summary. Tokyo: Ministry of Posts and Telecommunications, May.

Timmermans, Jeffrey. 1995. NTT plans to reduce its staff in move to thwart Japan's push for breakup. *Wall Street Journal* (November 9), p. A17.

Toyo Keizai. 1995. *Japan Company Handbook: First Section Firms*. Winter 1995 ed. Tokyo: Toyo Keizai Shinposha.

Umesao Tadao. 1963. Jôhô sangyô ron [Theory of information industries]. *Hoso Asahi* (January).

USITC. 1995. Global Competitiveness of the U.S. Computer Software and Services Industries. Washington, DC: U.S. International Trade Commission (June).

Valigra, Lori. 1994. Helping to Pave U.S. Information Superhighway. *Wall Street Journal* (September 26), p. B8.

Veblen, Thorstein. 1915. *Imperial German and the Industrial Revolution*. New York: Macmillan.

Vogel, Steven. 1996. *Freer Markets, More Rules: The Paradoxical Politics of Regulatory Reform in the Advanced Industrial Countries*, Ithaca, NY: Cornell University Press.

Watanabe, Teresa. 1994. Tide Turns on Mighty Tokyo Elite. *Los Angeles Times* (December 25), pp. A1, A13.

West, Joel. 1995. Where's the On Ramp? Puzzling over Japan's Information Future. *Tokyo Business Today*, 63(8): 42–44.

West, Joel. 1996. Utopianism and National Competitiveness in Technology Rhetoric: The Case of Japan's Information Infrastructure. *The Information Society*, 12, 3.

Yamada, Takahiro with Michael Borrus. 1992. *Change and Continuity in Japan's Telecommunications Policy.* Berkeley: Berkeley Roundtable on the International Economy, Working Paper 57.

Yamakoshi, Atsushi. 1995. White-Collar Work Performance in Japan: Implications for Restructuring. *JEI Report,* No. 27A (July 21), pp. 1–9.

Yamanishi, Ken. 1995. Petty Infighting at MPT and MITI Put Japan in Slow Lane. *Tokyo Business Today* (February), p. 9.

Yamazaki, Taketoshi. 1994. Cable TV Madness. *Tokyo Business Today* (November), pp. 6–9.

Yano Keizai. 1995. *Nihon Maaketto Shea Jiten.* Tokyo: Yano Keizai Kenkyûsho.

Zysman, John. 1983. *Governments, Markets, and Growth.* Ithaca, NY: Cornell University Press.

Korea's National Information Infrastructure: Vision and Issues

Kuk-Hwan Jeong and John Leslie King

Introduction

Information technology (IT) use has been promoted in Korea during the past decade by both government and segments of the private sector through a national computerization project called the National Basic Information System (NBIS) project, which began in 1987.[1] This project produced successes, but also suffered from weaknesses including insufficient funding, a lack of strong industry capability, decreasing government support and failure to stimulate domestic demand. These weaknesses generated a widespread consensus on the need to reform the NBIS project, and a second stage of the project was begun in 1992. Nevertheless, problems remained, and inadequate funding led to shortfalls in the expected benefits. Further reconsideration created a demand for new policy actions. This occurred at about the time the United States and Japan were announcing plans for a national information infrastructure (NII). The result was an effort to build a Korean NII, which has become known as the Korean information infrastructure (KII).

The KII movement arose from an established desire to exploit information technology and a new fear that a failure to build an information infrastructure would hurt Korea's basic industries to the point that they might not be able to compete in the global marketplace, leaving the nation farther behind the developed countries. This concern extended to production industries such as computers, telecommunications, components and semiconductors—all of which might be left behind by the global production system, with a subsequent loss of export and import substitution opportunities. In addition, there was concern that the consumer service industries would not be able to gain quick access to the latest technologies and would become less competitive.

The KII resembles both the original and new NBIS projects. Potentially it could repeat many of the same mistakes, especially those which arise from following a centrally coordinated plan in a field where more decentralized strategies would make more sense.

This chapter presents the evolution of the KII initiative from its beginnings in the NBIS project to its current vision. In the process, we identify the similarities and differences and strengths and weaknesses of the various projects. The NII is seen as a part of national economic policy to provide the tools for competitiveness, and thus economic development, in a globalized economy. This view is predicated on the belief that competitiveness will arise from the ability of each entity in the economy to develop, acquire and adapt new and state-of-the-art information and communications technologies as tools that will be available via information networks.

We begin with a brief history of Korean policies for economic development over the past three decades. The centrally coordinated economic plans performed well since the early 1960s, and this tradition has been transplanted to NII initiatives. In reviewing these initiatives we focus on the visions and goals of each project, their accomplishments and their implications for policy issues emerging as part of the NII initiative. Next we review the current structure of the computer and communications producers and users that form the building blocks of Korea's NII, plus Korea's plan for the NII, which was initially described in the April 1994 document "National Information Superhighway" and has evolved into the vision of the KII. We then analyze the critical factors that are expected to lead to the successful implementation of KII programs. Finally we discuss the future development of the KII, arguing that this initiative should emphasize both demand and supply strategies that reinforce one another for maximum leverage and synergy.

The Economic Development Strategies and the NBIS

Economic Development Plan

The KII arose from both the efforts of the NBIS project and the response of national policy leaders to NII initiatives in the developed countries, particularly the United States and Japan. Korea, like other countries, is eager to achieve competitive advantage through the use of information technologies. The KII initiative is part of Korea's well-established economic policy that is characterized by government-driven five-year economic development plans. There have been several five-year plans since the early 1960s. Most were executed very successfully, producing economic prosperity. These plans can be described as industrial policies targeting specific economic sectors, based on private sector investment and production, with a decisive role for the government. Strategic industries were targeted by specific legislation, as illustrated by the Industrial Machinery Promotion Act (1967), the Shipbuilding Industry Promotion Act (1967), the Electronics Industry Promotion Act (1969) and the Steel Industry Promotion Act (1970).

The economic policy of the five-year plans traditionally focused on supporting large enterprises. As a result, small and medium-sized enterprises (SMEs) were relegated to a disadvantageous position throughout the 1960s and 1970s, which resulted in weaknesses in the overall Korean economic structure. The high-technology industries such as IT were particularly hard hit since changes in technology development and applications occur so rapidly that small companies have advantages over large companies in responding to market opportunities, interacting closely with customers, having timely access to technology and market information, and producing new products. The Korean government realized the importance of SMEs in the 1980s, and made strengthening them a key economic policy goal. The Small and Medium Industry Promotion Act was enacted in 1982 in order to establish a fund for promoting SMEs and to build an industrial complex for SMEs. In 1986, the Small and Medium Industry Startup Promotion Act was prepared to help entrepreneurs start SMEs through tax incentives and financial support. Nevertheless, SMEs remained weak in Korea, not because of inadequate legal and administrative provisions of these acts, but mainly because the government was unprepared to pay the short-run cost of a structural adjustment to the economy.

Korean economic policy in the late 1980s and early 1990s began to shift toward economic liberalization and promotion of technology-intensive industries. This shift was brought about in part by recognition of the domestic and international pressures facing the country. The economic strategy reflected in the seventh five-year economic plan (1992–1997) can be seen as a response to problems that had accumulated during the decades of tremendous growth. Increasing public demands for a higher standard of living have been joined by radical increases in international technology competition and demands for market liberalization by trade partners. The seventh five-year plan adopted three major strategies: strengthening the competitiveness of industry, enhancing equity and balanced development, and pursuing internationalization and liberalization. Industry, the Korean leadership realized, can no longer rely on low wages for competitive advantage. Thus the 1992–1997 plan calls for human resources development and the promotion of technological development and innovation to keep pace with the Information Age.

The National Basic Information System

Korea's seventh five-year plan specifically emphasizes the information industry as a key sector. The NBIS project was not inaugurated as a product of this policy shift, but it was transformed by the shift. The NBIS project was Korea's first national project focused on IT use and production. It was created in the early 1980s when the Korean government began to realize that IT and its applications would play crucial roles as new national infrastructure. The objective of national computerization was to use IT for economic growth. It was believed that in the coming Information Age countries would require IT to be competitive in world markets, and thus IT would enable Korea to become a developed nation by the year 2000. The information revolution was expected to have the same kind of impact that the industrial revolution had in the 19th century. Many believe that if Korea had been exposed to economic developments during the industrial revolution, it would now be at the same level of economic development as the leading industrial powers. The economic and political hardships that Korea experienced in the first three quarters of this century would have been avoided. Thus keeping up in the new information revolution is essential for Korea.

The NBIS project initially focused on public sector computerization, with the objectives of creating a smaller and more efficient government, improving the daily life of citizens, and laying the foundations for the development of IT industries by stimulating initial markets. This strategy was also expected to raise the private sector's interest in the application of IT to internal business operations, allowing industry to follow the achievement of government computerization. Five major networks were planned as part of the NBIS: the National Administrations Information System, the Financial Information System, the Education & Research Information System, the National Defense Information System, and the National Security Information System. For security reasons, the latter two are run separately by the military and intelligence agencies, respectively. Because of the secrecy surrounding these systems, we will only discuss the first three systems.

The National Administrations Information System involved the computerization of the internal operations of government agencies and supported service delivery to the public. It included subsystems for residents, vehicles, homes and property, employment, customs and clearance, and economic statistics. The first stage of the project was completed in 1991. The government invested about U.S.$200 million in these six subsystems, mainly to install computers in local and central government offices and to develop networks and relevant software. The software and data requirements were often substantial. For example, the resident system included databases of personal information on the entire population over the age of 18 that were networked through central government offices and 3,700 local administrative offices. The first stage of the project (1987–1991) mainly involved developing the separate systems, whereas the second stage (1992–1996) emphasized integrating systems to allow sharing of information among government agencies, and to support new management systems for health care, postal services, marine transportation, intellectual property rights, weather information, government procurement and fishing.

The Financial Information System began as a data communication network involving banks. Korea's largest banks had computer networks in place by the late 1970s, but the smaller banks lagged behind. The Financial Information System was created to include the whole banking system. The planning and implementation process for this system was coordinated by the Confederation of Financial Institutions and its representative, the Financial Clearing House. In the second stage of the NBIS, other financial businesses such as securities and insurance began to expand the application of network technologies in their newly developed business areas.

The Education and Research Information System plan originally called for providing schools with computers and using them for teaching and administration. Universities, libraries and research institutes were also to be networked. During the first stage, investment was concentrated on providing PCs to primary and middle schools, with little success in networking education and research organizations. During the second stage of the NBIS, the network was to be developed. But this proceeded slowly, mainly due to tight budgets at the relevant ministries and weak demand for research and library networks. The slow development of Korea's NBIS research and education network provides an interesting contrast with the U.S. situation, in which higher education institutions have led the development of electronic networks, including the National Research and Education Network, which many see as a cornerstone of the U.S. NII.

Evaluation of the NBIS

The NBIS plan was to have several five-year terms, each building on the one before, and explicitly aimed at promoting IT use in Korea. In some areas this approach has been successful. For example, in the first stage of the National Administrations Information System (1987–1991) minicomputers (TICOMs) and PCs were installed in various administrative offices, and networks and relevant databases were constructed for internal operations and the provision of services to the public. The project succeeded in laying the foundations for further development of applications, especially in local administrative offices that deliver services to the public. For example, it is now possible for people to get a certificate of residence issued at any local office across the country, instead of having to report to a designated place. Since this certificate is the most frequently requested identification document in Korea, the number of people benefiting from this service is substantial. The Passport Issuing System, which was designed to speed up passport handling, is also being implemented nationwide.

Nevertheless, the NBIS strategy was unsuccessful in some areas because it was basically a supply-oriented enterprise that did not account for demand.[2] The central government maintained leadership in the process from the initial planning stage through implementation. Often the IT applications the project provided faced strong resistance from users simply because the applications did not support the established customs and cultural elements of government work.

Problems also arose from changes in the government's mechanisms of financial support for innovation. At the beginning of the project, about U.S.$200 million was earmarked in advance for the National Administrations Information System. This allowed the rapid start-up of the innovation process by avoiding bureaucratic entanglements over funding. By the second stage of the NBIS, the people controlling the national budget complained of a lack of easily identifiable returns from the large first stage, and they began to deny spending approval.[3] Project leaders were forced to submit requests to the national budget system prior to spending. This not only slowed the implementation of the plan, but also discouraged the development plans of individual agencies.

Next Generation NBIS (NGNBIS)

Radical changes in the organizational and technical environments of IT application areas emphasized agency strategies, but these did not keep pace. The framework for providing services through computer networks was not easy to develop in a manner that allowed the projects to keep up with rapidly advancing technologies. A new framework had to be created by rearranging regulations, organizations and financing mechanisms. Recognition of this need was reflected in a new vision called "Next Generation NBIS" (NGNBIS), which was prepared by the National Computerization Agency (NCA), which had been established to support the planning and implementation of the NBIS project. The NGNBIS plan identified areas of government services as targets for the application of a mix of rapidly advancing technologies. It was not submitted to the Ministry of Information and Communications as an official plan, but as a research report to be used as a reference in discussing future IT applications in the private and public sectors.

The services to be developed as part of NGNBIS were expected to act as market leaders for information traffic running on the national networks, giving the NGNBIS a key role in bringing the Korean information infrastructure into existence. NGNBIS was seen as the point of transition between the faltering NBIS and the emerging concept of information infrastructure. Applications like distance learning and remote medical diagnosis services were defined as part of NGNBIS and implemented as pilot projects to demonstrate the applicability of advanced technologies in the context of information infrastructure. The NGNBIS represented a turning point in Korean IT-related development, serving both as the extension of the earlier NBIS project, and as a response to concerns arising from the international discussion of the information superhighway and information infrastructure.

Existing Infrastructure and the KII

This section provides an overview of the structure of Korea's computer, telecommunications, cable television and multimedia industries and markets, all of which are critical to the future development of the KII. This section also describes the vision, strategies, programs and schedules for implementation of the KII plan.

Existing Information Infrastructure[4]

Computers
Table 1 shows Korean production and export of computers between 1993 and 1995. Most Korean computer production has been concentrated in personal computers; in 1994, PCs accounted for more than 90 percent of computer production. The PC industry has benefited from the strategic support of the government since

Table 1 Korean Computer and PC Production

	1993		1994		1995	
	Prod.	Export	Prod.	Export	Prod.	Export
All Computers	966	381	1,295	288	1,623	270
PCs Only	929	378	1,181	280	1,420	226

Unit: million U.S. dollars.

Table 2 Size of Korea's Domestic PC Market*

Year	1991	1992	1993	1994
Quantity	614	665	773	1,200

* in terms of PCs sold (thousand sets).

the mid-1980s when the NBIS project was introduced. More recently, the growth rate of PC production has started to slow down and overall computer exports have decreased.

Table 2 shows the number of PCs sold in Korea between 1991 and 1994. As part of the NBIS, the government encouraged computer use in homes as well as offices, with a goal of 10 million PCs in domestic use by the year 2000.[5] The plan estimated a use of 1.445 million PCs by 1990 (NCA, 1994), but a 64 percent growth rate between 1993 and 1994 suggests that the goal for 2000 will be met several years earlier than targeted.[6]

Korea's technological capabilities for producing computers are still weak. The government's strategy for developing the PC industry focused on domestic production of comparatively low-technology components such as memory semiconductors and motherboards, while high-technology components such as microprocessors were imported. Minicomputer development followed the strategy of copying core technologies under contract with an American venture-capital partner (Tolerant). The result was the TICOM I computer for use in the government systems projects of the NBIS. The TICOM I was also sold on the commercial market, and a consortium of four major electronics companies was formed to cooperate with ETRI, a government laboratory, in an effort to update the TICOM series. The TICOM project made modest contributions to the development of Korean computer technology, paving the way for further research and development, but the use of TICOM minicomputers remained limited mainly to the public sector.[7]

Telecommunications
Telecommunications service providers can be divided into three groups: general service providers, specific service providers, and value-added service providers. The first two operate their businesses with their own networks, whereas the latter group uses leased lines for value-added network (VAN) services. There are two network providers in Korea, KT (Korea Telecom) and Dacom.[8] KT provides telecommunications services and constructs, operates and maintains public telecommunications facilities. As a public corporation controlled by the government,[9] KT maintained its monopoly in the basic voice market until the middle of 1991, when Dacom began service in the international telephone market. The market for domestic long distance telephone service became a duopoly of KT and Dacom in January 1996. Dacom was originally established in 1982 as a monopoly to construct and operate public data communications networks, especially for the NBIS project. Since the early 1990s, however, the market for data communications services has been opened in the process of the liberalization of VAN services, and Dacom has been allowed to join the voice market to compete with KT.

Cellular telephone services were a monopoly of KMT (Korea Mobile Telecommunications Co.) until a second carrier, Shinsegi Telecom Inc., entered the market in early 1996. Paging services are provided by KMT and a number of private companies, each of which holds a local monopoly in a geographically designated area. The number of value-added network providers has grown since the liberalization of the market in 1990, accelerated by technology development and the broadening of applications in Electronic Data Interchange (EDI), electronic mail, computer reservation systems, etc.

An ambitious national program of investment in the availability and quality of communications networks during the 1980s eliminated the large backlog of demand for telephone lines, significantly improving the availability of telephone networks in Korea. As shown in Table 3, however, in terms of the number of telephone

Table 3 Telephone Lines per 100 People (1993)

Korea	U.S.	Japan	Germany	U.K.	France
38	53	47	46	47	53

Table 4 Korean Subscribers of Mobile Communications

	1993	1994
Mobile Telephones	472	960

unit: thousand sets.

Table 5 Korea's Telecommunications Service* Markets

	1990	1991	1992	1993	Average Annual Growth Rate
Sales (billion won)	231	308	497	668	96%
Number of Providers	99	130	173	227	76%

* includes VAN, DB, on-line data processing, voice-mail services.

lines per 100, people as of 1993 Korea was still behind the advanced countries. Mobile communications capabilities were even further behind: about one unit per 100 people in 1993, in contrast with 4.4 for the United States and 1.5 for Japan. However, the number more than doubled in 1994 (see Table 4), and it is expected to grow more rapidly since a second provider of mobile service was scheduled to begin business in the first half of 1996.

Prior to the convergence of computers and communications technology, voice communication was the major telecommunications service available in Korea. NII initiatives are based on the assumptions that the broader information services market is potentially very large, and that physical networks combined with terminals to produce services on demand will produce huge growth in demand. Network information services in Korea began with the NBIS project. Growth was slow at first, but as Table 5 shows, between 1990 and 1993, sales grew by 96 percent per year and the number of service providers grew by 76 percent per year on average. Further growth is projected, and could be accelerated as the new applications of the KII become available.

Korea's information service industry has been restructured by regulatory reform with the goal of increasing competition in the market and facilitating the provision of services enabled by new technology. To further advance network switching and transmission capabilities and to keep pace with the coming multimedia communications, the Korean government launched the Broadband Integrated Services Digital Network (BISDN) project. This project, which runs from 1992 to 2015, will mainly be carried out by KT. It is based on the success of the TDX switch project during the 1980s, which made a significant contribution to the national goal of one telephone per household. The BISDN project has made major investments in ATM switching technology and fiber optics, key technologies for high-speed networks for multimedia communications. The effects thus far are invisible, but the investment will continue (*Electronics Daily*, September 25, 1995). Major electronics companies have already joined in developing key technologies for this component of the future information infrastructure, either through contracts with foreign counterparts or by cooperation with ETRI.

Multimedia
At the beginning of the 1990s, some of small and medium-sized Korean enterprises began importing foreign CD-ROM titles and drives. Since then, multimedia products and equipment have attracted the attention of major companies that believe multimedia will play a key role in the coming information society. New business opportunities in education and entertainment are particularly important. Table 6 shows Korean sales of various multimedia products in 1994. Growth has been substantial in this sector, with sales quadrupling from 1992 to 1993, and tripling from 86.2 billion won (U.S.$108 million) to 251.8 billion won (U.S.$315 million) by 1994. The number of CD-ROM titles produced in Korea in 1994 was estimated at 2.9 million, slightly more than five percent of the worldwide production of 53.9 million. Sales of CD-ROM titles for educational purposes have been strong in the Korean market, reflecting parents' great willingness to pay for educational technology.

Table 6 The Korean Multimedia Industry

Product	1994 Sales (billion won)
Multimedia PC	94.5
CD-ROM drive	37.5
CD-ROM title	38.0
Sound card	51.4
Image card	25.0
Tools	5.4
Total	251.8

Cable television

Cable television is expected to play a major role in providing the network services envisioned in the KII, especially home shopping, news and entertainment programs. Cable TV is a precursor to publicly available, high-speed broadband networks. The cable industry was almost nonexistent in Korea until the early 1990s. KT launched a pilot cable television project in 1990 in a densely populated residential apartment complex in Seoul, and has subsequently extended service into other cities. The Korean government enacted the General Cable Broadcasting Act in 1991 to regulate cable operations and select service providers in three groups: program providers, network operators and system operators. In 1993, KT and KECO (Korea Electricity Corporation) were selected as network providers to construct physical networks with coaxial cables or fiber optics connecting 600,000 households by early 1995.[10] Fifty-four system operators were selected on a geographical basis. Each operator was allowed to provide individual subscribers in the designated local area with TV programs domestically produced or imported by 21 independent program providers. Each program provider must have its own special programming in music, movies, entertainment, news, sports, home shopping, religion, etc. The number of system operators is expected to double to 116 by the end of 1996, enabling all local areas to be completely covered by cable television service.

The Internet

Table 7 shows the number of Internet hosts[11] in selected countries. By July 1995, the number of host computers connected to the

Table 7 Internet Use (host computers in thousands, as of July 1995)

Korea	U.S.	Japan	Germany	U.K.	France
24	4,155	160	351	291	114

Source: Network Wizards (http://www.nw.com).

Table 8 Internet Use in Korea

	October 1994	October 1995
Commercial	3,131	13,644
University	6,524	12,554
Research	3,585	5,668
Organization	128	1,017
Government	37	80
Total	13,405	32,963

Source: NCA, October 1995.

Internet was estimated to be 6.6 million worldwide Almost two-thirds of host computers are located in the United States. NCA statistics on Internet use shows that the number of Korean Internet hosts in October 1995 had sharply increased to 33,000 from 13,000 in 1994 (see Table 8). This trend is expected to continue as commercial applications of the Internet become popular.[12]

The KII Plan[13]

Korea's vision for the 21st century and the NII
The Korean NII is based on a vision of information and communications infrastructure as a key factor in Korea's successful transition to an advanced economy. In this advanced economy, economic growth and market competition will be based on the creation, movement and application of information. Information infrastructure will also play a substantial role in achieving the national goal of a "transparent society" that is free from political and bureaucratic corruption. It is hoped that information technology will foster open processes of public administration and decision-making, and facilitate the simple, delivery of public services. Ultimately, information technology is expected to contribute to the vision of a small and efficient government.

The goal of Korea's information infrastructure initiative is the construction of an advanced national information infrastructure consisting of communications networks, Internet services, application software, computers and operating systems, and information products and services. The KII of the 21st century is expected to enable all Koreans to access information and communicate with anyone, anytime, anywhere. All information and communications services in voice, data and video will be provided easily, reliably, securely, in a timely manner and cost effectively.

Strategies
The establishment of the KII involves more than a plan to put additional cable in the ground and more computers into offices and homes. It incorporates the notion of a new social infrastructure, ranging from the establishment of a rich social and cultural environment to the development of hardware and software facilities that are conducive to a seamless flow of information. In order to achieve this, the general public must be prepared to use the new technologies and services so that they can benefit from the enhanced capabilities. Legislation that might unintentionally impede the use of new technologies to conduct business must also be reviewed and updated. The government is expected to be a leading user of the infrastructure to conduct administrative operations and deliver public services more effectively and efficiently, thus demonstrating the capabilities of IT applications. The government is also expected to create a favorable environment for financing that encourages investment and innovation.

The KII consists of high-speed government and public information networks. The New Korea Net-Government (NKN-G), funded by the government, will be constructed to provide government agencies and public institutions, including research organizations and universities, with information and communications services at a low cost. Application services and key technologies will be developed in collaboration with industry, universities and government laboratories. When these technologies and their applications have been tested and deployed over NKN-G, they will be commercialized on the New Korea Net-Public (NKN-P).

NKN-G

The NKN-G is intended to improve the efficiency of government operations and the delivery of public services. It is planned to connect central and local government agencies and various public organizations, including schools and libraries, by the year 2015, mainly through fiber optics. In the meantime, the facilities of service providers will be maximized. Standards for interconnectivity and interoperability with the existing computer networks will be created by the NBIS project as part of a program to create an integrated network. Construction and operation of the NKN-G will take place in three stages (see Figure 1): groundwork (1995–1997), diffusion (1998–2002), and completion (2003–2010). In each stage, network capabilities and switching technology are specified and the services that will be made available are identified in light of the continuing development of demand for services.

NKN-P

The objective of the NKN-P is to provide interactive broadband multimedia information services to users in the private sector by wiring offices and homes with fiber-optic cables. In the early stages of the plan, the NKN-P will target urban offices and apartments that are likely to have heavy traffic. Existing networks such as PSTN, PSDN, N-ISDN and the mobile communication networks will be integrated into the NKN-P. As with the NKN-G, the NKN-P will be implemented in three stages (see Figure 2).

Technology development and test-bed

The overall development plan for technology supporting the KII will be drafted stage by stage on the basis of forecasts of technology trends and the analysis of technology demands. The government is responsible for creating a hospitable environment for R&D investment and for conducting certain pilot projects to demonstrate or generate initial demand. Private industry will carry out most major R&D projects that have commercial prospects. The transfer of high technology from advanced countries is key to the plan, and private companies are encouraged to collaborate with foreign partners and to take part in joint research ventures. A test-bed will be established to evaluate various aspects of technology development,

Stage I (1995–1997): Groundwork

Transmission Network
   between 5 metropolitan areas: 622 Mbps–2 Gbps
   between metropolitan areas and 7 large cities: 622 Mbps
   between large cities and small–medium cities: 155–622 Mbps
Switching Technology
   data switching technology
   R&D and pilot project tests of ATM switching technology
Services
   high-speed Local Area Networks
   one-stop delivery for selected government services
   electronic library and museum service for selected areas
   remote diagnosis service, distance learning

Stage II (1998–2002): Diffusion

Transmission Network
   between 5 metropolitan areas: 2.5 Gbps–tens of Gbps
   between metropolitan areas and 7 large cities: 2.5 Gbps
Switching Technology
   ATM switching technology
Services
   super-high-speed interconnecting among LANs (above 155 Mbps)
   extending one-stop delivery for government services
   electronic library and museum service for extended areas
   remote diagnosis service, distance learning
   advanced services from geographic information system (GIS)

Stage III (2003–2015): Completion

Transmission Network
   networks for broadband multimedia services
   automation of network operation and maintenance
Switching Network
   enhanced switching enabling various multimedia services
Services
   HDTV image information service
   three-dimensional video conferencing service
   super-computer application service
   provision of government information by multimedia technology

Figure 1 Plan for NKN-G.

Stage I (1995–1997): Groundwork

Transmission Network
  interconnection of local telephone stations with 155–622 Mbps network
Switching Technology
  ATM-based multimedia services in metropolitan areas
Subscriber Loop
  fiber-optic cabling for large buildings with heavy traffic,
  densely populated areas
Services
  video conferences
  still-image picture phone services
  high-speed/resolution fax service
  expansion of ISDN services

Stage II (1998–2002): Diffusion

Transmission Network
  2.5–10 Gbps synchronous networks
Switching Technology
  development of ATM test network in large cities
Subscriber Loop
  full-scale supply of fiber-optic cables in apartment complexes
  and heavily populated areas
Services
  commerical services using ATM decentralized switching network
  test services using ATM switching network

Stage III (2003–2015): Completion

Transmission Network
  supply of optical transmission devices
Switching Technology
  integration of existing networks via ATM-based network
Subscriber Loop
  supply of fiber-optic cables to residential homes
Services
  ATM-based multimedia services
  HDTV-level video exchange services

Figure 2 Plan for NKN-P.

including R&D results of the KII. As part of the test-bed, fiber-optic backbone network of 2.5 Gbps was installed between Seoul and Daejon in 1995, and it will be gradually extended.

Policy Issues

The KII plan reflects the belief of the Korean government and industry that the key technologies of the NII will be powerful forces of competitive advantage in the developing global information economy. This issue is drawing considerable attention in Korea since economic signals suggest that Korea's competitive position in the world market is declining. For example, in the early 1990s there was a decrease in the production and export of Korean IT products (see Table 1), and domestic and overseas reports suggest a weakening of Korea's competitive position (Dedrick and Kraemer, 1995; WEF & IMD, 1994, 1995).[14] The current government has emphasized catching up in competitiveness in the global market, and IT and its applications are regarded as key tools in these efforts.

Many of the KII plan's strategy and action programs reinforce the importance and priority of information infrastructure. As with most NII initiatives, the KII initiative is concerned with the far-reaching economic and social ramifications of information infrastructure. Some of the planning is quite detailed; for example, the plans for the NKN-G and NKN-P identify the key enabling technologies required to achieve the desired services.[15] But overall, the KII plan is vague about how, when, and by whom it will be implemented. Development of the KII must be guided by an understanding of how networks will be designed, constructed and maintained in balance with existing infrastructure, as well as an understanding of how environmental factors must evolve for products and network services of the infrastructure to be efficiently utilized. Institutions such as the legal system must be properly aligned for effective deployment of the infrastructure and efficient utilization of its services. In addition, a long-term funding schedule for the KII project must be established. These issues have not yet been clearly addressed in the KII plan.

Perhaps the greatest challenge of the KII plan is achieving coordination among the parties with a stake in the process of network deployment and service provision. Different parties have different levels and kinds of risks and incentives to consider, and it is doubtful that any one scheme will meet all parties' needs. The KII will require coordination between the government and the private sector, among governmental agencies, between conduit owners and content providers, and so on. NII activities will also have an international dimension that the label "NII" tends to obscure. Coordination of NII issues will require smooth communication and interaction among countries whose welfare is dependent on effective interoperability of global information infrastructures.

Some of these issues surrounding the implementation of the KII are already known from the experiences of the NBIS project. In addressing these issues, we begin by analyzing the KII in terms of demand and supply orientations toward technological development policy.

Demand vs. Supply

Demand policy interventions have been widely regarded as more important than supply interventions in stimulating industrial technology innovation and application (King et al., 1994). The risk of misallocation of government or private resources is high when the demand side is not understood. Nevertheless, supply-side issues have often taken policy priority in technical projects requiring central coordination. Critics of the NBIS project pointed out that planning had focused mainly on the supply side, without considering sufficiently the established or potential demand, and the resulting services were not used as anticipated (see note 2). The key question on the demand side of the KII is this: What kinds of services and products merit the huge investments required by the KII programs? Unfortunately, this poses a dilemma. A number of IT-related industries such as computers and consumer electronics appear to have created their own demand, essentially making it impossible to predict demand until the supply is available.[16]

Supply and demand forces work together in the adoption and diffusion process of IT innovations. The dynamics of interaction between supply and demand also change, depending on circumstances such as the relative state of technical knowledge, the

availability of complementary and substitution factors, the character of the needs of society at any one time, and the market's
effectiveness in translating needs into clear demands (King et al.,
1994). The Korean government has failed when it has tried to force
active utilization of a system supported by public funding in the
NBIS project. The KII plan has attempted to take into account the
potential and actual needs of users in the drafting process, but
information on potential needs for IT innovations is so limited that
it is impossible for the plan to cover all possible needs that the
infrastructure might meet. The plan simply assumes that the rapid
advance of technology will stimulate new applications and new
demand.

Technologies and Standards

Technologically less developed nations such as Korea consider it
very important to catch up in advanced technologies. One way to
do this is through international cooperation in technology transfer, and the Korean government is very encouraging of private
sector collaborative research projects with foreign counterparts.
Technology transfer has long been an effective way of assuring the
assimilation of advanced technology, but international competition for technological hegemony has become so intense that
improving the level of technology consistent with the needs of the
KII could be very difficult. Thus new technology development
might be required in order to satisfy the demand for services and
products planned in the KII. The key from a policy perspective is
in figuring out how Korean industries involved in the KII can be
encouraged to take part in the process of developing technologies,
and assuming they do take part, accurately predicting the trend
and direction of technology development. Considering the rapidly
changing characteristics of IT, technology development programs
cannot be identified beyond the first stage of the KII plan (KIITF,
1995).

The adoption of technical standards is a key element in ensuring
the interconnectivity of existing and planned networks and the
interoperability of information systems and services.[17] The Korean
government has made a policy of developing original standards

that are internationally compatible, as well as accepting standards formulated in other countries. Korea has a free trade environment under the World Trade Organization, and standards are an important tool for fostering economic growth and competing for a share of the world market. However, the processes for establishing standards are complex and involve many organizations at both the domestic and the international level. The policy issues are sophisticated and hard to address, especially regarding the appropriate role of government in establishing standards. Government enforcement of standards can foster coordination among the parties at stake, but only at the risk of misallocating resources by pursuing standards that do not work well.[18]

Another important policy issue is the degree to which standards are domestically developed versus imported. One approach is to adopt external standards as soon as they are internationally accepted, and to get domestically developed standards adopted in the world market. The Korean government and industry examine standards developed by ISO/ITC/JTC1, as well as recommendations drafted by ITU-T that can be directly adopted or customized to become domestic standards. Korean industries are also encouraged to develop their own standards for situations in which international organizations do not provide adequate specifications or when those standards play an important role in protecting domestic markets. Of course, Korea would also like to make significant contributions to international standards development whenever possible.

A useful tool for establishing standards in Korea is identifying technical specifications created by user groups, especially in the public sector. For instance, the NBIS project developed technical criteria for several machines and network devices, such as multifunctional work stations, minicomputers (TICOMs), printers and local area networks (LANs). The procurement guidelines set by the user groups have provided an effective way to set standards in the KII, and user groups are now encouraged to participate actively in generating ideas for the direction of technology standards development.

There is a potential conflict in setting standards for intellectual property rights.[19] Korean industries have become interested in intellectual property rights as a result of developed countries' efforts to protect their own industries' R&D benefits. These rights have become a critical issue, and concern has grown as the owners of intellectual property have realized that they can increase their gains by manipulating the timing and outcome of the formal standard process. When there is more than one such player involved in a standard-setting effort, achieving consensus becomes difficult and slow, if not impossible. The importance of intellectual property rights to protecting producers' R&D investments in network devices and software is likely to grow as the convergence of technologies accelerates.

Network Expansion

The physical networks of the KII are scheduled to be constructed in three stages through the year 2015. The fiber-optic backbone networks will initially connect five metropolitan areas, each of which will be wired to nearby large and small cities. The capacity of the backbones as well as local connections to the small cities will be expanded at each stage. The fiber-optic network will be extended to individual homes (fiber-to-the-home, FTTH) in the final stage. The efficiency of deployment will ultimately depend on how fast the demand for network services increases. Lack of network capacity will hinder the growth of the information economy, but over capacity will generate serious inefficiencies for the KII builders.

The KII plan for network expansion is based on the supply-side view, but the question arises whether the supply model works in the context of network infrastructures.[20] The demand-side view sees the plan as too optimistic, citing the current low use of the Internet in Korean households as an indicator. Supply-side proponents claim that immediate adoption and deployment of digital fiberoptics will encourage consumers to find new applications. The debate on this issue is directly related to the investment priorities of government and industry, as well as the problem of constructing new networks that are in sync with existing networks. The KII guidelines state that existing networks will evolve into advanced networks, and eventually into the NKN-G and NKN-P. At the same time, the networks will be integrated with the existing PSTN, PSDN, N-ISDN and mobile communications networks. As an example of this approach, a number of public networks developed under the NBIS project will be reconfigured to transmit and switch text, audio and video so that they can be integrated into the NKN-G. While this looks very reasonable and simple, deploying high-speed networks based on the existing ones will not be easily accomplished given the high costs, complex technological development pathways, and the problems of estimating current and potential network supply to meet demand.[21]

Application Services

KII critics have raised questions about the usefulness of the high-speed networks envisioned in the plan given their high costs. The vast majority of identifiable consumer needs are readily met by existing capacities and technologies, so the urgent demand for extending network capacity is not obvious. Proponents of the KII often point to the Korean government's ambitious telecommunications investment plan of the 1980s to make up for the shortage of telecommunications service capacity. That strategy worked: Korea's infamous excess demand for telephone lines disappeared, and advanced information services such as data communications and VANs became available. This supply-side strategy benefited from the fact that demand for basic services was demonstrably clear, and the growing demand for data communications in developed and newly industrializing countries was generalizable to Korea.

The demand for advanced KII-based services is less obvious and less predictable. It is not clear that rapid advances in digital technologies and fiber-optic transmission systems, together with basic control software, will provide a platform on which applications will flourish. The KII's economic and political success depends on the creation of application services, but the strategies and policies necessary to encourage the private sector to invest in and create these new services are not clear.[22] At this point, the government sees a necessary leadership role for itself in the development of application services, and has focused on encouraging private sector investment through deregulation, privatization of public enterprises, legislation and so on.

The Korean government has been very active in the generation of service applications for NKN-G since 1994, the year the initial version of the KII plan was designed. Two directions are evident. One lies in developing pilot projects that demonstrate the feasibility of applying technologies to provide services to customers in remote areas. Three pilot projects initiated in 1994 provide public medical diagnostic service, education at the elementary level, and agricultural skills advice to remote areas. The remote elementary education system has since been extended to the college level.[23] In 1995, five more pilot projects were launched: telecommunications services for the handicapped; remote trading of agricultural products; remote retraining of industrial workers using university facilities; teleconferencing among cabinet members; and a remote court system. These projects are intended to demonstrate that state-of-the-art technologies can be applied to the existing activities of service providers and their clients, and to test the feasibility of applications running on the technology. The pilot projects also are intended to promote the efficiency of administrative operations and the convenience of delivering services to the general public.

The Korean government is also involved in developing applications for governmental agencies over the NKN-G. The KII Task Force collected 94 proposals for potential technology applications from various government agencies, and selected 36 projects for funding of about U.S.$20 million (16.2 billion won) during the initiation period in 1995. Planning is under way to support the systematic development of application services so that each application can successfully promote efficient agency operation, and thereby stimulate further demand for applications on the NKN-G.

Legal Structure

The basic law governing Korea's communications services until the early 1980s was the Telecommunications Act of 1961. In 1983, this was broken down into the Telecommunications Basic Act and the Telecommunications Business Act to separate the functions of policy formulation and business operations, and to take a step toward privatization. As technology convergence among computers and communications rapidly progressed in the 1980s, the 1986 Computer Networks Law was enacted to initiate the NBIS project.

The 1995 Informatization Promotion Act was passed to establish an efficient framework for policy formulation and effective support of R&D activities and information industries, all in preparation for the information society. This act requires the government to prepare action plans for informatization on an annual basis, and specifies the detailed items to be contained in these plans. It prescribes the organization of the top decision-making committee and its subsidiary body, specifies the missions of the public sector for the development of core technologies and their applications, and encourages promotion of information technology industries. Finally, it establishes the informatization promotion fund, stipulates the fund's sources and uses, and provides for the main body of its management.

The Informatization Promotion Act was initiated without regard to the KII plan, but it has developed a clear-cut relation to the plan. The act is to be accompanied by detailed regulations to enforce relevant policy decisions regarding the KII initiatives. Without these, the act cannot play a role in promoting informatization. Furthermore, the act is supposed drive Korea's computerization projects, replacing a corresponding part of the Computer Networks Law of 1986. The Informatization Promotion Act is to the KII what the Computer Networks Law was to the NBIS: a crucial clarifying and enabling input.

Costs and Funding Mechanisms

Cost estimation for IT projects is difficult because technologies advance continuously, enabling services to be provided over networks less expensively. Network-related costs decrease owing to rapid developments in enabling technologies such as fiber-optic facilities and signal-processing devices. Information service-related costs decline due to increasing competition, deregulation and economies of scale.

Nevertheless, the estimation of costs is necessary because the government must determine the investments required as part of establishing public consensus in support of the national project, and to help the parties with a stake in the KII to prepare their financing schedules. The establishment of the KII over the next 20 years is expected to cost 45 trillion won (U.S.$56 billion). Only a small portion of the total, 1.8 trillion won, or U.S.$2.25 billion, will depend on the public sector. This covers establishing test-bed and pilot projects, increasing public awareness of the information infrastructure, supporting development of core technologies as well as constructing the NKN-G and multimedia services delivered to the public over the networks. Application service providers and other private sector organizations will be responsible for financing the rest of the initiative.

The NBIS project experience showed that a preassigned fund for the National Administrations Information System was a major source of success in the project's first stage. The forced return to the normal budget process signaled a weakening of government support, and delayed the implementation of the government computerization projects in the second stage. Research was undertaken to show the payoffs from IT investments in quantitative terms, but the results were not conclusive. The Informatization Promotion Act provides a strong legal basis for making public IT investment necessary to the success of the KII plan, and prescribes the establishment of a fund large enough to support public IT investments. Although the act also specifies sources and uses for the fund, great controversy remains over how to finance the fund, what activities it will support, and who will manage it. The Ministry of Information and Communications is explicitly mandated to operate the fund. After years of effort to consolidate funding, several sources for the fund were listed in the law.[24] It is still not clear whether a fund large enough to finance the public activities will come out of the law.

Coordination between the Public and Private Sectors

The KII involves many stakeholders, and requires coordination among industries, governmental agencies, research institutes, universities and the general public. Korea's powerful tradition of central government coordination makes top-down planning of the KII somewhat easier than might be the case in more decentralized countries, but changes in the broader environment suggest that this is no longer the advantage it once was. Within the government itself power is becoming less centralized, and governmental agencies are becoming more autonomous and battling for influence over issues. A growing number of players outside the government have the power to influence policy, or ignore policies they do not agree with. Coordination between the private and public sectors and coordination within governmental agencies poses new challenges.

Strong government leadership in the past provided prompt solutions to serious conflicts among stakeholders. The government set goals and private industries ran their businesses in accordance with regulations. The government was able to enforce its strategies through effective tools such as special financing schedules, granting or withholding permission for particular firms to enter an industry, and the establishment of rules of competition in the market. This model was intended for the KII plan, but the trend toward liberalization and deregulation made that strategy unworkable except in a few cases, such as network deployment and funding of key technology research in which centralized government authority remains advantageous. It is also likely that the government's role in establishing technical specifications for network standards will remain key, though somewhat indirect, through coordinating and supporting the efforts of private companies.

The government is also being called on to support the KII by giving up some of its influence by removing regulations hindering privatization of public corporations, and redirecting its influence by setting fair rules of market competition. The government's responsibility is increasingly seen as that of maintaining a sound economic climate for private investment and a regulatory framework that encourages fair and open competition among equipment and service providers. The KII vision includes multiple networks with different functions, capabilities and patterns of ownership and use. Assuring the interconnectivity and interoperability of these networks is an important role of government at all levels, so that the maximum benefits of investments can be gained for both NKN-G and NKN-P.

There is increasing agreement that the traditional role of the Korean government in industrial and economic policy should change, but bureaucratic attitudes change slowly. For that matter, the private sector itself shows mixed feelings, preferring the liberalization of business environments, on the one hand, yet seeking continued direct government funding and regulatory support, on the other. The challenge facing Korea in the KII is how to create harmony between the government and the private sectors so that each can do what it does best, but it is not yet clear how that challenge will be met.

Committees and the Role of Governmental Bodies

The policy-making process in Korea has frequently been interrupted by bureaucratic rivalry among ministries with a stake in particular issues. The scope of information infrastructure cuts across several governmental bodies. Even if the government's role could be clearly constructed in balance with the private sector, the KII initiative would face considerable problems of coordination within the government. The process of legislating the Informatization Promotion Act illustrates this problem. As long as the implementation of the NBIS administrations information systems project was overseen by the NCB within the Executive Office of the president, things went smoothly. But when the National Computerization Board (NCB) was moved to a lower-status position in the government hierarchy, implementation of the project faltered.

This problem is recognized, and in an attempt to alleviate it, a high-level steering committee has been formed at the interministerial level to resolve controversies among government agencies involved in KII projects. The steering committee is headed by the prime minister, and includes the ministers of related ministries and representatives from the National Assembly and the Supreme Court. In addition, the Ministry of Communications (MOC) was reorganized into the Ministry of Information and Communications (MIC) in the 1994 to avoid past conflicts by consolidating authority. Nevertheless, resolution of the controversies in the KII plan will probably require a series of debates within the ministries. For example, proponents of IT projects tend to push for action given the successes in economic development in the past 30 years, but the Economic Planning Board (EPB), which controls the nation's budget office, is very conservative about allocating money for IT projects. The EPB has established guidelines for budget allocations based on cost-benefit analysis, and most analyses show IT projects in the public sector to have weak cost-benefit justification. Proponents of IT projects have conducted research to demonstrate the economic payoff or productivity impact of IT investments, but without much success. Should the EPB's conservative biases prevail, it is doubtful that the steering committee will decide in favor of the KII plan and might even block MIC's management of the Informatization Fund.

Similarly, the Ministry of Trade, Industry, and Energy (MOTIE) and MIC have clashed over which industries best represent the field of IT. MOTIE is responsible for industrial policy including the computer industries, whereas MIC regulates communications. MIC has gained management control over the KII plan through the Informatization Promotion Act and the 1994 reformulation of the central administration, but MOTIE argues that most equipment for networks, homes and offices specified in the KII plan falls under MOTIE's jurisdiction. MIC thus emphasizes a network perspective that puts it in charge, whereas MOTIE takes a manufacturing perspective that fits with its established authority in carrying out Korea's industrial policy.

Economic Benefits

The argument that the KII will accelerate economic growth claims that widespread use of IT will enhance productivity and competitiveness and increase the returns on investment in other capital goods. Furthermore, the IT industry itself can be a source of economic growth by creating new products and services. Unfortunately, this line of argument has grown less persuasive to those in charge of allocating money for KII-related projects in the public sector. The Korean private sector has invested heavily in IT applications, recognizing the implications for market competitiveness, but the government has been reluctant to allocate funds for IT projects on account of the "productivity paradox" reported during the late 1980s (Baily, 1986; Baily and Gordon, 1988; Brynjolfsson, 1993; NRC, 1994a). Great attention has been paid to clarifying the paradox in order to sustain the national consensus on the KII plan. In the process of drafting the plan in 1994, proponents of the KII cited research that explained the paradox in terms of measurement errors, a time lag for diffusion and mismanagement of IT (Brynjolfsson, 1993; Magnet, 1994; NRC, 1994a).

Proposed investments must be justified in light of their likely contributions to macroeconomic indicators such as gross domestic product (GDP) and job creation.[25] However, such predictions are difficult because they depend on innovations not yet developed and details of the plan that have yet to be created. It is more difficult to forecast the economic benefits of KII investments and regulatory reform than to predict, as in established macroeconomic practice, the consequences for GDP of changes in the tax rate or the monetary policy. Nevertheless, proponents of the KII plan have been under pressure to present quantitative evidence to support the anticipated benefits from IT investments proposed in the plan. In 1994, a task force was formed to draft a document to enhance public awareness of the KII initiatives. The Task Force, made up of specialists from NCA, KT, ETRI and other organizations, put great effort into the chapter on "Economic Impacts of the KII Initiatives." Using input-output analysis,[26] the Task Force estimated that a proposed investment of 45 trillion won would lead to the production of about 100 trillion won and 560,000 jobs by the year 2015. This report has improved public understanding of the KII initiatives and has reduced uncertainties concerning planned investments.

International Cooperation and the Asian-Pacific Information Infrastructure

Information technology is a global technology, produced and consumed in many countries. The concept of NII as developed in the United States and Japan has become a global concept. When the NBIS project was losing its driving force, the international dimension of IT helped raise concern that Korea not fall behind. NII services will clearly operate in a context of international connectivity, as use of the Internet demonstrates. Although information infrastructure has developed at different paces in different countries, the issues involved are global.[27]

The Korean government and Korean industries understand the implications of technology leadership for securing international market share in emerging network services. They are willing to make contributions to the new initiatives of the global information infrastructure (GII) and the Asian information infrastructure (AII), and even proposed the creation of an Asian-Pacific information infrastructure (APII) at the 1994 Asian-Pacific economic conference (APEC) summit meeting in Indonesia. In May 1995, the Korean government sponsored a meeting of top leaders in charge of communications and information industries to develop a concrete form for the proposed APII in the APEC countries. In that meeting, top officials from 17 APEC countries produced a document stating the purposes of the APII and the principles to be followed in its implementations. The APII vision includes construction of information infrastructure enabling interconnectivity and interoperability among member countries, promotion of technology cooperation, free and efficient circulation of information, development and exchange of human resources, and improvement of policy and the regulatory environment to support the regional information infrastructure. The APII will take into account individual countries' unique characteristics while promoting competition and private sector investment, protecting intellectual property rights, protecting privacy, and ensuring the security of data.

The Future of the KII

The KII was initiated in response to domestic and international challenges facing Korea in early 1990s. Although the NBIS project had made substantial contributions to IT use and production in Korea, it had lost its driving force because of reduced support from the government. Despite the recognized potential of IT use and its implications for efficiency and competitiveness, those in charge of public resource allocation could not find visible evidence that IT investments were paying off. What might have been a gradual decline in support for IT-related development projects was reversed when the NII proposals of the U.S. and Japanese governments caused Koreas leaders to worry that the global competitive advantages of Korean industries might weaken and the nation might be left farther behind developed countries if Korea did not respond with its own NII initiative. Thus the KII was born.

Considerable progress has been made in planning the KII, and one may be optimistic that key elements of the plan will be realized. More broadly, however, there are concerns over whether there will be sufficient actual demand for the services the KII will facilitate. It is widely believed that the NBIS project faltered in part because of its overemphasis on supply issues and insufficient concern over whether there would be adequate demand. More attention to demand factors has been part of the KII plan, but forecasting demand remains extremely difficult. To a considerable degree, therefore, the KII plan must proceed on the faith that demand will rise in response to supply.

Perhaps the most interesting long-term consequences of the KII concern the changes under way in the Korean tradition of economic and industrial policy intervention. The highly successful economic development practices of the last 30 years now seem to be at odds with key features of the evolving KII, NII and GII visions. Rather than taking the lead with highly centralized programs of funding, direction and regulation, the Korean government is increasingly pursuing less interventionist strategies such as deregulation, privatization of key industries and encouragement of competition. The government's interest and influence remain strong in key areas such as support for basic research, assistance in setting standards for information infrastructure and establishment of necessary international agreements to facilitate the APII and the GII. Nevertheless, the KII plan represents an important departure from a well-established and successful tradition, and might be an example for future economic development initiatives in Korea.

Acknowledgment

This chapter is a part of the result of joint study conducted under the collaborative research agreement between Korea's National Computerization Agency (NCA) and the University of California at Irvine's Center for Research on Information Technology and Organizations (CRITO).

Notes

1. The first computer used in Korea was an IBM 1401 installed by the Economic Planning Board (EPB) in 1967 to track and analyze the national census.

2. The employment information system, a subsystem of the National Administrations Information Systems, has been frequently cited as an unsuccessful example

due to the limited consideration of the demand side. One of the objectives of this subsystem was to apply IT in managing labor-management relations in the Ministry of Labor. The system did not serve this purpose effectively, but it turned out to be useful to have the labor market operate more efficiently by providing on-line information opportunities.

3. Identifying the impacts of IT investment has been an important issue in Korea in the sense that it determines the priority of the government budget allocation schedule. This issue is now being actively debated in terms of the so-called "productivity paradox." Popular explanations of the paradox that favor IT investment appear in both academic journals as well as the mass media.

4. Unless otherwise mentioned, data cited in this part describing the current capability of producing and using information technology are from the NCA's annual White Papers on national informatization from 1994 and 1995.

5. This policy goal was based on one terminal per household for the purpose of universal information service. It was similar to the goal of one telephone per household that was set in the early 1980s when an ambitious project was launched to eliminate the notorious excess demand for telephone lines. This goal was accomplished in 1987, when the total number of telephone lines exceeded ten million.

6. It should be noted that the total number of PCs sold is not the same as the number of PCs actually in use, since some of the newly purchased PCs are simply replacing obsolete ones.

7. Of 669 TICOM computers sold by 1995, only 76 had been purchased by the private sector. (New Media, February 1996).

8. Some public corporations have communications networks for their own business operations, such as, for example, the electric power company and highway maintenance company. While they are prohibited from providing commercial communication services to the general public, there has been a heated debate over whether they should be allowed to do so.

9. Privatization of KT was initiated by the EPB, which announced a privatization plan for public corporations in 1987. According to the plan, 15 percent of KT stocks were to be sold to the public in 1989, and additional shares sold annually until 1992, when the government would hold 51 percent of KT ownership. However, the process of selling shares on the stock market was very slow on account of a weak stock market, opposition from KT, etc. No shares had been sold by 1992, and only a very small fraction was sold to the public based on competing bid during 1993 and 1994.

10. The Association of Cable Broadcasting Firms announced in December 1995 that the number of Korean households subscribing to cable television had reached 500,000 by the end of 1995.

11. The number of host computers instead of users is taken as a variable representing the extent of Internet use since it is very difficult and sometimes meaningless to count the number of people on the Internet. Users do not

register in a central location before getting on the Internet. Furthermore, Internet providers do not register in one central location because they may be part of someone else's network. This means that counting the number of Internet users is probably impossible (P. Hoffman, 1994).

12. The number of hosts in commercial application surpasses that of academic use as can be seen in Table 8.

13. The plan for the KII has been revised by a series of meetings of the KII Task Force since its introduction in April 1994. The presentation of the plan in this chapter is based on the English version prepared by the KII Task Force for presentation to the 1995 International Conference on Computers and Communication.

14. There is also counterevidence, however. For example, NSF (1995) predicts that, in analyzing high-tech areas in Asian countries, Taiwan and Korea are the most likely to make the greatest impact in technology-related fields and high-tech product markets. The report also indicates that both economies have significant technological infrastructures in place that should serve to support further growth in high-tech industries.

15. The action plan does not intend to exhaustively list services and required technologies since this is not possible to do in advance. This is particularly true of increasingly sophisticated information technologies. It is difficult to predict the outcome of something that is changing so rapidly and seems to generate so many misconceptions as it evolves. Since the KII plan is supposed to be revised year by year taking the speed of diffusion of network services and technology development into account, the schedule for the available services will be changed accordingly.

16. Nobody could even imagine the present widespread use of computer technologies when they began to be used commercially in the early 1950s. As technologies have advanced, many of their most widely used application areas have come as a surprise.

17. KIITF (1995) places emphasis on standards by stating in the action plan for technology development that "[F]rom the early stage of R&D, concerted efforts will be given to standardization, including active participation in the international standardization activities" (p. 8).

18. One example of wasted resources pointed out in NRC (1994b) is the Government Open Systems Interconnect Protocol (GOSIP). "Indeed, past attempts to influence the process directly have not been effective. The attempt to force the use of OSI protocols by the promulgation of a federal government version, GOSIP, must be seen as a misguided attempt to exercise a governmental mandate. In the commercial marketplace, the contest between the OSI and TCP/IP protocol suite is over: the OSI market has largely disappeared, and vendors who invested enormous sums in trying to develop this market are understandably upset."

19. The logic behind the conflict is clearly explained in M. Shurmer and G. Lea (1995): "In the broadest sense, standardization and IPRs share the same economic objective—namely to ensure that society benefits to the full from the innovation. However, the approach adopted to achieve this objective is very different. IPRs are oriented toward producers and reflect the trade-off between the need to create sufficient incentives for innovation and the public good nature of an innovation once it has been discovered. Standardization, on the other hand, is much more consumer oriented and seeks to encourage a common platform whereby users benefit from enhanced competition and trade, (pp. 384–385).

20. The network construction schedule described in the section on the KII plan is based on the assumption that the future demand for network services will grow enough to require the planned capacity of networks in each stage.

21. The test-bed for the KII provides a tool for evaluating possible problems arising from the network evolution, though this is not the only objective of the test-bed.

22. As mentioned above, the objective of the report on NGNBIS was to identify service applications likely to be available that will also be able to create their own demand. This was based on the understanding that availability of application services would be a key factor to reviving the faltering NBIS project.

23. The remote college education system has been applied in the National Open University, which was established to deliver via broadcasting life-time educational services for residents of distant rural areas. Because of the nature of distance learning, the National Open University was selected as the most appropriate place to apply network technologies.

24. One source that had been initially discussed, but was ultimately excluded due to the objections raised by other ministries, was the proceeds from the sale of the government ownership of Korea Telecom, which is in the process of privatization. The sale's proceeds would make the biggest contribution to the fund.

25. For example, in January 1994, the Japanese Ministry of Post and Telecommunications (MPT) released a research report on the economic impact of proposed fiber-optic network deployment, estimating the size of the new applications market as 56 trillion yen (U.S.$560 billion) and the number of jobs created as 2.4 million by the year 2010. In the United States, the economic impact of proposed legislation on the NII was documented in June 1994 in "Economic Benefits of the Administration's Legislative Proposals for Telecommunications," which estimated the economic benefits to the nation that could be achieved through new legislative and administrative reform of telecommunications policy proposed by Vice President Al Gore. Furthermore, a report released in 1994 by the National Information Infrastructure Task Force (NIITF) states that the Computer Systems Policy project estimates that the NII will create as much as $300 billion annually in new sales across a range of industries. The Economic Strategy Institute concluded that accelerated deployment of the NII would increase GDP

by $194–$321 billion by the year 2007, and increase productivity by 20 to 40 percent; industry experts believe that the personal communications services industry, a newly created family of wireless services, could create as many as 300,000 jobs in the next 10–15 years.

26. The input-output analysis was adopted not because it was the best tool to estimate the economic consequences of IT investments but because it was the only one available based on the availability of data. In fact, the input-output framework could be the worst choice in the context of IT application since it is based on the clear division of various industries although it is highly probable that new industries will emerge and existing ones will disappear as the applications of advanced technologies evolve.

27. By global, we emphasize the value of technologies enabling the NII from the point of network connectivity. The word "global" does not deny the fact that each country's network activity reflects the unique characteristics of its local environment. For example, although the Internet was developed largely in the United States, Internet activity in Korea takes place under its own economic and regulatory framework.

References

Baily, M. N. (1986). "What has Happened to Productivity Growth?" *Science*, pp. 443–451.

Baily, M.N. and R.J. Gordon (1988). "The Productivity Slowdown, Measurement Issues and Explosion of Computer Power." *Brookings Papers on Economic Activity*, pp. 347–420.

Brynjolfsson, E. (1993). "The Productivity Paradox of Information Technology." *Communications of the ACM*, December, pp. 66–77.

Dedrick, J., K.L. Kraemer, and Dae-Won Choi (1994). *Korean Industrial Policy at a Crossroads: The Case of Information Technology*. Irvine, CA: CRITO, University of California.

Dedrick, J. and K.L. Kraemer (1995). "A Tale of Two IT Industries." *Electronics Business Asia*, February, p. 72.

Hoffman, P. (1994). *The Internet*. Foster City, CA: IDG Books Worldwide, Inc.

King, J.L., V. Gurbaxani, K.L. Kraemer, F.W. McFarlan, K.S. Raman, C.S. Yap (1994). "Institutional Factors in Information Technology Innovation." *Information Systems Research*, pp. 139–169.

KIITF (1995). *The Korea Information Infrastructure: Blueprint for Implementation*. Seoul: Korean Information Infrastructure Task Force.

Magnet, M. (1994). "The Productivity Payoff Arrives." *Fortune*, June 27, pp. 43–47.

NCA (1994, 1995). *White Paper on National Informatization*, 1994, 1995 (in Korean). Seoul: National Computerization Agency.

National Research Council (1994a). *Information Technology in the Service Society: A Twenty-First Century Lever.* Washington, DC: National Academy Press.

National Research Council (1994b). *Realizing the Information Future.* Washington, D.C.: National Academy Press.

National Research Council (1995). *The Changing Nature of Telecommunications/ Information Infrastructure.* Washington, DC: National Academy Press.

National Science Foundation (1995). *Asia's New High-Tech Competitors.* SRS Special Report, NSF 95-304.

Shurmer, M. and Gary Lea (1995). "Telecommunications Standardization and Intellectual Property Rights." In *Standards Policy for Information Infrastructure,* B. Kahin and J. Abbate, eds. Cambridge, MA: The MIT Press.

World Economic Forum (WEF) and International Management and Development Institute (IMD) (1994, 1995). *World Competitiveness Report.*

The U.S. National Information Infrastructure Initiative: The Market, the Net, and the Virtual Project

Brian Kahin

The U.S. information infrastructure, past, present, and future, is difficult for outsiders to understand. At one level, private-sector activity so outweighs that of the public sector that the situation in the U.S. defies comparison, even with the Western European countries with which the United States shares so many values and traditions. While other countries are focused on the politics of liberalizing the telecommunications sector, the United States is experiencing a market-driven frenzy that spans multiple sectors. Powerful industries with very different business models jockey for position and profitability, as old boundaries blur and new business models arise.

At another level, the federal government has played a critical role in seeding the advance of information infrastructure. In the name of national defense and scientific research, the government launched the Internet protocol suite and the Internet itself. The U.S. government still supports key central functions of the global Internet, and it still strongly supports basic research for information technology,[1] arguably the most competitive and freewheeling sector of the world economy.

This chapter explores the paradoxical role of the federal government as both a disinterested referee and an interested investor. It focuses on the Clinton/Gore Administration's efforts to shape and implement a broad *initiative* as a landmark in formulating national policy for advanced information infrastructure. But it makes the point that policy development has been overshadowed by radical and unanticipated developments in technology and the market-place.

These developments are not unique to the United States. The nature of the technology makes them globally accessible and implementable. The Web is conspicuously "World Wide," and its transformation of and by advertising, marketing, and customer relations is not limited by national borders.

The Initiative

The Clinton Administration officially launched the U.S. National Information Infrastructure (NII) initiative on September 15, 1993, with the publication of *The National Information Infrastructure: Agenda for Action*. Conceived as a broad, multifaceted approach to a complex set of problems and opportunities, the initiative has been a centerpiece of the Administration's technology policy, linking it to a wide range of economic and social issues.[2] Despite its prominent position in the Administration's policy agenda and a high-visibility advisory committee representing a broad spectrum of private-sector interests, the initiative has been managed through an unfunded ad hoc task force composed of representatives of executive branch agencies.[3] This flexible arrangement—in effect, a "virtual agency"—made it unnecessary to seek Congressional approval.

The NII initiative owed its ambitious agenda and high profile to Vice President Al Gore. As a senator, Gore sponsored a series of bills that were eventually enacted as the High Performance Computing Act (HPCA) of 1991. He introduced the Information Infrastructure and Technology Act of 1992 to extend the central themes of the HPCA into schools, libraries, health care, and manufacturing. Once elected Vice President, Gore was no longer bound by committee jurisdictions and was able to design the initiative as a general blueprint for the challenges of the information revolution.

Launched at a time of accelerating change in communications, computing, and publishing, the initiative recognized the need to address technological convergence not just between adjacent industries such as telephone services and cable television, but as a broader phenomenon generating unpredictable externalities and blurring boundaries among many different industries. It was a sweeping interagency effort that encompassed regulatory reform, strategic investment, information policy, and reengineering government operations. Because no new resources went into policy development for the NII initiative, it remained dependent on Gore and on the Department of Commerce, where much of the task force leadership was located.

The initiative was driven by two converging policy vectors: on the one hand, long-evolving efforts to increase competition in facilities-based telecommunications; and, on the other, a history of strategic federal investment in advanced computing and networking that gave rise to the Internet. This policy convergence is not explicit in the *Agenda for Action*, but we see it in the committee structure of the interagency Information Infrastructure Task Force (IITF) that was to carry out the agenda.

These dual roots contributed to early confusion about who would build the "information superhighway," illustrated by a well-publicized exchange between AT&T Chairman Robert Allen and Vice President-elect Gore in late 1992.[4] Gore had championed the development of the "National Research and Education Network" (NREN) as an evolution of the National Science Foundation's NSFNET and the research networks of other federal agencies. However, these were virtual networks assembled by contractors from leased lines and routers. They were significant not as stand-alone networks but by virtue of their role in the global Internet. As a practical matter, the NREN never became more than a component of the High Performance Computing and Communications Program (HPCC) that encompassed research on high-speed networking and participation in testbeds, as well as a set of funding strategies for advancing Internet connectivity in higher education. Calling it the "National Research and Education Network" was politically appealing, but it invited reading a more specific mission into the program than was possible, practically or politically.[5]

In March 1993, telecommunications industry executives issued a statement that sought to distinguish "production networks" from "experimental networks" and argued that the federal government should only subsidize experimental networks and certain users of production networks, not the network providers. This was in part a reaction to a controversy over the National Science Foundation's funding strategy for the NSFNET backbone.[6] However, it was also a legitimate reaction to the common, but unfounded, expectation that the federal government would build, hands on and from the bottom up, a dedicated National Research and Education Network.

At the time, telephone and cable television executives were focused on interactive television as the path to an advanced NII. They were not directly engaged with the Internet and did not understand how its many different aspects and services were continually evolving from experimental to "production."[7] Many saw the Internet as an academic toy that would not survive without the benefit of government backing. The computer industry, however, understood Internet technology and viewed it as an enabling platform. In general, computer companies had a greater appreciation for federal funding, especially since many could trace their own roots to academic research.

The communications and computer industries both saw a convergence on asynchronous transfer mode (ATM) as a common technology over the long run but differed significantly in their near-term view of information infrastructure. Telephone and cable companies focused on delivery of linear video on demand and variations thereof, collectively known as "interactive television." The computer industry, by contrast, was interested in a high level of functionality to support the widest variety of networked applications, known and unknown. The Internet protocol suite met this requirement, and although bandwidth was limited, the technology was scalable, and bandwidth could be added incrementally.

In the three years since the NII initiative was announced, a convincing business case for interactive television has not materialized, while the size of the Internet has continued to double every year. (See Figure 1.) Furthermore, the significance of the Internet as an enabling platform has been demonstrated by the meteoric rise of the World Wide Web as a new enabling platform on top of the Internet. As evidenced by a parade of public offerings and stock prices that bear little relationship to current earnings, the Internet

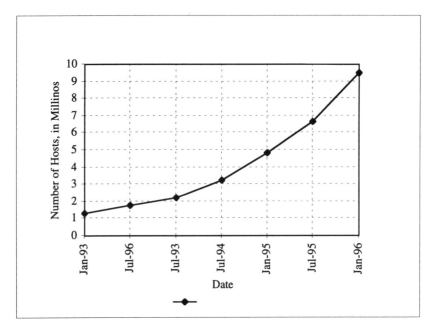

Figure 1 Growth of the Internet, as Measured by the Number of Hosts. Source: Network Wizards, "Internet Domain Survey, January 1996." [http://www.nw.com/zone/WWW/report.html], June 12, 1996

and the Web have become a favored arena for private investment. Even telephone and cable executives now see the untapped market of high-speed Internet access as offering a greater opportunity than invading each other's core business with conventional services or chasing after interactive television.

In January 1996, the long-sought and much belabored Telecommunications Act finally passed, promising to break down industry barriers and to fuel competition in new telecommunications technologies. January also marked the scheduled termination of the National Information Infrastructure Advisory Council, established by executive order at the time of the *Agenda for Action.* It appears that the interagency Information Infrastructure Task Force (which was not formally chartered to begin with) has largely ceased to function. As of this writing (June 1996), the IITF Web site stands unchanged since November 1995—basically still the gopher server set up in the fall of 1993 and now showing its age.[8]

Although the initiative may have faded, it was designed as a project, not an ongoing program. Some parts of the 1993 agenda were more successful than others, but as a whole, the initiative succeeded in raising awareness and understanding of important issues, both inside and outside the government. At its best, it provided momentum, direction, cross-fertilization and insight at a time when expectations of the federal government have been markedly diminished.

Industries and Infrastructure

Although Singapore launched the first national information infrastructure initiative a year earlier, the U.S. initiative staked out the issues as they would also be addressed by other large developed countries and international forums such as the International Tele-communication Union (ITU), the Group of Seven (G7),[9] and the Organization for Economic Cooperation and Development (OECD). Singapore's vision of an "intelligent island" befitted a small island state with a strong central government. The U.S. NII initiative, by contrast, expressed and illustrated the limited and increasingly self-effacing role of the public sector in the world's largest market economy.

The circumstances in the United States were and remain distinct from other countries, including other G7 countries. In the United States, private ownership of telecommunications infrastructure has been the rule. Federal and state agencies have been working for decades to increase competition in areas other than basic telephony, including private networks and "enhanced services." Spurred by new technology and the divestiture of AT&T, a variety of providers laid extensive networks of optical fiber in the 1980s. With prices for leased circuits typically one-fifth to one-third of prices in Western Europe and Japan, the United States presently has nearly two-thirds of the world's leased circuits.[10]

The importance of government support for ARPANET, NSFNET and other research networks is widely acknowledged, but the availability of relatively inexpensive leased lines also helps explain why 60 percent of the world's Internet hosts are in the United States.[11] The growth of private networks, large and small, fed demand for TCP/IP internetworking in companies that wanted their networks to interconnect. Demand for TCP/IP equipment advanced the technology and in turn brought down the cost of routers and software for the public Internet. Recently, the spectacular growth of World Wide Web technologies on the Internet has been pushing back into corporate networks, spurring the development of "Intranets" which use Web servers and clients for sharing information within the firm. Corporate "internets" have actually existed for years, but the Web-based transformation of internal communications has given them new prominence and a new name.

The United States holds a dominant position in the world computer market through leading positions in critical areas of innovation such as microprocessors and software. U.S. companies have consistently controlled roughly 70 percent of the total world market for software, custom and published. The computer industry (computer, software, and services combined) continues to grow at seven to eight percent annually compared with four to five percent for telecommunications services. (See Figure 2.)

The U.S. recording, television, and motion picture industries are powerful domestically and internationally. These industries are able to produce for a large integrated domestic market, which is supplemented by exports to other English-speaking countries. The ability to amortize production costs over these primary markets in turn provides extraordinary cost advantages in non-English-speaking markets. The strength of this sector (which has led some countries, such as Canada and France, to institute quotas and other defensive measures) leads the United States to take forceful international positions on copyright protection and market access.

In contrast to the international nature of the computer and entertainment industries, telecommunications is inherently local. Although there is increasing international trade in equipment, telecommunications remains a service industry characterized by enormous sunk investments in fixed assets, managed and regulated at local, state, or national levels. Since national governments are accustomed to playing a major role in telecommunications, just as they do in transportation, a policy focus on the "information superhighway" fits within the established realm of national government policymaking.

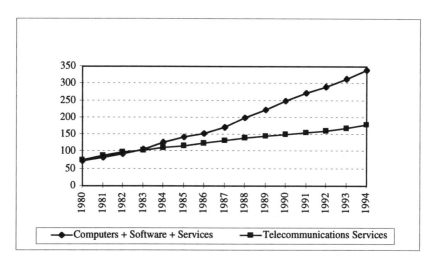

Figure 2 Worldwide Revenue of U.S. Telecommunications and Computer Industries, in Current (1995) Billion Dollars. Source: ITI Industry Statistics Programs, *1995 ITI Information Technology Industry Data Book*, Chapter 1, Table 1-2, p. 2.

Governments build highways even in the United States, where the government does not build telecommunications infrastructure. Al Gore's father, also a U.S. senator, sponsored the legislation for the federal Interstate Highway System, so the metaphor naturally appealed to the Vice President. It was a useful metaphor for a populace enamored of and dependent on automobiles. But the federal government's involvement in highway construction and its early role in creating the Internet suggested an exaggerated public role in the construction of the "information superhighway."

Significantly, the *Agenda for Action* does not use the superhighway metaphor but holds to "information infrastructure." The term implicitly links the familiar telecommunications infrastructure with content and suggests the ordering function of publishers and libraries. Unlike "information society," which is popular in Europe and Japan, "information infrastructure" does not posit an end state but a utilitarian framework in which a variety of individual and social goals can be pursued.

"Information infrastructure" conveys logical as well as physical infrastructure—i.e., not just telecommunications channels but a new kind of infrastructure that arises because computers enable information to be functional. In fact, digital information creates its own infrastructure. Information can be interpreted, applied, and configured by computers. Software defines networks. Networks can be built with databases of addresses and modified by editing the database. Text becomes searchable and networked. Although the *Agenda for Action* shies away from embracing the Internet (which is only mentioned once in the entire document), it emphasizes the importance of applications which are enabled by computers and computer networking. This expanded view of information infrastructure contrasts with the information superhighway model just as the richly enabling nature of the Internet contrasts with video on demand.

Political Economics of Content, Computing, and Communications

In the 1970s and 1980s, the Federal Communications Commission's "Computer Inquiries" sought to insulate new computer services from regulated telephony. By the 1990s, the computer industry was renowned as a hotbed of extreme competition and innovation. These characteristics became associated with the NII, even though telecommunications services and other NII industries remained characterized by relatively slow technological change, market concentration, and, in the case of local plant, regulation. In cable television, actual competition between systems in the same territory ("overbuild") is rare, and in 1992, the cable industry was reregulated at the national level in reaction to high prices. Broadcast television has been regulated on the grounds of spectrum scarcity, and the three major networks have been regulated as oligopolies. The motion picture industry has tended toward concentration because of the enormous costs of marketing new films. (In the 1940s, the Justice Department broke up vertical integration in the industry by divesting the major studios of their theaters.) Local newspapers have become de facto monopolies, except in the largest cities where there may be two newspapers with different readerships. Although other areas in publishing have been very competitive, mergers and acquisitions, often from outside of the publishing industry, have led to consolidation in recent decades. In all of these industries, the technology is ancient by computer industry standards.

Concentration in the media and communications sectors, the power of media to influence public opinion, and the potential for monopoly leveraging have led to restrictions on cross-ownership and service offerings. The regional Bell operating companies (RBOCs) that resulted from the divestiture of AT&T have been tightly constrained because of their secure, government-sanctioned monopolies and ability to use monopoly-derived profits in other markets. For example, the Modified Final Judgment[12] providing for the divestiture of AT&T precluded them from offering information services for seven years, and the 1984 Cable Act precluded most local telephone companies from offering cable television services.

The business models for telephone service, cable, broadcast television, and the local newspaper developed well enough in technological and regulatory isolation that many in the respective industries were reluctant to see the barriers disappear. The different industries often professed to welcome competition on a "level playing field," but the tilt of the field invariably depended on one's particular perspective. The business circumstances, regulatory frameworks, and policy values at stake were sufficiently dissimilar that it was hard to determine what was fair or "level" in specific cases, let alone as a matter of state or national policy.

Telephone service has been very much at the heart of this policy tangle, both because of the scale of the industry and the elaborate, institutionalized cross-subsidies. These cross-subsidies run in complex and interrelated ways from long-distance to local service, from business to residential users, and from urban to rural users. They reflect different aspects of the goal of "universal service" that complicates, and often frustrates, efforts to make the telecommunications industry more competitive.

The U.S. political system further exacerbates the situation. Telephone service is regulated at both the state and federal level. Local governments play an important role with respect to cable television, libraries, and education. At the federal level alone, there are a variety of players: the Federal Communications Commission (an independent regulatory agency), the National Telecommunications and Information Administration (a policy development agency in the Department of Commerce), the Justice Department (which initiated the breakup of AT&T), the State Department (which handles relations with the ITU), Congress, and the courts—including the Federal District Court of Judge Harold Greene, which maintained oversight of the terms and implementation of the AT&T divestiture until 1996.

Efforts to overhaul the Federal Communications Act of 1934 to reflect changes in technology began in the late 1970s, but the complex of competing interests and jurisdictions created a gridlock that broke only with the passage of the Telecommunications Act of 1996.[13] This breakthrough was achieved through bipartisan efforts that focused on bringing down the barriers to competition between cable television operators, local telephone companies, long-distance carriers, wireless services, and other new competitors. It happened because the convergence of technology and markets made regulatory distinctions untenable and because of growing conviction that only full-fledged competition would effectively drive prices down to costs.

The growing political influence of the computer industry was an important factor. The industry was not one of the established major stakeholders, but it had much to gain from lower costs for advanced communications costs. To make the case, the Computer Systems Policy Project articulated a vision that extended far beyond videoconferencing and interactive television to changes in work, learning, and the home as revolutionary as those enabled by the personal computer.[14]

The private-sector Council on Competitiveness chaired by Hewlett-Packard Chairman John Young (to be distinguished from the interagency White House Council of the same name chaired by Vice President Dan Quayle in the Bush Administration) also contributed to breaking the gridlock. The Council convened an interindustry working group that delivered a report on "Unlocking the National Information Infrastructure" in December 1993. The group reached consensus—except on the timetable for allowing the RBOCs to compete in the provision of inter-LATA service, which remained a principal point of contention in the legislative process over the next two years.[15] This would be resolved in the Telecommunications Act by assigning the FCC the task of determining whether an RBOC was facing effective competition in the local loop as determined by a 14-point checklist.[16]

Ascendance of Computing

Whereas the content industries have been apprehensive about the impact of a digital information infrastructure, fearful that it will undermine their intellectual property and disrupt established business models, computers and software are essential elements driving the new digital infrastructure. Publishing, entertainment, health care, manufacturing, libraries—all are seen as longterm growth markets by the computer industry, even though these markets may not be growing in their own terms.

This phenomenon is happening on a grand scale in communications. In fact, the Internet illustrates the "computerization" of communications because so much of its expanding reach, functionality, and value is in computers—routers, servers, and terminals. But whereas computers and the Internet do not directly threaten the core creative functions of the content industries, they do threaten to undermine and commoditize traditional communications services. This may look unlikely inasmuch as the sales volume of U.S. telecommunications carriers was $180 billion in 1995, while the Internet access market was less than one percent of that.[17] But the small size of the Internet access market reflects inherently low costs and the potential to undermine conventional pricing models for telephone service.

In the past, telephone companies have viewed Internet access as a small and uninteresting business. With the recent advent of Internet telephony and the imminent arrival of preferential routing, it threatens their core business. In the short term, if the telephone companies are able to market Internet access successfully, it may prove an inexpensive add-on to basic telephone service. In the longer term, the Internet confronts telephone companies with the pricing problems inherent in providing broadband service: how do you make it affordable without destroying the market for voice and other narrowband services? They face the prospect of an infrastructure as commoditized as personal computers, where they will find themselves chained to an obsolete asset base in an extremely competitive market.

The Divorce of Conduit and Content?

Anxiety about the future of telecommunications has led telephone companies to look longingly at content as a more enduring form of value that could help rationalize large investments in upgrading their physical infrastructure. "Content is king," it is often said. At least content creation is perceived as a glamour industry compared to commoditized and regulated telephony.

For their part, content companies have often sought to control distribution channels in order to assure access to markets and exploit economies of scope in vertical integration. However, this practice has been limited by antitrust action (motion pictures) and regulation (broadcast networks). Cable television systems, which originated as "community antenna television systems," actually integrated backwards into content development. The cable industry managed to maintain vertical exclusivity until the 1992 Cable Act required cable programming services to license to direct broadcast satellite (DBS) services such as Hughes' DirecTV. The ensuing success of DBS has motivated cable operators to look to providing Internet access out of fear that their core business may be threatened.

The earlier vision of interactive television as the "information superhighway" provoked speculation about big vertical mergers and alliances. The prospect of deregulation and expectations that they would be permitted to provide television programming spurred several of the seven RBOCs to pursue relationships with the content industry. U.S. West led the way, nearly merging with cable giant TCI, then entering into a complex partnership with Time-Warner, which has since gone sour. Other ventures have proved less fruitful.

The impulse to integrate content development and distribution may have made sense when distribution outlets were limited. However, in a competitive market where distribution opportunities abound, there is growing awareness that it may be self-defeating as a business strategy. It is not in the interests of distributors to have to accept inferior content from an affiliated provider. Nor is it in the interests of content providers to be bound to a particular distributor when they can get a better deal on the open market.

Initially, the vertically integrated cable television model took hold in online services with America Online, CompuServe, and Prodigy each offering exclusive content on their own proprietary systems. Some of these services objected when Microsoft announced its Microsoft Network, which a user could easily link to through an icon on the Windows 95 desktop. Did Microsoft's near monopoly in desktop operating systems give it an unfair advantage in exploiting economies of scope?

The question quickly lost its edge as the Internet undermined the exclusivity that online services were once able to command. The World Wide Web offered content providers the opportunity to publish on an open client-server platform and so deal directly with their customers instead of through an intermediary. What was an exclusive contractual chain has become an open and competitive market.

The collapse of the strategic rationale for vertical integration suggests the demise of a principal rationale for policy intervention, now that scarcity and barriers to entry are diminishing problems. Ironically, the abundance of low-cost options is the product of a standards-based environment traceable, if not attributable, to the federal investment in an open protocol suite and the interconnection practices that were essential for research networking.

The History of the NII Initiative

The definition of the National Information Infrastructure in the *Agenda for Action* is remarkable for its unreserved breadth. It encompasses everything that produces, contains, processes, or uses information in whatever form, analog or digital, on whatever media, as well as the people who develop information, applications, and services, construct facilities, and train users. National information infrastructures of this sort have existed from the dawn of recorded history (or at least since the development of the nation-state). The goal of the *Agenda for Action* is an "advanced NII"—not a bringing into being, but a transformation.

The "advanced NII" is only defined by example. The *Agenda for Action* begins by envisioning a device that combines a telephone, a TV, a camcorder, and a personal computer—the perfectly integrated advanced NII appliance. But there is no specifically defined goal, such as the Japanese goal of extending optical fiber to the home. The agenda does not include an "information superhighway" or "information society."

The term "national information infra-structure" first appeared in 1976 in *National Information Policy*, a report of the staff of the Domestic Council Committee on the Right of Privacy, chaired by Vice President Nelson Rockefeller. Remarkably, this report covered much the same subject matter as the Clinton/Gore NII initiative. But it posed questions without providing answers or a specific policy agenda. It recommended establishment of an "Office of Information Policy" in the Executive Office of the President, together with an interagency "Council on Information Policy." Although this recommendation was not implemented, the White House Office of Telecommunications Policy was later moved to the Department of Commerce to become part of the National Telecommunications *and Information* Administration (NTIA). Despite the "I" in NTIA, the agency has been almost exclusively concerned with telecommunications rather than information policy.[18]

The real momentum for the NII initiative would come later, beginning with the National High-Performance Computer Technology Act, introduced by Al Gore as a U.S. senator in October 1988. Following titles on "National High-Performance Computer Technology Plan" and "National Research Computer Network" came a short title, "National Information Infrastructure," which stated:

Under the direction of the Office of Science and Technology Policy, and in cooperation with the National Science Foundation, DoD, and other relevant agencies, there shall be developed an information infrastructure of services, databases, and knowledgebanks [sic] accessible through the research computer network. Such an infrastructure shall include—

• a directory of network users;

• improved access to unclassified Federal scientific data bases, including weather data, census data and remote sensing satellite data;

• provision for rapid prototype of computer chips and other devices using centralized facilities connected to the network, and

• data bases [sic] and knowledge banks for use by artificial intelligence programs.

Title III would reappear as the "digital libraries" component of later versions, but this information component would disappear before the High-Performance Computing Act finally passed in 1991. "National Information Infrastructure" was resurrected the following year as an umbrella concept that would reach its full flowering in the *Agenda for Action*.

The idea of a National Information Infrastructure played to a theme of national competitiveness that motivated the Clinton Administration's technology policy of February 1993 as well as the work of the Council on Competitiveness and others. It was advanced early on by the nonprofit Corporation for National Research Initiatives (CNRI), founded in 1986 by ARPANET pioneers Robert Kahn and Vinton Cerf. CNRI's case for information infrastructure as a national investment strategy[19] initially focused on research and high-end applications. But propelled by the expanding scope of the microcomputer revolution, the vision and constituency around an information technology-based investment strategy grew unremittingly.

Thus, the idea of a "National Research Network" propounded by the National Research Council in 1987[20] was repackaged by EDUCOM as the "National Research and Education Network." In 1989, the NREN was recognized as a principal component of the Bush Administration's High Performance Computing and Communications Program (HPCC), and it was formally enshrined in the second half of the High-Performance Computing Act of 1991.

The computer industry, through the Computer Systems Policy Project (CSPP), pushed aggressively to broaden the focus of the HPCC. Established in 1989 in response to protectionist policies that threatened to adversely affect domestic computer production, CSPP was set up not as a conventional trade association but as the CEOs of the 12 (later 13) largest computer companies acting in concert. CSPP, along with the American Electronics Association and other associations, strongly supported the High Performance Computing and Communications Program and Gore's High Performance Computing Act. Just after the High Performance Computing Act passed Congress, CSPP issued an influential report which called for a technology and policy foundation for "an information and communications infrastructure."[21] It recommended that the National Research and Education Network component of the HPCC be expanded to include research on "technologies needed to support broadly accessible and affordable networks." It also advocated research on technologies to support a much wider variety of applications. This recommendation would lead to a new component of the program, "Information Infrastructure Technologies and Applications," and to the bill introduced by Gore in July 1992.

In January 1993, as the Clinton/Gore Administration was taking office, the Computer Systems Policy Project issued a new report, *Perspectives on the National Information Infrastructure: CSPP's Vision and Recommendation for Action,* that advanced the agenda one step further. This document set out a vision for a future National Information Infrastructure very similar to what appeared in the *Agenda for Action* later that year. CSPP's recommendations included an NII Council with appropriated funds that would include public- and private-sector members. The recommendations also included a federal "implementation entity" that would combine oversight of the federal R&D agenda with developing strategies to overcome regulatory barriers to private-sector infrastructure deployment.

Policy Design for the NII Initiative

The kind of public/private-sector super-council that CSPP proposed is rare in the United States, and given a political climate that is skeptical of any new manifestations of government, it would have been difficult to establish a new agency. Instead, the Clinton Administration built on the model of the High Performance Computing and Communications Program, which had been set up as an interagency program in the Bush Administration before it was formally authorized by Congress in the High Performance Computing Act. The HPCC had worked well in coordinating the work and investments of the different agencies in advanced computing and networking. The Clinton Administration took this model one step further by setting up the NII initiative not as a program but as a project with an interagency *task force*. Unlike the HPCC, which was recognized in the federal budget as a crosscut of the participating agencies' budgets, the NII initiative did not appear in the federal budget at all.[22]

The Administration also established a conventional but high-profile private-sector advisory council (United States Advisory Council on the National Information Infrastructure, abbreviated as NIIAC) to be appointed by the Secretary of Commerce.[23] Initially limited by charter to 25 members, the NIIAC elicited such interest that it was expanded to 37 members.

The interagency Information Infrastructure Task Force debuted as the author of the *Agenda for Action*, its organizational structure outlined on a page at the end of the document. There were three committees: Telecommunications Policy, Information Policy, and Applications. The last was subsequently renamed Applications and Technology, and a crosscutting NII Security Issues Forum was added. Working groups were established under the committees with a number of additions over the following year and a half. (See Figure 3.)

The Committee on Telecommunications actually fit well within the charter of the National Telecommunications and Information Administration. However, the other two committees spanned traditional agency jurisdictions.

The Committee on Information Policy was not anticipated in CSPP's recommendations. Chaired by the Administrator of the Office of Information and Regulatory Affairs (OIRA) in the Office of Management and Budget (OMB), it was noteworthy because there is no common understanding of what "information policy" encompasses, despite the title of the 1976 Rockefeller Committee report. It usually includes privacy, dissemination of government information, access to government information (i.e., the Freedom of Information Act), and open meeting laws. With the exception of privacy, which spans behavior in both public and private sectors, information policy most often refers to management of information by the government. In the United States, intellectual property is not usually thought of as a branch of information policy, although the government processes patents and registers trademarks and copyrights. Although the organization of the Committee

September 1993

Telecommunications Policy
  Universal Service
Information Policy
  Intellectual Property Rights
  Privacy
  Government Information
Applications
  Government Information Technology

March 1995

Telecommunications Policy
  Universal Service
  Reliability and Vulnerability
  International Telecommunications
      Foreign Government/Foreign Corporation
      Participation in International Organizations & Standards Setting Bodies
      International Use of Research Networks
      Aid to Telecommunications Development
  Legislative Drafting Task Force
Information Policy
  Intellectual Property Rights
  Privacy
  Government Information
      Electronic Record FOIA [Freedom of Information Act]
      Scientific and Technical Information
Applications and Technology
  Government Information Technology
  Technology Policy
      Advanced Digital Video and NII
      NII Roadmap
      NII Services Architecture
      NII Standards Process
  Health Information and Applications
      Telemedicine
      Consumer Health Informatics
      Emergency Preparedness
      Issues
      Standards

Figure 3 IITF Committees, Working Groups, and Subordinate Working Groups.
Source: *Agenda for Action*; 3/24/95 IITF Fact Sheet.

on Information Policy may have suggested that the Administration would aggressively redefine information policy for the advanced NII, that did not happen. The three working groups set their own relatively narrow and pragmatic agendas.

The heart of the NII initiative as set out in the *Agenda for Action* is a set of nine principles and goals coupled with action items (see sidebar). A progress report on the long list of action items was reported on a year later[24]; a progress report for the second year (1994–1995) was drafted but not released.

Although much can be said about many of the agenda items individually, evaluating the initiative as a whole is difficult, especially since the application of resources to the initiative as such has been informal and quite modest. The initiative has remained a "virtual" program, coordinated by an ad hoc task force. NTIA has served as the secretariat for the NII initiative, but has received no funding for this function nor any new funding to support policy development in this expanded domain.

The Information Infrastructure Task Force has been staffed only to the extent that participating agencies have been able to assign their own staff, and available agency staff were often stretched thin by the proliferation of NII activities. Only a handful of key people, mostly in the Executive Office of the President, have fully understood the scope of the initiative and its relationship to developments in the private sector. However, the Clinton/Gore campaign in 1992 had promised to downsize the White House staff, subsequently limiting the Administration's ability to provide leadership.

As a virtual agency, the IITF was able to spring full blown into action. But over the long run, resource and staff limitations curtailed the development of the initiative. A policy case built on the powerful underlying externalities in information infrastructure was never attempted. Linkages between historically distinct policy domains were not developed. In one context, Gore envisioned a Tennessee schoolgirl accessing the collections of the Library of Congress; in another, concerns were expressed about publishers' needs for intellectual property controls. The *Agenda for Action* promised to "extend the 'universal service' concept to ensure that information resources are available to all at affordable prices." The policy problems in this ambitious item were never fully articulated

Headings from the *Agenda for Action*, Section V.

Principles and Goals for Government Action

1) Promote Private Sector Investment
a) <u>Action</u>: Passage of communications reform legislation
b) <u>Action</u>: Revision of tax policies

2) Extend the "Universal Service" Concept to Ensure that Information Resources Are Available to All at Affordable Prices
a) <u>Action</u>: Develop a New Concept of Universal Service

3) Promote Technological Innovation and New Applications
a) <u>Action</u>: Continue the High-Performance Computing and Communications Program
b) <u>Action</u>: Implement the NII Pilot Projects Program
c) <u>Action</u>: Inventory NII Applications Projects

4) Promote Seamless, Interactive, User-Driven Operation
a) <u>Action</u>: Review and clarify the standards process to speed NII applications
b) <u>Action</u>: Review and reform government regulations that impede development of Interactive services and applications

5) Ensure Information Security and Network Reliability
a) <u>Action</u>: Review privacy concerns of the NII
b) <u>Action</u>: Review of encryption technology
c) <u>Action</u>: Work with industry to increase network reliability

6) Improve Management of the Radio Frequency Spectrum
a) <u>Action</u>: Streamline allocation and use of spectrum
b) <u>Action</u>: Promote market principles in spectrum distribution

7) Protect Intellectual Property Rights
a) <u>Action</u>: Examine the adequacy of copyright laws
b) <u>Action</u>: Explore ways to identify and reimburse copyright owners

8) Coordinate with Other Levels of Government and With Other Bodies
Domestic:
a) <u>Action</u>: Seek ways to improve coordination with state and local officials
International:
b) <u>Action</u>: Open up overseas markets
c) <u>Action</u>: Eliminate barriers caused by incompatible standards
d) <u>Action</u>: Examine international and U.S. trade regulations

9) Provide Access to Government Information and Improve Government Procurement
a) <u>Action</u>: Improve the accessibility of government information
b) <u>Action</u>: Upgrade the infrastructure for the delivery of government information
c) <u>Action</u>: Enhance citizen access to government information
d) <u>Action</u>: Strengthen interagency coordination through the use of electronic mail
e) <u>Action</u>: Reform the Federal procurement process to make government a leading-edge technology adopter

let alone resolved. As noted, the Information Policy Committee did not attempt to rethink information policy as a whole but remained simply a home for three working groups with very different agendas.

In fact, given limited resources and the complexity of the issues, the structure of the IITF may have been too elaborate. Although some of the individual working groups may have enabled diverse agencies to share perspectives around a common table, priority was naturally given to producing tangible results. This required a narrow focus which left little room at the margin to explore underlying economics or the interrelationship of policy goals and objectives. Under these circumstances, the task force structure may have sometimes served more to disperse the issues than to address them coherently.

Nevertheless, the NII initiative was successful out of proportion to its resources in focusing public attention on the massive changes in communications and information technology and the potential for economic and social change. The Administration effectively exploited the "bully pulpit" of government to spur attention to a wide range of legislative, regulatory, and programmatic issues related to information technology and networking.

The vision of an advanced National Information Infrastructure promoted by a catchy metaphor (the "superhighway") unquestionably helped push Congress to enact telecommunications reform legislation. The pressure was powerful but informal; the Administration judiciously allowed Congress (even when it was under Democratic control in 1993–1994) to take the lead in crafting the legislation while the Administration kept beating the drum for the advanced NII. The Clinton Administration's formal contributions to the process were quite modest. It issued a short "White Paper on Communications Act Reforms" which included a proposal to add a new title for two-way broadband services, but it did not press the proposal.[25] Subsequently, the President's Council of Economic Advisors issued a short paper purporting to link the Administration's proposals to economic growth, but the paper was simply an illustrative model which assumed accelerated growth in the three basic components of information infrastructure (conduit, content, and computers).[26]

The initiative worked much more visibly on the applications side where there were many opportunities to publicize pioneering work without getting entangled in complex policy issues. Unlike NTIA on the telecommunications policy side, many of the agencies participating in the Committee on Applications and Technology (CAT) had substantial programmatic resources which could be brought to bear. The most active were those involved in high-performance computing and networking: the Advanced Research Projects Agency (ARPA) of the Department of Defense, the National Science Foundation (NSF), the National Aeronautics and Space Administration (NASA), and the Department of Energy (DOE). They were joined by the National Institute of Standards and Technology (NIST), which was expanding under the Administration's aggressive technology policy and whose director chaired the Committee on Applications and Technology.

These agencies produced or supported many reports and workshops which helped focus attention on the advanced NII and advance interindustry understanding of technological, business, and policy issues. In early 1993, before the *Agenda for Action* was issued, the High Performance Computing and Communications Program was expanded by executive action to include a fifth component: Information Infrastructure Technology and Applications. The new component merely enlarged the scope of the HPCC budget crosscut rather than adding a new funded program, but it answered CSPP's calls for broadening the focus of the HPCC.[27] Since it achieved some of what Gore had sought in introducing the Information Infrastructure and Technology Act of 1992, it mattered less that similar legislation introduced in the following Congress was never enacted.[28]

Just as HPCC applications already focused on "grand challenges" such as global climate change and human genome mapping, the IITA was designed to focus on common needs in education, libraries, health care, government services, and manufacturing—so-called "national challenges." The new program helped legitimize research investment in low-end applications where success might have broad and perhaps near-term payoffs.

This interest in "infrastructural" investment was reflected in the model advanced by the HPPC Program and the Committee on Applications and Technology showing generic *services* as the middle layer of a three-level NII, with *bitways* at the bottom and *applications* at the top. Under this model, the critical importance of generic services for leveraging information infrastructure development made them a funding priority under the IITA component of the HPCC. A landmark 1994 National Research Council report, *Realizing the Information Future*, advanced a similar vision. Funded by NSF, the report presented a compelling case for an open-architecture NII with a "common bearer service" based on the role of the Internet Protocol (IP) in the Internet.[29]

The Quest for Interoperability

These activities were concerned with how to achieve interoperability, which was explicitly recognized in the *Agenda for Action* as essential to the advanced NII. Here again, the Internet was recognized as a model because the processes for developing Internet standards had been so successful in advancing widespread use of the TCP/IP protocol suite, despite the fact that the competing OSI suite had been anointed for government use by NIST. This rift between the research agency practice and the official practice was addressed in the 1994 report of the Federal Internetworking Requirements Panel which acknowledged and legitimized the de facto success of the TCP/IP suite.

The success of the Internet processes convinced the federal research agencies that standards development in this fast-moving environment had to be anticipatory, iterative, and linked to the development of real products and services. However, over the past three years it has become clear that Internet standards will be driven increasingly by market forces, and that the role of university researchers and funding agencies will be diminished.

Although few people claim to fully understand all the technological, business, and legal dimensions of interoperability, it surfaces repeatedly as one of the central policy problems of developing an advanced NII. It is an issue where the strategic investment thread tangles with the competition policy thread and where the open traditions of the Internet clash with the proprietary interests of the computer industry.

In February 1994, CSPP took the lead in defining and addressing the problem in a report that focused on four "critical interfaces" in the NII: 1) appliance to network; 2) appliance to application; 3) application to application; and 4) network to network.[30] The report called for "open" specifications at these interfaces, defining open to include proprietary interfaces as long as they were available on reasonable and nondiscriminatory terms—and could only be changed with advance notice and public process. Although "public process" was not defined, this seemed to suggest a new way of handling proprietary standards, albeit only in the context of these few critical interfaces. Arguably, the extensive public beta-testing that Windows 95 underwent beginning later that year qualified as a public process.

CSPP did not specify how the requirements for open standards should be monitored or enforced. Early versions of the telecommunications reform legislation included provisions on interoperability, but Microsoft and some computer companies argued against FCC oversight of interoperability on the grounds that it could impinge on their intellectual property rights. The final version of the legislation only addresses interconnection. While interoperability is a necessary aspect of interconnection, the emphasis is different and the context is clearly limited to telecommunications services.

Because information infrastructure is characterized by strong externalities and economies of scale, network tipping—an irreversible shift in the market toward a single standard—may result. Microsoft's domination of the operating system and office applications software markets has become a conspicuous example. The lesson widely gleaned from Microsoft is that the unique economic characteristics of this environment argue for business strategies that emphasize market share over short-term profits. At the same time, the network tipping phenomenon raises the specter of monopolies more entrenched than telephone companies in the local loop.

The IITF did not tackle the policy issues between interoperability, different forms of intellectual property, and antitrust law. [31] However, the Committee on Applications and Technology has worked to broaden the scope of public debate on technological issues in the expectation that this would help advance a broad range of standards activities. Research agencies have continued to support the processes of the Internet Engineering Task Force, and anxiety over interoperability-related bottlenecks has been alleviated by the strong market demand for standards that are nonproprietary as well as open.

Telecommunications and Information Infrastructure Assistance Program

The only new funding program of the NII initiative, the NTIA-administered Telecommunications and Information Infrastructure Assistance Program (TIIAP), has played a catalytic role at a different level: local and regional implementation of infrastructure and applications. TIIAP has offered grants for collaborative, cost-shared pilot projects, especially in rural areas and inner cities and often with private-sector partners. However, it has been funded by Congress at such a modest levels—$26 million in FY1994, $36 million in FY1995, and $21.5 million in FY1996—that it has served more as a catalyst for collaboration than as a direct public investment in the NII. Ironically, its success on this score is probably best measured by the number of proposals received relative to the number funded. In FY1994, 92 applications were funded out of a total of 1,087; in FY1995, only 117 were funded out of more than 1,800 applications.[32]

Government Operations

One of the most visible accomplishments under the NII umbrella has been in the government's use of information technology for internal purposes and for dissemination of government information to the public. Here the initiative's objective of improving the government's management of information technology and information was bolstered by the National Performance Review, a government-wide reengineering effort, also under Vice President Gore's aegis, with the announced goal of "reinventing government."[33]

The first area of significant change, noticeable early in the first year of the Clinton/Gore Administration, was in the use of electronic mail. Many of the younger political appointees personally used email and promoted it as an efficient and cost-effective means of communication. The Administration's early emphasis on technology policy helped create a critical mass of users, inasmuch as the principal research agencies were longtime users of the Internet and electronic mail. By the end of 1993, Internet email was widely used in most agencies, enabling the federal government to appear as a leader in the adoption of new technology.

Over the following year, the federal government built on the infrastructure developed for email to become a leader in adopting and using the World Wide Web. The White House planned its own home page and urged other Executive Branch agencies to do the same. The White House Web site[34] was publicly unveiled in the summer of 1994, and it included a page listing the executive agencies, showing clearly which were linked (and therefore online) and which were not. The White House site was a public relations coup, especially among Internet users, and undoubtedly helped in a small way to leverage the growth of the Web.

After the Republican victory in the 1994 Congressional elections, Newt Gingrich, the new Speaker of the House, followed suit by mounting pending legislation on *Thomas* (for Thomas Jefferson, who donated his library to found the Library of Congress), an Internet-accessible system managed by the Library of Congress.[35] Congressional Democrats had been slow in making the legislative processes open to the Internet, which enabled Gingrich to score a public relations victory.[36]

Progress was also made in the management of information technology with passage of the Information Technology Management Reform Act of 1996 and the Federal Acquisition Reform Act of 1996.[37] The former required agencies to appoint chief information officers and required mission-oriented capital planning for technology investments, while the latter simplified a range of procurement practices and gave agency officials greater discretion. These reforms do not make the government the "leading-edge adopter" promised by the *Agenda for Action,* but they help the government keep up with the marketplace.

Encryption Policy

Cryptography policy has proved by far the most difficult and contentious NII policy issue for the Clinton Administration. The Administration has found itself in a stalemate between the interest of law enforcement and the National Security Agency in access to encrypted information around the world and industry's interest in marketing encrypted products to the world unencumbered by export controls. The software industry has been particularly outspoken, claiming that export restrictions severely limit its ability to compete in international markets where powerful encryption software is already available.

The Administration initially proposed a purportedly voluntary "Clipper Chip" with private keys to be held in escrow by government agencies. Massive opposition from civil libertarians as well as industry led to the abandonment of the Clipper Chip proposal. The Administration has subsequently proposed software-based key escrow systems with keys held by certified third parties. These schemes would remain voluntary within the United States but would provide an infrastructure in which encryption could be regulated worldwide. However, these proposals have met with similar resistance.

The Clipper Chip proposal did not originate from the Information Infrastructure Task Force, but encryption policy could not be separated from the goals of the NII initiative. The NII Advisory Council picked up the issue at its first meeting, and opposition to the Clipper Chip proposal was the first topic on which it expressed consensus. Later, a loosely chartered NII Security Issues Forum was formed within the IITF to interface with the Interagency Working Group on Encryption and Telecommunications, which was outside of the IITF structure.[38]

Intellectual Property

Intellectual property also proved a difficult issue. In this case, the Administration appeared to take sides in disputes that pitted one industry against another and publishers against users. The Working Group on Intellectual Property Rights produced a report in draft form as a "Green Paper" in July 1994 and a final "White Paper" in September 1995. While the overt message of the White Paper was that little in the Copyright Act needed to be changed, it was perceived by many as a legal brief for the content industry's view of the law, a perception aided by the fact that the Chair of the Working Group, the Commissioner of Patents and Trademarks in the Commerce Department, was previously a lobbyist for publishing interests.

The most prominent issue in the debate over the White Paper has been the extent to which intermediaries in a digital infrastructure, such as online services or Usenet servers, should be liable for infringements by their users. The White Paper argued for strict liability, even for incidental copying, on the grounds that such intermediaries are in a better position than publishers to police the behavior of users. Opposition to this view by carrier, Internet, and user interests stalled the legislation proposed by the White Paper.

The White Paper was the product of one of two action items under the heading of goal of protecting intellectual property in the *Agenda for Action*. The other action item, "explore ways to identify and reimburse copyright owners," promised to explore the need for standards in copyright management systems and the need for efficient payment systems. This item was not implemented, although the Working Group on Intellectual Property Right (in the White Paper) claimed this to be the responsibility of the Committee on Applications and Technology. This is perhaps a good example of an issue falling through the interstices of the IITF, as well as a case where a facilitative approach to standards development might have helped bring different industries together on a problem that spanned industry boundaries. By putting its entire effort into developing a legal position, the Administration ended up intensifying interindustry conflicts, as well as alienating some major supporters of its NII initiative.[39]

Universal Service

The *Agenda for Action* promised to "extend the 'Universal Service' concept to ensure that information resources are available to all at affordable prices." In an effort to fulfill this ambitious commitment, NTIA held a series of meetings around the United States in 1993–1994. However, it proved difficult to address the issue of universal service productively for communications beyond basic telephony. The problems of doing so were evident in the Internet, where access to the network required a computer, modem, software, and basic skills. The paradigm of a single provider offering uniform service through a simple, inexpensive handset clearly could not apply.

The *Agenda for Action* promised even more—that it would somehow reconcile the telecommunications concept of nationwide universal service to the traditional mission of the local public library. Superficially, this intractable policy problem appears to have been solved by the Web. At least for those able to get on, there is an abundance of information resources available for free!

The Global Information Infrastructure

Vice President Gore articulated a vision of the Global Information Infrastructure (GII) in a speech before an International Telecommunication Union conference on development in Buenos Aires in March 1994. The speech set forth the five principles in the Administration's recently released "White Paper on Communications Act Reform"—encourage private investment, promote competition, a flexible regulatory framework, open access, and universal service. These principles of course addressed facilities-based telecommunications rather than information infrastructure as a whole.

The charter for the U.S. vision, *The Global Information Infrastructure: Agenda for Cooperation*, appeared in February 1995 after a long gestation (just in time for the G-7 Conference on the Information Society in Brussels). The five principles still stood alone and intact. However, they were complemented by a second section on encouraging the use of the GII, which included a series of recommendations on information policy and applications. The operating

structure for the Information Infrastructure Task Force had become the organizing framework for the *Agenda for Cooperation*,
albeit not in recognizable form.

The focus on telecommunications can be explained in part by the
ITU context in which Gore broached the concept of the GII.
Domestically, the Administration had chosen to let Congress take
the lead on the telecommunications reform, but internationally,
the Administration was free to set the agenda. Of course, as a
practical matter, there was much less that could be done to define
and implement an agenda at the international level. Gore was not
advocating a program for the ITU but principles for liberalizing
telecommunications as a matter of national policy in other countries. The focus on telecommunications issues made sense because
those were issues that many countries were already addressing on
their own. Even though circumstances in the United States were
quite different because of the history of private-sector control,
many countries, and most developed countries, saw themselves
moving in the direction of private ownership and competition.

With the European Union picking up "Information Society"
issues under the Bangemann Commission and planning a G-7
ministerial conference on the same topic, the GII agenda moved
beyond facilities-based telecommunications. Many countries had
already defined public-sector roles in developing strategic technologies and in supporting information and communications
infrastructure for education, research, and other favored sectors.
With the Internet as an enabling platform, it was now possible to
collaborate on applications across national borders, and the G7
interest in the GII provided an occasion to do so.

But if agency resources for managing the U.S. NII initiative were
modest, agency resources for engaging in and coordinating any
sort of GII activities are virtually nonexistent. Even though the
Internet demonstrates that information is global and NIIs are
arbitrary subdivisions within the GII, it has proved even more
difficult to craft a coherent agenda for an advanced GII. In just the
past two years, the international landscape has been radically
changed by the emergence of the Internet as a common-denomi-
nator overlay infrastructure liberated from local facilities and
national regulation. But international policy development pro-

cesses are considerably more balkanized and less agile than the processes of the U.S. government.

The NII and the Republican Congress

Unlike conventional government programs, the NII initiative has been aimed at stimulating private-sector activity and at reducing government activity in favor of private enterprise. However, since provision of telecommunications services has always been a private-sector enterprise in the United States, liberalization has been somewhat less dramatic than in other countries. Telecommunications reform in the United States has not been a problem of privatization, but a problem of competition policy and reconciling open competition with the goals of universal service.

There is a different public/private-sector dynamic on the strategic investment side, where public investment for underlying technologies and for infrastructure development is seen as seeding private investment. The Clinton Administration inherited most of the technology-related investment programs but expanded the public-sector role with the approval and encouragement of CSPP and other high-tech industry organizations. When the Republicans gained control of both houses of Congress in the 1994 elections, this became a major partisan issue which threatened the survival of the Commerce Department.

The debate over the Commerce Department has not centered on the NII initiative per se. However, Republicans targeted NTIA, which continued to serve as the secretariat and point of coordination for the IITF and the NII Advisory Council. TIIAP, the one new program born of the NII initiative, was subject to continued debate on priorities, fluctuation in appropriated funds, and threats of rescission.

The Advanced Technologies Program (ATP), which cost-shares industry research on high-risk, enabling technologies, was often the focal point for attacks on what some Republicans described as "industrial policy." The ATP included a number of projects in information technology, as did the Technology Reinvestment Project (TRP), a Defense-led interagency effort designed to help defense industries reorient their technology base toward commercial technology. The TRP awarded substantial funds to information technology projects in its first year (1994), but shifted away after criticism from the new Congress that its grants were insufficiently related to defense needs.

While there has been some Republican criticism of the High Performance Computing and Communications Program (which is associated with Al Gore, even though initiated within the Bush Administration), there continues to be bipartisan support for basic scientific research and for the role the National Science Foundation has played in the development of the Internet. In fact, the Internet has become a conspicuous success story for the government's mission agencies, especially ARPA and NSF. While ARPA certainly did not intend or foresee today's vigorous Internet marketplace, NSF's method of funding the NSFNET beginning in the mid-1980s was remarkably open to commercialization.[40]

The Administration has quietly shifted secretariat responsibilities for the IITF from NTIA to NIST. That is, from a policy development home to an applications home, from the main Department of Commerce building (in the line of Congressional fire) to the NIST campus in Gaithersburg, Maryland (beyond the Beltway). As an agenda-driven project, the initiative had a natural life-cycle, which was undoubtedly shortened by the election of a Republican Congress and probably sealed by the death of Commerce Secretary Ron Brown in 1996. Many of the individual action items have played out in one form or another, so that the initiative is in need of reformulation. But realistically, this will not happen until after the 1996 elections—if the President and Vice President are reelected and if the initiative can be repackaged with a new vision.

Of course, the fading of the NII initiative as a project has not limited the Clinton Administration's interest in communications and information technologies and applications. In 1996, several initiatives were announced in primary and secondary education: A proposal for a Technology Literacy Challenge Fund which would require $2 billion in funding over five years; "California Net Day," which successfully engaged thousands of volunteers (including the President and Vice President) in wiring California schools; and "21st Century Teachers," a project engaging a number of education organizations in a voluntary program to better institutionalize technology in the schools.

The Administration has always been free to act outside of the IITF framework and has done so when the subject has demanded it. Encryption policy is one example. Following a March 1995 memorandum from Vice President Gore, the Department of Health and Human Services undertook an agenda of its own on health data standards, privacy, health information for consumers, and telemedicine. The Emerging Telecommunications Technology Act, which provided for the reallocation of spectrum used by federal agencies to the private sector, was passed before the NII initiative was announced.

Conclusion

The NII initiative as a whole has succeeded in focusing public attention on the transformative potential of information technology and networks and the need to develop a deeper understanding of their social, economic, and policy implications. It has also provided a useful framework for communications among federal agencies with diverse charters and perspectives, and it has spurred many of these agencies to communicate more effectively with their constituencies and with the general public.

There are a number of specific achievements that the Clinton Administration can point to, but there is no "man on the moon" by the which the NII initiative will be remembered. The Administration can claim a share of the credit for the Telecommunications Act of 1996, the culmination of a long struggle to draft a statutory framework for a competitive telecommunications industry. But with the passage of legislation, much of the action has moved to the Federal Communications Commission, an independent regulatory agency not formally part of the Administration.

The Republican victory in the Congressional elections in November 1994 took some of the wind out of an initiative that operated at the margin. While the Republicans did not oppose the initiative, they put the Administration on the defensive in a number of related areas. As an unfunded virtual project, the NII initiative was not directly affected, but some of the technology programs that had refocused on supporting the advanced NII were questioned and sometimes diminished by Congress.

In the three years since the NII initiative was announced, there have been sweeping changes in technology and the market. Speculation and debate on a future NII have been upstaged by the explosion of here-and-now Internet services, applications, and resources. The underlying policy issues remain, and indeed have grown in complexity and nuance, but they are overshadowed by the plethora of business opportunities playing out on the Internet.

Although many are wary of the Internet marketplace because so little money is being made, huge investments are being driven by the broad complex of expectations that stimulated the NII vision. The same profusion of externalities that argued for the initiative now drives the market for Internet services and software. Profits may be scarce now, but Microsoft is proof that spectacular success can be had, and that position and leverage are everything.[41] Netscape proves that giants can be surprised, that the quick can inherit position. And Java, from Sun Microsystems, shows that there are still surprises to be had....The metaphor of the highway has been overtaken by the mythology of the Internet. (See Figure 4.)

In 1990, technology policy in the form of federal investment strategy was shaping the Internet. Today, technology is driving the market, and the market is shaping the public perception and experience of information infrastructure. The policy development process struggles to keep up. How should federal agencies work with the private sector to foster networked applications in areas of public concern such as health care, education, libraries, and the environment? What do the externalities and scale economies driving the marketplace tell us? How are the old rules skewed in this vortex of accelerated competition? How can we, or should we, tailor antitrust and intellectual property to temper the maelstrom? What does the Web tell us about the flow of information? How do we inform it with labels and contracts? Will there be policy servers for all our needs and preferences?

If the NII were really an information superhighway, we would not have this difficulty. It would just be more of the same, only bigger and better. Rather, it is the extraordinary *functional* expansion of the Internet that keeps expanding the scope and play of these questions. It is the wealth of proliferating applications, each in its

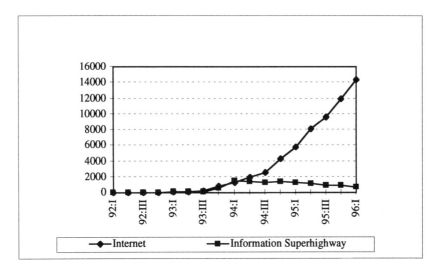

16000
14000
12000
10000
8000
6000
4000
2000
0

92:I 92:III 93:I 93:III 94:I 94:III 95:I 95:III 96:I

—◆—Internet   —■—Information Superhighway

Figure 4 References to "Internet" and "Information Superhighway" in the Top Fifty English-Language Newspapers. Source: Majpap Nexis Library Archive.

own domain of values, conventions, and institutions. It is the range and complexity of human interaction, enabled by the technology, the applications, and the market. Policy design and development, however expertly guided, just do not move this fast.

Then again, the market itself has never moved this fast. Within a growing investment community, the Internet is seen not only as the once and future NII, but as a vast frontier for innovation and enterprise. It is at once physical, logical, and institutional, an organic mesh of unfathomable richness and vitality. It bears an eerie resemblance to the marketplace itself—which, with the coming of electronic commerce, it promises to electrify in a reciprocal embrace.

Notes

1. See Committee on Information and Communications, National Science and Technology Council, "America in the Age of Information," National Coordination Office for High Performance Computing and Communications, March 10, 1995.

2. The Administration's technology policy was announced in *Technology for America's Economic Growth*, published in February 1993, a month after Clinton and Gore took office.

3. This meant that "independent agencies" such as the Federal Communications Commission and Legislative Branch agencies such as the Copyright Office could only participate as observers.

4. See John Markoff, "Building the Electronic Superhighway," *New York Times*, January 24, 1993, Section 3, p.1.

5. This tendency to reify network funding programs into networks and thereby cause confusion about federal roles and policies had already proved a problem for the NSFNET. See the author's chapter, "Information Technology and Information Infrastructure," in Lewis M. Branscomb, ed., *Empowering Technology* (Cambridge, MA: MIT Press, 1993), at pages 145–151.

6. The controversy concerned the award of a cooperative agreement that allowed a nonprofit corporation set up by IBM and MCI to operate the NSFNET backbone. See Office of the Inspector General, "Review of NSFNET," National Science Foundation 93-01, March 23, 1993.

7. Some divisions within the major long-distance carriers—AT&T, Sprint, and MCI—were involved in Internet technology. But Internet technology differed so radically from conventional telephony that few outside these divisions understood it or its implications. The regional Bell operating companies and other local exchange carriers were less technologically oriented and had correspondingly less interest in the Internet.

8. http://iitf.doc.gov. The Web site was maintained by the National Telecommunications and Information Administration as the IITF secretariat, a function that is reportedly shifting to National Institute of Standards and Technology. The "NII Virtual Library" site maintained by NIST for the Committee on Applications and Technology also points to NII resources: http://nii.nist.gov.

9. The G7 is comprised of Canada, France, Germany, Italy, Japan, the United Kingdom, and the United States.

10. ITU estimates for 1994 show 13.5 million leased circuits for the U.S. out of a world total of 20.4 million.

11. Estimated for January 1996. The exact figure is difficult to determine because most hosts in the United States use the three-letter top-level domains (.edu, .com, .org) that serve as global addresses, whereas hosts in other countries usually use the two-letter country code domains (.us, .uk, .jp). However, more companies outside the United States are seeking .com addresses, and approximately 20 percent of current .com registrations are for non-U.S. sites. Domain registration is administered by the Internic, which is operated by Network Solutions, Inc., under agreement with the National Science Foundation. Survey and analysis of hosts is conducted by John Quarterman (http://www.mids.org) and Mark Lottor (http://www.nw.com).

12. United States v. American Telephone & Telegraph Co., 552 F.Supp. 131 (D.D.C. 1982).

13. There were successful efforts to deal with cable television issues, first in the Cable Communications Policy Act of 1984, which was a reaction against local

regulatory practices, and then in the Cable Television Consumer Protection and Competition Act of 1992, which, in reaction to rising prices, mandated FCC regulation of cable rates.

14. Computer Systems Policy Project, "Perspectives on the National Information Infrastructure: CSPP's Vision and Recommendations for Action," January 12, 1993.

15. LATA = Local Access and Transport Area. Under the Modified Final Judgment providing for the 1984 divestiture of AT&T, local Bell operating companies could not provide toll service between LATAs.

16. Telecommunications Act of 1996, P.L. 104-104, Section 271(c)(2)(B).

17. Forrester Research estimates the Internet access market at $1.5 billion for 1995. The Maloff Company estimates $1.9 billion per annum as of April 1996.

18. An early NTIA effort to scope out a policy framework for information was published as *Issues in Information Policy*, Jane Yurow, ed., Washington, DC: NTIA, 1980. Since then, NTIA has rarely ventured into information policy.

19. See the prospectus of the Corporation for National Research Initiatives, *Building a Strategic Advantage in America*: "The United States has within its grasp the capability to mold this dependence [on computers and communications] into a powerful, strategic advantage through the creation of a national *information infrastructure* providing timely access to selected information and facilitating its rapid assimilation and use." [Emphasis in the original.]

20. *Toward A National Research Network*, (Washington, DC: National Academy Press, 1987).

21. Computer Systems Policy Project, "Expanding the Vision of High-Performance Computing and Communications: Linking America for the Future," December 1991.

22. Each year, beginning with FY 1992, a supplement to the President's Fiscal Year Budget has been prepared for the HPCC activities. The supplement includes an extensive narrative as well as the specific funds requested by agency. The annual supplements are posted by the National Coordinating Office for High Performance Computing and Communications at http://www.nco.gov.

23. Executive Order 12864 of September 15, 1993, *Federal Register*, Vol. 58, No. 179, September 17,1993.

24. Brown, Ronald H., Secretary of Commerce and Chairman, Information Infrastructure Task Force, *National Information Infrastructure, Progress Report, September 1993–1994,* (Washington DC: Department of Commerce, September 1994).

25. "Administration White Paper on Communications Act Reforms," undated [January 1994].

26. Council of Economic Advisers, "Economic Benefits of the Administration's Legislative Proposals for Telecommunications," Executive Office of the President, June 14, 1994.

27. Also in 1993, the National Science and Technology Council was formed as a high-level interagency coordinating body with a Committee on Information and Communications R&D (CIC) chaired by the Director of Defense Research and Engineering and the Deputy Director of the Office of Science and Technology Policy. The High Performance Computing, Communications and Information Technology (HPCCIT) Subcommittee of the CIC oversees the HPCC Program.

28. Similar legislation was introduced in the 103rd Congress by Congressman Rick Boucher (D-VA) and Senator Ernest Hollings (D-SC). Boucher's bill was H.R. 1757, the National Information Infrastructure Act of 1993, introduced July 15, 1993. Hollings introduced S. 4, the National Competitiveness Act of 1993, on January 21, 1993, just as President Clinton took office.

29. *Realizing the Information Future* (Washington, DC: National Academy Press, 1994).

30. Computer Systems Policy Project, "Perspectives on the National Information Infrastructure: Ensuring Interoperability," February 1994. Publication of the CSPP report was no small achievement because of the diversity of views within CSPP.

31. For an overview of the politics of interoperability, see Francois Bar, Michael Borrus, and Robert Steinberg, "Interoperability and the NII: Mapping the Debate," *Information Infrastructure and Policy*, Vol. 4, No. 4, 1995.

32. NTIA's analysis of the 1995 awards shows the following breakdown:

Application Domain	Total Award Amount	Number of Awards
Arts & Culture	$0.9 Million	1
Community Networking	$8.4 Million	28
Economic Development	$3.1 Million	12
Health	$4.7 Million	12
Higher Education	$4.2 Million	13
Human Services	$2.4 Million	9
Education	$5.6 Million	19
Library Services	$1.5 Million	8
Other	$1.0 Million	2
Public & Gov. Info.	$3.1 Million	7
Public Safety	$0.8 Million	5
State/Local Infra. Plan.	$0.2 Million	1
Totals	$35.7 Million	117

33. The pertinent recommendations are contained in National Performance Review, Office of the Vice President, From Red Tape to Results: Creating a Government that Works Better and Costs Less, Step 4: Reengineering Programs to Cut Costs, issued September 7, 1993, just before the *Agenda for Action* was announced. See also the supplemental report, *Reengineering Through Information Technology*, dated September 1993 but not publicly released until 1994.

34. http://www.whitehouse.gov.

35. http://thomas.loc.gov.

36. Congress passed legislation reauthorizing the Paperwork Reduction Act in 1995 as P.L. 104-13. Section 3506(d) codified principles on the dissemination of government information that had been incorporated into the revision of OMB Circular A-130 (58 F.R. 36070, July 2, 1993).

37. Both bills were included as amendments to the National Defense Authorization Act for Fiscal 1996, P.L. 104-106.

38. The name was changed to the Working Group on Cryptography Policy in 1996.

39. For a sense of the debate see the Web sites of the Creative Incentive Coalition (supportive of the White Paper) at http://www.cic.org and the Digital Future Coalition (critical of the White Paper) at http://www.ari.net/dfc.

40. See RFC 1192, "Commercialization of the Internet," Brian Kahin, ed., September 1990.

41. The spectrum of business models at work in evolving different levels of the NII is documented in the recent National Research Council report from the Computer Science and Telecommunications Board, *The Unpredictable Certainty: Information Infrastructure Through 2000,* (Washington, DC: National Academy Press, 1996).

Cultural Sovereignty, Public Participation, and Democratization of the Public Sphere: The Canadian Debate on the New Information Infrastructure

Marc Raboy

Debate over communication policy has been one of the dominant themes of Canadian social discourse since the early days of radio broadcasting. Communication, in Canada, has been seen variously as a binding force for national unity, a vehicle for social development, and an instrument of cultural affirmation. In contrast, policy has also sought to promote the development of Canadian communication industries. In this respect, more so than in Europe or the United States, where one or the other pole has conventionally dominated, in Canada communication has evolved according to the push and pull between economics and culture.[1]

The Canadian debate on the new information infrastructure, launched within weeks of President Clinton's 1993 announcement of the U.S. national information infrastructure (NII), has settled firmly into this historical mold. This chapter will explore the various facets of that debate with the historical context in mind, suggesting that the Canadian approach can be seen as a model for attempts to marry non market public policy objectives and market forces, with all pitfalls, in the framework of a stable democracy with a relatively robust economy.[2]

The development of a Canadian NII, it will be argued, can not respond only to technological or geopolitical imperatives but is also contingent on the extent to which the new initiatives correspond to a social demand. The question of how best to meet sociocultural objectives is part of the political equation of communications infrastructure development—or regulatory repositioning—in Canada, a country with a tradition of state intervention to promote an indigenous market and an indigenous culture.

General Background

The unfolding of the NII in Canada raises a number of public policy issues that will have to be faced by most of the advanced industrial nations.

Because of its historic tradition of policy intervention in the cultural and communication arenas, Canada has an established set of institutional practices for policy making that may be particularly appropriate for addressing national infrastructure issues in a variety of settings.

Among Canada's policy particularities are the principles that communication infrastructures constitute a cornerstone of the national cultural heritage, that the main instrument for carrying out cultural and communication policy is a mixed system of publicly owned and publicly regulated public and private industries, and that the participation of social groups is a central part of the policy making process.

Structurally, the Canadian NII debate has to be seen in the context of two pieces of legislation, the Broadcasting Act[3] and the Telecommunications Act,[4] of the activity of the agency charged with supervising and regulating both broadcasting and telecommunications under these two laws, the Canadian Radio-Television and Telecommunications Commission (CRTC).

The Broadcasting Act, first adopted in 1932 and last revised in 1991, is by far the more complex and elaborate of the two laws and gives some indication of the general tone of the debate. By virtue of this legislation, all broadcasting in Canada is declared to be "a public service essential to the maintenance and enhancement of national identity and cultural sovereignty."[5] Canadian broadcasting is deemed to be a single system comprising public, private, and community elements. It must be effectively owned and controlled by Canadians, make maximum use of Canadian creative and other resources, and serve the needs and interests and reflect the circumstances and aspirations of Canadian men, women, and children. These circumstances include equal rights, linguistic duality (En-

Government		Parliament	
Department of Industry	Department of Heritage	Broadcasting Act	Telecommunications Act
ad hoc committees (such as Information Highway Advisory Council, Mandate Review Committee)		CRTC	
	(public participation)		
	(industry lobbying)		

Figure 1

glish and French), the multicultural and multiracial nature of Canadian society, as well as the special place of aboriginal peoples within that society. The Act creates a publicly owned national broadcasting service, the Canadian Broadcasting Corporation (CBC), with a detailed mandate and provides for other public services in such areas as educational broadcasting (which falls under provincial jurisdiction). In the event of conflicting interests between public and private sector elements of the system, the objectives of the public sector are to prevail. The CRTC. an independent public authority, regulates and supervises the Canadian broadcasting system and oversees the implementation of the Broadcasting Act.[6]

The Telecommunications Act, adopted in 1993, starts from a similar position, declaring that "telecommunications performs an essential role in the maintenance of Canada's identity and sovereignty,"[7] and lists the objectives of Canadian telecommunications policy: to facilitate the orderly development of a telecommunications system that serves to safeguard, enrich, and strengthen the social and economic fabric of Canada and its regions; to make reliable and affordable services of high quality accessible to Canadians; to enhance the efficiency and national and international competitiveness of Canadian telecommunications; to promote the ownership and control of Canadian carriers by Canadians and to promote the use of Canadian transmission facilities; to foster increased reliance on market forces while ensuring regulation when required; to respond to the social and economic requirements of users; and to contribute to the protection of privacy. Since 1976 the telecommunications sector has also been regulated by the CRTC.

Legislative rhetoric aside, it is important to understand the scope of the telephone, broadcasting, and cable industries (see Table 1), the government objectives with regard to these industries, and public expectations of them.

The central feature of the Canadian broadcasting system is its public-private, mixed-ownership structure. The publicly owned CBC operates national AM and FM radio networks, over-the-air television networks, and 24-hour cable news services in English and in French, providing service even into the country's most remote northern regions. About 75% of the CBC's funding comes from an annual grant from Parliament, and the balance comes from television advertising (the cable news services are self-financed by cable revenues). After a decade in which the CBC struggled with a progressively shrinking public subsidy, its future financial basis was high on the national agenda following a major review of its mandate by a blue ribbon committee that reported in January 1996.[8] But it was still by far the largest single broadcaster, with an operating budget of around Can $1.3 billion in 1994 (see Table 2).

Private sector radio and television operate competitively wherever market conditions allow and are entirely funded by advertising revenues. Canada is one of the most highly cabled countries in the world, with a subscriber rate approaching 80 percent of total households, and the Canadian cable industry has been at the cutting edge of broadcasting development since the 1970s. More than a dozen Canadian speciality television services are currently available through cable companies, in packages structured by regulatory requirement to ensure priority delivery of Canadian signals and a favourable balance of Canadian and U.S. subscription services. As a matter of course, Canadian cable companies offer the main American network signals from bordering U.S. stations as part of their basic packages. At the time of writing, the CRTC had just licensed two Canadian satellite services, which hope to break into the cable-dominated market (see Table 3).

Table 1   Top Canadian Telephone, Broadcasting and Cable Companies (by revenue, Can$, 1994)

Company	Revenue	Principal Activity
Bell Canada	8,066,200,000	Telephone
Anglo-Canadian Telephone	2,565,400,000	Telephone
BC Telecom	2,319,600,000	Telephone
BC Tel	2,020,900,000	Telephone
Rogers Communications	1,482,755,000	Cable
Telus	1,387,345,000	Telephone
Can. Broadcasting Corp.	1,329,410,000	Broadcasting*
Le Groupe Vidéotron	646,340,000	Cable
Saskatchewan Telecom'ns	629,070,000	Telephone
Manitoba Telephone System	551,264,000	Telephone
Maritime Tel. and Tel. Co.	550,049,000	Telephone
WIC Western Int'l Communications	393,028,000	Broadcasting
Bruncor	377,658,000	Telephone
New Brunswick Telephone Co.	359,314,000	Telephone
Edmonton Telephones	311,766,000	Telephone
NewTel Enterprises	297,086,000	Telephone
Shaw Communications	288,789,000	Cable
CanWest Global Communications	273,396,000	Broadcasting
Newfoundland Telephone Co.	263,727,000	Telephone
Québec-Telephone	254,316,000	Telephone
Baton Broadcasting	253,346,000	Broadcasting
Standard Broadcasting	239,560,000	Broadcasting
CHUM	202,585,000	Broadcasting
Cogeco	194,612,000	Cable
Télébec	183,226,000	Telephone
CFCF	175,642,000	Broadcasting

*Includes Parliamentary grant of $955,000,000.
Source: *Report on Business* Magazine (July 1995).

Canadian broadcasting has several unique features: the Broadcast Program Development Fund administered by Telefilm Canada, a federal crown corporation that subsidises independent television productions destined for broadcast by both public and private sector broadcasters; a substantial inventory of Canadian documentary and feature films produced by the National Film Board of Canada; educational television broadcasters operated on a public service basis by provincial government agencies in several provinces; and a variety of community radio and television services

Table 2 The Canadian Television Economy (millions of Can$)

Public Spending on Television

Federal

Canadian Broadcasting Corp.	985
Telefilm Canada	95
National Film Board	66
Subtotal	1,146

Provinces

Educational television	230
Total	1,376

Commercial Television Revenue

Advertising

CBC	299	(1994)
Private TV	1,341	
Subtotal	1,640	

Cable Subscription

Basic	1,700	(1993)
Discretionary	471	
Subtotal	2,171	
Total	3,811	

Economy of Canadian Television, 1994

Public funding	1,376
Advertising	1,640
Cable subscription	2,171
Total	5,187

CBC, 1993–94

Spending on operations		*Revenue*	
Television	1,032	Parliament	955
Radio	325	TV advertising	299

Sources: CBC, Telefilm, and NFB Annual Reports for 1994; Statistics Canada, "Radio and Television Broadcasting 1992" (cat. no. 56-204) and "Cable Television 1993" (cat. no. 56-205); Association for Tele-Education in Canada, Creating Access to Tele-Education (ATEC, Burnaby 1993).

Table 3 Where Canadian Television Dollars Go

Public expenditure as percentage of overall economy of television:	27%
Average annual expenditure of a cabled household for basic service:	$300
Average annual expenditure by advertisers per television household:	$200
Average annual public expenditure per household for CBC television:	$123
Average annual public expenditure per household for Canadian television production via Telefilm:	$12
Average annual public expenditure per household for NFB production destined for television:	$8
Average annual public expenditure per Ontario household for TVOntario:	$36

Sources: CBC, Telefilm, and NFB Annual Reports for 1994; Statistics Canada, "Radio and Television Broadcasting 1992" (cat. no. 56-204) and "Cable Television 1993" (cat. no. 56-205); Association for Tele-Education in Canada, Creating Access to Tele-Education (ATEC, Burnaby 1993).

funded by various sources and organised to serve specific communities ranging from northern native settlements to urban college campuses.

In telecommunications, the market is characterised by a small number of dominant players, most of them grouped in a partnership known as the Stentor Alliance. By far the most important of these is Bell Canada, a subsidiary of Canada's largest industrial corporation, Bell Canada Enterprises. Until a Supreme Court decision in 1994 ruled that the federal government (and consequently its agency, the CRTC) had exclusive jurisdiction over telecommunications, regulatory authority was split, with the CRTC regulating the activities of "national" companies such as Bell and some provinces regulating the activities of companies operating exclusively in their territory. In terms of gross revenue, the telecommunications sector is roughly 8.5 times the size of the broadcasting and cable industries.

The current regulatory framework for telecommunications was established by a landmark CRTC decision, Telecom Decision 1994-19, announced in September 1994.[9] This decision introduced full competition in telecommunications markets, including local telephone service (long-distance competition had been introduced in June 1992), and began the process of removing barriers to telephone companies providing image-based information services. In principle, telephone companies, cable companies, and wireless service providers can all now offer voice, data, and video telecommunications services to local subscribers. In fact, cable companies have been lobbying for a moratorium on implementation of the new framework, and it is still unclear how the CRTC would respond to a telephone company application for a broadcasting license. In short, there is still some way to go before regulatory theory is confirmed in practice.

Obviously, like industries in other countries, a range of Canadian industries are concerned by the development of the new information infrastructure and the convergence of broadcasting and telecommunications. In the Canadian debate, the role that national cultural industries play in the political and social spheres, as well as in the economy, is central. In telecommunications, the issue is limited to the question of ownership (foreign ownership is currently capped at 33 1/3 percent). In broadcasting, foreign ownership was until recently restricted to 20 percent,[10] and Canadian content is protected by specific obligations and encouraged by various incentives in addition to production subsidies and publicly funded services. Film, publishing, record production, and creative activity benefit from various funding programs in addition to the access to broadcast distribution provided by Canadian content requirements. All of this points to (a) the importance of the Canadian position on the exemption of cultural industries from the general provisions of the Canada–U.S. Free Trade Agreement or FTA (carried over into the North American Free Trade Agreement, or NAFTA), (b) Canadian solidarity with the European position on culture in the 1993 General Agreement on Tariffs and Trade (GATT) talks, and (c) Canadian views expressed at the Group of Seven (G7) meeting on the global information infrastructure in Brussels in February 1995.

Antecedents of the NII Debate in Canada

The Canadian NII debate represents, in the words of one expert, "a new beginning for an old idea."[11] In a fundamental sense, it goes back to the 1960s and the creation of the federal Department of Communications (DOC), the launching of a domestic satellite program, and the decision to develop policy in the field of communications with an eye toward both cultural and economic concerns. National development and industrial development were to be the two poles of Canadian communications policy starting in 1969. The cornerstone of Canadian cultural policy was to be the broadcasting system, organised on a mixed public-private sector model, and closely regulated by an independent agency, the CRTC, to ensure both a strong Canadian presence on radio and television and the development of a strong domestic broadcasting industry. At the same time, communications policy aimed to develop communications infrastructure, mainly through the use of satellites—in some respects exporting the problem of national development north of the 49th parallel to the more comfortable reaches of outer space.[12]

One of the first acts of the new DOC created in 1969 was to set up a task force known as the Telecommission to examine the whole range of issues pertinent to a national telecommunications policy. According to scholar Robert Babe, "the DOC in these early years revised the past in attempts to incorporate communication technology into the Canadian creation myth, and moreover mythologized the future by positing nation building possibilities through communication technology."[13] Among other things, new communications technologies promised to enhance the possibility of fuller participation in public life; thus, in addition to investigating questions related to hardware and regulation, the Telecommission organised seminars and published reports on such themes as "Telecommunications and Participation." The results of the Telecommission studies were synthesised in a report entitled *Instant World*, published in April 1971.[14]

Instant World set the tone for the Canadian approach to communications development in the 1970s: continued public investment in hardware and infrastructure, subsidy and protective regulation of Canadian content, and regulatory convergence of broadcasting and telecommunications.

In its opening words the report noted, "Telecommunications policy may have to be re-shaped if full advantage is to be taken of the opportunities that technology affords and if socially undesirable effects are to be avoided."[15] The reshaping of telecommunications policy focused on the blending of broadcasting and telecommunications, consecrated in 1976 by the addition of regulatory responsibility for telephone companies to the Canadian Radio-Television Commission—thereafter known as the Canadian Radio-Television and Telecommunications Commission. (Regulation of common carriers had previously come under the authority of the Canadian Transport Commission and the Railway Act.) Whereas previously the CRTC had concentrated on the role of broadcasting as a vehicle for promoting cultural identity, it now began to view the Canadian public as consumers of broadcasting.

However, *Instant World* also introduced the idea of the democratic potential of communications. New telecommunications technology, the report stated, promised to transform broadcasting from a one-way medium "that treats viewers as largely passive homogeneous groups" into an interactive medium: "More and more people will then be able to decide for themselves what they want to watch and when they want to watch it and, still more importantly, to originate programs themselves." These prescient words foreshadow a later generation of similar promises.

As early as 1971, then, the government expressed the hope that new communications technologies could be harnessed both to deliver a more rationally organised system of services and to provide the framework for organising democratic communication to enhance the quality of participation in public life. *Instant World* highlighted these contradictory motivations driving the development of communications technologies in Canada.

But nothing happened. Countervailing pressures on the federal government following the work of the Telecommission led to an erosion of the political will to act. While the subject remained on the agenda throughout the 1970s and 1980s, Canada never formally adopted a national telecommunications policy, and as a result, policy evolved on an ad hoc basis and was couched primarily in terms of promoting culture and serving the public. Nevertheless, despite the positions taken in bilateral and multilateral trade negotiations such as the FTA, NAFTA, and GATT, foreign (largely American) content continued to flow through the veins of the Canadian communications system.

A 1981 DOC paper, *The Information Revolution and Its Implications for Canada*,[16] underscored the prevailing mythology, adding a new twist: Canada was not, in fact, in the world communications and information vanguard, as it had believed throughout the 1970s; in fact, Canada lagged behind and would have to jump on the train as it passed if it wanted to retain a competitive advantage in the global market. Acknowledging that communications technologies tend to erode national sovereignty, the DOC paper expressed no surprise at Canada's misgivings; at the same time, however, the paper accepted that the information revolution was "unavoidable": "Canada has no choice but to promote vigorously introduction of the new technology in order to maintain and increase its international competitiveness."[16]

Cultural policy was incorporated into this philosophy in the 1980s. A series of policy papers published in 1983 singled the DOC's shift to a cultural industries approach, as the rationale for public support of content development shifted from nation building to industrial growth. Over the next 15 years, the pivotal role of the CBC progressively dwindled, while public funds were used to create and nurture independent production of audiovisual products. Cultural nationalism continued to be the predominant theme of policy discourse, but actual policy programs focused on beefing up the industry side of the cultural industries equation. Officially consecrated as the preferred fuel of the Canadian distribution system, Canadian content kept pace with its global counterparts, and the government successfully kept culture off the table at the FTA talks.

Consistent with the historic Canadian policy stimulus of keeping pace with developments south of the border, the NII debate in Canada was launched early in 1993, within days of U.S. President Bill Clinton's announcement of the U.S. version. As a first step, the Canadian government commissioned a respected former senior official, Bernard Ostry, to study the question. He reported in early 1994.[18]

The central message of Ostry's report to the government was that the principal elements of an information infrastructure have been in place in Canada since the early 1970s and thus the "newness" of the new technology is only relative. Both the political issues and the obstacles to their resolution are exactly what they were a quarter century ago.

In fact, while the policy debate focused on developing an appropriate interface between technology and culture—what Canadian sociologist Thelma McCormack has called "the borderlines between two historic forms of knowledge and belief"[19]—technological development and cultural production in Canada had been harnessed to create new concentrations of corporate wealth and power oblivious to the social and cultural objectives encoded in legislation and regulatory policy.

If one were to take the NII debate seriously, to extend the argument of the Ostry report, the NII would have to be recognised as a public infrastructure, its use would have to be accessible to all, and, in consequence, it would have to be publicly regulated, in the public interest.

The Canadian NII Debate

The government's next initiative was to create an Information Highway Advisory Council (IHAC) in 1994 to propose guidelines for public policy. In early 1995, the government instructed the CRTC to conduct public hearings on regulatory changes necessitated by the convergence of broadcasting and telecommunications.

IHAC's mandate was to flesh out the government's three stated objectives: to stimulate the economy, to reinforce Canadian cultural identity, and to ensure universal access at affordable cost. These three sets of objectives corresponded to the parallel and at times overlapping interests of industry, the state, and civil society.

The Canadian debate since then has been characterised by a repositioning of actors around these three poles. The government and its agencies are interested in identifying appropriate new regulations and policies to meet public policy objectives within the new context. Meanwhile, industry has been scrambling to discover which sector will prevail; in the process, various industrial actors have proposed services that meet the needs of both consumers and the regulatory authority. The new infrastructure will require a new set of industrial/regulatory trade-offs, in line with the adjusted national policy. At the same time social groups are trying to determine what they want and need. The key question here has usually been articulated as: which of the two conventional models, broadcasting or telecommunication, is most appropriate for meeting social needs?

The CRTC convergence hearings, held in March 1995, reflected these divisions. The CRTC's report, published in May 1995, framed the new policy issues in a way that reflected the contradictions of the new context.[20] Earlier, in a decision announced in September 1994,[21] the CRTC had opened the door to industry competition, particularly to telephone-based development of image-delivery services. The decision was hailed by U.S. Federal Communications Commission (FCC) officials, who declared that Canada had, by this move, leaped ahead of the United States in adopting a bold deregulatory posture.[22]

But the CRTC has continued to promote the idea of a proactive approach to Canadian culture. While sensitive to the government's view that competition is the key to infrastructure development, the CRTC reported, "Exclusive reliance on market forces to shape the development of cultural products could well jeopardise the continued availability of Canadian voices and ideas on our communication systems."[23] Furthermore,

If Canadians are to benefit from increased choice, market entry should be regulated in a manner that contributes to the Canadian broadcasting system and the development of quality programming. It is therefore critical that we not ignore the economic limitations of our market, nor lose sight of what we have achieved, by embracing ill-defined promises of unlimited choice that often reflect more dogma than substance, more universal theory than Canadian reality.[24]

Under the heading of "Competition," the CRTC announced an important shift, from supporting cable as the main instrument of achieving the objectives of the Broadcasting Act (which it had reaffirmed in June 1993) to the new regulatory framework (announced in September 1994), which supports the development of competing distribution technologies, including video data transmission by telephone companies. Canadians want more choice in the packaging and distribution of broadcasting services; according to the report, combining telecommunication and information services competitively and accessibly is the key.

Meanwhile, the notion of culture was broadening, and scholars and policy analysts were increasingly talking about cultural development.[25] In the CRTC's view cultural development is articulated at the level of content, which is based on principles of shared national identity and public service. The Canadian system has developed mechanisms for promoting this notion: carriage rules for distribution systems, public support for production of Canadian programs, a licensing system to ensure that products reach markets. The CRTC has announced that it will focus on furthering the objectives of the Broadcasting Act; some new services such as video games will be taken out of the orbit of the Act if their purpose is not to promote cultural objectives. But the Telecommunications Act does not specify cultural or content concerns. What does this mean for new content-based services? New program services should, according to the CRTC report, contribute to the creation and presentation of Canadian programming by adhering to Canadian content and spending requirements similar to those that currently apply to existing services of the same type."[26] There is a consensus that all licensed distribution undertakings should make contributions to Canadian programming comparable to those currently required of cable.

With this as backdrop, a new policy framework for telecommunications and broadcasting is being developed; it will be overseen by a new political superstructure, the shape of which is not yet clear. Since 1993, responsibility for culture and communication has been shared between two ministers and two government departments: Heritage, responsible for national cultural programs and institutions such as the CBC, and Industry, which, not insignificantly, is heading the new information infrastructure initiative. The administrative separation of software from hardware leaves the future role of the CRTC unclear. Will there continue to be a public space for the interaction of social, economic, and state interests regarding information infrastructure issues?

The Canadian position taken at the February 1995 meeting of G7 ministers in Brussels was revealing in this regard. Promoting competition and affirming culture are not necessarily mutually exclusive, Heritage Minister Michel Dupuy told the gathering; the key is achieving balance. The information highway "has the most prestigious cultural showcase of all time. It will reach the largest imaginable audience and permit the most wide-ranging intercultural communication ever. We should therefore not treat the issue of content lightly but keep in mind that the Highway's vitality will depend on its programming, not on its technological infrastructure."[27]

It was necessary to make this self-evident affirmation in Brussels, where the initial agenda was set by the U.S. five-point program for the global information infrastructure (GII). Canada has known since the turn of the century what Europe has learned only much more recently: that the U.S. view that cultural production should be treated like any other business results in indigenous cultures being submerged in a tidal wave of American products. Canadian policy since the invention of radio has been geared toward ensuring countervailing forces where market possibilities do not suffice. In Brussels, Canada and the European members of the G7 added linguistic and cultural diversity to the GII program. It was not an innocent gesture. In the words of Michel Dupuy:

Neither a vehicle of cultural homogenization nor a mechanism for one kind of monopoly or another, [the information highway] must instead embrace a diversity of international perspectives and languages, for the benefit of all citizens. It should not thrive at the expense of national cultures and identities.... We must prevent the creation of any form of cultural monopoly on the information highway.[28]

Openness and diversity, not concentration and uniformity, are the official legitimating principles of Canadian protection of the domestic cultural industry. It is on this basis, for example, that Canadian ownership remains a central tenet of broadcasting and telecommunications regulation despite U.S. calls for free access to foreign invest. (Questioning the commitment to Canadian ownership in the interest of more rapid development and complete integration of the Canadian "branch" of the North American information infrastructure was one of the main recommendations of the IHAC report.)

Meanwhile, playing off a kind of good cop/bad cop routine, Industry Minister John Manley reminded the G7 ministers that Canada's telecommunications regulatory framework "places Canada at the forefront of countries with pro-market regimes."[29] The role of the Canadian state, however, was to promote a *Canadian* market. "In encouraging market forces, governments have a role to play in setting policy, partnering certain activities with private industry and addressing market failures."[30] Cultural nationalism and public policy objectives notwithstanding, this has been the driving motivation of Canadian communications policy since the creation of the CBC and introduction of the mixed, public-private broadcasting model in the 1930s.

Manley also called for going beyond the five principles adopted in Buenos Aires "to address the content that will flow through the pipe." Both ministers cited the degree of foreign penetration of Canadian cultural markets as evidence of an open, diversified communication system—76 percent of English television, 95 percent of theater-distributed films, 88 percent of records played on radio. In fact, reducing these percentages is the principal justification for Canadian policy.

IHAC's report, which was made public on September 27, 1995,[31] contained over 300 recommendations. The document, according to the Toronto *Globe and Mail*, "embrace[d] a pro-marketplace thrust" so prominent that the only non business representative on the council, Canadian Labour Congress Vice President Jean-Claude Parrot, felt compelled to state a dissenting opinion.[32] Among other things, the report recommended making competition the driving force on the information highway and liberalising foreign ownership requirements in broadcasting and telecommunications. The key idea, emphasised in several places in the report's 227 pages, was this: "In the new information economy, success will be determined by the marketplace, not by the government."[33]

The report's main emphasis on the likely benefits to Canadian industry of a pro-market policy approach was tempered by its embracing the traditional support for Canadian content and view of public broadcasting as promoter of Canadian culture and identity. A council subcommittee, the Working Group on Canadian Content and Culture, sought to revitalise this conventional ground of Canadian cultural policy: "Experience has shown that, while market forces alone may be sufficient to ensure rapid technological development, when the objective is to provide a broad and equitable range of intellectual and cultural *content*, these factors alone do not always suffice."[34] Synthesising the difference, the question becomes: what will drive the information highway, content and sociocultural objectives or hardware development and market demand?

The Working Group was studded with major cultural industry players, especially from the broadcasting/cable sectors—those with vested interests seeking to retain their policy advantage, a cynic might say. However, a paradoxical convergence of interests between industrial and cultural considerations provided a necessary antidote to the overall IHAC approach.

Although the Working Group's report was eventually published by Heritage rather than by Industry, most of its 20 recommendations were integrated into the IHAC report. These recommendations generally aimed to preserve and update the beneficial regulations and policies that have helped create and sustain Canada's cultural industries: "Canadian cultural policy must be reaffirmed and strengthened in relation to the new information infrastructure."[35]

The Working Group's pro-policy, pro-intervention (ultimately pro-protectionist) position was based on three critical assumptions: (a) the information highway is "a natural extension of the current broadcasting and telecommunication environments"; (b) "current cultural and broadcasting policies have been an essential component to current success, in the face of ferocious competition from numerically superior foreign sources"; and (c) "cultural and broadcasting policies must adjust to the changing relationship between consumers and producers in order to ensure success in the future."[36] For example, to stimulate creation and production of Canadian content, the group proposed navigational menu systems in English and French "to ensure universal access by all Canadians to all content."[37] Moreover:

As choice expands on the Information Highway, securing "shelf space" for Canadian content will be essential. However, to accomplish the objectives of the Broadcasting Act, Canadian content must also occur on a *prominent* shelf, at eye level. The challenge will be to establish clear rules for all distributors so that Canadian programming services retain "priority" in a real and effective manner.[38]

The extension of the conventional broadcasting model is implicit in proposals such as this one. Good for Canadian commercial producers of content and presumably good for Canadian consumers who will thus be helped to find their way on the Canadian side of the information highway, it does not ensure access in the sense implied by the telecommunications model or take advantage of the interactivity or connectivity that hold out the promise of bi directional communication or self-propelled uses of the system.

The limitations of the mainstream policy proposals have been underscored by citizens' groups such as the Public Information Highway Advisory Council (PIHAC), which argued before the CRTC's convergence hearing that promotion of the broadcasting model for the information highway would mainly protect entrenched interests, not empower users. Consumers are not demanding the information highway; rather, PIHAC argued, they are concerned about issues such as security, privacy, and access to the means of communication. The telecommunications and cable industries, meanwhile, are engaged in a "turf war, wrapped in the utopian rhetoric of 'third wave' ideologues."[39] They might have referred to the rhetoric of cultural nationalism as well.

PIHAC suggested taking the Telecommunications Act as a point of departure for the new infrastructure, maintaining the emphasis on the carrier-content distinction and nondiscriminatory access, with regulated rate-of-return-based tariffs and guaranteed access to essential services. While maintaining the principles of Canadian ownership of the conduit and public ownership of the spectrum, this proposal implied challenging capital interests, public policy assumptions, and accepted cultural policy.

In fact, a wide range of social approaches to the NII have emerged in Canada over the past two years. A consensus has developed around the notion that the federal government should establish mandatory infrastructure requirements, including a baseline of common key services, even within a framework of competition. A comprehensive study of consumer group input to the process refers to this as a "selective competitive model" based on a role for market forces and competition in some areas with a public service role in others. According to the author of this study, such a model "builds upon the Canadian tradition of a mixed public/private system, only with greater emphasis on policy initiatives favouring competition in selected areas and regulation ensuring affordability and access in others."[40]

Within this consensus, however, the study found an interesting range of distinctions between groups regarding the fundamental shape of the system. For example, "better informed consumer interests have a broader conception of ... 'communicative interaction' ... a user-controlled, fully switched, two-way system of communication which allows users to be information providers and participants, as well as consumers."[41] Consumers in rural and geographically remote areas prefer competition and choice in content but not in infrastructure provision. Some groups want to extend traditional community network services and public space (such as the community cable channel) to include data communications. In general, consumers apply a broad definition to the notion of Canadian cultural content. In addition to the "high culture" products produced by Canadian cultural industries, groups want to include "social and cultural information, data or communication activities produced by themselves or others (either individually or as groups) which is necessary to meet their daily social, educational, economic and cultural needs. It allows them to fully participate in society as consumers and as citizens."[42]

Toward a Hybrid Model of Public-Private Communication

In the current Canadian debate, "competition" and "culture," buzzwords used in the title of the CRTC's May 1995 convergence report, well describe the two dimensions of the issue: industrial (commercial-, business-, and consumer-oriented) and sociocultural (public interest-based and citizen-oriented). Policy design must take both of these dimensions into account if the NII is to be developed for the common good.

More than 1,000 organizations made submissions to the hearing leading up to the CRTC convergence report. Overwhelmingly, the accent was placed on content. Social actors are concerned about it; suppliers promise to offer it; distributors are vying to provide the best delivery system for it. The regulatory authority is also engaged in its own positioning: its raison d'être is to ensure that the system will remain open and receptive to indigenous content.

Content means different things in broadcasting and in telecommunications, which are based on two distinct models of communication, distinguished by different notions of access. Both are of considerable importance to social groups. From the perspective of democratization, the difference between the two models is critical. In the broadcasting model, emphasis is placed on the active receiver and on free choice, and access refers to the entire range of products on offer. In the telecommunications model, emphasis is on the sender and on the capacity to get one's messages out, and access refers to the means of communication.

The reception model of broadcasting is based on the notion of a shared culture. The sender's model of telecommunications is based on interactivity. From a regulatory perspective, the emphasis has been on content in broadcasting and on carriage in telecommunications. Until now, broadcasting and telecommunications in Canada have been regulated according to two sets of policy objectives, spelled out in the separate pieces of legislation examined above. The objectives follow a set of parallel lines, sometimes overlapping but not conflicting. However, the mechanisms that have been put in place to achieve these objectives are not necessarily appropriate for the new context, which will require a new set of policy measures. The CRTC is trying to sort all this out, to reconcile the historic differences between the two models, and to harmonise its regulatory framework.

Historically, Canadian communications policy has developed around the principle that communication is central to nation-building. The Canadian system has developed ways of promoting this principle, including: an emphasis on publicly owned and operated national institutions, carriage rules for distribution systems, public support for production of Canadian content, and licensing of services to ensure that products reach their markets.

Canadian broadcasting and telecommunications industries have flourished within this policy framework by providing services designed to meet national policy objectives. At the same time, the public service basis of communication has kept social preoccupations on the policy agenda. Today, industrial groups are positioning themselves according to their current market positions and the new services they expect to be able to offer. For social groups, however, the issues are less clear. Regulation of content, for example, is a means of meeting social and cultural objectives in the broadcast model, whereas it can be a means of gatekeeping and censorship in the telecommunications model. While industrial groups divide along the lines of competitive market positioning, social groups are situating themselves in the debate according to expectations based on different conceptual and instrumental approaches to communication.

In order for the new information infrastructure to realise its emancipatory potential, public policy will need to promote a new hybrid model of communication that combines the social and cultural objectives of both broadcasting and telecommunications and provides new regulatory mechanisms—drawn from both traditional models—aimed at maximising equitable access to services and the means of communication for both senders and receivers.

The industrial models being bandied about, meanwhile, are also hybrid models, but they are designed according to a different, industrial logic (reflecting the hybridization brought about by technological convergence). For example, the idea of paying as you go for consumer products such as movies and sports events applies a principle of telecommunications to cultural content that has hitherto been considered the purview of broadcasting. Conversely, the development of interactive entertainment activities and services such as teleshopping assumes that manipulating information in the act of consuming it is somehow inherently uplifting.

It is difficult to situate the public interest in this landscape, dominated as it is by promoters of various projects. Nevertheless, it is possible to identify the issues and, through them, certain public policy objectives: universal access for suppliers to distribution systems; interactive dialogue between users, affordable reception of consumer services, and publicly subsidised citizenship services.

In the CRTC discussion of universality, for example, it is recognised that the public interest requires rethinking traditional approaches to achieving social goals: "the policy objective of universal access at affordable prices will not be realised without some support"—that is, universal access will depend on a mix of market forces and public subsidy. The CRTC further suggests mandatory provision of at least one public access point in each community and requiring any new distribution undertaking to make "comparable contributions to outlets for community expression" on a par with what is presently offered by the community cable channel. Telephone companies be advised: "Parties wishing to operate new broadcasting distribution undertakings should come forward with innovative proposals for providing community expression, perhaps through incorporation of interactive community dialogue and vehicles for sharing information."[43] The CRTC (and the IHAC, via its Working Group on Content and Culture) also foresees tapping the revenues of the new system to fund Canadian services.

In Canada's particular context, cultural sovereignty remains an overriding concern. This implies maintaining foreign property restrictions and Canadian content requirements for licensed services. Cultural sovereignty objectives have historically been promoted through publicly owned public services, which implies reaffirming the public service, public utility basis of the national communications system. Meanwhile, another dimension is worth mentioning.

Whether Ottawa or the provinces should have jurisdiction over communication and culture is one of the recurring themes of the eternal debate over Canada's constitutional future. Not surprisingly, another alternative perspective comes from the domestic periphery of the Canadian communications policy environment— Quebec. Since the 1930s, Canadian constitutional law has awarded exclusive jurisdiction over communication (first broadcasting and more recently telecommunications as well) to the federal government despite periodic claims from the provinces (primarily Quebec). However, from the perspective of the NII, new potential uses overlap into areas of provincial jurisdiction such as education, health care and social services. "Repatriation" of powers in communication has been an issue in various constitutional reform packages since the 1970s. Temporarily stalled by Quebec's recent referendum on sovereignty—which would have resolved the issue dramatically—the federal-provincial push and pull is another particularity of the Canadian policy dynamic. In this context, it is interesting to look at Quebec's approach to the NII.

While the federal government's IHAC was studying the big picture, a Quebec committee was proceeding with somewhat less fanfare. The Quebec report, which came out in July 1995,[44] emphasises the information highway's potential impact on education, health care, and social services; the promotion of language and culture; the organization of public services; and, residually, the development of industry and export markets. Under "equality of access," the report states: "It is necessary to guarantee the right to information and knowledge for all citizens, without regard to their financial resources or their language of use, in order to avoid the division of Quebec society into two groups, those who have access to the information highway and those who do not."[45]

This is not to deny the obvious benefits to industry of such a policy, for as the report continues, "Facilitating accessibility in fact constitutes a way of stimulating demand for products and services."[46] Indeed, like its Ottawa counterpart, the Quebec committee that drew up this report was top-heavy with major industry players (some of whom served on both, providing an interesting example of the way the present constitutional arrangement enables some to butter their bread on both sides). But the difference is evident in passages in which the report develops notions such as the idea that building the information infrastructure should be seen as a "social investment" with economic benefits for future generations.

Characteristically, most of the legal and regulatory instruments required to orient the emerging technological environment remain under Ottawa's jurisdiction. Thus, while the federal government has the power to act on its advisors' report, the Quebec report includes the necessary recommendation that the Quebec government "use all means available to see that federal laws and policies regarding the information highway not only recognise the cultural specificity of Quebec but also allow Quebec to develop and reinforce it."[47]

In an age of globalization, one may be tempted to marvel at proposals that are contingent on a more active role for the state. But public attitudes toward collective institutions surely rank among the most significant markers of cultural distinction, and just as Canadians generally identify their social safety net, gun control, and the CBC as characteristics that distinguish their country from the United States, the Québécois continue to define their difference in terms of the French language, the decentralization of power, and the role of the state as the motor of social, economic, and cultural development.

In global terms, the various national NII debates point to the need to update the basis for legitimization of public policy intervention, to internationalise the issues identified through the local expression of social demand, and ultimately to develop new global regulatory mechanisms. In Canada at the moment, as in the United States, it is industrial offer rather than social demand that is driving the construction of the NII. In Canada, however, one has to factor in the "high policy" objectives and the particular set of jurisdictional disputes linked to the role of communication in constituting national identity, the role of cultural nationalism in legitimating the designs of industry, and the critical perspective put forward by social groups, with respect to both the substance of the project and the process surrounding its development.

In this context, the Canadian debate highlights the ongoing role of the state as the motor of industrial development and the organiser or facilitator of sociocultural development. For historical as well as pragmatic reasons, a sociocultural approach to communications policy persists in Canada (although the resources to support it may no longer be there). For Canadian society, this has meant the possibility of a public communicative space in which various social, economic and political discourses have been able to circulate—a space that, in its better moments, approaches the ideals of a democratic public sphere. The stakes of the current debate are no less than the maintenance, the flourishing, or the disappearance of this space.

Notes

1. For background on specific areas of Canadian communication policy, see Marc Raboy, *Missed Opportunities: The Story of Canada's Broadcasting Policy* (Montréal and Kingston: McGill-Queen's University Press, 1990); Robert E. Babe, *Telecommunications in Canada: Technology, Industry and Government* (Toronto: University of Toronto Press, 1990); Ted Magder, *Canada's Hollywood: The Canadian State and Feature Films* (Toronto: University of Toronto Press, 1993); Michael Dorland, ed., *Canada's Cultural Industries* (Toronto: James Lorimer, forthcoming). For general perspectives on Canadian communication policy, see Dallas W. Smythe, *Depen-*

dency Road: Communications, Capitalism, Consciousness, and Canada (Norwood, N.J.: Ablex, 1981); George Woodcock, *Strange Bedfellows: The State and the Arts in Canada* (Vancouver: Douglas & McIntyre, 1985); Stuart McFadyen, Colin Hoskins, Adam Finn and Rowland Lorimer, eds., *Cultural Development in An Open Economy* (Waterloo, Ontario: Wilfrid Laurier University Press, 1995).

2. For comparative purposes, see Robin Mansell, *The New Telecommunications: A Political Economy of Network Evolution* (London: Sage, 1993). The Canadian situation resembles what Mansell calls a "strategic evolutionary model," as opposed to one characterized by unregulated full competition.

3. Statutes of Canada, Broadcasting Act, 38–39 Elizabeth II, 1991, c. 11.

4. Statutes of Canada, Telecommunications Act, 40–41–42 Elizabeth II, 1993, c. 38.

5. Broadcasting Act, art. 3.

6. See Peter S. Grant, *The Annotated 1991 Broadcasting Act* (Vancouver: McCarthy Tétrault, 1991).

7. Telecommunications Act, art. 7.

8. Canada, Mandate Review Committee, *Making Our Voices Heard: Canadian Broadcasting and Film for the 21st Century* (Ottawa: Minister of Supply and Services Canada, 1996). The committee recommended that CBC be funded by a "communications tax" on cable and long-distance telephone revenues, instead of the current mixture of advertising and parliamentary subsidy.

9. Canadian Radio-Television and Telecommunications Commission, *Telecom Decision 1994-19* (Ottawa: CRTC, 16 September 1994).

10. In November 1995, allowable foreign investment in broadcasting holding companies was raised to 33 1/3 percent, to "bring the rules for broadcasting more into line with those in place for telecommunications firms." However, foreign ownership of any company holding a license for broadcasting programming continues to be restricted to 20 percent. See Canadian Heritage, "Government Moves to Increase Access to Investment Capital for Canadian Broadcasters," news release, November 23, 1995.

11. Bernard Ostry, *The Electronic Connection: An Essential Key to Canadians' Survival,* report to the Department of Industry (Ottawa: 1993, p. vi).

12. I am grateful for this insight to the work of Bram Abramson, a graduate student in communication at the University of Montreal, who is preparing a thesis on the role of the Canadian space program in the formation of national identity.

13. Robert E. Babe, "Media Technology and the Great Transformation of Canadian Cultural Policy," presentation to the conference on "Media Policy, National Identity and Citizenry in Changing Democratic Societies: The Case of Canada," Duke University (6–7 October 1995), p. 21.

14. Department of Communications, *Instant World: A Report on Telecommunications in Canada* (Ottawa: Information Canada, 1971). The Telecommission's

work was conducted under the leadership of Deputy Minister A. E. Gotlieb, later ambassador to Washington in the period leading up to negotiation of the Canada–US Free Trade Agreement, precursor to NAFTA.

15. Ibid., p. i.

17. Ibid., p. 96.

18. Ostry, *The Electronic Connection*.

19. Thelma McCormack, "Alt Dot Spicer Dot Ciao, Baby," presentation to the conference on "Media Policy, National Identity and Citizenry in Changing Democratic Societies: The Case of Canada," Duke University (6–7 October 1995), p. 1.

20. Canadian Radio-Television and Telecommunications Commission, *Competition and Culture on Canada's Information Highway: Managing the Realities of Transition* (Ottawa: CRTC, 19 May 1995).

21. Canadian Radio-Television and Telecommunications Commission, *Telecom Decision 1994-19*.

22. This view was expressed, for example, by the FCC's Donna Lampert at an international symposium on communication technology convergence in Montreal ten days after announcement of the CRTC decision ("La convergence des techniques de communication," University of Quebec at Montreal, 30 September 1994).

23. Canadian Radio-Television and Telecommunications Commission, *Competition and Culture on Canada's Information Highway*, p. 5.

24. Ibid., p. 6.

25. See, for example, Marc Raboy, Ivan Bernier, Florian Sauvageau and Dave Atkinson, "Cultural Development and the Open Economy: A Democratic Issue and a Challenge to Public Policy," *Canadian Journal of Communication* 19, no. 3/4 (1994), pp. 291–315. In that article, we define cultural development as "the process by which human beings acquire the individual and collective resources necessary to participate in public life" (p. 292).

26. Canadian Radio-Television and Telecommunications Commission, *Competition and Culture on Canada's Information Highway*, p. 33.

27. Michel Dupuy (Speech delivered at the G7 Ministerial Conference on the Information Society, Brussels, February 26, 1995).

28. Ibid., p. 42.

29. John Manley, "Universal Service Provision on the Information Highway" (Remarks delivered at the G7 Ministerial Conference on the Information Society, Brussels, February 26, 1995), p. 47.

30. Ibid.

31. Information Highway Advisory Council, *Connection Community Content: The Challenge of the Information Highway* (Ottawa: Minister of Supply and Services Canada, 1995).

32. Lawrence Surtees, "Competition on Information Highway Urged," *Globe and Mail*, 28 September 1995.

33. Information Highway Advisory Council, *Connection Community Content*, p. x.

34. Heritage Canada, *Report of the Canadian Content and Culture Working Group* (Ottawa: 1995), p. 1.

35. Information Highway Advisory Council, *Connection Community Content*, p. 123.

36. *Report of the Canadian Content and Culture Working Group*, p. 3. A slightly different version of this text appears in the IHAC report.

37. Ibid., p. 10.

38. Ibid., p. 12.

39. Public Information Highway Advisory Council, "Brief to the CRTC Hearing on Convergence" (Ottawa: 1995), unpaginated.

40. Andrew Reddick, *Sharing the Road: Convergence and the Canadian Information Highway* (Ottawa: Public Interest Advocacy Centre, 1995), p. 57.

41. Ibid., p. 23.

42. Ibid., p. 29.

43. Canadian Radio-Television and Telecommunications Commission, *Competition and Culture on Canada's Information Highway*, p. 46.

44. Comité consultatif sur l'autoroute de l'information, *Inforoute Québec: Plan d'action pour la mise en oeuvre de l'autoroute de l'information* (Québec, 1995).

45. Ibid., p. v. My translation.

46. Ibid., p. 37.

47. Ibid., p. 33.

Information Infrastructure Initiatives in Emerging Economies: The Case of India

Ben A. Petrazzini and G. Harindranath

Introduction

As the links between economic development and the availability of a national information infrastructure (NII) become more apparent, governments around the world have launched a variety of initiatives aimed at boosting their information-related capabilities. Developing countries have been slower than their more advanced counterparts in grasping the benefits of strong official commitment to an NII agenda. Several of them have, nevertheless, started to adopt radical and innovative policies to boost their communications infrastructure. India is one of these cases. Although events in India reflect a growing trend in developing economies, they also highlight the uniqueness of local economic, political, and socio-historical factors in shaping the rise and evolution of the NII in each nation.

India has embraced, since the early 1990s, significant economic reforms. Restructuring initiatives in telecommunications, informatics, and broadcasting are part of this larger shift in the socioeconomic paradigm that guides development in the South Asian nation. The breakup of state monopolies and the rise of competition and private involvement in the information and communications sector are the most outstanding features of a much larger and profound transformation that is affecting the price of telephone calls as well as the content of television programs.

This chapter explores in some detail recent government initiatives aimed at building an Indian NII. The first section lays out the international context in which the Indian case plays out. The second section attempts to identify the forces that are driving current government communications and information reform initiatives. The third section looks at recent telecommunications policies and their impact on ownership, market structure, and current and prospective infrastructure developments. The fourth explores changes in the informatics sector, analyzing policy implications in both hardware and software. The fifth section addresses the rapid transformations experienced by the broadcasting industry and the reactive policies articulated by the government in its attempt to guide transformations in this sector. In all three sectors (i.e., telecom, informatics, and broadcasting), the chapter lays out the institutional arrangements upon which the industries operate. The last section is an effort to assess the socioeconomic implications of the current Indian NII initiatives.

The Global Information Infrastructure

The global information infrastructure (GII) concept is broad and loose enough to encompass most aspects of a rising information-based global economy. The notion of the GII refers to an ever-expanding range of technologies, products, applications, and services that support the transmission of information on a worldwide basis. The profile and growth of the GII, however, are not evenly distributed across its various information and communications components. Older, more mature technologies such as broadcast television and telephone have a large worldwide installed base. However, their growth rates have slowed as markets with high purchasing power have become fairly saturated. New technologies and services such as the Internet and cellular phones have a small installed base but a steep growth curve (Figure 1). Moreover, while advanced nations have a well developed information infrastructure in place, in developing countries the NII is still far from being a reality (Figure 2).

There are some indications that the traditional communications infrastructure gap between developed and developing countries (based on the absolute number of basic telephone lines) is on the verge of narrowing. In the Asian Pacific region, for example, it is

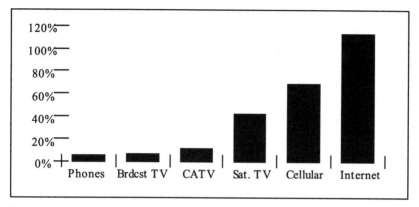

Figure 1 Annual Growth Rates of Elements of the Global Information Infrastructure, 1984–1994 (ITU).

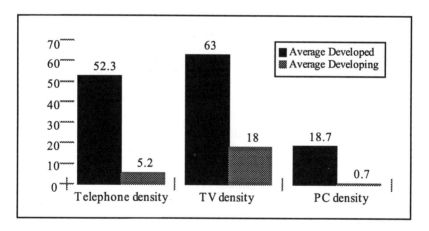

Figure 2 Information Infrastructure in Developed and Developing Countries, 1994 (ITU).

expected that the regional share of main telephone lines will progressively tilt in favor of low-income countries—particularly China and India. The ITU estimates that by the year 2000 developing countries in the Asia Pacific will account for approximately 65 percent of the region's total number of lines. This trend is not unique to Asia: developing countries worldwide are showing rapid expansion of their telecommunications networks.

But while the traditional communications gap narrows, a new one is rapidly opening up in more advanced computing infrastructure. By the mid-1990s, for example, the three most highly computerized countries in the world (the United States, Australia, and Canada) had an average of 23 computers per 100 people, while three of the main developing countries (Brazil, China, and India) had an average of only 0.38 computers per 100 people. In 1994, more than 90 percent of all data networks, 95 percent of all Videotex networks, and 98 percent of all ISDN networks were in developed nations. Similarly, in 1995 94.2 percent of all Internet hosts were based in developed countries.

This gap in the availability of information infrastructure and technology has its roots not in technological factors but in economic and social ones. Faced with considerable difficulties in achieving economic growth, governments in most developing countries have perceived telecommunications and related infocommunications services either as luxury items catering to the high-income strata of society or as part of the state machinery that serve national defense and political control. This perception, which informed public policy for decades, is being progressively replaced in most of the developing world by a recognition that information and communications infrastructure can play a crucial role in economic development.

The Driving Forces of the Indian NII

In an effort to overcome economic growth constraints, in the late 1980s most developing countries began to implement drastic economic reforms. Many current information infrastructure initiatives have developed out of these comprehensive economic reform packages.[1]

In the case of India this trend is fairly clear. Most of the restructuring of the information and communications sectors is closely tied to the sweeping economic reforms launched in the early 1990s by the Rao administration. The reform program was an attempt to overcome a serious decline in the performance of the national economy. Annual growth of the gross domestic product (GDP) had averaged 3.5 percent from the mid-1960s to the mid-1980s, increased to an average of 5.9 percent from 1985 to 1990, and then dropped dramatically to 1.2 percent during 1990–1991. In 1991 the fiscal deficit rose to an unprecedented 9.8 percent of GDP, while foreign exchange reserves dropped to levels below one month of imports, and inflation reached a peak of 17 percent in August.

In order to restore economic growth, the reform program focused on two main goals: increasing the share of private capital and exposing economic actors to market forces. More specifically, it liberalized the country's investment regime, allowing entry of both local and foreign private capital into sectors of the economy formerly reserved for the state. The reform program opened up international trade by eliminating licensing requirements on imports of intermediate and capital goods and by reducing tariffs for many items from approximately 400 percent to 60 percent. It devalued the rupee to increase exports and avoid capital flight and introduced significant changes into the tax system and the financial sector. Finally, a specific policy eliminated privileges and protection for state-owned enterprises, restructuring viable ones, liquidating others, and requiring most of them to become profit-oriented entities.[2]

To support this transformation, the government paid special attention to the country's national infrastructure, concentrating at first on restructuring the energy sector. However, by 1993, it became evident that, without a significant improvement in the communications and information infrastructure, India would not have a chance to integrate into the global economy (Sinha 1996). In May 1994, a new telecommunications policy that reflected this concern was officially launched. The introductory statement of the new policy argues that:

The new economic policy adopted by the Government aims at improving India's competitiveness in the global market and rapid growth of exports. Another element of the new economic policy is attracting foreign direct investment and stimulating domestic investment. Telecommunication services of world class quality are necessary for the success of this policy. It is, therefore, necessary to give the highest priority to the development of telecom services in the country. (Government of India 1994)

The fact that economic constraints triggered reform initiatives does not mean that the new policies were based on purely economic criteria. Politics and political considerations profoundly affected the reform process (Kohli 1990) and, more specifically, the development of the communications and information sector. Politics has always played a determining role in the profile and direction of NII policies. The new national telecommunications policy of 1994, for example, was strongly influenced by domestic and international political pressures. Decisions such as not to privatize the government Department of Telecommunications (DoT), the creation of telecom circles, the strong emphasis given to rural networks and local equipment in the licensing criteria, as well as the limits imposed on foreign investments are all products of political struggles or assessments of politically viable policies (Petrazzini 1996).

Beyond the pragmatic concerns of power politics and redistribution of national resources and wealth, the current policy reforms are part of a larger shift in the role of the state in developing societies. In the particular case of India, decades of sluggish economic growth and internal conflicts within the governing elite had led to a significant decline in the popular appeal of and support for state interventionism and central planning. To overcome this erosion of the power structure and decline in the legitimacy of public institutions, recent administrations have had to struggle to recreate and reinvent a role for the state and the governing elite in Indian society. Current economic reforms and the rise of new info-communications-related policies can be seen as efforts by the Indian state to regain its legitimacy and public support (Mody 1995).

India's NII Policy Initiatives

The Indian government has been divided as to how and to what extent the country needs to change its communications and information-related policies to build an NII. Some progressive sectors have been pushing since the late 1980s for sweeping changes, while others are still struggling to stop what they see as a frontal attack on the status quo and the socialist legacy of Gandhi and Nehru. For these and related reasons, the Indian NII agenda has developed in a piecemeal fashion and lacks an overall integrated framework. In some sectors, such as telecommunications and informatics, economic and fiscal constraints and the failure of former industrial policies have prompted the government to take a proactive approach to restructuring the sector. In others, including broadcasting, policies have unfolded in a reactive fashion, more as inevitable responses to uncontrolled events than as planned and genuinely official initiatives.

Telecommunications

Telecommunications services were launched in India in the early 1880s with exchanges in Calcutta, Bombay, and Madras. In 1947, when the country gained independence, the new government created the Post and Telegraph Department (P&T) and Overseas Communications Services. The national public network grew at a very slow pace both before and after independence. By the mid-1980s, with a teledensity of 0.45 main lines per 100 people, universal service goals were still closer to a national dream than a viable target.

In 1985, the administration of Rajiv Gandhi introduced the first significant institutional reform in the sector. Telecommunications services were separated from postal services, the DoT was created under the jurisdiction of the Ministry of Communications to provide telecom services, and the Telecom Board (now the Telecom Commission) was formed to develop policy for the sector. In 1986, further restructuring led to the creation of two new companies: Mahanagar Telephone Nigam Ltd. (MTNL) and Videsh Sanchar Nigam Ltd. (VSNL). While VSNL took charge of the DoT's international operations, MTNL took over the Department's local services in Bombay and New Delhi.[3]

Currently services are provided by the DoT, MTNL, and VSNL, but both MTNL and VSNL are under the institutional umbrella of the DoT. Policy is crafted through a complicated and sometimes obscure process in which the Ministry of Communications, the Telecom Commission, and the DoT have a say. Institutional boundaries and policy making responsibilities are not clearly defined among these institutions. Although the Telecom Commission has the upper hand on regulatory recommendations, the actual implementation of policies is usually the outcome of a political bargain that involves not only these three institutions but also the Prime Minister's office, the Ministry of Finance, and the Parliament. As in most democracies, these institutions often disagree on policies, slowing down any reform initiatives but providing legitimacy to the legislation that is implemented.

To de-politicize the current regulatory process somewhat, the government has passed a law transferring all regulatory functions in the sector to an autonomous regulatory body, the Telecom Regulatory Authority of India. This new agency will be a nonstatutory body operating under the jurisdiction of the Ministry of Communications, but it will presumably have considerable power and independence to buffer political influences from the executive branch, Parliament, and other interest groups.[4] The Authority's main tasks will include regulating everyday service provision and carrier operations, mediating among carriers and between carriers and consumers, and enforcing legislation. More specifically, it will address issues related to standards for technical compatibility of networks and applications, pricing mechanisms and regimes, and interconnection-related matters such as revenue-sharing agreements, access charges, and time frames for interconnection.

After the creation of MTNL and VSNL in 1985–1986, the reform initiated by Rajiv Gandhi lost momentum, and by the late 1980s it had completely stalled. While other countries in the developing world moved further down the reform road, India kept its telecom communications as a state monopoly.[5] By 1994, countries that had restructured their telecommunications sector (mainly through privatization and/or liberalization), such as Chile, Malaysia, and Argentina, showed considerable improvement in the development of their physical telecommunications infrastructure (Table 1).

Others countries with similar socioeconomic profiles, such as China, have not introduced sweeping reforms to the sector but have managed, through massive state investment, to expand their national telecommunications network. While both India and China had 0.60 lines per 100 people in 1990, by 1994 China had achieved a teledensity twice as high as India's. In the same year, China reported 38,666 km of installed fiber-optic cable while India had 15,834 km of installed fiber optics. In the case of mobile cellular telephones, China had surpassed three million subscribers by

Table 1 Number of Main Telephone Lines per 100 Inhabitants (ITU)

	1990	1991	1992	1993	1994
Argentina	9.55	9.78	11.12	12.22	14.14
Chile	6.53	7.89	9.43	11.01	11.00
Malaysia	8.93	9.99	11.24	12.62	14.69
China	0.60	0.74	0.99	1.47	2.29
India	0.60	0.67	0.77	0.89	1.07

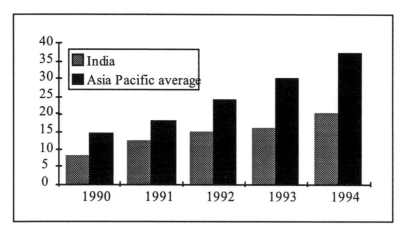

Figure 3 Growth of Main Lines (millions). Source: ITU.

1995, while in India the service was only being launched. India's network development remained slow not only vis-à-vis comparable cases but also when compared with the average main line growth in low-income countries in the region (Figure 3).[6]

By the mid-1990s India's physical infrastructure was slowly but increasingly undergoing a transformation . At the same time, radical changes were being carried out at the policy level. In May 1994, the Rao administration announced a sweeping telecommunications reform program and revised the eighth Five-Year Plan (1992–1997) accordingly, setting new expansion goals for both networks and services. In basic services, the revised plan aims at providing telephone service on demand by 1997, a public call office for every 500 persons in urban areas, and telephone services in all villages by the closing of the plan. Recognizing the strategic importance of value-added services for production and commerce, the new plan aims at providing all internationally available value-added network services (VANS) by 1996.

For the future of India's info-communications sector, however, the new telecom policies are far more important than the revision of the Five-Year Plan. The goal of building a national information infrastructure to support the growth of India's businesses and their competitiveness in the global economy is at the core of the government initiative. Aimed in the short term at giving a boost to the telecom infrastructure, the initiative addresses issues that are linked to broader information-related services and infrastructure. The new policy, for example, allows new telephone operators to cross traditional boundaries into the domains of multimedia services (e.g., cable TV, electronic banking, home-shopping, video-on-demand) and all value-added information and communications services.

Because the government was unable to cope with the financial requirements of developing a world-class infrastructure and because privatization of the DoT was quickly undermined by labor and political opposition, the Rao administration settled on a rather unorthodox combination of public and market arrangements. Under the new policy, private domestic firms are allowed to provide basic local telephone services in competition with the DoT and MNTL. Foreign firms can hold up to 49 percent of shares in the new private consortiums. The DoT and VSNL will maintain a monopoly over domestic long distance and international services for at least five years.

While paying particular attention to those aspects of telecommunications that would enhance national productivity, the government made a special effort to keep socially sensitive issues (such as universal service obligations and residential services at affordable prices) high on the official agenda. With the aim of avoiding "national cream-skimming" and the exclusion of unprofitable regions from the operators' networking plans, the government divided the country into 21 telecom circles for local basic fixed-network services and 18 circles for mobile cellular services. Under this scheme one private company would be licensed in each wireline circle and two companies in mobile circles.[7]

The government began to reform wireless services in 1992, inviting bids for supplying public mobile radio services in the four metropolitan cities of Delhi, Bombay, Calcutta, and Madras and paging services in 27 cities with over one million inhabitants. In late 1995, cellular licenses were granted to supply services in 18 other telecom circles throughout the country. In October 1995, India's first cellular services were launched in Delhi, Bombay, and Calcutta.[8] The market for VSAT services is also open to the private sector.[9]

VANS were liberalized in July 1992, and companies registered in India are permitted to operate under nonexclusive licenses for the provision of electronic mail, voice mail, data services, audio and videotext services, video conferencing, or any other new nonbasic service.[10] The DoT is not allowed to enter the VANS market, but other state-owned firms such as CMC (a company under the Department of Electronics) and VSNL have been granted licenses to operate in this segment of the market.[11] Along with CMC and VSNL, 46 other private companies signed letters of intent to provide VANS in 1994.[12]

The progress of networking in India had been slowed by the country's poor telecommunications infrastructure. The rapid growth in the informatics sector over the last decade and the liberalization of value-added services have opened the way for the expansion of national data and communications networks.

A considerable number of general and specialized networks are already in operation or in various stages of development. The most important among these in terms of both reach and technical sophistication is the National Informatics Centre Network (NICNET). This network provides computing and two-way data communications infrastructure for government departments and related agencies in order to facilitate development planning in the country. NICNET is a satellite-based network using 600 earth stations and connecting government agencies at the central, state, and district levels. The National Informatics Centre's 2,000 technical staff have also developed several applications in areas such as multimedia, medical data-bases, geographical information, and economic planning. Although a government agency, the National Informatics Centre is increasingly functioning like a commercial entity, distributing a variety of third-party software products as well as its own applications (see Nidumolu and Goodman 1993).

INDONET is a data network established and maintained by CMC Limited, a state-owned software and services company, for the community of computer users in India. This network provides distributed data processing facilities on an all-India basis to large organizations using CMC's computers for their data processing operations. Other specialized networks include SIRNET (the Scientific and Industrial Network), BTISNET (the Biotechnology Information System Network), and the SoftNET, which provides electronic mail, file transfer, and video conferencing for software developers.

The Educational and Research Network (ERNET) was initiated in 1987 by the Department of Electronics (DoE) to provide computer communications for India's academic and research community. Applications such as electronic mail, file transfer, remote login, and data-base access are some of the available services. Several local library networks such as BONET in Bombay, DELNET in Delhi, and CALIBNET in Calcutta are in various stages of completion (Arora 1992).[13] Thus, communications and data networks have begun to proliferate in India despite a slow and gradual beginning.

Internet access, although restricted to software developers, universities, and research institutions, has been available in India for several years through ERNET. The National Informatics Centre, which provides computer support to the government and public sector undertakings, has also begun providing limited Internet access to exporters and educational and research institutions. However, full-fledged Internet connectivity began only recently with India's long distance telecommunications carrier, VSNL, providing access initially to subscribers in the major cities.

The provision of Internet services by an apex organization such as VSNL has already caused problems. VSNL will be in direct competition with private value-added service providers, yet no discussions were held with private providers to plan for this major development. As a result, private service providers are not certain of the kinds of on line services they can provide through the Internet (Business India 1995, 125). Lack of coordination and political battles between the DoE, DoT, National Informatics Centre and VSNL may also slow down the growth of the Internet in

India. While the National Informatics Centre and the DoE are addressing the same market segment for Internet access through their respective networks and are thus in competition with each other, the DoT has continued to restrict the growth of the Internet because of its long-standing monopoly on telecommunications.

Industrial Policy and Defense

If the above network services represent a new policy challenge to the Indian government, telecommunications and informatics equipment policies have been a pervasive obsession of most administrations since the early 1970s. The goal of self-reliant industrialization in telecommunications and computing, that characterized the 1970s and 1980s have largely been replaced by the aim of generating foreign exchange required to pay for imports (Sinha 1996, 5).

Despite this abdication from preexisting industrial policies, support for a national manufacturing base still exists within the top circles of the Indian government. The clearest evidence of this is that "buy local" policies have made their way into the licensing criteria of new private operators. Higher points are granted to those bidders who include the use of locally manufactured equipment in their network construction plans.

Along with this "tame" industrial policy, defense and security issues have colored most of the new telecommunications plans. Although this may sound anachronistic, the official concerns seem justified if one takes into account current geopolitical disputes (e.g., with Pakistan), the rising military power of neighboring Asian nations (e.g., China), and the unsettled problem of domestic insurgency and ethnic friction in various states (Kashmir, Jammu, Nagaland, Mizoram, and Arunachal Pradesh)—not to mention the still vivid scars left by decades of foreign domination.

Informatics

Although telecommunications represent the basic foundation of the NII, in the Indian case, the informatics[14] sector has received greater policy attention and for a much longer time than telecommunications. As a result, India has a mature computer hardware industry as well as a technically sophisticated and globally competitive software services industry. The Indian approach to the development of the informatics industry has passed through a wide gamut of policy variations. Total dependence on multinational corporations in the 1960s and early 1970s gave way to almost two decades of protectionist regimes, characterized by import substitution, during the late 1970s and early 1980s (Grieco 1984; Subramanian 1992). Policy liberalization and the move toward more market-friendly policies in the 1990s have been accompanied by what both policy makers and industrial entrepreneurs term attempts at globalization of Indian industry in order to instill much needed competition and quality consciousness. To provide a holistic understanding of the changes in state informatics policy, we will first present an overview of the institutional arrangements for this sector and then examine the informatics sector against the background of macroeconomic changes over the decades.

Set up in 1971, DoE is the main governmental organization that is responsible for recommending and implementing policies for the informatics sector in India. During the 1970s and much of the 1980s, the DoE worked within the broad mandate of a restrictive import-substituting policy regime and thus administered a complex set of regulatory and licensing controls over local and foreign companies in this sector. During this period, the DoE was often preoccupied with protecting and expanding the role of state-owned informatics firms such as Electronics Corporation of India Ltd. at the expense of local and foreign firms in the private sector (see Evans 1992; Grieco 1984). However, with the adoption of liberalized industrial policies started in 1991, the DoE has managed to reinterpret its role as a facilitator and promoter of industry (see Evans 1992).

The DoE has been particularly proactive with regard to the software industry. For instance, it has established seven Software Technology Parks (STPs) in the country. Firms operating as STP units are 100 percent export-oriented and are entitled to a zero-tariff regime, competitive telecommunications facilities, and low taxes. In 1991, the DoE established an agency called Software Technology Park of India to manage all the STPs. The success of the STP scheme led to the establishment of a similar scheme for the electronics and computer hardware sector called the Electronic

Hardware Technology Park (EHTP) in 1993. Yet another organization called the Software Development Agency was established in 1986 to help coordinate software policy implementation, particularly in relation to software export.

India's Ministry of Commerce has also been instrumental in promoting software export activities since the late 1980s. In 1987–1988, the Ministry of Commerce sponsored the establishment of a separate Electronics and Computer Software Export Promotion Council with representatives from the Ministry of Commerce, the Ministry of Finance, and the DoE. The Council's primary function is to promote exports through the provision of market information and marketing assistance.

Apart from these nodal agencies, government-funded computing organizations such as the National Informatics Centre and the Centre for Development of Advanced Computing (C-DAC) play important roles in new technology development (see Nidumolu and Goodman 1993). C-DAC is at the forefront of new technology development: it has developed India's first 1 GFLOPS-parallel processor called PARAM and continues research and development in this area.

The Indian informatics industry has established two powerful, industry-wide associations, the Manufacturers Association for Information Technology and the National Association of Software and Service Companies, to lobby the government to safeguard the respective interests of the computer hardware and software segments. In the liberalized policy environment, the DoE and the MoC, through the Electronic and Computer Software Export Promotion Council, are increasingly cooperating with these two associations in order to provide broad support for the informatics sector.

The hardware industry

The Indian computer hardware industry (computer systems only) was worth U.S.$837 million in 1994–1995 (Table 2). The number of PCs produced in 1994–1995 was around 233,990, as against 7,500 in 1985.[15] Currently, India has a market for around 240,000 PCs a year. Despite the fact that the market has grown considerably in recent years, the number of existing PCs in India in the mid-1990s failed to surpass 1.2 million units. Liberalization has brought significant changes in the dynamics of the computer hardware market, yet local production based on indigenous designs continues.[16]

In the aftermath of independence, the development of India's electronics industry was closely aligned with defense and strategic concerns. Although this led to the discarding of static comparative advantages in favor of creating dynamic ones, especially in high technology areas, the resultant policy regime was essentially based on self-reliance and import substitution. A system of industrial licensing regulated the entry, expansion, diversification, and even exit of firms, thus encouraging firms to set up sub-optimal scales of production. Import licensing procedures and abnormally high customs tariffs protected the domestic industry from foreign competition and guaranteed good profit margins despite the low production volumes. Furthermore, high tariffs on the import of complete systems provided sufficient incentive for local manufacturing even though the actual import content of such systems was very high. While all this was aimed at building domestic technological capabilities—and there is evidence that some local firms did develop considerable capabilities in systems design—it also provided across-the-board protection to even inefficient firms operating with no concern for the relative costs of domestic and foreign production, or even quality.[17]

Active state intervention and involvement in production during these early years prompted a public sector company called ECIL to begin manufacturing computers in 1971. But ECIL could neither produce the technology entirely in India and make systems available at internationally comparable prices nor satisfy the growing demand for systems in the country. By 1978, private sector entrepreneurs had entered the computer manufacturing sector, and ever since they have accounted for the most of the computer production in the country.

To reflect the growing importance of a private sector informatics industry, India announced a relatively liberal computer policy in 1984 (Government of India 1984). By giving an impetus to public sector computerization and by permitting large-scale import of disassembled computer kits, this policy led to the mushrooming of

Table 2 Computer Hardware Production, 1985–1995 (in U.S.$ millions)

	Total computer systems production: exports	Total computer systems production: domestic	Total production of computer systems
1985	0.13	41.23	41.36
1988	5.33	118.06	123.39
1990	14.33	185.60	199.93
1991–92	6.70	322.63	329.33
1992–93	10.16	391.43	402.39
1993–94	5.06	530.00	535.06
1994–95	16.23	820.76	836.99

Source: DoE 1993; Dataquest 1993, 1994a, 1995.

computer hardware companies in the private sector. The downside of this policy was that by legitimizing the assembly business, it helped promote a large number of small entrepreneurs who lacked design skills and the investment necessary to build economically viable hardware manufacturing units.

By 1991, India's first-ever serious macroeconomic crisis made structural reforms inevitable, and Prime Minister Rao's government began a determined transition toward a policy regime that was less regulatory and more promotional in nature.[18] The 1991 industrial policy abolished the system of industrial licensing for the computer industry and liberalized curbs on foreign investment in Indian companies, thereby giving the green light to the entry of multinational corporations and a higher degree of competitiveness. Since then, the government has gradually accelerated the move toward globalizing the informatics industry through annual reductions in customs tariffs.

India's policies since 1991 have thus been qualitatively different from those of the previous decades; while the 1984 policy was aimed at giving a boost to computerization, the liberalization measures undertaken since 1991 have been explicitly aimed at globalizing the Indian informatics industry and making it internationally competitive. The new policy regime is built on a premise of mutual dependency and active collaboration with the global economy and its constituent units, be they states or global enterprises (Prahalad 1993), in contest to the desire for complete self-reliance characteristic of the 1970s and most of the 1980s.

Taking the Indian informatics industry as a whole, we find a concentrated structure, with the top 30 companies contributing nearly 75 percent of the industry's revenues. Despite such a concentrated structure, no Indian firm has been able to establish the economies of scale and the infrastructure necessary to become cost-competitive on the international market. Two important reasons for this are the small size of the domestic market for computer hardware (U.S.$821 million) and high tariff barriers over the last few decades that legitimized high-cost production.

A small market for a product that depends on production economies for competitiveness implies that the economies of scale in the Indian computer industry are low. While the firm selling the largest number of microcomputers in the country had an output of only 20,326 systems in 1994, the minimum efficient scale of output for microcomputers, as estimated by the World Bank, is around 50,000 (Dataquest 1994b, 48; World Bank 1987).

Apart from the small demand base, government policies can also be held responsible for having fragmented the licensed production capacities among several firms, leading to sub-optimal manufacturing units. Low scale economies have further implications, such as the inability to release significant resources for research and development. It has been estimated that the average research intensity of Indian computer firms is only around 3.08 percent, whereas large Japanese corporations such as Fujitsu have a research intensity of almost 10 percent (Bowonder and Mani 1991).[19]

The software industry

India's software industry is the fastest growing sector in the economy. The compound annual growth rate (CAGR) for the industry as a whole from 1989 to 1996 has been around 40 percent; the CAGR for the software export industry has been a very high 44 percent, while the domestic software industry showed a CAGR of around 36 percent over the same period. The U.S.$868 million Indian software industry consists of around 785 firms employing more than 125,000 people (Nasscom 1995; Financial Times 1995).[20] Of these, almost 425 are primarily oriented to the domestic market, while the remaining firms concentrate on exports (Table 3).

Table 3 Software Industry Revenues, 1992–1995 (U.S.$millions)

	Domestic	Export	Total
System and Application Software			
1992–93	56.87	4.67	61.54
1993–94	74.27	12.63	86.90
1994–95	136.50	56.00	192.50
Custom Software, Turnkey Projects, Consultancy			
1992–93	79.57	218.83	298.40
1993–94	101.70	316.00	417.70
1994–95	220.16	455.66	675.82
Total Software			
1992–93	136.44	223.50	359.94
1993–94	175.97	328.63	504.60
1994–95	356.66	511.66	868.32

Source: Dataquest 1994a,b; Nasscom 1995.

Software export promotion began as early as 1970 when the government started permitting import of computers for software export purposes. Since then, such imports have been gradually liberalized, but against stringent export obligations from importers. By the mid-1980s, as foreign firms increasingly turned toward India's low-cost, skilled software professionals, the government began to consider seriously the provision of infrastructure and incentives for software exports. A new software policy in 1986 permitted the import of the latest foreign designs and software development tools in order to enable the industry to produce world-class software for export (Government of India 1986). Unfortunately, the government failed to create and sustain a large domestic market for software and informatics applications, which could have provided the industry with immense opportunities for experimentation and learning. This in turn could have further helped the industry in its export efforts.

Another major initiative has been the Software Technology Park scheme, launched in 1990 to provide "motherly treatment" to companies and small entrepreneurs that cannot afford expensive communications facilities. Units in an STP are eligible for liberal importing of hardware and software tools, tax exemptions, and easy access to satellite links. Nearly 225 software units operate under this scheme.

In 1994–1995 alone, India exported software amounting to U.S.$500 million, and this figure is expected to rise to U.S.$1 billion by 1998 and to U.S.$4 billion by the turn of the century (Nasscom 1995, 16). Of total exports during 1994–1995, 39 percent were executed offshore within India and tele-commuted through high-speed, satellite-based data communication lines. The government's provision of high-speed satellite-based data communication links between clients and Indian firms as well as state-of-the-art computing facilities in the country's several STPs and export zones has greatly enhanced the ability of Indian software firms to undertake offshore software development (Harindranath and Liebenau 1995b). Such facilities are now being complemented effectively by private software companies that are establishing dedicated data communication and video conferencing links between their clients and themselves. More than 100 such data links now exist in the country, providing a fast, cost-effective, and secure means of transmitting data, software code, and intermediate output such as comments and queries from clients.

Almost half of all offshore development projects executed by Indian companies are in the realm of professional services, which includes customized or bespoke software development, application re-engineering, and systems integration. A high 81 percent of India's software exports go to the Organization for (OECD) countries, the United States, Japan, the United Kingdom, Germany, France, and Italy. American companies in particular have exploited opportunities provided by Indian software firms for offshore development, especially in the category of professional services, and have accounted for almost 60 percent of the total exports from India.

Outsourcing[21] software development to Indian firms has become particularly popular in the 1990s. A major reason for this is the substantial gap between the cost of local software development in the major information technology (IT) markets (North America, Japan, and Europe) and in the Indian market.[22] But it is also due to the increasing quality consciousness of Indian software firms,[23] the availability of highly skilled personpower trained in state-of-the-art technologies (such as computer-aided software engineering [CASE], fourth-generation languages, graphical user interfaces, object-oriented programming, client-server architecture, networking, and multimedia), and the ability of Indian firms to successfully manage large and complex projects involving 200–300 person-years.[24] India's expertise in software development extends through the entire range of activities from low-level data entry and contract programming to what are categorized as professional services, i.e., the provision of management information systems consultancy, application re-engineering for the Unix environment, systems analysis and design, custom software (also called bespokesoftware) development and implementation at the customer's site or offshore, maintenance, education, and training (Bhatnagar 1994; Brij 1994).[25]

The poor diffusion of informatics within India is largely a historical legacy. The protectionist policy regime not only emphasized computer hardware production instead of IT use but also made IT procurement an expensive and procedurally difficult proposition through elaborate import licensing measures. Moreover, the highly protected economy did not create conditions in which companies could gain competitive advantages through the use of IT. In particular, India's poor telecommunications infrastructure implied very low returns from IT, which discouraged corporate investment in the technology. Then again, Indian IT companies have not marketed their products in any meaningful way to increase awareness among people of the potential applications of this new technology, nor have users lobbied the IT industry through appropriate agencies or existing nationwide computer users groups for quality products and services and fair prices.

The attitude of senior policy makers and bureaucrats that computers were meant for social elites limited computerization within the government and administration. Furthermore, the use of IT in an economy with high levels of unemployment also presented the government with a politically and socially sensitive problem. Finally, an inadequate appreciation of the role of IT in improving administrative and business operations also helped keep administrators and managers away from the technology.

India's domestic software industry has also taken more time to develop than its export counterpart. On the one hand, this has been a consequence of government policy that promoted software exports while totally ignoring the need for a domestic software market. The problem was only compounded by policies targeted exclusively at computer hardware manufacturing. As a result, the attention of the government, industry, and users was aimed solely at computer hardware. Indeed, until recently, Indian users expected software to be bundled free with any computer hardware they purchased. Further negative fallout of this situation included rampant software piracy and the consequent neglect, until recently, of indigenous software development by the industry.

Although packaged software development is still in its infancy in India, a few firms manufacture products for banking, financial accounting, office automation, and word processing. Some Indian firms have also produced packages for engineering, manufacturing, CASE, database, project management, training, and utility applications. However, the lack of marketing clout has meant that these products have not met with much success even in the local market, with perhaps the sole exception of accounting and financial packages targeted specifically at the Indian user. This and the increasing popularity of imported software packages have forced many locally oriented firms to shift toward software exports.

The absence of any consistent effort to diffuse IT through either applications development for domestic use or the creation of a strong domestic market for software continues to be one of the major drawbacks to India's policies for the software sector.[26] As a result, almost four decades after the first computer entered the country in 1955, and after more than two decades of informatics policy, there are only around 1.2 million PCs in use in India and the entire Indian informatics industry contributes less than one percent of the country's GDP (see Harindranath and Liebenau 1995b).

Broadcasting

Broadcasting in India reflects the institutional and market arrangements and evolution of the Indian telecommunications sector. As a result of a variety of political, social and cultural issues, broadcasting was a state monopoly in India until the early 1990s. Since then, the sector has been progressively opened to private broadcasters. The dismantling of state-controlled television has led to a boom on both the demand and the supply sides of India's market. The number of viewers has skyrocketed and the number of broadcasters has kept pace with the expansion of the market. By mid-1995, there were 45.6 million television households, representing approximately 92 percent of India's 980 million inhabitants and making India the second-largest market in Asia.

Until recently, Indian television was provided on a monopoly basis by the Department of Broadcasting, which operated under the commercial name of Doordarshan.[27] The Department is part of the Secretary for Information and Broadcasting under the administrative supervision of the Ministry of Information and Broadcasting, and until 1975, it was part of All Indian Radio. Due to these institutional ties, Doordarshan suffered a number of constraints that undermined its entrepreneurial and creative capabilities (Rajagopal 1993, 98). Headed by a Director General, Doordarshan has a workforce of 27,000 public sector employees who are hired, paid, and promoted along the same lines as other workers in the Indian public sector. Or at least that was the case until the rise of competition. Since then, in an effort to reverse its rapidly shrinking market share, the company has begun hiring highly qualified professionals from the private sector. Nevertheless, its monopoly has been rapidly undermined since the advent, in the early 1990s, of satellite TV broadcasters and cable TV (CATV) operators.

Eroding further the exclusivity of state broadcasting, the Indian Supreme Court ruled in February 1995 that the airwaves were public and that state-run Doordarshan had no monopoly. Article 19[6] or the Indian Constitution allows monopolies in business activities. This clause, according to the court, limits Article 19(1-g), which is concerned with the right to trade and conduct business, but does not permit monopolies in activities—such as broadcasting—that are predominantly related to the right of expression and covered by Article 19 (1-a) of the Constitution.[28] The ruling considered that although the state has no constitutional right to maintain a monopoly on broadcasting, it should play an active role in regulating content and advertising.

The court's decision has had two significant institutional implications for the Indian broadcasting industry. On the one hand, it gave a green light to the innumerable private entrepreneurs who were attempting to enter into the sector, thus considerably changing the ownership and market share of India's electronic mass media. On the other hand, it gave rise to proposals for a new independent regulatory broadcasting agency, separating regulation from service provision at the state level.

The proposed regulatory agency, the Indian Broadcasting Authority (IBA), has already been endorsed by the government and will derive its powers from a new Indian Broadcasting Act, once it is approved by Parliament.

Until the mid-1990s, India had no specific broadcasting legislation. On the transmission side, the use of the radio spectrum was regulated by the 1885 Indian Telegraph Act, which stated that the airwaves are the property of the Union (i.e., federal) government. Content issues and freedom of speech were covered by the similar Cinematograph Act. The new sector-specific Indian Broadcasting Act will replace much of this legislation.[29] The IBA will deal mainly with issues related to content—namely, programming and advertising. Technical matters will rest in the hands of the Telecom Regulatory Authority. Unlike the Telecom Regulatory Authority, the IBA will have the power to grant licenses to prospective broadcasters. It will also act as a police agency, monitoring broadcasters' compliance with the current legislation and acting upon public complaints (carrying out investigations and applying penalties, including the termination of licenses). In institutional terms, the government plans to constitute the IBA along similar lines to the Telecom Regulatory Authority. It will probably be headed by a former Supreme Court judge and will probably include half a dozen members with legal and technical backgrounds along with respected artists, writers, and other eminent individuals. It will not include anybody actively involved in the broadcasting industry, although former broadcasters are not likely to be excluded.

In the early 1980s, television signals reached only 28 percent of India's urban population located in the four largest cities (Kishore

1994, 98). In 1982, India hosted the Asian Games, giving the domestic television industry a big technological boost. In 1983, the government launched the INSAT-IB satellite, which provided an important new platform for the industry's growth. By 1985, Indian television reached 53 percent of the population, growing to 62 percent in 1988, and passing the 90 percent threshold in the mid-1990s. The number of television transmitters multiplied from 19 in 1981 to nearly 400 in 1990 (Kishore 1994; Rajagopal 1993).

By the mid-1990s, however, satellite TV broadcasters still had to go through a rather difficult and convoluted process to reach Indian viewers. Since long distance telecommunications are a state monopoly, the government does not allow private TV operators to uplink signals to the satellites from which they broadcast their programs. To overcome government restrictions, Indian TV companies mail videotapes or send locally produced programs via international telephone lines to foreign destinations—mainly Hong Kong, the Philippines, Nepal, and Russia—and from there they are beamed to Asian and/or international satellites and then downlinked to viewers in India.

Despite these legal and infrastructure obstacles, the Indian television market has experienced a rapid growth of private broadcasters and CATV operators. During the Gulf War, Indian entrepreneurs set up illegal rooftop satellite dishes and downloaded CNN transmissions, which were then distributed to local subscribers. In 1991, the Hong Kong–based STAR TV network began regular satellite TV transmissions to India.[30] In its first six months of operation, STAR saw its viewership grow by 310 percent (Kishore 1994, 97). In late 1992, a new Bombay-based channel, ZeeTV, entered the market with a menu of local-language game shows, soap operas, and news programs. If STAR TV broke the ice in the Indian market, Zee triggered booms in both audiences and operators. By late 1994, ZeeTV claimed seven million subscriber households and 37 percent of the Indian prime-time audience, while the state-run Doordarshan attracted 28 percent of the viewership and other broadcasters and CATV shared the remainder of the market. Other smaller but rapidly growing channels are Jain TV (which became, in early 1995, the first 24-hour local-language service), Asia Television Network, Sun TV (a Madras-based Tamil language channel), and several other small broadcasters.[31]

CATV companies have also mushroomed throughout India to an estimated 60,000 operators in late 1994, serving approximately 12 million homes. The cable sector generates an estimated U.S.$450 million a year in subscription fees. Operators distribute a selected menu of programs downloaded from satellite broadcasting or videotaped from other sources.[32] CATV companies operated illegally until September 1994, when the government legitimized them in an effort to regulate the industry and raise tax revenues. CATV operators have come to play a key role in the industry due to their control of viewers and access to satellite-TV programming.

A number of other local and foreign groups are exploring ways to enter the Indian television market. The local Modi Group, which markets Walt Disney television programs, is planning to launch a sports channel and a pay-TV movie channel. Solomon International Enterprises has joined with U.S.-based Amritraj Entertainment to produce miniseries and feature films for the small screen and has made considerable investments in satellite channels. Ted Turner's group is entering the Indian market with the Cartoon Network and the TNT movie channel. Asian Television Network has entered a joint venture with Australian Television to provide an English-language channel and several others catering to India's main regional languages.

This flourishing of new broadcasters has been enhanced by legal and infrastructure developments. The February 1995 Supreme Court decision against Doordarshan's monopoly and the forthcoming Indian Broadcasting Act are two key pieces in this picture. The launching of India's locally designed and manufactured satellite, Insat-2C (which will offer TV broadcasting as well as business communications), and PanAmSat's PAS-4 (with a capacity of 120 channels of digitally compressed programming to be received in dishes less than one meter wide), will also have major economic and infrastructure effects on the sector.[33]

The appearance of competition has had a sobering effect on Doordarshan, which has rapidly gone from a dormant and dull company to an energetic and responsive broadcaster. Whereas in 1990 Doordarshan reached only 28 million households, by mid-1994 it covered 83 percent of the country, reaching more than 43 million households. In 1995, Doordarshan expanded its transmission to 13 channels; one of these channels broadcasts MTV programs, while several others cater to various linguistic communities. Doordarshan has also entered into a number of agreements with foreign content providers to enhance its programming,[34] and in April 1995, Doordarshan became the first Indian company to offer a movie channel.[35] Competition in the television market has not only shaken up Doordarshan and turned it into an innovative commercial operation but has also triggered a broader restructuring of the Indian content industry.

India's burgeoning broadcasting industry has lured an increasing number of advertisers, and in the mid-1990s, television advertising revenues are growing at an annual rate of 25 percent. This in turn has attracted the attention of several Indian newspapers and publishing houses that have diversified into the electronic media world. One of India's major publishers, the Hindustan Times Group, has entered a joint venture with the UK publishing and media conglomerate Pearson and the Hong Kong broadcaster TVB.[36] The new company intends to produce TV and video programming in various Indian languages.[37] Business India, a leading business publisher, has launched Business India Television (BITV) with three channels carrying news and entertainment. Relying on its already existing nationwide news-gathering infrastructure, BITV plans to become the first independent news network in South Asia.

The transformation of the broadcasting sector has also affected the Indian film industry. With most of its operations located in Bombay, the movie industry—commonly known as Bollywood— has in recent years seen its once flourishing business sharply curtailed by the rise of videocassettes and the shortage of cinemas. The booming world of television promises to revitalize Bollywood but also demands a shift in production to fit the small screen. A good example of this trend is that the Hinduja Group, one of the largest Indian film financiers, is migrating from film-only activities to a whole range of electronic media and communication ventures. Hinduja has formed the IndusInd Media and Communications Company, which is a holding firm for four subsidiaries: IN Cablenet, IN Vision,[38] IN Movies,[39] and IN Print.[40] In May 1995, the group announced the launching of a U.S.$169 million high tech cable television firm called IN Network. Like most Indian CATV firms, this company downloads satellite programming and distribute it to viewers through coaxial and fiber-optic cable.[41]

Telephone companies are not excluded from the television frenzy. The new telecom legislation allows private telecom operators to enter the CATV market. This official green light to cross traditional communication boundaries has led telecom companies, such as AT&T to join Indian firms in providing services such as video-on-demand, home shopping, interactive advertising, games and educational services. There is, however, no official plan to allow cable operators to enter the telecommunications market.

The economic implications of the recent developments in the Indian electronic media world are such that some Indian states are attempting to attract investments to the sector by giving tax exemptions to entrepreneurs who set up television studios. This has led to a mushrooming of program producers across the country.

Trends in and Implications of NII Initiatives

Some analysts close to the central administration have suggested that, if the Congress (I) Party remains in power, further changes will render the current initiatives mere preparatory steps to the real reforms. Although the reform process might continue to expand by the next administration, current initiatives to build an NII are already having a significant socioeconomic effect on Indian society. The following section explores the impact of Indian NII policy initiatives on economic growth, industrial production, and employment.

Economic Growth

India is well positioned to benefit from the rapid implementation of an NII. The service sector of the economy is growing rapidly and accounted for more than 40 percent of GDP by 1993 (Figure 4). The country is also endowed with a vast pool of technically skilled, English-speaking professionals. But to profit from these structural advantages and achieve sustainable economic growth, India needs telecommunication services of world-class quality. In this regard, India still remains at a considerable competitive disadvantage vis-à-vis other developing countries.[42]

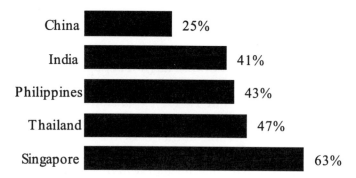

Figure 4 Services Share of GDP in Selected Asian Countires, 1993 (ITU)

One of the main reasons for Indian's competitive disadvantage is that prices for long distance and international telephone service will most likely remain high in the next few years due to DoT and VSNL's monopoly in those segments of the market.[43] Currently, prices for long distance and international services in India are higher than in other developing countries (such as Chile) that have introduced some form of competition into the market.

Furthermore, the expansion of VANS has been made difficult by high licensing fees. For instance, electronic mail providers have to pay an annual fee of U.S.$80,000 or U.S.$345,000 for a five-year license. For electronic bulletin board services, the fee is U.S.$38 per subscriber per year or a minimum fee of U.S.$46,900 per year.[44] The high cost of licenses will most likely be transferred to consumers in the form of high tariffs, which in turn discourage usage and represent an obstacle to low tariffs generated by economies of scale.

High tariffs might not present a major obstacle to the operations for large multinational corporations with strong financial backing and the prospect of large profits. But for small and medium-sized enterprises—which constitute the backbone of India's economy—the cost of information and communications services can become the determining factor for business survival. As the Indian economy opens and subsidies and privileges for local businesses fade away, the competitiveness and commercial prospects of small and medium-sized enterprises will largely depend on their production costs, of which communication costs form a central component.

In addition to the cost of services, there are more tangible infrastructure deficiencies that can hinder the building of a reliable and efficient national information infrastructure. The expansion of the DoT's long distance network has not kept pace with the growth of local networks. With the entry of fast-growing private operators in the local loop and DoT's expansion of its local networks to fight competition, the traffic at the national level will most likely encounter considerable bottlenecks in trunk transmission (Ravi 1995, 128).

The problem in the short run may be aggravated by the fact that the DoT will remain the only long distance operator but will face competition in basic services in all telecom circles. Some local analysts have argued that in its efforts to remain the dominant player in local markets across India, the DoT will shift resources to its local operations, not only hindering long distance network growth but also undermining the quality and diversity of national long distance services.[45]

Finally, one of the fundamental aspects of building an export-led national information industry is access to sophisticated, low-cost transmission facilities. However, India's national high-speed networks are still in their infancy. Although main telephone lines and computing support are growing rapidly, the country still has only limited access to other more sophisticated, low-cost transmission facilities such as ISDN. The difference in the cost of services provided via ISDN lines and conventional telephone lines (Table 4) is such that, in the case of developing countries such as India, the absence of ISDN networks could easily deter the rise of a national information service industry. In 1995, India still did not have any significant deployment of ISDN lines,[46] while digitization of the Public Switched Telephone Network (PSTN) had reached 53.9 percent of the switches only 29.8 percent of the transmission segment of the network.

Domestic IT Production

Although India's import substitution regime forced firms to manufacture computers domestically, indigenation proved impossible to achieve due to the rapidity of technological change and the

Table 4 Cost of Information Transfer, 1993 (U.S.$)

	Photograph[a] (1.0 MB)	Fax[b] (10 pages)	Data[b] (1.25 MB)
Conventional telephone lines	217.0	22.0	150.0
ISDN	12.1	4.8	9.9

a. Japan to UK. b. Japan to United States.
Source: ITU

nonavailability of locally made components.[47] With the coming of the new liberal economic agenda in the 1990s, the nature of computer hardware manufacturing in India began to shift from the classical approach of producing a good from the component level (i.e., vertical integration) to (a) either specialized manufacturing of some components (such as printed circuit boards, integrated circuits, and molds) wherein a firm has the advantage of volume or (b) the integration of purchased components, testing, and further value addition where possible (i.e., systems integration).

Despite lower tariffs, local Indian firms will find it increasingly difficult to compete effectively with illegal assemblers who pay no customs tariff.[48] This has put manufacturers at a relative disadvantage. Firms with international linkages have gained from tariff reductions since liberalization makes business with foreign partners easier. This has prompted Indian informatics firms to seek multiple linkages with foreign firms. For instance, each of the top 20 firms in the Indian informatics industry, including state-owned firms such as CMC and ECIL, has one or more joint ventures with international informatics companies. However, firms that have invested in setting up manufacturing facilities and building up design capabilities are having to make difficult choices about future strategies. Although idle or underutilized manufacturing capacities are causing problems, entrepreneurial firms are developing capabilities in software and making a transition from manufacturing to value addition through system integrations as their core business activity (Harindranath and Liebenau 1995a).

Although globalization will have a positive impact on informatics use in India due to price reductions and improvements in quality as a result of competition, it may affect the technical capabilities of some local firms. Import substitution forced these firms to painstakingly build up the capability to manufacture systems based on indigenous designs, often at great economic cost. Liberalization and the ready availability of foreign technology may lead to a gradual waning of such skills. Furthermore, these firms have traditionally invested some resources into in-house research and development, which has enabled faster technology absorption. However, the current policy environment has made these minuscule but locally relevant R&D investments economically unsustainable. While the shift from manufacturing to trading is certain to emphasize brand names at the expense of more substantive issues of technology development, the trend toward systems integration may yet represent an immensely important niche for Indian informatics firms. It may also be the only viable alternative for the very survival of the Indian computer hardware industry.

By contrast, the domestic software industry faces a good, but still unsettled, future. Although the sector has been growing rapidly in the 1990s, it still trails the export sector in terms of both revenue and government priority. However, liberalization and the ensuing globalization will increasingly make use of informatics to enhance competitiveness and productivity an imperative not merely for the Indian industry but also for the government and administration's ability to respond rapidly to the needs of an economy in transition.

Recent developments such as the reduction of customs tariffs on software imports to a uniform 10 percent and a May 1994 amendment to the Indian Copyright Law have the potential to boost domestic software development and IT use. Lower tariffs can help develop indigenous skills through greater exposure to international software as well as increased competition and can help reduce piracy, which has been a major disincentive to domestic software developers. The amended copyright law clearly determines what is legal and illegal in the copying of software, defines who an author is and what his or her rights are, and empowers the government to punish those who breach copyrights or engage in piracy. These changes should encourage software and applications (product) development for the domestic market.

The liberalization of the Indian telecommunications sector has led several software companies to target telecommunications software as a niche area. The opening of banking and financial services has also triggered the rise of customized software production. Both of these sector reforms will go a long way toward expanding the domestic market for IT. Indeed, there is now a growing recognition that a large domestic market for informatics can be utilized to develop and test indigenous software targeted at niche areas in the international software market (see Financial Times 1995).

A recent study estimated India's share in the worldwide outsourced professional services market to be at a high of 20 percent in 1991 (IDC and Maxi/Micro 1992, Volume 1, 21).[49] Compared with seven other countries (Israel, Ireland, China, Hungary, Singapore, Mexico, and the Philippines), India was the most attractive option for U.S., European, and Japanese companies seeking offshore development or international outsourcing partners (Udell 1993; Financial Times 1995). If this significant outsourcing opportunity is exploited by Indian industry, software exports will continue to maintain the highest growth rates among the various sectors of the Indian IT industry.

NII-Related Employment

Because India's information infrastructure industries are undergoing a process of transition and profound transformation, it is difficult to pin down with any accuracy the specific consequences that NII initiatives might have on information-related employment. Moreover, the results of research carried out in OECD countries that demonstrate some general trends in this industry do not seem applicable in developing countries such as India.

The size of the telecommunications workforce in many developed countries has seen a constant decline in recent years. In most cases, the convergence of technological innovation and market saturation for basic services has led to considerable labor cuts (OECD 1995). In most developing countries, the high growth rate of the domestic telecom market and still politicized labor policies have led instead to an increase in the number of people employed in the sector. This is particularly true in the case of India, where the total number of people employed in telecom services rose by more

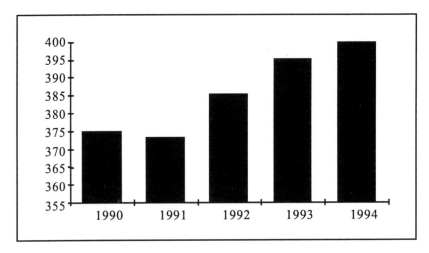

Figure 5   Telecom Employees in India (1,000s). Source: Department of Telecommunications, India.

than 25,000 between 1990 and 1994 (Figure 5).

Despite this increase in employment in recent years, one should not expect this trend to be sustained in the near future. However, it is also quite unlikely that telecom employment in India will suffer the sharp decline observed in OECD countries. The most likely scenario in the short- and mid-term is that employment in the Indian telecom sector will remain steady. A variety of factors support this forecast.

First, the DoT has not been—and will not be in the near future—privatized, which allows political criteria to remain important in the hiring and firing of state-owned telecom company employees. Second, as DoT, MNTL, and VSNL grow, the current low level of labor productivity—which can justify labor cuts—will most likely improve, rendering higher ratios of lines per employees and thus removing one of the main reasons for labor retrenchment.[50] Furthermore, the large number of new private firms entering the domestic telecom market may not only absorb the redundant workforce in the public sector but also provide new employment opportunities.[51]

Third, for the next few years the DoT will enjoy two sources of high revenues (long distance services and license fees—approxi-

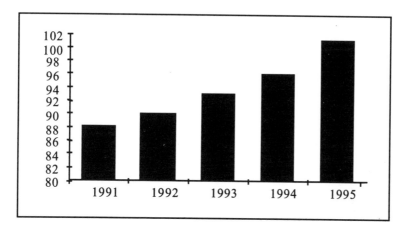

Figure 6 Estimated Demand for Computer Personnel in India (1,000s). Source: ITU.

mately U.S.$41 billion spread over a period of 15 years) that will allow the company to retain labor even at the expense of reduced efficiency and higher operating costs—if the state decides to do so for political and social reasons.

Although in the medium to long-term, the Indian telecommunications sector might face employment constraints, other segments of the info-communications sector—such as the computer and audiovisual broadcasting industries—are rapidly increasing their labor demand. In the Indian computer industry, for example, employment demand has been rising steadily since 1990 (Figure 6) and the industry is well positioned to become an important employer on a national basis.[52] As information services and content-based industries go global, the demand for low-cost, highly trained information professionals with English-language skills—such as those found in India—should increase even further, providing a considerable boost to India's labor market.

Conclusion

India faces the dawning of a new economic, political, and social era. Since the early 1990s, the country has experienced a paradigm shift in its national development strategy, moving from protectionism, self-reliance, and central planning to strategies that emphasize liberalization, global integration, and market-driven growth. Recent policy initiatives to boost the country's NII are part of these larger transformations of Indian society. In an effort to build a communications platform upon which a national information economy can flourish, the Indian government has introduced significant changes in the telecommunications, informatics, and broadcasting sectors.

To overcome the bottlenecks generated by a dearth of telecommunications facilities and services, the government has dismantled the long-standing state monopoly and invited private firms to deploy networks and provide basic and value-added services in the more than 20 telecom circles around the country. The cellular and value-added service markets have also been opened to the competitive entry of private operators. Developments in data networks and the Internet, although constrained by the limited availability of infrastructure, are nevertheless experiencing considerable growth induced by the liberalized telecommunications environment. Much of the transformation in this sector is guided by a group of government institutions including the Ministry of Communication, the Telecom Commission, the DoT, the Prime Minister's Office, and the National Parliament.

In the informatics sector (hardware and software), after following for more than two decades import substitution and self-reliance strategies, in the mid-1980s the government turned to more liberal policies allowing imported computer parts to support the hardware industry and, later, the import of advanced computers to boost the nascent software industry. In the early 1990s, the Rao administration went further, introducing reforms that abolished the system of industrial licensing and liberalized foreign investment in computer hardware. Meanwhile, in the software industry, the rapid growth of private firms has been enhanced in the 1990s with official export-oriented initiatives such as the STP scheme. These developments are progressively turning India's informatics sector into one of the key components of the country's emerging NII.

Changes in the broadcasting sector reflect general telecommunications trends with the difference that, in broadcasting, government policies have followed events rather than led them. Since the first satellite television broadcasts in 1991, this sector has seen a mushrooming of broadcasters and cable television operators. Television audiences and the number of households with television have grown dramatically, reaching more than 90 percent of the Indian population by the mid-1990s. The decline of state monopolies and the rise of private initiatives in television have brought a significant restructuring of the Indian content industry. Traditional firms in both the film and publishing sectors are diversifying and investing heavily in satellite and cable television as well as in the production of programs and on line information services. Private telecommunications companies on the verge of entering the Indian market are also venturing into content-related cable services.

For years, India (along with Brazil) provided leadership to developing countries on informatics and communications policy. Today, this South Asian nation again appears ready to supply the developing world with rich experience on how to build an NII.

Notes

1. A survey carried out by the ITU found that in most developing countries telecommunications reform initiatives were an integral part of larger national economic reform programs (Becher 1991).

2. Zagha et al. 1995; Bhagwati 1993; and Roy 1994.

3. The Indian government controls 67 percent of MTNL shares and 85 percent of VSNL shares. The remaining shares are floated in the stock market.

4. As the experience of other Least Developed Countries has shown, the autonomy of the body will largely depend on the political practices of the country and the legal instruments available to the agency.

5. Petrazzini 1995.

6. The quality of services has also been poor in India. In the early 1990s the waiting list included an average of 2.5 million unfulfilled requests, and faults per 100 main lines rose over 200.

7. Licenses are to be granted by the government initially for 15 years and can be extended for an additional 10 years.

8. Two companies operate in each city. Sterling Cellular and Bharti Cellular serve New Delhi, BPL Systems & Projects and Hutchison Max Telecom operate in Bombay, and Modi Telstra and Usha Martin Telecom provide services in Calcutta.

9. Hughes Escorts Communications Ltd., Comsat-Max, and Comnet have begun

operations attracting large users including the Bank of America, Philips India, and the Indian Stock Exchange to their growing customer base.

10. Unlike China, India has not had an explicit national initiative toward the development of high speed data networks. China has put special emphasis on the development of what it calls the golden projects. While the "golden card" and "golden customs" aim at supporting advanced electronic data transactions for banking and customs, the "golden bridge" plans to provide a nationwide basic infrastructure for voice, data, and video transmission. India has instead taken a market-driven, piecemeal approach. In China, the central government has developed, in addition to these three initial projects, at least six others oriented toward providing information infrastructure support to various sectors of the economy and society.

11. As of late 1995, VSNL supported a variety of value-added services, including Easynet data-base access, packet switching, electronic mail, commercial Internet access, electronic data interchange (EDI), remote login, store and forward fax, globally managed data networks, and file transfer. In addition, it was planning to incorporate in 1996–1997 services such as cargo community systems, ATM services, frame relay services and multimedia ISDN (Videsh Sanchar Nigam Ltd. 1995).

12. One of these companies is the powerful Business India Group, which owns the leading business magazine in the country and two of the top market research agencies and has now become a major e-mail and on line service provider. Ghosh, Rishab, "The Content Business," *The Indian Techonomist*, July 1995, 15.

13. Recently, India's Open University unveiled plans for a major communications network to link all distance education institutions in the country in order to serve over 500,000 students annually (Asian Age 1995).

14. The term "informatics" used here encompasses both computer hardware and software.

15. The bulk of the legal production of microprocessor-based systems was accounted for by systems based on 80386, 80486, and Pentium microprocessors (Dataquest 1994a; 1995).

16. Firms such as HCL-HP and Wipro continue to manufacture systems based on indigenous designs. A Pentium server designed by HCL-HP, a joint venture between HCL (an Indian company) and Hewlett Packard, was chosen by Intel to demonstrate the power of the Pentium chip at the 1993 Comdex computer show in the United States (HCL-HP 1994).

17. Firms like HCL (now HCL Hewlett Packard), Wipro Infotech (now Wipro), DCM Data Products (now DCM Data Systems), and ORG were able to manufacture computer systems based on original designs around Intel microprocessors in the 1980s. For instance, Wipro, India's second largest informatics company, became only the second company in the world, after Compaq, to develop an i386-based system, and immediately followed it with the world's first i386-based 32-bit minicomputer running the latest version of UNIX (see Brunner 1990).

18. It is interesting to note that the macroeconomic crisis also served as an opportunity to seriously begin a process of liberalization that would otherwise have been difficult, if not impossible, to handle politically and to establish a firm linkage with the global economy (see Bhagwati and Srinivasan 1993).

19. Research intensity is defined as the ratio of R&D expenditure to sales turnover in percentage terms (see Bowonder and Mani 1991).

20. This figure excludes software developed by data processing departments in several user firms. One industry report estimates the value of such software development at U.S.$161 million for the year 1992–1993 (Nasscom 1993, 37).

21. Outsourcing means contracting out software development and related activities to third parties, locally or abroad.

22. A survey by a team of British consultants in mid-1991 showed that the price differential between international (offshore) outsourcing and local development was between 30 and 50 percent (see Brij 1994, 52).

23. The quality maturity in terms of the Indian software industry can be measured by the fact that 25 Indian software firms have obtained ISO 9000 certification for quality processes, and 52 are in the process of obtaining such certification. Another example is provided by the Indian operations of Motorola, which is the only company in the world, apart from IBM's NASA project, that has obtained the Software Engineering Institute's Level 5 certification for quality maturity (see Nasscom 1995, 17).

24. India has the world's second largest English-speaking scientific labor pool in the world, next only to the U.S. It has the third largest university system in the world, with a growing pool of 3.5 million technical personnel and 1,670 educational institutions including engineering colleges, technical institutes, and polytechnics (see Frankel and Mazumdar 1993; Nasscom 1995, 15).

25. Indian software companies, such as HCL Ltd. were developing commercial Unix applications as early as 1983–1984 (Evans 1995, 168–170).

26. The domestic software market was worth U.S.$357 million in 1994–1995 (Nasscom 1995).

27. Doordarshan means "seeing distant images."

28. Ghosh, Rishab, "Monopolies and Free Speech," *The Indian Techonomist*, July 1995, 2.

29. Ghosh, Rishab, "Freeing the Airwaves," *The Indian Techonomist*, July 1995, 12.

30. Unable to control the transmissions, the government saw the development at that moment as the materialization of the long-feared "cultural invasion from the skies."

31. Jonathan Karp, "TV Times," *Far Eastern Economic Review*, 15 December 1994, 58.

32. Indian CATV operators, like several other Asian content providers, are notorious for violating program copyrights.

33. Chris McConnell, "PanAmSat expands DHS plans," *Broadcasting and Cable*, 27 March 1995.

34. In June 1995, for example, Doordarshan signed an agreement with CNN to broadcast live news to India 24 hours a day. In exchange, CNN will carry some content provided by Doordarshan, it will help the Indian company market its program to a global audience, and it will train Doordarshan's staff.

35. Doordarshan's movie channel broadcasts 16 hours a day of Hindi, English, and regional language films.

36. Interestingly, foreign investment is not allowed in the Indian press.

37. Amdur, Meredith, "Passage to India: Full Steam Ahead for TV," *Broadcasting and Cable*, 23 January 1995.

38. IN Vision plans to launch a CATV channel to be called Mumbai, which will provide original local information services and entertainment.

39. IN Movies already holds a 2,500-movie library which it plans to market to cable operators and video cassette libraries.

40. IN Print will publish specialized magazines for niche markets starting with *What's In*, a leisure magazine that will complement Mumbai's progamming.

41. Hinduja's projects are financed by IndusInd, a 39,000-shareholder financial group, and foreign partners from Europe and the United States. Uma Cunha, "Indians Brace for Hinduja Homecoming," *Variety*, 29 May 1995.

42. The telecommunications-related analysis of this section relies heavily on the paper by Petrazzini and Krishnaswamy delivered at the PICT International Conference on the Social and Economic Implications of Information and Communication Technologies, London, 10–12 May 1995.

43. This is one of the policy choices in which political pressures in favor of the status quo have come in conflict with the official aim of an NII that would support and enhance India's competitiveness in the global marketplace.

44. Department of Telecommunications 1994.

45. With the rapid erosion of high revenues in long distance and international transmission and the emergence of a myriad of infocommunications services, local services are being increasingly identified as the most profitable market in the coming years.

46. Six ISDN networks were being tested at the end of 1995.

47. An Indian-made computer has at least 64 percent import content (Verma 1993).

48. Nearly 18 percent of the total revenue from domestic microcomputer sales in 1993 went to the unorganized illegal assembly sector, also called the "grey market." This share is expected to increase to 30 percent by 1997 (Subramanian 1993).

49. According to this study, the world market for outsourced professional services would be worth U.S.$4 billion in 1996, and the market opportunity for

reengineering applications to client-server architectures would be worth U.S.$600 million by the same year.

50. The DoT employs over 400,000 people to administer a national network of 8.02 million lines, that is, 20.5 main lines per employee. In other developing countries in the region, the ratios of line per employee are: China 30, Thailand 84, and Malaysia 97, while in Brazil the ratio is 121 main lines per employee.

51. In the United States, for example, the number of employees in cellular companies has increased from approximately 2,000 in the mid-1980s to almost 60,000 in the mid-1990s. It is estimated that approximately 250,000 jobs have been created by the cellular industry if one takes into account related services and manufacturing (OECD 1995; ITU 1995b, 13).

52. This development in the Indian broadcasting sector reflects trends in the U.S. market, where the number of people employed in the cable television industry has increased fivefold from the late 1970s to the mid-1990s.

References

J. Arora, S. P. Kaur, H. Chandra, and R. K. Bhatt. "Computer Communication Networks and their Use for Information Retrieval and Dissemination: Basic Tutorial and Current Scenario of Networks in India," *Microcomputers for Information Management* 9 (1992): 41–261.

"Open Varsities Network to Reach Out to Millions of Students," *Asian Age* (25 November 1995).

Ernst Becher, *Restructuring of Telecommunications in Developing Countries: An Empirical Investigation with ITU's Role in Perspective.* (Geneva: International Telecommunication Union, 1991).

J. Bhagwati, and T. N. Srinivasan. *India's Economic Reforms.* (New Delhi: Government of India), 1993.

Jagdish Bhagwati,. *India in Transition: Freeing the Economy.* (Oxford: Clarendon Press), 1993.

S. Bhatnagar, "Outsourcing of Information Work: India's Experience in Exploiting the Global Market" (paper presented at the Seminar on Information Technology and Globalisation, London, May 1994).

R. Brij, "Software Exports: The European Opportunity," *Computers Today* (January 1994): 50–58.

Hans-Peter Brunner, India's Computer Industry: Policy, Industry Structure and Technological Change—The Last Road to Survival? (Ph.D. diss., University of Maryland, College Park, 1990).

"Internet is Here," *Business India* (3 July 1995): 117–125.

Dataquest. The Dataquest Top 20. *Dataquest* (July 1993).

Dataquest. The Dataquest Top 20. *Dataquest*, 1 August 1994(a); 16 August 1994 (b).

Dataquest. The Dataquest Top 20. *Dataquest*, 1 August 1995.

Department of Electronics. *Guide to Electronics Industry in India.* (New Delhi: Department of Electronics Data Bank and Information Division), 1993.

Department of Electronics. *New Computer Policy.* (New Delhi: Department of Electronics), 1984.

Department of Electronics. *Policy on Computer Software Export, Software Development and Training.* (New Delhi: Department of Electronics), 1986.

Department of Telecommunications. *Value Added Services Licensing Information.* (New Dehli: Ministry of Communication), March 1994.

Duncan, Emma. "The Tiger Steps Out: A Survey of India," *The Economist* (21 January 1995): 2–30.

Economic Intelligence Unit. *India.* EIU Country Profile 1993/94, 1994.

Evans, P. "Indian Informatics in the 1980s: The Changing Character of State Involvement," *World Development*, 20 (1) 1992: 1–18.

Evans, P. *Embedded Autonomy: States and Industrial Transformation.* Princeton, NJ: Princeton University Press, 1995.

Evanski, Leah et al. *Telecommunications Industry in India.* Michigan, IN: The William Davidson Institute, 1994.

Financial Times. "India's Software Industry: Special Report," *Financial Times*, 6 December 1995.

Frankel, M. and S. Mazumdar. "Hacking for Hire," *Newsweek*, 18 January 1993.

Government of India. *Indian Telecommunications.* Report by the Telecom Commission, Ministry of Commerce, 1994.

Grieco, Joseph M. *Between Dependency and Autonomy: India's Experience with the International Computer Industry.* Berkeley: University of California Press, 1984.

Guha, Ashok. *Economic Liberalization, Industrial Structure, and Growth in India.* New Delhi: Oxford University Press, 1990.

Harindranath, G. and Jonathan Liebenau. "The Impact of Globalisation on India's Information Technology Industry," *Information Technology for Development*, September 1995(a).

Harindranath, G. and Jonathan Liebenau. "State Policy and India's Software Industry in the 1990s." In: Khosrowpour M., ed. *Managing Information and Communications in a Changing Global Environment.* London: Idea Group Publishing, 1995(b).

IDC [India] and Maxi/Micro. *India's Software and Services: Export Potential and Strategies.* New Delhi: Department of Electronics, 1992.

Ingelbrecht, Nick. "Land of Opportunity or Wilderness of Confusion?" *Communications Week International*, 27 November 1995: 24–28.

International Telecommunications Union (ITU). *Asia-Pacific Telecommunica-*

tions Indicators. Geneva: ITU, 1995(a).

International Telecommunications Union (ITU). *World Telecommunications Development Report.* Geneva: ITU, 1995(b).

Kishore, Krishna. "The Advent of STAR TV in India: Emerging Policy Issues," *Media Asia* 21 (2), 1994: 96–103.

Lantzke, Hugh; Ashoka Mody; and Robert Bruce. "Telecommunications Reform in India: An International Perspective," *World Bank Informal Discussion Paper,* January 1992.

Ministry of Communications. *VIII Five Year Plan (1992–1997): Industrial Development for Telecom Sector.* New Delhi: Government of India, 1991.

Mody, Bella. "State Consolidation Through Liberalization of Telecommunications Services in India," *Journal of Communications,* March 1995.

Nasscom. *The Software Industry in India 1993–94.* New Delhi: Nasscom, 1993.

Nasscom. "India's Telecommunication: The Political Underpinnings of Reform," *Telecommunications Policy,* January 1996.

Nasscom. *Nasscom's India-Europe Software Alliance Seminar Report.* London: Nasscom, 1995.

Nidumolu, S. R. and S. E. Goodman. "Computing in India: An Asian Elephant Learning to Dance," *Communications of the ACM,* June 1993: 15–22.

Organization for Economic Cooperation and Development (OECD). *Restructuring in Public Telecommunication Operator Employment.* Paris: OECD, 1995.

Petrazzini, Ben A. *The Political Economy of Telecommunications Reform in Developing Countries: Privatization and Liberalization in Comparative Perspective.* Westport, CT: Praeger, 1995.

Petrazzini, Ben A. "India's Telecommunication: The Political Underpinnings of Reform," *Telecommunications Policy,* January 1996.

Petrazzini, Ben A. and Girija Krishnaswamy. "The Socioeconomic Impact of Telecommunications Reform in Developing Countries: India in the International Context." Paper delivered at the PICT International Conference on the Social and Economic Implications of Information and Communication Technologies, London, 10–12 May 1995.

Prahalad, C. K. *Globalisation: Pitfalls, Pain and Potential.* New Delhi: Rajiv Gandhi Institute for Contemporary Studies, 1993.

Rajagopal, Arvind. "The Rise of National Programming: The Case of Indian Television," *Media, Culture, and Society* 15, 1993: 91–111.

Ravi, N. "Can Private Operators Deliver?" *The Hindu Survey of Indian Industry,* 1995: 127–128.

Roy, Ramashray. "The Struggles of Economic Reform," *Asian Survey* 34 (2) February 1994: 200–208.

Sen, Pronab. "Telecommunications in India: Imperatives and Prospects," *Eco-*

nomic and Political Weekly, 29 October 1994: 2869–2876.

Sinha, Nikhil. "The Political Economy of India's Telecommunications Reforms," *Telecommunications Policy,* January 1996.

Subramanian, C. R. *India and the Computer: A Study of Planned Development.* Delhi: Oxford University Press, 1992.

Subramanian, L. "Hardware Market: The Bulls Take Off," *Dataquest,* December 1993: 110–113.

Telecom Commission. *Indian Telecommunications.* New Delhi: Ministry of Communications, 1994.

Telecom Commission. *National Telecom Policy.* New Delhi: Ministry of Communications, May 1994.

Udell J. "India's Software Edge," *Byte,* September 1993: 55–60.

Verma, R. K. "Electronics Hardware Technology Park: A Step Towards Globalisation," *Electronics Information and Planning,* March 1993: 278–291.

Videsh Sanchar Nigam Ltd. *India's Gateway to the World.* New Delhi: Government of India, 1995.

World Bank. *India—the Development of the Electronics Industry: A Sector Report.* Washington, DC: World Bank, 1987.

Zagha, Roberto, et al. *India: Recent Economic Developments and Prospects.* Washington DC: World Bank, 1995.

Brazil: Is the World Ready for When Information Highways Cross the Amazon?

Lee McKnight and Antonio J. J. Botelho

Introduction

In Brazil, emerging and advanced forms of digital infrastructure, such as the Internet and online information services, have been slow to develop. Only in 1995 did Internet access become available to individuals outside of a few university and corporate research centers. The Brazilian telephone system developed early in the postwar period, but penetration is lower than in other nations at comparable per capita income levels.[1] The number of digital phone lines, a prerequisite for many advanced services, is comparatively low, as is shown by Figure 1. Furthermore, it cannot be said that a national strategy toward information infrastructure exists; by 1996, a national debate has barely begun. Privatization and liberalization of telecommunications infrastructure have yet to be implemented. Commercial broadcast television, however, is widespread, and the leading firm in the media sector, Globo, ranks with the largest players worldwide. New media, such as cable and satellite television, have experienced rapid growth in the 1990s, although penetration is still low. Similarly, cellular telephony, at least in upper-income strata, has, despite a late start, rapidly grown from a luxury to a seeming necessity, spurred in part by the underdevelopment of the domestic terrestrial telecommunications infrastructure.

What accounts for Brazil's delay in responding to the growing worldwide movement to advanced information infrastructure? And now that the Brazilian political system, business community,

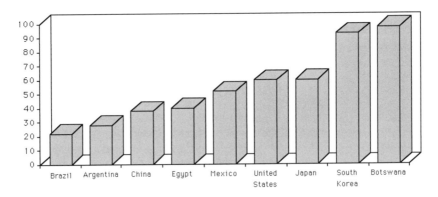

Figure 1 Brazil in Comparative Perspective: Percentage of Digital Lines (1992). Source: B. Regli from data in ITU (1994).

and social groups have begun to take the first steps toward development of a national information infrastructure, how may its structure and content differ from other nations? What challenges will Brazil present to the rest of the world as its cultural content and values become more widely accessible?

The popular stereotype of sexy Brazilian women on the beaches of Copacabana captures a challenge for the world. Content which may be considered indecent, offensive, or possibly even obscene in other countries is acceptable primetime viewing in Brazil. One step ahead of the morality ceilings of much of the developed world, Brazilian television has, for example, broadcast male nudity in primetime.[2] Attempts to restrict global access to this content would likely be seen by Brazil as foreign discrimination against its service exports. When the information highway crosses the Amazon, what will the world think? And, what will the world be able to do?

This chapter reviews the Brazilian information infrastructure context and provides comparative data to demonstrate the differences and similarities with other nations in Latin America, and in other parts of the world.

Brazilian Information Infrastructure Policy in the 1990s

The Brazilian political system traditionally has striven for national autonomy and self-sufficiency. This tradition has only recently given way to a more open attitude toward foreign investment and a reduction of barriers to trade. Import barriers had restricted significantly the growth of the Brazilian computer market. For example, barriers to trade in computer software and hardware were only lowered in the early 1990s, and are still present for some categories of goods. Although multinational personal computer and software companies expanded their presence significantly by 1995, only a few years earlier importation of computers was a criminal offense. And even now customs duties are prohibitive.

By 1996, the Brazilian political climate shifted tremendously. Import barriers have fallen and exposure of national industries and cultural institutions to foreign ideas, products, and services has changed public expectations. Cable television, satellite television, and cellular telephony are growing at a rapid rate, while more advanced wireless communications systems are beginning to be installed.

However, given vehement worker opposition to privatization across industrial sectors, and the gridlock on significant economic reforms within the Brazilian Congress, the pace and direction of regulatory change and industrial restructuring remain uncertain.

In areas such as harmonization of Brazilian protection of patents, copyrights, and trademarks with international norms, significant progress has been made even if large black and gray markets in counterfeit and pirated goods exists

With regard to the issues of cultural sovereignty, censorship, and freedom of expression, one may expect that Brazil will provide a haven for activities that are proscribed elsewhere, and think nothing of it. Since nudity and sexual content are widely accepted on primetime broadcast television in Brazil, it is unlikely that Brazilian Web sites will be void of similar material. Domestic restrictions on access, if they develop, may not conform to the standards promulgated by the United States—or Germany, Iran, China, or Singapore, to name a few more restrictive societies. If Brazilians in general do not consider such material offensive, how will they react to attempts by regulators in other countries to tell people what they can and cannot see in cyberspace? Why should they wish to harmonize with the far more restrictive (or prudish) norms and values of Americans, Germans, and Chinese?

International harmonization and cooperation in enforcing national policies on content censorship will likely be slow to develop. Technology-enabled restriction and mediation of information solutions are likely to develop more quickly than national policies develop and international rules can be harmonized. Nevertheless, developing, implementing, and enforcing technological means of mediating access to information are advancing rapidly, even if hacker attempts to circumvent these restrictions are also advancing rapidly. National policies toward information security technology (i.e., cryptography) will determine to some extent how this plays out in Brazil and other nations. But in this as in other areas of information infrastructure policy, Brazilian policies on security, export control, and encryption are either undeveloped or nonexistent. Rather, controls on imports were of greater concern until very recently.

Brazilian Information Infrastructure in the 1990s

Brazil is late in its consideration of options for telecommunications liberalization.[3] One could argue that this is an advantage in that there are lessons to be learned from the successes and failures of efforts in Latin America and elsewhere, as well as opportunities to be seized from emerging technological trends.[4] There are, moreover, significant differences among the different sectors that make up a country's information infrastructure. As technologies and markets converge and liberalization takes hold, the competitive dynamics of well-advanced sectors could make up for the laggard sectors and forge a uniquely strong and diverse Brazilian information infrastructure capable of meeting the social and economic challenges of the end of the century.

Telecommunications

At the outset, it should be noted that, despite Brazil's low penetration level, by any standard of economic performance or profitability, the national telecommunications operator Telebrás stands out: it was rated by *Fortune* magazine as the 22nd most profitable service firm in the world. Telebrás was the world's 20th largest public telecommunications operator (PTO) with U.S. $7 billion dollars in sales in 1995. Telebrás is a state-owned telecommunications service holding company which provides more than 90 percent of Brazil's telecommunications services. It controls 28 state operating subsidiaries providing local telecommunications service and Embratel, the country's only domestic and international long distance provider. Financial analysts predict Telebrás will have an annual growth in earnings of 25 percent, and it has made significant investments in its network, as is show by Figure 2. Nevertheless, the stunning business performance of Telebrás hides problems in the system that may impair its future growth and, more important, delay the development of a competitive Brazilian information infrastructure.

At the end of 1995, Brazil had 13.301 million telephone terminals for a population of about 154 million people.[5] This put Brazil in the 42nd position in the global rank of telephone density, behind its Latin American neighbors Argentina, Colombia, and Venezuela. The low number of lines per 100 people (1992) shown in Figure 3, even when contrasted to nations with comparable levels of economic development, suggests that the goal of universal service has not been met.

Although Telebrás may be partly to blame, one of the main reasons is Brazil's highly skewed income distribution. Only 27 million Brazilians, or about 18 percent of the population, have an annual per capita income comparable to levels in industrialized nations. Telephone density of this segment of the population is 41 per 100 inhabitants, similar to that of developed nations. Almost half of local subscribers do not generate sufficient income for Telebrás to cover costs, due to the unrealistically low government-regulated local tariffs. Only 30 percent of the lines generate profits, with basic services subsidized by long distance revenues (domestic and international).

The lack of political will within the Brazilian government to support investment in telecommunications constitutes another reason for the lag. Figure 2 demonstrates the level of investment in Brazilian telecommunications. From an all-time high of 3.28 percent of the gross National Product (GNP) invested in telecommunications in 1975, Brazil's investment level in 1994 hit rock bottom at 0.5 percent of GNP, and climbed back up to 1.2 percent in 1995 (when the GNP was U.S. $670 billion). Currently, Telebrás is

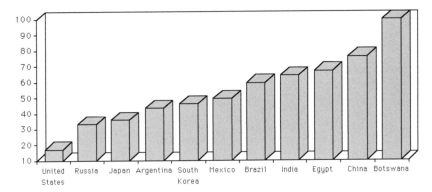

Figure 2 Brazil in Comparative Perspective: Investment as a Percentage of Telecom Revenue. Source: B. Regli from data in ITU (1994).

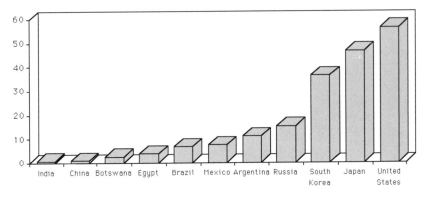

Figure 3 Brazil in Comparative Perspective: Telephone Lines per 100 Inhabitants (1992). Source: B. Regli from data in ITU (1994).

investing heavily in replacing copper wire with fiber optics. By the end of the century, Brazil's digital lines share is expected to reach 70 percent.

Estimated required annual investment in the Brazilian telecommunications sector is U.S. $6.5 billion, but the annual average of actual investment over the past decade has been less than half that amount. In fact, in less than a decade the government subtracted about U.S. $7 billion from Telebrás's investment capacity. Telebrás's investment program is funded mainly by high profits on long distance and international calls. The high cost of long distance calls depresses demand and inhibits national communications and economic development. Brazil has one of the lowest monthly basic

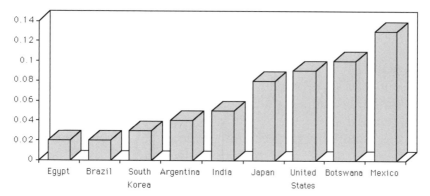

Figure 4 Brazil in Comparative Perspective: Cost of a Local Call (U.S.$, 1992). Source: B. Regli from data in ITU (1994).

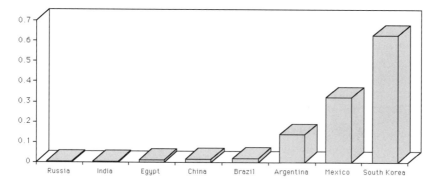

Figure 5 Brazil in Comparative Perspective: Mobile Telephone Subscribers per 100 Inhabitants (1992). Source: B. Regli from data in ITU (1994).

subscriber rates in the world and yet has one of the highest numbers of calls/pulses covered by the basic monthly subscription fee. The subsidized low cost of local calls shown in Figure 4 should encourage low-income subscribers to join the network. Due to tariff increases being held far below Brazilian inflation, local call rates had a negative growth rate of 70 percent over the period 1985–1993. But ultimately the unprofitability of local service restricts Telebrás's capacity to invest in network expansion. This in turn forces Telebrás to charge a high up-front price for a terminal, which has prevented most low-income citizens from getting a phone in the first place.

Moreover, the low number of digital lines that was mentioned above and is shown in Figure 1 raises the question of whether this investment is being appropriately targeted. The small share of digital lines in part reflects the fact that Brazil modernized its system earlier than other developing countries. The Brazilian telecommunications system faces the same difficulties as those of advanced nations in providing new services when the existing infrastructure has not been fully depreciated.

By other measures of advanced services and basic public services, Brazil also does not measure up well. The number of mobile subscribers in 1993 was still far below that of Argentina and Mexico (see Figure 5), which can be attributed to Brazil's late start in installing cellular telephone systems. When cellular service was finally introduced in Brazil, annual growth rates of cellular mobile subscribers were far higher than in most countries—close to 600 percent in 1992, and close to 100 percent in 1993. By 1994, Brazil had developed one of the largest installed bases of mobile cellular phones among middle-income developing countries. In comparison, on a per capita basis adjusted for the share of the population with comparable income levels, Brazil was among the top five. At the end of 1995, there were already 1.5 million cellular phones in operation and the sector's growth (30 percent) was above the global average.[6] According to Telebrás's ambitious cellular telephony plans for its affiliated state operators, this number should at least double in 1996 alone and reach 10 million at the end of the century. The strong demand for cellular systems bodes well for new wireless services in the Brazilian information marketplace.

Because of Brazil's skewed income distribution, only about 20 percent of households have telephone service. In fact, the vast majority of those without access to fixed telephone service fall below—generally well below—the income threshold estimated to be necessary to have access to the country's rather expensive service. In order to reach this large untapped market Telebrás and its subsidiaries have been experimenting with a variety of new technologies, ranging from wireless to satellite systems. In the state of Bahia, for example, a very-small-aperture terminal (VSAT) network supports fixed and cellular service between the state's hinterlands and its capital city, Salvador.[7] Telebrás also deployed a

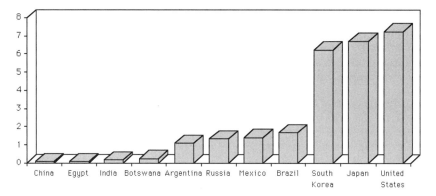

8
7
6
5
4
3
2
1
0

China | Egypt | India | Botswana | Argentina | Russia | Mexico | Brazil | South Korea | Japan | United States

Figure 6 Brazil in Comparative Perspective: Public Telephones per 100 Inhabitants (1992). Source: B. Regli from data in ITU (1994).

novel public 'virtual telephone' system, coupled with an innovative inexpensive calling card technology developed at its research and development (R&D) center, CPqD. In the state of Bahia, a virtual telephone system services 15,000 subscribers.[8] This public 'virtual telephone' system can be part of the answer to the challenge of extending universal service in Brazil while at the same time introducing competition and aligning prices with costs. Brazil has a comparatively low number of public telephones, as is shown in Figure 6. This makes the development of the virtual telephone system especially important if access is to be widened in low-income communities.

Computers

The Brazilian computer market has blossomed in the 1990s. The dismantling of a 20-year policy of market reserve (for domestic producers) in October 1992 and the reining in of inflation in mid-1994 set the stage for rapid growth. With continuously falling prices for personal computers, the market almost doubled between 1991 and 1995. Brazil is the largest information technology market in Latin America. In 1995, 600,000 computers were sold in Brazil and semiconductor companies also did a brisk business.[9] Brazil's annual national software fair, FENASOFT, with a public attendance of close to one million visitors, is by far the largest computer show in the world.[10] This dynamic behavior of the Brazilian computer and electronics markets, both dominated by American firms, will accelerate further due to the January 1995 implementation of the Southern Cone Common Market (Mercosur). Computers constitute the largest segment of Brazil's electronics industry, but other segments with a significant impact on the country's information infrastructure are also growing fast (see Table 1).

In the past few years, all major American computer hardware and software firms have established or considerably expanded industrial and marketing operations in Brazil in order to reduce the cost of their local products. For new foreign entrants such as the Acer Corporation of Taiwan, Brazil is their fastest growing market. Foreign computer distributors and value-added retailers have also flocked to the country in the past few years in expectation of booming sales and fat profits.[11]

In September 1995, the Brazilian government began privatizing the operation of Brazil's Internet. The preexisting academic National Research Network (RNP) is the system's infrastructure backbone. Connection operations were transferred from Embratel, the long distance operations subsidiary of Telebrás, to private firms and institutions, which were also charged with providing access to end users. In the first year, the government will invest about U.S. $11 million to expand the RNP. Research and educational institutions pay 50 percent of the regular tariff charged to private firms. An Internet Management Committee coordinates electronic-mail address distribution and regulates connectivity issues. Most of Brazil's academic institutions already have Internet access and are developing novel uses for it. For example, Brazil's foremost agricultural training school, the Federal University of Viçosa, has become the sole Internet provider for several nearby cities in the state of Minas Gerais and has linked all of its 1,300 computers in a local area network.

It is, however, principally in retail and banking automation that the use of computers is growing in Brazil. In 1995, the Brazilian commercial automation market was close to U.S. $100 million. The figure is small when one takes note that the retail business in Brazil racks up annual sales in excess of U.S. $30 billion, or seven percent of the GNP. The Brazilian business sector includes 600,000 estab-

Table 1 Brazil's Electronics Market (1995)

	Nationwide sales (U.S.$ millions)	Percentage growth from 1994 (%)
Electronic Data Processing	6,940	6.4
Office Equipment	404	3.2
Control & Instrumentation	1,060	3.7
Telecommunications	1,180	−1.7
Consumer Electronics	2,446	3.0
Semiconductors	1,134	5.3

Source: Adapted from Elsevier in Young (1995): 14.

lishments of which fewer than 1,000 have implemented some sort of basic retail automation. In other words, the annual potential market is at least three times the size of the current one. In banking automation, spurred by a decade of inflationary spiral, banks invested heavily in computerization, and in 1994, Brazil was AT&T's second-largest market for ATMs, behind the United States. The end of inflation, however, has not stopped Brazilian banks from continued investment in automation, this time prompted by rising costs and a new competitive environment. In 1995, for example, Banco Bradesco, Brazil's largest private financial conglomerate, invested U.S. $200 million to automate its branches and improve transaction processing.[12] Bradesco has also been a pioneer in the use of the Internet for banking services. It began auctioning off goods repossessed by the bank on its home page.

Television

The unparalleled interest of the Brazilian people in television produced national media giants including Globo, Manchete, and Grupo Abril. Globo programs are broadcast around the world, and are a significant export item. Some of the most popular programs are the telenovelas. In the 1990s, pay television as well as other cable and satellite television channels were developed by these and other

Brazilian firms and international producers. For example, the largest pay television network in Latin America (as of May 1996) is TVA in Brazil with 700,000 subscribers. Cable networks reached 51 cities and 2.5 million subscribers by 1995, of which 13 were actually MMDS, or wireless cable systems. The markets for televisions and VCRs together account for 60 percent of the U.S. $2.5 billion consumer electronics market. Established consumer electronics firms are growing at annual rates in excess of 50 percent, which has attracted the interest of emerging global giants such as the South Korean firm Goldstar, which invested U.S. $40 million in 1996 to produce television sets in Brazil. Firms such as Globo have been diversifying beyond broadcasting, not only into cable and satellite television, but also into cellular telephony and other information services. In the near future, the dynamic Brazilian media marketplace we expect will spill over onto the World Wide Web, which will enable a growing amount of Brazilian content to be available worldwide.

The Policy Context for Brazilian Information Infrastructure Development

One might surmise that the lack of competitive pressure and constitutional gridlock discouraged serious public discussion on the potential role of information infrastructure in Brazilian economic development strategies. But one should not ignore the benefits Brazil gained from having an integrated national telecommunications system. The innovative capacity of Brazilian telecommunications firms also should not be underestimated.

The inauguration of Fernando Collor as president in March 1990 promised to propel Brazil toward a more liberal political economy. Pressed by mounting investment deficits, the Collor administration set out to reform telecommunications institutions and markets. A cornerstone of the attempted reform was the relaxation of the laws regarding private and foreign participation in Brazil's constitutionally guaranteed state monopoly in telecommunications provision. Regarding industrial policy, the Collor government at the end of 1991 initiated an Industrial Competitiveness Program aimed at facilitating and accelerating the transition to a regime in which the private sector could play a much more vital role, following decades of state intervention in many sectors of the economy. In spite of the ouster of President Collor and the delay in implementation of reform under President Itamar Franco, the policy agenda set by the Collor administration continues to affect Brazilian telecommunications.

Brazil would like to have 25 million telephone lines installed by the year 2,000, 75 percent of which are to be digital. In the period 1992–1995, Telebrás planned to invest more than U.S. $3.5 billion and install 4.2 million new terminals, for a total of 13.5 million installed terminals. However, in light of the 6 to 9 million-line backlog, critics predicted that the number of installed lines would have to reach 27 million just to eliminate this backlog. In 1991, 479,000 terminals were installed. By 1996, one in five lines was digital and provided touch tone. In spite of significant progress in the 1990s, the failure of Telebrás to meet investment targets and increase access at a rate sufficient to reduce or eliminate the backlog increased public acceptance of the need for fundamental reforms, including privatization and liberalization of market access for domestic and international firms.

As was already noted, during the second half of the 1980s, the quality of Brazil's telephone services declined considerably. The comparative business success of Telebrás , as shown in Table 2, was not sufficient to overcome its problems in performance. The number of failed local calls, which was below average by international standards in 1980, increased to 25 percent of all calls in 1990. Telebrás telephone service quality indicators showed a decline by almost all counts. The number of crossed lines and wrong numbers continued to increase. In 1990, 30 out of 100 calls between Rio de Janeiro and São Paulo did not complete and about 40 percent of calls to other cities did not complete. The direct-dial long distance call completion rate fell from 49 percent in 1986 to 41 percent in 1990.[13] These poor figures increased doubts about the capability of the current telecommunications system to satisfy demand. Despite the ambitious goals described above, the pressure for reform of the structure of Telebrás and of the regulation of private telecommunications firms continued to grow.

The installation of a line in Brazil cost U.S. $4,570 in 1992 against an international average of U.S. $2,500 partly due to the higher price of telecommunications equipment in Brazil.[14] The price

Table 2 Telecommunications Companies Business Performance (1993):
Brazil, Mexico and Argentina

	Telebrás	Telmex	Telecom Argentina	Telefonica
Access Lines per Employee	119	107	98.2	110
Revenues (millions of U.S.$)	5,900	6,185	855	1,598
Operating Income (U.S.$ millions)	535	2,952	373	243
Net Income (U.S.$ millions)	308	2,633.1	221	144
5yr Earnings Growth Rate	n/a	14.7%	23.5%	24.9%
5yr Cash Flow Growth Rate	n/a	15.7%	16.7%	18.9%
Debt to Total Capital	38.2%	12%	28%	18%
Main Lines (Total, millions)	9.9	6.5	1.6	2
Main Lines (1991–1992 Change)	8.1%	12.1%	n/a	12.7%
Year of Privatization	n/a	1990	1990	1990

Adapted by B. Regli and A. Botelho from Shearson Lehman, Global Telecommunications Report, Issue 1 (1993); Goldman Sachs' World Telephone Industry Overview (1993); World Telecommunication Development Report (1994)

charged for a line dropped dramatically in the mid-1990s, and is now as low as $1,300, and the actual cost of the line may now be near the world average of $2,500, which is significant progress. The cartelized manufacturers of telephone exchanges argue that the cost per terminal remains high in Brazil because they are forced to buy locally a number of inputs and components such as copper at prices above world market rates. The size and recent growth rates of Brazilian electronics markets are shown in Table 1.

The pressure for change first acknowledged by the Collor administration stemmed from the state's fiscal crisis, dwindling investment capital, rising unmet demand, and declining quality of services. The evidence that Brazilian telecommunications was lagging behind its Latin American neighbors was growing. As Table 3 shows, in 1994 Brazilian telephone density was less than in Argentina, Chile, and Mexico. Further, as Figure 7 shows, growth over

Table 3 Brazilian Telecommunications: A Comparative Summary

	Population (millions)	GDP ($millions)	GDP per Capita ($)	Main Telephone Lines	Density
Argentina	33	129	4,000	3,680	11.1
Chile	14	31	2,340	1,213	8.9
Mexico	90	287	3,260	6,573	7.5
India	880	241	285	6,800	0.8
South Korea	44	283	6,540	15,865	36.3
Brazil	156	421	2,740	10,260	6.8

Source: ITU, 1994.

time in Brazilian telephone density has been weak. This is explained in part by Figure 8, which illustrates that changes in Brazilian telephone tariffs fell far behind inflation. For the regional telephone companies, the uneconomic local telephone rates eliminated incentives for expansion of the national telecommunications infrastructure.

The Collor (and now Cardoso) administration recognized telecommunications as a key infrastructure which must be improved for the government's economic policy to succeed. The Collor administration based its strategy for the sector on its March 1991 National Deregulation Program. Any proposal for change in the existing institutional telecommunications regime confronted the state mandate for basic telecommunications services. The Brazilian Telecommunications Code of 1962, codified by the 1988 Constitution, recognizes the public interest in the provision of basic telecommunications services, though whether this constitutional provision mandates a publicly owned monopoly system is disputed.

One of the policy linchpins of Collor's liberalization strategy toward the telecommunications sector was Decree 99.179 of 1990, which opened to private capital community telephone programs, information services, private telecommunications exchanges in residential and business buildings, and cellular mobile phone services. Only in 1994 did Telebrás begin to actively pursue these now permissible public-private partnerships for the accelerated development of local telecommunications systems. The Collor

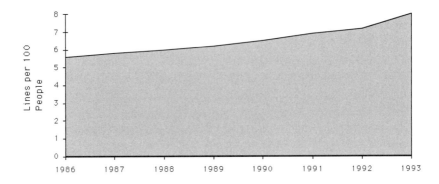

Figure 7 Brazil: Telephone Density (1986–1993). Source: Adapted by B. Regli and A. Botelho from Neuman et al. (1994) and Telebrás.

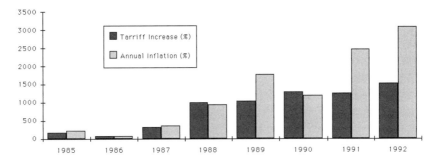

Figure 8 Brazil: Tariff Increases vs. Inflation Rates. Source: Adapted by B. Regli and A. Botelho from Neuman et al. (1994).

administration abolished the Ministry of Communications (Minicom) and created the National Communications Secretariat (SNC) under the Ministry of Infrastructure.[15] In mid-1990, the government issued, as part of the so-called Collor Plan I, a provisional measure (*Medida Provisória* No. 151) with the objectives of: 1) regionalizing management of the Telebrás system, with the creation of seven regional operating companies (from the 33 regional pole companies existing at that time),[16] resembling the Baby Bell institutional model; and 2) opening telecommunications services markets to private national and foreign companies, including long distance service, cellular mobile phones, paging, cable television, telecommunications infrastructure development, and private data services.[17] The restricted basic services monopoly was preserved, while state companies were allowed to compete in the value-added services market. The measure was approved by the congress, with the suggested creation of two regional companies in the Northeast instead of one as proposed in the presidential measure, and the preservation of the Embratel status quo.

However, because the management and operation of the local operating companies had become a clientelist bonanza for local politicians, the implementation of the measures never took place. The fall of the Collor government over corruption charges removed the impetus for reform. The center-left political bloc in congress strongly opposed the measure, arguing that it violated the congressionally sanctioned state monopoly on telecommunications embodied in the 1962 National Telecommunications Code, and represented presidential interference in an exclusive prerogative of congress under the 1988 Constitution. The Collor administration's strategy was to interpret liberally the legal provisions regarding the state monopoly. In this view, there is no link between the concession of a right to operate a telecommunications service and the ownership of equipment or the network used, thus allowing these to be installed, leased, franchised, or operated by the private sector. The government expected the liberalization measures to attract upwards of U.S. $1 billion in new foreign investment to the sector. In fact, little foreign investment was made since the new policies were not implemented. The announcement in August 1994 of Telebrás' plans for facilitating private investment in Brazilian telecommunications systems finally implemented some of the Collor policies for local network construction.

In the two years of the Collor administration, despite the intractable federal budget deficit, sensitive sectors such as oil (Petrobrás) and telecommunications (Telebrás and Embratel) were excluded from the government privatization program. They were considered sacred cows not to be touched, lest opposition from nationalists derail the entire liberalization agenda. With the ouster of Collor on corruption charges, the impetus for reform was momentarily thrown off track. Over the past decade's deep economic crisis in Brazil, both Embratel and Telebrás repeatedly ranked among the top firms in terms of performance in Brazil, public or private. For example, Telebrás shares performed very well on the São Paulo stock market in 1991 when it had revenues of U.S. $1.6 billion, 82 percent higher than in the previous year.

Because the Brazilian Constitution adopted in 1988 does not allow for the outright privatization of public utilities, it has been argued that a constitutional amendment is required for the privatization of Telebrás and Embratel. Interpreting the constitution is not an exact science, and another reading of its language would consider state regulation of telecommunications to be all that is required, not outright public ownership. In any case, the issue is not just ownership but also management structure and flexibility. Another problem for the privatization of Brazilian telecommunications is how to assess the true value of a company like Telebrás, which practically controls Brazil's national and international telecommunications. By mid-1992, it was estimated that a Telebrás privatization sale could fetch U.S. $10 billion on international stock markets.

At the local level, emerging entrepreneurial companies and state governments are already taking advantage of opportunities created by the regime changes.[18] The local regional telephone companies (referred to as the pole operating companies), particularly the larger ones in the Southeastern region (Telesp, Telerj, Telemig, Telepar), seek to shape Brazil's future telecommunications policy. Traditionally, the pole companies provided private residential service and business lines. Since 1988, they have also installed point-to-point networks within their geographic area. In the emerging institutional regime, the regional operating companies, or pole enterprises, are likely to acquire considerable managerial and budgetary freedom from the holding company, and face significant competition.[19]

Conclusion: Information Infrastructure Challenges for Brazil and the World

Privatization of telecommunications facilities alone does not assure information infrastructure development. In fact, two out of three high achievers of the 1980s according to the International Telecommunication Union (ITU) were publicly owned telecommunications operators in South Korea and Turkey. The trend of the 1990s, however, is toward entrusting private corporations with responsibility for infrastructure development, in the hopes that private firms will be more responsive to market and user needs. What is clear is that the economic and social benefits of advanced information infrastructure will not be widely available to Brazilians if the national telecommunications system is not restructured. Brazil has lacked the political will to consider telecommunications a critical strategic infrastructure investment. As we noted above, Table 3 illustrates where Brazil is in comparison to peer nations such as Argentina, Chile, Mexico, India, and South Korea. Brazil has roughly 10–20 percent fewer telephones per capita than nations which have comparable income levels such as Chile and Mexico.

Telebrás plans to enter into partnerships with private sector firms to finance telecommunications projects. This is a step in the right direction, but falls short in its political and economic reach. In the economic area, the rosy predictions of two million new lines installed with private capital by the end of 1995 was an unrealistic target. The inauguration of President Fernando Merique Cardoso in March 1995 was welcomed by advocates of liberalization and privatization, but progress has remained slow. In addition, the Brazilian Congress, for similar reasons, is likely to delay approval of partnership projects and privatization initiatives. Regional politicians seeking to wrestle control of the telecommunications sector away from the federal government risk promoting the disintegration of the system as the centrifugal forces against Brazilian federalism gain speed. The slow pace and the fiscal crises of states have given regional governments an incentive to take the lead in privatizing telecommunications systems and authorizing new telecommunications services.

The economic uncertainties that have surrounded the Brazilian economy for the past decade because of the inflationary spiral have not yet completely disappeared despite the short-term success of the Real Plan. The Real Plan was named after the new Brazilian currency, the Real, which was introduced in 1994. The principal feature of the plan is its emphasis on fighting inflation and stabilizing the value of the currency. Political uncertainties, dominated by struggles for position prior to the upcoming presidential election of 1998 and the crisis of the legitimacy of the congress, may still hold numerous surprises for Brazil's political economy. Moreover, the political failure of the Collor administration dragged down the liberalization discourse, tarnishing its political identification. The Brazilian Congress will still have to approve individual partnership projects, which may discourage foreign investors. The Brazilian bureaucracy is caught up in this political and economic turmoil, struggling to protect its turf and reinvent itself to survive according to the political winds of the moment, a delicate task whether the political outcome is a hurricane or a small tornado. The deterioration of the telecommunications equipment trade balance may spark a nationalist fire whenever it is deemed useful by forces defending the status quo.

Brazil's technological and marketing capabilities in telecommunications are roughly complementary to those of large international companies in that they are concentrated on the mass provision of low-end services and batch provision of customized medium- to high-end services. The stunning success of Telefonica of Spain in the privatization of some of Latin America's main markets laid bare the critical importance of low-cost solutions optimized to local conditions and market elasticity of demand. The gradual growth of interest among large Brazilian engineering firms in the telecommunications sector further strengthens Brazil's comparative advantage in these segments, as their project management and installation skills are largely transferable to telecommunications. In spite of the relative strength of Brazilian firms in these sectors, the imbalance in exports and imports in the hardware sector, as is shown in Figure 9, increases the importance from a macroeconomic point of view of increasing Brazilian software and information services exports—such as on-line telenovelas?

The Brazilian markets for wireless technology, virtual telephony, and information services are indeed promising. More important, there is a clear fit between the needs and the technology. The telecommunications growth rate over the past couple of years has been on average twice that of GDP. São Paulo's mobile cellular market reached 250,000 subscribers by the end of 1994, taking off from zero in 1993. There is a large, undeveloped rural telephone market, which could be aggregated around small urban communities. Similarly, only 19 percent of the residential market and 53

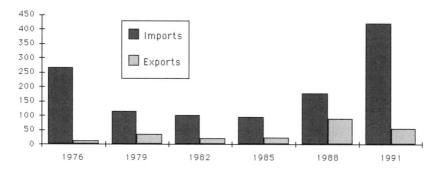

Figure 9 Brazil: Telecom Equipment Imports and Exports, 1976–1991 (U.S.$ millions). Source: Adapted by B. Regli from data in ITU (1994).

percent of the business market (mainly small and medium-sized businesses) have access to the telephone today. Despite the geographic size of Brazil, 75 percent of its population inhabit urban areas where wireless local loop technologies could be an effective low-cost alternative to digging up streets and stringing wires. Wireless technologies (MMDS) are also being used for cable television distribution in a number of cities, as discussed above.

Eventually, one would expect that Brazilian telephone tariffs will be adjusted to provide a reasonable return on local as well as long distance and international services. This will likely include a slight increase in local phone charges and significant reductions in long distance and international rates. Costs as well as revenues should be adjusted. An increase in operating company productivity could reduce the need for significant changes in basic local rate structures. The markets should be shared with private companies in order to bring in the required capital and accelerate the introduction of new, low-cost technologies and services.

A new business and regulatory structure could enable Brazil to capture the benefits for society and the economy of enhanced universal service and networked information transaction capabilities. The virtual telephone system, wireless local loop, and Internet-based wireless, wireline and satellite services are particularly promising applications of advanced information technology to the challenges and opportunities of Brazilian information infrastructure development. Brazil is already a strong content producer, but has not yet gotten much of that content into cyberspace.

Fernando Henrique Cardoso was elected president of Brazil in October 1994. After taking office in 1995, he moved cautiously to restart the process of privatization and liberalization, not only for telecommunications but also for other economic sectors. The economic plan based on the Real currency reform carried out by the Franco government has enabled inflation to be contained since July 1994. The Cardoso administration is pursuing a strategy for information infrastructure development based on wireless and Internet technologies, partnerships, and global alliances. The extension of universal service to additional communities and lower-income groups throughout Brazil may eventually be possible.

However, in spite of the profitability of Brazilian public telecommunications operators, the dynamism of the Brazilian commercial broadcasting industry (led by media powerhouse Globo and its risqué telenovelas) and the emergence of new services such as cable and satellite television, cellular telephony, and Internet access, problems remain. The risk of a return to hyperinflation hovers over prospective domestic and foreign investors. Powerful social and economic forces make fundamental change in the regulatory framework for telecommunications difficult. With the gradual emergence of a Brazilian information infrastructure perhaps things will change—or perhaps not. When the information highway crosses the Amazon, whose cultural values will prevail? And whose commercial interests will be served?

Notes

1. For more information on the current state of Brazilian telecommunications infrastructure, see Neuman et al. (1994); Botelho et al. (1997); Del Fioretino (1996); and Dutta-Roy (1996).

2. See the insightful analysis in López-Pumarejo (1995). A far-ranging cultural assessment of television in Brazilian society is Kottak (1991).

3. The following section of this chapter is based on Neuman et al. (1994); and Botelho et al. (1997).

4. A first assessment of pioneering experiences in Latin America can be found in Rammamurti (1996).

5. See Del Fioretino (1996) and Dutta-Roy (1996) for recent reports of similar data which may not agree exactly with the numbers cited here. Primary data sources unfortunately are inconsistent and subject to some interpretation. The data presented in this chapter are our best estimates at the time of this writing.

6. For comparison, in 1991 there were only 13,500 cellular phones.

7. See Blair (1995).

8. See Lerner (1995). The 'virtual telephone' concept is to provide typically low-income subscribers with personal electronic voice mailboxes, even if they do not own a telephone. The subscriber can call from a public telephone to retrieve his or her messages. The inexpensive and durable calling card technology is an important element in maintaining the reliability of the system, since there are no coins in the telephone, vandals have little financial incentive.

9. Klebnikov (1995); Young (1995).

10. Fallows (1995).

11. Kepp (1994); Hubbard (1994).

12. Power et al. (1995).

13. In the same period, the rate of obtaining a dial tone fell from 95 percent to 88 percent. On the positive side, over the same period, requests for telephone repair per 100 telephones declined from 5 to 4.7 and the service to repair rate remained stable at around 85 percent.

14. Hobday (1990), pp.184–185.

15. By 1994, the Ministry of Communications was back in existence, or rather, renamed yet again.

16. It has been argued that this measure was aimed at further breaking down the strong professional esprit de corps that exists in the Embratel and Telebrás system by making the affiliate companies more amenable to regional political influences. The proposed regional companies would start from widely different installed bases of terminals (in 1,000s): North (Amazon), 490; Northeast, 1,738; Center, 2,316; South, 2,203; São Paulo, 4,494; and Southeast, 2,288.

17. Presidential decree on "Regulation of Limited Services," July 17, 1991.

18. For example, in Londrina, Paraná state, a local company called SERCOMTEL entered into an agreement with Ericsson do Brasil for the installation of a mobile cellular phone service valued at U.S. $7.2 million.

19. Already in 1989, the declining investment capacity of Embratel and the trend toward deregulation had wrested away Embratel's monopoly over telex maintenance service and modem supply, which were taken over by private companies. Firms were also permitted to develop intra-enterprise data communications.

References

Barros, Lins de, and Henry British, eds. 1989. *História da Indústria de Telecomunicações no Brasil* (História Geral das Telecomunicações no Brasil—Cadernos da TELECOM I) Rio de Janeiro: Associação Brasileira de Telecomunicações—TELECOM.

Blair, Michael. 1995. "New VSAT Networks Benefit Brazil and Mexico," *Satellite Communications* 17 (April).

Botelho, Antonio Jose J., Jose Roberto Ferro, Lee W. McKnight, and Antonio C. Manfredini Oliveira. 1997. "Telecommunications in Brazil," in Eli Noam, ed. *Telecommunications in Latin America* (Oxford: Oxford University Press).

Capellaro, Jorge José V. 1989. "História da Indústria de Equipamentos de Telecomunicações no Brasil: Dos primórdios até a segunda metade da década de 70," in Barros and British (1989), pp. 137–148.

Del Fiorentino, Luiz. 1996. "Telecommunications in Brazil," *IEEE Communications*, 34(5) (May), pp. 34–39.

Duarte, Luiz Guilherme, Joseph Straubhaar, and Joseph Stephens. 1992. "Audiences, Policy, Technology and 'Cable' TV in Brazil," paper presented to International Communication Association annual meeting, May 21–25.

Duch, Raymond M. 1996. "Privatizing the Economy —Telecommunications Policy," in *Comparative Perspective* (Ann Arbor: University of Michigan Press, 1991).

Dutta-Roy, Amitava. 1996. "Special Report: Brazil. Telecommunications," *IEEE Spectrum*, 33(6) (June), pp. 36–42.

Graciosa, Hélio Marcos M. 1988. "Telecommunications Research and Development in Brazil," mimeo.

Graciosa, Hélio Marcos M. 1991. "Evolução da Forma de Atuação do CPqD," mimeo, Versão 1. (March 21).

Graciosa, Hélio Marcos M. 1989. "Pesquisa e Desenvolvimento na Telebrás—O CPqD," in Barros and British (1989), pp. 137–148.

Graciosa, Hélio Marcos M., Luiz Del Fiorentino, and Robert S. Goodrich. 1991. "Strategic Management of Telecommunications R&D in Brazil," manuscript submitted for publication at *International Journal of Technology Management*.

"El hilo de la modernidad." 1989. *Vision* (Bogota), (March 25), pp. 6–7.

Hobday, Michael. 1990. *Telecommunications in Developing Countries—The Challenge from Brazil* (London and New York: Routledge).

Hobday, Michael. 1986. "Telecommunications—A 'Leading Edge' in the Accumulation of Digital Technology? Evidence from the Case of Brazil," *Information Technology for Development* (March 1), pp. 32–40.

Hobday, Michael. 1984. *The Brazilian Telecommunications Industry: Accumulation of Microelectronics Technology in the Manufacturing and Service Sectors* (Rio De Janeiro: Instituto de Economia Industrial, Universidade Federal do Rio de Janeiro, Texto para Discussão No. 147).

Hubbard, Holly. 1994. "Latin American Distribution Channel Borders on Change," *Computer Reseller News* 578, 587 (May 16), p. 50.

Informationweek. 1995. "Brazil's Better Conference," 537 (July 24), pp. 51–54.

Kepp, Michael. 1994. "High-tech Bedfellows," *Business Latin America*, 29 (16) (April 25), p. 6.

Klebnikov, Paul. 1995. "A World to Conquer," *Forbes*, 156 (3) (December 4), pp. 256–257.

Kottak, Conrad P. 1991. "Television's Impact on Values and Local Life in Brazil," *Journal of Communication*, 41 (1), pp. 70–87.

Lerner, Norman. 1995. "Brazilian Telephone Company Uses Octel Voice Platform to Deliver 'Virtual Telephone' Service," *Telecommunications* (Americas Edition), 29 (7) (July), p. 65.

López-Pumarejo, Tomás A. 1995. "The Stripper and the Chief of State: About the Male Nude in the Brazilian Soap Operas," *Archivos de la Simoteca*, 21 (2) (October), pp. 184–197.

Matos, Gustavo. 1991. "País une iniciativa privada e tecnologia sofisticada para modernizar telecomunicações," *Indústria e Produtividade* (September 24), pp. 5–10.

Medeiros, Armando L. 1989. "A ITT e a Indústria Brasileira," in Barros and British (1989), pp. 184–187.

Ministerio da Communicacoes. 1993. *Normas de Atribucoes de Faixas de Frequencias no Brasil.* (Brasilia: Secretaria de Administracao de Radiofrequencia, Ministerio da Communicacoes, N-006/90).

Nassif, Luís. 1992. "A privatização da Telebrás," *Folha de São Paulo* (May).

Neuman, W. Russell, Lee W. McKnight, Jose Roberto Ferro, and Antonio José J. Botelho. 1994. "Brazilian Telecommunications in Transition: A New Strategy for Competitiveness," RPCP technical report, Massachusetts Institute of Technology (August 31, 1994).

Perrone, Fernando. 1992. "Communication Systems in Latin America," paper presented to International Communication Association annual meeting, (May 21–25).

Petrazzini, Ben A. 1995. *The Political Economy of Telecommunications Reform in Developing Countries: Privatization and Liberalization in Comparative Perspective.* (Westport, CT: Praeger).

Power, Keith, et al. 1995. "Out of the Shadows," *Computer World* (Global 100 Supplement) (May 1), pp. 40–43.

Rammamurti, Ravi, ed. 1996. *Privatizing Monopolies.* (Baltimore: The Johns Hopkins University Press).

Schmitz, Hubert, and Jose Cassiolato. 1992. "Fostering Hi-Tech Industries in Developing Countries," in Hubert Schmitz and Jose Cassiolato, eds. *Hi-Tech for Industrial Development: Lessons from the Brazilian Experience in Electronics and Automation.* (New York: Routledge), pp. 1–20.

Sussman, Gerald, and John A. Lent, eds. 1991. *Transnational Communications: Wiring the Third World.* (Newbury Park, CA: Sage).

Tapia, Jorge Ruben B. 1984. "A Política Científica e Tecnológica em Telecomunicações," *Revista de Administração*, 19 (January/March), pp. 101–111.

Telebrás, various documents.

Teleguia—O Guia Completo das Telecomunicacoes. 1984/85. (São Paulo: Telepres).

Wajnberg, Salomão. 1989. "A Indústria de Equipamentos de Telecomunicações no Brasil: Da segunda metade da década de 70 até hoje," in Barros and British (1989), pp. 47–81.

Young, Lewis H. 1995. "Latin America: A Growing Marketplace, but Risky Business," *Electronic Business Buyer*, 21(3) (March), pp. 13–14.

National Information Infrastructure in Developing Economies

Eduardo Talero

This chapter presents a conceptual introduction to the broad topic of the role of national information infrastructure (NII) in developing economies. It proposes a definition of the NII that reflects the special concerns and priorities of this group of countries. It presents an argument for the role and importance of the NII in socioeconomic development, provides examples of NII initiatives, and describes the potential scope of NII strategies in developing economies.

Introduction

Because of its potential impact on economy and society, NII is receiving attention worldwide, but its role is not the same in industrialized and developing countries. Three key differences are the primacy of infrastructure use over technology production, the importance of strategic information systems, and the need for direct, measurable impact on economic growth. The purpose of this chapter is to prime the discussion on national information infrastructure as a special public policy concern in countries with low or middle per capita income.[1]

I will use the term "developing economies" for convenience. It denotes the group of countries in which the fight against poverty, malnutrition, infant mortality, illiteracy, gross social and income inequality, poor administration of justice, inefficient government, and environmental degradation is most pressing. The term does not imply homogeneity in any other respect or that other economies have reached a preferred or final stage of development.

The term "information system" denotes an information-based social capability, and as such it encompasses not just the technology—hardware and software—and the content, or data, but also the organization, incentives, procedures, and people involved. In high-income economies, certain basic capabilities such as the regular production of macroeconomic statistics are often taken for granted. Behind them, however, are complex arrangements of people, technology, organizations, and procedures that are often lacking in developing economies.

The term "strategic information systems" refers to a certain kind of system of central importance to economic activity. For example, a payments clearance and settlement system and a public financial management system are strategic necessities for sound macroeconomic management and transaction efficiency in a growing economy. Such systems represent new forms of national infrastructure because, like roads or utilities, they have major economies of scale, require substantial sunk costs, are non-tradeable, and underpin other economic activities.

Which systems have this strategic importance is of course determined by each country. There is, however, a core group of strategic information systems that all countries must put in place for continued economic development. Included in this group are systems that:

• facilitate general economic activity (national statistics, geographic information, and judicial administration systems);

• enable the functioning of financial markets and the development of the private sector (property, land, and business registry systems; payment clearance and settlement systems; financial institution oversight systems);

• improve delivery of infrastructure services (air transport control, vehicle registration, port operations, and utility management systems);

• increase trade and global competitiveness (trade facilitation and customs administration systems);

• manage the macroeconomy and government (planning and

budgeting, debt management, civil service payroll, tax administration, and expenditure management systems at both national and local levels);

• combat poverty (social security, basic education, and primary health care systems);

• build human capital (school, university, and research networks; sectoral information systems for education and health); and

• preserve the environment (natural resource inventory, geographic information, environmental monitoring, industrial/commercial licensing, and regional planning systems).

I will define NII as the telecommunications networks and strategic information systems necessary for sustainable economic development. This definition accommodates both the development concerns of developing economies and the economic growth and social welfare concerns of high-income economies. It is not incompatible with the concept of the "information highway," but it connotes structural economic importance that the information highway concept lacks. NII denotes both something existent that underpins current economic activity and something new that must be put in place to sustain emerging forms of economic activity.

In contrast with other definitions of NII, the above definition excludes the appliances (telephones, computers) and the human resources associated with the use of the infrastructure. This is done not because these two elements lack importance in the policy dialogue on NII, but because in economic terms they are complementary rather than integral elements of the NII. In the case of appliances, economic decisions do not involve substantial economies of scale, considerable externalities, or large sunk costs. In the case of decisions on human resources, a different set of policy considerations applies that shares more with the objectives of the NII (increased income levels and improved quality of life) than with the NII itself.

The Importance of NII in Developing Economies[2]

If the NII is conceived as consisting of both telecommunications networks and strategic information systems, it assumes extraordinary importance for developing economies. NII is a new instrument created through revolutionary advances in information technology that societies can now use for the developmental challenges they face. From this perspective, NII is far more fundamental to a developing economy than, say, a broadband facility to the home is for a high-income economy. A quick overview of some of the principal challenges of development will illustrate this.

Fighting Poverty

So far, information technology has played a modest role in the arsenal of weapons with which societies fight poverty. Can information infrastructure be deployed to improve living conditions and income levels? As an illustration, World Bank studies have shown a close association between illiteracy levels and national income.[3] Reducing illiteracy is thus a key aspect of the fight against poverty; it is also one that is directly manageable through improved education delivery assisted by information technology.

Other indicators of poverty can also be improved through communications and information systems. The provision of basic services such as primary health care, family planning, basic education, nutrition, and drinking water, for example, is largely dependent on information handling by both suppliers and recipients of services. Programs such as social security, public employment schemes, and food pricing and distribution policies also require information systems for effective analysis and implementation. For example, a structural adjustment loan by the World Bank to Morocco includes the development of an information base to strengthen poverty assessment, to design future programs, and to track progress in reducing poverty.[4]

Reducing the Isolation of Rural Areas

Since a large proportion of the poor live in rural areas, this challenge is closely related to the fight against poverty. In Côte d'Ivoire, for example, 86 percent of the poor lived in rural areas in the mid-1980s, while in Ghana the figure was 80 percent.[5] Declining costs and new technologies are combining to bring rural telecommunications within reach of normal market mechanisms, thus promising to reduce the isolation of the rural poor. A recent rural telecommunications study found

significant downward pressure on the cost per line, though there is a wide range of costs depending on potential subscriber distribution and density. In the ideal environment, where subscriber densities in excess of 0.1 per sq. km can be achieved within 40 km of an urban center, capital costs can be as low as U.S.$1,000 per line using wireless loop technology. This kind of service can be commercially feasible if annual revenues per line are in the U.S.$400 range.[6]

When policy allows small private operators to provide rural telecommunication services, as in the case of Indonesia, private investment and telephone service expand rapidly.

Educating More People and Supporting Lifelong Learning

Education pays. Rewards to an individual for an educational investment include increased employment options, higher income, and better future prospects. Education is the best route to improved status for women worldwide. The need for continued education and training persists throughout a person's career. To export low-value-added goods and services, a country needs a labor force with good-quality primary education, including language skills; for high-value-added exports, it requires advanced and lifelong training of the labor force. Information systems have supporting roles in education—efficient administration, low-cost delivery, and production of appropriate educational materials. Computer-based training, moreover, is an effective tool for lifelong learning.

Education correlates with employment, income, and opportunity. In industrial countries, the well-educated are more likely to be employed. In the United States in 1989, unemployment was 9.1 percent for persons with high school or less education and 2.2 percent for those with college degrees. In Japan, these figures were 7 percent and 2.3 percent. The well-educated earn more, and the gap is widening. In the United States in 1980 the earnings gap was 31 percent; in 1988 it was 86 percent. The well-educated land jobs that provide them with more training; the uneducated are locked out of opportunities to improve their skills.[7]

Making Governments More Efficient, Accountable, and Transparent

Large productivity increases in government services are possible with information systems that increase the speed, volume, quality, transparency, and accountability of transactions. Government work is by its very nature highly information-intensive in terms of data collection, archiving, dissemination, and processing. Well-designed information systems can become major instruments of public policy—powerful tools to implement, enforce, and evaluate policy reforms.

Increasing the Effectiveness of Economic Reforms

Economic reforms often fail during implementation due to weak compliance. When information systems are designed in conjunction with reforms, monitoring and facilitating compliance is easier and reforms are more likely to be effective. Through information systems it is possible to embed policy reforms into institutional processes and transactions, which can then be readily monitored and audited.

Singapore, for example, has a fundamental goal of developing an open, export-oriented, market economy and since the early 1980s has supported this goal through the creation of information systems. Tradenet, the resulting system, has become a key vehicle for implementing the country's trade policies. Today this system connects all participants in international trade transactions through electronic data interchange and allows government agencies to exercise their oversight role unobtrusively.

Monitoring and Protecting the Environment

Environmental monitoring, inherently data-intensive, is made more effective by using information technology, particularly geographic information systems. These systems are increasingly inexpensive, and the data captured are of lasting value beyond their initial use. International cooperation in monitoring of pollution and natural resources is fostered by environmental networks. Information technology also provides effective tools for regional planning based on dynamic modeling.

In the Philippines, land resource maps were developed for the entire country, demonstrating that useful national land resource data could be compiled in a short time at low cost. The project produced map coverage and national, regional, and provincial statistics within one year for about U.S.$1.7 million.

Promoting Small and Medium-Sized Enterprises

Small and medium-sized enterprises (SMEs) are vital engines of job creation. They are quick in bringing new products to market, getting into and out of fast-changing niche markets, and setting up spin-off companies. In the information industry itself, SMEs play a key role in production and diffusion of information technology. For example, in Africa today small firms are pioneering Internet access services as a commercial venture, and where policy allows, as in Indonesia, India, and Ghana, microenterprises are finding ways to provide telecommunications services for profit. The needs of SMEs can be addressed through self-sustaining service systems and networks for training, technical cooperation, accounting, purchasing, marketing, banking, and government licensing.

Participating in Global Trade

If the goods and services of developing countries are not globally competitive, their national and international markets will evaporate under attack from better suppliers in other parts of the world. Cheap and efficient customs procedures are one necessity. Electronic exchange of trade transaction data and the access to global databases of trade opportunities are becoming even more important. Trade facilitation systems and production and distribution systems based on electronic data interchange have emerged as powerful mechanisms to reduce processing time and increase performance of the entire value chain in international trade.

The State of NII in the Developing Economies

Developing countries are of course heterogeneous. No general descriptors of progress in deploying NII are completely adequate, and data are difficult to obtain, particularly on strategic information systems. What follows is therefore a series of illustrations of how developing countries are progressing in the task of deploying NII.

Telecommunications Services and Reform

There is a positive correlation between economic development and telecommunications density, and some studies even claim that a causal relationship exists in both directions.[8] Telecommunication networks provide a platform for innumerable forms of economic activity. In developing countries, access to telecommunications infrastructure is generally inadequate, and progress depends on policy reforms not yet widely implemented. Yet there is an opportunity to leapfrog—new technology can provide better, cheaper links to subscribers, and competing global operators can provide low-cost long distance connections. Developing countries can deploy telecommunications for lower costs per capita than in the industrialized world.

For basic telephone service, the gap between industrial and developing countries is still large but narrowing. In 1988, developing countries had about 75 percent of the world's population, about 16 percent of world production, but only about 12 percent of telephone main lines. Industrial countries averaged about 32 main lines per 100 inhabitants; developing countries, only 1.5.[11]

Many developing countries are deploying telecommunications infrastructure at a fast pace (see Table 1). Between 1969 and 1988, they almost doubled their share of the world's telephone lines, from 7 percent to 12 percent. While China's economy is growing at over 10 percent per year, telephone lines are increasing at more than 20 percent and telephone traffic at about 70 percent per year.[12]

While there is wide agreement that policies favoring private ownership and competition are effective in meeting growing demand for quality telecommunications services, debate rages over the pace of reform and the best policy mix to attract the large investments needed. In a continuum between state monopoly at one extreme and full market competition at the other, numerous options are possible through combinations of approaches such as commercialization, operating licenses, second operator entry, competition in value-added services, privatization, and regional mo-

Table 1   Rate of Increase of Telephone Lines in Selected Economies, 1983–1993

	Growth of Telephone Lines (%)
Angola	1.5
Ghana	2.7
United States	2.9
Japan	3.1
Russia	6.3
Brazil	6.3
Hungary	8.3
Mexico	8.6
India	11.7
Indonesia	13
Chile	13.3
Egypt	15.1
China	21.3

Source: World Bank.[9]

nopoly licenses. Ultimately, each country must choose its own path according to political and market forces. Most state monopolies have failed to meet the telecommunications needs of developing countries. A notorious example of this failure is the extraordinary waiting times for a new telephone line in many developing countries.[13] This is one reason why the World Bank usually recommends starting a reform path toward private competitive provision of telecommunications services.

A policy, legal, and regulatory environment that attracts private sector investment appears to be a necessity rather than a choice for developing economies. Of the approximately U.S.$60–90 billion per year needed to build up basic telephone networks in these economies (including the Commonwealth of Independent States and East Central Europe), up to 50 percent must come from private sources. Internal cash generation can provide up to 40 percent, while only 10 percent will be available from public sources.[14]

Extraordinary advances in fixed access technologies (wireline or wireless connection of the household or business to the national telephone network) create a rich set of possibilities for developing economies. For many technologies, investment costs per subscriber start around U.S.$2,000 at densities of 10 subscribers/km^2 and decrease to U.S.$500 and less at densities of over 1,000 subscribers/km^2. Wireless local loop technologies, which are most appropriate for areas of low and medium (but uniform) density (1–100 subscribers/km^2), have payback times of six to seven years and internal rates of return between 8 and 12 percent.[15]

Penetration of Computing and Networking Technologies

Worldwide annual sales of personal computers (PCs) exceed 50 million units (by comparison, 35 million passenger cars are sold annually). An estimated 300 million PCs of all kinds are now in use. Because of falling costs, microcomputers are accessible to even very small businesses and households in developing economies, and they can be found now everywhere in the world. Developing country markets provide an increasing share of the revenue of large corporations such as IBM.

With a growing installed base of computers in these economies, there is a multiplier effect on information technology–related products and services, and new possibilities for exports are created. Software production from companies in Bangalore, India, yields annual exports worth U.S.$300 million (as of mid-1994). Approximately 150 of 600 Indian firms operate on global contracts only, mainly from the United States and Europe. Before 1989, few Indian firms worked internationally. Citicorp, Microsoft, Oracle, and others now have software operations in India. Most firms have leapfrogged traditional software development approaches to the latest programming technologies, such as object-oriented development and client-server systems.[16]

Networking in developing economies is also advancing apace with deployment of telecommunications infrastructure. Table 2 shows the Internet connectivity scenario for developing countries at the end of 1995. Internet connection costs ranged from U.S.$100,000 for a basic, 50-user electronic-mail connection to

Table 2 Internet Connectivity in Developing Countries

	Countries Connected	Countries Not Connected	Total Countries
Low Income	34	21	55
Lower Middle Income	61	9	70
Upper Middle Income	33	7	40
Total	128	37	165

Derived from: Lawrence H. Landweber and the Internet Society.

U.S.$1 million+ for over 10,000 subscribers and full connectivity.[17] These costs are substantial but increasingly within the range of academic institutions, government agencies, and—most promising—private Internet service providers. Countries such as India, Brazil, Chile, Egypt, Russia, and South Africa have enough Internet connections to participate in global networking on a plane approaching those of the United States and Europe.

A growing number of special-purpose national and international networks such as Healthnet, Commercenet, Cetcol (Colombia—science and technology), Reuna (Chile—academic), and many others are reaching developing countries and helping to make the concept of the global village a reality. Through the Internet, in 1995 the World Bank polled the views of senior professionals from 21 countries as input for the development of an institutional strategy on the global information infrastructure.

Strategic Information Systems

Strategic information systems are fast being deployed in developing economies. The World Bank, for example, lends U.S.$700–900 million per year to developing economies for public expenditure management systems, national statistical systems, tax and customs administration systems, sectoral information systems in health and education, payment clearing and settlement systems, management information systems for ministries and public enterprises, geographic information systems, debt management systems, and the like.

There is no doubt of the importance that governments attach to deploying strategic information systems. Serious constraints, mainly in human resources and institutional capacity, may slow down their progress,[18] particularly in the poorest countries of Africa, but developing countries almost without exception have realized that deployment of strategic information systems is a necessity rather than a choice for national economic development. As they grapple with implementation problems, an extraordinary opportunity exists to design NII strategies that remove constraints to successful deployment.

An idea of the magnitude and importance of strategic information systems can be derived from the Indonesian effort (in April 1996) to inventory the main strategic information systems being developed in the public sector. It was found that these systems span 33 different government agencies, ranging from the country's national planning agency to the Ministry of Industry and Trade and the Environmental Impact Agency. The current investment budget for development of these systems is on the order of U.S.$243.4 million.

Developing an NII Strategy

Revolutionary advances in information and communications technologies have two concurrent and complementary impacts on developing countries. First, they open up extraordinary opportunities to accelerate social and economic development. Second, they create a pressing need for policy reform and investment to capitalize on the new opportunities and to avoid deterioration of international competitiveness.

Policy reform and investment are needed to move countries into a different kind of economy—the information economy—in which information is the key factor of production, trade and investment are global, and firms compete globally on the basis of knowledge, networking, and agility. This agenda also leads countries into a new type of society—the information society—that is quite different from an industrial society. An information society is better informed, more competitive, less stable, and more able to address individual needs; it can also be less centralized, more democratic, and friendlier to the environment.

Both the extraordinary development opportunities and the need for policy reform and investment are of direct concern to governments and to the private sector, including nongovernmental organizations. The private sector is the primary engine of the information economy. Government has a fundamental role as a catalyst for change, as policymaker, and as guarantor of a level playing field. Public/private sector partnerships are therefore being formed in many nations to develop NII strategies that exploit the link between information and socioeconomic development.

Components of an NII Strategy

There is no such thing as a standard outline for an NII strategy, but five components are often included:

• *Strategic goals and target dates* around which to rally the energies and resources of society.

• A *target portfolio of investment projects* to develop and put in place the NII. This portfolio consists of projects to expand the telecommunications networks and projects to deploy the strategic information systems that the country needs for its developmental priorities, such as the TradeNet system in Singapore.

• A set of *policy and legal reform proposals* to create an information-friendly environment[19] and to remove constraints on implementation of the NII projects above.

• A *strategy for developing the human resources* for the information age, through appropriate education and training policies and institutions.

• An agreement on *responsibilities* for implementation financing, oversight, and participation.

Roles and Responsibilities

Formulation of a national strategy should ideally be demand-driven and achieved through a broad-based participatory process because the NII cannot be deployed effectively without the active cooperation of all stakeholders. The following groups need to be represented in formulating the strategy, for the reasons given:

• The government usually needs to mobilize other stakeholders to participate, to organize and (often) lead the preparatory work, and to play a central role in formulation of the strategy, as a policymaker and regulator.

• The demand side of the NII, including the productive and service sectors as well as sectoral government ministries, is the primary user of the NII and the major stakeholder in the formulation of a related strategy.

• The private sector, both national and international, has a key role as supplier of investment, finance, and technical services for the NII.

• The telecommunications industry has a vital interest in the sectoral policy reform, investment, and service objectives likely to be part of the NII strategy.

• Nongovernmental organizations have increasingly important roles as providers of services in society, particularly to the poor, and can contribute an important perspective on how the NII can help solve social problems.

• Scientists and educators provide input on the technological, scientific, and human-resource implications and requirements of the NII.

• International experts from the private sector and from international financial organizations can contribute a global perspective and an objective, nonpolitical point of view. They can also facilitate financing of follow-up investments.

Strategy Formulation Process

A growing number of countries are developing explicit NII strategies. Singapore, Taiwan, and South Korea did this in the early 1980s with astonishing results. China, Japan, and Tunisia followed in the late 1980s, and Mauritius, Australia, and the United States have done so recently. Presently, countries as diverse as Indonesia, Thailand, Jordan, and Vietnam are in the process of developing explicit NII strategies.

Most countries belonging to the Organization for Economic Cooperation and Development (OECD), notably Australia and the

United States, developed their highly advanced NIIs without explicit strategies. Among developing countries, Chile is well advanced into the development of its NII without reliance on an explicit national strategy. These countries relied instead on general open economic policies and aggressive privatization of their telecommunications sectors.

When strategies are explicitly formulated, two possible starting points are increasingly combined. A country can start by examining the priority needs and major opportunities in the economy and fashion a national strategy to satisfy the needs and capitalize on the opportunities. This is what Singapore, Taiwan, Korea, and Mauritius did. Alternatively, a country can start by looking closely at its existing information infrastructure initiatives and fashion a strategy to remove constraints on these initiatives and accelerate their successful completion. Indonesia is considering this approach, which may be well suited to large economies.

Other aspects of the strategy formulation process are more or less common. Wide participation, particularly from the private sector, is clearly a best practice. A high-level steering committee or advisory group is needed to ensure speed and objectivity in the strategy formulation process. A series of analytical studies are required to gain understanding of current resources, problems, opportunities, and needs and to formulate tentative policy reform and investment proposals. Finally, one or several high-profile workshops are commonly held to raise awareness among NII stakeholders, reach consensus on the strategy, and gain commitment for its implementation.

The strategy formulation process encompasses three broad phases: awareness-raising, analysis, and decision-making. Steps in each phase vary in nature, order, and scope in different countries; some of the most important ones are described below and summarized in Figure 1.

1. *Identify the strategic opportunities and needs for information and communications in the economy.* Using existing macroeconomic development plans and sectoral assessments, identify the opportunities and needs for telecommunications infrastructure and information related to the key national development priorities. Examples of such opportunities and needs are: (a) trade performance levels

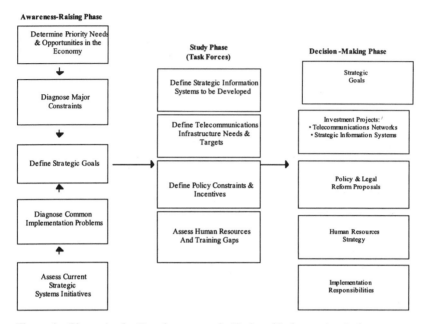

Figure 1   Phases in the Development of a National Information Infrastructure.

achievable with electronic trade facilitation and the possible economic gains from removing critical bottlenecks such as slow port operations; (b) socioeconomic gains achievable from large increases in telephone service penetration, particularly in small towns and rural areas; (c) impetus to municipal development from modern planning and management systems; (d) gains in educational or literacy levels achievable through distance education and computer-aided education; and (e) social and economic gains from performance improvements in the SME sector through modernization of administrative and production systems.

2. *Assess the current strategic information systems projects in the country,* their scope and importance, their budget and status, and the common constraints and difficulties they encounter.

3. *Formulate strategic goals and target dates for the NII.* These are goals around which to rally the energies and resources of society. An example of such a goal from the United States: to create a seamless web of communications networks, computers, databases, and consumer electronics that will put vast amounts of information at

users' fingertips. An example from Singapore: to create the first developed city of distinction in the tropics, a city of gracious living and a cultured society.

4. *Define the strategic investments needed to achieve the stated goals.* For telecommunications infrastructure, this definition includes target service levels, type of services (basic telephony, broadcasting, value-added services), service standards, broad institutional setup (who owns? who operates? who regulates?), order-of-magnitude investment cost, and financing strategy. For strategic information systems, the definition includes broad objectives and descriptions of each system, order-of-magnitude investment cost, and financing strategy.

5. *Agree on policy, legal, regulatory, or institutional reforms* needed to eliminate constraints on widespread access to telecommunications and information services in society and to complete and sustain strategic investments. The prime examples of such reforms are ones that restructure the telecommunications sector to allow increasing forms of market discipline in service provision. Other examples include intellectual property legislation, liberalization of technology markets, public information and contracting policies, regulatory reforms to guarantee fair competition in telecommunication services, subsidy or exclusivity policies to foster private investment in rural telecommunications, incentives for the adoption of technology and for the supply of technical consulting services, and establishment of professional accreditation, metrology, and standards boards.

6. *Assess the knowledge and skills required in the workforce to implement the NII strategy and formulate related education policies and institutional reforms.* The NII requires researchers and technicians across the spectrum of information technologies, a workforce skilled in the use of these technologies, and a general population capable of operating electronic appliances and computers and able to consume information products intelligently. Appropriate education and training policies and institutions need to be proposed to develop these human resources.

7. *Determine responsibilities for implementation and oversight of the NII strategy.* One of the most important benefits of wide participation in

strategy formulation is to gain visibility and accountability for the subsequent strategy implementation effort. Toward this end, responsibilities, sources of funding, participation in projects, and oversight should be negotiated. This applies not only to strategic investment projects but also to the policy and legal reform tasks included in the strategy.

Conclusion

The NII plays an increasingly important role in economic development. As technology advances, this infrastructure underlies more of the economic activities on which sustainable socioeconomic growth hinges. In particular, it affects the capacity of countries to maintain their long-term international trade performance. Faced with these changes, developing countries need to implement an accelerated agenda to revitalize telecommunications markets, modernize information-related policies and laws, create incentive systems, and support institutions appropriate for an information economy. Additionally, developing countries need to launch a major investment program to deploy the telecommunications networks and strategic information systems that make up the NII.

The very same technological advances that create this pressing reform and investment agenda provide the tools for its successful implementation, particularly through the empowerment of the private sector and the strengthening of market mechanisms. Rapidly decreasing costs and the proliferation of new transmission and switching technologies, for example, make it possible to open the telecommunications sector to competition and private ownership. Computing and networking technologies, accessible now even to microenterprises and small civic organizations in developing countries, make possible an increase in economic activity and in participatory decision-making.

Facing up to the challenges of the information revolution requires decisive and well-coordinated action. Developing countries are therefore formulating explicit NII strategies for this purpose through unprecedented joint action between government and the private sector. Guided by such strategies, developing countries can reduce the income gap that separates them from developed countries and pursue their own, unique development paths.

Notes

The views expressed in this chapter are entirely those of the author and should not be attributed in any manner to the World Bank, to its affiliated organizations, or to members of its Board of Executive Directors or the countries they represent. Portions of this chapter have been excerpted from internal World Bank papers that may be published in other forms.

1. Economies are divided into the following categories according to 1993 Gross National Product [GNP] per capita, calculated using the *World Bank Atlas* method: low income, U.S.$695 or less; lower-middle income, U.S.$696–U.S.$2,785; upper-middle income, U.S.$2,786–U.S.$8,625; and high income, U.S.$8,626 or more. See World Bank, *The World Bank Atlas, 1996*, Washington, DC: World Bank, 1996.

2. Excerpted from Eduardo Talero and Phillip Gaudette, "Harnessing Information for Development, A Proposal for a World Bank Strategy," World Bank discussion paper No. 313, (May 1996).

3. World Bank, *The World Bank Atlas*, p. 15.

4. World Bank, *Implementing the World Bank's Strategy to Reduce Poverty—Progress and Challenges* (April 1993), p. 22.

5. Ibid., p. 10.

6. Intelecon Research & Consultancy Ltd, "Options for Rural Telecommunications Development," Final Report, unpublished report to the World Bank, April 1995.

7. Adrian Wooldridge. "Survey of Education," *The Economist*, November 21, 1992.

8. Andrew Hardy. "The Role of the Telephone in Economic Development." *Telecommunications Policy*, Vol. 4, No. 4 (December 1980).

9. World Bank, "Performance Indicators for the Telecommunications Sector," internal report, May 1995.

10. Pyramid Research Inc., "Analysis of Telecommunications Investment and Financing in Less Developed Countries," internal report to the World Bank, May 16, 1994.

11. Robert Saunders, Jeremy Warford, and Bjorn Wellenius. *Telecommunications and Economic Development*, 2nd edition (Baltimore, MD: Johns Hopkins University Press for the World Bank, 1994).

12. World Bank/IFC, "Telecommunications Sector Background and Bank Group Issues," February 16, 1994.

13. World Bank, "Performance Indicators for the Telecommunications Sector," internal report, May 1995.

14. World Bank/IFC, "Telecommunications Sector Background and Bank Group Issues," February 16, 1994.

15. Telecon/Nokia, "Access Technology—Life-Cycle Economies Study," internal study for the World Bank, June 1995.

16. Michael Richardson, "Closer Ties Could Create an Important New Regional Axis," *International Herald Tribune,* January 29, 1994; "Singapore to Expand in East Asia," *International Herald Tribune,* January 31, 1994.

17. World Bank Africa Regional Office, "Internet Toolkit for Task Managers," internal report, January 1996.

18. Antoun Moussa and Robert Schware, "Informatics in Africa: Lessons from World Bank Experience," *World Development,* Vol. 20, No. 12 (1992).

19. An information-friendly environment requires that information and communications markets are open and well regulated, that the primary responsibility for investment and service provision rests with the private sector and the government has primarily a regulatory role, and that public information policies as well as laws protecting investment, intellectual property, and individual privacy exist and are enforced.

Information Superhighway Policy in France: The End of High Tech Colbertism?

Thierry Vedel

Introduction

Is there a French vision, strategy, or policy for the Information Superhighway (IS)?

The question may sound surprising, as the French state has long demonstrated an inclination toward high tech ventures and a propensity to launch *grands projets*. Yet, this kind of state entrepreneurship, often termed "high tech colbertism," may be vanishing with the IS.[1] Compared with previous activity in support of telematics, cable TV, or high-definition TV, France's first steps in the IS domain appear somewhat modest: the government has restricted its role to accompanying private initiatives. In this sense, French IS policy may indicate a smooth, though radical, shift in government-industry relations, from *dirigism* (administrative guidance) to pragmatism.

It also seems that, with respect to the IS, France has refrained from presenting itself as an "exception": French IS policy takes place within a framework designed at the European level. Most of the arguments put forward to justify the move forward the information society replicate ideas, laid down in European reports. However, the integration of France within the EU and the acceptance of the single market have not been fully achieved. While the current rhetoric about the IS illustrates France's apparent alignment in the global economy, IS implementation may cause new fracture lines. In particular, the definition of universal service may reveal or catalyze social, cultural, and political concerns that so far have been not been dealt with by the public authorities.

Background and Motivations: A Reactive Policy

It was only in January 1994 that the IS was put on the French political agenda by the Minister of Communication, Alain Carignon. One month later, on February 22, the Prime Minister, Edouard Balladur, commissioned Gérard Théry, who had been Director General of Telecommunications (i.e., head of France Télécom) from 1974 to 1981 and is known as the father of Minitel, to write a report on the IS. This move was clearly a reaction to initiatives taken in the United States—the national information infrastructure policy of the Clinton administration—and at the EU level—especially the European Commission White Paper on Growth, Competitiveness and Employment published in June 1993 and the European Council's December 1993 decision to commission a report on the development of information infrastructures (the so-called Bangemann Report on the information society issued in June 1994).

Although a first draft of the Théry Report was available in July 1994, it was only at the end of October 1994 that an IS policy was designed. In addition to personnel changes in the French government, this delay reflected internal political conflicts such as competition within the government for leadership on IS policy and the opposition of France Télécom to the Théry Report. On October 27, 1994, an interministerial committee made public the French policy for the IS. Along with the objective of gradually connecting all French people to the IS by 2015, the government decided to launch trials. The deadline for the selection of these trials was set in January 1995 so that the government could better devise its position in view of the Group of Seven (G-7) leading industrialized countries summit on the IS, which took place in Brussels on February 25–26, 1995.

A Policy Constrained Mainly by External Factors

The French government's move toward the IS was not primarily the result of internal pressures from the industry[2] but rather stemmed from external factors. First, the development of the IS in the United States was perceived both as a sign that the IS is the inevitable future of communications and as a threat. The French government traditionally fears American domination of the information market, a market deemed not only very profitable but also an essential part of the French identity. Not surprisingly, coming at the same time as difficult GATT negotiations and conflicts about cultural exception, the Clinton-Gore National Infrastructure Initiative (NII) initiative revived old concerns about the protection of French culture. As distinguished experts argued, if France did not have an active IS policy, the French people would soon be obliged to get information through American databases, as is already the case on the Internet.[3]

Second, the European agenda for a single market also led the French government to adopt an IS policy. Under President François Mitterrand, France demonstrated a constant commitment to European unification that changes in government have not altered. When the EC White Paper was released, it was seen as just another step on the road to a united Europe, and its rationale and proposals were accepted without real discussion in France. That the development of trans-European networks was an essential component in the making of a single market and would help to maintain growth, secure competitive advantages, and create jobs was seen as almost a truism. The political significance and the societal impact of this policy were not really taken into consideration.[4] Moreover, the decision to fully liberalize the European telecommunications market by January 1998 (see below) obliged France to upgrade its infrastructure to limit penetration by foreign companies.

While external factors dominated, some internal factors also affected the French move toward the IS. As in the United States, although in a different fashion, the IS is a new frontier, in the sense of a political program that serves to mobilize people toward a better future. A few months before the 1995 presidential election, Prime Minister (and candidate in the election) Edouard Balladur described the IS as perhaps "one of these stars which, if they do not give a meaning to modern life, shape it in a different way. The IS crystallizes hopes and dreams which are already becoming real. Like the infrastructure programs of the 50s and 60s, like the new frontiers that many times humanity has sought to conquer, IS can rally enthusiasm, mobilize and bring together energies."[5]

In some way, the government was trying to make use of the "interpretative flexibility"[6] of the IS. As with all new technologies, the IS can be the object of multiple interpretations and associated meanings, social visions, or patterns of use. It is a vague enough concept to accommodate various, and even conflicting, interests.

Overall, French IS policy is mainly reactive—even defensive—and driven by economic and industrial considerations. As with previous high tech developments, the main issue is not what people need and want and the social utility of new infrastructures but the position of French industry on the world market.

The Trend toward Telecommunications Liberalization

Since 1987, the EC has steadily pushed for the liberalization of the European telecommunications market. A series of directives has gradually opened the European market to internal competition: terminals (1988), value-added telecommunication services (1990). An additional step is the European Council's decision in June 1993 to liberalize voice telephony and infrastructure by January 1, 1998.

Most member-states have modified their national legislation accordingly. Although it was not required by the Commission's telecommunications policy, many have also begun to privatize (at least partially) their public telecommunications operators (PTOs) in order to prepare them for new market conditions (see Appendix).

In France, the liberalization of telecommunications has been on the political agenda since 1986. While the cable TV market was opened to private operators as early as September 1986, a first attempt to introduce a tiny dose of competition in the provision of telecommunications services failed during the summer of 1987 because of union opposition. In 1990, a law was passed that partially and gradually liberalized two segments of the telecommunications market: mobile services and value-added services.[7] Yet, the telecommunications infrastructure remains a France Télécom monopoly. However, private networks are allowed as long as they are not open to a third party.

Over the years, the French government's position on telecommunications liberalization has changed. Until 1994, France resisted the EC push toward liberalization. Since then, France has speeded up the liberalization of its telecommunications, sometimes ahead of European deadlines. This shift followed a report prepared by Bruno Lasserre, head of the Regulatory Directorate at the Post and Telecommunications (PTT) Ministry. Lasserre argued—and convinced the government—that France Télécom's monopoly could not resist technological progress and the liberalization of mobile and satellite communications. He advocated an early demonopolization of French telecommunications in order to prepare the public operator for a tougher environment and to foster the emergence of new, stable (and French) actors (Lasserre 1994).

In fall 1995, the French government released an orientation paper for future telecommunications legislation in view of the 1998 European liberalization. In January 1996, the PTT Minister, François Fillon, introduced a bill that was adopted by the French parliament in spring 1996. All telecommunications services will be open to competition. Licenses will be granted by the PTT Ministry. Universal service—comprising nationwide provision of telephone service at affordable rates, information service, telephone books and telephone booths—will be provided by the public operator France Télécom and any other willing operator. Competitors will share in the costs of universal service through payment to a special fund. Finally, an independent regulatory agency will be established to monitor operators' activities, administer the universal service fund, and solve conflicts among operators.

In 1990 France Télécom was transformed from a government department into a public corporation and fully separated from the Postal branch. The privatization of France Télécom remains a highly sensitive issue, discussion of which has been postponed several times. Privatization is supported by the public operator's top managers as a means to deal with competition but is opposed by the unions and employees who want to keep their civil service status. In summer 1994, a report on the future of France Télécom submitted to the government by former France Télécom chairman Marcel Roulet called for selling a minority share of the public operator while maintaining employees' civil service status. This strategic reform was not endorsed by Prime Minister Edouard Balladur, who decided to drop the privatization effort. The government argued that privatization should follow completion of the liberalization of the market rather than precede it. However, after the election of Jacques Chirac as President, France Télécom's privatization was put on the government agenda again.

Visions and Goals

The European Framework

The White Paper on Growth, Competitiveness and Employment: The critical role of trans-European networks in the single market

The White Paper on Growth, Competitiveness and Employment, prepared under the active direction of Jacques Delors and released in June 1993, is certainly *the* key document for understanding the European approach to the IS. Not only did it pave the way for subsequent EU actions, it also articulated a cognitive map of the challenges facing Europe and shaped a framework within which member-states designed their strategies and policies.

The White Paper presents a straightforward picture of Europe's economic crisis, characterized by the highest unemployment rate since 1945 and a decline in position vis-à-vis the United States and Japan with respect to market shares, research and development, and the capacity to design and launch new products. "Insufficient progress in adapting the structures of the Community's economy to the changing technological, social and international environment" is identified as the main in factor this crisis (p. 49).

The White Paper's aim is not to justify the necessity of the single market already enacted by member-states. The single market is considered to be a living reality (with the outstanding exception of the free movement of people) that allows firms to benefit from economies of scale, reduce their administrative and financial costs, and cooperate more efficiently with one another (p. 57). The White Paper examines ways "to make the most of the internal market" and to boost competitiveness. With this in mind, it calls for two main actions:

• *Building trans-European networks* in the fields of transport, energy and information. Such networks are seen as "the arteries of the single market" and the "lifeblood of competitiveness." Their malfunction is reflected in lost opportunities to create new markets and hence in a level of job creation that falls short of Europe's potential (p. 75).

• *A redirection of research and development activities* to encourage broader cooperation among European firms and public research centers, especially in the fields of information technology and biotechnology.

The White Paper also provides a vision of the information society that can be summed up in three ideas. First, the information society is an inevitable process, "not a technological dream for the next century." This process has started in the United States and will gain ground in Europe. Second, the information society will have large and long-term effects comparable to those of the first industrial revolution. It has the potential to answer the new needs of European societies. Finally, compared with its leading competitors, Europe has comparative advantages including a powerful telecommunications industry and Europe's cultural diversity.

Overall, the White Paper's vision of the information society is deterministic, optimistic, and economic. The information society cannot be rejected or even slowed down. One can only adapt to the change and try to direct it so that negative effects will be avoided or minimized. The White Paper underlines the economic benefits that the information society will bring but does not really address societal issues. Especially striking is the White Paper's insistence on the urgency of actions to be taken and its denial of social debate on the impact of the IS: "The first economies which successfully complete this change [to the information society] in good condition will hold significant competitive advantages.... In any event, it would be fruitless to become embroiled in a fresh dispute about the machine age" (p. 23).

The Bangemann Report on the Information Society: Faith in the marketplace
In June 1994, *Europe and the Global Information Society*, a report prepared by the High-Level Group on the Information Society chaired by Martin Bangemann, was presented to the European Council at Corfu. This report had been requested in the White Paper to help with establishing priorities, deciding on procedures, and defining the resources required for the information society.

The Bangemann Report considers the information society to be a technology- and market-driven revolution that will create new social and economic opportunities. To turn these opportunities into benefits, the report calls for a break with past practices (public money, financial assistance, subsidies, *dirigism*, protectionism) and for a new regulatory environment allowing full competition. This regulatory framework should also deal with issues of intellectual property rights, privacy, encryption, and media ownership. The report also addresses a major problem in Europe's IS policy. While competition can overcome market fragmentation along national lines, it may create a *technical* fragmentation. That is why the plea for competition is complemented by a call for interconnectivity and interoperability.

The Bangemann Report has often been presented as a liberal document[8] and, indeed, it is. However, despite its faith in market forces, the report emphasizes that competition alone cannot provide the critical mass necessary to obtain adequate returns on investments. Thus, the report recommends launching experimental applications that will create a virtuous circle of supply and demand. Specifically, the report advocates an action plan based on ten initiatives linking public and private interests: teleworking, distance learning, a network for universities and research centers, telematic services for small and medium-sized enterprises, road traffic management, air traffic control, health-care networks, electronic tendering, a trans-European public administration network, and city ISs.

Following the Bangemann report, the EC adopted an action plan in July 1994 that was organized along four themes:

• review of the telecommunications regulatory framework in order to provide a fully liberalized environment;

• development of networks, applications, and new services though European pilot projects;

• study of the social and cultural impact of the information society; and

• promotion of the information society.

Meanwhile, the Fourth R&D Framework Program for the period 1994–1999 was also launched. This program embraces all community-supported R&D activities. About 30 percent of its funding will be devoted to projects related to information technology and communications. In contrast to previous programs, a new line was added to support targeted socioeconomic research; however, this effort represents less than one percent of funding.

The French Vision

The Breton Report on Teleservices: The impact of the IS on employment
The Breton Report was commissioned by the French government to assess the impact of new telecommunications services (such as teleservices and telework) on employment. Prepared by Thierry Breton, strategic director of the French computer group Bull, and released in June 1994, the report first underlines the growing importance of services in modern economies. Even during the last decade, this trend has been impressive (see Table 1). However, productivity gains have mainly taken place in the manufacturing sector. The use of new information and communications technology should be encouraged

in the service sector in order to enhance productivity and create new jobs.

According to the Breton Report, the market for teleservices—i.e., all value-added services supplied via communications networks, including cable television—represented around Fr 30 billion in 1993. The report estimated that this market would be worth Fr 90 to 190 billion by 2005, with Fr 30 to 50 billion for services to domestic users. Online information services could grow up to 16 percent a year in France over the next decade. Related employment would grow from 65,000 persons in 1995 to at least 170,000 in 2005. But the overall impact on employment would not necessarily be positive since teleservices may destroy traditional jobs and facilitate off-shore relocation of industries.

The bulk of the growth will come from business services, including teleworking, telebanking, and distance management of computer systems. However, telemedicine and distance education could also grow rapidly of the government supports their development. The report suggests that the development of telework in the public sector and a reduction in the rates of France Télécom would help teleservices take off. It also notes that a major obstacle that must be addressed is the fair distribution of revenue among services providers.

While sharing the overall rationale of the White Paper, the Breton Report expresses some dissent on the timing of innovations. In Breton's view, the information revolution will take place over four or five decades since people need time to adapt to and take advantage of new technologies. There is therefore no urgency for the public authorities, which should assess the social effects of new communications and information technologies before taking action. Another difference with the Bangemann Report can also be noted: Breton considers state support to be necessary in the domain of educational and health services.

The Théry Report on the IS: Forward to the past?
The Théry report, published in September 1994, bears some similarity to the White Paper and the Bangemann Report: it assumes that the development of the IS is inevitable and will be global. Since the world's leading economic powers are committed to deploying the IS, it is urgent that France take similar action. Like the White Paper and the Bangemann Report, Théry emphasizes "the multiplying effect that the superhighways will have on the competitiveness of enterprises and the

Table 1 Employment in France by Sectors (in millions)

	1982	1990
Agriculture	1.760 (8.20%)	1.250 (5.60%)
Manufacturing	7.345 (34.2%)	6.690 (30.1%)
Services	12.360 (57.6%)	14.290 (64.3%)
Total	21.465	22.230

Source: Breton Report

development of service activities, which constitutes a formidable opportunity to create jobs." Finally, Théry stresses that public authorities should ensure real competition not only in the service sector but also in the software field. However, the liberalization of telecommunications should not lead to a "crumbling" of European forces.

Gérard Théry's plan for the IS rests on three main proposals:

• *All French households and firms should be connected to the IS by 2015.* Access to the IS must be universal in order to allow equal access among citizens and avoid discrimination between the poor and the rich, urban and rural areas, professional users and domestic users.

• *The IS necessitates a massive development of fiber-optic links.* Four to five million French households and businesses should be connected as soon as possible. ATM technology should be put into general use and new software be designed for instance with the support of venture capital companies.

• *Experiments should be initiated immediately.* Pilot projects are intended to stimulate partnerships, test new services, and assess technical problems.

The costs of setting up a fiber-optic network in France would amount to Fr 150 billion over 20 years. According to Théry, this would be less than twice the cost of maintaining and upgrading the existing telephone network, estimated at Fr 5 billion a year.[9] Théry thinks that the major hurdle en route to the IS is the cost of related software, which would boost the total investment to Fr 450 billion.

Théry's plan shares at least four common features with the Minitel plan implemented in France during the 1980s:

• *A voluntarist approach.* The Minitel plan, like the IS relies on the idea of the stimulating role played by public authorities in the dialectics content/conduits. Infrastructures have to be developed for a demand to emerge. The public operator should play a key role in setting up the network because it alone has the financial capacity to implement the needed investment and because it is committed to universal service. However, in contrast to the Minitel plan, the role of the public operator in the IS development should not be exclusive.

• *The importance of experiments.* This notion seems to be taken directly from the Minitel plan. Between 1978 and 1981, experiments in videotex services were conducted in France. This approach turned out to be very positive: it allowed technical improvements, the formation of partnerships, and the progressive design of an appropriate regulatory framework through negotiations among the actors involved. Experiments also familiarized the French people with the concept of videotex and contributed to the social legitimization and political acceptance of Minitel (one of the aims of the experiments was to assess Minitel's social impact and utility). However, such a societal concern does not appear in the Théry Report on the IS. Instead, it focuses on the economic viability and technical feasibility of applications.

• *The model for information provision.* The Minitel plan is based on the notion of a transparent network—the network as a marketplace—that permits users and information providers to "meet" simply and freely. Any user can access any information provider; any information provider can offer services. The network operator facilitates contacts but does not play any other role (such as the selection of users or information providers). In this model, there is no hierarchy of services, no permanent commitment on the part of users. This concept of information provision is also present in the Théry report which opposes reliance on integrated and segmented systems of services, each one linking specific network operators and information providers (as in the United States where Compuserve, Prodigy, America Online, and other providers coexist).

• *Partnership between public and private interests.* The Minitel system relies on cooperation between the public operator—which runs the network—and private information providers operating the host computers and applications. In the same way, the development of France's IS should be based on joint action by public authorities and the private sector, including both small and medium sized enterprises and large corporations. The government must act as the driving force, particularly with regard to public service missions.

Strategies and Policies: From Dirigism to Pragmatism

The Changing Role of Government

Although it endorsed the Théry Report's presentation of the IS's challenges, the French government did not adopt the action plan that the report proposed. In contrast to previous policies on new communications and information technologies (such as videotex and cable TV), the French strategy for the IS designed at the governmental council of October 27, 1994, does not rest on a *grand plan* with clear and quantitative objectives, a central role for the public telecommunications operator, and a binding schedule. Instead, the French government has called for private initiatives under a trials process. As Director General for Industrial Strategy Didier Lombard put it: "We have reined in our Colbertist instinct."[10] The role of the government has been limited to:

• *Adaptation of the regulatory framework.* The aim is to allow more competition while maintaining basic principles such as universal service, the protection of privacy, and social cohesion.

• *Stimulation of new markets and services.* Public administrations are expected to launch applications that will create a virtuous circle within which the IS can develop.

• *Organization of a public debate on the stakes of the IS.* This debate will probably aim primarily at the promotion of the information society.[11] It is doubtful that it will deal with the social impact of the IS: research programs on this topic have not been started undertaken as was the case when the videotex plan was introduced.

Overall, the French IS strategy illustrates a shift in the conception of the government's role. The government is expected to act as a conductor that gives political impetus to the IS, mobilizes actors, and creates favorable conditions for them by adjusting regulations. This conception mirrors the action plan designed by the EC in July 1994 (see above) while being more limited with respect to public awareness campaigns and support for research and development activities. The state is meant to be modest and flexible,[12] no longer *dirigist*.

This move from dirigism to pragmatism can be explained by structural and conjunctural factors:

• *the liberal stance of the government,* which is based on both economic and political considerations. Whereas a natural monopoly once existed, technological change has made it financially possible to diversify networks and operators. In a democratic society, free choice of carrier is intimately linked to freedom of speech and creation.[13]

• *the cable plan syndrome.* Despite huge investments, the French cable plan has had disappointing results. Almost 15 years after its launch, only six million homes are linked and only 1.6 million actually subscribe to cable TV services. This failure has frequently been attributed to the dirigism of the public authorities, who initially imposed unrealistic technical options, and a regulatory framework that was too constraining.[14]

• *the lack of public resources.* As the state budget deficit increases, it is difficult for the government to devote large amounts of money to projects such as the IS. In a period of economic crisis with around 3.5 million people unemployed, it appears more important to direct government action to job creation.

• *the reluctance of France Télécom to play a central and instrumental role in the IS.* As will be developed later, France Télécom has anticipated the liberalization of French telecommunications and does not want to commit itself to projects that could hamper its future profitability.

Pilot Projects

In November 1994, the French government issued a call for trial proposals. This call was purposely open to any kind of technical or commercial proposal. The main criteria for selection were the "economic, technical, industrial and financial viability" of the projects.

On February 28, 1995, a first roster of 49 projects was selected out of 635 proposals. While 81 projects were definitely rejected, it was decided that another 218 would require technical, financial, or regulatory changes and would be reviewed again in six months. Among those put on hold were projects proposed by the French cable operators Générale des Eaux and Lyonnaise des Eaux, which planned to offer telephone service over their cable systems. The government initially argued that such a service could not be offered, even on a trial basis, without changing French legislation, an objective that, the government did not want to meet ahead of the EU's 1998 deadline. On October 16, 1995, and on March 27, 1996, the government selected additional projects. Projects submitted by cable operators that had been initially rejected were this time approved.

Altogether, 244 projects were accepted, which represented a Fr 4 billion investment.[15] The government decided to devote Fr 270 million in 1996 to finance up to 30 percent of these projects. It is expected that complementary subsidies will come from European funds (especially from the Telematics Program). It is striking that France Télécom is involved in many of the selected trials as either the main developer or a technical partner. Regional authorities are also involved in many projects, with a special emphasis on educational and social services (see Table 2).

In parallel, in February 1996, the government introduced a bill in the Parliament to establish a specific regulatory framework for trials. This bill, which was passed on March 26, 1996, allow networks and services that are not permitted under current law such as telephony on cable TV networks, teleports facilities, and Microvawe Multipoint Distribution Systems. However, these rights will be limited in time (five years) and in space. If trials will primarily serve to provide technical and commercial information to operators and service providers, an assessment of their social impact is also planned.

France Télécom's Strategy: The End of the *Grand Projet* Model?

Although segments of the French telecommunications market have been open to competition (notably, mobile telephone and value-added services), France Télécom is by far the dominant actor in the telecommunications sphere. In 1994, its total revenues amounted to Fr 130 billion, its net profit to Fr 4.8 billion[16] and its investments to Fr 35.7 billion. Yet, the public operator has dramatically changed over the last few years.

In many respects, France Télécom is no longer the powerful actor that it used to be. Following its transformation into a public corporation in January 1991, France Télécom underwent a complex process of regarding its employees according to actual functions. This created a climate of suspicion within the organization, which hampered its dynamics. The separation of the operating and regulatory functions also affected France Télécom. Although it has maintained close links with public authorities (especially the Ministry of PTT), France Télécom has less influence on French telecommunications policy than previously. More important, France Télécom does not seem to have a clear strategy for the future, or more exactly, it is hesitating between different strategies. On the one hand, France Télécom is tempted to get into the competition, to look for new markets in France and abroad, to be a "real enterprise." On the other hand, France Télécom is still marked by its public service and monopoly traditions. Its top managers do not know how to make the conflicting choice between the exciting, motivating, but uncertain and unstable promises of new markets and the familiar, but outmoded, routines. Some people within the organization point out that France Télécom only works well when it has a *grand projet,* such as the catch-up telephone plan of 1975, the Minitel program of 1978, or the cable plan of 1982. Whereas former heads of the public operator, such as Gérard Théry, could be portrayed as captains of industry fascinated by technical excellence, France Télécom's present top managers are more concerned with profit margins, cash flow, and other financial indicators.[17]

France Télécom's unofficial reaction to the Théry Report has been rather negative. It refused the imposition of imposed binding, costly, and unrealistic provisions such as quantitative objectives or deadlines (as was the case with the cable plan of 1982). It also disagreed on most of the report's proposals. Thus, according to France Télécom, the cost of providing fiber to the home would be too high for residential users until 2005 at least (Guieysse et al. 1995). In its view, a better option would be fiber to the curb or fiber to the building, depending on the area. France Télécom also objects to a voluntarist approach. It maintains that the market for information services is narrow and mostly

Table 2 Examples of Pilot Projects

National platforms
- ATM network.
- RENATER 2 (network linking universities and research centers).
- Education network (linking primary and secondary schools in 13 regions).

Regional platforms (12 are proposed by regional authorities)
- CRISTAL project piloted by *Conseil régional d'Alsace*: Building up a network linking all cities and universities in the region. Will provide access to job listings, social security information, regional information, etc.
- Project sponsored by *Conseil régional Midi Pyrénées*: Access to the Internet and exchange of teaching experiences among schools.

Services
- BATRU (Bringing ATM to Residential Users) piloted by France Télécom (Brest/Lille): ATM network to provide videophone and online banking and retail services using regular telephone lines.
- Multicâble (Paris, 2,500 households): "Electronic village" with telephone service, access to the Internet, online information, shopping services on cable tv. Similar trials will take place in Annecy (8,000 households) and Nice (5,000–10,000 households).
- Teleport (Roubaix).
- MMDS (Haute-Vienne, Corse).

Sources: Personal interviews, December 1995

professional and that only some users will be able to afford to link up with the IS in the short term. The approach should therefore be market-driven. Finally, it seems that France Télécom wants to get rid of the Minitel model for information provision. In the view of its officials, the impossibility of selecting and controlling information providers resulted in the overall poor quality of the Minitel system and its deteriorated image on account of a few controversial services. It also created additional costs with no corresponding benefits.

Clearly, France Télécom's preferred IS strategy is to focus on specific applications and groups of users (vs. a universal approach) and to develop closed partnerships with selected service providers.[18] This move is already apparent in a number of projects that France Télécom has undertaken through its subsidiary France Télécom Multimédia (see Table 3). But such a strategy may create an unprecedented problem for regulatory authorities. Since France Télécom will remain the dominant carrier in the near future, it will be necessary to ensure that other service providers have fair access to the public operator's network and enjoy the same conditions as its partners.

Cable Operators' Strategies

Almost 15 years after the launch of the cable plan and an overall investment of Fr 35 billion, France had no more than 1.6 million cable subscribers at the end of 1995 (see Table 4). Cable operators are suffering big losses (estimated at Fr 2 billion in 1994). In February 1995, the major French cable operator (a subsidiary of the Caisse des Dépôts) left the business and its systems were taken over by the Compagnie Générale de Vidéocommunication and France Télécom Câble.

These undesirable outcomes can be attributed to several factors. The technology initially chosen for cable systems (star architecture and fiber optics) has proven to be costly and cumbersome.[19] The programming initially offered on cable was not attractive. The major cable operators, which are subsidiaries of public utility companies, tended to consider cable TV as another public utility and did not do any marketing. Only when investments were made in specific programs for cable channels did consumer interest in cable TV grow. Finally, numerous and cumbersome regulatory constraints apply to cable. For example, cable channels have to be licensed. Since cable operators failed to get such licenses for Arabic channels, they lost many subscribers among the French Muslim population (which has turned to satellite reception).

Cable operators have welcomed the government's support for the IS. They see it as a unique opportunity to start providing new services. Cable operators are especially interested in the regulatory changes that the IS policy could bring about in telephone services, from which they are currently excluded. Trial projects from cable operators, including video-on-demand, access to online information services and the Internet, as well as telephone service, have been accepted by the government. However, the two-way capacities of current cable systems are questionable. To allow real interactivity, structural modifications and an upgrading of systems will be required. It is not clear how this investment will be financed given the situation of cable operators. The costs of the technology and the low penetration suggest that the introduction of new services on cable will proceed slowly, and most likely in areas in which business users are concentrated.

Table 3 Selected France Télécom Multimedia Pilot Projects

Type of Service	Partners
Information for consumers (Magic Yellow Pages)	Office d'Annonces (subsidiary of Havas)
Online information and transaction services (France en ligne)	Bellanger, Fillipacchi Groups
One-stop shopping for business travel	Havas, Hertz
Video games	Sony, Lyonnaise Communications
Video-on-demand, near-video-on-demand	TF1
Online information services, shopping, banking (Multicâble)	Lyonnaise Communications

Source: Busson 1995

The entry of cable operators into telecommunications services is backed by local authorities. In France, cities authorize the creation of cable systems. This responsibility allows local authorities to barter with cable operators for the development of services that are useful to local communities or to the management of their own facilities (Dupuis 1995). However, since cable has appeared in France, cities have not been very active in using cable systems. At best, local officials have tried to foster the development of municipal channels with the idea of exerting influence on their constituencies. The use of cable systems for other purposes (access to administrative information, social services, educational channels, etc.) has been marginal. The move toward the IS might change this situation. Some local officials have realized that the governmental initiative creates the conditions for a new assessment of the role, impact, and regulation of telecommunications networks in cities. With this prospect, a number of local authorities have decided to take part in the IS pilot projects.

Media Groups' Strategies

Compared to their U.S., British, and German counterparts, French

Table 4 The Growth of Cable TV in France (in thousands)

	Homes passed	Homes connected
1988	957	93
1990	2,776	514
1992	4,662	1,048
1994	5,802	1,617

Source: Agence Câble and Association des villes câblées

media groups are somewhat weak. They are characterized by low multimedia integration, insufficient turnover or profits to undertake huge investments and the lack of an international dimension.[20]

French national television stations, like other European broadcasters, enjoy a great advantage in the provision of new services. Their transmitter networks provide almost universal coverage of the population, so they can quickly reach a critical mass of consumers. Moreover, the provision of new services over terrestrial networks does not require the construction of a new infrastructure: costs will be concentrated in production facilities and digital decoders. Yet despite these advantages, French broadcasters' IS strategies are rather timid. France Télévision (the public TV company) and TF1 (the major commercial TV company) have both announced plans to launch digital services in the near future. France Télévision is also preparing the launch of France Télévision Interactive in partnership with the media group Havas and the electronics company Thomson to provide services with some level of interactivity through a return path based on the telephone and the Minitel.

Canal Plus, which operates a pay-TV channel with four million subscribers, is more dynamic. It has set up a multimedia subsidiary and unveiled plans to pour several million francs into the creation of multimedia products, including video games and cultural products, targeting the global market. It has also signed a 30-year partnership with the German media group Bertelsmann to jointly develop pay-TV and interactive services such as video-on-demand in Europe.[21] Around Fr 2 billion will be devoted to these projects over the next three years. The deal will be complemented by two joint ventures to develop the required digital technology and to buy broadcasting rights for programs.

The French electronics and publishing group Matra-Hachette is carefully expanding its multimedia activities on both sides of the Atlantic. In Europe, Matra-Hachette is setting up together with France Télécom an interactive video games cable TV channel, Ludo Canal, and has announced the launch of a cable TV channel for women based on its best-selling women's magazine, *Elle*. Matra-Hachette is especially active in the production of CD-ROM titles. In the United States, its subsidiary Grolier has sold two million copies on CD-ROM of its popular school encyclopedia over the last five years.

As for Havas, the other major French publishing group, its multimedia plans and global strategy are unclear. Havas has a difficult choice to make. It is linked both to France Télécom and to Canal Plus, which are competing in various fields, including the technology for digital pay-TV.

It is also interesting to note that Bull, France's major computer manufacturer with an revenue of Fr 26 billion in 1995, is scarcely involved in IS developments. Over the last 15 years, Bull has gone through numerous internal restructuring and experienced big losses (Fr 22.1 billion from 1989 to 1995). After attempting to develop its personal computer branch by buying Zenith, Bull is now concentrating on services and Unix servers.

Institutional Structures for Coordination and Implementation: Between State and Market

IS Policy Making in France: Policy Arenas and Majors Actors

The IS puts four different policy arenas into contact with each other: the electronics industry, print media, audiovisual media, and the telecommunications industry.

The electronics industry has been open to competition for a long time. There is no barrier to entry; regulatory constraints are weak or nonexistent and mostly related to consumer protection (e.g., safety standards). Public policy in this field has mainly comprised subsidies aimed at fostering domestic companies. On occasion, projectionist measures have been taken by setting standards or certification processes.[22]

The French print media have been governed by the principle of freedom of speech since the end of the 19th century. Nonetheless, some regulatory constraints apply, though they are essentially structural and intended to limit concentration in order to ensure pluralism of opinions.

The audiovisual media (broadcasting and cable TV) were part of the French state apparatus until 1986, when private channels and cable operators were allowed.[23] The regulation of audiovisual media is considerably stronger than that of the press. Regulations are both structural (e.g., concentration ceilings, licensing justified by the scarcity of the spectrum) and behavioral (content regulations aimed at ensuring the promotion of French culture). In addition, in the broadcasting field there is a neat separation between policy making (under the authority of the Ministry of Communication) and regulation, which is the responsibility of an independent agency.

The telecommunications industry was until 1990 a de facto monopoly run by a state body. Public policy in this field was shaped by neocorporatist relations between the domestic manufacturing industry and the public operator.[24] Since 1990, the market has been partially open to competition and the separation of operating activities and regulatory functions has been completed.[25] However, policy making and regulation continue to fall under the responsibility of one single body (the Ministry of PTT).

French IS policy making involves several governmental bodies. The main player is the Ministry of Industry, Post and Telecommunications,[26] within which two departments share the responsibility for IS policy. The *Direction Générale des Postes et Télécommunications* (DGPT) sets the regulations for the telecommunications and IS sectors and defends French positions in international forums (such as the International Telecommunications Union and the European Council of Telecommunications). The *Direction générale des stratégies industrielles* (DGSI) promotes the competitiveness of French industries in France and abroad. The DGSI also oversees the IS pilot projects.

So far, this division of labor has worked out without major conflicts, which is surprising given the differences in background of the two departments. Coming from the PTT world and closely linked to the operating activities of France Télécom until 1990, the DGPT has often been portrayed as interventionist and marked by the monopoly culture of the telecommunications sector, while the DGSI has more of a tradition of *faire faire* (having things done by others) by orienting private initiatives through subsidies. A rivalry similar to that between Japan's Ministry of Post and Telecommunications (MPT) and Ministry of International Trade and Industry (MITI) would not have been surprising. That this did not occur can be explained by several elements: (a) the separation from France Télécom has precipitated a change of staff and led to new methods and approaches; (b) as an emancipated entity, the DGPT has sought legitimacy and authority by demonstrating its independence; and (c) a liberalizing mood has overtaken the French telecommunications sphere since 1993.

The other two major players in IS policy are the Ministry of Culture—which supervises the film industry, museums and libraries, frames copyright and intellectual property policies; and more generally deals with any issue related to the promotion or the defense of French culture—and the Ministry of Communication, which is primarily in charge of setting regulations for the broadcasting and print media. So far, these two ministries have not been very involved in IS policy because its focus has been on the development of infrastructure rather than on content matters. However, in the longer term, the government is likely to face the challenge of reconciling contradictory industrial and cultural goals. While liberalization and competition are the key words in the policy on telecommunications infrastructure and services, the French approach to content is fundamentally projectionist and interventionist.

Governmental coordination is traditionally achieved in France through interministerial committees, in which interested ministers meet under the chairmanship of the Prime Minister or his/her representative. Most of the time, the Minister of the Budget is present and has an important say in decisions. On occasion, when important decisions are to be made, interministerial committees are chaired by the President of the Republic.

For the IS, such an interministerial committee, the *Service des Industries de Communication et de Service* (SERICS), has been set up on a permanent basis. Its work is complemented by a working group, the *Groupe Inter-Industrie* (GII), in which representatives of industry, public bodies and local authorities address specific topics such as teleworking, electronic payment or online administrative information. It is important to note that, in contrast to previous high tech policies, no special structure has been created to design, coordinate, or implement the

French IS policy.[27] The institutional vacuum for the IS is further evidence of the state's withdrawal in the domain of high tech policies.

IS Regulation in France

France's IS will involve the regulation both of telecommunications and audiovisual services and of infrastructures, which currently fall under the responsibility of two different bodies, the *Conseil supérieur de l'audiovisuel* (CSA) and the *Direction générale des postes et des télécommunications* (DGPT). The CSA is an independent regulatory agency that issues licenses to private over-the-air TV stations, private radio stations, cable TV systems (but not operators), and TV channels on cable networks. It also allocates frequency channels for broadcasting uses. The DGPT issues licenses for telecommunications networks and services that do not fall under the state's monopoly.

This regulatory structure has been criticized because of the lack of independence of the DGPT and the overlapping of responsibilities of the two bodies. The DGPT is part of the Ministry of PTT, which is also responsible for telecommunications regulations. Furthermore, although France Télécom has become a public corporation and is no longer part of the Ministry of PTT, the DGPT has been suspected of maintaining close links with it. For these reasons, there have been frequent demands for an independent regulatory agency that would, on the one hand, allow a clearer separation between policy making and the interpretation and implementation of policy and, on the other hand, ensure fair competition among operators when the telecommunications market is fully liberalized. The new law on telecommunications will allow such a move.

Whether some categories of services fall under the authority of the CSA or the DGPT is not always perfectly evident. In some cases, it may be necessary to obtain two licenses to operate one service. For example, while cable systems are authorized by the CSA, the DGPT issues licenses for the operation of telecommunications services on cable, except for those related to TV (e.g., conditional access to video programming), which fall under the CSA's authority. This has led to territorial conflicts between the two regulatory bodies, which might become more acute with IS—as was apparent during the drafting of the regulatory framework for IS trials (CSA 1995).

There is no serious thinking in France about ways in which telecommunications and broadcasting regulators could cooperate. In the United Kingdom, which faces the same problem, some have argued for a single "economic" regulator for the whole communications sector supplemented by a "content regulatory body" concerned with matters of taste and decency (Cave 1995).

IS Policy Making and Implementation at the European Level

The task of governmental coordination is much more intricate at the European level given the fragmentation of policy making. At least three kinds of coordination are required:

• *among different Directorates General within the EC,* so that a clear plan of action can be proposed by the Commission to the Council;

• *coordination among memberstates within the European Council of Ministers,* which must agree on common objectives and principles; and

• *coordination among the Commission, the European Council of Ministers, and the European Parliament,* which is necessary for a directive to be adopted.

At the Commission level, the definition of European IS policy involves several Directorates General (see Table 5). Conflicts between Directorates may arise from their different priorities and approaches. Traditionally, there is opposition between DG IV (Competition) on the one hand, and DG III (Industry) and DG XIII (Telecommunications, Information Market, and Exploitation of Research) on the other. DG IV is primarily concerned with creating competition and abolishing monopolies or dominant positions; it sees the development of the IS as best achieved through the invisible hand of the marketplace. DG III and DG XII put more emphasis on public intervention (standards setting, financial assistance to research and development programs, etc.) to help construct a coherent pan-European infrastructure.

The difference in approaches is more striking when content matters come into play. The contrast between the Bangemann Report (largely in line with DG IV) and the Audiovisual Green Paper that was sponsored by DG X (Information, Communication, Culture and Audiovisual), both published in 1994 (EC, 1994), is eloquent testimony to the conflicting values and approaches that exist within the Commission. To reach basically the same goal (a strong European industry that

Table 5 Directorates Involved in European IS Policy

DG III	Industry
DG IV	Competition
DG X	Information, Communication, Culture, and Audiovisual
DG XII	Science Research and Development
DG XIII	Telecommunications, Information Market, and Exploitation of Research
DG XV	Internal Market and Financial Services

can resist an exogenous threat), the Bangemann Report puts its faith in market mechanisms, while the Green Paper underlines market failures and calls for intervention to secure desired ends (Collins 1994).

IS implementation also raises various coordination problems at the European level. For example, directives are not directly applicable to member-states but must be incorporated into national laws. If European regulations are not transposed into national legislation at about the same time, the entire coherence and dynamic of the European regulatory thrust can be altered. Administrative cooperation between member-states is also necessary to achieve effective and equivalent enforcement of rules. This is a critical point. The implementation of regulations designed at the European level can be significantly hampered if there are cross-national variations in the detailed interpretation of rules or in the practices of regulatory agencies.

In order to fully and effectively liberalize the telecommunications market, the Bangemann Report suggested the creation of an independent European regulatory authority that would take charge of licensing procedures, interconnectivity and network access, and universal service funds. While this move is supported by many industry representatives, its political acceptance by all member-states is uncertain. National regulation has sometimes been used by member-states to adjust European rules to their specific needs. Moreover, the creation of a European regulatory body would be one more step toward a political unification that is still strongly rejected by some countries.

Coordination by the EC or by Industry?

Since the development of the IS in Europe will depend on private initiatives, some kind of coordination is also necessary among European businesses. If such coordination fails to be provided, there is a risk that market forces will lead to a duplication of effort (for example in terms of R&D), which may hamper European industry's competitiveness, or to conflicting standards, which may inhibit consumer demand for new products or services. Without minimal coordination within the industry, the fragmentation of the European market along national lines will merely be replaced by fragmentation along corporate lines.

The EU traditionally encourages industry coordination through research and development programs that foster cooperation, dissemination of results, training, and mobility of researchers among European firms. The EC set up a new instrument for the IS, the Information Society Project Office (ISPO), in December 1994. The aim of ISPO is "to support, promote and advise private and public initiatives related to the development of the information society." Its main objectives are:

• to help industry and consumers make optimal use of the instruments and resources provided by the Commission;

• to act as a broker of ideas and experience by disseminating and sharing information on the development of new applications; and

• to facilitate the launching of relevant international cooperation and the establishment of new partnerships.

In some cases, European firms have designed their own coordination structures, of which the European Multimedia Forum is one outstanding example. The Forum was set up during the summer of 1994 by a group of more than 30 Europe-based telecommunications, computer, electronics, publishing, and television companies to encourage cross-industry synergy and partnerships, facilitate the exchange of information, and act as an intermediary between businesses and government.[28] Another example is the Digital Video Broadcast (DVB) group in which 145 European enterprises, television stations, and satellite operators are participants. The DVB group agreed on a common encryption code and a two-year code of good conduct starting in 1995 for digital TV broadcasting.

Occasionally, existing interest groups may also act as forums for coordination and present public authorities with proposals for action. Two major business organizations, the European Employers Federation (Unice) and the European Round Table (ERT)—which involves 39 leading European entrepreneurs—have fulfilled this function by publishing reports on telecommunications.[29]

Industry coordination typically faces two conflicting problems: free riders on the one hand, and too broad a membership on the other. In the first instance, if significant actors refuse to join the coordinating group, agreements that can be reached have little operative value.[30] In the latter case, useful agreements cannot be reached because of the diversity of interests, or, if decisions are made, they are purely formal.

While most industry leaders lament the lack of industry coordination, which impedes Europe's competitiveness, opinions are split on whether the EU or the private sector should coordinate the development of the IS in Europe. The Internet model is attractive to some who argue that there would be no need for a central planning or coordinating authority and that the IS could grow as a network of networks by the successive addition of building blocks. However, it is not clear that the Internet model can apply to the IS. The Internet was able to develop as a self-regulated network largely because it was backed by a closed community that shared common goals and values. In contrast, the IS will involve a broader range of actors and conflicting interests. While the industry is able to coordinate technical problems, its ability (and willingness) to regulate social issues (e.g., undesirable content) is uncertain.

NII Services, Present and Future: Is There Life after Minitel?

The Minitel Industry

At the end of 1995, France had about 10,000 different service providers offering 25,000 services through some 4,200 host computers. In 1994, total revenues of service providers amounted to Fr 3.1 billion for videotex services and Fr 1.3 billion for audiotex services.

According to a February 1993 survey,[31] 21 percent of French service providers are independent, specialized companies (so-called electronic publishers) for which information provision via Minitel is the sole or primary business. These companies provide 50 percent of the services available on the Minitel system. The other service providers are public administrations or public bodies (36 percent), which use Minitel to have a more direct relationship with citizens; private firms (38 percent), which mainly use Minitel as a way of advertising their products or services; and broadcast or publishing companies (5 percent).

Since Minitel was first introduced, the videotex industry has experienced impressive growth and exhibited a tendency toward concentration that is apparent in the diminishing number of host computers. The top 20 host computers provide about 20 percent of the services; they account for 40 percent of Minitel traffic and one-third of service provider revenues. Many of the independent electronic publishers have been taken over by banks and communications enterprises. Only the most innovative, which have accumulated technical expertise in a variety of areas (software, graphics, host computers management), have been able to survive in the long term.

Minitel Usage Patterns[32]

The interest of Minitel users has remained focused on the same hierarchy of services. Minitel's electronic directory is by far the service that the greatest number of people use. Following in popularity are three other services: banking (account information, information on financial investments), transportation (timetables, plane or train reservations), and shopping. Some services have experienced a decline in user interest, including services provided by the print media, messaging services, and games.

While the number of connections to Minitel has remained stable (around fifteen per month), usage time has declined: after reaching a peak in 1987 of 93 minutes per month, usage per Minitel dropped to 67 minutes per month in 1994. This trend can be explained by several factors:

• a learning effect; as they become more familiar with videotex services, users are able to get the information they need more quickly;

• changes in the user population; the propensity of early users to consume services is higher than that of late adopters;

• an increase in services rates since 1987; and

• a growing lack of interest in Minitel services, especially among people who have PCs. In order to stop this trend, France Télécom has open new access gateways to Minitel, allowing high speed transmission and the provision of enhanced services.[33]

The Low Penetration of the Internet and Other Online Services

Beyond Minitel, other online services are underdeveloped in France. Despite huge press coverage, only about 200,000 individuals (half of them academics) used the Internet at the end of 1995. Commercial online services such as Compuserve, Delphi, and America Online had fewer than 30,000 subscribers in France (and only about 250,000 in Europe). These figures do not necessarily indicate that the French are content with Minitel but reflect various commercial and technical obstacles to accessing other online services.

While French academics are able to access the Internet via a specialized network (Réseau National de Télécommunication pour la Recherche, or RENATER, which is subsidized by the government), the general public depends on commercial access providers, of which a dozen now exist in France. Access rates have steadily declined over the last two years, but remain high: typically Fr 100 a month with a few hours of free usage plus the cost of communication to access provider's host computer and the subscription to commercial services. This situation is likely to change with France Télécom's commitment to providing national access to the Internet at the cost of a local telephone call.

More generally, the development of online services in both France and Europe as a whole is hampered by several problems. First, the number of PCs equipped with modems is still low (see Table 6). This is a legacy of the monopoly period when modems fell under the public operator's jurisdiction and were considered part of their network.[34] The base of potential users is therefore narrow, which makes it difficult to recoup investments. Second, the diversity of languages and the fragmentation of markets in Europe are serious obstacles to the launch of genuine European services. Third, European online services must meet the EC's requirement that they do not represent any obstacle to competition. On this ground the Commission has recently opened an investigation concerning the creation and operation of the Luxembourg-based Europe Online service.[35]

Lessons from Stone Age Telematics[36]

With its low speed, poor graphics, and dumb terminals, the Minitel system is certainly not a good indicator of what the information society will be like in the future. However, with a ten-year history, a significant base of users, and a genuine market situation (services are sold and not free), the Minitel experience can provide useful lessons on social needs with respect to information services.

The Christmas toy effect. During the first months of usage, users generate heavy traffic directed to a great range of services. After this discovery period (which lasts around two months), most users tend to rationalize their consumption and focus on a few services; they also become much more sensitive to the value for money of services.[37]

The importance of a trigger service. Minitel's electronic directory was a magnet service that drew people into the Minitel galaxy. It attracted new users to Minitel, familiarized them with the system and eventually got them to use other services. It is likely that electronic mail is playing a similar role in the development of the Internet.

The declining importance of communication activities in comparison to information retrieval. While messaging services played an instrumental role in the growth of Minitel traffic, they tended to decline over time. Communication services (forums, messaging services, chatlines, etc.) primarily fascinated users during the discovery period of Minitel.

The marginality of advertising within services. Advertising did not develop within general Minitel services. Attempts to provide cheap services financed by advertising have generally failed. This may be due to the format of Minitel services (pages that contain little information, poor graphics). However, a number of companies have developed their own services to advertise their products (often complementing TV or magazine commercials).

The crucial role of advertising for services. The long-term viability of services depends less on their specific value than on their notoriety. Service providers that do not constantly advertise their brand and offerings quickly fail. If broadcast media services are doing well, it is mainly because of the impact of the commercials that they regularly air for their own services.

The failure of the print media in packaging information services. Print media services did not succeed when they tried to play a packaging/editing function for other services. Along with the decline of traffic experienced by print media services, this suggests that the concept of videotex as a kind of electronic newspaper has not been successful.

Table 6 Communications Equipment in French Households in 1995

Equipment	Penetration rate
Television	95%
multiple sets	35%
Telephone	95%
Videocassette recorder	60%
CD player	60%
Video game station	35%
Minitel	35%
PC	20%
with CD-ROM	5%
with modem	3%

Source: Author's analysis

Issues and Propects for the Future

Which Conduits Will Carry Information Services?

Is building a brand new network necessary to develop the IS in France? This question constantly permeates the debate surrounding the IS and has been answered in different ways. "High tech Colbertists" call for a new infrastructure because they put the technical coherence of the network above demand. Their approach assumes that new infrastructure will create a demand for new services. It is also shaped by an egalitarian vision of the information society in which everybody should benefit from new technological developments.

For France Télécom, however, network developments should be incremental and linked to market niches. When demand appears for specific services, new infrastructures can be created. Only some categories of users would really need IS in the short term, but certainly not the "bike riders" (i.e., small users).[38]

The approach of French cable operators to the IS is mostly driven by their desire to get into telephone service rather than an overall vision of the information society. Their IS strategy is currently limited to upgrading their systems in specific areas.

Major actors in the content industry have adopted or prepared strategies that reveal that they remain uncertain about how they will provide their services in the future. While they envision the use of different kinds of telecommunication networks, multimedia companies continue to invest in products such as CD-ROMs, PCs software, and digital video disks as well as movie theaters. The Minitel industry even expressed some doubts about the necessity of building an IS. According to a Minitel representative, it would be enough to increase the speed of the Minitel network and to adapt modems to international standards (an investment estimated at Fr 200 million!) so that Minitel terminals could be replaced by PCs.[39]

What Is the Demand for Information Services?

The answer to the question of the conduits depends on the nature, range, and number of services to be carried on the IS as well as on the categories of users to serve, two elements which are still unclear. Will there really be a demand for online information? Do people really need the large quantities of information promised by the IS? Market estimates for information services vary greatly. The problem with such estimates is not so much their contradictory results as their conception of demand. The social dynamics shaping the demand for and uses of information services are rarely taken into account. For instance, much of the current IS vision is an extrapolation of how the Internet is presently used. But the professional characteristics of Internet users and their specific social environments are often neglected. This may lead to misinterpretations (such as the assumption that there is a global information market).

As recent research has shown, the introduction of information and communications technologies into homes involves a complex process based on gender and age-related factors and constrained by material factors such as the level of disposable income or the amount of space available for shared or private use. The economics of the IS will largely depend on the ability of operators and service providers to understand the "moral economy" of households (Silverstone et al. 1992).

Universal Access

Public authorities and politicians regularly insist on the necessity of providing everyone with access to the information society. Universal access to the IS as proposed by the Théry report has been endorsed by the French government. The Group of Seven also endorsed it at its Brussels meeting: "governments will have to preserve provision and access to services to all citizens (universal service), promote equal opportunity for all in the information age, and preserve and encourage the diversity of the content of information, in particular concerning its cultural and linguistic aspects." Yet one may wonder how universal access will be implemented and financed effectively. Is it not just lip service being paid to the liberalization of telecommunications?

Above all, it must be kept in mind that the concept of universal service was not originally shaped by social goals but linked to the telephone industry's need for an integrated market that would generate economies of scale. Theodore Vail, the founder of the Bell system in the United States, championed universal service as an ideal because it furthered his drive to achieve political support for the elimination of competition and the establishment of a regulated monopoly (Mueller 1993, p. 365). Only in the 1960s did the universal service concept take on an egalitarian shade when competition and antitrust lawsuits threatened to unravel the Bell system. Universal service then became a convenient defense for the preservation of the Bell system (Sawhney 1994). Much of the talk about universal service is rhetorical: its social glamour and appeal are exploited by groups only when it furthers their private agendas.

While the definition of universal service may appear simple to understand, a variety of meanings and expectations are associated with the concept. When the French use the term, it is likely that they do so in a different sense from Americans or EU bureaucrats. Yet until December 1995, many French people saw universal service as just a modern label for the old concept of public service. They understood universal service as encompassing social or political goals (what the French call *missions d'intérêt général*). The public debate over the industrial action of November and December 1995 put an end to this confusion and led the French government to commit itself to defending the *service public à la française*. In the telecommunications field, this means supporting various tasks that serve the general interests of society such as internal security and defense, basic research, public telecommunications training centers, and the development of rural or remote areas. This definition will have a tremendous impact on the development of competition in French telecommunications: new entrants will be expected to make a Fr 25 billion annual contribution to finance the *service public* charges.[40] It might also further complicate negotiations at the European level on the harmonization of the telecommunications regulatory framework.

Universal service can cynically be considered a trade-off between telecommunications operators and governments, in which the former provide a sort of social net in exchange for being granted greater freedom in their market. From this perspective, operators would define universal service as reaching the equilibrium point where the political acceptance of liberalization is maximized and the associated social costs are minimized. As a result, the scope of universal service will depend on the telecommunications politics that exist in a given country.

Yet universal service may be more than a mere token payment to enter a liberalized market. The definition of universal service introduces a critical moment in the creation of the IS because it raises the question of people's fundamental needs and the hierarchy of values that exists in any society. As such, it can reveal or catalyze social, cultural, or political concerns that have not been seriously addressed by policy makers. The outcome of this process is uncertain: some groups or countries may be using it to voice their dissent or challenge current IS policies. For instance, a "right to isolation" was recently asked for in France.[41] Although marginal, this claim expresses a reaction to an information society in which anybody can be reached at any time. Other demands of this sort may appear. If they are granted, universal service could, ironically enough, lead to a local disintegration of the global concept of the information society.

A Lack of Political and Ethical Vision

In both Europe as a whole and in France, liberalization is often said to be the key to the IS. But one may wonder whether the IS is not just a code name for liberalization.

As Volker Schneider has pointed out (Schneider 1995), there are two differences between the European debate on the IS and the NII initiative in the United States. First, the American initiative gives greater emphasis to the societal potential of the IS (e.g., its possible contribution to democratic life or to education) than the European policy, which is more driven by commercial interests. Second, the American policy process is more open than the European one. In the United States, a much more diverse array of interests has access to the various policy arenas via public hearings and institutionalized representation on the NII advisory council. European policy has been shaped more "secretly" and restricted to technocratic expert committees with a clear overrepresentation of commercial interests. Only recently has representation been broadened through the establishment of the European Information Society Forum in which experts and qualified persons from different countries address social and political issues.

The lack of democracy in European steps toward the information society has been underlined on several occasions. During the G-7 meeting in Brussels in February 1995, a countersummit was convened by about 30 French and Belgian organizations, including trade unions and the Belgian Greens, to denounce the lack of democratic debate surrounding the cultural, political, and social stakes of the information age. Participants, who included academics, artists, and members of the European Parliament, lashed out at the important role industrialists play in shaping the society of the future. On March 23–24, 1995, the Council of Europe held a colloquium on electronic democracy that criticized the EU for not adequately addressing the impact of the information society on political life. These groups are not radically opposed to the IS. They not only emphasize only the risks of the information society but also recognize its potential benefits. In other words, while policy makers and industry focus on the technical shaping of the information society, there is also demand for social shaping.

The diffusion of information services depends not only on technical infrastructure but also on social infrastructures. If we are to move to an information society, it will not suffice to upgrade networks, ensure their technical interconnectivity and interoperability, or change regulatory arrangements. Social structures also have to be adjusted.

The task is not easy in France. As the social crisis of November and December 1995 demonstrated, French society is not yet fully prepared for a global economy. The vote on the Maastricht Treaty and subsequent polls have shown that a significant number of French people are reluctant to embrace the single market and the single European currency. As Jacques Delors put it: "*Si les élites ont leur tête dans le monde global, la population a encore les pieds dans le territoire national*' (While elites have their mind on the global world, people still have their feet on national territories).

Compared to the United States, where the IS is the object of emphatic declarations, IS policy in France clearly lacks a political and ethical vision that could encompass current IS developments within a broader social project and help mobilize people. Beside their economic rationale, French public statements on the IS demonstrate a very poor, nonexistent, symbolic content and do not provide a vision for the future. Even in the sphere of rhetoric, which is supposed to be the prime locus of politics, the French government has withdrawn. Could it be that the French do not want to have a dream?

Appendix: State of Telecommunications Privatization in Europe (end of 1995)

Country	Public telecommunications operator	State of privatization
Belgium	Belgacom	49.9% in progress.
France	France Télécom	Partial. Postponed to 1996 due to union opposition.
Germany	Deutsche Telekom	25% planned for mid-1996. An other 25% two years later. Privatization to be carried out through a subsequent increase of capital, while the German govern ment would retain its shares until the year 2000.
Greece	OTE	6–8% planned in 1996. Previous attempts to privatize 49% and then 25% failed due to political and union opposition.
Italy	STET	Planned for 1996.
Ireland	Telecom Eireann	Sale of 35% planned.
Netherlands	Koninklijke PTT Nederland (KPN)	30% privatized in 1994. Sale of another third in progress. Gov ernment does not intend to reduce its stake to less than one-third before 2004.
Portugal	Portugal Telecom (PT)	25–30% planned for 1996.
Spain	Telefonica	12% sold in fall 1995, which reduces the state's stake to 20%.
Sweden	Telia	Planned by 1997.
United Kingdom	British Telecom	100% completed.

Source: Author's analysis

Notes

This paper is part of a comparative study on NII in the US, France, Japan, Korea, and Singapore sponsored by CRITO (University of California at Irvine) and the Korean National Computerization Agency.

1. The notions of grand projet and high tech colbertism refer to the development model for French high tech industries (the space industry, telecommunications, aeronautics, the nuclear industry). It designates a type of government-industry relations involving a complex of actors—public administrations, public research centers, public operators, private manufacturers—linked together by common values and goals and based on huge public procurement (see Salomon 1987, Brenac 1991, Cohen 1992). French elites—*les grands corps techniques*—play an instrumental role in this linkage by providing communication channels and sharing the same technical culture. (see Vedel 1984).

2. For reasons explained below, France Télécom did not lobby in favor of the IS.

3. "I cannot stand the idea that someday I will have to read the catalogue of Le Louvre Museum in English on an American database," said Michel Serres, a famous philosopher, on a TV show.

4. In particular, the question raised by the Bangemann Report of "whether the information society will be a strategic creation for the whole Union, or a more fragmented amalgam of individual initiatives by Member States" (p.5) was not addressed.

5. Closing statement at the Conference on IS organized by the French Ministry of Industry, Paris, December 1994. Note that, in French, the plural is used to designate the IS.

6. On the notion of interpretative flexibility, see Pinch and Bijker (1984) and Bijker and Law (1992).

7. Loi du 29 décembre 1990 relative à la réglementation des télécommunications. depending on their nature, services are either fully liberalized, or submitted to a licensing process.

8. Lorente (1995) argues that, in an unexpected way, the Clinton-Gore Agenda for action puts much more emphasis on the role of the state than does the Bangemann Report.

9. France Télécom experts strongly disagree with Théry's figures and provide costs estimates considerably higher: up to FF 30,000 to equip each household with fiber to the home.during the first years

10. Colloquium on "Les autoroutes et services de l'information." Paris, December 7, 1994.

11. I use the future tense since this debate has so far not taken place (with the exception of a one-day conference devoted to the presentation of government policy).

12. Eloquent evidence of such flexibility is that applicants for trials were asked to indicate in their proposals what regulatory, technical, or financial provisions they would need from public authorities.

13. José Rossi, Minister of Industry, Post and Telecommunications, and Trade, at the Colloquium on "Les autoroutes et services de l'information." Paris, December1994.

14. On the French cable plan, see Vedel and Dutton (1990).

15. For the full list of pilot projects selected by the French government, see the Ministry of PTT Web site: http:// www.telecom.gouv.fr/

16. Not including the 14,9 billion FF "contribution" that France Télécom has to make to the state budget.

17. With the prospect of possible privatization, such management is indeed indispensable, given France Télécom's debts. In September 1995, France Télécom Chairman Marcel Roulet was replaced by Michel Bon. It is interesting to note that for the first time in the company history, the new head is not a telecommunications engineer, but comes from the food distribution sector.

18. Personal interviews, July 1994 and November 1995. See also Busson 1995.

19. Cable operators have now turned to coaxial or hybrid systems.

20. With the notable exception of Canal Plus, a pay-TV station. Canal Plus's annual revenues amount to FF 10 billion and its net profits to FF 1 billion. Canal Plus is also an integrated group with subsidiaries in decoders manufacturing, TV and film production, and satellite operation. Canal Plus has developed its pay-TV activities in Belgium, Germany, Spain, Poland,and various African countries.

21. Bertelsmann and Canal Plus are already partners in Premiere, a German pay-TV channel.

22. In 1984, foreign VCRs had to be cleared through customs in Poitiers, a medium-sized city 400 km from Paris without an international airport. This delayed the penetration of foreign equipment for a while.

23. Loi du 30 septembre 1986 relative à la liberté de communication.

24. On neocorporatism in general as well as in France in particular, see respectively: Schmitter and Lehmbruch 1979; Wilson 1987.

25. Loi du 2 juillet 1990 relative à l'organisation des Postes et télécommunications; loi du 29 décembre 1990 relative à la réglementation des infrastructures et services de télécommunications.

26. The title and responsibilities of this ministry may change depending on the government. It is only since 1988 that the Ministry of Industry has supervised telecommunications and postal activities. However, most of the time, the Minister of Industry is associated with an adjunct Minister for Post and Telecommunications (known as *Ministre délégué* or *Secrétaire d'Etat*). It should also be noted that from May to September 1995 there existed a Minister of Information Technologies and Post (who had the same responsibilities as the former and current Minister of Post and Telecommunications).

27. In the case of videotex, a Commission comprised of representatives of ministries and interest groups and MPs was established to survey and assess telematics trials. In the case of the cable plan, a *Mission Câble* (task force for cable) was set up to foster cable projects, disseminate regulatory and technical information, and contribute to the sharing of experiences.

28. Members include: the Association of Commercial Television in Europe (which groups private TV stations), British Telecom, Canal Plus, Compaq, the European Publishers Council, France Télécom, ICL, Mercury, nCube, Oracle, Philips, Silicon Graphics, Sony and Thomson.

29. The ERT, which is chaired by Carlo De Benedetti, the head of Olivetti and a member of the Bangemann group, stressed that the current liberalization process within the EU is too slow. Unice's June 1994 report, Making Europe More Competitive—Towards World Class Performance, called for an overhaul of the European public sector, including the privatization of telecommunications, postal, energy, transport, and social services.

30. This was the case of the DVB: four of the largest TV companies (TF1, CLT, BBC, and ITV) did not endorse the agreement for a common encryption standard.

31. Survey commissioned by GESTE (a service providers association).

32. This section is based on the author's analysis of France Télécom data published in *La Lettre de Télétel et Audiotel.*

33. Unfortunately, only a few services are available through gateways open to PC users. And the other high-speed gateways require the purchase of a specific modem.

34. In Germany, a license used to be required for modems.

35. Investigation is examining the following aspects: fair access by other online services to the publications controlled by Europe Online's founders, the potential for other groups to offer content under conditions similar to those enjoyed by Europe Online's founders, and the existence of noncompetition agreements with third companies.

36. For further developments on the politics and lessons of Stone Age telematics in France, Germany and the United Kingdom, see Vedel et al. 1995.

37. This Christmas toy effect probably comes into play for the Internet. However, it does not have a global impact as long as additional users continue to join the network.

38. This metaphor was used by fomer France Télécom Chairman, Marcel Roulet: "Bike riders do not need highways."

39. Antoine Beaussant, "Les éditeurs télématiques français sont prêts pour l'après-Minitel," *Le Monde,* November 2, 1994, p.13. Beaussant, the head of GESTE, an information providers association, also criticizes the hype about the IS and the Internet. "The Minitel has been providing for years a variety of services which are just being discovered on Internet (...). We in France have known the cyberpizza for ten years," he writes ironically.

40. *Le Monde,* January 10,1996, p. 20.

41. Yves Lasfargue, representative of the CFDT, a French trade union, at the

Conference on Les autoroutes et services de l'information organized by the Ministry of industry, Paris, December 7,1994.

References

Bijker, Wiebe E., and Law John (eds.), 1992. *Shaping Technology/ Building Society: Studies in Sociotechnical Change.* Cambridge, MA: MIT Press.

Brenac, Edith, 1991. "La grande technologie entre l'Etat et le marché." Actes du séminaire international des 8–9 novembre 1990, Université Pierre Mendès-France, Grenoble.

Breton, Thierry, 1994. *Les téléservices en France. Quels marchés pour les autoroutes de l'information?* Paris: La Documentation française.

Busson, Alain, 1995. "France Télécom et les autoroutes de l'information: le client, le service et la technologie." *Communications & Strategies,* no. 19, 3ème trimestre, pp. 95–116.

Cave, Martin, and Mark Shurmer, 1995. "Business Strategy and Regulation of Multi-media in the UK." *Communications & Strategies,* no. 19, 3ème trimestre, pp. 117–140.

Cohen, Elie, 1992. *Le colbertisme high tech. Economie des télécom et du grand projet.* Paris: Hachette.

Conseil Supérieur de l'Audiovisuel, 1995. *Avis du CSA sur le projet de loi sur les autoroutes de l'information.* Paris, October 24.

Collins, Richard, 1994. "Convergence between Telecommunications and Television. Technological Change, Regulatory Lag and the Case of Satellite Television in the European Commudnity." Paper presented at the Symposium international sur la convergence des techniques de communication, Université du Québec à Montréal, September 29–October 1.

Dupuis, Patrick, 1995. "Téléservices et collectivités locales. Nouvelle société ou nouveaux marchés?" *Pouvoirs locaux: Les cahiers de la décentralisation,* no. 25, June, pp. 19–24.

European Commission, 1993. *Growth, Competitiveness, Employment. The Challenges and Ways Forward into the 21st Century* (The White Paper). Brussels.

European Commission, 1994. *Strategy Options to Strengthen the European Programme Industry in the Context of the Audiovisual Policy of the European Union* (The Audiovisual Green Paper). Brussels.

Guieysee, Michel, Lionel Levasseur, and Etienne Turpin, 1995. "Du chalcolthique aux grands boulevards de l'information: techniques, services et économie du multimédia." *Communication & Strategies,* no. 19, 3ème trimestre, pp. 141–172.

High-Level Group on the Information Society, 1994. *Europe and the Global Information Society. Recommendations to the European Council* (The Bangemann Report). Brussels.

Lasserre, Bruno, 1994. *Quelle réglementation pour les télécommunications françaises?* Report prepared for the Minister of Industry, Posts and Telecommunications, and Trade. Paris, March.

Lorente, Santiago, 1995. "Similarities and Differences between the Gore Report and the Bangemann Report." Paper presented at the International Conference on "The Social Shaping of IS—Comparing the NII and the EU Action Plan," Bremen, October 5–7.

Ministère de l'Industrie, des Postes et Télécommunications et du Commerce Extérieur, 1994. *Les autoroutes de l'information. Appel à propositions.* Interventions et débats de la journée d'information du 19 décembre. Paris.

Ministère de l'Industrie, des Postes et Télécommunications et du Commerce Extréieur, 1994. *Les autoroutes et services de l'information,* Actes du colloque du 7 décembre. Paris.

Mueller, M., 1993. "Universal Service in Telephone History: A Reconstruction." *Telecommunications Policy,* 17, pp. 352–369.

Pinch, Trevor J., and Wiebe E. Bijker, 1984. "The Social Construction of Facts and Artefacts, or How the Sociology of Science and the Sociology of Technology Might Benefit Each Other." *Social Studies of Science,* 14, pp. 399–441.

Sawhney, Harmeet, 1994. "Universal Service: Prosaic Motives and Great Ideals." *Journal of Broadcasting & Electronic Media,* 38(4), pp. 375–395.

Schneider, Volker, 1995. "Different Roads to the Information Society? Comparing the US and European Approaches from a Comparative Public Policy Perspective." Paper presented at the International Conference on "The Social Shaping of IS—Comparing the NII and the EU Action Plan," Bremen, October 5–7.

Silverstsone, R., E. Hirsch, and D. Morley, 1992. "Information and Communication Technologies and the Moral Economy of the Household." In R. Silverstone and E. Hirsch (eds.), *Consuming Technologies* (London: Routledge).

Schmitter, Phillip, and Gerhard Lehmbruch (eds.), 1979. *Trends toward Corporatist Intermediation.* London: Sage.

Théry, Gérard, 1994. *Les autoroutes de l'information. Rapport au Premier Ministre.* Paris: La Documentation française.

Vedel, Thierry, 1984. "Les ingénieurs des télécommunications. Formation d'un grand corps." *Culture technique,* March. pp. 63–75.

Vedel, Thierry, and William Duton, 1990. "New Media Politics: Shaping Cable Television Policy in France." *Media, Culture and Society,* 12, pp. 491–524.

Vedel, Thierry, Graham Thomas, and Volker Schneider, 1995. "Lessons from Stone-Age Telematics. What Can We Learn from Videotex and Audiotex Experiences in Europe?" Paper presented at the 23rd Telecommunications Policy Research Conference, Solomon, MD, September 30–October 2.

Wilson, Franck, 1987. *Interest-Group Politics in France.* Cambridge: Cambridge University Press.

Public Policy and the Information Superhighway: The Case of the United Kingdom

Andrew Graham

Introduction

This chapter discusses UK policy related to the development of an information superhighway (IS). The first part sets the context by describing the telecommunications and media markets in the UK and highlighting how they have changed in terms of both delivery mechanisms and patterns of consumption. The second part provides the policy background with regard to telecommunications and broadcasting. The third part gives an account of the main policy developments toward the IS itself. The fourth part discusses the main policy issues that have arisen in the UK. The Appendix provides a summary of the main regulatory institutions in the UK that are relevant to the IS.

Some further introductory remarks may be helpful. First, a Conservative government has been in power in the UK continuously since 1979, and its economic philosophy has rested heavily on privatization, liberalization, and a belief in the merits of consumer sovereignty operating via market forces. Policy toward the IS therefore needs to be seen not in isolation but as part of a far wider program. Second, the government established a policy framework designed, at least in part, to encourage the development of cable, and by 1994 the cable industry was growing rapidly. Nevertheless, it started from near zero. Thus, even by 1994 the UK cable industry was still tiny (less than 3 percent of total telecom revenue, making the UK cable sector smaller than those of almost all other European Union (EU) countries and minute in comparison with that of the

United States). Third, although the government has begun to move broadcasting toward a greater reliance on consumer sovereignty, UK broadcasting continues to be strongly influenced by public service considerations, dominated by national channels, and free at the point of use (this being one major reason cable television penetration in the UK remains so limited).

These points about market forces, the liberalization of telecommunications, and consumer sovereignty in broadcasting are relevant to later discussion. The fourth part of this chapter takes up the questions of whether UK policy toward the IS has shown an excessive reliance on market forces, whether liberalization was the best way to promote the infrastructure, and whether content on the IS can be left entirely to consumer sovereignty.

The last general point to keep in mind about the UK is that there has been almost no debate about the goals or purposes of the IS. There are two reasons for this. One is the single party dominance of the government for the last 16 years: most of the important discussion has been *within* the governing party and *within* government departments. Moreover, since all Conservatives support the market in general (a consensus that even the opposition parties no longer challenge), much of the argument is merely a question of degree. The other is that, for much of the Conservative Party, competition and choice are both means and ends. Policy needs no other justification beyond the fact that it increases competition. Nevertheless, muted though the debate has been, it is not *just* about the extent of the market. In broadcasting, at least some of the debate is about high culture versus popular culture or about national interest versus individual interest. There are also Conservatives who support free competition and wish UK firms to play a global role, two aims that are not always complementary. However, it is helpful at the outset to see policy as primarily driven by a strong desire to liberalize and to promote competition, inward investment, open trade, and free capital markets. Yet, simultaneously, policy is constantly being constrained by countervailing tendencies, including both political/ideological influences and the force of circumstances.

The Telecommunications and Media Markets in the UK

In considering policy toward the IS it is useful to set the market context. This section discusses how the telecommunications and media markets have been changing and identifies the main companies involved. Tables 1 and 2 summarize the main changes, from the early 1980s to the present. Table 1 focuses on delivery mechanisms, and Table 2 on patterns of consumption.

The Main Structural Changes: Delivery and Consumption

Along with those of all other countries, the UK's telecommunications industry mechanisms and media markets have been transformed in recent years by technical change in delivery. Table 1 shows that in 1981 the UK had two public telephone operators (and one of these, Kingston Communications, operated only in Hull), whereas today there are some 30 (or more than 150 if all the cable companies are included). In 1981 there were three television and about 60 radio stations, whereas today there are at least 37 television channels and more than 200 radio stations. Moreover, if the proposals for digital terrestrial television broadcasting currently before Parliament proceed, the number of television channels could rise in the next year or so to more than 50. In 1981, almost no homes were connected to cable television; today there are a million (or about four percent of households).

Consumption has also changed. Table 2 summarizes household consumption of communication and media products and compares these figures to those for consumer durables. There has been a significant increase in the proportion of households with telephones (from 75 percent in 1981 to 91 percent in 1994), and whereas in the early 1980s very few households had video recorders and almost none had CD players or home computers, the percentages with these items by 1994 were 77 percent, 47 percent, and 24 percent respectively. It is important, however, not to over emphasize the change. Only the rise in video recorders is out of the ordinary. The rate at which households in the UK have been purchasing CD players is parallel to the increased popularity of microwave ovens, and the growth of home computer purchases, after an initial jump, is currently slower than those of deep freezers, central heating, or tumble dryers in the past.

In an interesting paper looking over a longer period, Milne (1994) finds that in the UK adoption of telephones proceeded at a similar rate to central heating, and that the UK has lagged behind

Table 1 Communications and the Media: Delivery

	1981	1995
Fixed Service Telephone Operators	2	150+
Telephone Lines[a] (millions)	18.17	28.35
BT		27.07
Mercury		0.24
Cable		0.87
Kingston		0.17
Cellular Telephone Operators	nil	4
Homes Passed by Cable	neg.	5.0m[b]
Homes Connected to Cable	neg.	1.0m[b]
TV Channels	3	3
Radio Stations	60+	200+
Daily National Newspapers	9	11
Sunday Newspapers	7	10

a. As of March 31.
b. July 1995.
Sources: OFTEL, BBC, CCA, ITC, Social Trends.

the United States by as much as 25 years in the spread of telephones. Moreover, in the UK, as elsewhere, both telephone ownership and computer ownership are strongly correlated with income (Policy Studies Institute, 1995). Such observations are warnings both about how fast the move to an IS might be and about how incompletely it might be adopted.

It is also noticeable that the expansion of the means of delivering material to consumers has not had a dramatic effect on habits. The number of people physically attending events such as Wimbledon or the Grand National has either remained unchanged or risen over the last decade. Of course such national events often have persistent excess demand, but total visits to places where excess demand is not usually a problem, such as the National Gallery or the British Museum or Madame Tussaud's, have also increased substantially. Still more striking is that the time spent watching television has hardly changed at all, that the readership of newspapers has only declined slowly, that the number of videotapes rented per week did not change from the mid-1980s to the early 1990s, and that the number attending cinemas, after falling rapidly from the 1950s to the 1980s, has since been *rising*—slowly, judged from total

Table 2 Communications and the Media: Consumption

	1981	1984	1991	1994
1. Consumer Durables: Percentage of Households with:				
Video Recorder	n.a.	24	68	77
CD Player	n.a.	n.a.	27	47
Home Computer	n.a.	9	21	24
Telephone	75	78	88	91
Microwave Oven	n.a.	n.a.	55	67
Deep Freezer	49	61	83	88
Central Heating	59	66	82	85
Tumble Drier	23	29	48	50
2. Expenditure[a] (%)				
Radio and TV, etc	1.3	1.6	1.2	1.1
Books & Newspapers	1.4	1.4	1.3	1.3
Education	0.9	0.8	1.1	1.3
Other Recreation	4.8	5.1	5.1	5.1
Total Rec. Ent. & Ed.	9.2	9.2	9.7	9.9
3. Cinema Attendance[b]	n.a.	38	61	69[c]
4. Newspaper Readership (millions)				
Daily	31.8[d]	29.8[e]		27.4[f]
Sunday	33.2	32.8		30.9

a. Percent of total consumers' expenditure.
b. Percent of population making "occasional" visit.
c. 1993. d. 1983. e. 1986. f. 1993–1994.
Sources: Social Trends, General Household Survey

attendance data, but dramatically, as measured by the proportion of the population that attends occasionally (see Table 2).

Such relative stability of habits could have two different implications for the IS. On the one hand, it could be that consumers are rationally resistant to new technology while the entry costs in time, effort and expenditure are high. We need to remember that for many people computers are still viewed today as cars were in the 1920s—as something to be indulged in only by experts or by people with a strange fascination with the inner workings of machines. On the other hand, even after computers have become more physically accessible, more reliable, and more user friendly, consumers might still prove resistant to the new technology.

There is, of course, a major point that data on consumption cannot show. Much direct observation suggests that the main impact of the IS may be less on which goods and services are produced than on how they are produced, where they are produced, and how they are sold. Examples are everywhere. Business communication by fax and e-mail has partly replaced traditional methods; in the financial services sector, significant reductions in employment are occurring in the UK (and elsewhere) as direct banking and direct insurance replace the physical branch network while in manufacturing and distribution, direct marketing and teleshopping are fundamentally recasting the economy. But while examples abound, good data measuring the degrees of substitution are hard to obtain.

The Major Companies

In the early 1980s the major telecommunications company was British Telecom (BT), while in the media the BBC, the ITV, companies and the major newspaper groups were predominant. In the 1990s, these have been joined by cable companies (see Table 4) and satellite broadcasting. However, as Table 3 shows, neither the aggregate call revenue of the cable companies nor the total expenditure on satellite broadcasting is yet especially large in comparison with either BT's revenues or various other forms of expenditure on the media.

Table 3 has two limitations. First, satellite broadcasting revenue has been growing very rapidly since 1993. Second, the table does not allow for overlapping ownership or display the pressures toward convergence created by the new technology. Table 5 (from Robinson 1995) deals, to some extent, with the second of these problems by showing the market shares of the main companies in the media market taken as a whole. The first column gives the market shares that result from combining the different activities in terms of "reach" (the number who see or read a particular prod-

Table 3 Communications and the Media: Revenue and Market Shares

A. Media	Revenue, 1993 (£m)	% of Media
Terrestrial TV	2930	19.6
Satellite	471	3.2
Radio	556	3.7
National Press	2762	18.5
Regional Press	2342	15.7
Consumer Magazines	1460	9.8
Books	2699	18.1
Cinema	361	2.4
Video Rental and Sales	1171	7.9
Theaters	216	1.4
Total	14,968	100.0

B. Communications	Retail Call Revenue, 1994/5 (£m)	% of Communications
BT	4,790	84.3
Mercury	704	12.4
Kingston	29	0.5
Cable	119	2.1
Others	42	0.7
Total	5,683	100.0

C. Reference Items	1994 (£m)
Total UK Consumer Expenditure	428,084
UK Consumer Expenditure on Recreation, Entertainment, and Education	42,584

Sources: Robinson (1995), OFTEL, CSO.

uct); the second column gives the shares based on revenue, and the third column on simple time use. Several other studies have been done in the UK showing additional measures. However, for reasons developed elsewhere (Graham 1995b), it is doubtful whether such figures are much help to public policy. In particular, any combination uses arbitrary weights and any aggregate figures of this kind fail to reflect the fundamentally different purposes of commercial firms and public service broadcasters.

Table 4 UK Cable Operators, Ranking by Equity Ownership, 1995

	Homes Passed (thousands)
TeleWest	3,757
Nynex	2,502
Bell Cablemedia	1,904
CableTel	1,630
Diamond	868
General Cable	843
Comcast	752
Videotron	712
Singapore	619
Telecential	614
Eurobell	337
Caledonian	195
IVS	139
British Telecom	120
English Cable Enterprises	106

Source: Cable Communications Association.

Table 5 Market Shares of Top 12 Media Companies, 1993

	Reach	Revenue	Simple Time Use
BBC	26.0%	17.5%	44.9%
(ITV Network)	9.6%	16.0%	25.4%
Channel 4	8.5%	3.6%	5.6%
News International	7.2%	11.6%	4.5%
Daily Mail	5.7%	6.5%	1.2%
Daily Mirror	5.1%	6.0%	1.8%
United Newspapers	4.6%	5.7%	1.1%
Carlton	3.2%	5.3%	8.0%
Pearson	2.5%	5.3%	1.2%
Granada	2.4%	4.1%	5.8%
Guardian Media	2.0%	1.6%	0.2%
Capital Radio	1.5%	0.3%	3.9%
Conrad Black	1.0%	3.3%	0.4%
Total Share of 12 Companies	69.7%	70.8%	78.7%

Notes: Reach: proportion of number of viewers, listeners, and readers of all media products in a given time period (week). Revenue: share of revenue of all media companies in a given year. Simple Time Use: proportion of time spent consuming media products in a given period.
Source: Robinson 1995.

The Policy Background: Telecommunications and Broadcasting

Telecommunications Policy

UK telecommunications policy has had a major influence on policy toward the IS. Indeed, it almost *is* the policy. At the very beginning of the Conservative government's first serious policy statement on the IS in 1994 was the statement that "the UK enjoys a real advantage over its main international competitors: because of the [telecommunications] regulatory and policy framework."[1] What then was this framework, and are the strong results claimed for it justified?

The fundamental features of UK telecommunications policy according to the government have been "privatization and then market liberalization begun in 1984 and further developed in 1991 as a result of the review of the telecommunications duopoly."[2] However, to these must be added two features that the government chooses not to emphasize. First, there is conduct and price control regulation (based on the retail price index less an efficiency factor, or "RPI minus X"), and second, there is what might be called "assisted" competition. The strength of both of these is determined by the regulator, the Office of Telecommunications (OFTEL), also established in 1984. Evidence suggests that regulation of prices has been particularly important and strongly complementary to the other three approaches (Armstrong, Cowan and Vickers 1994).

Although the evolution of this policy is well known, a brief chronology is given in Table 6 and a summary of the main developments is as follows. The publicly owned monopoly supplier of fixed telephone networks, British Telecom, was privatized in 1984. At the same time, the fledgling competitor Mercury, first licensed in 1982, was licensed for a further 25 years with the guarantee that no other suppliers would be licensed before 1990. This step was judged necessary to give Mercury the incentive to take on the incumbent. Mercury, however, made few inroads into BT's market between 1984 and 1990, and BT continued to totally dominate residential lines and local calls.

At the same time, the government tried to encourage a cable television industry. Eleven pilot franchises were awarded in 1983, and in 1984 the Cable Authority was established to administer the

Table 6 Main Developments in UK Policy: Telecoms

1982	Mercury licensed to run a Public Telephone Operator
1983	Government announces forthcoming duopoly in fixed-network telecom operations
1984	Telecommunications Act (licenses Mercury and creates OFTEL)
1984	Privatization of British Telecom (51 percent of the shares sold)
1984	Cable and Broadcasting Act sets up Cable Authority
1989	Liberalization of resale of leased capacity on telecom lines within the UK
1989	Government selects three consortia to provide digital cellular phone networks, or personal communication networks (PCNs)—Mercury PCN, Microtel Communications, and Unitel
1991	White Paper *Competition and Choice: Telecommunications Policy for the 1990s* ends the duopoly of BT and Mercury and allows cable companies to provide telephone service in their own right
1993	(September) Mercury One-2-One launches PCN service
1994	(November 17) BT announces home services experiment at same time as US West is raising funds
1995	(July 26) OFTEL publishes a new regime for competition, *Effective Competition: Framework for Action*
1995	(July) OFTEL publishes consultative document, *The Future Regulation of Premium Rate Services*, which proposes separate charges for conveyance and call content and that PTOs should introduce plans to achieve such "unbundling" by the end of 1996
1995	(August 7) OFTEL publishes consultative paper on the future regulation of broadband switched mass-market (BSM) services, *Beyond the Telephone, the Television and the PC*
1995	(October) Leader of the Labour Party announces understanding with BT
1995	(December) OFTEL publishes its consultation document on universal service, *Universal Telecommunications Services*

franchising process and to regulate and promote the industry. However, cable television failed to establish itself at this stage because firms were small, the City proved reluctant to finance them, and there were changes in depreciation allowances that reduced cash flow.

The upshot of these two developments was that when the government came to review telecoms policy in 1990, neither Mercury in practice nor the cable companies potentially presented any serious competition to BT (certainly not in the local loop). Moreover, the government was criticized, with some reason, for having replaced a nationalized industry with a private monopoly. As a result, the 1991 White Paper *Competition and Choice: Telecommunications Policy for the 1990s* recommended major changes. The domestic telephone market was opened to other operators (including non-EU companies). In terms of the IS, the most important change was that cable companies were allowed to carry telephone services in their own right (not just as agents of BT or Mercury, as had been the case), while public telephone operators (PTOs) were still restricted from conveying or providing entertainment.

At the time, the UK was the only country in the world where cable companies were allowed to carry telephone calls while the national telephone company was not allowed to carry television. The result was an explosion of interest in cable. The companies entering the British cable market, many of them from the United States, included both telephone and cable television companies, and each was keen to learn about a new market while still able to operate from its traditional base. In the following three years, the number of homes connected to cable television quadrupled and telephone connections by cable companies, which were nil in 1991, grew to over 300,000 by January 1994, and to one million by July 1995.

Notwithstanding the arrival of the cable companies and their importance in the local loop within particular areas, BT continues to dominate both traffic and total lines, and in the market as a whole the power of the incumbent has been such that the government has been forced to retain a significant degree of regulation (in fact, the regulator, OFTEL, has recently been trying to update its power in ways that give it more rather than less influence). OFTEL's main impact comes via its control of prices. It is allowed to set a formula that requires a basket of BT's prices to rise by less than the retail price index (RPI). This formula, known as "RPI minus X," has been progressively tightened (the "X" was increased from –3% in 1984 to –4.5% in 1989, to –6.25% in 1991, and to –7.5% in 1993). In addition, OFTEL has been developing the policy of "assisted competition," i.e., giving a degree of protection to the cable companies via a lower contribution to the so-called "access deficit" charge. This charge is the cost to BT that arises from restrictions on BT's charges to customers for line connection and line rental—restrictions imposed, in part, in the interest of achieving universal service.

Three aspects of this history of telecommunications policy are important to subsequent policy toward the IS. First, there is the continuing conscious attempt to "promote" competition by encouraging the cable companies. Second, and intimately related to this, is the ongoing dispute over whether BT should be allowed to provide and convey entertainment services over its lines. Currently BT may provide video-on-demand but not broadcast services. What is at issue here is whether the cable companies will build their infrastructure if BT is allowed to carry identical material over its infrastructure and thus whether the cable companies plus BT, or just BT alone, will be the main carriers of the new services on the IS. It may well be that the demand will only justify one highway and that the desire to promote competition on the highway, understandable as that is, is inconsistent with the highway being laid down in the first place. Third, there is the critical fact that, despite cable's rapid expansion, its market share remains small compared with BT's. As discussed later, BT remains sufficiently dominant for the opposition Labour Party to have reached an arrangement with it in which permission to provide entertainment is used as the lever to persuade BT to provide networks for free to public places.

Broadcasting Policy

Broadcasting policy in the UK has implications for policy toward the IS for three main reasons. First, for many years to come, most people will continue to receive the majority of television services via this broadcasting source. This is especially so in the UK where there is a well-established national framework of channels providing what is generally considered high quality broadcasting that is free at the moment of use. In other words, regardless of whether broadcasting is considered part of the IS, it will certainly be a large source of information.

Second, the vibrancy of the UK's national terrestrial channels (which are about to be expanded to include digital terrestrial) affects the number and quality of alternative systems such as cable and satellite in quite complex ways. The presence of a good quality national broadcaster might, for example, raise the quality of the whole system and yet at the same time constrain the expansion of broadband switched communications or multi-channel broadcasting. The size, the direction, and even the desirability of such effects can be disputed, but what cannot be ignored is that broadcasting, and thus broadcasting policy, influences IS policy.

Third, British broadcasting is especially important to a debate that is only now beginning about what regulation, if any, should apply to the content of the IS. In the UK, a sharp distinction exists between the regulation of broadcasting and the regulation of the press: the first is regulated in significant ways by statutorily appointed bodies, and the second is virtually free of direct regulation (though not of the influence of a wide range of laws; see Appendix). The question is therefore which of these models (if either) will predominate in the case of the IS. UK policy on broadcasting provides some pointers.

Table 7 provides a summary chronology. The relevant starting point was the major inquiry set up by the government, the Peacock Committee (Cmnd 9824). This inquiry was charged with examining the future financing of the BBC but chose to interpret its remit as the future of broadcasting. The idea that captured the imagination of the Peacock Committee was the suggestion of the economist and commentator Peter Jay that broadcasting is nothing more than electronic publishing. Thus, once there is no technical scarcity of channels (either because of satellites, digital broadcasting, or fiber-optic cables), the Committee thought that "no regulation would be necessary, save that to maintain standards of taste and decency."[3] Consistent with this, the Peacock Committee also recommended a gradual transition to a more competitive delivery structure. The number of channels available via terrestrial, cable, and satellite broadcast were all expected to expand. Most fundamentally, apart from some minimal qualifications, the demand for particular channels, or even particular programs, was to be decided by consumer sovereignty in the market via a transition to subscription channels or pay-per-view.

In practice, the shift to consumer sovereignty in the intervening decade has been much smaller than the Peacock Committee or the

Table 7   Main Developments in UK Policy: Broadcasting

1986	Peacock Committee report Financing the BBC
1988	White Paper *Broadcasting in the '90s: Competition, Choice and Quality*
1989	Sky Television begins direct broadcasting by satellite
1990	Broadcasting Act. ITC replaces IBA, allows non-EU companies to control cable franchises and introduces local delivery service licenses in place of the existing franchise system
1990	British Satellite Broadcasting begins broadcasting
1990	Merger of British Satellite Broadcasting and Sky Television to form BSkyB
1993	(August) Cable Television Association argues that video-on-demand requires a local delivery service license under the Broadcasting Act of 1990
1993	(September) ITC states that video on demand would not fall within the purview of the Broadcasting Act of 1990
1994	Publication of House of Commons National Heritage Committee report on *Sports Sponsorship and Television Coverage*
1994	In *The Future of the BBC: Serving the Nation, Competing World-Wide* the government publishes its proposals for the renewal of the BBC Charter due in 1996.
1995	(May) Publication of White Paper *Media Ownership: The Government's Proposals* discussing the convergence of technologies and the need to define a "total media market" and to relax cross-media ownership rules
1995	(August) Publication of White Paper *Digital Terrestrial Broadcasting: The Government's Proposals* (London HMSO) (see December) with proposals for digital terrestrial broadcasting via multiplexers with 12-year licenses and no fixed date for switching off analogue
1995	(December) Publication of Broadcasting Bill in the House of Lords (HL Bill 19) incorporating revised proposals on digital terrestrial broadcasting and cross-media ownership

then government (led by Mrs. Thatcher, it should be remembered) either expected or hoped. There are five main reasons for this: (a) the ethos of public service broadcasting, (b) dissimilarities between the press and broadcasting, (c) the concern of the government not to damage (at least not too obviously) the widely recognized success of the BBC (and allied to this the BBC's potential as a global player in the world media market), (d) the slow development of cable in the 1980s; and, linked to this, (e) considerable uncertainty about the appropriate moves to be made by either the private sector or the government in a period of rapid technical change.

The influence of the public service ethos and the confusion within the government about the direction in which to go can clearly be seen in the debate and publications that followed Peacock. The House of Commons Home Affairs Committee third report, *The Future of Broadcasting* (1988), said that, from its outset, British broadcasting has been dominated by the principles of public service broadcasting. This has implied a strong concern that broadcasting should be used for the national good rather than for the benefit of particular interest groups; it should be universal in its reach, free at the point of use, free from government intervention in its day-to-day affairs and in the content of its programs and committed to informing and educating as well as entertaining and to promoting quality programs with high technical and artistic standards that extend the public tastes rather than take it as given.[4] Still more important was the evidence of Minister of State Tim Renton, who added that these principles were expected to guide the commercial channels as much as the BBC.[5] Such arguments directly conflict with allowing or encouraging the provision of broadcasting to be driven purely by consumer sovereignty.

The government also found that Jay's analogy between the press and broadcasting has proved more complicated than it at first seemed, in large part because of the intrusiveness of television. Almost without choice, television is in the home, with anything available to be seen by anyone. This characteristic has been associated with public concern over the "quality" of television (the government was forced to amend its 1990 legislation to allow more of a role for quality in the allocation of licenses) and with public demands for content regulation (especially of sex and violence) far more stringent than for the press.

Broadcasting has also proved to be different from the press in two other ways, at least in the UK. First, the view that having paid the television license fee residents should be able to see national events and national sports for free has proved highly resilient. At the time of writing (January 1996), Parliament is debating whether to restore the special position of the national broadcasters to bid for such events and whether to increase the number of such events. Second, there continues to be concern about the special importance of television in a democratic society and about the complex relationship between the power of television and ideas of community and citizenship (Graham and Davies, 1992).

A third strand, of increasing importance as large mergers among media companies are occurring, is the concern that UK broadcasters should be large enough to compete internationally. Broadcasting and the media are increasingly being seen as areas in which the UK might have a comparative advantage and which should therefore be promoted not for the sake of consumer welfare or cultural goals but for industrial goals.

Much has changed since Peacock. The number of channels has increased, and satellite and cable television have expanded from a negligible amount to some 15 percent of the British market (in terms of broadcast time). Satellite television, in particular, has grown because it has escaped (or was allowed to escape) most of the regulations of the 1990 Broadcasting Act. Nevertheless, the result has been that far more traditional broadcasting has been left in place than might have been expected in 1986.

Two facts here are of particular significance for policy toward the IS. First, in terms of *delivery*, terrestrial broadcasting remains dominant. Second, in terms of *content*, much of the history of UK broadcasting policy in the last 20 years is the playing out of the conflicts between public interest considerations, consumer sovereignty, and the aims of industrial policy. As the media are increasingly seen as both a commodity to be traded and an additional tool of industrial policy, conflicts concerning industrial policy in particular are growing. Thus it is hardly surprising that the IS is beginning to display similar conflicts.

The IS: Main Policy Developments

The IS became part of the public debate in the early 1990s within the context of a liberalization of telecommunications and considerable uncertainty about the future of broadcasting. However, the sudden interest in the IS in 1993 and 1994 (largely because of American initiatives and the explosive growth of the Internet) obscures the fact that UK policy in this area has been emerging over a longer period.

Early Beginnings

As early as 1981, Prime Minister Margaret Thatcher had appointed
Kenneth Baker Minister for Information Technology, and in 1982
a report from the Information Technology Advisory Panel (ITAP),
set up under the umbrella of the Cabinet Office, recommended the
development with private sector financing of a UK cable network
that would carry information and other services as well as entertainment. A "Micros in Schools" scheme was also launched in 1982,
which was designated IT year. Mrs. Thatcher and Mr. Baker both
saw the new technology as central to maintaining the UK's international competitiveness (a theme that has reappeared forcibly in the
1990s). Mr. Baker also established the Alvey Committee to look at
advanced IT. In 1983, a second ITAP report pointed out that,
within IT, "emphasis has been on the T and not on the I,"[6] The
report commented on the convergence of publications, films, and
news services and urged that attention be given to an expanding
"tradable information sector." Note again the industrial emphasis.

The result of all this activity was that, following the recommendations of the Hunt Committee (Cmnd 8679), the government
established the Cable Authority in 1984 and began to offer franchises. The Economic and Social Research Council, one of the
UK's research-funding bodies, also began supporting a ten-year
Program on Information and Communications Technologies.
Building on research carried out in the 1970s, the UK also expanded the network connecting most of its institutions of higher
education and research—the Joint Academic Network (JANET)
linked 200 academic sites by 1983 and was formally launched in
1984.

UK Policy and the IS in the 1990s

UK policy was slow to catch fire, however. As explained above, the
cable experiment of the mid-1980s had little impact. In addition,
ministers changed and little was done to promote JANET or to link
it to the commercial world (with the result that, until as late as 1993
or 1994, electronic mail remained little used outside the academic
community). For whatever reason, policy from the late 1980s to the

early 1990s appears to have been almost wholly absorbed with telecommunications and broadcasting. The result was that after the flurry of activity from 1982 to 1984 there was no substantial government policy statement on the IS until as late as November 1994. Moreover, this statement came *after* the passing of the High Performance Computing Act and the National Information Infrastructure Act in the United States in 1991 and 1992, *after* the 1993 Delors White Paper promoting the idea of a "common information area" throughout the European Union, *after* the Bangemann Report of May 1994 (and its follow-up in August 1994), *after* the House of Commons released its report on *Optical Fibre Networks* in July 1994, and *after* the Internet had become headline news. While thinking may have been continuing within the government, the public impression was of a government reacting to events elsewhere and lacking either energy or direction in this area. [7]

The House of Commons publication, in particular, criticized the Government for "not sufficiently encouraging the development of the most advanced infrastructure and services" and for a "lack of a clear sense of vision."[8] More specifically it recommended that the government lift the restrictions on PTOs providing entertainment services "on a franchise by franchise basis at specified future dates, subject to the principle that all cable franchises should be exclusive for seven years from the granting of the original licenses; and that the Government should make clear that all restrictions on PTOs conveying or providing entertainment will be lifted by the end of 2002, provided that the PTOs permit fair and open access to their networks."[9] The Committee was also concerned that the government should ensure that "all public institutions such as hospitals and schools are connected to broadband networks as soon as possible"[10] and said that one way in which this might be achieved would be by making the lifting of the restrictions on PTOs conditional upon adequate links to public institutions—a bargaining chip that the Labour Party later picked up.

The government, however, rejected these suggestions. Instead it eventually set out its own position in the Command Paper *Creating the Superhighways of the Future: Developing Broadband Communications in the UK* (November 22, 1994). This paper emphasized that the 1991 White Paper on telecommunications continued to provide the best framework for developing internationally competitive

Table 8 Main Developments in UK Policy: Information Superhighway

1979	Computer Board and Science and Engineering Research Council set up the Joint Network Team at SERC's Rutherford Appleton Laboratory to initiate a networking program for the UK academic community
1982	Information Technology Advisory Panel (ITAP) report recommends the development of a UK cable network carrying information and other services as well as entertainment financed by the private sector
1982	(October) Report of the (Hunt) Inquiry into Cable Expansion and Broadcasting Policy (Cmnd 8679)
1983	JANET (the Joint Academic NETwork) links 200 academic sites (the official start is 1984)
1983	White Paper *Development of Cable Systems and Services* proposes a privately financed cable television industry
1985	BT launches Integrated Services Data Network (ISDN)
1992	(May) Planning for the pilot network for SuperJANET begins with six selected sites (Cambridge, Edinburgh, Manchester, Imperial College, Rutherford Appleton Laboratory, and UCL)
1993	(March 11) SuperJANET starts life when BT delivers the 140 Mbps for the pilot network
1993	(August) Cable Television Association argues that video-on-demand requires a local delivery service license under the Broadcasting Act of 1990
1993	(September) ITC states that video-on-demand would not fall within the purview of the Broadcasting Act of 1990
1993	(December) Presentation of the Delors White Paper, *Growth, Competitiveness, Employment: The Challenges and Ways Forward into the 21st Century*, promotes the idea of the EC as a "common information area"
1994	(May) Bangemann Report published (see August)
1994	(June) Publication of CCTA consultative report, *Information Superhighways: Opportunities for Public Sector Applications in the UK*
1994	(July) Publication of House of Commons Trade and Industry Committee report *Optical Fibre Networks*
1994	(August) Follow-up to Bangemann Report published by the EC, *Europe's Way to the Information Society: An Action Plan*
1994	(September) JANET and other commercial Internet service providers announce a common interconnection point—a single high-capacity line to the central hub LINX (the London Internet Neutral Exchange) links everyone

Table 8 (continued)

1994	(November 10) Launch of Government Information Service on the Internet
1994	(November) BT announces home services experiment at same time as US West is raising funds
1994	(November 22) UK government sets out its policy on the IS (including its reply to House of Commons report) in a command paper, *Creating the Superhighways of the Future: Developing Broadband Communications in the UK*
1994	(December 9-10) European Council meeting in Essen discusses the "information society" and stresses the role of the private sector in building and financing information infrastructures
1995	(February 25-26) Special Meeting of the Group of Seven on the IS is held in Brussels. Agreement reached on 11 collaborative pilot projects to demonstrate the potential of the IS
1995	(March) Department of Trade and Industry (DTI) launches pilot scheme to help secondary schools connect to the Internet
1995	(April) Government announces that many departments will publish their press releases on its Web site (open.gov.uk)
1995	(April 24) DfE publishes consultation document *Superhighways for Education*
1995	(May) Publication of White Paper *Media Ownership: The Government's Proposals* (London HMSO) Cm 2872 (see December) discussing the convergence of technologies and the need to define a "total media market" and to relax cross-media ownership rules
1995	(May 22) White Paper *Competitiveness: Forging Ahead* (Cm 2867) announces that there will be a "major Information Society initiative" in the autumn.
1995	(July 18) Labour Party special conference on the IS and publication of policy document *Communicating Britain's Future* (see October)
1995	(July) OFTEL publishes consultative document *The Future Regulation of Premium Rate Services,* which proposes separate charges for conveyance and call content and that PTOs should introduce plans to achieve such "unbundling" by the end of 1996
1995	(August) Publication of White Paper *Digital Terrestrial Broadcasting: The Government's Proposals* (Cm 2946) with proposals for digital terrestrial broadcasting via multiplexers with 12-year licenses and no fixed date for switching off analogue
1995	(August 7) OFTEL publishes consultative paper on the future regulation of broadband switched mass-market (BSM) services, *Beyond the Telephone, the Television and the PC*

Table 8 (continued)

1995	(October 3) Leader of the Labour Party announces understanding with BT
1995	(November 13) Government publishes *Superhighways for Education: the Way Forward*. Funds of £10 million (including private sector) to be made available
1995	(December) OFTEL publishes its consultation document on universal service, *Universal Telecommunications Services*
1995	(December 14) DTI publishes Report of Multimedia Advisory Group focusing on intellectual property rights, standards, education, and health
1995	(December 19) House of Lords Select Committee on Science and Technology announces establishment of subcommittee on the Information Superhighway: Applications in Society and the taking of written and oral evidence

communications in the UK and that local delivery services for broadcasting services should continue to be awarded on an exclusive basis (i.e., that BT could bid for cable franchises but not carry television services on its own network). It also appointed Ian Taylor, Parliamentary Under Secretary of State for Trade and Technology, to a new coordinating role drawing on advice from senior industrialists.

In a further interesting development, this was the first Command Paper made available over the Internet on the Government Information Service. It was not, however, the first government publication of any kind to do so. The CCTA (which runs the Government Information Service) had published a consultative document about the IS in June 1994 and made its official launch on the Internet on November 10, 1994. The Treasury immediately made its press releases available on its server, but the press releases of many other departments were only accessible from commercial data-bases. Moreover, White Papers and other government publications appeared on the Internet in an apparently random way. [11] The number of government departments with home pages has been growing ever since, but even now not all departments have them. Nor is there any obvious pattern in how frequently information is kept up-to-date. Most surprising of all is that, at the time of writing, the government has still not decided whether *Hansard* (the official record of the House of Commons) is to be available on the Internet. This confusion about what information should be made available, where, to whom, and at what price, if any, is a matter returned to below.

The core elements in public policy thinking at this stage were subsequently set out by Ian Taylor in evidence to Parliament in January 1995. He emphasized the following: (a) a stable regulatory framework is essential (in particular the 1991 White Paper on telecom policy); (b) developments "should be private sector led"; (c) policy should "encourage competition in infrastructure and services"; (d) the UK liberalization of telecommunications provided an example "that the rest of Europe is now following"; and the next step was to focus on content and applications "for which customers are really prepared to pay." [12]

Recent Developments

Despite a slow start, the UK has been moving rapidly, and from late 1994 to the present (January 1996) there has been a flurry of activity by the government, the opposition, the regulatory authorities, and actual and potential users related to the advancement of the IS (Table 8 provides a chronology of the most important events).

The government has produced four major policy statements one covering media ownership (proposing that as a result of the convergence of the press and broadcasting, the former rules restricting cross-ownership should be relaxed); a statement on digital terrestrial broadcasting (including proposals for six multiplexers with 12-year licenses, which would be taken up by new players as well as by existing national broadcasters, but with no fixed date for switching off analogue); a white paper on competitiveness proposing that there should be a major information society initiative in the autumn of 1995 (though, by January, 1996, this had still not occurred); and a statement on "Superhighways for Education: The Way Forward." The last of these discussed extending SuperJANET into schools (but made no recommendations) and estimated that about 2,000 schools and colleges would be connected to the Internet by the end of 1995 (i.e. about one in every 15). At a more concrete level, this document also included 23 pilot projects that were to be evaluated with the help of government funding. The projects chosen include assistance to students with special needs, links to schools in rural areas, a foreign language training course bringing together schools in four different European countries, and training and research in multimedia.

The government has also increased the number of its publications put out on the Internet (though coverage is still not complete), and at the end of the year the DTI published its *Report of Multimedia Advisory Group* focusing on intellectual property rights, standards, education, and health.

The Labour Party, for its part, has held a special conference on the IS and published a policy document, *Communicating Britain's Future.* This document supports the proposals of the House of Commons (discussed above) that BT be allowed to provide entertainment beginning in 1998 but expects in return that BT and others will establish a program to provide broadband communications to the "whole country—as far as is practicable." The Labour document also proposed "a single 'Ofcom' to regulate the whole communications infrastructure and ... a revamped ITC to regulate content provision." and that the "definition of issuing copies in existing copyright law be specifically extended to include digital distribution through the new electronic networks." In addition, at the subsequent Labour Party Conference, the Leader of the Party, Tony Blair, devoted a significant part of his speech to the IS and the role that it could play in improving education and training and in making the UK competitive internationally. His speech also announced the achievement of an understanding with BT according to which, in return for early permission to provide entertainment services, BT would connect schools, hospitals, colleges, and libraries free.

The regulatory bodies were equally active, especially OFTEL. In July 1995, OFTEL published a consultative document, *The Future Regulation of Premium Rate Services,* which proposed separate charges for conveyance and call content and that PTOs should introduce plans to achieve such "unbundling" by the end of 1996. They followed this with a document on a new regime for competition, *Effective Competition: Framework for Action,* and one on the future regulation of broadband switched mass-market (BSM) services, *Beyond the Telephone, the Television and the PC.* The latter document clearly signaled OFTEL's intentions to be the regulator of these new markets. Perhaps most significantly, in December 1995 OFTEL published a consultation document on universal service, *Universal Telecommunications Services,* which proposed a third-party body to run a Universal Service Fund financed by contributions in proportion to basic network service revenues. The necessary costs were estimated £50–100 million and the contribution rate at 0.5–0.8 percent of telecom revenues.

Major Policy Issues

Three groups of questions stand out. First and foremost, there are questions about the emphasis in all government statements on the merits of liberalization, market forces, consumer sovereignty, and competition. This emphasis has dominated telecommunications policy and has been the one consistent theme in UK policy toward the IS. The questions are whether this emphasis is justified and whether such exclusive reliance on the market is sufficient.

Second, there is the relative lack of debate in the UK on the purposes or long-run goals of the IS. While there has been consultation, there has been no equivalent of the U.S. discussion of, for example, an entertainment model versus a democracy model. It has been taken for granted that the market should be the prime determinant and that customers through their choices would decide the outcome. Is this possible or does the government inevitably have to have a view of the longer run—even if only by omission?

Third, there is the regulatory structure. The government has emphasized that it believes that the right regulatory regime is in place. However, in practice, a number of large unresolved questions remain. What should be done about cross-media ownership (on which a bill is still before Parliament)? And what regulation, if any, should apply to *content* on the IS?

In the chronology of UK policy (see Table 8) one other point emerges. In the late 1980s and early 1990s, JANET and SuperJANET continued to be developed, but information technology and the IS virtually disappeared from public debate from the mid-1980s to the mid-1990s. Was this an opportunity wasted? Or was policy more continuous that it seems to have been? These are important questions, but they are beyond the scope of this chapter.

The Efficacy of the Market

The government's heavy reliance on competition and its exclusive focus on the benefits of the market, raise a number of questions. First, was it the right policy to attempt to induce competition in the local loop? Much of the government's policy on telecommunications since 1991 has rested on providing positive help to the cable industry to enable it to compete with the incumbent. Yet if the local loop is, in the present state of technology, a natural monopoly, this will decrease production efficiency. In testimony before the House of Commons Committee, Dr. Hartley, Director of the Cambridge University Computing Service, for example, argued that there was little point in duplicating infrastructures, particularly "if we are having difficulty establishing even a *single* fiber local loop" (emphasis in the original). [13] On the other hand, the *threat* of entry can be a powerful stimulus to reduce costs, and even if production inefficiency occurs, it might be more than offset by gains in consumption efficiencies. Unfortunately, economic modeling of these alternative regimes has not yet produced clear answers about where the balance of advantage lies.

The government, however, is in no doubt. In the 1994 Command Paper it not only maintained that the UK was ahead of the rest of Europe and the United States in terms of liberalization but, looking back over the whole period to 1984 and at the real fall in telecommunications prices, the growth in capacity, and the other beneficial changes that had occurred stated that "the spur *to all this progress* was the original decision to liberalize infrastructure and services" (emphasis added). [14] Liberalization and the subsequent competitive pressures have undoubtedly played their part, quite possibly an important part, but this statement takes no cognizance of (a) the fact that until 1991 there had not been competition but a duopoly; (b) the fact that, even since 1991, there is still, at best, a duopoly in the local loop; [15] (c) the presence of a tough regulatory regime (a policy instrument that is independent of liberalization and that the government had been forced to extend and to use more severely than anticipated); and (d) technical change on a massive scale (much of which would also have been independent of liberalization and some of which was certainly independent of the UK).

The second major question concerning the role of the market is whether the government has adequately allowed for a variety of other market failures. For example, the House of Commons Report called on the government to ensure that all public sector institutions should be connected to broadband networks as soon as possible, yet in reply the command paper explicitly stated that "it is ultimately for budget holders in public bodies and institutions to judge whether the benefits of these services merit their participation."[16] There was no awareness here of the possibilities of network externalities, critical mass, economies of scope, economies of scale, or public goods. Yet without a recognition of at least the first two of these, what the government has elsewhere called the "excellent SuperJANET" would never have been built.

The third question is whether there has been a conflict within the government's own position. Much of the time it has used the words "competition" and "competitiveness" as if they were interchangeable. Yet they have quite different implications. The former refers to the idealized state of competition of the many, whereas the latter is often a coded reference to the need for UK firms to be large in global terms. For example, in July 1994, when the government published its proposals for the renewal of the BBC Charter due in 1996, it said that the BBC should "evolve into an international multimedia enterprise,"[17] and in its 1994 highway paper it welcomed the fact that BT was one of the "world's largest players" and was "forming strategic alliances in order to compete at the global level."[18] Similarly, in its review of media ownership the government stated as one of the major reasons for more readily allowing mergers that UK media companies needed to establish themselves as "large players in overseas markets".[19]

There is more at stake here than a matter of words. Is the IS either at the infrastructure level or at the content level going to be characterized by small-scale firms with reasonable ease of entry and thus by plentiful competition? Or will it be an industry characterized by economies of scale, scope, and agglomeration, making dominance its natural state? I have suggested elsewhere [Graham, 1995a, 1996] that I expect both to occur, but this has consequences for public policy that the government does not seem to have thought through.

The final question about the reliance on the market is whether it is possible to establish a technologically neutral regime. Such a regime sounds desirable in principle, but in practice it is difficult to establish. Moreover, there is no such thing as a regime that is wholly neutral towards long-range goals. The UK experience illustrates the problem. In telecommunications, there was a regime shift in 1991 toward cable, which was clearly unattractive before that date yet more attractive afterward. Similarly, in broadcasting, the decision to leave nondomestic satellite television outside the domain of the 1990 Broadcasting Act had significant effects.

Equally important at the moment (January, 1996) is the debate about the regulation of conditional access systems for digital television. These systems represent potential control points, or "gateways" on the IS. It will therefore make a considerable difference whether public policy views such systems as, at one extreme, proprietary or, at the other extreme, "essential facilities." Should any broadcaster be able to travel via any gateway in the interests of diversity of view and competition or should a single owner be able to control the gateway in the interests of maximizing investment?[20] The crucial point here is not the direction in which any particular decision goes but that these decisions have major effects on the long-range structure of the industry.

The Long-Range Purposes of the IS

What the long-range structure of the IS should or might be cannot be analyzed without a discussion of purpose. If its purpose is primarily to deliver entertainment, and especially unswitched entertainment, then the IS may be able to be asymmetrical, i.e., broadband in one direction only. In that case, terrestrial or satellite broadcasting would be viable forms of delivery. Such a system might even work for "top-down" versions of education (particularly if there were some "upstream" capacity, e.g., via a phone line).

However, if the goal is *communication* (including good quality visual communication) then there have to be broadband switched networks, and in the present state of technology that means wires or fibers. UK policy gives the impression of being slow to face this choice, and UK debate on the IS has given little attention to long-range purposes. The 1994 paper spoke of "working with the private sector *to articulate a clear vision*" (emphasis in the original),[21] but, as noted above, this only came in the wake of initiatives abroad and after the explosion of interest in broadband communications. Moreover, more than a year later the follow-up publication, *Multimedia Industry Advisory Group: Report*, is merely a collection of papers from the subgroups with no discussion, let alone endorsement, by the government.

The Structure and Goals of Regulation

In all discussion of the IS the government has emphasized the procompetitive stance of the 1991 Telecommunications Act, seeing this as the crucial element in a stable regulatory environment. However, this is not sufficient. A major feature of the IS is that it is creating the convergence of telecommunications, computing, broadcasting, and publishing. As a result, the regulatory frameworks of the press, on the one hand, and broadcasting, on the other, are also relevant.

The UK regulatory structure in these areas is complex, but at a minimum the following issues need to be addressed. First, there is the question of whether the structure of the regulatory authorities themselves should be redesigned. As noted above, the Labour Party has advocated that the existing structure, which follows "industry" lines, should be replaced by "an 'Ofcom' to regulate the whole communications infrastructure and ensure fair competition, and a revamped ITC to regulate content provision."[22] In other words, "vertical" regulation would be replaced by "horizontal" regulation. In practice, the existing regulator for telecommunications, OFTEL, has been staking out its claim for a wider remit. Many of its publications in 1995 (see Table 8) can be seen as occupying the regulatory vacuum that the explosion of broadband communications is creating. An additional question about the regulatory structure is that of national versus international regulation. Should there, for example, be an FCC for the European Union as the European Commission has suggested? It is hardly surprising that this is a topic that the Conservative government hopes will stay well off the agenda at least until after the next general election.

Second, there is the question of the goals of regulation. The UK media, like the media in many other countries, are regulated both because of political concerns (in particular the need for diversity and plurality in a democratic society) and because of traditional economic concerns about market dominance. How these two very different concerns should be handled as the media converge is one of the main issues currently before Parliament. Yet, amazingly, the government White Paper on media ownership stated that "interactive multimedia services . . . are not covered by this document."[23] This is not a sustainable position.

Equally unsustainable is the government's position on universal service. So far the government has emphasized that the major contribution to universal service should come from progressively cheaper telephone services. Beyond this, the position was left on hold in the November 1994 Command Paper. It would, the government said, "be premature to try to assess the extent to which new services will become available on a commercial basis."[24] This is in sharp contrast to the United States, where one aspiration of the national information infrastructure initiative is universal access to e-mail within a decade and where there is an active discussion of the IS's implications for democracy (Anderson, Bikson, Law and Mitchell 1995). In addition, as noted, the Labour Party has announced its understanding with BT; the European Commission has published a Theme Paper, held public hearings, and issued a draft Interconnection Directive; and OFTEL has proposed a Universal Service Fund. In any event, there is now an active debate on universal service. In addition to the work by OFTEL useful contributions have come from Analysys (see Gray 1995) and Murroni and Collins (1995).

Third, there is the question of what model for content regulation should apply to the IS. Putting it simply, the UK offers two different approaches. As Curran (1995) states, "The press is organized as a free market, broadcasting as a system of public regulation." Remembering always that the IS is a global development, not something restricted to the UK, should the IS follow either of these models or develop a new position?

On this last point there are several arguments that have not been given sufficient prominence so far in the debate about the IS. The three central points, elaborated in greater detail elsewhere (Graham and Davies 1992; Graham 1995a; Graham 1995b; and Graham 1996), are as follows:

1. Information as a commodity has many special characteristics. There is the well-known problem of pricing information, but to this must be added that preferences may be endogenous, that information once published can be either a public good (most knowledge) or a public "bad" (e.g., the knowledge of how to make chemical weapons), and that information is not retractable—once something is known, it is virtually impossible for it to become unknown.

2. The media play a special role in a democratic society. Beyond the familiar argument about its power, what needs to be considered is that the media serve as one of the main arenas in which "common knowledge" is constructed, and common knowledge is a prerequisite for rational debate.

3. At present, my expectation is that, if left to the market, the IS will develop in two directions. One part of it is likely to consist of a small number of large, commercial information providers (almost certainly wielding a degree of power undesirable in a democratic society and possibly charging excessive prices for important information). Alongside this there is likely to be a public-domain system, but with highly fragmented, incomplete, and possibly unreliable information.[25]

For all three of these reasons, public policy must address the content of the IS. Such public policy should, I suggest, follow two routes. First, it should build on the helpful distinction made by the Williams Committee[26] between "censorship" and "restriction." The point is that television offends people more than books do because it is more intrusive and more public. If, therefore, the problem with content is the offense it causes, then the appropriate remedy is to restrict its intrusion, not to ban it. Clearly there is much here that could be built on in the case of the IS. One-to-one e-mail, narrowcasting, and broadcasting are all at different points on the spectrum. Pure text messages might also be seen as different from still video clips, which in turn might be regarded as different from a full audio-video sequence.

Second, public policy needs to think hard about what kinds of information are core contributors to the democratic process and then ensure that these are provided. The right way to do this, I suggest, would be via a variety of public or not-for-profit organizations establishing a presence on the IS and pursuing similar purposes to those of UK public service broadcasters or of public libraries and museums in the nineteenth century. Note, here again there would be no censorship but an extension of choice via a positive form of intervention.

It is far too soon to say how these issues are likely to settle down. UK policy is currently at something of a turning point. The Labour Party has shown itself willing to talk seriously to BT and to propose new regulatory structures, and it is explicitly committed to spreading the benefits of the new technology as widely as possible. It is also more open on the question of European integration. On the other hand, the Labour Party shares the view of the present government that investment in the IS should be made primarily by the private sector, and it is far more persuaded than in the past of the merits of competition and the need to work alongside the private sector instead of opposing it. How these influences will play themselves out remains to be seen.

Conclusions

UK policy toward the IS has been primarily driven by two goals. The first has been the objective of liberalizing the telecommunications infrastructure. The Conservative government has made a great deal of progress in this direction, especially in the supply of equipment and in competition over long-distance calls. However, the power of the incumbent, BT, has been such that the government has been forced to maintain and extend the power of the regulator, to introduce "assisted competition," and to generate a set of conditions that, at least in the early 1990s, were exceptionally attractive to the cable companies. That telephone prices have fallen substantially in real terms and that aggregate investment has grown significantly are not in doubt, but it is far less clear that overall investment in the infrastructure has also benefited. The desire for direct competition in the local loop may have been (and may still be) inconsistent with maximizing investment in that part of the infrastructure.

The second objective of the government has been to increase consumer sovereignty in both telecommunications and broadcasting. Here, especially in broadcasting, developments have been less rapid than the government had hoped. Moreover, the government has not articulated a clear vision for the IS. Major questions can also be raised about whether such exclusive reliance on the market is justified.

For the future, much remains to be decided and the problems are complex. However, even within a primarily market environment, it is essential to think hard about long-term purposes. It may also be useful to realize that different goals need different (and separate) policy instruments and to distinguish the regulation of the infrastructure from regulation of content. It may be necessary to focus on the traditional negative aspects of regulation at the infrastructure level, e.g., preventing abuse of dominance. At the services and content level, there may be need to prevent abuse of the IS as well as a need for positive intervention (e.g., via the presence of institutions with public interest obligations) to provide the "common knowledge" and the reliable and impartial information upon which democracy depends.

Appendix: UK Regulatory Institutions Relevant to the IS

Telecommunications

The main regulatory body is the Office of Telecommunications (OFTEL), established by the 1984 Telecommunications Act. OFTEL is a nonministerial government department. The Director General has the duty to ensure that holders of licenses comply with the license conditions and advises the Secretary of State on licensing. He or she also has the power to deal with anticompetitive and monopolistic practices. Within the function of promoting competition, OFTEL has special responsibility for regulating certain BT services.

The British Approvals Board for Telecommunications (BABT) is responsible with OFTEL for approving equipment.

The Department of Trade and Industry issues licenses for telecommunications on the advice of OFTEL.

Broadcasting

The BBC is regulated by the obligations placed upon it by the Royal Charter, which covers both its television and radio services. The current Charter is due for renewal in 1996.

All other television is regulated by the Independent Television Commission (ITC), established by the 1990 Broadcasting Act, which licenses all non-BBC television—including cable and local delivery services, independent teletext services, and domestic and foreign satellite services—available to viewers in the UK. It also enforces license conditions and has the duty to ensure fair and effective competition and to ensure that a wide range of television services is available throughout the UK and that, taken as a whole, they are of a high quality and appeal to a variety of tastes and interests. The ITC operates statutory codes of practice covering a wide range of matters such as impartiality, the portrayal of violence, privacy, and crime.

All non-BBC radio is regulated by the Radio Authority, established by the 1990 Broadcasting Act. The Radio Authority has codes similar to the ITC's.

The Broadcasting Complaints Commission adjudicates complaints of unjust or unfair treatment in sound or television programs and unwarranted infringements of privacy in, or in connection with, the obtaining of material included in such programs. This function extends to all sound, television, licensed satellite, and cable programs.

The Broadcasting Standards Council (BSC) acts as a focus for public concern about violence, sex, and standards of taste and decency. It covers both radio and television and monitors programs broadcast into the UK from abroad. It has statutory powers under the Broadcasting Act of 1990 that require the codes of the

BBC, the ITC, and the Radio Authority to be consistent with the BSC's code.

The Press

The British press is often described as unregulated. This is true in the sense that there is no statutory body with overall responsibility—though there is a self-regulatory body, the Press Complaints Commission. Nevertheless, items published in the press may be influenced by numerous pieces of legislation. Collins and Purnell (1996) state that freedom of expression in the UK may be lawfully restricted under common law (notably the laws of confidentiality and defamation) and the provisions of numerous statutes, including:

Obscene Publications Acts of 1959 and 1964

Contempt of Court Act of 1981 (revelation of sources)

Police and Criminal Evidence Act of 1984 (revelation of sources)

Video Recordings Act of 1984 (video classification)

Public Order Act of 1986, formerly the Race Relations Acts of 1965 and 1976 (incitement to racial hatred)

Malicious Communications Act of 1988 (material distributed by mail)

Official Secrets Act of 1989

Prevention of Terrorism (Temporary Provisions) Act of 1989 (revelation of sources)

Broadcasting Act of 1990 (especially Section 10)

Football (Offenses) Act of 1991 (indecent or racist chants)

Criminal Justice and Public Order Act of 1994 (right to assemble, video classification)

Cross-Media Ownership

The press and broadcasting are also subject to normal monopoly and merger legislation and a complex set of rules on cross-media ownership defined by the Broadcasting Act of 1990 (though "nondomestic" satellite services are exempt from this part of the Act).

Acknowledgments

Research for this chapter has been undertaken with the support of the Economic and Social Research Council (Award L126 25 1017). In addition I would like to thank Peggotty Graham, Martin Cave, and Richard Collins for helpful comments on an earlier draft. I am also grateful to Veronica Sardon, Claire Smith, and Andrea Woodhouse for research assistance. Any errors that remain are my own.

Notes

1. Cm 2734 para 4.

2. Cm 2734 para 4.

3. Cmnd 9824 para 477.

4. House of Commons Home Affairs (1988) paras 12–13.

5. House of Commons Home Affairs (1988) para 24.

6. ITAP (1982) p. 10

7. The impression of government running to catch up was reinforced when on January 25 1995, Ian Taylor said in evidence to the House of Commons," the Government is a good deal more advanced than it was three months ago."

8. House of Commons Trade and Industry (1994) para. 132.

9. House of Commons Trade and Industry (1994) para. 108.

10. House of Commons Trade and Industry (1994) para 115.

11. This was hardly surprising, as each Department was left free to decide its own use of the Internet (letter of November 11 from Chancellor of Duchy of Lancaster to Maurice Frankel, Director of the Campaign for Freedom of Information).

12. House of Commons Trade and Industry Committee (1995) *Minutes of Evidence* 25 January

13. House of Commons (1994) para 69.

14. Cm 2734 para. 5.

15. Mobile phones represent a third potentially important competitor. However, until recently, their coverage has been limited and the quality not reliable enough for data communications.

16. Cm 2734 para 12 p. 29

17. Cm 2621.

18. Cm 2734 para 93.

19. Cm 2872 para 5.21

20. These issues are discussed further in Graham, 1995b.

21. Cm 2734 para 34.

22. Labour Party 1995 p.8

23. Cm 2872 para 1.2

24. Cm 2734 para 76.

25. In practice there would be likely to be a degree of arbitrage between these two. Commercial suppliers might package public domain information, and individuals might copy, legally or otherwise, commercial material. However, this would not remove the basic distinction.

26. Cmnd 7772.

References

Anderson, R., et al. 1995. *Universal access to email: Feasibility and societal implications*. Santa Monica: RAND.

Armstrong, M., S. Cowan and J. Vickers. 1994. *Regulatory reform*. Cambridge, MA: MIT Press.

Bangemann Report. 1994. *Europe and the global information society: Recommendations to the European Council 26 May*. Report of the High Level Group on the Information Society.

Cable Communications Association. 1995. *The Case for Cable*.

CCTA. 1994. *Information superhighways: Opportunities for public sector applications in the UK*.

CCTA. 1995. *Report on ISs*.

Cm 1461. 1991. Department of Trade & Industry. *Competition and choice: Telecommunications policy for the 1990s*. London: Her Majesty's Stationery Office.

Cm 2621. 1994. Department of National Heritage. *The future of the BBC: Serving the nation, competing world-wide*. London: HMSO.

Cm 2734. 1994. Department of Trade & Industry. *Creating the superhighways of the future: Developing broadband communications in the UK*. London: HMSO.

Cm 2867. 1995. *Competitiveness: Forging ahead*. London: HMSO.

Cm 2872. 1995. Department of National Heritage. *Media ownership: The government's proposals*. London: HMSO.

Cm 2918. 1995. Department of National Heritage. *Privacy and media intrusion*. London: HMSO.

Cm 2946. 1995. Department of National Heritage. *Digital terrestrial broadcasting: The government's proposals.* London: HMSO.

Cmnd 7772. 1979. *Report of the Committee on Obscenity and Film Censorship.* London: HMSO.

Cmnd 8679. 1982. *Report of the (Hunt) inquiry into cable expansion and broadcasting policy.* London: HMSO.

Cmnd 8866. 1983. Home Office & Department of Industry. *The development of cable systems and services.* London: HMSO.

Cmnd 9824. 1986. *Report of the (Peacock) Committee on Financing the BBC.* London: HMSO.

Collins, R. and J. Purnell, eds. 1996. *Reservoirs of Dogma.* London: Institute for Public Policy Research.

Congdon, T., A. Graham, D. Green and B. Robinson. 1995. *The cross-media revolution: Ownership and control.* London: John Libby.

Curran, J. 1995. *Policy for the press.* London: IPPR.

Delors White Paper. 1993. *Growth, competitiveness, employment: The challenges and ways forwards into the 21st century.* COM(93) 700 Final. December 5, 1993.

Department for Education. 1995. *Superhighways for education: Consultation paper on broadband communications.* London: HMSO.

Department for Education and Employment. 1995. *Superhighways for education: The way forward.* London: HMSO.

Department of Trade & Industry. 1982. *A programme for advanced information technology: The report of the Alvey Committee.* London: HMSO.

Department of Trade & Industry. 1995. *Report of Multimedia Advisory Group.* London: HMSO.

European Commission. 1994. *Europe's way to the information society: An action plan.* ED Cons Doc 8791/94, COM(94) 347.

European Council. 1994a. Industry/Telecommunications Council Press Release 9561/94 (Presse 197). September 28, 1994.

European Council. 1994b. Telecommunications Council Press Release 10633/94 (Presse 233). November 17, 1994.

European Council. 1994c. European Council meeting on 9 and 10 December, Presidency Conclusions. SN300/94.

Graham, A. 1995a. Public policy and the IS: The scope for strategic intervention, co-ordination and top-slicing. In *Managing the information society*, R. Collins and J. Purnell, eds. London: IPPR.

Graham, A. 1995b. Exchange rates and gatekeepers. In *The cross media revolution: Ownership and control*, T. Congdon et al. London: John Libby.

Graham, A. 1996. Evidence to the House of Lords Inquiry into the Information Superhighway. (forthcoming).

Graham, A. and G. Davies. 1992. The public funding of broadcasting. In *Paying for broadcasting*, T. Congdon et al. London: Routledge.

Gray, N. , ed. 1995. *Universal service obligation in a competitive telecoms environment.* Cambridge, UK: Analysys Publications.

House of Commons National Heritage Committee Fourth Report. Session 1993–94. *Sports sponsorship and television coverage.* House of Commons papers 189-I & II. London: HMSO.

House of Commons Trade and Industry Committee Third Report. Session 1993–94. *Optical fibre networks.* House of Commons papers 285-I & II. London: HMSO.

House of Commons Trade and Industry Committee. 1995. *Minutes of evidence.* January 25, 1995.House of Lords. 1995. *Broadcasting bill.* HL Bill 19. London: HMSO.

ITAP. 19183. *Making a business of information: A survey of new opportunities.* London: HMSO.

Labour Party. 1995. *Communicating Britain's future.*

Milne, C. 1995. A telephone in every home? Benefits for all from the information society? In *Managing the information society*, R. Collins and J. Purnell, eds. London: IPPR.

Murroni, C. and R. Collins. 1995. *New issues in universal service obligation.* London: IPPR.

OECD. 1994. *Privacy and data protection: Issues and challenges.*

OFTEL. 1994. *A framework for effective competition.* London: OFTEL.

OFTEL. 1995a. *Beyond the telephone, the television and the PC: Consultative document.* London: OFTEL.

OFTEL. 1995b. *Universal telecommunications services.* London: OFTEL.

OFTEL. 1995c. *Effective competition: Framework for action.* London: OFTEL.

OFTEL. 1995d. *The future regulation of premium rate services.* London: OFTEL.

OFTEL. 1995e. *Market information.* London: OFTEL.

OPCS. 1995. *Living in Britain: Preliminary results form the 1994 general household survey.* London: HMSO.

OPSS. 1994. UK government joins the Internet. Office of Public Service and Science News Release 234/94. November 21, 1994.

Policy Studies Institute. 1995. *Barriers to telephone ownerhip.* London: Policy Studies Institute.

Robinson, B. 1995. Market share as a measure of media concentration. In *The cross media revolution: Ownership and control*, T. Congdon et al. London: John Libby.

Multimedia: Germany's Third Attempt to Move to an Information Society

Herbert Kubicek

Three Attempts in 20 Years

The phenomenon that is known in the United States as national information infrastructure or the information superhighway has begun to be discussed in Germany in terms of multimedia and the information society.[1] There are historical reasons for the differences in terminology which also express some differences in the goals being pursued and how they are being pursued.

In Germany, the term information superhighway, or *Datenautobahn*, is used by the media and in literature, but does not appear as a general heading in official government or parliamentary documents. Highways are a controversial issue in Germany, conjuring up associations of traffic jams and environmental pollution. A debate on introducing tolls on the Autobahn has raised criticism because of the additional financial burden it would impose on working people and because of privacy concerns. Moreover, the construction of the Autobahn started as a prestigious infrastructure project of the Nazi regime, thus depriving it of a positive historical association as well.[2]

The term infrastructure is associated in Germany with state investment, monopolies and bureaucracies. But the federal government, in accordance with the requirements of the European Commission, is going to dissolve monopolies in several areas, including telecommunications, railroads and, to a certain extent, roads. Another reason to avoid the term infrastructure is that in the

1970s and 1980s, the federal government tried to initiate and accelerate Germany's transformation into an information society via an infrastructural approach that used the state-owned telecom monopoly Deutsche Bundespost to build an innovative infrastructure that far exceeded demand in order to create new markets for services and hardware. In both attempts, computer networks and cable television were on the agenda, and there were high expectations for data communication. But in both cases, a push for cable television was the only result.[3]

In 1974, the Social Democratic government set up a Commission for the Development of Technical Communication to determine which communication services were "economically sensible" and "socially desirable." The main focus was on data communication and two-way cable television, new technologies that had just been introduced in the United States. The Commission was skeptical about the demand for commercial television and recommended some pilot projects. It was also skeptical about the diffusion of data communication and asked for trials with telefax and telex-oriented services instead. But Deutsche Bundespost started a joint venture with German computer manufacturers to set up universal data communication services (Datel-services). This early attempt at a public-private partnership was a big flop.[4]

In 1984, the Conservative government launched a joint program to coordinate the developments and grants programs of several ministries (BMFT 1984). Deutsche Bundespost was to invest about DM500 billion within 20 years to upgrade the analog telephone network to a switched broadband network with fiber-optic lines to every single home in Germany (BPM 1984). At the same time, Deutsche Bundespost started to build a one-way cable TV network on coaxial cable. There was a big dispute about fiber versus copper which at its core was really about data communications versus television. While today the cable television network reaches 47 percent of all German households and has increased the number of available channels from three to about 30, the plans for fiber to the home as the regular subscriber line were very quickly abandoned and have only been taken up again with the renewal of the telephone network in the former German Democratic Republic (GDR).

Again today, television and data communications are expected to create big markets and improve life. But once again, the main result may only be a multiplication of TV channels. This time the battlefield is called multimedia, a term which I will attempt to define in the following section. The various markets from which multimedia is expected to emerge will be described in the third section, followed by an overview of the main policy issues in the fourth section. Finally, the fifth section offers a look at possible future developments.

Multimedia as the Convergence of Technologies and Markets

In technical terms, multimedia is defined by three characteristics (Booz, Allen and Hamilton 1995, p. 27):

- interactive use, as compared to passive reception of television programs;
- integration of static and dynamic media (i.e., text and data combined with audio and video sequences); and
- digital storage and transmission using compression technologies.

There is broad agreement that these technological developments allow for or will lead to the merging of the following previously separate technologies and markets:[5]

- the technologies of data processing, telecommunications and broadcasting at the network level;
- technologies and markets for terminal equipment (PCs, video recorders and/or set-top boxes); and
- markets for content (software, games, broadcasting and publishing).

Despite the consensus on this process of convergence, its ultimate impact is far from clear. While some people, mainly from the computer industry, assume that the computer will take over the functions of the television set and video recorder, others, mainly from the consumer electronics industry, predict that the television set will take on the functions of an on-line computer terminal. In terms of networks, there is a similar debate over the upgrading of cable television networks with back channels or upgrading the telephone network through digitalization, thus repeating the fiber versus coaxial dispute of the early 1980s.

In this ongoing discussion it is not at all clear what convergence really means. The range of markets considered when predicting multimedia growth varies a lot. According to a study by Booz, Allen and Hamilton, the multimedia markets for pay TV, on-line services and CD-ROM and the respective equipment are expected to rise to DM 20 billion (i.e. U.S.$14 billion) in the consumer segment and to DM 10 billion in the business segment (multimedia servers, video-conferencing, etc.) in the year 2000 (Booz, Allen and Hamilton, pp. 47 and 50). Tom Sommerlatte of Arthur D. Little predicts a growth of the European multimedia market from U.S.$1.5 billion in 1994 to U.S.$37 billion in 2000. It is hoped that this growth will create ten million new jobs (Sommerlatte 1995, p. 22).

My suggestion is to consider the markets for networks and basic services, for equipment and for content as three separate markets of supply for multimedia systems as defined in the technical sense.

The multimedia market itself comprises at least three different markets which are to some extent complementary but also compete with each other. So far, the only profitable one is the CD-ROM market; narrowband on-line services are just taking off; and not until at least the year 2005 will interactive broadband services, in particular video-on-demand and interactive television, be profitable.

Bertelsmann, the largest German media firm, has projected the growth of these three markets. Their forecast of a DM 1.5 billion turnover for on-line services in Germany in 2000 does not seem very ambitious at first glance. However, this estimate is based on a forecast of the diffusion of PCs and other equipment, particularly modems, that is very ambitious. The percentage of German households with PC modems is expected to grow from 2 percent in 1994 to 27 percent in the year 2000, and the percentage of households with a PC is expected to double to 45 percent; Bertelsmann assumes that the current large differences between Germany and the United States will decrease considerably until the year 2000.[6]

These predictions resemble those made in the 1970s and early 1980s. When videotex[7] was introduced in Germany in 1983, it was predicted that it would have three million subscribers by 1990, but only 260,000 had signed up at that time (Kürble 1995, p. 10). One of the reasons for this high error rate is that the special character of on-line services, which Kürble calls experience goods, has been neglected. The problem with this kind of goods is that consumers have to buy them in order to evaluate their benefits. Therefore most consumers are very cautious. In addition, the new media have to be compatible with consumers' established behavior patterns of media use. Therefore videotex was not accepted at all as long as the television set with a special hardware decoder was the only terminal possible. The number of subscribers went up when a software decoder was offered and PCs could be used as terminals.

The following section will examine those markets from which multimedia goods might emerge. The final section will examine the extent to which earlier experiences have been taken into consideration in today's predictions and political concepts.

The Present State of and Future Developments in the Markets for Multimedia[8]

As defined in the previous section, various multimedia markets will emerge from the combination of elements from the three markets of origin:

• telecommunications networks and basic services;
• telecommunications terminals and multimedia equipment; and
• value-added services and content.

Telecommunications Networks and Basic Services

Until 1989, the German market for telecommunications networks was a monopoly controlled by the state-owned Deutsche Bundespost, which ran the network and all the services on it. Telephones and modems were part of the network, and could only be rented from Deutsche Bundespost. Deutsche Bundespost never produced terminals but had the authority to license them. In 1989, competition was allowed for any kind of terminal and any kind of service except basic telephone service. Two licenses were granted for nationwide networks for mobile communications.

Table 1 The German Market for Telecommunications Networks and Services
(Schwab 1995 and 1996)

Market Volume	1993 (billion DM)	1994 (billion DM)	Change 1994 : 1993
Within the monopoly	44.0	50.2	+14%
• Telephone service	*42.6*	*48.1*	*+13%*
• Leased lines	*1.4*	*2.1*	*+50%*
Deregulated services			
• Mobile communications	3.5	5.5	+57%
Deutsche Telekom	*2.6*	*3.7*	*+42%*
Others	*0.9*	*1.8*	*+100%*
• Satellite communications	0.1	0.1	0
• Other deregulated services	8.3	5.1	−39%
Data transmission services by			
Deutsche Telekom	*2.8*	*3.3*	*+18%*
German telecommunications services market	55.9	60.9	+9%
Telecommunications services by Deutsche Telekom	52.2	57.2	+9.5%
Market share of Deutsche Telekom	93%	94%	—

The member-states of the European Community have decided to introduce full-fledged competition for telecommunications networks and telephone services by the end of 1997. So-called alternative networks, which so far have only operated for internal use by public utilities and the German railway company, will be allowed to operate for third parties even before this date.

Germany's overall market for public telecommunications networks and services had a volume of DM 55.9 billion in 1993 and DM 60.9 billion in 1994[9] (see Table 1). The annual turnover of Deutsche Telekom was DM 64.9 billion in 1994 (versus DM 59 billion in 1993) including sales of equipment. Thus Deutsche Telekom covers almost the whole market for telecommunications networks and basic services. It is worth noting that there was a high growth rate

Table 2 Size of German Telecommunications Networks (Schwab 1996)

	1993	1994
Telephone lines (millions)	37.0	39.2
ISDN basic access lines	281,000	509,000
Connections to Deutsche Telekom data-exchange networks		
datex-L (circuit-switched)	23,000	c. 20,000*
datex-P (packet-switched)	86,500	92,600

* My estimate.

within the monopoly, whereas deregulated services, except mobile communications, declined.

Telephone Service and Basic Networks

The telephone network is still Germany's largest network in terms of number of lines and turnover. The growth of telephone lines from 1993 to 1994 was greater than the number of all existing data exchange lines at that time (see Table 2).

The digitalization of the entire telephone network will be completed by 1997. Deutsche Telekom's long-distance network has the most fiber-optic cable in the world (100,000 km). However, diffusion to the customer has been very slow. In 1989, a broadband switching network (VBN) was introduced for video-conferencing and high-speed data transmission, but the most subscribers it reached was 1,000 (Eutelis, pp. 21f). VBN was followed by two broadband services, Datex-M (34–140 Mb/s) and B-ISDN (155 Mb/s), which together have about 14,000 subscribers. In 1996, Deutsche Telekom will introduce ATM access, which offers full compatibility between local area networks (LANs) and the public network (Eutelis, pp. 37ff). But experts do not expect large increases in broadband services in the near future. Zoche predicts 20,000–25,000 subscribers by 2000. However, the reconstruction of the telephone network in the former GDR introduced 1.2 million fiber-to-the-home lines there by the end of 1995, though they are currently used for narrowband applications only.

Table 3 Mobile Communications (Subscribers per 1,000) (ZVEI/VDMA 1995; Mobilfunk News 5/96)

	C-net	D1	D2	E+
1 Jan.1993	772	75	105	—
1 Jan.1994	800	481	495	—
1 Jan.1995	724	872	850	30
1 Nov.1995	688	1,312	1,370	142
1 Apr. 1996	620	1,600	1,635	252 (E1)

Mobile Communications

The effects of deregulation can be observed in the market for mobile communications. Until 1992, Deutsche Telekom also held the monopoly for mobile communications, which included two very old networks and the analog mobile communications network called C-net introduced in 1985. In 1992, the German government granted two licenses for a GSM-standard digital network to a consortium headed by Mannesmann (a heavy industry, engineering, computing, and telecommunications conglomerate) and to a 100 percent subsidiary of Deutsche Telekom, DeTeMobil. In 1994, a third license was granted for a cellular mobile communications network called E+net to a consortium headed by Vebacom, an electricity company, and Thyssen Telecom, a major steel firm.

As Table 3 demonstrates, so far the private and the public competitors are fairly evenly matched in this new market.

Cable and Satellite Television

Deutsche Telekom claims to own and operate the largest cable TV network in the world. It is a one-way distribution network constructed completely of coaxial cable. Since its start in 1984, cable TV networks were built up under the telecommunications monopoly. Deutsche Telekom only granted local licenses for building or marketing subnets in certain residential areas. By the end of 1994, 23.2 out of 33.4 million German households (69.5 percent) had access to cable, but only 14.6 million subscribed (43.7 percent) (Eutelis 1995).

Table 4   New Providers of Telecommunications Networks in Germany

	Alliance with	Relation to Electricity Supply	Access to Telecom Infrastructure
Vebacom	Cable&Wireless	Preussag	E+ Mobile Communic. 1.2 million cable-TV subscribers
Mannesmann RWE Telliance	CNI, AT&T	RWE	D2 mobile communic. 4,300 km fiber optic lines
VIAG InterKom	British Telecom	Bayern-werk	4,000 km fiber optic lines
Thyssen Telekom	Bell South		E+ Mobile Communic. 2,000 km fibre optic lines

Cable television's competitors are direct-broadcast satellites that broadcast almost all the channels available on the cable network plus many more.[10] The biggest satellite broadcaster, ASTRA, reaches between 5 and 7.7 million receivers (Blume and Wahl 1995). Between 1995 and 1997, a new generation of satellites, Astra 1 E, F and G, is being introduced with the capacity to digitally broadcast about 500 television and radio channels. Ten percent of the cable and satellite households are expected to switch to digital technology by the year 2000.

New Providers

Now that Germany's third telecom reform is under way, it is rather obvious which companies will enter into competition with Deutsche Telekom (see Table 4). The experts only give a chance of success to existing companies that have access to some cable infrastructure. There are five companies that meet these conditions (Gerpott 1996); three of them belong to conglomerates that also own electricity companies that have their own telecommunications infrastructure.

Another big player is Deutsche Bahn AG, the German railway company, which owns 3,200 km of fiber-optic lines (ZVEI 1995). This company, which is wholly owned by the German government, was looking for a partner to buy 49.9 percent of the shares of the new offshoot DBKom. After the first round of selection, Mannesmann Eurokom, RWE Telliance and Viag Interkom were still in, but Vebacom did not meet the criteria.

There is also Deutsche Netz AG, which was founded by seven regional electricity firms, and many municipal utilities are starting to market their networks and rights of access. It is most likely that they will become partners or suppliers of the national providers. Most observers expect that only two national providers can survive the competition with Deutsche Telekom.

Telecommunications Terminals and Multimedia Equipment

Investments in network infrastructure are expected to create demand for new terminal equipment. Markets of origin for multimedia equipment include PCs, televisions and VCRs, CD-ROM drives and the traditional telecommunications terminals, in particular modems, but also telephones, which might be exchanged for picture phones.

The size of the submarkets in terms of turnover is quite different. For 1993, the following figures have been reported:[11]

• telecommunications terminals: DM 2.7 billion;

• PCs for private households: DM 4.0 billion;

• CD-ROM drives: DM 1.0 billion; and

• televisions and VCRs: DM 10.3 billion.

When discussing different options for convergence, it should be kept in mind that the market for television equipment is larger than all the other terminal markets for private households put together.

Telecommunications Equipment

Of the German telecommunications market's DM 75.3 billion turnover in 1994, DM 60.9 billion (81 percent) came from services and only DM 14.4 billion (19 percent) from equipment, which had decreased from 26 percent in 1992. In the whole market for equipment, which includes switching and transmission technology for networks and cable as well, terminals account for almost 20 percent (Schwab 1996). Deutsche Telekom continues to dominate the market as its most important customer. It purchases more than 90 percent of the switching and transmission technology and 80 percent of all terminals (Landtag 1995, p. 140). On the production side, only two companies (Siemens and Alcatel SEL) are still important; the others are losing market shares because they cannot adapt to the technological dynamics and the increased international competition.

Although production of and national demand for German equipment are declining, exports have gone up from DM 5.8 to 8.7 billion, leading to an export balance of DM 3.2 billion (Schwab 1996, p. 392).

Personal Computers

Data on personal computers vary quite a bit. In most cases there is no definition of what is considered to be a computer (e.g., some figures include computer game stations). In 1994, 3.1 million PCs were sold in Germany, two-thirds to businesses (ZVEI 1995). Altogether 12 million PCs were installed that year (ZVEI), with five to seven million of them in households (Bisenius 1995; DM 1995). The market volume for private households is estimated to be about DM four billion (Booz, Allen and Hamilton 1995, p. 63). According to Middelhoff (1995), German households are lagging behind U.S. households, but the gap is expected to become much smaller (Table 5).

A similar lag is also reported for the number of PCs per capita; while there are 12 PCs per 100 inhabitants in Germany, there are 30 in the United States (IdW September 95).

According to other sources, 1.1 million German households (3 percent) had CD-ROM drives in 1994; this number was expected to increase to 3.1 million (9 percent) by the end of 1995 and to 9.6 million (28 percent) in 1998 (Peters 1995, p. 95). According to a survey of 15,000 Germans at least 14 years of age, there would be 2.3 million CD-ROM drives and 2.0 million modems in German homes by the end of 1995.

Table 5 Diffusion of PCs, Modems, and CD-ROMs in Germany and the United States

Households with	Germany 1994	U.S. 1994	Germany 2000	U.S. 2000
PC	22%*	37%	42%	48%
modem	4%**	17%***	21%	28%
CD-ROM	2%	10%	20%	32%

* According to other sources 14–30% (Blume and Wahl, p. 30) or 17 (DM, p.2)
** According to an MGM Study 7–10% (p. 21)
*** According to other sources 8–10% (Bisenius 1995, p. 251)

Televisions and VCRs

Television has a much higher penetration rate than PCs or CD-ROM drives in private households. In 1993, there were 32 million televisions installed with an annual market volume of DM six billion, and 22 million VCRs with a market volume of DM 4.3 billion (Blume and Wahl, 1995, p. 16; Booz, Allen & Hamilton 1995).

In 1996, set-top boxes will come on the German market. This technology is necessary to receive pay-per-channel and pay-per-view TV because it decodes the scrambled signals. Set-top boxes also modulate digital television signals for reception by analog televisions. In addition, they provide data for invoicing and some menu choice and help functions. Two different systems have been developed by competing alliances centered around Bertelsmann and the Kirch Group.

Set-top boxes will cost about DM 1,000. It is expected that the market for digital TV of this kind will grow rapidly, reaching 3.5 million German households (10 percent) by 2000 (Schrape 1995).

Value-Added Services and Content

More than the other markets, the content market depends on language. Since English is spoken in so many countries, Hollywood and other U.S. media producers can export a lot of product. German is the native language of 100 million people and the largest language in the European Union (Middelhoff 1995). However, this dominance is not reflected in all areas of the European content market.

Table 6 Markets of Origin for Multimedia Contents

	Turnover 1993 (DM billion)
Newspapers and Magazines	
advertising	12.0
other revenue	11.4
Books	20.0
Movies	10.0
Television and Radio	
advertising	9.0
other revenue	8.7
Video Rentals and Sales	1.7
Computer Games	1.5
CD-ROMs	0.3
On-line Information Services and On-line Data Bases	
Consumer On-line Services	0.2
other services	0.8
Whole Market for Media Content	75.6
Share of Advertising	27.8%
Share of Consumer On-line Services	0.3%

The market for multimedia content is often differentiated by technology—i.e., off-line (CD-ROMs, electronic books), on-line services, interactive televisions. The predictions of high growth rates and the political significance attributed to multimedia are based on the assumption that an increasing share of traditional mass media content will shift to a multimedia format. Table 6 shows the structure of the markets of origin for multimedia content. It is worthwhile taking a closer look at these different submarkets.

CD-ROM, Computer Games, and Video

Even if the technical definition of multimedia is interpreted broadly to include CD-ROMs, computer games, consumer on-line services and video cassettes, this market area does not even reach 5 percent of the media market.

The German market for CD-ROMs is growing fast. There were 6,000 titles available in 1994 compared to 3,500 in 1993. Bertelsmann predicts an increase in revenues from DM 300 million in 1994 to DM two billion in 2000 for the consumer segment, and an even higher increase for the professional segment. However, DM 300 million is not very much on the media market, even compared to video and computer games. The markets for videos and films must also be considered (Booz, Allen and Hamilton 1995). In 1993, German video sales (DM 1.2 billion) exceeded cinema revenues (DM 1.1 billion). From 1991 to 1994, revenue from video sales and rentals remained almost constant. However, within this market there has been a shift from renting to buying. Revenues from video rentals declined from DM 1.0 billion in 1991 to DM 0.7 billion in 1994, while they increased for video sales from DM 0.6 billion to DM 1.0 billion in the same period (Bisenius 1995, pp. 248). If video rentals are indicators of the potential demand for video-on-demand, this is not very encouraging.

The German market for computer games, including proprietary play stations and software, is estimated to be about DM 1.5 billion, of which at least two-thirds are covered by Sega and Nintendo (Booz, Allen and Hamilton 1995, p. 35). The share of CD-ROMs is slowly increasing, however.

Television and Radio

It is generally assumed that multimedia will customize television to individual preferences and make it even more attractive. While expectations for video-on-demand have been greatly reduced, there is still the hope that pay-per-channel, pay-per-view and near-video-on-demand will fill the hundreds of channels created by the digitalization of cable and satellite television and reach large market shares.

In Germany, this assumption has to be analyzed within the context of the general development of TV and radio broadcasting during the last ten years. There have been fundamental changes in this regard. Until 1984, Germany had only ten regional public broadcasting stations which provided three radio programs and one regional television program each and contributing to one national program (ARD, Arbeitsgemeinschaft der Rundfunkanstalten Deutschlands). There were also two national radio stations and one national public television station (ZDF—

Zweites Deutsches Fernsehen). All these institutions were legally established by the Bundesländer (states) and are financed by a monthly lump-sum fee for every television and radio set in accordance with a state treaty among the state governments.

Since 1984, however, private radio and television stations can apply to the state authorities for regional or national licenses to broadcast. Within ten years production value climbed from DM 6.4 billion to DM 17.7 billion.[12] Commercial television suppliers came from the publishing business and from abroad, in particular Luxembourg. In 1993, there were about 15 nationwide commercial television channels. However, the three largest cover 85 percent of the market for TV advertising. The fourth largest (Premiere) was the only pay channel available at that time.

The market volume in 1993, according to one source, was DM 10.1 billion for commercial and public television, and DM 4.2 billion for radio (Booz, Allen and Hamilton 1995, p.43). According to another source, it totaled 17.7 billion including private television with DM 4.45 billion, private radio with DM 0.77 billion, and public broadcasting with DM 12.52 billion. Of these revenues, advertising accounts for 91 resp. 96 percent in private television and private radio, compared to 9 percent in public broadcasting (Kors and Boeckelmann 1995).

Public and private radio and TV stations are sourcing production out to private production companies; the volume was DM 2.37 billion in 1993. Since 1993, commercial stations have become profitable in Germany and are changing the markets for TV production and advertising: When commercial stations started, almost all the movies and programs that they broadcasted had been bought on the international market. Today, two-thirds of the programming of Radio Luxembourg are its own productions or specially ordered productions. Thus commercial stations are becoming the main customers for the German television production business, accounting for about 60 percent of turnover (DM 1.3 billion) in 1993.

But the most important factor in the economics of television is advertising. Of the total market volume for advertising in the media (DM 23.4 billion in 1994), television's share was 38 percent (DM 9 billion) (Debus 1995, p. 247). Although the advertising market is still growing, it will not be easy to finance the many new TV channels that are expected to start broadcasting through an increase in television's share.

The other option is pay TV. Germany has not yet had much experience with pay TV. Until recently, Premiere was the only German pay-TV channel. The monthly rate is DM 40, leading to revenues of DM 330 million in 1993 and DM 410 million with 850,000 households subscribing in early 1995 (Kürble 1995, p. 34). In 1995, MTV shifted to pay TV. The Kirch Group has announced plans to start up to 50 digital pay-TV channels by the end of 1996. The high expectations for pay TV in Germany are based on U.S. developments. U.S. pay TV revenues increased from $149 million in 1988 to $327 million in 1992, with 20 million households (26 percent) subscribing.[13]

Newspapers, Magazines and Movies

Another important market of origin for multimedia content encompasses the print media and films. This market provides content for CD-ROMs and on-line services. The German market volume in 1993 was DM 23.4 billion for newspapers and magazines,[14] DM 21.0 billion for books and DM 10.0 billion for movies.[15] Forecasts for the year 2000 assume that ten to 20 percent of the print media market will be covered by electronic media (i.e., DM 4–8 billion). But again, one has to take into account that 50 percent of the turnover in the whole market for newspapers and magazines comes from advertising and that it is not at all clear how advertisements will be placed in interactive media.

On-line Services

Most difficult to analyze is the German market for on-line services. Whereas Middlehoff expects revenues of DM 1.5 billion in the year 2000, an MGM market study predicts DM 3.5 billion. But only three years ago, on-line services did not even earn DM 0.5 billion. As already mentioned, the history of on-line services in Germany is one of exaggerated predictions.

Until recently, there was only one general on-line service available in Germany and this was provided by Deutsche Telekom. Bildschirmtext (the German videotex system), introduced in 1980, was originally accessible only via the television screen and a hardware decoder (see Thomas, Vedel and Schneider 1992). After two field trials, between 1.1 and 2.3 million households were predicted to subscribe in 1988, and Deutsche Telekom expected 4.8 million by 1994–1995. The millionth subscriber, however, only signed up at the end of 1995. During the past decade, the technology and the name of this service have changed several times. Today, T-Online works like the U.S. on-line services with extended multimedia features. Deutsche Telekom distributed one million multimedia-software decoders on CD-ROM free of charge to its subscribers and others in September 1995. Until recently, T-Online's only competitor was Compuserve, which started operating its English-language service in Germany in 1989 (ZVEI/VDMA 1995).

In 1995, two big German publishing firms announced their own on-line services. Bertelsmann, the largest German media conglomerate, started a joint venture with America Online to operate a German version called AOL Deutschland which is expected to have 3.5 million German subscribers by the year 2000. And Burda entered into a joint venture with the French publisher Hachette (*Elle*) and the British publisher Pearson (*Financial Times*) to set up Europe Online, located in Luxembourg and offering its services in English, German and French (MGM 1995, pp. 54 and 63). They expect 100,000 subscribers after one year and one million after five years. Axel Springer Verlag, Germany's second-largest publishing company, was also negotiating to participate. However, in December 1995 this joint venture dissolved before the full service had started.

Microsoft has also begun to introduce a German version of Microsoft Network in Germany. Microsoft expects to attract 10 percent of the users of Windows 95 (200,000–300,000 in Germany) in the first year (MGM 1995, p. 85).

All the new services initially planned to set up their own proprietary networks with about 180 entry nodes each. But by the end of 1995, they all announced that they would use the Internet instead. However, it is still not clear how they are going to charge subscriber fees.

Until 1994, the Internet in Germany was almost exclusively used in universities and research institutions. As of early 1995, Germany had 1,600 networks out of 50,000 worldwide with 1–1.5 million potential users. In July 1995, the World Wide Web had 150,000 users in Germany compared to an estimated 2.2 million worldwide (Eutelis 1995, p. 45 ff). According to ZVEI/VDMA, there were 351,000 Internet accesses in Germany by the end of 1995. Meanwhile, T-Online and the other on-line services provide access to Internet services, e-mail and the Web, accounting for about 1.2 million potential subscribers. A recent survey reported a penetration rate of 3 percent of German households. In addition, there were about 200 commercial local mailboxes and about 600 commercial on-line databases.

There is not much statistical information available about the suppliers of content behind these providers of on-line services. Although there are 6,000 German commercial databases, no figures about their turnover are available. The European Commission published the following data about the turnover of German providers of electronic information services (Table 7).

Differentiated by content, 80 percent of the world market for on-line services is devoted to financial services, 15 percent to other business services (legal, marketing, etc.) and only 5 percent to consumer services.

Although in 1994 Bertelsmann was the second-largest media enterprise in the world (with revenues of DM 18.4 billion, behind Time Warner with DM 24.1 billion and ahead of Viacom with DM 15.4 billion),[16] German firms have not played an important role in the market for on-line services. Although the volume of the German market was estimated to be one billion ECU in 1992, German providers had revenues of only 285 million ECU.

But this might change. In November 1995, Axel Springer Verlag and Deutsche Telekom announced that they were joining America Online and Bertelsmann. Deutsche Telekom would take over America Online shares while Bertelsmann and Springer wanted to buy shares of T-Online. However, this joint venture must be approved by the German antitrust authority.

Preliminary Summary

The different markets of origin from which multimedia might emerge produce almost DM 150 billion in revenues. However, there are differences between these three markets. The largest is the market for content (DM 75.6 billion), of which print products

Table 7   Revenue of Providers of Electronic Information Services (Schwuchow 1995)

Information Services (Volume in Million ECU)	Germany 1992	European Union
On-line	216	3,644*
Audiotext	10	97
Off-line	59	473
Total	285	4,213**

* 2 billion ECU from Reuters alone; ** approx. 9,300 for the United States.

account for 57 percent. Video rentals and sales, CD-ROMs, on-line information services and computer games together add up to only 0.1 percent.

The second-largest is the market for telecommunications networks and basic services with DM 63.5 billion. The telephone service, still under the monopoly of Deutsche Telekom, has a share of 82 percent of this market. Data communication services still play a very minor role.

The market for terminal equipment including telephones, modems, PCs, televisions and VCRs with DM 18 billion is relatively small. Televisions and VCRs have a share of 57 percent of this market.

Looking at the structure of these markets it is not at all evident how they may grow to DM 20 billion for the consumer segment in the year 2000 as predicted by Booz, Allen and Hamilton (1995, p. 50). Even if we include PCs and CD-ROM drives, the multimedia market in 1994 only had revenues of DM 5 billion. There is no indication of where an increase in demand of 400 percent within six years may come from. But the industry and its consultants maintain a supply-oriented position and are urging the government to remove all the likely impediments to the growth of this sector. The greatest barriers to investment and new services are said to be the telecommunications monopoly and the restrictive broadcasting law (Booz, Allen and Hamilton 1995; Sommerlatte 1995).

Key Policy Issues

In the late 1980s and early 1990s, the German federal government seemed rather reluctant to take the lead in the process of socioeconomic structural change. It did not react immediately to the Clinton/Gore initiative in 1993 or the Bangemann initiative in 1994 despite criticism from German industry of the lack of technology policy at the federal level. Only late in 1994 did the federal government announce that it planned to organize and intensify the dialogue between industry, science and the state on research, technology and innovation.[17] Early in 1995, Chancellor Helmut Kohl convened the Council for Research, Technology and Innovation, which comprises 20 representatives from universities, industry and trade unions as well as four federal ministers and one state minister (from Bavaria).

The first topic that the council addressed was the U.S. and EU challenge, and thus it focused on Germany's route to the information society. In December 1995, the council submitted a report to Chancellor Kohl.[18] The federal government also initiated a working group on the reform of Deutsche Telekom as well as a series of meetings with representatives of the states to address the reform of the broadcasting law. All three initiatives have been integrated into a report by the federal government called *Info 2000: Germany's Path to the Information Society* (BMWi 1996). This report was due out in late 1995, but was published only in February 1996 because of conflicts of authority among federal ministries as well as between the federal government and the states. *Info 2000* closely parallels the report of the Council of Research, Technology and Innovation.

Telecommunications Deregulation

As previously discussed, the deregulation of the German telecommunications monopoly occurred in three stages. After stage two, Deutsche Telekom became a public company. Its shares are now being floated, but it retains a monopoly on network and basic telephone services until the end of 1997. The deregulation of these remaining monopolies is the focus of the third phase of telecom reform. In autumn 1995, the federal Minister for Post and Telecommunications submitted a first draft of a telecommunications law that was introduced in the Bundestag in early 1996 and will be passed before summer 1996.[19] The main reason for this strict timetable is that the new regulatory environment will be an important factor in determining the price of Deutsche Telekom equities on the stock market. As the telecommunications law has to be approved by the Bundesrat, the upper house of parliament representing the states, which is currently controlled by the Social Democratic Party (SPD), the federal government is trying to get SPD consent to this reform in the Bundestag and the states. Whereas the Social Democrats in the Bundestag have joined the governing coalition in sponsoring the bill, the Social Democrats in the Bundesrat rejected several points.[20]

There is no longer any controversy over whether there should be competition in all markets. Even the Post and Telecommunications Workers' Union no longer opposes deregulation. But there are different ideas about how competition should be regulated and by whom.

Market entry
The draft bill tries to make market entry as easy as possible. Licenses are only requested for providing transmission facilities for telecommunication services to be used by the public and public telephone services based on private networks. To provide any kind of telecommunications service using networks of other providers, there is no need for a license but only the obligation to register with the federal Regulation Office. Licenses may be granted by auction or tendering. In general, there is no restriction on the number of licenses except if there is a shortage of the available spectrum.

Universal service
The draft bill defined universal service as the "minimum offering of telecommunications services for the public, for which a certain quality level is defined and to which all users must have access at an affordable price independent of their living or business location. While telephone services and transmission lines have to be defined as universal service, telecommunications services may be defined for which there is a general demand and which are indispensable as a basic supply for the public" (§ 17). The federal government can introduce a directive which must pass both the Bundestag and the Bundesrat to define as universal services those telecommunications services that require a license and meet the other criteria. The

directive has to specify the minimum quality standard and price, or the yardstick for defining the price. A second draft directive that met with the approval of the Social Democratic Party in the Bundestag defines as universal service:

• voice telephone service with ISDN features;[21]

• directory inquiries and editing of directories;

• provision of public telephones and facilities for emergency calls; and

• provision of transmission facilities.

An affordable price is defined as being no higher than the average price that private households outside cities with more than 100,000 inhabitants pay on December 31, 1997. Only if the federal Regulation Office receives information that shows that in a regional market a telecommunications service defined as universal service is not adequately provided, may it put a universal service obligation on a provider of this service who has a dominant market position according to the competition law. If such a provider can demonstrate that this obligation entails additional costs, the Regulation Office may refund the difference. This subsidy is financed by contributions from only those licensed providers of universal services with a market share greater than 5 percent of the national market for the service.

These definitions have been criticized by the SPD-governed states and the Green Party as being too narrow. They want ISDN to be defined as universal service and want every network and service provider to contribute to a Universal Service Fund.[22]

In contrast to the U.S. Telecommunications Act of 1996, Germany's plan offers no option for reduced rates for public institutions or special groups of users. There is not even an obligation for the Regulation Office to monitor service provision and accessability. As the Council of Research, Technology and Innovation has stated, there is a strong belief that market forces will supply everybody with telecommunications services at an affordable price and that government intervention will only be necessary if it turns out that this is not the case in certain areas.

Public right of way

The draft telecommunications bill gives the federal government the right to use traffic routes intended for public purposes free of charge for telecommunications lines. Furthermore, the federal government is authorized to pass this right on to organizations licensed to offer telecommunications networks. When making use of this right the concerns of the local community have to be considered. The Council of Research, Technology and Innovation has made the same recommendation. However, associations of local governments claim the right to make decisions and to market their public rights of way, and they have received the support of the Bundesrat, which wants the draft bill to be changed.

The Regulation Office

The federal Ministry for Post and Telecommunications is the regulatory body that governs telecommunications in Germany. However, the draft bill proposes the dissolution of this ministry. Some functions would be transferred to other ministries and a new Regulation Office would be created under the control of the Minister of Economic Affairs to carry out the main regulatory tasks. The Regulation Office would not be an independent office, but rather a suborganization of the ministry.

The Regulation Office would have to supervise the implementation of the telecommunications law, including registration of providers, distribution of licenses, decisions on numbering systems as well as privacy protection, security control and provision of access to those authorities permitted to engage in wiretapping.

Within both the federal government and the telecommunications industry some people still question the necessity of a separate Regulation Office for telecommunications, and argue that there is only a need for control of competition, which could be exercised by the General Antitrust Office. It is still open how the boundaries against the authority of existing offices such as the Antitrust Office and the Data Protection Office will be drawn.

Reform of Broadcasting

In accordance with the German Constitution, which grants full legislative power in cultural affairs to the states, broadcasting falls within the jurisdiction of the states. However, the states ratified a state treaty that created a unified funding system for a nationwide network of public broadcasting stations. According to this treaty, broadcasting is the "production and distribution of presentations of any kind in words, sound and pictures intended for the general public." As far as radio and television are concerned, each state has a media office that determines the distribution of frequencies and monitors the provisions of the state's broadcasting law.

In the early 1980s, when Bildschirmtext, the German videotex system, was introduced, there was a consensus that this type of service also falls within the cultural jurisdiction of the states. A separate state treaty regulated this medium, but did not require licenses or a new regulatory organization.

During the late 1980s and early 1990s, several German states reformed their broadcasting law and introduced a differentiation between broadcasting (radio and television) and quasi-broadcasting communications. For example, according to the State Media Law of Baden-Württemberg, broadcasting is defined as the distribution in a structured time sequence for the simultaneous reception by the general public, even if the signals are scrambled; whereas quasi-broadcasting communications are defined as either the transmission of text, pictures, movies or sound presentations from one storage facility on individual demand (broadcast on demand, e.g., videotex), or the distribution of a larger number of objects of this type with the possibility of individual choice (broadcast by access, e.g., videotext). The law requires licenses and a set of obligations for broadcasting programs. A service by access must also be licensed, but the provision of quasi-broadcasting communications on demand only has to be declared to the state media office. In both cases, there are some requirements concerning advertisements and privacy in particular that the media office supervises.

When Compuserve entered the German market in the late 1980s, there was no debate about its legal status. But as the debate on multimedia has grown, broadcasting law has become one of the most urgent policy issues. Several studies claim that video-on-demand does not fall within the scope of the broadcasting state treaty, but that the continued uncertainty about its legal status holds back companies from investing in this market (Booz, Allen and Hamilton 1995, pp. 89–94). The Council on Research, Technology and Innovation defines broadcasting very narrowly and assumes that on-line services and video-on-demand are completely comparable to buying or renting videos without any impact on the general public and thus should be treated like any other goods or services. This point of view coincides with that of the European Commission. The Council has suggested restricting the concept of broadcasting to the traditional electronic mass media and creating a common regulatory framework for multimedia services that would cover issues of privacy and property rights, and protect consumers and children. The federal government submitted a draft multimedia law in March 1996.

The states and the state media offices oppose this attempt by the federal government to take over legislative authority from the states. The state media offices have agreed on a so-called negative list naming those services that do not require licenses according to broadcasting law, including electronic mail, telemetry, electronic catalogues, telebanking, reservation systems, video-conferencing, and distance learning. They have also proposed less restrictive regulation for services such as teleshopping, video-on-demand and telegames. In reaction to the federal initiatives, they have begun consultations on an on-line state treaty to update the old videotex state treaty.[23]

Recently, the first German home-shopping television channel was the subject of controversy among the state media offices. This conflict demonstrated that the prime ministers of the states use different yardsticks depending on the location of the applicants for licenses to attract or keep media enterprises within their states.

Intellectual Property Rights

Germany's present law on intellectual property rights was passed in 1965 and covers the use of digital work in general. The Council on Research, Technology and Innovation has stated that the main principles are still valid but that some issues need to be clarified, such as whether individual on-line access falls within the concept of public use, which so far requires several recipients. Another issue concerns the compilation of multimedia works (e.g., CD-ROMs).

While the editor has to get consent to use any single picture or line of text, there is no protection for this special compilation. In general, there is consensus that a reform of German intellectual property law has to take place in accordance with European law. The European Commission has submitted a draft directive on computer software and databanks.[24]

Privacy, Security and Other Provisions

Existing privacy laws at both the federal and state level were developed for the sphere of centralized computing with the particular goal of protecting the individual citizen against a government that, by pooling data from different areas, could create comprehensive profiles of citizens without their knowledge or consent. However, in the present era of decentralization and networking, these traditional provisions no longer work effectively. The Council on Research, Technology and Innovation recommends a shift from organizational procedures of registration and supervision to technical measures such as encryption, authentification and so forth. In accordance with the data protection officers, the Council demands the option of paying anonymously for electronic services with prepaid cards or other procedures. There is also broad consensus that data security has to be improved. The technical means to encrypt messages with a combination of public and private keys are available. But it is still not clear how issues like the creation and administration of public keys should be organized.

Another issue concerns consumer protection and the protection of children and young persons. As mentioned earlier, the Council of Research, Technology and Innovation recommends dealing with these issues in a federal multimedia bill but does not specify any rules. The Bavarian state prosecutor's recent investigation of Compuserve revealed the complicated situation with international services and the Internet. Some observers argue that the rather low interest and reluctance of many companies and private households to connect to the Internet is related to this lack of control in comparison with traditional mass media.

Public Institutions

Neither the debate on telecommunications reform nor the debate on broadcasting reform gives particular consideration to public institutions. Rather, the trend is toward liberalization, deregulation and privatization. Commissions and programs that deal with the reform of the public administration and public schools do not address new technologies.

The Council on Research, Technology and Innovation has stated that Germany is lagging behind the United States and many West European countries in information and communication technologies in education, and a cooperative effort by federal, state and local governments, industry and foundations is required to close the gap. In December 1995, Deutsche Telekom announced a program to connect schools to ISDN and T-Online with expected turnover of DM 35 million in 1996. The federal Ministry of Education, Science, Research and Technology added another DM 23 million. But the German computer industry is still reluctant to participate. The industry association has stated that there is currently one PC for every 63 pupils and that providing two computer rooms for 20 pupils in each school will require investments of DM 7 billion. Governments would have to spend this money, which signifies only 0.09 percent of the public budget over five years. If governments would provide one multimedia PC for every two pupils, DM 22 billion would be needed, and 10,000 jobs would be created (ZVEI/VDMA 1995). However, at the same time it has turned out that the public budget deficit in 1996 is DM 60 billion larger than expected. Therefore there are no discretionary funds available for any additional public programs.

Pilot Projects

As there is so much uncertainty about the technical feasibility, costs and demand for multimedia applications, everybody wants pilot projects. On one level, there are the Bangemann and Group of Seven (G-7) industrialized countries application projects in several areas that build upon existing infrastructure and/or research and development programs.[25] On another level, Deutsche Telekom and some states have pilot projects to test options for digital audio and digital video broadcasting (DAB, DVB) including interactive television.

Almost all of the official multimedia pilot projects in Germany (listed in the appendix) build upon the existing one-way cable television network. Only a few plan to use fiber-optic lines. But their starting date has been postponed several times and the number of participants has declined. During 1995, great skepticism surfaced over whether fiber-to-the-home will pay off during the next ten years. The content providers in these pilot projects are the big media firms that also own the commercial television channels and invest in on-line services. It is not yet clear whether the main development will be a large increase in the number of TV channels or the broad diffusion of on-line services. It might be that television will win as it did twice before.

A Look into the Future: The Alliance of Media Conservatism

So far it is very difficult to draw conclusions about the outcome of Germany's telecommunications and broadcasting reforms and how this in turn will influence the diffusion of various multimedia services. There is no doubt that the business sector will profit from telecommunications deregulation and will gain access to any technology it demands. But how will private households be affected? In somewhat simplified terms, there are two main alternatives for the dominant technological infrastructure that will be available to the German public: 500 TV channels in a digitalized cable and satellite TV network, on the one hand, and an interactive network like the Internet, on the other. These types of networks offer very different services. According to the vision of the information society, only the Internet option would be appropriate. But it is still not clear that this will be affordable for the majority. Nor are there grounds to assume that this is the option that the majority of users wants. Finally, it is not likely that the main players will push this alternative. What is more likely to develop is a conservative alliance of users and suppliers of electronic media.

Conservative Users

Although Prognos, a well-known Swiss economic research institute, expects a growth of Germany's PC penetration rate from 14 percent in 1993 to 40 percent in 2000 and 80 percent in 2010 (Prognos 1995), other experts assume that the market is already saturated.

Although media use is constantly changing, its structural features are rather consistent. The amount of money spent on mass media as a percent of private consumption has been 4 percent for private households since 1970. The distribution of this budget among the various media has not changed very much either (Kürble 1995).

The mass media have taken a long time to integrate themselves into the everyday routine. None of the so-called new media have become mass media yet; they have only been adopted by a rather small segment of society. In addition, to realize the predicted growth rates of multimedia, millions of people would have to change their everyday habits. This sort of transformation only happens if there is some kind of pressure or if there are great benefits.

One of the problems of new telecommunications or information services is that their benefits cannot be judged without using them. Although diskettes are distributed free, a PC and a modem are still required, creating a high barrier just for a trial subscription. This means consumers have to buy equipment without first being able to make a cost-benefit evaluation.

While the predictions for growth of interactive media assume that most Germans want to be more interactive, several surveys show that this is not true for the majority. When asked about the preferred kind of television, only 20 percent named video-on-demand, while 58 percent preferred pay-per-view. Kürble (1995, p. 36) explains this by the greater transaction costs connected with finding the video one wants in a complex set of offerings. Pay-per-view provides more discretion than traditional television, but is still quite similar. In addition, only 20–30 percent said that they were at all willing to pay for watching movies on television, and only 5 percent would be willing to pay between DM 21 and 50 per month. There are also empirical indicators for a limited level of activities in media use. The sales of video recorders are stagnating and the average number of videos rented per month is going down (Kürble 1995, p. 29).

According to a recent study commissioned by a consumer magazine, 4 percent of German households (1.3 million) say they will buy a computer (DM 1995); the general consumer analysis for 1994 assumed that only 1 percent of households intended to buy a computer in the next year, while 5 percent were undecided and 94 percent definitely would not (Grudzinski 1996). It also has to be noted that 60 percent of all PCs in Germany are in households with a monthly income of more than DM 5,000 which only 20 percent of all households have (DM 1995, p. 9).

While Prognos assumes that PCs will reach a higher penetration rate than cable television, H. W. Opaschowski, a well-known specialist on leisure behavior, predicts that "the future train is heading toward more diversified TV instead of PC communications" (1995, p. 31). According to his study, there is no evidence that young people are shifting from TV to PCs. They watch television, listen to the radio and read books as often as people of other ages, but they also listen to CDs, watch videos, play computer games and use the computer more frequently. And the main competitor for on-line interaction is still real life interaction (dancing, shopping, sports, etc.) (see Table 8).

According to this study, there is no generation of computer kids growing up in Germany since only 18 percent of young people regularly use a computer.

Conservative Suppliers

Big players might take a deep breath and start trying to change the media behavior of millions of people, but it seems that in Germany they prefer the easier route of continuing their present business strategies.[26]

As mentioned in the preliminary summary—the three markets of origin for multimedia—i.e., telecommunications, terminal equipment and content, produce almost DM 150 billion in revenues. In the telecommunications market, Deutsche Telekom is the only big player with a market share of 94 percent, covering telephone services, data communication and cable television networks.

Table 10 Media Use in Germany (Opaschowski 1995, p. 8)

Previous week's activities, per 100 persons (n = 2,600)	All Germans	14–24 years old
TV	86	82
Newspapers, magazines	68	49
Radio	64	66
CD, Music Cassettes	34	66
Books	33	36
Videos	19	36
Encyclopedias	9	12
Computers	9	18
Video games	5	12

In the content market with its volume of DM 75.6 billion, there are three big players, the media firms Bertelsmann (18.4 billion) and Springer (4 billion) and the film distributor Kirch (4 billion). The market for terminal equipment is much smaller and has no dominant player.

And indeed, federal government's policy is heavily influenced by Deutsche Telekom, Bertelsmann, Springer and Kirch.

From the point of view of these media giants, the digitalization of cable and satellite TV offers a much less uncertain business opportunity: pay-per-view and some special-interest TV channels, financed by advertising, do not require an investment in infrastructure. The movies they own can be marketed without much additional effort, while the markets for narrow or even broadband on-line services are much riskier.

Although this is true for Bertelsmann, Springer and Kirch, one might argue that Deutsche Telekom should be interested in increasing traffic on the telephone network. However, this company has invested its cable TV network, which reaches almost 70 percent of German households, but only 44 percent have subscribed so far. If new programs encourage these households to subscribe, then it would be more profitable to invest in them than in additional hours of data communications. Furthermore, Deutsche Telekom has to react to the digitalization of satellite television in order not to lose cable customers. How little Deutsche Telekom is trying to promote on-line services was demonstrated by the tariff reform of January 1, 1996, which increased local charges by almost 100 percent. Using an on-line service with a modem for half an hour costs DM 2.40 ($1.65). Using the Internet gateway of T-Online during that time costs an additional DM 1.80, raising the price to $2.90 for 30 minutes. After strong protests, some reductions have been announced for private customers at the end of 1996, but it is not certain that the pending telecommunications reform will keep local tariffs down. If there is no universal service obligation for carriers other than Deutsche Telekom, they will mainly compete for business customers, thus forcing Deutsche Telekom to lower business rates and perhaps charge even more for local calls by private customers.

Trends Can Change

If we assume that commercial companies prefer an incremental approach to diversification, there is a high probability that they will put major emphasis on new television channels. This might lead to multimedia in a special sense, but has little to do with the visions of the information society. In comparison with the United States, Germany has far less experience with computers, electronic bulletin boards, etc. But even more important, Germany has no strong computer industry, and the only big company, Siemens-Nixdorf (SNI), only became interested in the consumer market in 1995. But SNI still has much less political influence than Bertelsmann and Kirch. Politicians depend on the media. And Leo Kirch is a close personal friend of Chancellor Kohl.

High diffusion rates of computers and on-line services to private households will not become a reality in Germany unless the political agenda changes and explicitly considers the need for a broader concept of universal service, special access for public schools and libraries, and a closer connection between technological innovations and institutional reforms (e.g., in public administration).

The hope for economic growth and new jobs in telecommunications, computers and multimedia is based on the assumption that there will be a massive and rapid diffusion of these technologies. Multimedia is expected to become a mass media comparable to the print media and television within a few years. But the mass media as we know them today are the outcome of a very long process of cultural institutionalization. The newspaper and book market not only derives from technological innovations and a rather liberal press law; it would never have grown to its present size in the industrial countries without the establishment of public school systems and compulsory education. Some analysts already predict disappointment in 1996 after the great multimedia euphoria of 1995. One has to wait and see what kind of creativity this disappointment will set free. It might lead to even stronger calls for deregulation or a more balanced approach to introducing competition within a framework of modernized public institutional infrastructures.

Notes

1. The term "information society" comes from the initiative of Commissioner Martin Bangemann of the European Commission. See *Europe and the Global Information Society* (Brussels: 1994).

2. See Helmers, Hoffmann and Canzler (1995).

3. See Mettler-Meibom (1986) and Kleinsteuber (1995).

4. See Scherer (1985), pp. 368ff.

5. For example, see Middelhoff (1995), Booz, Allen and Hamilton (1995) or Sommerlatte (1995).

6. There are similar differences concerning the access to other networks. There were 48 telephones per 100 inhabitants in Germany compared to 60 in the United States in 1994; 3.1 compared to 9.3 for mobile communications. Out of 100 households, 47 had access to cable TV in Germany and 65 in the United States (see ZVEI/VDMA 1995).

7. The term videotex is mainly used in Europe and denotes a special kind of on-line services which were started by the PTTs in the early 1980s. Many of them used a graphical interface from the start. For an international comparison, see Bouwman and Christoffersen (1992).

8. Most of the data reported in this chapter are estimates. Where available, differences between sources are noted.

9. Cable TV networks are not included in these statistics. The annual turnover for cable TV of Deutsche Telekom is estimated to be about DM 2.6 billion.

10. For a more extensive analysis see Kleinsteuber (1995).

11. See Schwab (1995), Middelhoff (1995), and Booz, Allen & Hamilton (1995).

12. See Kors and Boeckelmann (1995) for this section.

13. *Telephony*, May 2, 1994.

14. According to Booz, Allen and Hamilton (1995), p. 47. According to the Deutsche Institut für Wirtschaftsforschung, revenues in 1992 totalled DM 20 billion for newspapers and DM 15.5 billion for magazines.

15. Revenues for German books and movies in 1992 estimated by the Deutsches Institut für Wirtschaftsforschung (1996).

16. In 1995, Bertelsmann dropped to third place behind Walt Disney Productions.

17. *Bericht der Bundesregierung zur Intensivierung des Dialogs zwischen Wirtschaft, Wissenschaft und Staat zur Forschung, Technologie und Innovation*, BT Drs. 12/6934.

18. Der Rat für Forschung, Technologie und Innovation, *Informationsgesellschaft: Chancen, Innovationen und Herausforderungen. Feststellungen und Empfehlungen* (Bonn: December 1995) (http://www.kp.dlr.de/BMBF/rat/).

19. Gesetzentwurf der Fraktionen der CDU/CSU, SPD und FDP: Entwurf eines Telekommunikationsgesetzes (TKG). German Bundestag, 13th Session, Document 13/3609, January 30, 1996.

20. Empfehlungen der Ausschüsse zum Entwurf eines Telekommunikationsgesetzes (TKG). Bundesrat Document 80/1/96, March 22, 1996.

21. This official definition is misleading. It does not mean ISDN service, but rather an analog subscriber line to a digital switch offering features such as calling line identification or call redirection.

22. For the different positions see the contributions in Kubicek et al. (1996).

23. Entwurf der Rundfunkreferenten der Länder für einen Staatsvertrag über neue Mediendienste, March 1, 1996.

24. Directive 91/250/EWG, May 14, 1991; and ABl. EG No. C 156, June 23, 1992.

25. For a list of references to these projects see: http://infosoc.informatik.uni-bremen.de/NII/contact/html.

26. See also Kleinsteuber (1995).

References

A list of European political programs and pilot projects is provided by the Telecommunications Research Group of Bremen University at http://infosoc.informatik.uni-bremen.de/nii/contact/html.

Bisenius, J.C. "Multimedia Online—Trends und Perspektiven." In *Multimedia Online: Content, Technology, Projects*. Proceedings September 27–28, 1995. Stuttgart: Bisenius Teleconsult, pp. 247–258.

Blume, H. and Wahl, T. *Auf dem Weg in die Informationsgesellschaft: Fakten und Argumente 1994/1995*. Cologne: Deutsche Forschungsanstalt für Luft und Raumfahrt, April 1995.

BMFT (Bundesministerium für Forschung und Technologie). *Informationstechnik: Konzeption der Bundesregierung zur Förderung der Entwicklung der Mikroelektronik, der Informations- und Kommunikationstechniken.* Bonn: BMFT, 1994.

BMWi (Bundesministerium für Wirtschaft). *Die Informationsgesellschaft: Fakten, Analysen, Trends.* Bonn: BMWi, November 1995.

BMWi (Bundesministerium für Wirtschaft). *Info 2000: Deutschlands Weg in die Informationsgesellschaft.* Bonn: BMWi, February 1996.

Booz, Allen and Hamilton. *Zukunft Multimedia: Grundlagen, Märkte und Perspektiven in Deutschland.* Frankfurt/M.: Institut für Medienentwicklung und Kommunikation, 1995.

BPM (Bundesministerium für das Post- und Fernmeldewesen). *Konzept der deutschen Bundespost zur Weiterentwicklung der Fernmeldeinfrastruktur.* Bonn: BPM, 1984.

Debus, M. "Anhaltende Dominanz der Fernsehwerbung." *Media Perspektiven* (June 1995), pp. 246–257.

Der Rat für Forschung, Technologie und Innovation. *Informationsgesellschaft: Chancen, Innovationen und Herausforderungen. Feststellungen und Empfehlungen.* Bonn: BMBF, December 1995. (http://www.kp.dlr.de/BMBF/rat/)

DM. *Multimedia-Studie: Expertenband.* Munich: 1995.

Europe and the Global Information Society. Recommendation to the European Council (Bangemann Report). Brussels: 1994.

Eutelis Consult. *Baustelle Information Highway Deutschland: Status und Perspektiven.* Ratingen: July 1995.

Gerpott, T.J. "Alternative Carrier im deutschen Telekommunikationsmarkt." In Kubicek, H. et al., eds. *Neue SpieleróNeue Regeln: Jahrbuch Telekommunikation und Gesellschaft*, Vol. 4. Heidelberg: Hüthig, 1996, pp. 34–49.

Grudzinski, W. "Der Verbraucher allein zu Haus: Multimedia aus der Sicht einer Werbeagentur." In Kubicek, H. et al., eds. *Neue Spieler—Neue Regeln: Jahrbuch Telekommunikation und Gesellschaft*, Vol. 4. Heidelberg: Hüthig, 1996, pp. 130–136..

Helmers, S.; Hoffmann, U.; Canzler, W. "Die 'Datenautobahn.'" *Forum Wissenschaft*, Vol. 12, No. 1 (1995), pp. 10–15.

IWD (Informationsdienst des Instituts der deutschen Wirtschaft). *Computer-Einsatz—Globales Gefaelle.* Vol. 29, January 13, 1994, p. 1.

Kleinsteuber, H.J. "U.S. National Infrastructure vs. German Digital Television." Paper prepared for a conference on "Social Shaping of Information Highways," October 5–7, 1995. (http://infosoc/informatik.uni-bremen.de/nii/)

Kors, J. and Boeckelmann, F. "Wachstumsbranche Rundfunk: Produktionswert und Beschäftigung nach 10 Jahren Privatrundfunk in Deutschland." *Tendenz* (January 1995), Bayerische Landeszentrale für neue Medien, pp. 4–15.

KtK (Kommission für den Ausbau des technischen Kommunikationssystems). *Telekommunikationsbericht.* Bonn: Bundesminister für das Post- und Fernmeldewesen, 1976.

Kubicek, H. et al., eds. *Neue Spieler—Neue Regeln: Jahrbuch Telekommunikation und Gesellschaft,* Vol. 4. Heidelberg: Hüthig, 1996.

Kürble, P. *Determinanten der Nachfrage nach multimedialen Pay-TV-Diensten in Deutschland.* Diskussionsbeiträge No. 148. Bad Honnef: Wissenschaftliches Institut für Kommunikationsdienste, 1995.

Landtag von Baden-Württemberg. Report and Recommendations of the Inquiry Commission, *Entwicklung, Chancen und Auswirkungen neuer Informations- und Kommunikationstechnologien in Baden-Württemberg.* Document 11/6400, October 1995.

Mettler-Meibom, B. *Breitbandtechnologie.* Opladen: Westdeutscher Verlag, 1986.

MGM. *Marktübersicht Online-Dienste.* Munich: MGM 1995.

Middelhoff, T. *Zukunft Multimedia: Globale Informationsinfrastrukture und neue Märkte.* Bertelsmann Briefe 134, Supplement. Gütersloh: 1995.

Opaschowski, H.W. *Medienkonsum.* Hamburg: B.A.T.-Freizeit-Forschungsinstitut, 1995.

Peters, Falk. Statement to a hearing of the Bundestag Committee for Post and Telecommunications on the Subject of Multimedia. September 20, 1995.

Prognos AG. *Digitales Fernsehen: Marktchancen und ordnungspolitischer Regelungsbedarf.* Munich: Bayerische Landeszentrale für Neue Medien, Vol. 30, 1995.

Riehm, U. and Wingert, B. *Multimedia: Mythen, Chancen und Herausforderungen.* Mannheim: 1995.

Scherer, J. *Telekommunikationsrecht und Telekommunikationspolitik.* Baden-Baden: Nomos Verlag, 1985.

Schneider, V. "The Governance of Large Technical Systems: The Case of Telecommunications." In La Porte, T.R., ed. *Responding to Large Technical Systems.* Dordrecht: Kluwer 1991, pp. 18–40.

Schneider, V. and Werle, R. "Policy Networks in the German Telecommunications Domain." In Marin, B. and Mayntz, R., eds. *Policy Networks.* Frankfurt/M. and Boulder, CO: 1991, pp. 97–136.

Schrape, K. "Kultur und Professionalisierung von Mediendienstleistungen." In Bullinger, H.J., ed. *Dienstleistung der Zukunft.* Wiesbaden: Gabler 1995, pp. 253–274.

Schwab, R. "Netze, Dienste, Marktvolumina im statistischen Überblick." In Kubicek, H. et al., eds. *Neue Spieler—Neue Regeln: Jahrbuch Telekommunikation und Gesellschaft,* Vol. 4. Heidelberg: Hüthig, 1996, pp. 398–404.

Schwuchow, W. *Die deutsche Informationswirtschaft im internationalen Vergleich.* 1995. http://www.nordwest.pop.de/bda/nat/w/w/presse/10.html

Sommerlatte, T. "Neue Märkte durch Multimedia: Chancen und Barrieren." In Eberspächer, J., ed., *Neue Märkte durch Multimedia*. Munich: Springer Verlag, 1995, pp .16–30.

Thomas, G.; Vedel, T.; and Schneider, V. "The United Kingdom, France and Germany: Setting the Stage." In Bouwman, H. and Christoffersen, M., eds. *Relaunching Videotex*. Dordrecht: Kluwer, 1992.

Zoche, P. Statement on multimedia of the Fraunhofer-Institut für Systemtechnik und Innovationsforschung at a hearing of the Bundestag Committee for Post and Telecommunications. September 20, 1995.

ZVEI/VDMA. *Fachverbund Informationstechnik im VDMA und ZVEI: Eckdaten zur Informationsgesellschaft. Informations-Infrastrukturen im internationalen Vergleich.* Frankfurt/M.: December 1995. (Also in English: http://www.kp.dlr.de/BMWI/gip/fakten/)

The Information Welfare Society: An Assessment of Danish Governmental Initiatives Preparing for the Information Age

Annemarie Munk Riis

"Clearly there will be as many information societies as there are societies. All countries should not try to charge down a single path emulating the perceived leaders in technological development at any moment in time. Rather each society will want to use the new technology and service opportunities to serve its particular priority needs and values, and so help to shape its future."—William H. Melody (1995)

Introduction

A highly educated work force, an innovative and flexible production force and an efficient welfare system have contributed to Denmark's position as one of the richest countries of the world. Whether Denmark will be able to maintain this position in the Information Age, when ever more sophisticated technology is making the world shrink and computers and networks are creating the potential for entirely new information and production processes, has been widely discussed in the 1990s. Like many citizens of other industrialized nations, many Danes fear that the new technological regime will lead to a further loss of jobs. Others foresee that Denmark will benefit from the technological transition and gain competitive advantage if it constantly pushes to be on the cutting edge of technology applications.

If one examines some of the prerequisites for succeeding in the Information Age, Denmark's prospects seem promising. Having made discriminating investments in its educational and communications infrastructure, Denmark is poised to take a leading position in rapidly evolving, knowledge-intensive, high-wage industries. Despite a tiny population of five million, Denmark has a well-developed technological infrastructure with a high penetration of fiber optics and high-speed broadband services. Furthermore, advanced information technology has found its way into Danish industries and into the public sector, and over 30 percent of Danish households are equipped with a computer. Danish industry has traditionally demonstrated a profound ability to reorient production to new competitive conditions. This competency is indeed useful in building up an information society based on knowledge and technology-extensive production of goods and services.

In the postwar years, Denmark grew rich not by playing a role in the leading sectors of the world economy, but through flexible specialization in niche products. As a result, Denmark's per capita gross domestic product (GDP) of U.S.$26,204 is one of the highest in Europe. Surpassed only by Luxembourg within the European Union (EU). The public sector accounts for about 60 percent of GDP, and for 30 percent of total employment. The importance of the public sector in Denmark is second only to that of Sweden. The Danish economy is highly fragmented, with half of all firms in the manufacturing sector employing fewer than 20 people, and only five percent employing 200 or more people. (By comparison, U.S. manufacturing firms with fewer than 20 employees accounted for only eight percent of the manufacturing work force in the mid-1980s). In 1995, Denmark's unemployment rate was about nine percent, which was one percent lower than the average unemployment rate in the European Union, but significantly higher than the U.S. unemployment rate of about six percent.

The Danish government, industry and labor unions are strongly committed to jointly meeting the challenges and opportunities of the new competitive international order. A November 1994 report of a working group of specialists from government, academia, the telecommunications and electronics industry, consumer organizations, the labor movement and other sectors recommended a strategy for developing an information society in Denmark. This strategy built on distinctive Danish values such as openness, democracy, equity and responsibility for all people in society, and it stressed that the information society should preserve and underscore the aims of the welfare state by offering new opportunities for citizens and securing social stability. This major emphasis on social issues and public sector applications of information technology (IT) reflected Denmark's status as a welfare state with egalitarian values, or as the report stated, "the country is characterized by some basic—and often tacit—values. Our social consciousness reaches far, we care for our welfare society. The distribution of income and wealth is not as uneven as in most other, comparable countries" (Ministry of Research and Information Technology, 1994, p. 25). On the basis of these recommendations, in early 1995 the Danish government issued its strategy for the future of the information society.

The aim of creating an information society in Denmark is neither narrowly focused on providing the best conditions for commercial stakeholders nor exclusively directed at liberalizing the telecommunications market, as is the case in other countries. The use of the term "information society" rather than "national information infrastructure" reflects a broader conception of the challenge and opportunities posed by the Information Age. For Denmark, the myriad possibilities of technology are primarily linked with what they can do for society at large rather than the business opportunities they can create for commercial stakeholders. This is partly because Denmark has no large-scale commercial stakeholders supplying IT equipment such as computers and telephones. Furthermore, Denmark has no tradition of large-scale industrial policy projects, and instead focuses on providing a favorable business climate for the country's many small and medium-sized businesses.

To reach its goal, the Danish government believes that market forces should not be left alone since they will not provide socially optimal solutions. Two main approaches are at the core of the Danish strategy for developing an information society: the enhanced use of advanced technology and networking in the public sector (i.e., in education, health care, libraries, traffic and government services), and the early breakup of existing telecommunications monopolies. Denmark's early use of technology in the public sector (which accounts for 60 percent of GDP) proved to be an effective catalyst of innovation and competitiveness in private industry (e.g., in the production of health care equipment). By opening the telecom market, the government aims to enable Denmark to provide the world's most advanced and cheapest telecommunications services, which would allow the Danish consumer, private industry and the public sector to enjoy low-priced, advanced services that would improve the quality of life and create new jobs, particularly in the service sector. Other key themes in the Danish debate on telecommunications policy include privacy, the future of universal service, businesses' use of networks and the relationship between jobs and information technology.

Political Visions and Actions: Info-Society 2000

In 1994, the Danish Ministry of Research and Information Technology issued the report *Info-Society 2000* which proposed a Danish strategy for the Information Age. This report marked the first steps toward a radical upgrading of the political priority given to the broader development of an information society. It had been drafted by a committee of experts representing a wide range of ministries and government agencies, consumer interests and industry associations and chaired by former Minister for the Environment Lone Dybkjær and a high-ranking civil servant, Søren Christensen (see Figure 1).

The Dybkjær-Christensen Report proposed that the Danish government should develop a comprehensive strategy that could put Denmark on the cutting edge of the development toward an information society and would ensure that new technology "was a source for economic development and enhanced quality of life through increased openness and interchange of information as well as better public and private service." The report stressed that "the market forces should not be the only forces involved" (p. 24) and called for state and local authorities to do their share of the work in building an information society in Denmark. Nonetheless, the report did recognize that a significant part of the development toward an information society was controlled by market forces.

The committee agreed that Denmark should not simply copy other countries' approaches to the Information Age, but should instead create a distinctly Danish model based on Danish values that had developed since the establishment of the egalitarian

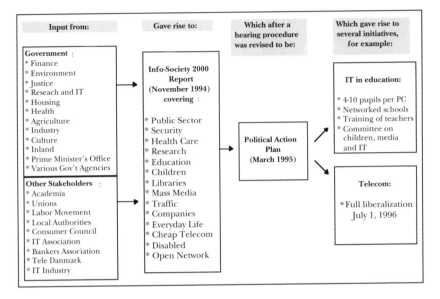

Figure 1   The Danish Model: Players, Strategy and Actions.

welfare state. The committee proposed a set of core values that the Danish strategy should build on in order to secure future economic growth and enhance the quality of life for all Danes. In particular, information technologies should:

• secure free access to and exchange of information;

• support democracy and individual influence;

• contribute to personal development;

• make the public sector more transparent and facilitate the delivery of better services;

• support disadvantaged members of society; and

• strengthen the international competitiveness of Danish companies as the basis for the Danish welfare system.

The report's comprehensive proactive strategy proposed 14 areas for action, primarily focused on the public sector (see Figure 1). Each field of action was analyzed in detail, and both principles for the Danish approach and specific initiatives were proposed. The report was circulated for comments in all Denmark's ministries and a number of government agencies, as well as business organizations and companies. *Info-Society 2000* immediately attracted the attention of all levels of society and became a government best-seller.

In March 1995, based on the recommendations of *Info-Society 2000*, the Danish government submitted to parliament a statement on the objectives of its strategy and a political action plan for 1995.[1] The action plan ("From Vision to Action: Info-Society 2000") largely adopted the proposals of the Dybkjær-Christensen Report and set out a range of initiatives to be implemented in 1995.

Figure 1 illustrates the Danish cooperative policy process for the information society project, concentrating on two fields of the strategy—IT & education; and deregulation of the telecom sector[2]—to illustrate how the process works.

It is fair to say that the action plan was generally welcomed by the public as well as by private industry, although many wondered how many of the initiatives would be financed. Fearing that the government initiative would be interpreted as a state-led crusade, the 1995 action plan stated in the introduction "this is not a kind of Soviet five-year plan with every detail being fixed for the coming years. Nor is it a traditional lump-sum plan with millions of kroner earmarked for each initiative. There is no need for this" (Ministry of Research and IT, 1995, p. 15). The budget for 1995 provided DKK 35 million (U.S.$6.1 million), and the action plan stated that the initiatives would generally remain within the overall state budget and that a reallocation of the approximately DKK 10 billion (U.S.$1.75 billion) for IT in the public sector would help fund the initiatives. Nevertheless, the 1996 budget increased the amount committed to DKK 291 million (U.S.$51 million) for information society-related projects. Despite this increase, the government's strategy is still being criticized for not committing enough funding to achieve its ambitious goals and for not devising specific budgets for public/private funding of the initiatives. Copenhagen has also been criticized for not carrying out a cost-benefit analysis (Melody, 1995).[3]

Although the financing of many of the initiatives in the 1995 action plan remained unresolved, several projects were launched in the course of 1995. Since the strategy concentrated on the public sector's use of IT and advanced networking, most of the initiatives and success stories were found there. The main achievements as of February 1996 are listed below:

- A government-funded (DKK 40 million/U.S.$7 million) Virtual Center for IT Research that connects departments of various universities by networks was created. Its aim is to upgrade and enhance Danish IT research, especially in software.
- An IT Security Council that debates security and privacy issues related to the information society was established.
- Denmark became the first country to allow public institutions to shift to purely electronic processing and filing.
- Denmark became the first country to introduce a national electronic-mail directory backed by all Danish e-mail providers.
- Stage one of the telecom liberalization was finalized on July 1, 1995.
- Political agreement was reached on achieving the full liberalization of the telecommunications sector by July 1, 1996.
- A trilateral summit of labor market parties and the government was held to discuss future requirements of the information society, education policies, trade policy and eventual public support for reorganization of companies aiming at using IT efficiently.
- Thirteen spearhead projects were launched in ten municipalities with the aim of creating more efficient public service and improving communication between the populace and the administration.

Clearly, the first year of the information society strategy has put Denmark in the fast lane in preparing for the Information Age. However, it will take many more years before the mission is completed and the results can be measured. Nonetheless, some of the elements of this strategy merit closer examination.

Social Concerns and Economic Gains

One initiative that successfully supports the Danish welfare state and also provides good business opportunities focuses on increasing the use of IT in the health care sector. There are three benefits of using IT applications in the health care sector: 1) increased health care quality and access through improved clinical processes; 2) reduced costs because of improved productivity; and 3) enhanced competitiveness of the nation's medical technology industry.[4] A focal point of the Danish strategy for the information society is thus to build a better public health sector with more efficient treatment. Projects for image transmission through the telecommunications networks have been initiated at various hospitals, and a special, government-funded test case has been set up in the city of Odense. The Ministry of Health in cooperation with county councils, municipalities and other players in the health care sector prepared an action plan for the establishment of a health network based on the MedCom Project. The aim of this project is to make all general practices, hospitals, pharmacies and so forth electronic before the year 2000.[5]

Denmark has not set up a large-scale support scheme for the medical technology sector, or for any other strategic sectors. The Danish strategy refrains from inaugurating any special programs aimed at developing large-scale Danish production of IT. Quite on the contrary, only two out of 12 broad fields of action focus directly on the commercial side of the information society. Moreover, these initiatives focus solely on the user—i.e., industrial use of e-mail, electronic data interchange (EDI) and other advanced network technologies. One can, however, identify several initiatives that indirectly have a positive influence on the business environment. For example, the strategy emphasizes that it is crucial to increase the effort towards creating a knowledge-intensive society stressing the importance of education and training; this factor is believed to have significantly stimulated Danish industrial competitiveness. It has become increasingly obvious that Denmark's high-wage work force has to be able to compete on the world markets by providing knowledge-intensive goods and services. The information society strategy's emphasis on human resources thus mirrors the general Danish conclusion that Denmark's niche in the new competitive international order is to produce "hyperspecialized" quality goods and services by using technologically advanced production processes (Lindholm, 1995). Manufacturing processes must be highly flexible as product life cycles get shorter and innovation races faster. These conditions require both a highly educated work force and an efficient method of organizing production.

The Decision-Making Process in the Telecommunications Sector

In 1994, the *Danish Ministry of Research and Information Technology* (which was created by the new coalition government) was allocated overall jurisdiction of information technology and became responsible for the government's IT policy and for telecommunications.[6] The creation of the new ministry marked a significant political upgrading of IT matters in Denmark.

The *National Telecommunications Agency* (Telestyrelsen) of the Ministry of Research and IT is the center of government expertise on telecommunications. It is in charge of regulatory and administrative functions in the telecommunications sector, including preparatory legislative work, the administration of licenses and frequencies, inspection, type approval, specifications, supervision and control. In preparing executive orders for the minister the Agency involves a wide range of organizations (e.g., the Consumer Council, trade unions, industrial associations, labor).

The Telecommunications Board (Telenævnet) serves as board of appeals on decisions of the National Telecommunications Agency on certain telecommunications issues related to exclusive and special rights holders. Within the government, the *IT Forum* is a coordinating forum where representatives of all the ministries can discuss the common IT strategy and the interrelated IT initiatives of various ministries. In 1995, the Minister for Research and IT established the *IT Security Board*, which has the task of pointing out the risks facing society from the increased use of IT[7] (i.e., the Board assesses issues like security, data protection, the paperless office and the national identification card). The *National Advisory Council on Telecommunications* (Telerådet) advises the Minister of Research and IT on issues presented to the minister for comment. The Advisory Council also takes up issues on its own accord and has all questions regarding a number of areas of telecom regulation presented before final decision are made. The Advisory Council includes representatives of 35 private and public bodies, including the new operators in the Danish telecom market such as France Telecom and Telia.

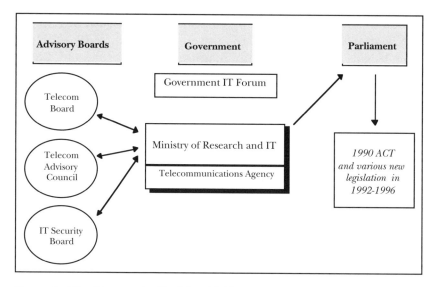

Figure 2   The Cooperative Decision-Making Process in Telecommunications.

In sum, it is fair to say that in Denmark close cooperation exists among government, industry and consumers in the field of telecommunications, which reflects the government's clear aim that "the public sector should interact with the private sector on a forceful strategy for Denmark's development towards the information society and take the lead in the efficient use of information technology" (Ministry for Research and IT, 1994). The role of the state is thus to consult industry and consumers on important matters and to provide a favorable framework for Danish businesses to operate in. In other words, the state is supportive rather than directly interventionist. The government instead concentrates its efforts on using advanced technology in its own affairs (re-engineering public administration, finding new ways of providing government information, improving health care and education, etc.), which has a positive impact on the private sector.

The cooperative nature of the Danish decision-making process has so far avoided creating significant problems in the field of telecommunications. Danish trade unions generally look positively on the introduction of new technologies in the work place. Kraft and Bansler (1993) state that it is surprising to outside observers how willing the Danish trade unions are to appreciate the perspective of management regarding Denmark's competitiveness in the international economy. Competitiveness and innovation are the watchwords for both the national unions and management, which is why the introduction of IT in the workplace has not been disturbed. Denmark is therefore unlikely to experience major battles over the information society strategy: all parties are committed to maintaining industrial peace since it drives the welfare state and supports rising standards of living. Consequently, at an early 1996 meeting between the labor market parties and the government it was again emphasized by all parties that the development of the information society needs to be managed through proactive strategies stressing: 1) the development of human resources; 2) innovation and research; and 3) public-private cooperation (Ministry of Research and IT et al., February 1996).

The Danish telecommunications liberalization process has been criticized for being too close to the Ministry. It is argued that in order to preserve its authority in the field of telecommunications, the Telecommunications Agency's ties to the Ministry and the political system need to be released (Fischer-Madsen, 1995). In the still more competitive market it is not considered optimal that the Minister for Research and IT continues to get involved in specific cases about tariff regulations and so forth. The UK approach with OFTEL as an independent regulator has often been pointed out as a more appropriate model. If Denmark adopted that model, the Ministry could operate solely on the political and legislative level, leaving specific decisions on tariffs, licenses, price controls, etc., to the independent regulator.

The main problem related to the Ministry's authority is that the state still owns a majority of shares in Tele Danmark (51 percent), and that the highest-ranking civil servant in the Ministry, the permanent under-secretary, is a member of Tele Danmark's board. The 1990 Telecommunications Act mandates that the government appoint six of Tele Danmark's 12 board members, including the chairman and the deputy chairman, who are under special obligation to "inform the minister of any company business that might interest him." The permanent under-secretary is blamed for not being able to both represent the shareholders' interest and secure fair competition for Tele Danmark's competitors. Sonofon, Tele Danmark's competitor in mobile communications, has complained that the regulator does not provide a level playing field in the global system of mobile communications (GSM). Indeed, it is a regulatory paradox that authoritative and operational tasks are so tightly intertwined (M. Andersen, 1995).

Telecom Liberalization

The Political Agreement on the Telecommunications Structure of June 22, 1990 (Act 743/90), established the framework for the liberalization of the Danish telecom market. The first step was to establish a strong Danish telecom provider—Tele Danmark—which was a concessionary holding company for the regional telephone companies (KTAS, Jydsk Telefon, Fyns Telefon, TeleSønderjylland) and the international operator, Telecom. The idea was to build a strong company, in Danish hands, which could survive in a fully liberalized environment. Tele Danmark was granted monopoly rights on telephone service, telex, mobile and paging services, data transmission services and the provision of leased lines. Gradually Tele Danmark's exclusive right to provide services was restricted: e.g., in 1991 mobile communications was duopolized, and in 1993–1994 the provision of X.25 was liberalized. In 1994, Denmark endorsed the EU decision to introduce competition based on common European regulation of the entire telecommunications sector by January 1, 1998.

However, in 1995, Denmark leaped ahead of the EU in deregulating telecommunications: on April 6, 1995, an understanding was reached among the political parties on a two-stage strategy for the implementation of the future Danish telecommunications policy. Stage One, which took effect on July 1, 1995, implied that Tele Danmark's exclusive rights to transmit radio and TV signals and to establish broadband in local areas were lifted. Moreover, just before the finalization of Stage One the Minister for Research and IT issued a proposal in June 1995 for the full liberalization of Danish telecommunications: "Real Competition—the Road to the World's Best and Cheapest Telecommunications."[8] In December 1995, political agreement set the deadline for full liberalization as July 1, 1996, overtaking the EU deadline by 18 months.

The full liberalization in Stage Two will entail the introduction of new legislation in two phases. In the first phase (to be completed during spring 1996), the Danish Parliament will pass legislation

Table 1   The Final Stages of Danish Telecom Deregulation 1995-1996

Stage 1 (July 1, 1995)

1. Normalization of the hybrid network: Tele Danmark's right to transmit radio and TV programming via the nationwide telecommunications network was lifted.
2. Liberalization of local broadband networks: Tele Danmark's right to establish broadband networks in local areas (e.g., within the boundaries of a municipality) was lifted.
3. Establishment of private networks: The possibility of establishing internal infrastructure within companies or between closely related companies was improved and the establishment of private networks was facilitated.
4. Lowest tariffs for broadband connections: Charges for using broadband connections, both of the 140 Mbit/s and 34 Mbit/s categories, were reduced by 65 percent on average. This means that Denmark has the world's lowest national standard tariffs for broadband connections.
5. Improved conditions for mobile operators: Special rights in the mobile services area were extended to cover direct interconnection between mobile networks in Denmark and abroad.
6. Political constraints on Tele Danmark's organization no longer apply

Stage 2a (July 1, 1996)

1. Universal service obligation: All users were guaranteed access to telephone services (including ISDN) and leased-line services at diminishing maximum prices.
2. Full liberalization in the infrastructure field
3. Provisional framework for interconnectivity
4. Establishment of an independent telecommunications supervisory authority and effective appeal bodies
5. Promotion of further competition in the mobile sector
6. Competition in the telecommunications sector
7. Radio and transmission network
8. Telecommunications companies granted the right to provide radio and TV broadcasting services

Stage 2b (Autumn 1996)

1. Consumer interests
2. Regular interconnectivity regulation
3. New radio frequency legislation
4. New legislation in the telephone number field
5. Rights of way, access to buildings, erection of masts, etc.

Source: Ministry of Research and IT (1995b, 1996c)

deregulating all segments of the telecommunications market; in the second phase (autumn 1996), it will pass legislation on broader issues, such as consumer rights, right of way, access to buildings and interconnectivity (see Table 1).

Danish Initiatives in the EU Context

Denmark's information society initiative is clearly influenced by the actions of the European Union. In 1994, a group of leading industrialists under the chairmanship of Commissioner Bangemann issued the so-called Bangemann Report which emphasized the need to build an efficient information infrastructure in Europe. The conclusions of the report gained support from the European Commission which responded to the Bangemann group's findings in July 1994 with an action plan: "Europe's Way to the Information Society: An Action Plan." The Commission thus increased awareness of the need to speed up the liberalization of telecommunications in Europe and to provide an efficient information infrastructure throughout Europe.

The EU member-states agreed on liberalizing telecommunications and cable television by January 1, 1998. The Infrastructure Green Paper, which was published in two parts in late 1994 and early 1995 (European Commission, 1994 & 1995), was primarily concerned with the basic principles of and timetable for liberalization, but it also addressed particular issues such as universal service, interconnectivity and interoperability, employment and the information society. The European Commission also set up several programs to support the development of a European information society by funding the use of information technologies and networks (e.g., health care networks, telecommuting, distance learning). The Advanced Communications Technologies and Services (ACTS) project, for example, proposed to move beyond research into commercial production of advanced network technologies, applications and services.[9]

Infrastructure and the Penetration of the Information Society

Compared to those of the United States and various European countries the Danish telecommunications infrastructure is fairly advanced and well developed. Denmark has 3.06 million access phone lines in operation, and its telephone penetration per 100 inhabitants is one of the highest in the EU (see Table 2). Thanks to favorable demographics, low prices and effective marketing, mobile telephone penetration stood at 16 percent in January 1996, which is one of the highest rates in the world, though not exceptional by Nordic standards. The total growth in mobile subscribers from 1993 to 1994 was 80 percent. The trunk network was fully digitized; however, only 46 percent of the local exchange lines were digitized. The lack of digital switches meant that intelligent network services such as itemized billing and toll-free numbers were not introduced until 1993 although these services had been common in many other European countries for years.

In 1994, 1.7 million Danish homes (76 percent) had cable television—one of the highest ratios in the European Union. Furthermore, the use of computers in private homes was only surpassed by the United States. In 1994, 32 percent of Danish homes were equipped with a computer; by the beginning of 1996, the penetration rate was estimated to be as high as 50 percent. The aggregate power of a nation's installed base of computers gives an indication of how well the country adapts to new information technology. In terms of the installed base of computer power, Table 2 reveals that the United States is far ahead of other countries. However, Denmark is one of the front-runners in Europe. In terms of per capita computer sales, which indicate the renewal of the computer base, Denmark is ahead of most other countries. However, when it comes to using computer networks, the Danes still have a long way to go: in 1993, as few as 1.4 percent of the population owned a computer that was connected to a network via a modem. And in 1995, it was estimated that only 35,000 Danes were connected to the Internet (less than one percent of the population). However, a number of Internet providers have established themselves in Denmark since mid-1995, and a boom in use of the Internet is expected in 1996. Moreover, the portion of Danish offices equipped with a computer—85 percent—is significantly higher than the average 55 percent in the EU.

A report on information technology issued by the Organization for Economic Cooperation and Development (OECD) in 1994

Table 2 Indicators of Preparedness for the Information Age

	Denmark	US	Germany	UK	France
Phone lines per 100 inhabitants (1993)[c]	59.1	55.2	46.3	46.4	53.1
Mobile phone penetration per 100 inhabitants (1994)[a]	10	NA	2.9	5	1.5
Digital switches, % of total (1993)[a]	46	NA	32	63	83
Computer penetration, % of households (1994)[c]	32	44	16	26	20
Computer sales, ECU per inhabitant (1993)[d]	588	531	365	349	358
Computer power, MIPS per inhabitant (1992)[d]	240	516	NA	217	180
Modems per 100 inhabitants (1993)[b]	1.4	NA	0.4	NA	0.9*
Cable TV penetration, % of households (1994)[a]	76	67	61	13	26
IT investments, % of GDP (1993)[d]	2.71	2.87	1.91	2.38	1.98
% of this investment in IT services	48	33	40	40	45
IT work places, % of all office employees (1993)	85	NA	61	57	57

Sources: a. Mercer (1994); b. IDC (1993); c. IDC (1994); d. Erhvervsredegørelsen (1994).
* Minitel not included

showed a significant correlation between per capita GDP and IT spending, which certainly applied in the case of Denmark. The wide use of IT-dependent production methods and the extensive utilization of IT in the public sector are reflected in high—and growing—IT spending. Danish IT investments in 1993 amounted to 2.71 percent of GDP, which in the European context was only surpassed by Sweden. Denmark's high level of IT investment reflects a significant proportion of investment in IT *services*—i.e., education, consultancy, technical services and value-added network services (voice mail, e-mail, EDI, video conferences, etc.).

Another way of determining a country's readiness for the Information Age is to look at computer literacy and corporate use of IT. The World Competitiveness Report for 1993 issued by the World Competitiveness Forum compared these two factors in 38 countries (based on a opinion survey conducted by the World Economic Forum); Denmark ranked second in both categories.[10]

The Danish Communications, Information and Computer Markets

Communications—Tele Danmark's Crumbling Monopoly

When Tele Danmark was founded in 1990, the state owned 90 percent of its shares. In 1993, however, the state's ownership of the company was reduced to 51 percent.[11] The restrictions on Tele Danmark's organizational structure were loosened in April 1995, when a political agreement allowed Tele Danmark to create a more business-oriented organizational structure. Denmark's regional telecom companies subsequently merged with Tele Danmark, and Tele Danmark reached an agreement with the trade unions that, until 1997, no employees would be made redundant as a consequence of changes in the organizational structure, and that there would be no major redistribution of jobs among various parts of the country.

Tele Danmark's revenues increased in the early 1990s, reaching DKK 18 billion (U.S.$3.1 billion) in 1994. The 1994 distribution of revenues (see Table 3) reveals that apart from international projects,[12] Tele Danmark did not engage in any new business areas (e.g., Internet provision, advanced value-added services) contributing to revenues. Still, the lion's share of the income came from business areas with low competition, making the provision of domestic wireline telephone service—for which it still had exclusive rights—Tele Danmark's core business.[13]

Mobile telephone and paging services comprised the fastest growing area of business for Tele Danmark in 1994, accounting for eight percent of revenues. The Danish market for mobile services has a duopoly; the Telecommunications Act of 1990 established that the Ministry of Research and IT could license the provision of one additional wireless network to compete with Tele Danmark. In 1991, the ministry awarded this GSM license to Sonofon, creating fierce competition between Tele Danmark and Sonofon in the mobile market. The Danish mobile market is expected to grow substantially over the next few years, with a mobile penetration rate of 20 percent predicted for 1997 (McClelland and Bright, 1995). Tele Danmark presently controls 60 percent of the mobile market.

Although Danish telecommunications were liberalized gradually, it is fair to say that the Danish telecom market is not competi-

Table 3 Revenues in Tele Danmark's Areas of Business (1994)

Business area	% of revenues	Degree of liberalization
Domestic calls	40	low/medium
International calls	16	low
Mobile telephone services	8	medium
Leased lines	5	zero
Business and installations	14	high
Service center	4	medium
Data communication	2	high
Cable television	2	high
International projects	2	high
Others	7	high

Sources: Tele Danmark (1995); Ministry of Research and IT (1995b)

tive. Tele Danmark maintains its dominant position, with a 90 percent share of the market. However, many international telecom companies are positioned to enter the Danish market when it is fully opened to competition in July 1996. The Swedish company Telia and France Telecom have been present in the Danish market since 1995, and Unisource, AT&T and the Uniworld alliance have expressed interest in selling telecommunications services to large Danish companies with a high level of international telecommunications traffic. Telia appears interested in becoming a general supplier of telecommunications services (including infrastructure) in Denmark, with a market share objective of 20 percent (Ministry of Research and IT, 1995b). In addition, the Danish State Railway (DSB) has a nationwide network of fiber-optic cables for signaling control and internal communication that it could utilize for telecom transmission. Studies show that DSB, if allowed, is in a position to sell—at a very low marginal cost—its excess capacity at rates well below Tele Danmark's (Kristiansen et al., 1991). This is true despite the fact that in 1995 Denmark—according to the OECD—had one of the lowest telecom rates in the OECD. Only Finland and Iceland had lower tariffs on telephone calls via the PSTN for domestic business services. For residential calls Denmark was the fourth cheapest country in the OECD, and third for both leased lines and mobile telephone services with prices half the average level in the OECD countries.[14]

In 1993, Mercer Management Consulting issued a report assessing the competitiveness of Tele Danmark's domestic network infrastructure. The study benchmarked Tele Danmark's network against those of 15 other operators, and concluded that Tele Danmark's network was able to meet any competitive threat. Mercer thus recommended a smaller infrastructure investment budget than first planned by Tele Danmark (Insead, 1995), and suggested that Tele Danmark should focus more on service-related investment programs (toll-free services, calling cards, etc.). This recommendation contrasted with the European Commission's 1992 review which concluded that infrastructure investment was most important. The Mercer study also concluded that Tele Danmark would face serious problems with early deregulation: revenues were predicted to fall by six percent annually, and it estimated that by the year 2000, 30 percent of Tele Danmark's revenues would be captured by competitors (Insead, 1995).[15]

In sum, Tele Danmark's biggest challenge prior to full deregulation is to manage the new competitive situation in the soon-to-be liberalized market. With the largest shares of revenues still flowing from well-established businesses such as national and international telephone services that will be opened to free competition in July 1996, Tele Danmark can expect to lose revenues to new competitors who are predicted to target Tele Danmark's core business areas.

Cable Television

The Danish cable industry is very fragmented, with more that 10,000 networks in operation (Mercer, 1994). Until the first stage of the liberalization process (July 1995) only Tele Danmark, municipalities and nonprofit organizations were allowed to transmit radio and TV programming on the national telecommunications network, and Tele Danmark had the exclusive rights to transmit radio and TV signals across municipal borders. However, in 1994, TV transmission contributed only two percent to Tele Danmark's revenues, although the company had about 50 percent of all cable subscriptions. Most other cable networks are owned by municipalities, which, if large enough, operate their own networks. The largest cable operator after Tele Danmark is Stofa, which manages (but does not own) approximately 25 networks nationwide with an estimated market share of 20 percent. This consortium includes Cox Enterprise and GN Store Nord A/S.

As of July 1995, Tele Danmark's exclusive right to transmit radio and TV programming was lifted to allow unrestricted transmission or provision of services via the network over lines leased from Tele Danmark. This step lifted all restrictions on the use of leased lines and paved the way for service providers who wanted to use the telecommunications network for services that combined transmission of programming with other services interactive services (like e.g., video on demand) (Ministry of Research and IT, April 1995 Agreement).

The Internet

An estimated 35,000 Danes are connected to the Internet and there are 17 Internet and on-line services providers in Denmark which are mostly Danish companies. The big U.S. on-line service provider CompuServe also offers Internet connections. DENet is the Danish research community's part of the Internet network to which the Danish Computer Center for Research and Education (UNI-C) provides access. However, during 1995, business customers also began connecting to the Internet via UNI-C and on January 1, 1996, DENet was split into separate research and a business networks. The research network was upgraded from a 2 Mbps net to a high-speed network of 34 Mbps. The government co-funded the establishment of the high-speed backbone and Tele Danmark won the procurement (KommUNICation, Dec. 1995). Internationally, the Danish network is connected to Stockholm (the Nordic network center) from where there are 34 Mbps high-speed connections to the United States and connections to Paris, London and Munich will be built during 1996.[16]

Information: Broadcasting and Cable Television

The Scandinavian countries were among the last OECD members to abandon long-standing monopolies for public service broadcasters and to allow advertising on radio and television. In 1983, the incumbent, state-subsidized Danmarks Radio (DR) lost its television and radio monopoly and foreign channels were allowed to be received in Denmark, and in 1988, an additional license for a terrestrial, largely advertising-funded television channel was granted to TV2. DR and TV2 (and TV2's regional channels) fulfill the public service obligation since they are non-commercial, not directly owned by the state, and provide the public with a broad spectrum of quality programs.

In 1994, Danish households were able to receive on average nine TV channels, including many foreign cable and satellite stations such as MTV, CNN and BBC. However, Danish TV3 was the most popular channel after DR and TV2. There is now strong competition among broadcasters, and both TV2 and DR are under pressure, finding it difficult to maintain their previously high ratings. This has led to discussions about the appropriateness and extent of financing via the license system. The debate about the future of DR and TV2 as public service channels has been particular intense, and in a world where electronic media is increasingly dominated by international channels and producers, the Danish government deems it vital to preserve the Danish culture and language to continue to support a public service function in radio and television.

Although Denmark has the disadvantage of being a small market and a small language area, the breakup of DR's broadcasting monopoly increased the national market for production of television programs and a large number of production companies have subsequently been established. However, trans-national giants like Time Warner control a large share of the Danish entertainment market, and there is no expectation of an increase in the number of Danish-language TV channels. A much-discussed question related to content development is the issue of copyright. *Info-Society 2000* argued that if Danish production is to survive in a situation where international (mainly U.S.) supply is overwhelming and available at relatively low prices, it should be made possible to recycle Danish productions in various forms of distribution. Thus the Danish Media Commission is working on how to recycle content without undermining the economics of production.

On-line Services

Politiken, the largest Danish daily newspaper, offers an on-line service with news and other information databases. In early 1995,

Tele Danmark, together with GiroBank and the two main daily newspapers, introduced another Denmark-based on-line service, Diatel, which provided a wide range of services from 70 different service providers, including home shopping and home banking. In February 1996, the original Diatel company, with only 12,000 users, was closed down; however, its on-line service continues under the ownership of Tele Danmark, which shifted Diatel's technological platform to the Internet. Tele Danmark aims at becoming Denmark's biggest provider of Internet services by the end of 1996, and is developing an Internet payment system in the Danish language and a Danish version of Netscape for its customers.

Multimedia

The main Danish publishers are involved on a small scale in producing multimedia CD-ROMs in the Danish language. However, there is a lag in the expertise needed to develop multimedia content. Denmark has no well-developed industry exploiting the opportunities of developing new technologies for the Internet, and there is no Danish tradition of developing general-use software products. The focus of Danish software producers has mainly been on specially tailored software for single customers. Thus there is debate about publicly supporting a coordinated effort to develop Danish multimedia competence to enable Danish firms to produce both Danish and foreign-language multimedia products. There is talk about a government-funded Danish Media Lab (after the MIT Media Lab model) that could spur interaction between private industry and public research institutions in order to develop general multimedia systems as well as multimedia products for hospitals, education, leisure, and so forth (Ministry for Research and IT, 1996b).

Computing: Lack of Hardware Production

OECD statistics reveal that Denmark has no significant production of office, computing and accounting (OCA) machinery. In 1989, less than one percent of Denmark's GDP came from this sector, whereas in Germany, OCA contributed six percent, in France the sector accounted for 5.3 percent, and in the United Kingdom and the United States this sector contributed 3.5 percent to GDP. These figures certainly show that Denmark is not a significant player in the computer market. However, at the same time the generally low figures for the OCA contribution to national GDPs reveals that the sector is not one of the most important to any country. What is important is the impact OCA products have on the related service sectors and on productivity (OECD, 1994).

When looking at trade performance, Denmark's OCA market share is similarly insignificant (less than one percent of the world export market), and it is decreasing (OECD, 1994). In 1990, Denmark's comparative advantage in OCA was the lowest among the OECD countries; however, Denmark's degree of specialization was increasing and Danish firms were gaining competitiveness in niche markets (OECD, 1994). Danish IT companies are generally very small and are not competitive in products that demand economies of scale and enormous R&D budgets (e.g., consumer electronics, chip production). Thus, Danish IT companies focus on niche segments of the IT market, developing fairly advanced, specially tailored products. Denmark's advanced public and private sector demand provides an important basis for the development of products such as radio navigation equipment, mobile communications, loudspeakers, hearing aids,[17] medical measuring instruments, etc. In these products Denmark holds significant market shares and a trade surplus. In 1991, these niche markets contributed 1.6 percent of Danish exports and 11 percent of its trade surplus.

In 1993, the total revenues of the Danish IT, telecommunications and electronics sectors amounted to DKK 85 billion (U.S.$15 billion). IT services accounted for a major share of the DKK 46 billion revenues of the IT sector. This was mainly due to the high demand for services in the public sector, the financial sector and the agricultural sector as all sectors increasingly make use of IT.

Advanced Computing Systems

Denmark, via its advanced use of IT in the private and public sectors, has showed some success in developing large-scale efficient systems such as the Danish electronic debit card, Dankort. Dankort is unique in being a common system for *all* financial systems in

Denmark. It was introduced in 1993 and in August 1994 there were 2.5 million cardholders out of a total population of 5 million (Ministry of Research and IT, 1994). Despite the national success of Dankort, there has been no export of the system. Nevertheless, this advanced and early use of IT in banking has strengthened expertise and innovation within the highly specialized, advanced IT services, telecommunications and software of the banking sector. In other words, Denmark has developed expertise based on the extensive use of IT in payment transactions which it has parlayed into export of banking systems, despite the fact that Denmark does not otherwise have a competitive advantage in this field (Falch and Skouby, 1995).

* * *

The above descriptions reveal that the division of the IT markets into communications, information and computing is too crude. In the Information Age, only a few goods and services fit neatly into one of these three sectors. The picture has indeed become much more complex, and the dividing lines between sectors are becoming increasingly blurred as companies from the three sectors have begun to compete in each other's markets. This involvement of most actors in hybrid activities is what makes policy design for information societies so complex.

The Effectiveness of the Danish Information Society Approach

In the early 1990s, many governments unveiled large-scale visions for national information infrastructures, promising the public access to a wide range of new technological wonders. In contrast to most of these rhetorically rich—but often empty—promises, the Danish strategy has been one of profound exploration of the special opportunities the Information Age offers Denmark supported by an ambitious action plan. Melody (1995) asserts that the Dybkjær-Christensen Report is a "brilliant contribution" to the international literature on the information society, and stresses two particular strengths of the Danish model compared to other countries' strategies. First, through its focus on the application side (as opposed to technology supply as in, for example, the United States and the United Kingdom), the Danish strategy is much more concerned with how society at large can reap benefits from the Information Age. Second, the Danish strategy to a much larger extent acknowledges the many areas where the public sector can play a significant role by cooperating with private industry and being a key user of advanced technologies.

Denmark is better positioned to use IT strategically than most countries because of its small size, well-developed infrastructure and highly educated and independent workforce tailored for the flat network organization of the future. Moreover, Denmark is especially favored because it has recognized the importance of having advanced users of IT in all corners of Danish society; the government has pro-actively acknowledged the importance of letting the public sector be a lead user of IT; and Denmark has accelerated the liberalization of the telecommunication sector ahead of the EU.

It is fair to say that the Danish information society strategy is being pursued in a very ambitious and systematic way, carrying the actions much further than most other countries. The government has recognized the profound impact of the technological revolution on the Danish society, and that technology alone will not point the way or fulfill the dreams of deliverance. Technology is socially constructed; its character and implications depended on how it is organized, supplied, accessed and utilized in the context of corporate strategies, market structures and public policies. The Danish government (in cooperation with industry and consumer organizations) has decided to actively influence the development path for the Danish information society, arguing that the goal of society-wide gains from the technological revolution will not be reached by adopting a purely free-market model. Louis Branscomb once pointed out that "the Internet is egalitarian for those who are on it; it is elitist for those who can not use it, or do not have access to it." (Branscomb, 1994). This point was what the Dybkjær-Christensen Committee—and later the Danish government—had in its mind when designing its plan for the Info-Society 2000.

If the Danish model works—i.e. if it provides the right market incentives—it could very well lead to an extraordinary explosion of new opportunities for wealth creation and personal empowerment across Danish society. The mission's key mechanisms are briefly evaluated below.

Advanced Danish Users

From the outset, the Danish strategy has had the goal of preserving and underscoring the special Danish values of equity, democracy and openness, as well as high standards of living, and is committed to both engaging the whole population in the information society and enhancing Denmark's competitiveness. Indeed, these two aims are not contradictory: building a society of advanced users of information technology will not have a positive impact on competitiveness. Interaction between users and producers of new IT goods and services will be a major stimulus to technological change and economic growth. Thus the ubiquity of the information society is more than a social welfare issue: it is a strategic economic issue for the evolution of Denmark's competitiveness and economic growth. This mechanism is based on the foundation of small and medium-sized Danish companies with the ability to innovate and diffuse new technology.

Many scholars (Linder, 1961; Porter, 1990; Andersen & Lundvall, 1988; Bar & Borrus, 1993) have emphasized the importance of user-producer relations in the innovation process by arguing that national demand is a prime determinant of competitive advantage in countries—like Denmark—where growth is assumed to be innovation driven. Indeed, the Danish mission of universal IT use and networking could very well prove to be an effective tool for creating user-producer linkages that can significantly influence the Danish innovation path. By stimulating the pervasive use of new advanced technologies the government can create a user-active paradigm, where lay users (i.e., households, schoolchildren) can also make a contribution at different phases of the IT innovation process. By aiming at securing equal access to the information society for the whole population, the Danish model thus prevents the risk of excluding large segments of the economy from contributing to the discovery process (see, e.g., Bar, 1995).

Government as a Lead User

There are several actions that governments can take to enhance the development of the information society. The most prominent is facilitating innovation at the user-producer interface. Not surprisingly, empirical evidence suggests that government's direct role is greatest when it is itself an important user, and that public procurement has its greatest impact when technology is newly emerging (Rothwell, 1994). The Danish plan's emphasis on the public sector as a user of advanced IT thus is likely to positively influence Danish innovations in advanced technology. Historically, the public health system has acted as a demanding and sophisticated user of technology, thereby honing the competitiveness of Danish firms in this sector. Employing increasingly advanced IT and networking in health care in all likelihood will positively influence Danish competitiveness in producing advanced medical technology. In the same way, the Danish government's plans to increase its demand for advanced IT systems for educational purposes, traffic control, cultural networks and so forth will positively stimulate economic growth.

To ensure the necessary process of experimentation and learning, government policy should also encourage exploratory use among targeted user populations of special economic significance such as small businesses. Corporate networking experience suggests that experimentation and learning play an essential role in network development. Some elements of the network portfolio, such as private networks of large manufacturing corporations, support that learning process on their own (Bar, 1995). Small and medium-sized businesses often cannot afford such experimentation and would thus benefit from government assistance schemes. Assistance to small companies should include training potential users so that they can develop sufficient skills to participate in experimentation with new technology and networking. Also field trials exploring the support of interfirm linkages such as EDI should increasingly be funded by the Danish government in order to speed up the development of the Danish information society.

Furthermore, the Danish strategy should focus more on getting IT and networks into public schools and adapting the educational system to technological developments. There is demand for further cooperation between government and industry especially in renewing the educational system. Detailed cost-benefit analyses need to be carried out and a dialogue on how the government can achieve computer literacy among all students is called for.

Liberalization of Telecommunications

Denmark's decision to move ahead of the EU in deregulating the telecommunications industry is critical since having a telecom sector characterized by growth and innovation is of great importance to the competitiveness of the Danish business community. The government's objective of providing Danish users with the world's best and cheapest telecommunications services is certainly ambitious. However, if fulfilled, it could positively influence companies with growth potential connected with new and innovative IT applications as well as the broad range of small and medium-sized companies for which access to cheap, advanced services is crucial for future growth. Households will also benefit from the introduction of competition in telecommunications, since deregulation encourages the supply of a broader range of services at diminishing prices.

In 1996, the Danish parliament will pass legislation supporting the introduction of full competition in telecommunications. This legislation must be worked out very carefully if it is to balance the important dimensions of consumer protection, universal service obligations, interconnectivity and competition. Moreover, it is critical to ensure the National Telecom Agency's independence from the Ministry of Research and IT, in order to separate control of telecommunications from the political system.

Notes

The author gratefully acknowledges the very constructive comments of Heather Hazard and Brian Kahin.

1. The government aimed at issuing a yearly action plan.

2. The use of IT in schools and the deregulation of telecommunications were among the most politically controversial issues in Denmark in 1995. The possibility of developing electronic national identification cards and the security

and privacy issues linked to this initiative also attracted interest as many people feared that it would lead to a "Big Brother" state.

3. For example, the lag of public funding for the use of computers in primary schools was widely criticized, and the goal of having one computer for four pupils (instead of 40 computers per pupil as in 1994) was attacked for being far too ambitious if no additional funding was committed. The cost of this "IT & Education" initiative was estimated between DKK 1 and 2 billion ($180–360 million).

4. An increased effort is expected to further the existing competitive advantage of Danish medical technology companies. Previous Danish studies show that the advanced Danish health system has acted as a competent and demanding user of hospital instruments, thereby honing the strong competitiveness of Danish firms in the sector (Andersen and Lundvall, 1988). Analysts predict that the information technology market in health care could be the biggest growth market for IT providers in the 1990s, exceeding $20 billion by the turn of the century (*The New York Times*, October 21,1995).

5. In 1996, only DKK 10 million ($1.75 million) of public funds were committed to this project; however, it was expected that considerable gains from rationalization would help finance the project.

6. Danish television and broadcasting have their own set of regulations and regulators in the Ministry of Culture that deals with TV services, information content, public service and commercial radio and TV, etc. The telecommunications regulations govern provision of services. As the lines between these two elements become blurred there is a growing need for a common set of rules in broadcasting and telecommunications in order to avoid unequal competition between the converging sectors. Danish regulators are awaiting the Danish Media Commission's report addressing many of the questions related to the future of the broadcasting system.

7. Apart from the permanent boards several ad hoc working groups have been formed. on issues such as EDI, multimedia, privacy, etc.

8. The Minister stated that the main objective of deregulation was to obtain cheaper telecommunications services in Denmark, and that the future legislation should "reflect the political aim of guaranteeing all users continued access to certain basic telecommunications services at steadily falling maximum prices, thus giving the message to the rest of the world of 'best practice'. Further, important consumer interests (improved consumer protection with regard to billing, complaints procedures, etc.) should be considered. General legislation on competition and consumer protection (and its principles) should be given higher priority, combined with the necessary regulation specific to the sector."

9. Another program aims at developing the European multimedia markets; a special Multimedia Educational Software Task Force has been set up; and the multi-year INFO2000 program is designed to stimulate the development of a European multimedia content industry and to encourage the use of multimedia

content in the emerging information society. Furthermore, the Fourth Framework Program committed substantial funding for research and development in IT.

10. Although the use of IT in Danish companies is high compared to other countries, Danish industry has not reaped the full benefits of employing advanced technologies. A recent study of the Danish grocery, construction, transportation and banking sectors shows that these sectors could benefit immensely from a more widespread use of electronic data interchange (Henten and Skouby, 1995). In 1995, the Danish government initiated a campaign to stimulate the use of EDI and e-mail in Danish firms.

11. In April 1994, Tele Danmark was successfully floated on the New York Stock Exchange. It was the largest Danish share issue ever, as well as the largest international share issue on the New York Stock Exchange: 63 million new B shares were sold to private and institutional investors in Denmark and abroad.

12. Tele Danmark is actively involved in international enterprises. In 1994, Tele Danmark started integrated data and telephone network services in Hamburg, Germany, and joined the British Telecom/MCI consortium Concert. Furthermore, the company is engaged in several cable projects, particularly in Central and Eastern Europe, with interests in cable links in Poland and Lithuania, and also in major international submarine links with Russia. Tele Danmark participates in mobile networks in Ukraine, Hungary, and Lithuania, and on February 1, 1996, the consortium of Polkomtel S.A. in which Tele Danmark is a participant was awarded one of the two GSM licenses in Poland. Moreover, Tele Danmark recently teamed up with Ameritech Corp. and Singapore Telecom to acquire a 45.9 percent stake in Belgacom S.A. (the national telecommunications operator of Belgium), which was approved by the European Commission on February 29, 1996.

13. Not until January 1996 did Tele Danmark become seriously involved in Internet provision, for example.

14. The OECD figures were widely disputed by, for example, the Danish Consumer Council, which claimed that the figures did not reflect the real telecom rates which where higher due to Tele Danmark's high subscription rates, etc.

15. However, according to Chief Executive Hans Würtzen, Tele Danmark does not fear competition in international business, which he believes would at worst cause limited damage to Tele Danmark, noting that "one hundred of our largest customers only account for slightly more that 10 percent of our revenues, and no single customer accounts for more that 1 percent of our revenues" (McClelland and Bright, 1995).

16. From 1990 to 1995, the Nordic network connections increased their speed by an average of 166 percent per year, while the price only increased about 50 percent per year. In other words, bandwidth price per Mbps decreased by 35 percent annually.

17. Denmark had a 36.2 percent market share in trade of hearing aids with OECD countries, South Korea, Taiwan, Singapore and Hong Kong.

References

Andersen, M. M. (1995). Udviklingstendenser i reguleringen af telekommunikation i Danmark—om reguleringens nødvendighed og nødvendighedens regulering. *Informationssamfundet til debat—Antologi on Danmarks muligheder i Informationssamfundet.* M. Falch. Lyngby, Center for Tele-Information.

Andersen, O. E. (1995). Medieudbud og medieforbrug i Danmark. Copenhagen, Medie Udvalget (The Media Commission).

Andersen, E.S. and B.-Å. Lundvall (1988). Small National Systems of Innovation Facing Technological Revolutions: An Analytical Framework. *Small Countries Facing the Technological Revolution.* C. Freeman and B.Å. Lundvall. Pinter Publishers.

Branscomb, L. (1994). Balancing the Commercial and Public-Interests Visions of the NII. *20/20 Vision: The Development of a National Information Infrastructure.* Washington D.C.

Bar, F. (1995). Information Infrastructure and the Transformation of Manufacturing. *The New Information Infrastructure. Strategies for US Policy.* W. Drake. New York, Twentieth Century Fund: 55–75.

European Commission (1994). Europes Way to the Information Society. Brussels.

Falch, M., Ed. (1995). *Informationssamfundet til debat—Antologi om Danmarks muligheder i Informationssamfundet.* CTI's rapport. Lyngby, Center for Tele-Information.

Fischer-Madsen, A. (1995). Hovedlinier i dansk telepolitik. *Informationssamfundet til debat—Antologi on Danmarks muligheder i Informationssamfundet.* M. Falch. Lyngby, Center for Tele-Information.

Henten, A. (1995). Danmark i det internationale informationssamfund. *Informationssamfundet til debat—Antologi on Danmarks muligheder i Informationssamfundet.* M. Falch. Lyngby, Center for Tele-Information.

Henten, A. and K. E. Skouby (1995). EDI Development in Denmark: Grocery Industry, Construction, Transportation, and Banking. *Social and Economic Implications of Telecommunications.* Skouby. et.al. Lyngby, Center for Tele-information.

Henten, A., K. E. Skouby, et al. (1995). European Planning for an Information Society, Center for Tele-Information: 1–23.

High Level Group on the Information Society (1994). Europe and the Global Information Society—Recommendations to the European Council. Brussels.

Insead (1995). Tele Danmark (A): The Transformation Challenge. A Case Study. Insead, Fontainbleau, France.

Jensen, J. F. (1995). Multimedier og teknologiudvikling. København, Rapport udarbejdet for Statsministeriets Medieudvalg. (Multimedia and development of technology).

KommUNICation (1995/96). Various Issues. Danmarks EDB-center for forskning og uddannelse (UNIC), Copenhagen.

Kraft, P. and J. Bansler (1993). "Mandatory Voluntarism: Negotiating Technology in Denmark." *Industrial Relations* 32(3): 329–342.

Lindholm, M. (1995). Det virtuelle Danmark. *Informationssamfundet til debat— Antologi on Danmarks muligheder i Informationssamfundet.* M. Falch. Lyngby, Center for Tele-Information.

McClelland, S. and J. Bright (1995). "Expecting Competition." *Telecommunications* (International Edition) v29(3) (March 1995): 35–37.

Melody, W. (1995). "Toward a Framework for Designing Information Society Policies." Center for Tele-Information: 1–24.

Mercer Management Consulting (1994). *Future Policy for Telecommunications Infrastructure and CATV Networks: A Path Towards Infrastructure Liberalisation.*

Ministry of Business and Industry (1994). Erhvervsredegørelse. Copenhagen. (Annual statement on the Danish industry).

Ministry of Research and Information Technology (1994). *Info-Society 2000.* Copenhagen, November 1994. (http://www. fsk.dk/).

Ministry of Research and Information Technology (1995a). *From Vision to Action.* Copenhagen, March 1995. (http://www. fsk.dk/).

Ministry of Research and Information Technology (1995b). Bedst og billigst gennem reel konkurrence. Temaoplæg om dansk telepolitik. Copenhagen. July 1995. (Best and cheapest through real competition).

Ministry of Research and Information Technology (1995c). Agreement on the Total Liberalization of the Telecommunications Sector in Denmark, mid-1996. Fourth Supplement to the Political Agreement on the Telecommunications Structure. Copenhagen.

Ministry of Research and Information Technology (1995/96). Various press releases. (http://www. fsk.dk/).

Ministry of Research and Information Technology (1996a). Electronic Filing. Current Possibilities and Recommendations. Copenhagen.

Ministry of Research and Information Technology (1996b). Et dansk medialab! Et multimediacenter i Danmark. (A Danish Medialab! A Multimedia Center in Denmark). Copenhagen.

Ministry of Research and Information Technology et al. (February 1996). *Tripartite meeting on the Information Society,* Copenhagen.

OECD (1994). *Information Technology Outlook.* Paris, OECD/Information Computer Communications Policy.

OECD (1995). Communications Outlook. Paris, OECD/ Information Computer Communications Policy.

Rothwell, R. (1994). Issues in User-Producer Relations in the Innovation Process: The Role of Government". *International Journal of Technology Management* Vol 9: 629–649.

Schoof, H. and A. W. Brown (1995). Information Highways and Media Policies in the European Union. *Telecommunications Policy* 19(4): 325–228.

Skouby, K. E., M. Falch, et al. (1995). *Social and Economic Implications of Telecommunications.* Lyngby, Center for Tele-Information.

Søndergaard, H. (1995). Public Service i dansk fjernsyn—begreber, status of scenarier. Copenhagen, Medie Udvalget (The Media Commission).

Tele Danmark A/S (1994). Annual Report. Århus.

Tengroth, L., L. N. Jørgensen, et al. (1995). Telecommunications in Scandinavia. *International Financial Law Review* Jan 1995: 9–14.

Information Liberalization in the European Union

Shalini Venturelli

The debate over the role of transnational regulation and the basis of union among peoples and nations in the European Union (EU) bears profoundly on competing conceptions of the information infrastructure revolution and the struggle to define a policy design for the Information Age. There are three dominant regulatory visions shaping the information sector in the EU: the liberal, the public service, and the nationalist. Proponents of each vision are engaged in a struggle for dominance over the policy design of information liberalization. The political and policy resolution of the conflict has resulted in combining elements across models, even where those elements may be incompatible. The consequence of the struggle between competing visions of a European information society is leading toward construction of a very different and separate path to liberalization.

This chapter examines the European approach to information liberalization in terms of competing regulatory visions and underlying political and cultural factors that determine the distinctiveness of the EU's information infrastructure initiatives in at least three areas: (1) the meaning and application of competition policy and the policy design of a particular European form of a competitive market; (2) the rights of the communications industry vs. the rights of individual users; and (3) the future role of the state (national or transnational) in regulating the communications market. The chapter will attempt to assess the structural barriers to full liberalization of the European communications market arising from the conflict between the regulatory models and the resulting different path adopted by EU initiatives.

Models of Communication Regulation in the European Union

Since the early 1980s, the growing integration of the global economy and the expansion of trade liberalization have challenged the very basis of European policy toward the communications sector. Within the EU, telecommunications and audiovisual policies, for instance, have evolved as powerful sites of conflict not only between rival political and social interests but also among three rival paradigms of how the European Union ought to approach the design of the information society: the liberal model, the public service model, and the nationalist or culturalist model. Liberalization initiatives launched by the European Union have challenged national traditions of communications policy and law. Yet these traditions are proving quite resistant and have transformed, in reverse, the framework of information liberalization at the European level.

The application of more liberal policies in European communications markets and the EU's effort to create greater competition (Commission of the European Communities, 1995a) require a significant redistribution of power from the public to the private sector. For this reason, EU proposals for information liberalization have turned into a debate over the long-term political objectives of constructing a transnational communications order in Europe. For instance, political resistance to full privatization of public telecommunications monopolies and the creation of competition in communications infrastructure and content sectors appears as a set of national conflicts over two views (Collins, 1994; Morgan, 1989) of the role of the state: one advocating intervention (dirigisme) in the market, and the other advocating nonintervention or minimal market intervention (liberalization). However, just as liberalization has often been oversimplified as a minimum regulatory approach when, in fact, it is most often re-regulatory, *dirigisme* is frequently reduced to a phenomenon of French history, which obscures the real nature of European opposition to full liberalization. Consequently, the debate over the role of the state in the communications sector is far less about a choice between interven-

tion and nonintervention, than it is a contest among three principal forms of intervention and which social model ought to prevail
over the information infrastructure.

The Liberal Model

National regulatory traditions in EU member-states traditionally
follow the public service and/or the nationalist models for organizing the structure of communications as public utilities. Using
either public interest or national/cultural rationales, European
countries have created government agencies to manage information services under virtual monopoly conditions. Thus the liberal
model of regulation in the EU does not originate in policy traditions at the level of member-states, but in the mandate to create a
single market for goods and services granted to the European
Commission[1] by the 1957 Treaty of Rome (Commission of the
European Communities, 1993a). However, it was not until the
1980s that the Commission started to draw on its constitutional
power under Articles 90, 85 and 86[2] of the Treaty to develop a
framework for introducing privatization, deregulation and competition into the European communications market. Article 90 forms
the legal grounds for enforcing privatization and competition
policies in the single market[3] and gives the EU wide-ranging and
direct powers for legal and regulatory action. Articles 85 and 86
bestow upon the Commission the authority to block abuse of
monopoly power and to prevent barriers to market entry.

While there is no specific mandate in the Treaty dealing with the
communications industries as with other sectors such as transportation and the environment, the Court of Justice of the European
Communities[4] (ECJ) ruled in 1985 to assimilate communications
policy into the competition provisions of Articles 85 and 86 of the
Treaty with the British Telecommunications decision (*Italy v.
Commission*, 1985). In 1991, the ECJ widened application of Article
90 to extend the Treaty further to cover the communications sector
with the Court's landmark judgments in the so-called "Terminal
Equipment" (*France v. Commission*, 1991) and "Services Directive"
(*Spain v. Commission*, 1992) cases. This juridical trend has fortified
the Commission's statutory and regulatory jurisdiction[5] to shape

the structure of transnational communications networks and content, and even allows that EU legal and policy actions take precedence over national communications laws.

Throughout the 1990s, and especially since 1992, the European liberal model for the information infrastructure has produced a set of sweeping liberalization proposals that are dramatic relative to the European context of traditional public sector control and constraints in virtually every area of the infrastructure and content industries. A mountain of statutes and policy rulings has emerged at the European level from the extension of the Treaty to cover the communications market. The quantity and complexity of the process of legal production to create a single market in communications networks and information services can be confusing, especially when overlaid upon even more fragmented structures of national laws governing this sector. Nevertheless, it is suggested here that the entire body of EU communications policy and law can be distilled to a set of core measures bearing the greatest potential for determining the climate of investment, the structure of competition, and the character of information services in the future broadband, multimedia environment. Based on these criteria, a European liberalization framework can be said to rest upon ten significant initiatives:

1. *Distribution*: The commercialization and transnationalization of program distribution networks, beginning with television (Commission of the European Communities, 1989).

2. *Content Policy*: Development of legal and constitutional grounds for extending strong content regulation in television programming to new audiovisual and multimedia services on any distribution network, regardless of the form of technology (Commission of the European Communities, 1995c, 1995d; European Parliament, 1996). The principle of strong content regulation may be antiliberal but remains an important characteristic of the European approach to the information society, and it is drawn from both the public service and nationalist regulatory models (discussed below).

3. *Copyright*: Creating a particular European approach to intellectual property rights on the information superhighway that extends the economic rights of industry in some forms but delimits those

rights in other forms by tilting in favor of the individual rights of artistic labor (Commission of the European Communities, 1995h, 1993e, 1993f, 1992a). The approach to content ownership rights in a multimedia environment results from a specific balance between the liberal and public service models of regulation (discussed below).

4. *Information Services*: The immediate liberalization of all telecommunications services (value-added, data communication, private network services, etc.), except for basic voice telephony which must be opened to competition by 1998 (Commission of the European Communities, 1995b, 1994b, 1990b).

5. *Open Access*: Promoting equal and fair access to the network infrastructure by establishing the principle of open access to networks, interworking and interconnection controlled by monopolies, whether public or private (Commission of the European Communities, 1990c).

6. *Competition*: Establishment of general, legal and economic principles for the application of competition rules in telecommunications, including those communications sectors not covered by other Commission statutes (Commission of the European Communities, 1995g, 1993d, 1991a).

7. *Alternative Infrastructures*: Liberalization of alternative network infrastructures such as the excess capacity of utilities and transportation industries that can be utilized to develop high-speed corporate networks in Europe in addition to generating pressure on national carriers to lower tariffs (Commission of the European Communities, 1995b, 1994b).

8. *Cable*: Liberalization of cable TV infrastructures entitling cable operators to carry telecommunications services in competition with telephone companies (Commission of the European Communities, 1995f, 1994b).

9. *Mobile Communications*: Liberalization of mobile and personal communications network infrastructures that allows use of own and third-party infrastructures to create internal links within digital mobile cellular telephone networks (Commission of the European Communities, 1994c).

10. *Satellite Communications*: Liberalization of satellite communications networks that remove current restrictions on infrastructure within satellite networks in order to stimulate the use of satellite communications in the EU (Commission of the European Communities, 1996).

This ten-point framework radically alters the climate for private investment in the development of European information industries and in the transnationalization of communications networks in Europe. Yet, full liberalization, such as with voice telephony even after 1998, remains highly questionable owing to the persistence of the public service and nationalist regulatory models. These models are grounded in political and cultural factors which appear to preserve and maintain the structural position of national information carriers, producers and distributors, and to strengthen the role of the state—that is, of EU law and policy and of national governments—in shaping and molding the social parameters of the European communications market.

The Public Service Model

The public service idea that competes against strict liberalization and delimits its scope in the European Union is far more useful to understanding European differences over the role of the state and public policy in the communications sector than the more conventional explanation of *dirigisme* or "interventionism." The contrast between the liberal and public service models allows a better assessment of the problems of European information liberalization than the false presumption of conflict between *dirigisme* and liberalism with respect to state intervention.

The conflict over deepening the union of European states through a framework of laws and regulations can be understood as a contrast between the idea that the route to liberal democracy is by way of a community based on public service, on the one hand, as opposed to either liberal or nationalist models, on the other. Assumptions about the economy and society in the public service policy approach stress the priorities of the legal system to guarantee the institutional arrangements of public communications networks and services first for all citizens, and only second for market players. The public service model requires that the central principle of modern free societies comprises not merely the rights of private investors, competitors and the functioning of the communications market, but also the rights of citizens to comprehensive information services and access to the communications network.

The public service approach to information liberalization describes not only the French policy tradition but also that of several other states, including, for example, Belgium, Italy and Germany (Mansell, 1993; Lasok & Stone, 1987; David & Spinosi, 1973). The concept has evolved since the French Revolution, but especially in the period from the end of the 19th century to the 1930s as embodied in the corporatist organization of social sectors such as railroads and utilities that are held to be basic to the common interest of all members of a democratic society. The principle of public service is not merely a policy convention, but is constitutionally grounded in the French Constitution (1946) and in those of other member-states. More significantly, however, the public service model of regulation and the statutory responsibility it implies is explicitly provided for in two separate constitutional provisions of the European Union. The first is the social cohesion requirement of the Treaty of Rome:

The Community shall have as its task . . . to promote throughout the Community . . . a high level of . . . social protection, the raising of the standard of living and quality of life, and economic and social cohesion and solidarity among Member States (Article 2 of the Treaty of Rome, Commission of the European Communities, 1993a).

The second constitutional provision for public service is enshrined in the social progress clause of the Maastricht Treaty (a 1992 treaty to revise and extend the powers of the institutions of the European Union):

The Union shall set itself the following objectives: to promote economic and social progress which is balanced and sustainable . . . through the strengthening of economic and social cohesion . . . (Title 1, Article B of the Maastricht Treaty, Commission of the European Communities, 1993b).

These provisions underscore the role of Community law in guaranteeing the general welfare of European citizens. Needless to say, the public service sections of the EU constitution are in direct conflict with more liberal sections elsewhere (Articles 85, 86, and 90, at the very least, of the Treaty of Rome) that put forward a Community mandate to create laws for achieving greater liberalization of markets by reducing barriers to competition and investment.

What exactly is the central focus or the driving concern of the European model of public service regulation? As Bauby and Boual (1994, p. 11) explain, it rests on the recognition that key socio-economic sectors, such as communication, should be exempt from sole governance by market processes in order to permit universal access to certain public goods and services that contribute to the minimum threshold of human need and equality in economic, social and cultural areas. It is grounded in the assumption that the self-regulatory conditions of modern democracies are only possible if the law guarantees the minimum basis for defining the rights of citizens to have access to network infrastructure and communication services. This approach seeks to oblige the state to maintain access to basic goods and services and represents a fundamental departure from the assumptions of liberalization. The basis of the liberal model, by contrast, is the argument that modern market societies require little or no political-legal intervention, thereby creating a favorable climate for capital investment and private innovation through which social needs will be automatically and naturally addressed.

The "common interest" interpretation of communications policy under the public service model requires that the individual's need for access to a minimum threshold of communication infrastructure and services is identical to other basic necessities such as health care, education, public libraries, or utilities such water and electricity. The criterion for applying this policy approach arises if a society—whether local, regional, national or transnational—determines that a public good or essential service, whether already existing or new, cannot be satisfactorily provided by the private market (see discussion of the evolution of "social citizenship" in Europe in Meehan, 1993; Dahrendorf, 1994; Dyson, 1980). The essential characteristic of this "good" could proceed from a strategic common interest, or a fundamental condition of equity or social cohesion, and it is mandated for all by an act of law or through processes of regulation.

The public service tradition of regulation continues to play a central role in shaping the future structure of communications networks and information services in the European Union, and it frequently provokes disagreements with other countries and regions of the world (e.g., the United States) that view public service regulation as a trade barrier to foreign competitors. There are at least five principal forms in which public service regulation defines the unique character of information infrastructure initiatives in the EU:

1. *Universal Service.* This is among the most politically sensitive conditions of European communications regulation, and it will only be maintained, strengthened and extended in the digital age. The EU is attempting to harmonize all the national approaches and set the universal service obligation at a very high standard in the post-liberalization and post-privatization period. This contrasts dramatically with the more market-oriented solutions sought in recent U.S. legislation that veer away from imposing non-commercial obligations on the communications industry (see U.S. Congress, 1996). The guarantee of the principle of universal service in advanced stages of the information society includes setting up an extensive regulatory framework for tariffs and quality of service, establishing procedures for consumer monitoring, defining access for all social sectors, establishing funding mechanisms, and including provisions for higher thresholds of minimum services with continued advancement of the broadband network (Commission of the European Communities, 1995b, 1995e, 1994b). Clearly, such an extensive initiative delimits the scope of strict liberalization not only at the European level but also within member-states such as France and Germany, where non-commercial obligations in the interest of universal service are considered a necessary precondition for achieving political consensus on the privatization and liberalization of the communications industries.

The emphasis on universal services reflects the public service concern that transnationalization of the liberal model will be destructive to the social order of European societies. There even exists a broad political will to resist EU information liberalization initiatives if they prove weak on the question of universal service or if the standard is set too low on the question of what constitutes minimum services. From France and Germany to the Nordic states, demands are emerging for a higher standard coupled with strong mechanisms for enforcement.

2. *Competition Policy*: The EU is adopting a far more re-regulatory approach to competition than recent legislation in the United States (U.S. Congress, 1996) which instead constrains the legitimate authority of government regulation over the information sector. Pressures are evolving in the European Parliament, the European Court of Justice, from member governments, and from a growing number of transnational public interest groups to interpret competition in the evolving digital multimedia network as a direct product of the degree of antitrust enforcement under Community law (Commission of the European Communities, 1995g, 1994i, 1993d, 1992b, 1991a). In other words, the demand for anti-concentration measures driven by a more public service oriented concept of competition policy will mean relatively stronger constraints on commercial alliances, joint ventures, partnerships, and mergers. However, the stricter application of antitrust rules through increased regulation will be waived for communications carriers, providers, and distributors who perform services (frequently non-commercial or low-profit services) in the public interest as part of their cost of operation. Under the public service regulatory model, services performed in the public interest—for example, in the areas of public opinion formation, education and training, or nondiscriminatory access—allow certain communications entities to be exempted from antitrust or competition law. In either instance, in order to meet the criteria of the public service regulatory model, industries must agree to either restrain their size and thus their profitability and freedom to consolidate capital ownership structures and reduce risk, or else assume an array of less profitable public interest obligations.

3. *Content Policy*: Achieving diversity and pluralism in information services in the broadband multimedia domain is seen by the EU (particularly the European Parliament) and by member-states as a matter of fundamental importance to the future of European democracies. The Nordic states have strongly advocated regulation

for diversity and pluralism in the EU policy agenda, while the German constitution at both the federal and state levels practically mandates content regulation for every communications sector. The German Constitutional Court has pressured the European Court of Justice and the Commission to uphold information services as a fundamental right of citizens—that is, a human right to diversity and plurality of information. Both the left and the right of European politics and significant social interest groups support the principles. Thus the public service principle of a right to receive information is likely to be extended to cover all advanced information services, as is evident in a number of recent measures (Commission of the European Communities, 1995c, 1995d, 1992b; European Parliament, 1996). The public service model therefore substantively demotes the First Amendment right of the communications industries to be free of content regulation in favor of the First Amendment right of individuals to receive and have access to information services.

4. *Copyright Policy and Law.* Rules governing copyright are central to the development of new information services and to the investment climate for interactive multimedia content. While the liberal model favors the contractual, economic rights of exploiters, the public service model favors the noncontractual, inalienable civil rights of the artistic creator such as the rights of paternity, integrity, and pursuit. The public service model shrinks the economic rights of third-party exploiters, thus reducing the guarantee of unrestricted ownership of content and compensation from exploitation for communications businesses investing in content production, packaging, and distribution. While the EU has attempted to harmonize European copyright laws to assure the content industry a transnational liberal model of copyright, it has been unable to do so without considerable integration with national public service approaches to copyright like those prevailing in Germany, France, Italy, and Belgium (Commission of the European Communities, 1995h, 1993e, 1993f, 1992a). There is broad political and social consensus in Europe for retaining the public service approach to copyright, but few advocates, other than the international content industries, of a liberal model of laws governing who owns information and who should benefit from its exploitation.

5. *Consumer Protection*: Proposals to protect the rights of consumers by restricting socially harmful content, providing basic educational programs for children, shrinking the limits of advertising (which forms the commercial basis of private sector content distribution), requiring citizens groups to be represented on the governing boards of the infrastructure and content industries, or transforming information services into a civil right are constantly arising in the European Parliament, in Community actions, and in the rulings of the European Court of Justice (Commission of the European Communities, 1995b, 1995c, 1995d, 1995e, 1995g, 1994b, 1993c, 1993d, 1992b, 1990a; European Parliament, 1996, 1994, 1989b). The greater the EU priority for consumer rights under the public service model, the lower the priority of unconstrained commercial freedom for communications industries under the liberal model. The balance achieved between the two approaches in European communications policies at any particular time, and on any single issue, will determine market conditions for investment and competition in a given communications sector.

The question of basic public service rights in the Information Age, not only in terms of telecommunications or infrastructure, but also in content and other sectors (Commission of the European Communities, 1995e), is to be addressed far more comprehensively for European-wide applicability as part of the 1996 Intergovernmental Conference (IGC) to revise the Maastricht Treaty. Both the French and German governments would like commitments to the public service model to be written into the constitution of the European Union as a safeguard against the further expansion of the liberal model.

But the greatest pressure for strengthening the public service model emanates from the European Parliament where firmer legal and constitutional foundations for preserving this regulatory model are being developed as part of a long-term process of constructing a piece-by-piece legal framework. The European Parliament has notified the Commission on numerous occasions that the regulatory boundaries of the multimedia age must not preclude development of the broadband network for public, non-commercial applications at the same time as the network gives full license to commercial applications. The European Parliament's efforts to establish a "communication right" as a fundamental political/civil right of European citizens is probably the most critical of all European initiatives for influencing the direction of the information society. This could have global implications if adopted elsewhere.

This direction in Community law can be detected for the first time in the Commission's Green Paper (policy proposal) on "Television Without Frontiers" (Commission of the European Communities, 1984) that preceded the directive to transnationalize program distribution networks (Commission of the European Communities, 1989). The Green Paper assessed the relation between principles of free expression and free trade in order to develop some rationale for a link. It concluded that free expression rights form an integral part of the Community's central mission to create a single market, and far from being a coincidental linkage, relations between Article 59 on free movement of services in the Treaty of Rome (Commission of the European Communities, 1993a) and freedom of information constitute a source for enriched development of both human rights and trade law.

Since then, the European Parliament and the European Court of Justice have each moved to assimilate a more extensive basis for free expression rights into the EU's constitutional framework by adopting the European Convention on Human Rights (ECHR), international human rights treaties and conventions, common constitutional principles drawn from member-states, and by the accumulation of human rights case law (Commission of the European Communities, 1993g; European Parliament, 1989a, 1989b). Currently, legal protection for communication rights at the EU level principally derives from an appeal to Article 10 of the ECHR. This basis has been upheld in several cases in which the European Court has emphasized "the pre-eminent role of the press in a State governed by the rule of law" (*Castells v. Spain*, 1992). While this form of ruling may serve as reasonable grounds on which to protect the First Amendment rights of the communications industry from regulatory intervention, that defense may have been undermined by the European Court's parallel ruling that clearly emphasizes a public service approach to interpreting freedom of expression in the Community:

[it is] . . . incumbent on the press to impart information and ideas on matters of public interest. . . . Not only does the press have the task of imparting such information and ideas: the public also has a right to receive them. Were it otherwise, the press would be unable to play its vital role of 'public watchdog' (*The Observer and Guardian v. the United Kingdom*, 1991).

This formulation of freedom of expression is not a negative right as in the United States, but a more extensive positive right to *receive* information and to be informed which elevates the communications rights of citizens over the communications rights of industry. It is not likely that this highly significant trend can be reversed or effaced since it is now constitutionally grounded in Article 10 of the ECHR, which grants the positive communication right to all individuals as a human right:

Everyone has the right to freedom of expression. This right shall include freedom to hold opinions and to receive and impart information and ideas without interference by public authority and regardless of frontiers. This Article shall not prevent States from requiring the licensing of broadcasting, television or cinema enterprises (European Convention for the Protection of Human Rights and Fundamental Freedoms, 1950, Article 10, para. 1).

By granting not only the right of conscience and speech, but also the right to receive information, Article 10 generates a positive claim that citizens can exercise on European law to guarantee their rights against the competing claim of freedom from obligation asserted by information content providers. Thus European law confers a more extensive right to individuals (i.e., listeners, viewers and users); it provides communications policy with a positive legal foundation to allow states to regulate to advance a non-commercial common good and not merely to advance a free market; and it imposes a constitutional obligation on producers, providers and distributors of communications content by holding them to public service standards of adequacy, sufficiency and plurality of information in the development of advanced information services for the digital network.

The EU has thus succeeded in transferring the public service model to the policy design of the information age and in fusing this model to the constitutional framework of union and integration. The approach defines the form of liberalization, and the political and legal terms of the communications market; but when further combined with a third, nationalist model of regulation, the European information society promises additional complexity to those seeking a strictly liberal direction.

The Nationalist (or Cultural) Model

There is a significant divide between the public service model of communications policy and the nationalist or culturalist approach. They are based on distinctly opposed fundamental assumptions concerning the communications rights of individuals and industry, the role of government policy, and the function of the communications sector. At the same time, the vision of the national or cultural collective as a basis for regulating public communications is also opposed to liberalization's market-based criteria which favor greater freedom for investment and innovation independent of the state.

The cultural-nationalist model stresses content policy over infrastructure policy. Communications industries are regulated to require communications content that celebrates the cultural exclusiveness of the collective as contrasted with the universal service conditions favored by the public service approach, though it should be noted that what divides the two is even more substantive since a cultural argument for the communications industries is not necessarily identical to a democratic argument of information equality. The relationship between the liberal and nationalist models in the politically sensitive sector of content policy is evident in the tension between liberal versus nationalist initiatives toward the information superhighway, particularly in the concrete manifestations of the positions of the United Kingdom, on the one hand, and those of France and Belgium, on the other, toward influencing the policy framework of the European Union.

The nationalist model advocates the social community as an expressive rather than a political or economic unity. This unity expresses a unique, irreplaceable, frequently "pure," cultural form that must be sustained and handed down in some untainted form

(Gellner, 1983; Anderson, 1983). The expressivist conception of communication law defends the idea of culture as its own "form" driven to some realization, which must be freed from external constraints—such as competing or alternative cultures—in order to discover the indefinable thread that guides it. The logic of this view of communications therefore suggests a purity of content that must be defended against polluting cultural strains that must be excluded or even eradicated in order to release the forces of cultural self-realization or the unique form embedded within the expressive unity. This was precisely the reasoning articulated in the early stages of the European Community's justification for transnationalization of audiovisual production and distribution:

The audiovisual sector is of great importance to the cultural identity of peoples, regions and nations. It is also a rapidly growing sector of the world economy, significant in its own right and with considerable multiplier effects on other cultural sectors (European Parliament, 1989a, p. 8).

Earlier nationalist reasoning formed the political premise for the "Television Without Frontiers" Green Paper (Commission of the European Communities, 1984) in this classical cultural syllogism:

European unification will only be achieved if Europeans want it. Europeans will only want it if there is such a thing as a European identity. A European identity will only develop if Europeans are adequately informed. At present, information via the mass media is controlled at the national level (Commission of the European Community, 1984, p. 28).

The "unquestionable cultural significance" (Commission of the European Communities, 1993c, p. 120) of program production and distribution has also been pointedly stressed by a president of the European Commission:

. . . the culture industry will tomorrow be one of the biggest industries, a creator of wealth and jobs. Under the terms of the Treaty we do not have the resources to implement a cultural policy; but we are going to try to tackle it along economic lines. It is not simply a question of television programmes. We have to build a powerful European culture industry that will enable us to be in control of both the medium and its content, maintaining our standards of civilization, and encouraging the creative people amongst us (Jacques Delors, see European Parliament, 1985, p. 64).

The momentum behind the expressivist conception of a transnational information infrastructure has been strong enough to cause a significant change in the Community's narrow economic mandate, granting constitutional authority to shape the communications market as a cultural realm. Article 128 of the Maastricht Treaty provides legal grounds for the European Commission and other institutions of the EU, including the European Court of Justice, to intervene in the cultural domain. The political and regulatory significance makes this provision worth quoting in its entirety (emphasis has been added):

TITLE IX: CULTURE

1. The Community shall contribute to the flowering of the cultures of the Members States, while respecting their national and regional diversity and at the same time bringing the common *cultural heritage* to the fore.

2. Action by the Community shall be aimed at encouraging cooperation between Member States and, if necessary, supporting and supplementing their action in the following areas:

• improvement of the knowledge and dissemination of the *culture and history of the European peoples*;

• conservation and *safeguarding of cultural heritage* of European significance;

• non-commercial cultural exchanges;

• artistic and literary creation, including the *audiovisual sector.*

3. The Community and the Member States shall foster cooperation with third countries and the competent international organizations in the sphere of culture, in particular the Council of Europe.

4. The Community shall take cultural aspects into account in its action under other provisions of this Treaty.

5. In order to contribute to the achievement of the objectives referred to in this Article, the Council:

• acting in accordance with the procedure referred to in Article 189b and after consulting the Committee of the Regions, shall adopt incentive measures, excluding any harmonization of the laws and regulations of the Member States. The Council shall act unanimously throughout the procedures referred to in Article 189b.

• acting unanimously on a proposal from the Commission, shall adopt recommendations.

(Commission of the European Communities, 1993a, Maastricht Treaty, Article 128, p. 89, emphasis added).

These developments testify to the importance the EU attributes to the audiovisual sector as the most central of the cultural industries—an importance perceived as relevant not only to the idea of content production and distribution as an agency of social cohesion (Commission of the European Communities, 1993c, pp. 120–121), but also to the perception that program production and the information industry comprise prime agencies in the regeneration of economic growth (Commission of the European Communities, 1994a, pp. 11–14). What seems evident here is that a cultural model of regulation is being combined with the liberal approach, which in turn argues for the communications sector as an engine of economic growth with power to recreate a new industrial age. A certain form of liberalization has therefore fused with the Community's notion of content creation as a cornerstone in the embroidering of self-proclaimed, exclusive national cultures into a unitary European identity. The Community's synthesis of liberalism and nationalism is best summed up in the following declaration:

The audiovisual sector has enormous potential to generate wealth and create jobs, as well as being essential to Europe's cultural life (Commission of the European Communities, 1994b, p. 17).

According to Gellner (1983), the argument for the cohesive power of culture is nationalist especially when it presupposes that the body politic or the nation and an exclusive cultural form are congruent. That is to say, the formulation of cultural uniqueness employed to fuse the collective into a nation serves in fact to justify the legitimacy of social and political institutions, thereby replacing the communications sector's function of enhancing information needs in a democracy and a free market with the function of enhancing integration and cohesiveness of a cultural form.

The idea of European cohesion is framed in a nationalist matrix of communication policy that ascribes to the circulation of program forms the strategic function of forging a sense of Europeanness as a unique identity. The development of European content policy touches on the question of union as well as economic enlargement. Yet these separate aims obscure the profound difficulty in reconciling the Community's jurisdiction in enhancing the conditions of transnational commerce with the aim of promoting the construction of pan-European nationalism. Former Commission President Jacques Delors may be credited with discovering a working concept that allows the liberal model to be applied to the cultural sphere. In his speeches (European Parliament, 1985) and policy proposals (the "Delors White Paper," Commission of the European Communities, 1993c), Delors identified the economic basis of cultural production, specifically content and program production, as a justification for state—i.e., Commission—intervention.

Although the 1957 Treaty of Rome (Commission of the European Communities, 1993a) provides no specific grounds for Commission action in support of cultural policy, it could be construed as a basis for regulating cultural forms as commodities or services—i. e., as activities conducted for remuneration—thus rendering legal any Commission instrument designed to create a common market in information content. This was the approach to adoption in 1989 of a Commission statute establishing a single market in broadcasting, the "Television Without Frontiers" Directive (Commission of the European Communities, 1989) which proposed to regulate an economic activity whose form was judged as cultural. A Green Paper on broadcasting that preceded the directive by several years justified establishing Community authority over the structure of communications networks that are dominant content or programming carriers in the public realm:

Contrary to what is widely imagined, the EEC Treaty applies not only to economic activities but, as a rule to all activities carried out for remuneration, regardless of whether they take place in the economic, social, cultural (including in particular information, creative or artistic activities and entertainment), sporting or any other sphere (Commission of the European Communities., 1984, p. 6).

Based on the evolution of a cultural approach to program content, it is argued here that a nationalist model of communication regulation will influence development of the European information society in two significant areas:

1. *Content Distribution Policy as Cultural Policy*: The Community's emphasis on creating a European cultural identity that transcends national cultural borders has been translated into a series of communications policy initiatives advocating a shared culture through audiovisual forms. In the language of the EU, such policies "will strengthen the Europeans' sense of belonging to one and the same Community" (Commission of the European Communities, 1988, p. 52). Ministers of culture of member-states have gone even further to propose expansion of transfrontier audiovisual distribution networks as "one of the top priorities of a European cultural policy... part of the concept of a 'people's Europe' " (Commission of the European Communities., 1988, p. 49). The communications dimension of the single market offers a key rationale in the development of a European cultural policy (Commission of the European Communities, 1990a, p. 52), and to this extent, as Robins & Morley (1992) and Collins (1994) argue, EU policy increasingly recognizes that questions of culture, politics and identity are at the heart of the European project.

This recognition has led the European Commission and European Parliament to strengthen rules governing majority European content as a percentage of distributed programs and to close all loopholes that permitted more liberal national policies in some states to allow content distribution industries to circumvent European content carriage rules (Commission of the European Communities, 1995c, 1995d, 1994h; European Parliament, 1996).

2. *Content Production Policy as Cultural Policy*: The public service model of communications policy tilts in favor of the political, information and consumer rights of individual citizens, thereby granting secondary status to the First Amendment and commercial freedoms of communications industries. But the nationalist model, like the liberal model, favors the rights of industry over individuals. The essential difference relates to the nationalist concern for protecting and enhancing the market share of domestic content producers and national carriers, whereas a strictly applied liberal model advances the interests of market players over the public service claim of individuals, but without biases regarding market sectors or particular private entities.

In the period leading up to as well as after 1998, EU policies grounded in nationalist reasoning are actively influencing the design of information liberalization in favor of European industries, whether in the content or infrastructure sectors. Initiatives to strengthen the market position of European content producers and the creation of a trans-European content production industry include: public funding of programs and multimedia information services that attract international publics; consolidation of European content producers and distributors to form larger entities for competing against multinational content industries; and the protection of the market position of national infrastructure networks or national carriers so that they will be well-positioned to construct integrated national fiber-optic networks for delivery of advanced information and interactive multimedia services (Commission of the European Communities, 1995b, 1995c, 1994b, 1994d, 1994e).

For example, a joint initiative of the Commission and the European Parliament has led to the draft of a comprehensive agenda for developing the European multimedia content industry that covers companies involved in the production, development, packaging and distribution of information (Commission of the European Communities, 1995c). This "multimedia policy" unites European concern for cultural policy, social policy, economic policy and technology policy. Its foremost objectives are to push for strengthening the European content production industry, make new information services contribute to growth and employment, and make certain advanced information services contribute to the social and cultural development of European citizens. Multimedia services are thus being assimilated to broader industrial as well as cultural/social goals, a process that is seen as a means of promoting essential underlying goals of cultural heritage. The EU is treating the multimedia content sector as an opportunity to design a new legal framework for extending the cultural policy goal of majority European-produced content to the broadband network. It seems evident at this juncture that cultural goals in the multimedia sector will exceed anything the EU has accomplished thus far in either the television or film sectors.

For all these reasons, European content production policy is not completely identical with industrial policy, as it is sometimes mistakenly—and all too hastily—defined in multilateral disagreements over the liberalization of communication. This is because initiatives to strengthen the market position of European content

producers in the post-liberalization period also serve as a cornerstone of Community action to buttress indigenous cultural expression and the continuity of a particular cultural form of society
(*European Report*, 1995) . From a market standpoint, the national-
ist/culturalist regulatory model erects a dense barrier of external,
noncommercial burdens on new entrants, thereby distorting the
processes of actual competition and circumscribing a highly political and nationalist matrix for the future of competition in a
liberalized, trans-European information market.

The particular configuration of the liberal, public service, and
nationalist models of information liberalization confers a uniqueness on the European communications market that is not necessarily evident in initiatives emerging in the United States, Asia or
elsewhere. The combination of assumptions and actions of each
model point to a separate path for information liberalization in the
EU.

A Separate Path to Liberalization

The conflict month the three models of communications regulation have led the European Union to a critical stage in the process
of liberalization. The foundation for future development of the
European information market has been established in the core ten-
point liberal framework outlined above, and a clear momentum
has developed. Investors now have a firm basis upon which to plan
entry and expansion into the European communications market.
Yet EU member-states such as Germany, France and even the
United Kingdom are advocating very different paths to liberalization in national policies and European law. Analysis of the basis of
the public service and nationalist regulatory models has illumi-
nated the conflicting traditions shaping the future of liberalization. The underlying political and social factors in these traditions
point to at least six reasons for taking an alternative path to
information liberalization in the EU, described below.

Securing the Social Model

Across all European states, from the West to emerging democracies
in the East, a broad political and social consensus has emerged

regarding the complex functions of the communications sector and its vital connection to the persistence of evolved European social models. These models differ from the U.S. approach to the economy and society because they describe a very distinct tripartite balance between the state, the players in the market economy, and the broader society of citizens and interest groups. Because the United States historically regarded the state, in principle, as a threat to personal and commercial freedom, the government's role in determining the competitive, cultural and social environment of the communications sector has been kept to a minimum (relative to other countries). This is not the case in the European Union, where, despite the creation of a common market, the social consensus of postwar Germany, and even more so in the Nordic states and on the left and right of the political divide in France, Belgium and Italy, continues to impute a very different meaning to liberalization. In these countries, the democratic state and legislative institutions are regarded by all significant political and social groups as the guardians and defenders of a unique inherited social tradition of solidarity and "common interest" regulation according to which the communications market is at the very top of the list of sectors vital to the continuity of the social model. The information superhighway debate has only further consolidated Europe's post-Cold War commitment to the public service model and thus to application of advanced information services and technologies to this larger sociopolitical end.

Preserving National Culture

European nations and EU law have increasingly sought to strengthen not only social solidarity but also the cohesion of cultural, national and European identities. Cultural cohesion is thought to be largely preconditioned on a vast range of public service and cultural functions performed by all communications industries, whether in the public or private sector. Currently a complex structure of noncommercial obligations applies to every type of communications entity from network carriers and operators to content producers and distributors. Elimination of the existing structure of obligations (from universal access to cultural content carriage requirements) rationalized under a more liberal model or derived from liberalization pressures in multilateral trade negotiations is seen by Europeans governments, political parties and interests groups as a threat to the future basis by which cultural and national traditions can continue into the 21st century.

Conserving the Social Democratic Tradition

Industry, workers, interest groups, politicians, journalists, intellectuals and opinion leaders in Germany and the Northern European member-states, in addition to France, assert the firmly held conviction that the survival of a special tradition of democracy is at stake and endangered under particular liberal models of information liberalization. This democratic tradition is indeed distinctive from the American political tradition in terms of separate constitutional bases, diverse institutional structures and differing assumptions about the rights, duties and obligations of citizens and their relationship to the democratic state. The implications of this tradition for the legal basis of information rights in the Information Age have already been explored under the public service model.

The Dominance of Public Law

During the past century of successive information revolutions, a separate legal tradition known as public law has regulated the communications sector in most European states. This legal tradition is resilient and gives every sign of continuing to oversee, define and govern this sector in the age of multimedia interactive networks. Public law in European states such as Germany, France, Sweden, Denmark, Italy and Belgium is highly integrated with public policy, jurisprudence and legislation. It derives from constitutional law rather than from civil, contractual, private or common law. Public law frameworks that constitute the foundation of the public service regulatory model have profoundly shaped the design of the information society under EU communications statutes and the legal jurisprudence of the European Court.

The European public law tradition has empowered national governments and now the EU as a transnational legal entity to design comprehensive public interest, sector-specific legal frameworks. The tradition allows the state to actively shape sectors affecting in particular the constitutional rights (as opposed to economic or commercial rights) of citizens to receive information, cultural forms and the guarantee of social inclusion. Since the early days of telephony and broadcasting, communications industries have always fallen within the scope of public law. Thus, new privatization initiatives to transform the status of public monopolies will not alter the established public law responsibility of states or EU institutions to the communications sector; instead, they merely shift the mechanisms from direct public administration and ownership of industry to strengthened legal parameters defining commercial freedom, market behavior and service operation of public stock and private corporations. Accordingly, the regulatory path evolving in the EU for the information sector will necessarily differ from that of the Anglo-American, common law/civil law countries.

Fear of Rising Unemployment

Consistent with the generally consensual rather than competitive approach to society and economy shared by European democracies and by the consensual requirements of integrating European policy and law, the European path to information liberalization will depart from that in the United States because of the profound concern with the social costs of structural unemployment and the fear of additional unemployment in the Information Age. Liberalization of the communications sector will not be achieved in Europe—though it may be expressed as a principle—if it is seen to increase unemployment. This is evident in the consensus between the left and right in European politics, in the intense focus on unemployment brought to every level of the European policy agenda by member-states from both the north and the south, and in the public outcry in all segments of society and the economic market.

A Separate Approach to Competition

The EU's approach to information liberalization has taken a separate path from the United States because the combined effect of all preceding political and social conditions add up to an unconventional way of interpreting the meaning of competition in the communications sector. Under new liberalization initiatives emerging at the national and transnational levels, EU competition policies are being designed to achieve virtually opposite goals.

On the one hand, the market is being structured to facilitate open network and interconnection regimes against the national monopolies, as well as to lower other barriers to market entry for new carriers, providers, and packagers. On the other hand, however, competition policy is being applied to secure more entrenched national goals, such as preserving the market share and economic scale of privatized national carriers so that they can compete more effectively at the global level. National carriers will therefore continue to be required to perform a range of noncommercial functions, ranging from comprehensive universal service to strengthening and extending content regulation over information and entertainment services in the broadband environment. Similarly, at the European level, competition policy under EU law is clearly forcing the liberalization of alternative infrastructures (such as cable TV). However, the EU remains silent on compelling the national carriers to agree to interconnect with the very same alternative infrastructures. This is largely because large member-states such as Germany have not yet arrived at a political consensus on diminishing the dominance of national carriers like Deutsche Telekom. For these reasons, among many others, EU competition policy in the information sector will continue to be colored by public service and nationalist concerns that will shape the application of competition in contradictory ways.

This chapter has assessed some of the critical political and social factors driving the European approach to information liberalization. These conditions deriving from the conflict of regulatory models are seldom factored into economic analysis of the European communications market, yet they comprise the central factors determining the structure and form of the information society in Europe. Foreign entrants seeking to expand operations in the European information market need to take into account the special political and social conditions underlying each of the regulatory models governing this sector in order to develop effective investment and marketing strategies. Such conditions provoke new ways of thinking about communications markets in different regions of the world. An understanding and exploitation of these conditions in the changing European communications market will make the difference between short-term entry and long-term staying power.

Notes

1. The Commission of the European Communities ("Commission") is the Community institution responsible for enforcing the Treaty Establishing the European Community (Treaty of Rome and all subsequent versions such as the Maastricht Treaty), and for initiating and proposing Community legislation.

2. Article 90 of the Treaty of Rome:
   1. In the case of public undertakings and undertakings to which Member States grant special or exclusive rights, Member States shall neither enact nor maintain in force any measure contrary to the rules contained in this Treaty, in particular to those rules provided for in Article 6 and Articles 85 to 94.
   2. Undertakings entrusted with the operation of services of general economic interest or having the character of a revenue-producing monopoly shall be subject to the rules contained in this Treaty, in particular to the rules on competition, in so far as the application of such rules does not obstruct the performance, in law or in fact, of the particular tasks assigned to them. The development of trade must not be affected to such an extent as would be contrary to the interests of the Community.
   3. The Commission shall ensure the application of the provisions of this Article and shall, where necessary, address appropriate directives or decisions to Member States.

Article 85 of the Treaty of Rome:
85(1) The following shall be prohibited as incompatible with the common market: all agreements between undertakings, decisions of associations of undertakings and concerted practices which may affect trade between Member States and which have as their object or effect the prevention, restriction or distortion of competition within the common market, and in particular those which:
(a) directly or indirectly fix purchase or selling prices or any other trading conditions;
(b) limit or control production, markets, technical developments, or invest-ment;
(c) share markets or sources of supply;
(d) apply dissimilar conditions to equivalent transactions with other trading parties, thereby placing them at a competitive disadvantage;

(e) make the conclusion of contracts subject to the acceptance by the other parties of supplementary obligations which, by their nature or according to commercial usage, have no connection with the subject matter of such contracts.

85(2) Any agreements or decisions prohibited pursuant to this article shall be automatically void.

85(3) The provisions of paragraph 1 may, however, be declared inapplicable in the case of: . . . [any agreement] . . . which contributes to improving the production or distribution of goods or to promoting technical or economic progress, while allowing consumers a fair share of the resulting benefit, and which does not:

(a) impose on the undertakings concerned restrictions which are not indispensable to the attainment of those objectives;

(b) afford such undertakings the possibility of eliminating competition in respect of a substantial part of the products in question.

Article 86 of the Treaty of Rome:

Any abuse by one or more undertakings of a dominant position within the common market or in a substantial part of it shall be prohibited as incompatible with the common market in so far as it may affect trade between Member States. Such abuse may, in particular, consist in:

(a) directly or indirectly imposing unfair purchase or selling prices or other unfair trading conditions;

(b) limiting production, markets or technical development to the prejudice of consumers;

(c) applying dissimilar conditions to equivalent transactions with other trading parties, thereby placing them at a competitive disadvantage;

(d) making the conclusion of contracts subject to acceptance by the other parties of supplementary obligations which, by their nature or according to commercial usage, have no connection with the subject of such contracts.

3. The single European market has been created through a rolling program of 279 legislative measures that the Community agreed to adopt and implement by the target date of December 1992. The package of measures originated in the European Commission's *White Paper on Completing the Internal Market* (Commission of the European Communities, 1985) adopted by member-states in Milan on June 28 and 29, 1985. The aim of creating a single market through the removal of all barriers to the free movement of people, services, goods and capital within the EU is not new. The obligation to remove such barriers dates back to the inception of the Community itself, but the effect of the 1992 deadline was to give new political impetus to the process. A greater focus on communications as part of the single market in services has emerged from this initiative.

4. The Court of Justice of the European Communities, based in Luxembourg, is the supreme arbiter of Community law. The Court has three main roles: first, to rule on the legality of Community legislation or acts of Community institutions; second, to rule on alleged breaches of the Treaty by member-states or Commu-

nity institutions; and third, to rule on questions of Community law referred to it by national courts. The Court is assisted by a Court of First Instance, which deals with appeals, among other issues, against the European Commission's antitrust decisions.

5. It is important to note that, under the Community's legislative and policymaking structures, in the majority of cases, policy and formal legislation is finally agreed by the ministers of the member-states, meeting in the Council of Ministers (the "Council"). Proposals for such policy and legislation, however, may only be made by the Commission, taking into account the opinion of, and amendments of such proposals made by, the European Parliament. The Council may not initiate legislation itself, and in all but exceptional cases, the Commission may not adopt binding legislation. It is just such an exception in the field of competition policy that has been of key importance in the liberalization of telecommunications.

References

Anderson, B. (1983). *Imagined communities.* London: Verso.

Bauby, P. and Boual, J. (1994). *Pour une citoyenneté Européenne: Quels services publics?* Paris: Les Éditions de l'Atelier.

Castells v. Spain, European Court of Justice judgement of 23 April 1992, Series A, No. 236.

Collins, R. (1994). "Unity in diversity? The European single market in broadcasting and the audiovisual, 1982–92." *Journal of Common Market Studies,* Vol. 32, No. 1, pp. 89–102.

Commission of the European Communities (1996). Proposal for a European Parliament and Council Decision on an action at a Union level in the field of satellite personal communications services in the European Union (96/C 15/07, OJC, January 20, 1996).

Commission of the European Communities (1995a). Chair, Mr. Jacques Santer's conclusions, G-7 Ministerial Conference on the Information Society, Brussels, February 25–26, 1995. Office of the President of the European Commission, Brussels.

Commission of the European Communities (1995b). Green Paper on the liberalization of telecommunications infrastructure and cable television networks, part 2: A common approach to the provision of infrastructure for telecommunications in the European Union, (COM(94) 682 final, January 25, 1995).

Commission of the European Communities (1995c). Proposal for a Council Decision adopting a multi-annual Community programme to stimulate the development of a European multimedia content industry and to encourage the use of multimedia content in the emerging information society (COM(95) 149 final, June 30, 1995).

Commission of the European Communities (1995d). Proposal for a European Parliament and Council Directive amending Council Directive 89/552/EEC on the coordination of certain provisions laid down by law, regulation or administrative action in Member States concerning the pursuit of television broadcasting activities (COM(95) 86 final, May 31, 1995).

Commission of the European Communities (1995e). Proposal for a European Parliament and Council Directive on interconnection in telecommunications with regard to ensuring universal service and interoperability through application of the principles of Open Network Provision (COM(95) 379 final, July 19, 1995).

Commission of the European Communities (1995f). Commission Directive of 18 October 1995 amending Directive 90/388/EEC with regard to the abolition of the restrictions on the use of cable television networks for the provision of already liberalized telecommunications services (95/51/EC, OJL No. L 256/49).

Commission of the European Communities (1995g). Draft Commission Directive amending Commission Directive 90/388/EEC regarding the implementation of full competition in telecommunications markets (95/C 263/07, OJL No C 263/6).

Commission of the European Communities (1995h). Green Paper on copyright and related rights in the information society (COM(95) 382 final, July 19, 1995).

Commission of the European Communities (1994a). "Europe and the global information society," Bangemann Task Force Report to the European Council. *Cordis*, Supplement 2, July 15, 1994, pp. 4–31. Brussels: European Commission, DG XIII/D-2.

Commission of the European Communities (1994b). Green Paper on the liberalization of telecommunications infrastructure and cable television networks, part 1. October 25, 1994. Brussels: European Commission, DG XIII.

Commission of the European Communities (1994c). Green Paper on a common approach in the field of mobile and personal communications in the European Union, (COM (94) 145).

Commission of the European Communities (1994d). Green Paper on strategy options to strengthen the European program industry in the context of the audiovisual policy of the European Union, April 7, 1994. Luxembourg: Office for Official Publications of the European Communities.

Commission of the European Communities (1994e). Report by the think-tank on the audiovisual policy in the European Union, March 1994. Luxembourg: Office for Official Publications of the European Communities.

Commission of the European Communities (1994f). MEDIA guide for the audiovisual industry, 10th edition, June 1994. Brussels: DG X, Commission of the European Communities.

Commission of the European Communities (1994g). Opinion on the proposal for a Council decision amending Council decision 90/68/EEC concerning the implementation of an action programme to promote the development of the European audiovisual industry, MEDIA 1991–1995, 94/C 148/02 (OJL No C 148/3, May 30, 1994).

Commission of the European Communities (1994h). Communication from the Commission to the Council and the European Parliament on the application of Articles 4 and 5 of directive 89/552/EEC, television without frontiers (COM(94) 57 final).

Commission of the European Communities (1994i). Transparency of media control: Study for the European Commission, DG XV by the European Institute for the Media, November 1994. Brussels: Commission of the European Communities, DG XV.

Commission of the European Communities (1993a). "Treaty establishing the European Community (signed in Rome on March 25, 1957)," in *European Union: Selected Instruments taken from the treaties*, Book 1, Vol. 1, pp. 91–669. Luxembourg: Office for Official Publications of the European Communities.

Commission of the European Communities (1993b). "Treaty on European Union (signed in Maastricht on February 7, 1992)," in *European Union: Selected Instruments taken from the treaties*, Book 1, Vol. 1, pp. 11–89. Luxembourg: Office for Official Publications of the European Communities.

Commission of the European Communities (1993c). White Paper on growth, competitiveness, and employment: The challenges and ways forward into the 21st century (the "Delors White Paper"), (COM(93) 700 final).

Commission of the European Communities (1993d). Communication from the Commission to the Council, the European Parliament and the Economic and Social Committee on developing universal service for telecommunications in a competitive environment (COM(93) 543 final, November 15, 1993).

Commission of the European Communities (1993e). Council Directive of 29 October 1993 on harmonizing the term of protection of copyright and certain related rights (93/98/EEC; OJL290/9, November 24, 1993).

Commission of the European Communities (1993f). Council Directive of 27 September 1993 on the coordination of certain rules concerning copyright and rights related to copyright applicable to satellite broadcasting and cable retransmission (93/83/EEC; OJL 248/15, October 6, 1993).

Commission of the European Communities (1993g). *The European Community and human rights*. Luxembourg: Office for Official Publications of the European Communities.

Commission of the European Communities (1992a). Council Directive of 19 November 1992 on rental right and lending right and on certain rights related to copyright in the field of intellectual property (92/100/EEC; OJL 346/61, November 27, 1992).

Commission of the European Communities (1992b). Green Paper on pluralism and media concentration in the internal market: An assessment of the need for Community action (COM(92) 480 final).

Commission of the European Communities (1991c). Communication of the Commission of 26 July 1991 concerning guidelines on the application of the EEC competition rules in the telecommunications sector, (OJ C233, September 6, 1991).

Commission of the European Communities (1990a). *The European Community policy in the audio-visual field*. Luxembourg: Office for Official Publications of the European Communities.

Commission of the European Communities (1990b). Commission Directive on competition in the markets for telecommunications services (90/338/EEC).

Commission of the European Communities (1990c). Council Directive of 28 June 1990 on the establishment of the internal market for telecommunications services through the implementation of open network provision (90/387/EEC; OJ L192/10, July 24, 1990).

Commission of the European Communities (1989). Council Directive of 3 October 1989 on the coordination of certain provisions laid down by law, regulation or administrative action in member states concerning the pursuit of television broadcasting activities (89/552/EEC; OJL 298/23, October 17, 1989).

Commission of the European Communities (1988). *The audio-visual media in the single European market*. Luxembourg: Office for Official Publications of the European Communities.

Commission of the European Communities (1984). "Television without frontiers": Green Paper on the establishment of the common market for broadcasting especially by satellite and cable. (COM (84) 300 final).

Dahrendorf, R. (1994). "The changing quality of citizenship," in B. van Steenbergen, ed., *The condition of citizenship*, pp. 10–19. London: Sage.

David, R. and Spinosi, C. J. (1973). *Les grands systèmes de droit contemporains*. Padua, Italy: CEDAM.

Dyson, K. (1980). *The state tradition in Western Europe*. Oxford: Martin Robertson.

European Convention for the Protection of Human Rights and Fundamental Freedoms, Rome, November 4, 1950, in *European Convention on Human Rights: Collected Texts* (1987). Dordrecht, The Netherlands: Martinus Nijhoff.

European Parliament (1996). Galeote Quecedo-Hoppenstedt Amendments to the Proposal for a European Parliament and Council Directive amending Council Directive 89/552/EEC (A4-0018, February 14, 1996).

European Parliament (1994). Constitution of the European Union. Committee on Institutional Affairs, February 9, 1994, EP A3-0064/94.

European Parliament (1989a). Report on the European Community's film and television industry (the De Vries Report), January 9, 1989, PE 119.192/final.

European Parliament (1989b). Human rights and the European Community: Nationality and citizenship. Report for the European Parliament, October 1989.

European Parliament (1989c). Human rights and the European Community: Conference Acts. Strasbourg, November 1989.

European Parliament (1985). Jacques Delors' address to the opening of the European Parliament, March 12, 1985, Commission programme for 1985, Debates of the European Parliament.

European Report (1995). "Commission unveils MEDIA II and calls for financial muscle," No. 2015, pp. 4–5, February 11, 1995.

France v. Commission, ECJ judgement of March 19, 1991, C-202/88, ECR 1223, "the Terminal Equipment case."

Gellner, E. (1983). *Nations and nationalism.* Oxford: Basil Blackwell.

Italy v. Commission, ECJ judgment of March 20, 1985, case 41/83, 1985. ECR p. 873.

Lasok, D. and Stone, P. A. (1987). *Conflict of laws in the European Community.* Abingdon, UK: Professional Books Ltd.

Mansell, R. (1993). *The new telecommunications: A political economy of network evolution.* London: Sage.

Meehan, E. (1993). *Citizenship and the European Community.* London: Sage.

Morgan, K. (1989). "Telecom strategies in Britain and France: The scope and limits of neo-liberalism and dirigisme," in M. Sharp and P. Holmes, eds., *Strategies for new technology,* pp. 19–55. London: Philip Allan.

The Observer and Guardian v. the United Kingdom, ECJ judgement of November 26, 1991, series A, No. 216.

Robins, K. and Morley, D. (1992). "What kind of identity for Europe?" *Intermedia,* Vol. 20, No. 4–5, pp. 23–24.

Spain v. Commission, ECJ judgement of November 17, 1992, C-271, 281, 289/90, "the Services Directive case."

U.S. Congress (1996). Telecommunications Act of 1996, Public Law No. 104, 104th Congress, February 8, 1996.

European Information Infrastructure Policy Making in the Context of the Policy Capacity of the European Union and Its Member-States: Progress and Obstacles

Milda K. Hedblom and William B. Garrison, Jr.

The framework of the global information infrastructure (GII) rests on the capacities and concrete actions of individual countries and groupings of countries. The European Union (EU) champions common action for the creation of a European information infrastructure. To a large extent the policies proposed and partially adopted for the European information infrastructure fold into GII goals. Yet support for common information infrastructure policies varies widely among EU members, and the capacity of the EU's institutions to implement far-reaching policies is also uncertain.

This tension will be examined by looking at the implementation of policies in the information and telecommunications sectors and the capacity of the EU to formulate and adopt common policy for a European information society. European information society goals necessarily touch on GII goals, but it must be recognized that telecommunications—which is a core element of an information society—has been and remains one of the more contentious policy areas both among member-states and in EU/U.S. relations.

Despite this aura of controversy, the EU and many individual countries have recognized the necessity to accelerate movement toward an information society, in large part because of the awareness that a strategic competitive edge in the world economy increasingly seems to depend upon the availability, use, and exploitation of information. For those countries and economic sectors with a history of significant involvement in electronics, computers, multimedia, and telecommunications, timely achievement of an information society is a matter of prime importance.

Acknowledging this, the EU–through the Commission–launched a strong push to adopt a common strategy for the creation of a European information society based on a European information infrastructure. The main objective of that strategy is to bridge individual initiatives being pursued by EU member-states.

Principal EU Information Infrastructure Initiatives

The current push by the EC toward Union-wide liberalization of the telecommunications and information sectors springs from the June 1994 report of the Bangemann Group, *Europe and the Global Information Society: Recommendations to the European Council.*[1] Asked by the heads of government of the EU member-states for views on the future course of these sectors, this panel of high level representatives of industry and government recommended specific measures designed to create needed infrastructure for information and telecommunications services.

The report called for a break from the pervasive government intervention that has characterized these sectors in the European economy. Instead, the report advocated initiatives to promote partnerships between the public and private sectors with private industry providing the driving force for change. In addition, the report concluded that traditional monopoly provision, most often through state-owned or state-directed entities, must end. A regulatory system must be created for these sectors that, in a post monopoly environment, will support and enable the rapid emergence of new competitive infrastructures and services. Accompanying that change in regulatory structure is the need to reduce disparities in national regulatory regimes and requirements that disrupt or retard the development of a true internal market across the Union.

The EC's response to the Bangemann Report was the promulgation of an Action Plan addressing four areas. (a) new proposals for regulatory and legal frameworks related to telecommunications and information services, legislation and regulations to protect intellectual property rights and privacy, controls over media concentration, and rules for free movement of television broadcasts within the Union; (b) common action on networks, basic services, content, and applications; (c) common policies on the social,

societal, and cultural aspects of the information society; (d) identification of market stimulants to support the mass consumerization
of information services and systems. [2]

The first implementation stage of the Action Plan was a Green
Paper on liberalization of telecommunications infrastructure,[3]
which was promulgated in two phases in late 1994 and early 1995.
The first phase posited the principle that where the provision of
telecommunications services is open to competition, there should
be free choice of the underlying infrastructure used by service
providers to deliver services. The EC proposed the removal of
restrictions on the delivery of satellite services, on the provision of
already liberalized terrestrial services over alternative infrastructure networks, and on the provision of links with mobile networks
to support competitive mobile services.

In the second phase, the EC outlined consultations on several
areas of regulatory policy. The Green Paper addressed the scope of
universal service, the need for a common approach to identifying
its cost and the creation of common financing mechanisms to
ensure the continuation and development of universal service in a
competitive environment. The EC identified the need for a clear
and stable regulatory environment governing interconnection,
based on principles of open access. The need for a common
approach on licensing and for an overall Union-wide framework
for permissible license conditions was identified. The EC called for
fair competition based on full application of EU competition rules
in a manner that will provide a clear and predictable environment.
The EC also addressed issues such as comparable and effective
access to third-country markets; the need for common EU policies
in international fora; and employment, social, and societal issues
flowing from a liberalized environment.

Between publication of the two phases of the Green Paper, the
Council met in November 1994 and addressed several relevant
issues. It deferred action on an EC proposal to allow near-term
competition over alternative networks but did accept January 1998
as the deadline for full liberalization and the introduction of
competition in voice services. The Council also deferred action on
the EC's proposal for a directive on satellite networks and services.

Since that 1994 Council meeting, the EC has taken several
important actions to establish conditions for achieving full liberal-

ization by 1998.[4] Within days of the Council's meeting, the EC issued a proposal to liberalize mobile services and to end monopoly provision of these services. Mobile operators are to be allowed to use alternative networks, including their own. Every member-state must license at least one alternative mobile operator by 1996. Mobile operators are to be allowed to offer any combination of fixed and mobile services. This proposal was adopted as a directive through the EC's exercise of its powers over state-controlled industry sectors under Article 90 of the Treaty of Rome; it became effective as of January 1996.

The EC also invoked Article 90 to adopt a directive allowing use of cable television networks as alternative infrastructure.[5] As in the case of mobile services, consideration of this directive had been deferred by the Council at its November meeting. In addition, the EC adopted an amendment to an earlier directive on satellite services to require mutual recognition of satellite service licenses and to liberalize access to space segments.[6]

During 1995, the EC introduced and adopted additional proposals addressing several key issues: revising open network provisioning (ONP) to cover voice telephony;[7] competition terms and conditions, interconnection, licensing, and universal services;[8] and mobile and personal communications services.[9]

The draft licensing directive will require member-states to adopt procedures designed to enable new providers of telecommunications services, if they meet certain conditions, to start operations immediately instead of having to wait. Member-states are not allowed to limit the numbers of new entrants except to insure the efficient use of the radio spectrum (as in the case of mobile services). A new body, the EU Telecommunications Committee, is to establish authorization procedures that will enable companies licensed in any member-state to operate throughout the Union.

In November 1995, the Council adopted the proposed directive extending ONP to voice telephony. A state-controlled national telephone operator can no longer be both managed and regulated by the same governmental body. ONP rules on leased lines would apply not only to established national operations but also to providers with significant market power, defined as 25 percent of the relevant market. The directive requires national telephone operators to give notice of users' rights service, tariffs and charges, etc. The directive also empowers the EC to intervene to rationalize regulation when important differences are found in the regulation of voice service among the member-states.

The proposal on terms and conditions of competition was discussed by the Council in November 1995 and referred to the Parliament for action.

Principal Technology Programs Pertinent to Information Infrastructure Initiatives

The first of the cooperative research and development programs to address the information and telecommunications sectors was the European Strategic Program for Research and Development (ESPRIT). ESPRIT was designed to provide a framework for industrial cooperation in research and development. The first phase was approved in December 1982 and formally initiated in 1984; it covered a four-year term, ending in 1988.

During this first phase, fundamental milestones were achieved in the Europeanization of these sectors.[10] The traditional international collaboration among national telephone operators carried out through European organizations such as the Conference of European Postal and Telecommunications Administration was determined to be insufficient for the achievement of ESPRIT's goals. A framework was developed to incorporate other interested parties, primarily universities and telecommunications equipment manufacturers. The expansion of the ESPRIT collaboration to include these players fostered the examination of national industrial policies that had retarded Europe-wide technological development.

The Task Force on Information and Telecommunications Technologies was created in 1984 within Directorate General (DG) XIII to provide policy analysis and evaluation of the sectoral technology projects being developed through ESPRIT. As these projects evolved, the scope of the Task Force's policy work expanded to examining infrastructure requirements, market policies, and educational and social issues and to evaluating parallel or comparable areas of concern or action in Japan and the United States. The work of the Task Force during this period laid the foundation for the EC's campaign to end fragmentation of information and telecommunications by national markets and to create an internal market across the Union.

Because of the broad reach of the ESPRIT program and because of the needs identified in the first phase, a more focused program of cooperative development for improved telecommunications infrastructure was initiated. The RACE program specifically addressed advanced telecommunications networks, particularly broadband networks. Network operators, manufacturers, software designers, university-based researchers, and laboratories cooperated to develop broadband technologies. While ESPRIT II addressed microelectronics, information processing, advanced computer systems, and peripherals, RACE concentrated on the telecommunications infrastructure required to enable advanced information technologies to reach the broadest markets.[11]

The work carried out under RACE formed an integral part of the telecommunications policy work of the EC as it identified parameters that regulatory policy must address if advanced communications services were to be developed and delivered by European industries. In its first phase, RACE concentrated on evaluation of technological options for advanced networks. In its second phase, the work shifted to preparation for the introduction of integrated broadband communications.

However, the focus on broadband networks was eventually seen as too narrow.[12] During 1995, the EC's work in advanced communications policy shifted toward services and the removal of technical and operational barriers to improved and advanced services. User-driven experimentation and trial projects are now the primary interest. Areas such as intelligent networks, mobile and personal communications services, and integrated services technology are grouped with others under the rubric of Advanced Communication Technologies and Services (ACTS).

In December 1994, the Regional Information Society Initiative (RISI) was launched under the ACTS program as a follow-up to the Bangemann Report.[13] RISI is oriented toward applications and is charged with promoting cooperation in teleworking, distance learning, university and related research networks, telematic services, telemedicine, tele-administration, teletraffic management, telemeasuring, teleshopping, etc. Cooperative undertakings are to be implemented on a regional basis with emphasis on projects designed to stimulate local economies. Local RISI steering groups oversee the projects under the direction of an Inter-regional Information Society Management Group made up of representatives of participating regions and appropriate EU officials.

In keeping with subsidiarity and the promotion of regional application projects, member-states are encouraged to undertake comparable programs to promote the information society. An example is the Dutch Electronic Highways Action Program, begun in 1994, which addresses policy areas for liberalization and establishes demonstration projects for advanced telecommunications and information services. [14]

The RISI program has proposed a schedule for liberalizing telecommunications infrastructure, satellite services, and spectrum. It has called for loosening unnecessary or restrictive statutes governing the development and use of electronic services. Adoption of a definition of the public domain for electronic information has been proposed for services that should be the responsibility of government. Interconnection standards, security and privacy protections, and intellectual property rights are being assessed.

Under the RISI program, demonstration projects must have realistic chances for commercial deployment. New services provided through cable television systems are being explored, and airports and cargo ports are being encouraged to extend services as "information ports." Study is under way of the legal changes required to establish an "information freeport" in order to encourage trade in information and communications services.

Intellectual Property Rights Development

The EU has undertaken to develop intellectual property rights as part of its information society initiative in ways that take account of technology and electronic communication. If the information society is to develop successfully, the new services and products being created must be able to benefit from a more coherent regulatory framework at the national, Union, and international levels. One element of a coherent regulatory framework is the adaptation of the legal environment for intellectual property.

The movement toward a more coherent regime began with the EC's 1988 Green Paper[15] which resulted in a number of Directives: the Software Directive, 1991, on the legal protection of computer programs;[16] the Rental Rights Directive, 1992, on rental rights and lending rights and on certain rights related to copyright in the field of intellectual property;[17] the Cable and Satellite Directive, 1993, on the coordination of certain rules concerning copyrights and on rights related to copyright being applicable to satellite broadcasting and cable retransmission;[18] and the Term of Protection Directive, 1993, harmonizing the term of protection of copyright and certain related rights.[19]

The Software Directive requires member-states to protect computer programs by copyright as literary works within the meaning of the Berne Convention on the Protection of Literary and Artistic Work. Protection of computer programs extends to preparatory design material, but the ideas and principles that underlie any element of a computer program, including those that underlie its interfaces, are not protected. A computer program is protected if it is original in the sense that it is the author's own intellectual creation; no other criteria are to be applied to determine its eligibility for protection.

The Rental Rights directive requires the member-states to protect authors' and producers' rights to control the rental or lending of original or copied copyright works, such as records, videos, or film. Non-profit libraries are excluded. Significant exceptions are created for private, reportorial, teaching, scientific, and ephemeral use.

The 1993 directive on harmonization of copyright and related rights for satellite and cable TV retransmissions had the primary goal of insuring payment for the holders of such rights. Since 1995, broadcast rights must be obtained in the country of origin, not of destination. For cable TV, broadcast rights must be negotiated through cooperative bodies representing various categories of rights holders.

The directive on harmonization of duration of copyright and related rights (photographs and posthumous works) provides that from July 1, 1995, all works subject to copyright protection in the Union will be protected for 70 years after the death of the author. In the area of audiovisual and cinematic works, rights will extend for 70 years after the death of the last survivor among the principal director, the script author, the dialogue author, and the music composer.

A major next step in harmonization of areas affected by the information society is the formal adoption by the Council of Ministers of the Directive on Legal Protection of Data-bases.[20] This is a relatively innovative EU-wide copyright protection for data-base creators and investors throughout the Union. It aims to combat piracy and unauthorized use of information through its main feature, which is a new exclusive economic right protecting the substantial investments in time, money, and effort of data-base manufacturers. This protection will last 15 years from the finalization of a data-base even if the contents do not qualify for the standard copyright protection—giving the maker the right to prohibit the extraction or reuse of the data-base's content by third parties. However, member-states will be able to grant certain exemptions from the right, notably extraction of information for private use and teaching. In addition, the directive provides for the harmonization of copyright law applicable to the structure of both electronic and paper-bases manufactured in the EU. This protection may be extended to data-bases manufactured in third countries if their legislation provides a similar level of protection for EU firms.

The EU has also issued a Green Paper[21] taking up broad issues in copyright and related areas triggered by the Bangemann Report.[22] Work on the EU's copyright Green Paper and its progeny took place in the context of copyright reports in the United States,[23] two MITI reports on the management of rights to multimedia products and moral rights in Japan, and the French Sirinelli report on multimedia.[24]

The Green Paper has set the terms for EU discussion on copyright in the digital environment. As a whole it does not seek a sweeping reform of intellectual property policy on the European level. In this view it was corroborated by the Law Advisory Board which observed that "No pressing need for immediate action and reform...seems to exist."[25]

Nevertheless, five fields of regulation were examined which in themselves are intended to strengthen the protection of intellectual property in the emerging digital networked environment. The first regulatory field involves the question of whether a digital communication is a restricted act of communication only in the country where it arises and therefore subject only to its laws or it is subject to the laws of all the member-states. A second regulatory question arises in the field of exhaustion of rights (or first sale doctrine under U.S. law). Should the principle that rights of distribution be exhausted after physical copies of a work are first put into circulation apply to transmissions over a network? And should the principle of exhaustion be limited to the EU member-states?

The third field of regulation is the most important of all: how should the EU define economic rights, reproduction, communications to the public, and broadcasting in the electronic network environment? A related issue attaches to the management of multimedia rights given that a multimedia producer may use fragments of other works numbering in the thousands. What should be the level of obligation of the producer in regard to licenses or permissions? Lastly, the Green Paper considered the matter of regulating copyright protection through Europe-wide technical identification.

The most notable feature of the Green Paper was the extent to which it looked at the question of intellectual property rights from the right holder's perspective, which highlighted the problems that arise for the copyright industries in the evolving digital environment. There was less concern about the rights or problems for others in the information chain such as libraries, universities, and end users. The task remains for the EU to take into account the legitimate interests of all parties.

EU Policy Capacity

The concrete actions taken by the EU in the telecommunications and information sector need to be examined in the context of general Union policy making. The EU policy environment is complex, partly due to the distribution of powers under the treaties, partly due to the institutional profile, and partly due to the distribution of powers among the member-states, including political power, sectoral power in telecommunications and information industries, and the overall economic power of member-states.

The distribution of powers under the treaties and their proper characterization are the subject of extensive discussion and debate.[26] The EU is a peculiar hybrid, part international organization and part intergovernmental organization. In legal terms, its existence derives not from a constitutional pact but from an intergovernmental compact, the Treaty of Rome, and subsequent treaties. As a rule, treaties devise systems of checks and balances whose main function is to keep the powers of the organization they set up under control. The various treaties of the EU reflect this desire to limit, but they also take a pioneering approach by introducing substantial elements of regional integration.

Thus the EU has created a novel system of government in which significant federal elements, represented by the EC, the European Parliament, and the European Court of Justice, coexist with the European Council and the Council of Ministers in whose hands ultimate power still firmly rests.[27]

Power sharing is expressed in an arrangement whereby in some areas the EU is assigned full competence to act on behalf of member-states, in some areas competence is shared so that both the EU and individual member-states can act, and in still others the member-states remain fully responsible.

Shared competence characterizes at least some of the policy making for telecommunications and information initiatives. This began somewhat slowly in the early 1980s but has now steadily expanded and accelerated. It is important to note that the direct involvement of the EU in shaping internal information and telecommunications policy originated in external concerns, was carried along by single market concerns, and is now supported by an emerging consensus at the highest levels of politics and industry.

The possibility that the health, shape and direction of this sector might become a serious concern to the EU first arose at the 1980 Dublin summit. The EC identified the need to respond to U.S. and Japanese trade in high tech goods and services, particularly in the field of telecommunications. At that point, this need was stated largely in terms of the goal of increasing the European share of world trade in telecommunications goods and services.

Over the course of the next decade, the EU dramatically redirected its prime orientation away from an external trade response to a far-reaching reassessment of internal infrastructure capabilities both from the trans-European perspective and from the perspective of individual countries. Both external and internal factors account for this shift.[28] Paramount among the external factors was the breakup of AT&T, which demonstrated that telecommunications need not be structured as a natural monopoly. Internal factors included the impact of powerful EC leadership, which led to the launch of the internal market program, an increasing high level of dissatisfaction with the state of telecommunications services among business leaders, and a sharpened understanding in Brussels of the critical importance of the sector for other economic and market goals.

In 1987, the EC issued a landmark Green Paper with the twin goals of achieving an efficient regional network structure and strengthening the private sector for competition.[29] This opened the door to an intensive elaboration of policy that inevitably brought to the surface the most difficult problems in transforming the telecommunication and information landscape within the EU. These problems included the role of Postal Telegraph and Telecommunication Administrations (PTTs)–leveling the playing field for new entrants and restructuring 12 previously distinct industries to support pan-European services. The numerous proposals made by the EC and the steps taken by the Council have been shaped by these key problems, though not to the exclusion of all others.

Since 1990, the scope of EU authority in this sector has steadily enlarged; the particulars of this enlargement are striking. The Maastricht Treaty formally recognized the importance of trans-European networks by assigning to the Union a priority task of promoting and supporting the rapid development of such networks not only in telecommunications but also in transport, electricity, and gas.

While some of the problems in the area of telecommunications and information exhibited unusual dimensions—such as the extraordinary fiscal and political importance of state-sector PTTs— the policy strategy chosen by the EC and Council was familiar. This strategy involves incrementalism, issue fragmentation, and hierarchical analysis in order to develop and resolve the least difficult issues first.[30] An example of this approach is the 1986 directive to harmonize the testing and certification of equipment with Union-wide guaranteed connection rights to public networks and the sponsorship of the European Telecommunications Standards Institute.[31]

By 1994, several key factors—the confidence of the EC, the backing of the Court, powerful pressures from European industry, the impact of rapidly changing technology, and significant strides made in other countries (notably the United States) on broader information infrastructure goals—led to the launching of the 1994 EU program.

EU Policy: Progress and Obstacles

A distinguishing feature of the EU policy environment is that it occurs in a variety of both formal institutional and informal venues, including special high-level task forces with reporting duties, intra-EU consultative and advisory bodies, and international intergovernmental meetings and programs of cooperation.

Apart from the will of the EC and its ability to navigate the shifting tides of pro- and anti-Brussels sentiment among its member-states, the most critical feature of the EU policy process is the extraordinary role of the Court of Justice. It is clear that the Court's main endeavor has been to "fashion a constitutional framework for a quasifederal structure in Europe."[32]

Since the Treaty of Rome failed to state squarely whether Union law prevailed over member-state law, it was left to the Court of Justice to lay down that marker. It did so in Costa v. Enel,[33] stating that the member-states had "created a body of law which binds both their nationals and themselves." Other expansions followed, and it is reasonable to view the Court of Justice as the preeminent integrating force through the early 1990s. But what about the future?

The importance of Article 90 to the expansion of a regional telecommunications and information regime based on open networks and competition is evident from the several examples of its use described above. However, the more aggressively it is invoked, the more certain a challenge will arrive at the door of the Court. The Court's earlier activism on behalf of expanded powers for the EU took place in a very different internal political and legal environment than now exists. The Court conducted its business for some decades more or less out of sight and out of mind thanks to the benign neglect of the media and the relative indifference of national political leaders. Today, under the Single European Act and the Maastricht Treaty, the European Parliament's influence on lawmaking is enlarged, but that enlargement does not make it a coequal with the other institutions.[34] Nevertheless, there is a decided sense in which the EU is now on the path to making key decisions by political rather than legal means. Therefore the next steps in the telecommunications and information policy process will be more fully subject to the inevitable hazards of the political give-and-take in the Council and Parliament as well as in the informal policy venues populated by mobilized interests. The general shift toward political decision making is likely to lengthen and roughen the road toward an effective European information infrastructure.

In terms of policy making that supports both the EU information infrastructure and the goals of the GII, the most consistent center of activism has been the EC. Although its proposals have often been too ambitious for the political environment and its timetables beyond the reach of the Council's political will, especially in view of the difficulties of the monopoly operators of member-states, one of the factors enabling the EC's success has been pressure for change arising from two directorates simultaneously–DG XIII for telecommunications policy and DG IV for competition policy.

However, a new question now touches on this joint focus: to what extent will telecommunications problems migrate to other spheres? Some have pointed to the competition policy Directorate and the External Trade Directorate as likely destinations. To the extent that the goals of current directives (such as interconnection and fair competition) can be achieved, the resultant industry landscape should present questions that will fall under the authority of the competition Directorate.

This does not pose a serious problem to progress in principle, assuming problems are dealt with adequately. But in the real world of policy process, such a transition is likely to be highly disturbing to the balance of bureaucratic relations. In view of the importance of EC leadership in this complicated and technical area, a weakening of its internal capacity could only in the end prove an additional obstacle to the timely emergence of the information society in the European arena.

Informal Policy Process

One of the hallmarks of EU policy process is its high dependence upon an extraordinary variety and depth of contacts, consultations, meetings, programs of cooperation, and task force activities. This is in addition to the institutional work of the EC in developing agendas and the work of the Committee of Permanent Representatives in developing policy possibilities for the Council. [35]

There are strong examples of the unusual importance of the informal policy process to the telecommunications and information sector, including the work of the group of top-level representatives of industry and government from across the Union convened by Martin Bangemann, ECer for Telecommunications. The group's call for a break with the past European inclination toward pervasive governmental intervention and its advocacy of initiatives involving private and public partnerships to stimulate markets created an unusual aura of legitimacy and sense of urgency to which the EC responded with great dispatch. A second case worth considering since it is so closely linked to the GII process is the series of U.S.-European meetings that took place in 1992 to address issues of cooperation and competition in telecommunications, proceedings without fixed agendas or action obligations. Initiated and supported by the DG XIII, these meeting have served as important vehicles for discussing differences and developing the common interests supporting the evolution of the GII initiative at the Brussels summit in 1995. These discussions became increasingly important as the degree of crossmarket penetration by transborder companies reached new highs in the telecommunications and information sector during the first half of the 1990s, with every expectation of more to come. The participants often debated highly contentious issues outside the meetings.

The atmosphere is conveyed by a joke told by Michel Carpentier, then ECer for DG XIII, at the opening of the 1993 Rome round of meetings: Two mountain climbers are walking through a forest. Suddenly they come upon a large, hungry-looking bear. The first climber takes off his hiking boots and changes into his running shoes. His friend looks at him and says, "There's no way you can outrun the bear; what's the point of trying?" His friend replies," I don't have to run faster than the bear; I just have to run faster than you."[36]

What Happens Next?

The road ahead is by no means clear of obstacles, and the EU's desire to take its place as an important pillar in the GII program is highly contingent on whether it can overcome these barriers.

The plan to liberalize voice competition has been confirmed by the constituent bodies of the EU, but opportunities abound for the entrenched telephone operators to slow the process down and to delay introduction of meaningful competition. The Council's preference to elaborate a regulatory framework before introducing competition and to reach agreement on expansion and financing of universal telephony presents many opportunities to tie up the deliberative process. The terms and conditions for competition must be resolved more directly in the political arena by bureaucrats, politicians, politically powerful incumbent operators, and other interested parties.

This leads one to conclude that full liberalization will not occur expeditiously and therefore the spread of the benefits envisioned in the plans for an information society and the GII will be delayed. If the EC proves unable to enforce the 1998 deadline for full liberalization, the EU will be at risk of never attaining the critical mass cited in the Bangemann Report.

Nonetheless, the inexorable pace of technological innovation and crossmarket penetration that has driven this industry's evolution toward competition may ultimately win out. If enough member-states adopt full liberalization, soon it will be very difficult for others to delay past 1998. Such a development would bear some similarity to the expected implementation of the European Monetary Union in that inauguration by a few would likely increase the need for the remainder to find their way in.

Despite the diffuse environment in which the information society in Europe must develop, the EC's programs of regulation and technology promotion constitute a comprehensive approach to the challenges of this sector. The analysis and policies set out in the Bangemann Report, the Action Plan, and the Green Papers provide insightful explication of the social and economic importance of the industry. Taken together, the EU's directives, legislation, and cases provide a corpus of legal and public policies that reveal the tensions and the potential gains that will characterize information infrastructure development on both the national and the global level in the future.

Notes

1. *Europe and the Global Information Society: Recommendations to the European Council,* May 1994; adopted by the European Council in June 1994.

2. *Europe's Way to the Information Society: An Action Plan* (Com. 347 final).

3. Green Paper on Liberalization of Telecommunications Infrastructure and Cable Television Networks, Parts I and II, 1994/1995.

4. Com/94/492, November 22, 1994.

5. Amendment to Directive 90/388/EC, 95/51/EC.

6. Amendment to Directive 90/388/EEC, 94/46/EC.

7. Draft amendment to Directive 90/388/EEC, December 6, 1995.

8. Draft amendment to Directive 90/388/EEC, July 19, 1995.

9. Draft amendment to Directive 90/388/EEC, June 21, 1995.

10. Report of ESPRIT Review Board, SEC (89) 1348 final.

11. Final Report on Phase I of RACE, Com (93) 118.

12. RACE 1994, DG XIII/B-46.

13. Regional Information Society Initiative, DGs XIII & XVI, December 1994.

14. Actie-programma Electronische Snelwegen, van metafoor naar actie, URL:http://www.nic.surfnet.nl/nap/.

15. Green Paper on Challenges of Technology, 1988.

16. Council Directive 91/250/EEC of 14 May 1991, O.J. No. L 122, 17/05/91, p. 42.

17. Council Directive 92/100/EEC or 19 November, 1992, O. J. No. L248, 06/10/93, p. 15.

18. Council Directive 93/83 EEC of 27 September 1993, O. J. No. L 248, 06/10/93, p. 9.

19. Council Directive 93/98/EEC of 29 October 1993, O.J. No. L. 290, 241/11/93, p. 9.

20. Eurocom, March 1996.

21. http://www.ispo.cec.be/infosoc/legreg/com95382.doc.

22. Europe and the Global Information Society: Recommendations to the European Council, May 1994; adopted by the European Council, June 1994.

23. http://www.uspto.gov./web/ipnii/ (PDF, Microsoft Word 6.0 or zippered PostScript) or gopher://ntiant1.ntia.doc.gov:70/00/papers/documents/files/ipnii.txt (ASCII format).

24. Industries culturelles at nouvelles techniques. Paris: La Documentation française (fax +33 1 40 15 72 30). ISBN 2-90917-17-8.

25. http://www2.echo.lu/legal/en/pr/reply/general.html#HD_NM_1.

26. Robert O. Keohane and Stanley Hoffmann, in Keohane and Hoffmann, eds., *The New European Community: Decisionmaking and Institutional Change* (Boulder, CO: Westview, 1991), pp. 10–15; Philip, in Andrew Duff, John Pinder, and Roy Price, eds., *Maastricht and Beyond: Building the European Union* (London and New York: Routledge, 1994), pp. 123–139.

27. Laffan, in Alan W. Cafruny and Glenda G. Rosenthal, eds., *The State of the European Community*, vol. 2: *The Maastricht Debates and Beyond* (Boulder, CO: L. Rienner Publishers, 1993), pp. 35–39.

28. Dizard, in Cafruny and Rosenthal, eds. *The State of the European Community*, vol. 2, pp. 328–330.

29. Thatcher, *European Public Policy*, Vol. 4, No. 1, p. 212.

30. Kate Lodge, *Social Sciences Yearbook* (Harlow, UK: Longman, 1993), \pp. 2–26.

31. Dizard, in Cafruny and Rosenthal, eds. *The State of the European Community*, vol. 2, p. 323.

32. Mancini, in Keohane and Hoffmann, eds., *The New European Community: Decisionmaking and Institutional Change*, p. 178.

33. Case 6/64, European Court Reports, (ECR), p. 585.

34. Mancini, in Keohane and Hoffmann, eds., *The New European Community: Decisionmaking and Institutional Change*, p. 189.

35. Laffan, in Cafruny and Rosenthal, eds. *The State of the European Community*, vol. 2, pp. 35–45.

36. *Cooperation and Competition in Telecommunications: Proceedings* (EIC and Center for Media Law, 1993), p. xv.

Approaches for Maximizing GII Impacts on Sustainable Development

Thomas R. Spacek

Introduction

The European Commission (EC) has established a "working circle of experts" to compile a report on the role of the Information Society in achieving sustainable development. The working circle consists of twelve experts on the environment, social development, economics, and the Information Society selected by the EC. The initial version of this chapter was prepared as a contribution to the first meeting of the working circle at a workshop sponsored by the EC in Brussels on December 12–13, 1995.

Since sustainable development has become one of the principal policy objectives of the European Union (EU) countries, an objective of the working circle of experts is to recommend "lines of action" (such as research projects) for the EC to pursue in concert with industry, national and regional governments, academia, and environmentalists to further explore the contributions of the Information Society to sustainable development. An additional objective is to provide the rationale for pursuing each recommended research project. The intent of this chapter is to contribute to these objectives. Pursuing the recommended research projects will generate both qualitative and quantitative evidence to form a sound base and the impetus for the EC and EU countries to accelerate the development of the Information Society.

Although the concept of sustainable development is not precisely defined, background material prepared by the working circle organizers included the following:

With the Maastricht Treaty a "harmonious and balanced development of economic activities, sustainable and non-inflationary growth respecting the environment"[1] has become one of the principal policy objectives of the European Union. The principle of sustainable development given by the Brundtland Commission is that "current generations should meet their needs without compromising the ability of future generations to meet their own needs."[2] Linking economic and social development to improvement of the environment is a first step in that direction. However, making the concept of sustainability precise and easily applicable in practice has proved difficult.

The transition to the Information Society must be shaped to contribute to the goal of sustainable development. Title XII of the Union Treaty commits the Community to contribute to the establishment and development of a trans-European telecommunications network. The goal of transforming its fragmented national networks into a truly European communications network has been extensively discussed, and a more precise scope of Union action in this field has been defined.[3] At present, the development of trans-European services and applications, supported by advanced communications networks, has become the objective of Community action in this domain.

Innovative use of new communications services will also enable the emergence and growth of industries which will create new employment and which at the same time offer substitutes for travel and transport of goods, a major shift towards less material-intensive production and consumption, trade and value generation. Such changes can significantly reduce the environmental impact of industrial and commercial activities and thus make a considerable contribution to sustainable development.[4]

This chapter focuses on the intersections among three classes of issues identified by the EC: sustainable development issues, Information Society issues, and technology and infrastructure issues (see Figure 1). Work in the field of sustainable development often forecasts far (as much as hundreds of years) into the future to address slowly changing impacts in areas such as population and the environment.[5] To complement such approaches, this chapter will use an approach that is designed to be both practical and meaningful; beginning with today's information infrastructure and applications together with a vision of an advanced National Information Infrastructure (NII) and Global Information Infrastructure (GII) as the goal, the chapter discusses changes that need to be made and steps that need to be taken to make major strides toward achieving this vision in the next five to ten years. The chapter also suggests that the goals of sustainable development be explicitly taken into account while addressing the many key NII/ GII issues that are yet to be resolved. This perspective takes into account experiences in the United States to date as the information/communications industries continue to converge and become increasingly competitive. With the EU countries' ongoing progress toward privatizing telecommunications industries and increasing competition, many of the experiences of the United States may be worth exploring and many of the issues concerning NII and GII initiatives being addressed are likely to be relevant to Europe.

Following a brief background discussion, this chapter will address the issues shown in Figure 1. The discussion will focus on four areas included in a questionnaire developed by the working circle organizers:

1. perceptions of sustainable development;

2. interrelationships among sustainable development, the Information Society, and technology and infrastructure;

3. approaches to achieving sustainability via NII/GII applications; and

4. lines of action.

Background

The existing U.S. NII consists of a wide variety of networks and applications including wireline and wireless telephony, 800 and 888 based (toll-free) information services, cable TV, the Internet, on-line services, and others. These networks, either separately or in some cases jointly, provide transport and access to a wide array of useful information as well as computing and communications applications that are socially and commercially beneficial. As we look forward to an advanced NII as articulated by the Council on Competitiveness,[6] the Computer Systems Policy Project (CSPP),[7] and the Clinton/Gore administration,[8] questions remain as to whether the full vision of this advanced NII will require more than the extension of existing networks and applications to multimedia forms. In particular, one must address the issue of full, seamless

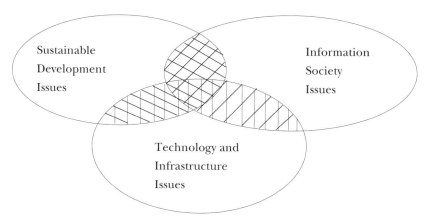

Figure 1

connectivity and interoperability among networks and the associated applications that will form the next generation NII.[9] These interoperability issues are addressed separately in an earlier paper by the author.[10]

The United States does have a voice telephony NII today, and one can view the Internet as a model for a data (or perhaps broader) communications NII. Telephony, the Internet, or perhaps other existing network approaches represent good starting points from which an NII may evolve; however, these may not naturally evolve into an NII as envisioned by the Council on Competitiveness, the CSPP, the Clinton/Gore administration, and others. Although business and technology convergence is taking place in the communications/information industries, it is not at all clear that current market forces will be viewed by major players in these industries as creating the incentive for making necessary investments and cooperative agreements to evolve the current array of networks in a way that will achieve such a vision.[11]

The three key NII visions referenced above are quite similar in intent although they differ somewhat in emphasis based on the authoring organizations' perspective. Since the visions are so similar, just one will be quoted here. The "Vision for a 21st Century Information Infrastructure" of the Council on Competitiveness states that: "The infrastructure of the 21st century will enable all Americans[12] to access information and communicate with each other easily, reliably, securely, and cost-effectively in any medium—voice, data, image or video—anytime, anywhere. This capability will enhance the productivity of work and lead to dramatic improvements in social services, education, and entertainment." This infrastructure will consist of: "a set of widely accessible and interoperable communications networks; digital libraries, information databases and services; easy-to-use information appliances and computer systems; and trained people who can build, maintain and operate these resources." Some additional characteristics of an NII are listed in Appendix 1 to help make the term somewhat more concrete.

Significant efforts aimed at realizing the common vision of an NII are being carried out by telecommunications service providers, the Internet community, the computer industry, information providers, telecommunications equipment manufacturers, cable companies, wireless providers, satellite systems, and others. There are several activities focused on bringing these efforts together. The Harvard Information Infrastructure Forum, which has previously focused on policy issues related to the NII in the United States, has expanded its focus to include GII issues. The Cross-Industry Working Team focuses on NII architecture, technology, services, and applications issues. In addition, Bellcore and others are working on key standards and technologies, including the next generation of the Internet Protocol, ATM, and SONET. Hopefully the activities aimed at bringing these efforts together will result in an NII/GII characterized, where appropriate, by cooperation, partnership, and competition.

Questionnaire Issues

Perceptions of Sustainable Development

The value of the NII/GII is realized only through the applications it provides that are used by people to perform specific tasks, whether they involve gaining knowledge or purchasing a product—people receive value from using applications, not from the infrastructure itself. The degree to which NII/GII applications help improve the economy, meet societal needs, and/or help the environment is the degree to which the NII/GII achieves the goals of sustainable development. The "or" part of the "and/or" is important. For example, a particular educational application may meet the needs of a rural school district (or, for that matter, any school district in a less-developed country) yet may be neutral or even have a negative impact on the economy in the short run, for example, if the cost of reaching the rural area exceeds the local educational community's ability to pay. Trade-offs of this sort will be common in developing a policy framework for a country's (or a union of countries') NII. In the overall picture, however, the costs and benefits of an NII/GII must contribute positively to the economy, society, and the environment if the NII/GII is to contribute to sustainable development.

If the vision of an NII/GII is going to be realized and if the NII/GII is to be broadly available to schools, libraries, businesses, homes, etc., a large investment will be required in information appliances (e.g., computers, set-top boxes, HDTVs), information content (e.g., digitizing textbooks), network infrastructure (e.g., greater bandwidth to the home, faster switches), and support (e.g., awareness, training). Estimates for the U.S. network infrastructure alone range from $100 billion to $400 billion. The wide range likely results from varying assumptions about fiber deployment. No one industry or organization, including the federal government, can pay for the needed investment. Multiple organizations will need not only to invest but also to provide the variety of skills required to achieve an NII/GII.

To ensure that an NII/GII contributes toward the goals of sustainable development, the planning, development, and implementation of an NII/GII need to be guided by a policy framework that must:

• encourage an NII/GII based on market-driven products and services;

• support societal needs—recognizing that market forces alone may not create the incentive for the private sector to make the investment needed (e.g., in K-12 education, rural areas, or for particular applications such as environmental monitoring) but that those needs must be met;

• motivate the private sector to begin investing, perhaps up to hundreds of billions of dollars over many years, and provide an opportunity for a reasonable return on investment;

- result in an economically sustainable system to provide for the ongoing development, improvement, and growth of an NII/GII;
- help ensure affordable universal access, maximum inter-connectivity, and user-friendliness;
- promote the collaborative environment characteristic of the Internet today; and
- address intellectual property, copyright, security, and privacy issues.

How can this be accomplished? Some key aspects of a solution framework are noted in Appendix 2.

Interrelationships among Sustainable Development, the Information Society, and Technology and Infrastructure

As mentioned above, sustainable development is concerned with a wide range of issues related to economic improvements, societal benefits, and environmental quality. These issues include air and water pollution, depletion of certain natural resources, improved education, and inflation rates, among others. All issues in this class (whether or not related to the GII) are included in the Sustainable Development Issues circle in Figure 1. The Information Society can be defined as: (a) people and organizations with evolving communications and information access needs, (b) services and applications that can be used to meet those needs, and (c) the information content itself. Information Society issues include intellectual property rights, security, privacy, censorship, the value of information, and the value and usefulness of particular applications, among others. All issues in this class are represented by the Information Society Issues circle (regardless of any particular technology and whether the issues are related to sustainable development). Finally, there are many issues involving communications technology and infrastructure and the firms that provide network services using the infrastructure; these issues include costs, network design, alternative technologies, performance, reliability, availability, investment incentives, and interoperability, among others. All issues in this class are contained in the Technology and Infrastructure Issues circle.

This section focuses on the shaded areas in Figure 1 where the circles intersect. Although each circle represents a different class of issues, as described above, it may turn out that all Technology and Infrastructure issues overlap with Information Society issues. In this case, the nonshaded area of the Technology and Infrastructure circle may be null.

We will start with an observation about complementarity and then focus the rest of this section on problems that need to be resolved where potential conflicts exist between and among the overlapping circles in Figure 1. The observation is that the Information Society and Technology and Infrastructure mutually support Sustainable Development by *enabling* the vision of an NII/GII to be *realized* through the availability of useful *applications,* many of which can improve the economy, meet societal needs, and help improve the environment. There is the potential for NII/GII applications to make contributions to sustainable development that could otherwise not be made. So perhaps we should not only ask, "What are the possible contributions of the Information Society to sustainable development?" We may also want to ask, "Since the NII/GII has potential for major contributions to sustainable development, how can we vector the evolution to an advanced NII/GII to maximize these contributions?"

One way to maximize contributions to sustainable development is to encourage development of two types of applications: (a) those aimed at sustainable development itself, e.g., environmental monitoring, and (b) those applications that can have a major impact on sustainable development, e.g., distance learning and tele-commuting. Applications will be addressed in more detail below.

The fact that there are many issues yet to be resolved in evolving to an advanced NII/GII provides further opportunities for maximizing its contributions to sustainable development since the goals of sustainable development can be explicitly taken into account while resolving these issues. This concept should be kept in mind as we look first at the intersection among all three circles in Figure 1 followed by a look at the bilateral intersections.

Although there are many potentially conflicting issues in the intersecting areas of Figure 1, we will address just a few key issues in each area.

Issues at the Intersection of Sustainable Development, the Information Society, and Technology and Infrastructure

At the confluence of the three circles is the issue of defining universal access and universal service. In Appendix 1 we describe universal access as universal availability—anyone who wants to connect to a network that is part of the NII can do so at an affordable price. In voice telephony, universal service can be easily defined. In addition to everyone, or almost everyone, having a telephone at an affordable price with the ability to make a call, the definition could include other capabilities such as 911 emergency service. In an NII/GII environment, defining universal access and service becomes more complex. What line speed must everyone be able to afford? Must multimedia services including voice, data, and video be available in every home? If so, must access be bidirectional and symmetrical? What applications are part of the universal access/service definition? Does everyone need a sophisticated computer in his or her home to have equal access to services? Are we creating a society of information "haves" and "have nots" if some people cannot afford the latest technology and applications that others can afford?

These are all interesting but complex questions. Because the answers are difficult does not mean we should slow efforts toward reaching the goal of an NII/GII. Reaching the vision will likely be a slow process in any event. The capabilities that need to be made available to everyone should be some minimal set of services and applications (yet to be defined in the United States). Initially, more sophisticated capabilities can be made available to everyone in community centers such as libraries. Over time, as competition increases, technology prices decrease, and new applications arise, the minimal set of services can be adjusted upwards, and perhaps the more advanced services of that future time can be made available in community centers. Clearly precautions should be taken so that the Information Society does not widen the gap between rich and poor. However, precautions should also be taken not to hinder competition, innovation, or democracy. The fact that some people will be able to afford more than others should not be a reason to slow the development of an NII/GII. On the whole, the characteristics of an NII/GII are likely to lead to greater equality in the abilities of people at different ends of the economic spectrum to have access to information and improved forms of interpersonal communications than they have today. Similarly, the benefits of access to sophisticated networking capabilities will be available to individuals and small businesses which cannot afford to own a network, as many large businesses can.[13]

A second issue at the intersection of the three circles involves the potential conflict between (a) meeting societal needs in areas where market forces may not naturally provide the incentives for the investments required to meet those needs and (b) the fact that large investments by the private sector are needed to make the vision of an NII/GII a reality and that market needs and an expectation of a profitable return are appropriate incentives to drive such investments. To avoid this conflict requires a combination of a policy framework that provides incentives for the private sector to invest in a way that both meets reasonable profitability expectations and addresses societal needs together with a regulatory framework that appropriately motivates (or at least does not deter) investment and open, fair competition.

A third issue involves the amount of interoperability among networks and applications that is needed to create the capabilities envisioned for an Information Society and to reap the benefits that contribute to sustainable development. This third issue is a key issue in the sense that if this issue is not addressed, there will not likely be an NII/GII as envisioned, and thus a discussion of its contributions to sustainable development will have little meaning.[14]

Issues at the Intersection of Sustainable Development and Technology and Infrastructure

As we move toward increasingly competitive information/communications industries and strive toward the goals of an NII, many approaches to achieving these objectives have been proposed.[15] A common theme in many of the proposals involves open competition at all layers of the Open System Interconnection protocol stack and an ability for "anyone" (particularly new entrants) to operate profitably at any layer of the stack. Although the intent appears to be sound, the economics of the proposals must be carefully examined. Assume there is open competition and no regulation. Consider a set of telecommunications firms that offer competitive transport services at the low levels of the stack using their facilities. These firms are likely to have large sunk costs and large amounts of excess capacity on many of their fiber-optic facilities. When these firms compete, they may at first price to recover their sunk costs and realize a return on their investment. However, any incremental revenue a firm would gain by selling its excess capacity would increase its profitability. To attract customers to use the firm's excess capacity, the firm lowers it prices (this is similar to selling an otherwise empty airline seat). Competing firms do the same, and prices spiral downward toward marginal costs. The firms do not recover sunk costs and find themselves in an unstable, unprofitable situation. Firms can potentially differentiate themselves in the marketplace through service quality and other marketing parameters; however, with bandwidth becoming more of a commodity, attempts at such differentiation may reduce the number of firms in the marketplace but will likely yield a number of firms with high-quality service still in the above quandary.[16]

Solutions to this problem could include having a regulated monopoly operate at the bottom of the protocol stack or creating a regulatory framework that provides the incentives for these firms to compete, meet service standards, and price in such a way as to recover sunk costs and gain a fair return on their investment. Potential solutions also may be possible via pricing arrangements such as long-term contracts. Other solutions, less palatable to some since they appear to be less competitive, would allow competing firms to offer more vertically integrated services without having to unbundle transport services and sell them to non-facilities-based providers. Such a solution would still involve a number of competing firms but would not facilitate "anyone" becoming a telecommunications services provider unless they had the means to operate facilities. While solutions that reduce barriers to entry (such as the costs of large facilities-based networks) may be preferred, such solutions must ensure that the firms operating at the lower levels of the stack can recover their sunk costs and earn a return on their investments.[17]

Issues at the Intersection of the Information Society and
Technology and Infrastructure

The ease of access to information enabled by the NII/GII's technology and infrastructure raise key intellectual property, security,
and privacy issues. For example, electronic information technology makes it easier to reproduce and distribute information of
value without compensating the owner of the information. Similarly, the proliferation of electronic information as well as electronic business and personal transactions and communications
makes it more difficult to protect private information from unscru-
pulous eyes. With respect to intellectual property, current laws
need to be examined to determine whether they provide adequate
protection in an electronic environment; if they do not, revisions
need to be made. Interestingly, although technology may have
generated security and privacy concerns, technological solutions
to those problems are currently being addressed, and solutions that
will satisfy security and privacy needs for the preponderance of
applications are close at hand.

Another issue being debated is whether to develop one-way or
two-way network capabilities (e.g., to deliver entertainment video
to the home). Clearly, for many NII/GII applications, some degree
of upstream transmission is needed, and in some cases a high
degree. This then shifts the debate to whether symmetric or
asymmetric bandwidth is needed. An argument for symmetric
bandwidth is the NII/GII goal espoused by some that "anyone" can
be an information content provider; thus the technology infrastructure should provide for the ability to send large amounts of
data (e.g., video transmissions) from every home, small business, or
other access site. Two arguments against symmetric bandwidth are
that (a) the typical content provider's usage is asymmetric and
indeed most users are likely to be either heavy senders or heavy
retrievers of information, but not both, and (b) an individual who
desires to be a content provider can rent server space from a
provider with adequate bandwidth and need not have high bandwidth available at his or her home. Asymmetric bandwidth seems to
meet people's needs for the preponderance of NII/GII applications. Although symmetric bandwidth perhaps can be made available for purchase, it does not seem to be so essential as to be part

of the minimal set of services included in the universal service array.

A related issue is whether entertainment video will be the demand driver for NII/GII infrastructure development aimed at the mass market or whether the demand will be generated by new advanced forms of interpersonal communications, access to information, and cost reduction technologies. Over the past few years there seems to be a shift in thinking on the part of some U.S. players to a belief that the latter will more likely be the driver than the former. The technology and architecture of the NII/GII as well as the applications available to the mass market may vary widely depending on how the above issues are viewed by those players making the infrastructure investment decisions.

Issues at the Intersection of Sustainable Development and the Information Society

Some key issues in this area involve the value of information content. In the United States the federal government plans to give away government information, for example to enable people to increase their participation in the democratic process through electronic availability of pending legislation. The rationale includes the observation that the taxpayers have already paid for the generation of the content. The "giving away" may not be totally free, since there may be a charge for the incremental cost of preparing the information for electronic access. However, there are firms already in existence that add value to government information by organizing it in various ways, printing the organized material, and selling it for a profit. Will these firms' business be affected since the government is "competing" with them?

Apart from government information, information content in general offers a wide range of value that content creators or providers can sell, for which the price over time will be dependent on the customers' willingness to pay. In addition, organizing, synthesizing, critiquing, and analyzing content can add value. Should firms be permitted to take free or relatively inexpensive content owned by others, add value to it in one or more of these ways, and resell it? Clearly this touches on the intellectual property issues raised earlier. It would appear that pricing mechanisms could be worked out by which the content creators are fairly compensated and the resellers make a profit based on the market's willingness to pay for the value they add. Of course, content creators could also choose to provide additional value and compete with resellers. This issue is not unlike network service providers and resellers operating at different levels of the protocol stack.

Unless the information content issues are worked out, it will be difficult to have a sustainable mechanism for creating content, compensating the content creators, and making information available to the populace in a way that enhances the economy and society.

Approaches to Achieving Sustainability via NII/GII Applications

An NII/GII includes applications in the areas of health care (e.g., telemedicine), education (e.g., distance learning), digital libraries, intelligent transportation systems, interactive entertainment, advanced telecommuting, business applications (e.g., electronic commerce, intelligent manufacturing, resource sharing), and others. There are existing applications, experiments, and trials in each of these areas. But what characteristics distinguish future NII/GII applications from local area networks (LANs) or local computing applications? An NII/GII application eliminates distance. It facilitates the formation and functioning of virtual communities without the need for the physical presence of community members. Some of these communities may otherwise not have formed. It provides for remote access to a wide variety of information sources. Furthermore, applications can be shared in an NII/GII as opposed to being available only in niches. Thus, for example, if a pilot education project in Brussels were successful, it could be readily available in other parts of Europe as well as throughout much of the world. In addition, functionalities are shared in an NII/GII. For example, remote diagnosis in health care and distance learning in education may have many application and network functions in common (such as video telephony) that can be shared, resulting in reduced costs.

It is precisely these distinguishing characteristics of NII/GII applications that give rise to tremendous potential contributions of the Information Society to sustainable development.

One can easily envision specific implementations in each of the NII/GII application areas listed above that could contribute greatly toward sustainable development. For example, consider a business application whereby two competing firms electronically share expensive phototypesetting equipment. In the area of health care, in addition to emerging telemedicine applications and their clear potential for contributions to sustainable development, many beneficial applications already exist—for example, in the United States. the National Library of Medicine has a publicly available on-line Internet service and the National Institutes of Health have a similarly available Internet service for cancer and AIDS information. Telecommuting is being considered by many firms as a means of complying with environmental laws in several states in the United States that require reductions in automobile commuting miles by 25 percent or more over a short number of years. Many aspects of intelligent transportation systems (ITS) have been demonstrated in pilot tests in several areas in the United States, and nationwide deployment is being planned. These plans rely heavily on the NII in general and the telecommunications infrastructure in particular. Contributions of ITS toward sustainable development include increased traffic safety, reduced air pollution, improved productivity, reduced monetary and resource expenditures for highway construction, and reduced traffic congestion. (See Appendix 3 for examples of the potential impact of applications on sustainable development.)

The examples could go on and on, and the benefits of the Information Society to sustainable development are almost limitless—depending mostly on creativity and an entrepreneurial spirit. Potentially, these benefits could be severely limited by economic distortions due to an inappropriate regulatory environment, or perhaps a lack of government incentives to catalyze investments by the private sector, especially in areas in which market forces alone may not lead to investments required to meet certain societal needs.

Lines of Action

As requested by the EC, the following are specific suggestions of lines of action for the EC to pursue in concert with industry, national and regional governments, academia, and environmentalists to further explore the contributions of the Information Society to sustainable development:

1. Identify key NII/GII issues that have not yet been resolved, including those discussed above, and develop a framework to address these issues in a way that explicitly takes into account the goals of sustainable development.

2. Identify NII/GII applications aimed directly at sustainable development, e.g., environmental monitoring, and applications that can have a major impact on sustainable development, e.g., distance learning and telecommuting. For each NII/GII application: (a) identify, describe, and if possible, quantify its impacts on the social, economic, and environmental aspects of sustainable development; (b) anticipate potential "rebound effects"[18] caused by the application and describe, and if possible quantify, the impacts of each potential rebound effect identified;[19] develop ways to shape the application development (or the information infrastructure development) to reduce or eliminate potential rebound effects; develop approaches to reduce these effects in ways separate from the information society/infrastructure itself, and if possible, quantify the reduced or eliminated rebound effects; (c) describe, and quantify if possible, how the application narrows the gap between more developed and less developed countries and between information "haves" and "have nots."

3. There are many synergies among NII/GII applications and their use of a common communications infrastructure (see, for example, "Approaches to Achieving Sustainability via NII/GII Applications" above). These synergies can significantly increase the contributions to sustainable development well beyond those described for the individual applications in suggestion (2) above. Describe specific synergistic effects and, to the extent possible, quantify their increased contributions to societal, economic, and environmental aspects of sustainable development.

4. Develop a policy framework to begin the process of creating appropriate incentives (investment incentives, a regulatory structure, etc.) for evolving to an advanced NII/GII in a way that contributes significantly toward sustainable development goals.

Pursuing these research projects will generate both qualitative and quantitative evidence to form a sound base and the impetus for the EC and EU countries to accelerate the evolution toward the Information Society.

Appendix 1: Characteristics of an NII

Some characteristics of an NII include:

• Meets urgent societal needs: An NII must meet urgent societal needs and maximize benefits to the public. Areas needing particular emphasis are K-12 education, lifelong learning, libraries, health care, manufacturing productivity, the environment, and job creation.

• Market-driven applications: Additional applications should be market-driven to assure that investments made in the infrastructure will enable applications and services that meet customer needs and provide a fair return on investment.

• Maximum interoperability and interconnectivity: Networks with different characteristics must work together smoothly and seamlessly.

• Universal access: Universal access means universal availability—anyone who wants to connect to a network that is part of the NII can do so at an affordable price.

• Global interconnectivity: The infrastructure should provide a gateway for international connectivity as the Internet and phone system do today.

• User-friendliness: Universal access, including access by those who are not computer literate, will require the development of standardized, user-friendly interfaces.

• Provides a framework for continued development, growth, and improvement in an ongoing economically sustainable way: An NII must be planned, designed, and developed to generate sufficient revenue for investment in research and development in new technologies so that it can grow, improve, and prosper over time.

Note that the last characteristic listed is quite important but often ignored when characterizing an NII.

Appendix 2: Some Key Aspects of an NII/GII Policy Framework

To ensure that an NII/GII contributes toward the goals of sustainable development, the planning, development, and implementation of an NII/GII need to be guided by a policy framework that meets requirements listed earlier in this paper. Some key aspects of such a policy framework include the following (note that the first three bullet items have been broadly accepted in the United States, but not necessarily in many other countries):

• The private sector provides services.

• Government serves as a promoter and catalyst by providing leadership in telecommunications policy, keeping standards processes fair and open, collaborating in technology development, and providing incentives (e.g., appropriate tax treatment) for the private sector to invest in the NII/GII.

• Government should focus its funding support not on network providers but rather on key network user communities (e.g., K-12 education). Thus, the government should not build, own, operate or subsidize networks that offer services in competition with commercial network service providers. As used here, the term "commercial network service providers" includes telecommunications providers, many of the Internet mid-level networks, commercial resellers of network services, and others. This funding focus allows the public, for-profit companies, and not-for-profit companies to use commercial networks, while deserving user communities can receive government support for access to and use of such networks.

• There are some cases, such as for national security purposes, when it may be appropriate for the government to develop or subsidize private networks or private virtual networks. Clearly the government, or for that matter anyone, may choose between a private network solution or purchasing network services from commercial providers that use public switched or routed networks. Often that choice is based in large part on whether commercial providers offer services that meet the customer's needs in an economical way. With new data communications services and technology (e.g., SMDS, Frame Relay, SONET, ATM), increased internetworking capabilities, and increased competition in the emerging NII/GII, the results of such customer needs and economic analyses will likely lead to the customer choosing services offered by competing commercial providers.

However, in cases where the government does develop or subsidize networks, access to such networks should be limited to meeting the requirements of the government agency's mission. In addition, network services or excess capacity on such government networks (or the government-funded portion of networks such as subsidized logical networks) should not be resold in competition with commercial network service providers. Reselling network services or excess capacity on a government-funded network in competition with commercial network service providers, say, to local businesses, may at first glance have some appeal (for example in offsetting some of the often high ongoing costs of operating, maintaining, and upgrading the networks, servicing users, etc.). However, this appeal will actually significantly hamper the development of an NII/GII and work against such key NII/GII characteristics as universal access at an affordable price. The rationale for this hampering effect follows.

Resale of a subsidized good in competition with commercial providers will cause a significant disincentive for the private sector to invest in the NII/GII. Recall that making the NII/GII vision a reality will require the private sector to invest perhaps hundreds of billions of dollars. In addition, this type of resale will cause some customers to migrate to the subsidized networks, resulting in the fixed costs of commercial networks being spread over a smaller base of customers, potentially raising their prices. Hence, what might initially appear to be an appealing way to offset some costs of government networks will actually hamper the development of an NII/GII and cause the development that does occur to do so in a way that will not be economically sustainable.

• Other areas that are appropriate for government support include: (a) new network technology development and testbed networks; (b) research into user-friendly access to and use of networks as well as training (significant effort in these areas is essential for use in K-12 education, by parents and teachers, and in the mass market in general); (c) research on middleware; and (d) research into new applications and services.

• Regulatory reform is needed so all players have an equal opportunity to compete. Competition will lead to low prices.

• The decision-making process for government programs should be open. It would be especially helpful to get users and providers involved in order to ensure value to consumers and ultimately the feasibility of implementation.

• There needs to be cooperation among government, educators, industry and users—not only for NII/GII development but also to find innovative ways to support K-12 education, libraries, services for rural areas, etc.

Requirements for realizing the vision of an NII/GII include a large investment by the private sector, meeting urgent societal needs and maximizing benefits to the public, and providing an opportunity for a fair return on the total investment by selling market-driven applications and services. To achieve these requirements, all stakeholders must understand each other's views, and the proper mix of cooperation and competition must be struck. The framework presented does not address all NII/GII issues (e.g., security and privacy), but it does provide a meaningful structure for cooperation among all stakeholders to achieve the above requirements in a way that will provide for the development, growth, and improvement of an economically sustainable NII/GII.

Appendix 3: Examples of the Potential Impact of Applications on Sustainable Development

Currently, various trials and pilot projects are developing useful information on the ability of modern computing and communications technologies to support telebusiness in a range of application domains. Three examples are described below, and their short-term benefits are presented. In each case, the projects build upon current strengths to solve current problems and generate continuing benefits over a long span of time. This incremental approach, which does not require massive reengineering or reorganization, may play a vital role in the transition of the global economy from the manufacturing age to the information age. Dematerialization is a natural consequence of trends exemplified by these examples:

reductions in transport and the savings that result from elimination of redundant equipment and processes will reduce the consumption of energy and materials. Longer-term impacts are hard to predict, but issues that are relevant for the longer term are raised.

Telemedicine

The Texas Telemedicine Project linked major public and private providers of health care in Austin, Texas, with a 22-bed hospital, a renal dialysis center, a community mental health center, and a prison infirmary 65 miles away. A detailed financial analysis for the period April 1991 to April 1993 showed substantial savings from reduced travel expenses, reduced telephone expenses, elimination of redundant personnel, lower ambulance charges, and elimination of redundant diagnostic testing. Indirect (unmeasured) savings included reduced family travel and reductions in lost productivity. The direct financial savings amounted to 14 percent of conventional costs and implied a payback period of 2.6 years.

The major benefits of this project were the cost savings as well as the ability to treat prison inmates without incurring the medical and security risks inherent in transporting prisoners to and from a distant medical facility. These benefits are available today and will grow as the health care industry adopts and deploys available technology.[20]

Environmental Issues

Supercomputer Systems Engineering and Services Company (SSESCO), a small business in Minnesota, has developed a 3-D graphics visualization product, the Environmental WorkBench, which it markets to scientists and engineers working interactively with environmental data. SSESCO is working with the San Joaquin Valley Air Quality Study and the Atmospheric Utility Signatures, Predictions, and Experiments Study to examine scenarios for controlling ozone emissions in California. According to study participants, the Internet has played a key role in the project's progress and its role will expand in the future.

The major benefit demonstrated by this project is the ability of the Internet to bring together scarce talent that is geographically dispersed (team members are in Pennsylvania, Colorado, California, Minnesota, and New York) to work on a pressing social issue, air pollution. The benefits of this project will be obtained in the short run as a better understanding of ozone emissions leads to better laws controlling air pollution.[21]

Education

Students Investigating Today's Environment (SITE) is an educational project in Idaho that uses the Internet to provide students with the support they need to learn more about the environment and the sciences that can be used to study it. Students collect water from the Snake River for testing in school labs and are assisted by scientists at the Idaho National Engineering Laboratory (INEL) in designing appropriate study frameworks and analyzing the data.

The major benefit is the creation of a trained pool of protoscientists who have developed the interests and the skills needed for a career in environmental science. The use of the Internet is critical: students in remote parts of Idaho can gain access to a limited pool of talent at INEL. Greater social benefits will be obtained in the medium term as the current crop of student participants enters the work force with the skills necessary to tackle difficult environmental issues.[22]

Long-Term Issues

The ability of communications networks to overcome the barrier of distance may well increase the ability of people to live in comfort and safety in remote locations. Proximity to good schools, hospitals, libraries, and shops may not be as important in the future as it is today. While overcoming the barrier of distance may reduce the pressure on urban environments, it may create new pressures on virgin territories that are not currently settled because they are far from the conveniences of urban centers. The movement to suburbs may be replaced by a movement to more remote locales. The social and environmental impacts of this migration may need to be better understood.

Notes

1. "Maastricht Treaty, Title II: Provisions Amending the Treaty Establishing the European Economic Community with a View to Establishing the European Community," European Community, Maastricht, February 1992.

2. Gro Harlem Brundtland et al., *Report of the World Commission on Environment and Development: Our Common Future* (New York: United Nations, 1987).

3. European Commission, *Towards the Information Society: An Action Plan* (Brussels: European Commission, 1994).

4. Background material prepared by the working circle organizers at the European Commision.

5. H. Benking, G. W. Brauer, et al., "A Robust Path to Global Stability: Tough but Feasible," paper presented at the 14th World Conference of the World Futures Studies Federation, Nairobi, Kenya, July 1995.

6. Council on Competitiveness, *Vision for a 21st Century Information Infrastructure* (Washington, DC: Council on Competitiveness, 1993).

7. Computer Systems Policy Project, *Perspectives on the National Information Infrastructure: CSPP's Vision and Recommendations for Action* (Washington, DC: CSPP, 1993).

8. Information Infrastructure Task Force, *The National Information Infrastructure: Agenda for Action* (Washington, DC: Department of Commerce, 1993).

9. Computer Systems Policy Project, *Perspectives on the National Information Infrastructure: Ensuring Interoperability* (Washington, DC: CSPP, 1994).

10. Thomas R. Spacek, "How Much Interoperability Makes an NII?," paper presented at the Interoperability and the Economics of Information Infrastructure Workshop sponsored by Harvard Information Infrastructure Project, Clinton Administration's Information Infrastructure Task Force, and others, Roslyn, VA, July 1995. Also in Herbert Kubicek et al., eds., *Jahrbuch Telekommunikation und Gesellschaft* (Heidelberg: R.v. Decker, 1996), pp. 144–150.

11. Policy statement by CEOs of 14 major telecommunications U.S. firms. (Morristown, NJ: Bellcore, 1993). Thomas R. Spacek, "Building Consensus for a U.S. National Information Infrastructure: A Telecommunications Industry Perspective," in Dru Mogge et al., eds., *Association of Research Libraries Proceedings of the 123rd Meeting: The Emerging Information Infrastructure: Players, Issues, Technology, and Strategy* (Washington, DC: Association of Research Libraries, 1994), pp. 39–46; also in *Educational IRM Quarterly* Vol. 3, No. 3/4: (Spring/Summer 1994), pp. 37–40. 7 RBOCs, *An Infostructure for All Americans: Creating Economic Growth in the 21st Century* (Washington, DC: RBOCs, 1993).

12. One can view each country (or in some cases, groups of countries) in the world having a vision of its "network of networks" or NII and a timetable for evolving toward that vision. A GII then consists of a "network of NII networks" within which the NIIs of countries throughout the world interconnect and

interoperate. For this to occur, the timetables, technologies, and capabilities of each country's NII do not have to be the same; however, common protocols need to be followed.

13. Henry C. Lucas, Hugues Levecq, Robert Kraut, and Lynn Streeter, "France's Grass-Roots Data Net," *IEEE Spectrum* (November 1995).

14. I address this issue in Spacek, "How Much Interoperability Makes an NII?"

15. David Clark, "Interoperation, Open Interfaces, and Protocol Architecture," paper presented at the NII 2000 Conference sponsored by the National Academy of Sciences, Washington, DC, May 1995. Computer Science and Telecommunications Board of the National Research Council. *Realizing the Information Future— The Internet and Beyond* (Washington, DC: National Academy Press, 1994).

16. Padmanabhan Srinagesh and Jiong Gong, "Economics of Layered Networks," paper presented at the NII 2000 Conference sponsored by the National Academy of Sciences, Washington, DC, May 1995. Hal Varian, presentation at the same conference.

17. Ibid.

18. People working in the area of sustainable development contend that technological improvements, even those aimed at reducing the use of resources, often become excessively consumed and unintentionally end up causing a net increase in resource use in the same or other areas (see Benking et al., "A Robust Path to Global Stability"). This is referred to as the "rebound effect."

19. The idea of anticipating and trying to negate rebound effects up front may be novel in the field of sustainable development. It is the author's understanding that studies have been performed after the fact to quantify actual rebound effects of some technological innovations but that anticipating the effects and attempting corrective actions before the technological innovation is implemented may not have been tried previously.

20. Britton Berek and Marilyn Canna, "Telemedicine on the Move: Health Care Heads Down the Information Superhighway," *American Hospital Association Hospital Technology Feature Report* Vol. 13, No. 6 (1994), pp. 1–65.

21. Kent Steiner, "Cleaning Up California's Air Through the Internet," in Martha Stone-Martin and Laura Breeden, eds., *51 Reasons: How We Use the Internet and What it Says About the Information Superhighway* (Lexington, MA: Farnet, Inc., 1994), pp. 23–24.

22. Bob Beckwith, "Students Investigating Today's Environment," in Stone-Martin and Breeden, eds., *51 Reasons*, pp. 81–82.

Will the Global Information Infrastructure Need Transnational (or Any) Governance?

Walter S. Baer

"Just as human beings once dreamed of steam ships, railroads and superhighways, we now dream of the global information infrastructure that can lead to a global information society."—U.S. Vice President Al Gore, Brussels, February 25, 1995[1]

Introduction

There is now general recognition that telecommunications and information technologies and their applications are having important effects worldwide. As a result, much of the attention that previously was focused on development of national information infrastructure (NII) now turns toward the even broader concept of a global information infrastructure (GII).

The technologies, markets and investment patterns propelling the GII are changing much faster than are the rules and institutions that traditionally have governed these activities. How these rules and institutional arrangements evolve will strongly influence the pace of investment, trade, innovation and infrastructure development within and among nations. This chapter examines three contrasting evolutionary paths: (1) continued reliance on national regulatory regimes; (2) acceptance of negotiated arrangements principally among private sector stakeholders; and (3) strengthened GII roles for regional and international institutions.

What do we mean by the GII? Although there is still no standard definition, most visions of the GII incorporate several large communications and information components. First are the national telecommunications infrastructures: the telephone, private point-to-point, wireless, satellite, cable TV and broadcast networks. Although privately owned in the United States, in many countries these networks are owned primarily by government entities. Next are the international cable facilities: initially bundles of copper wires, then coaxial cables, and now optical fibers. They typically are owned and operated by consortia of national carriers. Then come the international satellite networks: satellites operated by the intergovernmental consortia, Intelsat and Inmarsat; the regional satellites largely (but not entirely) owned by government carriers; and the increasing number of commercial communications satellites providing international telecommunications and broadcast services.

The GII also includes computer equipment, software and services, as well as the network standards, protocols and interfaces necessary to interconnect them. In addition, one should add applications, information and entertainment content, and human capital components of the GII.[2] Summing up these components, the International Telecommunication Union (ITU) estimates that revenues of the global information industry totaled U.S.$1.35 trillion in 1993, or 5.6 percent of world gross domestic product (GDP).[3]

The GII stakeholders thus comprise a wide range of private sector suppliers of communications and information products and services, government-owned communications carriers, content providers and others who want access to networks, large and small users, and a variety of national and international governmental agencies. Reaching agreement among such stakeholders on the technical, economic, access and content issues surrounding information infrastructure has been very difficult at the national level, as preceding chapters in this volume describe in detail. Consensus becomes even more difficult to achieve when the actors and issues are transnational.

Transnational Trends Driving the GII

The forces driving the GII are inherently transnational:

• Technological advances;
• Increasing demand for services;

- Multinational suppliers and users; and
- National and transnational competition.

Technology

The prime motive force is, of course, technology. Advances in the basic technologies of communications and information processing have driven the information revolution throughout the 20th century. Figure 1 shows the exponential growth of computational power per unit cost—a phenomenon that is expected to continue for at least the next 20 to 30 years.[4]

New satellite systems under development will deploy constellations of satellites in low- or mid-earth orbits to communicate directly with handheld mobile terminals. These global mobile personal communications systems (GMPCS), such as Iridium, Globalstar and ICO Global (a commercial subsidiary of Inmarsat, an intergovernmental satellite consortium), will provide voice and data connectivity anywhere on earth. Their initial launches are planned before the end of the decade. Fiber-optic technology is also continuously improving. New international fiber cables, such as the Fiberoptic Link Around the Globe (FLAG)[5] and the Africa ONE network,[6] will greatly expand capacity and offer better quality of service both on existing heavily trafficked routes and in emerging markets.

Technology has also brought forth new network concepts, like the Internet, which is an interoperable worldwide network of networks. The Internet is now available in more than 100 countries and is expanding particularly rapidly in Asia, Central and Eastern Europe and the former Soviet Union.[7]

Increasing Demand

Beyond technology, the GII is driven by economic and political changes. Growing national economies and burgeoning international trade spur the demand both for basic information services—telephone and television—and for new services such as wireless, facsimile, electronic mail, and access to the Internet. The global market for telecommunications services was estimated at more

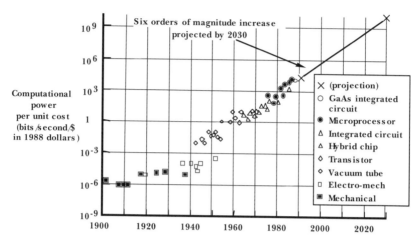

Figure 1 A Century of Computing.

than U.S. $500 billion in 1995 and is growing at double-digit rates. It will double by the year 2000. In the United States, information products and services as a share of personal consumption expenditures increased from 9.9 percent in 1980 to 12.5 percent in 1992.[8] Worldwide demand for wireless services grew by about 45 percent a year between 1989 and 1992.[9] And the number of Internet hosts worldwide has nearly doubled each year since 1990 and now totals more than ten million.[10]

Multinational Stakeholders

Leading private sector suppliers and customers of communications and information services are increasingly multinational. Most multinational firms are sophisticated political actors and can mobilize political resources at the national level in many countries to promote their own interests. On GII issues, however, it is often less clear precisely what interests should be pursued, or what alliances should be forged, in which political forums. Firms may find their interests aligned with competitors or customers in one market or region, and diametrically opposed in others.

As technologies and services proliferate, multinational corporations are also looking for single points of contact—"one-stop shopping"—for their telecommunications needs. As a consequence, major national carriers are forming international alliances to offer worldwide services to their large customers.[11] Some of these international groupings include:

- Concert: British Telecom, MCI
- Global One: France Telecom, Deutsche Telekom, Sprint
- Uniworld: AT&T, Telia (Sweden), PTT Telecom (Netherlands), Swiss PTT, Telefonica (Spain)
- World Partners: KDD (Japan), Singapore Telecom, Uniworld, Telstra (Australia), Unitel (Canada)
- Cable & Wireless: Mercury (UK), Tele2 (Sweden), Hongkong Tel, Optus (Australia), Bell Canada

Moreover, the new global mobile personal communications systems each involve international consortia including satellite manufacturers and carriers:

- Iridium: Motorola, Lockheed Martin, China Great Wall, Khrunichev (Russia), Korea Mobile Telecoms, STET (Italy), Vebacom (Germany)
- Globalstar: Loral, Qualcomm, AirTouch, Alcatel (France), France Telecom, DACOM (Korea), Deutsche Aerospace, Vodafone (UK)
- ICO Global: Inmarsat, Comsat, GM Hughes, Ericsson (Sweden), KDD (Japan), Singapore Telecom and more than 30 other Inmarsat signatories
- Odyssey: TRW, Teleglobe (Canada)
- Orbcomm: Orbital Sciences, Teleglobe (Canada), Technology Resources (Malaysia)

Assembling these consortia is essential for obtaining spectrum frequencies, aggregating demand and securing financing.

Competition

The fourth major driver of the GII is greater competition in telecommunications at both the national and international levels. Until perhaps 15 years ago, telecommunications services were considered natural monopolies that would be best provided by a single national carrier. In most countries this has been a state-owned public telecommunications operator (PTO). But in the

Country	PSTN Local	PSTN Trunk	PSTN Int'l	X.25 Data	Leased Lines	Mobile Analog	Mobile Digital
Australia	D	D	D	D	D		C
Austria							
Belgium				C			
Canada		C		C	C	RD	D
Denmark				C		D	C
Finland	C	C	C	C	C	D	D
France				C		D	D
Germany				C			C
Greece							C
Iceland							
Ireland				C			
Italy				C			D
Japan	C	C	C	C	C	RD	C
Luxembourg				C			
Netherlands				C			D
New Zealand	C	C	C	C	C	C	C
Norway				C			D
Portugal			D	C	C	C	C
Spain				C			
Sweden	C	C	C	C	C	C	C
Switzerland							
Turkey							
United Kingdom	C	C	D	C	C	D	C
United States	PC	C	C	C	C	RD	C

C   Competition Permitted   D   Duopoly   R   Regional   P   Partial

Figure 2   Telecommunications Competition in OECD Countries. Source: OECD 1994.

1980s, the United States and the United Kingdom permitted competitors to build long distance facilities and compete with the incumbent PTO. A handful of other industrialized countries— including Japan, New Zealand, Australia, Sweden and Finland— have followed, and the European Union has mandated that its members (with a few exceptions) must allow competition by January 1, 1998. Most countries belonging to the Organization for Economic Cooperation and Development (OECD) permit competition for cellular telephone and value-added services (see Figure 2).

Competition brings both net economic benefits and some real (primarily political) costs, which are discussed elsewhere.[12] From the GII perspective, national competition stimulates investment in the information infrastructure, reduces prices, and increases usage of telecommunications and information services. It also brings foreign carriers and other new players into these markets, either as partners with or rivals to the national PTO. Multinational alliances and transnational joint ventures among carriers are growing in importance.[13]

The growth of global markets and multinational telecommunications service suppliers challenges the existing order even in countries that are trying to retain their national PTO monopolies.

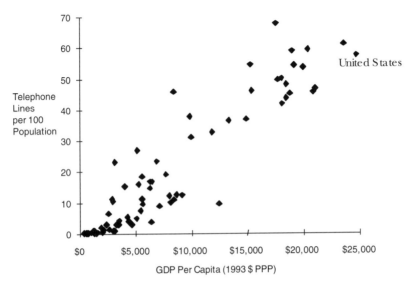

Figure 3   Telephone Lines vs. GDP. Source: ITU.

International callback services, in which callers in a high-tariff country can use a carrier in a low-tariff country to place their international calls, provide one good example. Despite efforts by many national governments to make these services illegal and shut down the companies offering them, the callback business keeps expanding.[14] National governments find it very difficult to enforce their regulations on commercial firms operating outside their borders or in cyberspace.

A Basic Conflict: Transnational GII Forces vs. National Regulatory Regimes

This discussion points out some basic conflicts in GII development between international and national imperatives. On the one hand, the technologies are inherently transnational, major equipment and service providers are becoming multinational, and users want cheap, reliable global connectivity. On the other hand, the telecommunications sector is still governed by national regimes, international organizations are relatively weak, and large gaps remain between developed and developing countries. Figure 3 shows the tight correlation between national GDP and telephone availability;

even larger gaps between rich and poor countries exist for Internet access and other advanced information services.[15]

How can such conflicts be resolved, or at least dealt with constructively? In February 1995, representatives of the seven wealthiest industrialized countries plus the European Union (G-7) met in Brussels and proposed the following core principles for GII development:[16]

- Promoting dynamic competition;
- Encouraging private investment;
- Defining an adaptable regulatory framework;
- Providing open access to networks;
- Ensuring universal access to services;
- Promoting equality of opportunity;
- Promoting diversity of content; and
- Encouraging participation by developing countries.

But turning these core principles into working realities raises many complex and practical issues (see Table 1); these are discussed for individual countries in the various chapters in this volume.

In many of these categories, current national policies are not consistent with the G-7 core principles for the GII. For example, despite the U.S. government's call for more open markets throughout the world, the United States still limits foreign investment in U.S. telecommunications networks to less than 50 percent, and investment in television broadcasting to less that 25 percent.[17] Other governments that retain national monopolies over international calling are trying to outlaw international callback services based in countries that permit competition. A number of countries, including Iran, Saudi Arabia and China, restrict their citizens' access to satellite television broadcasting or the Internet.[18] And issues surrounding content on television or on the Internet are highly contentious today in a great many countries.[19]

Alternative GII Governance Regimes

Looking forward as the GII evolves, there are three broad governance approaches to dealing with the core principles and the

Table 1 Major Issues Surrounding Development of the GII

Technical coordination issues

- Spectrum allocation and assignment;
- Assignment and coordination of geostationary orbital slots;
- Interoperability, security and other network standards;
- Interconnectivity arrangements and revenue sharing; and
- Coordination of research and development, prototypes, field tests.

Economic and investment issues

- Market entry and licensing;
- Foreign direct investment;
- Competition policies;
- Intellectual property rights;
- Dispute resolution; and
- Development assistance.

Access, service and content issues

- Access to networks by content and service providers;
- Affordable access by users;
- Privacy, security, encryption policies;
- Government content controls; and
- Obscenity, indecency, libel, slander, defamation.

specific issues listed in Table 1: (1) continue to rely principally on national regulation; (2) accept negotiated arrangements among nongovernmental stakeholders; and (3) strengthen international institutions. We consider them in turn as alternative "regimes"; that is, a "set of principles, norms, rules and decisionmaking systems for governing international relations."[20]

Rely on National Regulation

This is the "business as usual" scenario, which extends national regulation and governance to cover the GII and involves the least political change from the status quo. In most countries, national regulatory regimes evolved as part of the system of national monopoly PTOs and have worked reasonably well within that framework for governing international communications and information flows. That framework includes bilateral arrangements among carriers for interconnecting international traffic and sharing revenue. Although the spread of information technology has clearly weakened national powers to control international commerce, it does not mean the end of national sovereignty or of national regulation of telecommunications and information services.[21] Indeed, strong coalitions of PTOs, regulators, standards bodies and various national interest groups exist to champion continued national authority over GII investments and operations.

However, national governance regimes often are poorly matched to the transnational technologies, multinational stakeholders and global markets that increasingly characterize the GII. This seems especially true for the licensing and related competition issues identified in Table 1. For example, several global mobile personal communications systems have been approved for launch by regulatory authorities in the United States and the United Kingdom. These systems must presumably obtain operating licenses in other countries to provide services to customers, but negotiating individual country licenses will likely prove difficult in some cases, particularly if the incumbent PTO is not a part of the GMPCS consortium. At the same time, it may be difficult for a national authority to block service to individuals in that country who have legitimately purchased a GMPCS receiver someplace else. GMPCS takes the international callback concept one step further and illustrates the problems national regimes will have in regulating inherently transnational systems.

Extend "Nongovernmental Governance"

Governmental organizations find it increasingly difficult to keep up with technical and market changes in the information and communications sectors. Multinational suppliers and users also are finding ways to bypass PTO monopolies and restrictive national regulations, as illustrated by the growth of private VSAT networks, international callback services and the Internet. As a consequence, the nongovernmental stakeholders—both for-profit firms and independent nongovernmental organizations (NGOs)—are developing their own de facto standards, procedures and business arrangements for transnational information and communications flows.[22] These include new alliances and consortia among firms, national associations and industry groups that previously operated separately and often competitively.[23]

Perhaps the best current example of "nongovernmental governance" is the Internet Engineering Task Force (IETF), which develops and implements de facto technical standards for the Internet.[24] Like the Internet itself, the IETF has no official governmental charter or formal membership requirements. Rather, it comprises a series of working groups formed to deal with specific technical problems and to come up with implementable solutions to them. Membership in the IETF working groups is open to any interested individual; there explicitly are no institutional memberships. Each working group conducts its business over the Internet and in open face-to-face meetings. Technical solutions emerge from consensus among the working group members rather than through voting or other formal procedures, and are implemented wholly on a voluntary basis.

The keys to the success of the IETF are its open processes, its dedication to incremental and implementable results, and the legitimacy it has developed among the key actors. While it is not obvious how broadly the IETF model might be used to deal with other GII technical and nontechnical issues, it does serve as an impressively successful contrast to slow-moving, formally chartered international standards bodies. For technical coordination and the development of protocols in fast-moving areas such as electronic commerce, negotiations among nongovernmental stakeholders seem more likely to lead to early workable results than formal intergovernmental agreements.

More generally, nongovernmental governance may be the default scenario for the GII. Informal agreements among multinational stakeholders will stimulate global infrastructure investment and make new services available quickly, at least to customers who can pay for them. At the same time, it may exacerbate the gap between rich and poor nations (and individuals) in their access to GII facilities and services.

Strengthen International Organizations

Given the difficulties national regimes face in dealing with the GII, it is natural to look for possible multinational approaches to achieving the goals stated in the G-7 core principles or resolving specific GII issues. Regional organizations represent one approach.

The European Union is seeking to develop common policies and actions for its member-states on such diverse information infrastructure issues as telecommunications network interconnectivity, television broadcast content quotas and satellite GMPCS licensing. Although the division of roles and powers between the European Union and its member states is still a contentious policy issue,[25] Europe seems clearly moving toward the concept of a strong regional, European Information Infrastructure.[26] In contrast, countries in the Asian Pacific region are considering purely voluntary coordination of some infrastructure-related trade practices, such as common electronic customs documents, through the Asia-Pacific Economic Cooperation (APEC) and other regional organizations.[27]

Strong models of international governance in telecommunications are provided by the international satellite treaty organizations, Intelsat and Inmarsat. The Intelsat Interim Agreement of 1964 essentially gave Intelsat monopoly powers over international commercial satellite communications.[28] The Agreement required potential competitors to "coordinate" with Intelsat by fully disclosing their plans and providing assurance that Intelsat would suffer no economic harm from their entry. While these provisions may have made sense 30 years ago in an era of PTO natural monopolies, they do not in today's more competitive environment.[29] Intelsat is in the process of restructuring to try to meet the growing threats from competing satellite and fiber-optic systems; whereas Inmarsat, a second international satellite treaty organization, has recently set up a new for-profit subsidiary, ICO Global, to operate a global mobile personal communications system in competition with other multinational consortia. Both organizations are undergoing major structural changes, and consequently neither Intelsat nor Inmarsat provides a good institutional model for dealing with GII issues.

A number of other existing international organizations have stakes or interests in the GII issue areas outlined in the previous section. They are shown in Table 2 and discussed below.

Technical coordination

The International Telecommunication Union, which is a specialized agency of the United Nations, and the International Organization for Standardization (ISO), a nongovernmental federation

Table 2 International Organizations with GII-Related Charters

GII Issue Area	International Organizations
Technical coordination	
Spectrum allocation	ITU
Geostationary orbital slots	ITU
Technical standards	ITU, ISO
Interconnectivity arrangements	ITU
R&D, prototypes, field tests	ITU
Economics and investment	
Market entry and licensing	OECD, G-7
Foreign direct investment	OECD, G-7
Competition policies	OECD, G-7
Intellectual property rights	WIPO, WTO
Dispute resolution	WTO
Development assistance	WB, ITU
Access, service and content	
Access to networks by service providers	
Affordable access by users	
Privacy, security, encryption	ITU
Government content controls	
Other content issues	

Organizational key: ITU, International Telecommunication Union; ISO, International Organization for Standardization; WIPO, World Intellectual Property Organization; WTO, World Trade Organization; OECD, Organization for Economic Cooperation and Development; G-7, Canada, the European Union, France, Germany, Japan, Italy, United States and United Kingdom; WB, The World Bank

of national standards bodies, have traditionally served as the officially sanctioned developers and coordinators of international standards for telecommunications and information technologies. However, despite recent reform efforts,[30] the bureaucratic structures and formal processes of these agencies hamper their ability to keep up with rapidly changing technologies and markets.[31] As described in the previous section, private firms and nongovernmental entities increasingly are making their own arrangements for technical coordination.

As a consequence, one should have relatively modest expectations for the future roles these international organizations will play in the development of GII technical specifications, standards and protocols. Their primary function may best be to provide forums for discussions and negotiations among national government, NGO and private sector stakeholders as they address these issues. This is the stated purpose of the World Telecommunication Policy Forum established by the ITU at its plenipotentiary conference in October 1994.[32]

In addition, the ITU can continue its useful roles of publishing international technical standards and protocols, coordinating international spectrum allocations and registering geostationary satellite orbit slots. Making this information widely available and easily accessible via the Internet is important to speeding up the ITU's internal processes, as well as to expanding participation in the GII by governments, businesses and NGOs.[33] The ITU could also establish an international clearinghouse for information about GII-related R&D programs, pilot projects and proven applications.

Over time, a streamlined, energetic ITU could provide an institutional framework for improving the satellite orbital slot and frequency assignment processes,[34] coordinating international numbering plans, or coordinating national licensing of GMPCS satellite systems. These involve more economic and political questions than technical ones, however, so that a broad consensus for action must be achieved before the ITU can function effectively as a coordinating or implementing organization.

Economic and investment issues
The G-7 countries have taken the lead in exploring the GII concept and identifying problems that must be addressed.[35] Promoting competition and encouraging private investment are the first two of the G-7 core principles listed. Similarly, the Organization for Economic Cooperation and Development, composed of representatives of the industrialized countries, has called for increased infrastructure competition as a way to promote faster economic growth.[36] Neither the G-7 nor the OECD has any formal powers or governance authority; however, they can make recommendations that subsequently are incorporated in more binding international agreements.[37]

The World Trade Organization (WTO) was established on January 1, 1995, as the successor to the General Agreement on Tariffs and Trade (GATT). It provides the principal legal and institutional foundation for the international trading system, including the General Agreement on Trade in Services (GATS); and, as such, it is expected to play an important role in resolving disputes among nations over GII investment and competition issues. The WTO also oversees the Agreement on Trade-Related Aspects of Intellectual Property Rights (TRIPS), which is based in part on the preexisting conventions of the World Intellectual Property Organization (WIPO), a UN specialized agency. However, the WTO has neither the charter nor the expertise to exercise broader regulatory authority over the GII. The ITU, in fact, could be a useful source of technical advice and expertise to the WTO on GII-related matters.[38]

The World Bank and other multinational lending agencies are heavily involved both in financing information infrastructure projects in developing countries,[39] and in helping these countries develop their own regulatory capabilities. The ITU, through its Telecommunication Development Bureau, provides technical assistance to developing countries, and it is currently seeking through a newly authorized WorldTel organization to offer financial assistance in building information infrastructure.[40] Information infrastructure investments are attractive to a growing number of private investment funds,[41] but countries must establish effective national institutions for governing the telecommunications and information sectors in order to attract new investment, extend services and participate more fully in the GII.

Expanding access to the GII
International organizations today play minor roles in the GII access, service and content issues listed in Tables 1 and 2. These are generally dealt with at the subnational, national or (for Europe) regional levels.

One way that international organizations can support broadened participation in the GII is to help institutions and individuals in all countries connect to the global Internet. While conceived by and initially developed for technically sophisticated elites, the Internet now has much wider usage and appeal. The cost of Internet access has dropped dramatically (although high tariffs for Internet connections remain a problem in many countries), and its principal applications—electronic mail and the World Wide Web—are relatively easy to use. Moreover, connecting to the Internet requires very little, if any, central planning by national governments or PTOs. Through the Internet, government agencies, universities, NGOs and businesses in developing countries can connect to each other and to the larger international community. Individual access is less feasible in countries that lack basic telephone infrastructure, but some public access can be provided through government agencies, schools and private entrepreneurs.

Many specialists in international organizations recognize the opportunity to build stronger international communities through the Internet, and a few small programs, such as the World Bank's *Info*Dev, are under development. Still, the traditional approach of most international organizations is to work from the top down through established government or PTO organizations, many of which fear the economic, political and social reverberations from more open communication and access to content on the Internet. Yet the greatest opportunities lie in small-scale, bottom-up support to schools, universities, NGOs and entrepreneurial businesses that want Internet access. The Internet is today the principal manifestation of the GII and seems destined to expand in both scale and influence. The international community, through the G-7, OECD, World Bank, ITU and other UN agencies, could be a stronger source of technical and financial assistance to connect government, nonprofit and business organizations to the Internet and thus enable them to participate directly in the GII.

Summary and Conclusions

Governance of the GII seems one element of a larger shift of authority from the political to the economic realm.[42] Today, the private sector clearly drives GII development, as technological advances spur the growth of global markets for telecommunications and information services. The major suppliers and users of GII services are multinational organizations that seek rapid liberalization of restrictive national policies. National and international governance structures are not keeping pace with the technological and market changes that are occurring. As a consequence, GII governance in the near term seems likely to be characterized by negotiated arrangements among private sector, NGO and national government stakeholders.

This does not mean that national regulations will soon be subordinated to such nongovernmental agreements. The three alternative regimes presented in this chapter are not, of course, mutually exclusive. They will evolve simultaneously, intertwined and strongly interacting. The key stakeholders, whether they be corporations, business associations, government agencies, consumer/user groups or other NGOs, will pursue a mix of national, bilateral, multilateral and privately negotiated strategies. How these strategies will play out over the next several years is not yet clear. What is clear, however, is that the national government strategies and policies for information infrastructure described in this volume must increasingly take into account transnational arrangements among diverse, nongovernmental actors.

There is now no consensus for international regulation or governance of GII activities, nor is there likely to be one in the near future.[43] History suggests that to be effective in any aspect of governance, international organizations must have: (1) clear objectives and authority; (2) the support of major stakeholders; (3) timely decision-making processes; (4) an expert and results-oriented staff; (5) real enforcement powers; and (6) adequate financial resources. The international organizations involved in the GII today fall short along one or more of these dimensions. Nevertheless, international organizations can play constructive roles in technical coordination, recommending sound economic and investment policies, resolving GII-related trade disputes among countries, and providing technical and financial assistance for infrastructure development and Internet/GII access. Moreover, it seems important to begin discussion and debate now on the potential roles of international organizations in coordinating or even overseeing some GII functions as the global information infrastructure expands.

Notes

1. Remarks by U.S. Vice President Al Gore, G-7 Ministerial Conference, Brussels, Belgium, February 25, 1995.

2. This conforms with the U. S. government's description of the GII in Al Gore and Ron Brown, *Global Information Infrastructure: Agenda for Cooperation* (Washington, DC: U.S. Government Printing Office, February 1995). See also the U.S. Government description on the World Wide Web, at <http://nii.nist.gov/whatgii.html>.

3. International Telecommunication Union, *World Telecommunication Development Report, 1995*, Figure 1.4, available on the World Wide Web at <http://www.itu.ch/WTDR95/>.

4. Current RAND estimates; also see Hans Moravec, *Mind Children: The Future of Robot and Human Intelligence* (Cambridge, MA: Harvard University Press, 1988).

5. Thomas Welsh, Roger Smith, Haruo Azami and Raymond Chrisner, "The Flag Cable System," *IEEE Communications Magazine* (February 1996), pp. 30–35.

6. William C. Marra and Joel Schesser, "Africa ONE: The Africa Optical Network," *IEEE Communications Magazine* (February 1996), pp. 50–57.

7. Current data on the Internet are available at the Internet Society's site on the World Wide Web, at <http://www.isoc.org/isoc/>.

8. *World Telecommunication Development Report, 1995*, Figure 1.1.

9. International Telecommunication Union, *World Telecommunication Development Report, 1994* (Geneva, Switzerland: ITU, 1994), p. 35.

10. Data from the Internet Society, available on the World Wide Web at <http://www.isoc.org/ftp/isoc/charts/90s-host.txt>

11. Douglas Galbi and Chris Keating, *Global Communications Alliances: Forms and Characteristics of Emerging Organizations* (Washington, DC: Federal Communications Commission, 1996).

12. Walter S. Baer, "Telecommunications Infrastructure Competition: The Cost of Delay," *Telecommunications Policy* (May/June 1995), pp. 351–363.

13. Galbi and Keating, *Global Communications Alliances*. However, some observers worry that these alliances may lead not to greater competition but to regional cartelization or monopoly. See, for example, Yoshiko Kurasaki, "Globalization or Regionalization? An Observation of Current PTO Activities," *Telecommunications Policy* (December 1993), pp. 699–706.

14. Michael J. Scheele, "You Can't Beat the Price," *Telephony*, March 20, 1995, pp. 65–72.

15. *World Telecommunication Development Report, 1994* and *1995*.

16. "Full Text of Chair's Conclusions," G-7 Ministerial Conference, Brussels, February 27, 1995.

17. Liberalizing U.S. restrictions on foreign direct investment was brought up in the congressional debates over the Telecommunications Act of 1996, but no consensus in favor of liberalization was achieved.

18. B. Gabbard and G. S. Park, "The Middle East Meets the Internet" (Santa Monica, CA: RAND, 1996).

19. See, for example, Leslie Helm, "Asia Wary of Being Wired," *Los Angeles Times*, February 3, 1996, 1ff. For current commentary on this fast-moving topic, see the weekly column on the World Wide Web by Madanmohan Rao, "International Internet Newsclips," at <http://www.iworld.com/netday/NATW.html>.

20. Peter F. Cowhey and Jonathan D. Aronson, *Managing the World Economy* (New York: Council on Foreign Relations Press, 1993), p. 13.

21. For a discussion of the impact of technology on national sovereignty, see Eugene Skolnikoff, *The Elusive Transformation* (Princeton, NJ: Princeton University Press, 1993), pp. 224–226.

22. For example, the specifications for the first Local Area Network—Ethernet—were developed in the late 1970s by Xerox, Intel and DEC and became de facto world standards. Specifications for frame relay transmission were developed around 1990 by Cisco Systems, DEC, NTI and Stratacom, bypassing the formal national and international standards bodies. See "The New Public Network," *Data Communications* (November 1994), pp. 60–66.

23. See, for example, the joint position paper by the European Association of Business Machines and Information Technology Industry (EUROBIT), the U.S. Information Technology Council (ITI), and the Japan Electronic Industry Development Association (JEIDA), "Global Information Infrastructure (GII): Industry Recommendations to the G-7 Meeting in Brussels," Brussels, January 27, 1995. Another example is the Global Information Infrastructure Commission (GIIC), formed in 1995 "to promote private sector leadership and transnational cooperation on information infrastructure development." The GIIC includes top executives from telecommunications and information companies in North America, Europe and Japan.

24. David Crocker, "Making Standards the IETF Way," Association for Computing Machinery, *StandardView*, Vol. 1, No. 1 (1993); Anthony M. Rutkowski, "Today's Cooperative Competitive Standards Environment For Open Information and Telecommunication Networks and the Internet Standards-Making Model," paper presented at the Standards Development and Information Infrastructure Workshop, Harvard University, June 1994.

25. See the companion chapter in this volume, Milda K. Hedblom and William B. Garrison, Jr., "European Information Infrastructure Policymaking in the Context of European Union and Member States Policy Capacity: Progress and Obstacles."

26. The drive toward a common European approach to information infrastructure was spurred by publication of the Bangemann Report, *Europe and the Global Information Society: Recommendations to the European Council*, Brussels, June 1994.

27. Julia Lowell, "APEC: A New Model for International Economic Cooperation?" Thirteenth International Law Symposium, Whittier Law School, Whittier, CA, March 18, 1996.

28. *Agreement Establishing Interim Arrangements for a Global Commercial Satellite System (Interim Agreement)*, signed August 20, 1964, 15 UST 1705, TIAS No 5846.

29. Leland L. Johnson, *The Future of Intelsat in a Competitive Environment* (Santa Monica, CA: RAND, N-2848-DOS/RC, 1988); Henry Ergas and Walter S. Baer, *Future Structural Options for Intelsat: An Issues Paper* (Santa Monica, CA: RAND, MR-668-CIRA, 1995).

30. Audrey L. Allison, "Meeting the Challenges of Change: The Reform of the International Telecommunication Union," *Federal Communications Law Journal*, Vol. 45, No. 491 (1993); Donald J. MacLean, "A New Departure for the ITU," *Telecommunications Policy* (April 1995), pp. 177–190.

31. Anthony M. Rutkowski, "Multilateral Cooperation in Telecommunications" in William I. Drake, ed., *The New Information Infrastructure* (New York: The Twentieth Century Fund Press, 1995), pp. 223–250.

32. Tim Kelly, "ITU: Global Regulator or Policy Forum?" *Intermedia* (August/ September 1994), p. 39. The first meeting of the World Telecommunication Policy Forum, scheduled for October 1996, will focus on "Global Mobile Personal Communications by Satellite." See International Telecommunication Union, *Resolution 1083*, Geneva, ITU Document c95/115-E, 1995.

33. See, for example, "Delay in ITU Process Concerns FCC Official," *Telecommunications Reports*, March 18, 1996, p. 32. An earlier and, fortunately less currently applicable, account of the ITU's reluctance to embrace the Internet for dissemination of technical documentation is found in Carl Malamud, *Exploring the Internet: A Technical Travelogue* (Englewood Cliffs: NJ, PTR Prentice Hall, 1993).

34. The current first-come first-served process has permitted the tiny Kingdom of Tonga to register orbital slots which it then leases to commercial satellite operators; furthermore, it has no provisions for resolving disputes. Proposals for reforming the process include nonrefundable filing fees; "use-or-lose" provisions; auctions; and binding arbitration procedures. See Robert M. Frieden, "Satellites in the Global Information Infrastructure: Opportunities and Handicaps," *Telecommunications* (February 1996), pp. 29–33.

35. Ministerial and summit conferences on the GII and Global Information Society have been held in Naples (July 1994), Brussels (February 1995), Halifax (June 1995) and Johannesburg (May 1996).

36. Committee on Information, Computer and Communications Policy, "The Benefits of Telecommunication Infrastructure Competition," Paris, Organization for Economic Cooperation and Development, September 1994.

37. Kalypso Nicolaidis, "International Trade In Information-Based Services: The Uruguay Round and Beyond," in Drake, ed., *The New Information Infrastructure*, footnote 35, p. 415.

38. This suggestion is also made by Bruno Lanvin, "Why the Global Village Cannot Afford Information Slums," in Drake, ed., *The New Information Infrastructure*, p. 213.

39. The World Bank has established a new program for developing countries, *Info*Dev, to promote and facilitate "widespread access to information services, and . . . exploit information technologies for poverty alleviation and sustainable

development. . . ." See "Operational Guidelines," Information for Development Program, Washington, DC, The World Bank, October 20, 1995.

40. See the feasibility study for WorldTel by McKinsey & Company, "Closing the Global Communications Gap," Geneva, International Telecommunication Union, 1995.

41. Andrea Anayiotos, "Infrastructure Investment Funds," in *Private Sector* (Washington, DC: The World Bank, December 1994), pp. 29–32.

42. James N. Rosenau, "Governance in the Twenty-First Century," *Global Governance*, Vol. 1, No. 1 (1995), pp. 13–44.

43. See, for example, Monroe E. Price, "The Market for Loyalties: Electronic Media and the Global Competition for Allegiances," *The Yale Law Journal* (December 1994), pp. 667–705.

"We are still at an early, frontierlike stage in the overarching competition among global voices, and as a consequence, the underlying consensus—the market-shaping impulse that is at the root of media law—does not exist. Familiar instruments of change—banks, giant telephone companies, international trade organizations—are beginning to find their way. Being more plastic, they mediate transborder markets ..., responding to economic and political forces, providing technical and financial assistance, assuring step-by-step change. Since sovereignty is a difficult thing to cede, candidates for greater international power, such as the ITU, face the obstacle of reluctant sponsors. At some point, in the not-too-distant future, participants in the global market for loyalties will require a stronger regulatory presence, a global hand, invisible or not. But that time is not yet here." (p. 702)

Regional Development and the Information Society: The IRISI Initiative as a Pilot Project of the European Union

Wolfgang Kleinwächter

The Inter-Regional Information Society Initiative (IRISI), launched by the European Commission in November 1994, brings an interesting new element to the worldwide development toward a global information society. IRISI began as a pilot project in six European regions that are confronted by a particularly deep economic structural crisis: Northwest England (United Kingdom), Valencia (Spain), Nord pas de Calais (France), Piedmontee (Italy), central Macedonia (Greece), and Saxony (Germany). These regions have joined together within the framework of IRISI to pool their energies and to exchange practical experience with the aims of (a) minimizing the expenditures of public and private money on costly individual pilot projects and (b) maximizing the benefits of local and regional innovations by reducing development costs, increasing markets, and managing the social and cultural consequences of the transformation from an industrial society to an information society.

IRISI is a public framework that does not provide funds but offers contacts, information exchange, and networking opportunities to public and private partners with similar interests. Although it was initiated by the European Commission and the regional governments, IRISI takes a bottom-up approach by attempting to stimulate local and regional public and private players to look forward and to seek new creative partnerships in a broader European context. IRISI was established by the six founding regions to serve as a "learning experience". Within 15 months of its launching,

IRISI had become a functioning network increasingly attractive to other European regions. In April 1996 the regions of western Finland and the Styria region of Austria joined the network, and other regions are expected to follow.

At a time when goverments around the world have to both reduce spending and meet the challenges of the information age, IRISI could produce interesting innovations that could be applicable beyond the European Union (EU). Its non hierarchical approach and decentralized organization reflect the general tendencies of the information revolution as well as the global shifts in power from the traditional national level both upward and downward. While on the one hand political strategies and economic operations are becoming more global, on the other hand many of the elements that are crucial for the establishment of an information society are determined regionally or locally.

The Regional Dimension of the Information Society

The regional dimension of the information society is evident in many key areas. The global information infrastructure, the material backbone of the information society, comprises a network of mainly regional and local nets: local area networks (LANs), metropolitan area networks (MANs) and wide area networks (WANs). Without the local "last mile" the global information superhighway will not reach the customer. Although more and more students utilize global knowledge and information resources and travel around the world, education and training, the prerequisites for meeting the challenges of the information age, are organized and regulated mainly regionally. This is true at both the primary and secondary level as well as at the level of the higher education. Health care and transport, obviously two of the main fields for telematics application, are the responsibilities of local or regional public administrations. Meanwhile, local and regional public administrations themselves are becoming increasingly "informatized" and serve as the primary users (and often also providers) of new services. Small and medium enterprises that are locally or regionally based are becoming more competitive because their flexibility allows them to use the global networks to compete with transnational corporations on world markets by building virtual factories and using the electronic marketplace.

In the news media sector, while there is CNN International on one side, local and regional print and electronic media are of growing importance on the other. People want to know what is going on in the world, but what is happening next door and across the street is much more important to their daily lives. The same trends can be seen in the fields of entertainment and culture. Today television series, films, music, and the arts easily cross the frontiers of time, space, and language. *Baywatch, Schindler's List,* and the Beatles revival are found everywhere from Rio de Janeiro to Warsaw to Sydney. At the same time, the local cultural scene, including traditional folk culture, local entertainers, and regional popular art, is as important as Woody Allen or Madonna to the local inhabitants. Despite global Coca-Colonization people will not give up their national cultural sovereignty. After enjoying a hamburger at McDonald's they will listen to a local band playing traditional folk music. Taken together, global and local culture constitute the intellectual enviroment of individuals.

Communications no longer recognizes frontiers either political, economics, or legal. But there exist communication "areas," constituted by history, tradition, culture, language, personal contacts, and daily life experiences. An example from Germany: Bavaria is quite a different region from Northrhine Westphalia, as is Saxony. They have different histories, different habits, and even different dialects. All belong to the German nation-state, but there is more communication flow within these regions than between them. And regardless of overseas vacations and access to global computer networks, people identify themselves primarily with their local and regional environment, for example, as "Bavarians" or "Saxonians."

Regions can be considered a kind of laboratory in which many facets of the transformation to an information society can be integrated, tested, and monitored. This transformation will also be a step toward a new civil society in which the individual citizen is the key actor. Teledemocracy makes sense first of all on the local level. The citizen of the twenty-first century, who will travel easily through cyberspace, clicking from continent to continent, will spend 85 per cent of her or his lifetime within a physical radius of about 150 miles from where she or he is living, working, learning, loving, shopping, and relaxing.

Economically the transition from the industrial society to the information society is accompanied by a shift from a provider-oriented economy to a user-oriented economy. In addition, users are local actors. Whether a consumer will buy or reject individualized multimedia products (global brands) or spend money on value-added services that are globally available at any time will depend to a high degree on regional public awareness. If my neigbor has it, I need it! If my friend does it, I have to do it, too!

Globalism and regionalism are not mutually exclusive. Rather, they are two sides of the same coin. The new information society will be built both from the top down and from the bottom up. Directives by senior governments officials or decisions by CEOs of transnational corporations will channel worldwide developments and create the political conditions and legal frameworks for building the global information society. But the global information society will be constructed first of all by numerous local grassroots actions that will have global implications. The provider of new global services needs local markets. The local user is looking for global brands.

The information society is growing like a tree: the branches of a tree grow higher and higher, its roots grow deeper and deeper. Both elements belong together. A tree would not be a tree if the branches were fighting with its roots and vice versa.[1]

Europe's Regional Approach to the Information Society

The EU agreed in the Maastricht Treaty to give the principle of subsidarity a central place in future policy making. Subsidarity means that the nation-state and the regions will have a decisive word in key issues of importance to themselves. This includes a certain degree of sovereignty for the regions. The aim of this principle is to guarantee diversity and pluralism within the EU in spite of "Brussels centralism." This principle also applies to policy on the development of the information society. According to Jacques Delors in the *White Paper on Growth, Competitiveness and Employment* published in Decmber 1993, "the move towards an information society is irreversible, and affects all aspects of society and interrelations between economic partners. Creation of a common information area within the Community will enable the Community fully to seize their opportunities.[2] This study was followed by the launching of a high level commission with the mandate to study the implications of the information revolution for Europe.

In May 1994 the Bangemann Commission (named after Commissioner for Telecommunications Martin Bangemann, who chaired the group) produced a report titled *Europe and the Global Information Society*, which made numerous recommendations to the European Council.[3] The Bangemann report, which mainly reflected the industrial point of view (the members came from Siemens, IBM, Alcatel, Olivetti, and other companies), was endorsed at the EU summit in Corfu and put forward to the European Commisssion. It was followed by numerous activities, including the launching of the Commission´s Action Plan, *Europe's Way to the Information Society*[4] in July 1994, the establishment of the Information Society Project Office (ISPO) in Brussels in December 1995, calls for proposals by several promotional programs in this field (Telematics Application Programme [TAP], Advanced Communication Technology Services [ACTS], and Information Technology [IT]) in 1995, and the launching of the Information Society Forum in July 1995 with support from the European Parliament. A new program called INFO 2000 was adopted by the EU at its summit in Madrid in December 1995. Another high level expert group, under the guidance of Padraig Flynn, the EU Commissioner for Employment and Social Affairs, was established to analyze the social and job implications. In January 1996 the expert group presented an interim report *Building the Information Society for Us All*, in which Flynn emphasized that a "cohesive Information Society" should be first of all about people. "We must put people in charge of the information, not let it be used to control them."[5]

The regional and local aspect of the information society played an important role in all of these activities. The EU sponsored a "telecities" initiative through which more than 60 large European cities are cooperating in the development of information society projects that are especially needed in urban areas. The call for proposals for the Telematics Application Programme in March 1995 promoted initiatives for multimedia services in rural areas and for digital towns. Futhermore, immediately after the adoption of its Action Plan, the European Commission invited regions from six EU member states to investigate the possibility of launching a regional initiative, which became known as Inter-Regional Information Society Initiative (IRISI).

The Inter-Regional Information Society Initiative (IRISI)

In accordance with the principle of subsidiarity, the European Commission wanted to stimulate bottom-up development to promote the implementation of the recommendations of the Bangemann report on the regional and interregional level. IRISI was created for this purpose.

The idea behind this initiative was very simple: if regions develop their own strategies and pilot programs, they will gain experience that will be useful for other regions. Even if there are local and regional differences, the global nature of the transformation toward the information society will confront all regions with many similar problems and barriers to implementation. An organized exchange of experiences and best practices and the stimulation of interregional cooperation to launch pilot projects could produce innovative ideas, create new partnerships, and avoid continuous reinvention of the wheel—to the benefit of the more than 200 regions represented on the Committee of the Regions of the European Parliament. Networking among the six pilot regions could also produce practical experience in how such cooperation could be organized technically (multilateral phone and video conferences, electronic file transfer, virtual working groups and seminars, etc.)

Three months after the adoption of the EU Action Plan, the six regions of northwest England, Nord pas de Calais, Saxony, central Macedonica, Piedmontee, and Valencia decided to form a common framework and to take the lead in regional development toward the information society. All of these regions have been facing severe problems associated with the reconstruction of declining industries, unemployment, and the need to develop new skills as well as the economic and social problems of integrating rural areas into core economic activities. They all see the economic and social transition to the information society as a challenge that provides the opportunity to catch up in terms of economic competitiveness, core economic activities, employment, and quality of life. Furthermore, the deep crisis of traditional industries in these regions offers the opportunity to leapfrog directly into the technologies of the twenty-first century.

On November 28, 1994, before the European Summit held in Essen, the six regions signed a memorandum of understanding in Brussels.[6] The objective of IRISI as defined in Article 2 of the memorandum is "to promote universal acces to the opportunities and advantages of the information society with a view to generating new employment opportunities, improving quality of life, and addressing the challenge of structural adjustment and sustainable development." The six regions agreed to cooperate with one another by systematically sharing experience and information and by jointly implementing new applications and services.

IRISI's specific aims include the following:

• acting as a catalyst for the development of the information society through support for the introduction of advanced telematics applications and services throughout the region, utilizing advanced telecommunications and information networks;

• establishing a partnership among the public sector, the private sector and social organizations and between the urban and rural areas of the regions to identify demands for new applications and services and to assess their economic feasibility in relation to user needs and market demand;

• promoting a wider awareness of the potential uses of new applications and services and to ensure that their use reflects a balance between economic competitiveness and social needs, contributing both to employment growth and to improving the quality of life and the environment; and

• providing a platform for the exchange of information and experiences, both within the region and with other regions of Europe participating in this initiative and involved in developing the information society.

Priority fields for regional actions and for interregional cooperation include, among others, telecommuting, distance learning, university and research center networks, telematics services for small and medium-sized enterprises and municipal information highways.

The IRISI Structure

IRISI is not a traditional hierarchical institution but is instead organized as a decentralized network. At the regional level, a regional information society steering group (RISSG) with high-level representation from all the key organizations in the region oversees and coordinates development in each of the six regions. A Regional Information Society Unit (RISU) assists the Steering Group in fulfilling its task. In addition, regional working groups have been established for the varions fields of applications. The main tasks of the regional bodies include: the creation of public awareness, the development of regional strategies, the initiation of pilot projects, networking within and among regions, demonstration and dissemination of information, documentation of experiences and achievements, and the promotion of transnational and inter-regional cooperation.

At the inter-regional level is an IRISI Management Committee, in which each region is represented by one member and which coordinates regional activities. The Management Committee reviews the strategies and action plans of the regions, evaluates recommendations for further actions, organizes IRISI events such as interregional workshops and conferences, and has established 12 inter-regional working groups addressing nearly all topics relevant to the information society. An IRISI Network Bureau based in Brussels assists the Management Committee and works with the European Commission and its various directorates general and programs. The IRISI Management Committee is chaired by a president who is elected, on a rotating basis, for a six-month period. Technical assistance for both the regional and inter-regional institutions has been provided for a pilot phase of 18 months by the European Commission, in particular by DG XIII (responsible for telecommunications) and DG XVI (responsible for regional development).

Fifteen months after its launching, the IRISI network was operational. In all six regions the steering groups and units had been established and regional strategy and action programs had been developed and presented to the public for discussion. The IRISI Management Committee, established in January 1995, holds regular telephone conferences with periodic meetings in Brussels. The IRISI Network Bureau, after an open call for tenders, started operations in May 1995. The first IRISI workshop concerning regional strategy development was held in Leipzig (Saxony) in May 1995, followed by an IRISI seminar on inter-regional cooperation in Lille (Nord pas de Calais) in June 1995. The First Annual IRISI Conference on Strategies to Build the Information Society in the Regions took place in Torino (Piedmontee) in October 1995 with the participation of about 300 experts from the six pilot regions and other regions of EU member states.[7] During the Directoria Conference of the European Commission held in Brussels in December 1995, the six regions presented their initial experiences to a gathering of representatives of more than 100 regions from all over Europe. In February 1996 an IRISI Information Day was organized in Brussels for members of the European Parliament and representatives of the European Commission. Regional IRISI conferences with participation from the other regions took place in Thessaloniki in November 1995 and in Manchester in March 1996. In April 1996 an IRISI Secretary General was nominated to manage the day-to-day activities of the growing network.

The IRISI home page on the World Wide Web, managed by the Piedmonte region, includes details about the inter-regional and regional IRISI institutions and provides their mailing addresses, phone and fax numbers, and electronic mail addresses. Each region has its own home page in both English and the national language that presents its strategies and action plans, projects, and other regional information. The presentation of projects is, where appropriate, combined with invitations for cooperation. If someone in one region is looking for a partner for a pilot project, she or he can easily obtain an overview of similar projects in the other regions. With one click, she or he can initiate communication with potential partners on their experiences, best practices, and possible joint actions. The IRISI home page also provides an overview of European Commission programs and is linked to each other with e-mail connections. Electronic file transfer and telephone and video conferences are speeding up communication among the varions committees, working groups, and project partners.

Regional Strategies and Action Plans

In the memorandum of understanding, the six regions agreed to develop an outline strategy and an action program within the pilot phase. The outline strategy was to include an analysis of the baseline situation, with an evelution of strengths, weaknesses, opportunities, and threats from both a regional point of view and a long-term perspective. The action plan was to include concrete pilot projects.

During the Torino conference, the six IRISI regions presented their regional strategies and action plans.[8] The inter-regional working groups began to develop inter-regional projects for 1996 on public awareness, small and medium-sized enterprises, a virtual academy, municipal information highways, and other topics. All the projects are demand driven, user-oriented, and organized from the bottom up. IRISI does not provide funds, but it offers a useful framework, a bridge where partners can find each other, come together, and identify common interests.

When the six regions presented their strategies and action plans at the Torino conference, they discovered that despite regional differences they shared similar problems on the road to the information society.

The following key issues can be drawn from the six strategy documents:

1. The development of a local and regional information infrastructure is a precondition for the promotion of multimedia and telematics applications. Existing networks have too many bottlenecks and the tariffs are too high. Liberalization and competition among networks should be flexible and user-oriented, and bandwidth should be available on demand.

2. Public awareness is crucial to reaching a critical mass of users for new and innovative services. While large companies and academic institutions in the six regions are well aware of the potential of the information economy and are intense users of new and value-

added services, not more than seven percent of the population is on the Internet, and the majority of public administrators and small and medium-sized businesses have no real idea about the information society in general and the special value of on line service and new telematics applications in particular. For most small and medium-sized enterprises the new services create more costs than benefits. Their managers do not trust the reliability of the new systems, and they are not yet sufficiently qualified to use or produce online services. Public administrators have objections concerning security matters and data protection. They are also neither equipped nor qualified to become users of new services or, even more important, service providers for their citizens.

3. Training and education are also key issues in all six regions. Only a small number of primary and secondary schools are already online. Although college students learn how to use a computer at university, often those who have learned by playing with the computer at home and are online in their leisure time have a better knowledge of the latest achievements of the information revolution than their teachers.

4. Although multimedia and telematics applications are still in the infant stage, there are many innovative ideas and pilot projects. On the one hand, transnational corporations are involved in pilot projects in some regions (e.g., Siemens in Saxony, Olivetti in Piedmontee, IBM in Valencia, France Telekom in Nord pas de Calais); on the other hand, however, small and medium-sized enterprises represent more than 70 percent of the economy of the regions, and they very often do not have the capital resources to start a new multimedia service or introduce a new application. Although the underlying principle of the Bangemann Report that the private sector should take the lead and that taxpayers' money should not be wasted, are widely acknowledged in the six regions, pilot projects involving small and medium-sized businesses need public funding.

5. The medium- and long-term consequences of the information society, particulary concerning employment, the democratic rights of citizens, information security, and cultural sovereignty, are not at all clear. Although all six IRISI regions see in the new information economy a chance to create new jobs, there is also a fear that

the number of jobs that will be lost as a result of increasing informatization will be higher than the number of new jobs.

The six regions have found different solutions to developing a regional strategy and organizing a regional platform. In Valencia, a private OVSI Foundation has been established that involves about 30 key regional players including public institutions. In Northwest England, a number of local authorities and private businesses have joined the Northwest Partnership which is supported by the Duke of Westminister. Piedmontee has launched the Torino 2000 Program with a series of telematics applications. Saxony has established the "Saxon Information Initiative, and sixteen pilot projects including a teleport, a teleschool, a virtual technology transfer center, and an interactive video service project have been initiated and will be implemented within the next two years. In Nord pas de Calais working groups are the main orgaizational structure. The regional initiative in central Macedonia is advaced mainly by the regional government, OTE (the state-owned phone company), and the University of Thessaloniki.

Although their organizational structures differ, the six regions take very similar approaches, and they share the following conclusions:

• Liberalization and competition are needed for both telecommunications networks and services to improve the information infrastructure and to reduce tariffs for services.

• There is a need in public awareness campaigns (including workshops, conferences, publications, exhibitions, and demonstrations of best practices) not only for the experts but also for the benefits of ordinary people.

• Special lifelong training programs, in particular for small and medium entrepreneurs and public administrators, must be established.

• Schools must be linked to the Internet, and new programs for primary and secondary schools must be developed.

• Public funds should be made available to initiate pilot projects, especially for small and medium-sized enterprises.

• The public interest, from universal service to data protection, should be taken into consideration.

• The social and cultural consequences of informatization should be analyzed, in particular as far as employment is concerned.

• Synergy should be encouraged by developing intra- and interregional cooperation.

All regional action plans comprise a number of pilot projects aimed at implementing the strategic objectives. The pilot projects cover the whole range of applications mentioned in the Bangemann Report and the IRISI memorandum of understanding and include health care projects, telecottages, distance learning, municipal information highways, training, the introduction of an electronic cash card, electronic tendering, telecommuting, virtual technology transfer centers, interactive video services, and even an Internet vineyard in the wine region of Piedmonte.

The majority of the projects concern training, education, small and medium-sized enterprises, and public administration. Telecommuting projects or entertainment efforts such as video on demand are rare and are considered low priority. While the dearth of efforts in the field of entertainment is understandable (since all video on demand experiences so far from Orlando to the German Telekom pilot projects in Berlin or Stuttgart have produced negative results and Europeans already have acces to more than 50 national and international television channels and have no real need to add another 150), the limited number of telecommuting projects has raised some concerns.

At the Torino conference, the inter-regional working group on telecommuting discussed this issue and discovered that there are many different concepts of telecommuting, ranging fom outsourcing jobs from big companies to the home to constructing telecottages in rural areas to stimulating entrepreneurial ways to look for jobs on in the Internet. There are also many uncertainties concerning the social consequence of telecommuting, from the danger of a loss of personal contacts to social security. None of the IRISI regions has yet been able to demonstrate the creation of truly new jobs through increased informatization.

The six regions have entered into negotiations with DG V of the European Commission (responsble for social development) to develop a special research program to analyze the social implcations and labor market consequences of regional developments toward the information society; a contract was signed in March 1996. IRISI will enter into an interactive dialogue with the Commission's high level group of experts, the Flynn Commission and the interim results of the IRISI study will be included in the forthcoming EU Green Book on the social implications of the information society.

Perspectives

IRISI is not a new membership organization with a heriarchical structure but an open network. According to Article 10 of the memorandum of understanding, the six IRISI regions "seek the extension of the Inter-Regional Information Society Initiative to one region per member state and subsequently to all regions who wish to participate."

DG XVI, encouraged by the success of the regional approach to the information society, has issued a call for proposals under Article 10 of the European Regional Development Fund for another 20 regions to develop strategies and actions plans as well as pilot projects. More than 50 regions in Ireland, Finland, Sweden, Portugal, Austria, Denmark, the Netherlands and elsewhere have submitted proposals. Decisions will be made in fall 1996. In a March 15, 1996, letter to the IRISI president, EU Commissioner for Telecommunication Martin Bangemann encouraged IRISI to broaden its partnership and to include more regions in the network. The regions of western Finland and Styria in Austria have meanwhile been invited by the IRISI Management Committee to participate in IRISI projects.

IRISI offers a lot of benefits. It gives regions easy access to experiences: best pratices can be exchanged via the network. IRISI also stimulates innovative ideas and experiments, helps to find effective, creative and commited partners, help to reduce project development costs through cooperation and avoidance of duplication, and supports small and medium-sized enterprises in their search for new and fruitful markets.

During the regional IRISI conference in Manchester March 13–15, 1996, the Management Committee adopted the IRISI Manchester Statement, which summarizes IRISI's experiences.[9] In the statement the six regions reconfirm their long-term commitment to the information society, summarize their conclusions, invite other regions to join IRISI, and recommend that the European Commission should continue its support for this regionally oriented bottom-up approach.

The Manchester conference will be followed by a series of 12 inter-regional workshops that will make recommendations for regionaly oriented actions in the relevant fields of applications. Regional IRISI conferences will take place in Leipzig in May 1996, in Alicante in June 1996, in Thessaloniki in October 1996, in Liverpool in December 1996, and in Lille in February 1997. The conferences are linked with exhibitions and demonstations of pilot projects. They are open to representatives of other regions. An IRISI Summer School on regional telecommunication policy will be organized in September 1996 in Alicante, and the second annual IRISI Conference in scheduled for October 1996 in Thessaloniki.

IRISI is a learning experience. It is a new approach to multilateral actions. Not only that regions are legally bad defined, there is also a new and challenging subject and a new organizational structure that has to be tested out. There is no precedent for this kind of interregional cooperation. Moreover, there is no guarantee that this joint effort will produce only success stories.

After IRISI's first year, there were still a lot of open questions. While there is no disagreement that regions can learn from each other, IRISI offers concrete experience in implementing complex projects with partners from different cultural backgrounds. Early starters have a competetive advantage in the information economy, and speed is a crucial element in meeting the challenges of the Information Age. IRISI is a fast train that is moving at 155 Mbit/sec into the 21st century.

Notes

1. Alvin Toffler, *Powershift: Knowledge, Wealth and Violence at the Edge of the 21st Century* (New York: Bantam Books, 1990).

2. *White Paper on Growth, Competitiviness and Employment*, Brussels, 5 December 1993, p. 109.

3. Europe and the Global Information Society, Recommendations to the European Council, Brussels, 26 May 1994.

4. *Europe's Way to the Information Society: An Action Plan*, Brussels, 17 July 1994,

5. *Building the Information Society for Us All, First Reflections of the High Level Group of Experts*, Interim Report, Brussels, January 1996, p. III.

6. Memorandum of Understanding of the Regional Information Society Initiative, Brussels, 28 November 1994.

7. Claire Shearman, Summary Report on the IRISI Conference in Strategies to build the Information Society in the Regions, Torino, 5–7 October 1995 .

8. The following outline strategies are available from the IRISI home page <http://wevserver.tag.uk/taish/pubs/ukinfosoc/iris.htm>.

9. IRISI Manchester Statement, Manchester, March 15, 1996.

Materials from the Special Session on Information Infrastructures

OECD

Foreword

The main purpose of the Special Session on Information Infrastructures ("Towards Realisation of the Information Society") of the ICCP Committee held 3–4 April 1995 was to identify the main issues confronting governments and business in this regard, by examining the economic and social impacts of information infrastructures, the development of new applications and the markets for them, the requirements for regulatory frameworks for national and global information infrastructures and the principles governing the transition to global information infrastructures and the development of global information society. Following the G-7 Ministerial conference on the Information society of February 1995, there has been a movement towards consensus among OECD countries of these main principles. The Special Session started the process of building on these principles and movement towards their further elaboration and eventual implementation. This document regroups the rapporteur's report of the Special Session prepared by Professor Jens Arnbak and Mrs Jolien Ubacht (Delft University of Technology, The Netherlands), the Chairman's closing statement, two Secretariat papers prepared for the occasion by Dimitri Ypsilanti, Yvonne Walhof and Jeremy Beale and the Programme.

Part II: Rapporteur's Report

I. Introduction

A message voiced by the ICCP with increasing conviction during its first ten years of existence is the need for structural and policy changes and more suitable regulatory frameworks, in order to increase the economic and social benefits of new information and communication technologies (ICT). The early recognition by the ICCP of the future significance of the germinating convergence of the telecommunications, computing and broadcasting sectors has positioned it well for a closer examination of optimum conditions for the transition to a more knowledge-based international economy.

With the mounting political interest in the novel concept of Information Infrastructures (II) since 1993, a new impetus has been given to the examination of appropriate policy actions and their socio-economic consequences. A mandate was given by OECD Ministers in 1994 to consider this concept in the wider perspective of the Organisation's ongoing work on technology, productivity and employment. In keeping with the multilateral traditions of the OECD, many member states emphasised the need to consider the related issues in a global context, including non-OECD countries.

A Special Session of the ICCP was convened for this purpose at the OECD in Paris, 3–4 April 1995. It thus took place in the wake of the G-7 Ministerial Conference dedicated to the Information Society and having reached agreement on 11 international pilot projects in the area of networked multimedia services. Frequent references to this Ministerial Conference in Brussels, to the joint APEC/PECC/OECD Symposium in Vancouver on "Building the Foundation for the 21st Century" (both held in February 1995), and to the several other international meetings held on this subject in the last year, were made at the Special Session of the ICCP. The ICCP Chairman, in his Welcome Address, summarised the emerging general principles for development of global information services and the underlying infrastructures as follows:

- competition
- co-operation

- diversity
- openness
- safeguards

These five broad principles are also recurrent in the national policy plans and action programmes recently adopted or proposed for the II in many OECD countries. Clear differences in national emphasis exist, but governments nevertheless one and all declare positive views on the general possibilities and promises of ICT.

The following account of the results of the Special Session summarises the main questions and the evolution of tentative answers. This approach will allow readers not having attended the Special Session to identify the important common points at issue in the ICCP work on II. Such an agenda-setting approach is more fruitful at the initial stage of this programme, which is planned to be finalised in due time for reporting to the 1996 OECD Ministerial meeting. As a consequence of this synthetic approach chosen by the rapporteur, he accepts the sole responsibility for all omissions or factual errors in this account.

II. Source material

Many countries made their national Information Infrastructure plans or policy papers available to participants in the Special Session. Differences in emphasis are evident and can be understood from the domestic economic and social situation and, notably, the perceived national strengths. The cultural traditions and institutional arrangements in each individual country, not least in the area of broadcasting and other audio-visual services, also play a role. A very useful overview and comparison of the various national initiatives and policies for Information Infrastructures in 11 OECD countries is found in a background document for the meeting (Annex B to this paper). This review also includes the corresponding policy positions of the European Union and the G-7. It is divided into four specific parts, matching the agenda set for the Special Session. (See Annex C.)

In addition to this structured background material on national policy, the Secretariat provided a policy issues paper posing a range of questions for possible discussion at the Special Session (Annex A) and, in addition, a total of 17 Room Documents were available to participants in the Special Session. Many of these documents contained submitted material not accommodated in the four sessions. A few Room Documents were closely related to oral presentations by individual speakers; moreover, a number of other speakers made copies of their speaking notes available.

III. The Notions of (Information) Infrastructure

At the present early stage of international deliberations, the Special Session showed that a clear common notion—let alone definition—of the II has yet to emerge in OECD countries: Some countries put more emphasis on the capacity of networks, while others see new services and applications as the key area of interest. Very substantial parts of the world must still give absolute priority to the evolution and penetration of public telephony. Some countries now possess a ubiquitous narrowband infrastructure for telephony and data communications, plus various analogue broadband networks for one-way delivery of audio-visual programmes; these highly developed countries look for wider and more integrated service perspectives as their penetration of personal computers rapidly approaches 50 per cent of all homes.

The term 'infrastructure' until recently referred to fixed collective installations and logistic facilities necessary to support and supply operations of a country, or even an alliance of countries. However, the meaning of this word has widened in recent years to designate the supporting systems of any specific organisation—be it public or private, large or small. This modern trend results in less emphasis on the shared and universal use associated with the classical notion of public infrastructure. For example, computer firms now advertise their local area networks as the proper 'infrastructure' to satisfy the specific business interests of a particular organisation. But many national telecommunications acts still apply the very same word for the integral body of fixed transmission and switching facilities underlying the universal public supply of communications services in a certain geographical area. Still, there is also considerable variation between the legal definitions of the extent of public telecommunications infrastructure in different

OECD countries. The different positions and regulation of specialised domestic networks for delivery of audio-visual services, such as broadcast transmitters and cable television networks, illustrated this point most clearly—a matter of potential importance for delivery of multimedia services in the future Information Society.

Appropriate regulations for the dynamic ICT markets may thus seem to require more precise, but at the same time flexible notions of (public) information infrastructure. This view was stated in several presentations and interventions at the Special Session. The need for a clearer description is most strongly felt in two areas: (i) where new demarcation lines are to be traced between retreating monopolistic supply and more competitive market arrangements, and (ii) when safeguards for fair and equitable interconnection arrangements between an incumbent operator and new market entrants are to be laid down. In addition, many countries are reviewing the extent of the Universal Service Obligations to be imposed on the operator(s) of the national II.

Given the strong emphasis put on market initiatives for developing a national II by many OECD countries, and the common desire for international principles, it appears necessary to give priority to a clear and consistent description of the activities which fall within the scope of the II. Hence, common principles or reference models for the II were seen as a priority by many participants.

Of of the most embracing descriptions of Information Infrastructure is that found in the United States, whose policy vision of the II comprises four areas, which extend far beyond the classical concept of infrastructure, i.e., as confined to the underlying physical foundation for specific operations. The four areas are described as follows in "The National Information Infrastructure, Agenda for Action" (1993):

(1) thousands of interconnected, interoperable telecommunications networks; (2) computer systems, televisions, fax machines, telephones and other information appliances; (3) software, information services and databases (e.g. "digital libraries") and (4) trained people who can build, maintain and operate these systems.

The US infrastructural concept thus includes the network terminals and other private appliances in homes and offices. It also covers information content—so far clearly separated from the infrastructural conduit in US regulatory tradition—and even human intelligence. It was related to a "beehive" model of the future Information Society.

Clearly, such an organismic metaphor contrasts strongly with the classical engineering perception of public infrastructure, which puts the emphasis on predictability, procedures, and *efficiency of delivery*—in short, on a more mechanistic model of infrastructure. This view has matured in the administrative environment of the public service and hence has often been based on *a priori* principles of codified law and conformance with technical standardisation, particularly in continental Europe. An organismic view of infrastructure, on the other hand, puts more emphasis on *adaptability, processes and effectiveness of delivery*, and so may thrive better in the learning process on competitive markets.

It is tempting to over-emphasise such differences in order to appreciate fully the tremendous task confronting the ICCP Committee in developing a consistent view on the development of information infrastructures, especially in a global context.

IV. The Economic and Social Context of Information Infrastructures

A matter of considerable socio-economic concern in most OECD countries is the rapid loss of employment in manufacturing industry, both in absolute terms of number of jobs and measured as a percentage of total gainful employment. Many observers see this as evidence of the predicted post-industrial trend towards a service- and knowledge-based economy in the Information Society. Several speakers and discussants at the Special Session addressed the question of how to create a sufficient number of new jobs to compensate for the losses occurring in the manufacturing industry, and for the jobs eliminated where monopolistic supply of telecommunications infrastructure is exposed to market forces. Further OECD research in this area was urgently requested by the representative of the Trade Union Advisory Committee of the OECD, who like other speakers referred to the recent loss of jobs in the European telecommunications industry due to increased competition and relocation of jobs between national economies. It was generally acknowledged that traditional statistical methods do not offer the data needed to analyse fundamentally new structural trends, such as the changes of the nature of jobs, the structure of work, and the re-location of particular jobs within and between national economies.

Rapid structural changes appear to be taking place in national economies built on the traditional foundations of the manufacturing Industrial Society. With the globalisation of trade, newly industrialised countries (NICs) and some Eastern European countries can now bring their lower cost structure to bear in international competition. This, in turn, leads to higher economic growth and consumption in these countries. Therefore, the loss of employment in the manufacturing sector of OECD countries does not merely reflect the increased industrial competition from outside, but also the emergence of markets able to attract production facilities and other investments from OECD countries. In the area of ICT, all these new trends add up to a rapid exodus of the production of electronic consumer goods from OECD countries, which may retain only corporate headquarters and special facilities, including R&D-centres, and the regional distribution and service centres for their domestic market. This, in turn, explain the shift in strategic focus away from hardware production towards service creation and software production in many OECD countries.

Loss of jobs can also occur in (physical) infrastructural activities. A number of source documents and speakers refer to the—often substantial—lay-off of personnel by telecommunication operators who must become more efficient in the face of competition, or who have completed a major installation or refurbishment programme. In particular, many jobs have been eliminated in the areas of cable laying, maintenance of (electromechanical) switches, and the many auxiliary activities no longer seen as core business by most operators (e.g., canteen facilities, transportation, hardware-oriented R&D). Often, such activities have been outsourced, so the net loss of jobs may be less. In addition, many jobs have arisen from new operator activities, such as wireless (cellular) networking, service creation, quality assurance, customised billing, etc. It is generally noted that standard labour statistics do not adequately capture these quantitative and qualitative shifts in employment. This problem adds a very speculative element to the present balance of creation and elimination of jobs in the ICT sector, but cannot be solved in isolation within this sector.

In any event, the major structural changes in the ICT market give rise to a strong demand for new skills and, hence, for a new approach to vocational education at all levels. The Special Session was reminded that economic growth in the past has been more accelerated in an environment of general literacy and a creative plurality of views than by strongly focused technological innovation and strict media rules, particularly in times of structural change. There was, however, little reference at the Special Session to general content aspects of the II. This may be considered surprising in view of the widely held opinion that provision of information content and access to information services will be the most promising markets.

V. Network Structures and Market Strategies.

The present, rather vague notions of Information Infrastructures referred to in Sect. III were reinforced by the much clearer views on evolving markets and (corresponding) network structures advocated in several presentations. Several speakers and discussants referred to 'layered' structures of service provision, either as a basis for analysis of market segmentation or in order to develop regulatory frameworks. We consider the regulatory aspects further in Sect. VI.

Figure 1 shows one such reference model of communication and information service infra- structures, with four layers of service provision. In analogy with the Open Systems Interconnection (OSI) model and the various proprietary models adopted by computer manufacturers, the higher layers require services from the lower layers. The bottom layer comprises the provision of the transport infrastructure of transmission links; these require 'rights-of-way', radio-frequency assignments, or other special rights based on licensing by public authorities. At the next layer, one or more network operators provide the routing capacity to connect users to each other during a communication session, by appropriate switching of transmission links in the bottom layer. Routing may also connect users to the providers of value-added services, located at the third layer from below. These value-added service providers

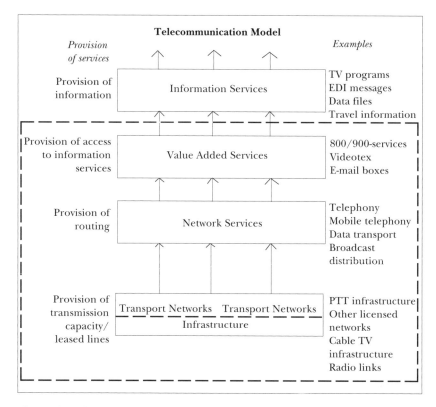

Figure 1 The layered model for telecommunications and tele-information service provision.

enhance the value of the 'bare' network service by offering access to free-phone (800-) services, electronic-mail boxes, Internet, videotex, etc. The kiosque of the French Minitel system is a classical example of a separate third-layer provision of access, which includes the ability to charge for information (video programmes, database files, banking and travel services, and so on) delivered by separate content providers. These belong at the topmost level of the layered model.

While the available services and precise regulatory borders in such a layered model vary from country to country, it was pointed out that certain economies apply at each layer. Thus, the lower layers are burdened with considerable economies of *scale*, because of the high costs of physical infrastructure. Unfortunately, this will remain true in the event of fibre 'highways' to the home. Hence, only a few large operators are sustainable in this 'transport industry', either because of formal monopolistic restrictions justified by universal-service obligations, national security, etc., or simply because of the economic reasons, which may hinder new local entrants. On the other hand, the 'content industry' also enjoys economies of *scope*. Its revenues can be raised either by globalisation in one particular service niche or by a suitable synergy, such as bundled provision of different national services. Thus, a plurality of specialised business strategies and providers may be feasible at the highest layer. Although this is an area subject to traditional government interventionist policies for public media, including broadcasting, it was argued that the market developments at this layer are 'uncontrollable' or, at least, unpredictable.

Often, the role of R&D is to change the network economies and service costs incurred at the different layers. Pre-competitive R&D-programmes may not merely have a technical impact on network architectures, consumer products and open standards; the most successful programmes can also result in major changes in the operators' economies of scale and scope and, hence, in the market structure. For instance, new wireless technologies improve the economy of the sparingly used, but costly, local loop to individual subscribers and, hence, could affect the classical paradigm of (local) telephone monopolies still adhered to in most OECD countries. Europe's pre-competitive GSM research programme eventually resulted in the introduction of competition between mobile operators. Such wireless innovations may call for economic principles for more efficient assignment of scarce radio frequencies than the administrative procedures in force in many countries.

Several speakers and discussants reiterated that there is a gap between the present cost of modern equipment borne by operators, and their pricing of the corresponding services. This gap can be very wide in the absence of effective competition. The erratic pricing of broadband leased lines, which may vary by an order of magnitude between operators in OECD countries, was particularly criticised as a serious obstacle to development of global information infrastructures for advanced multimedia applications. Arguably, this could also result in national handicaps, both for modern government services and for new business applications, and would need to be addressed clearly in plans and policies for realisation of the Information Society: Market-driven applications will evade those countries where service providers or users have to foot operator bills considered non-competitive or even unreasonable. Access to alternative broadband infrastructure, including specialised networks of railway and utility companies and cable-television networks, is foreseen in the national II plans of several OECD countries. Ongoing R&D programmes on wireless multimedia service provision might also open new channels to users.

It was observed that a layered structure, similar to that displayed in Fig. 1, also exists in the computer sector. At the lowest layer, hardware platforms and terminals connected to the network will dominate; at the higher layers, software-related products and services are found. The convergence of computing and communications ('telematics') will result in a 'Siamese-Twin' relation between these two layered structures, it was argued. Still, the situations in the two sectors are not completely parallel: The significant economies of scales in production and delivery of hardware in the *computer and terminal sector* are hardly reflected in national monopolistic regulation, but rather in the rapid market shake-outs and concentration of manufacturing in the NICs. Conversely, geographical relocation of infrastructural activities at the lowest layer of national *network operations* appears virtually impossible, for physical and economical—if not legal—reasons. On the other hand, many OECD countries now appear to focus more on higher-layer software/content activities which could, in principle, quite easily be relocated to the NIEs or other countries, given appropriate local programming and marketing skills and access to modern international networks. It would appear crucially important for OECD countries to maintain the leading edge in such skills and in advanced network availability, since content/software activities could, in principle, become nomadic once a Global Information Infrastructure is in place.

In conclusion of such strategic considerations, one speaker outlined four likely market options for operators and service providers, namely to:

a) enhance or expand present domestic network(s)

b) add new services and features to existing networks

c) expand into traditional networks/services elsewhere (as a mega-operator or niche player)

d) move into value-added services or content provision.

These strategies correspond to different movements towards vertical or horizontal integration in the layered structure in Figure 1. It will be a matter of competition policy and other regulatory principles to determine when these options should be encouraged or prevented, and how the increasing number of competitive players must co-operate to maintain interconnectivity and universal service in the new circumstances.

VI. Towards Common Regulatory Frameworks

The Special Session was warned that establishing regulatory barriers between converging economic sectors, such as broadcasting and telecommunications, will be in vain. This might pose problems for countries with traditional segregated regulation, but to limit political intererence governments may also need to decide between regulation by government or by a separate governmental authority. In some countries, the responsibility for policy for the Information Society falls to many different government Ministries, in view of public domains such as culture, communications, education, etc.

Some EU Member states also advocate an intermediate phase prior to full liberalisation in 1998, during which alternative infrastructures would become available to third parties.

Speakers from several countries agreed that content and carriage issues become increasingly intertwined, partly because of the market tendency towards vertically integrated Information Infrastructures covering most or all the service layers in Figure 1. Broadband infrastructures other than broadcast networks are still largely non-existent, it was pointed out. But speakers from other countries appeared unconvinced about the institutional feasibility of joint regulation of content and carriage. As stated by one speaker, many aspects of business, social and cultural life contain user patterns which are "invisible to government". Government should rather act as a model user itself. Countries also stressed the need for multilateral international agreement on flexible principles for open global infrastructures more strongly than any problems with convergence of national broadcasting and telecommunications. Countries are also considering institutional arrangements for regulation at a distance from government to reduce political interference.

Much business frustration is indeed caused by the fact that liberalisation or divestiture of communication infrastructure and services often results in complex transition rules, additional regulation and an increasing number of legal disputes with competitors or the State. However, the discretionary powers of an independent regulator were also seen as objectionable by some business users and operators. The fundamental question here seems to be whether 'liberalisation' can be a synonym for 'deregulation' in the area of II.

Another set of commercial problems related to the development of the II is experienced with the Internet. As pointed out by a number of speakers and discussants, this successful international network of networks does not yet comply with elementary, but essential requirements for security, privacy and recognition of intellectual property rights. This could frustrate the creation of networked information markets, where suppliers and users of information will be confident to 'meet' and trade electronically with each other. The need for international harmonisation in this area has to be addressed.

A third area requiring consideration is the need for international standards for the II, to allow easy interconnection of networks and interoperability of services across borders. This is a field where considerable differences seem to exist between the policy views held in OECD Member states: In the EU and Japan, more formal policies for standardisation are in place than in the US. However, this is not strange in view of the much larger home market in North America where, moreover, the existence of the Bell system ensured the informal adherence to unified network interfaces and protocols until divestiture of AT&T in 1983. In practice, this history has given the US a leading edge in the development of procedures for interconnection and equal access in a competitive, but technically harmonised environment. The more monopolistic, but technically fragmented PTO networks and the smaller home markets in the smaller OECD countries give them a stronger incentive to standardise new systems such as GSM and the future II.

In conclusion, the Special Session thus demonstrated a clear and urgent need for discussion of main principles and reference models for the II. In the multilateral OECD context, such principles and models should apply to global infrastructures and service provision, in order to provide common guidance for interconnection rules and transparent regulations of national markets. Governments will need to act rapidly to ensure that their national policies facilitate private initiatives and the pilot projects agreed at international level. Building the reference models on harmonised principles will improve economies of scale and scope, both for new initiatives and for basic telecommunication service. This will reduce the inevitable uncertainties of demand, supply and investments in novel markets, and so allow a wider reach of services in the future Information Society. According to the Chairman of the Working Party on Telecommunications and Information Services Policy (TISP), the agenda of the ICCP and its working parties should be determined by the need to attract investors in the II. Quality of services will be a key concept to create the confidence to invest in new markets.

In closing the Special Session, the ICCP Chairman reminded participants that government policies need to reflect the emerging consensus on international principles. In the present economic situation faced by OECD countries, this is of particular importance in view of the longer term economic and social potential of the Information Society.

Part III: Policy Issues [DSTI/ICCP(95)9]

The ICCP's Special Session on Information Infrastructures will examine the economic impacts and policy issues raised by the development of information infrastructures (II) and international, or global information infrastructures (GII). This paper aims to provide an overview of the issues and to help stimulate and focus discussions at the meeting. In particular, the paper outlines in brief an introductory analysis of the following issues:

• the economic and social impacts and benefits which the development of new applications and information infrastructures can provide, and the issues which governments need to confront and overcome in order to realise these benefits;

• the driving forces behind and barriers to the development of information infrastructures for large-scale demand and supply of new network applications integrating voice, data and video services;

• the regulatory and policy measures which governments need to take to optimise the benefits of national information infrastructures;

• the implications of these issues for international information infrastructure development, and the specific impact of information infrastructures on international relations.

Inevitably, there is overlap between these issues, but it is hoped that each session will fully develop a particular perspective on the issues which will interlock with and build on discussions in preceding sessions.

Session 1: The Economic and Social Impacts of Information Infrastructures

The recent interest in information infrastructures has been based on their perceived potential to increase productivity, stimulate economic growth and create employment in new activities. This is a pressing matter at a time of high unemployment in many countries and increasing international competition. For growth to occur in advanced, value-added areas, the costs of communication and information inputs which are their lifeblood need to come down. Otherwise, general economic anaemia will set in.

As ubiquitous infrastructures for a range of other activities, communications infrastructures are far-reaching in their ability to affect the workings of society. Nevertheless, their impact in different areas is varied, and there is legitimate concern that the increases in productivity in existing sectors which new information infrastructures can help achieve will fail to be offset by demand for and growth in new service areas. Additionally, there are fears that the qualitative impact on employment practices and social activities will be negative. In addition, negative impacts are likely to accumulate in the short term as a result of transition costs and learning effects, compared to the longer term when the net positive economic and social gains can be expected to be more evident. Analysis therefore needs to be brought to bear on how the broad social and economic impacts of developing information infrastructures are unfolding.

Supply and demand relations between firms are changing fast through the implementation of information services and multimedia products, particularly when combined with the introduction of information infrastructures. In particular, the development of just-in-time forms of delivery, automated inventory and stock control, and customer billing arrangements have undermined the arms-length structure of traditional market relations and facilitated vertical interlinkages between firms in different sectors. While firms have been able to gain a much greater awareness of and responsiveness to different customer tastes and consumption patterns as a result, labour relations are being restructured in the production and delivery of goods and services (re-engineering and downsizing).

The impact of information infrastructures on employment is not simply direct and quantitative, but also indirect and qualitative. For many OECD countries, the creation of new services, or the enhanced packaging and delivery of existing ones, is potentially the most rewarding result of developing information infrastructures. Other information and entertainment sectors can gain from the possibilities offered by new applications to improve their flexibility of demand and supply, improve utilisation of labour and natural materials, and lower costs and more efficiently utilise support services. This potential provides the possibility of new jobs being created to offset those lost by improved productivity being brought about in other sectors. However, such an outcome requires the development of mass markets for service applications, and this depends upon overall macroeconomic relations of demand and supply being sustained.

In this context, it is appropriate to evaluate the immediate role that governments can play in supporting the accelerated development of information infrastructures. Retraining of the workforce is particularly important in an economy where skills are being made redundant at a more rapid pace. The closer relationship between customers and their suppliers within a broad competitive market framework also changes the nature of commercial relationships. In addition, the vertical interlinkages of previously unrelated sectors means that the appropriate placement and effects of incentives for R&D, employment and information generation and distribution anywhere along the chain of supply is fundamentally more difficult to ascertain. A key issue which needs to be addressed in order to define effective policy responses is, therefore, *how* to measure these different impacts of information infrastructures and multimedia services. Existing statistical categories and data collection procedures are often inadequate for monitoring and keeping pace with the changes involved.

In the longer term, the impact on society of information infrastructures and applications is expected to include fundamental changes in working habits and work location, access to information, leisure and social interaction. Whether these impacts will be socially disruptive or beneficial will depend on the rate and manner of implementation of new applications and network diffusion and on adjustments in human behaviour. Even though these matters are long term, governments need to consider the social, educational and welfare policies which can support a smooth transition path.

A related issue is the public provision of services such as education and healthcare, and the way in which these need to be re-defined to take into account the development of information infrastructures. These services have traditionally been provided on an universal basis in most OECD countries. As information infrastructures are adopted for delivery and operational purposes (e.g. tele-medicine and distance learning), it is important to consider the extent to which public subsidies are needed for their support, and the relative roles of the public and private sectors in organising the inputs and outputs of these services. At the same time, because these questions raise issues of network utilisation and efficiencies, they touch upon universal service issues traditionally associated with cross-subsidies in telecommunications.

Questions which need to be addressed include:

• What measures do governments need to adopt in terms of (re)training programmes, establishment of seed-finance for SMEs, and information dissemination in order to boost the beneficial impact of information infrastructures on society and the economy?

• Where will labour shedding occur and where and how will employment increase and change? How should government efforts differ for different sectors of the economy?

• What measures may government take in terms of restructuring the relationship between public provision of such services as education and healthcare, on the one hand, and private sector-led information infrastructure development, on the other, in order to maintain social standards of living?

• What measures should governments take to better monitor and measure developments and the impacts of information infrastructures and related applications?

Session 2: Market Development and New Applications

Market and technological forces are currently driving private sector investments in the development of network services which integrate voice, data and video technologies. A wide range of factors will determine the success of these services and the importance of each of them will depend on the type of network application involved. Some of these factors include pricing structures, standards, and the legal and regulatory frameworks for the development and use of applications. The success of many, though, will also depend on their rate of diffusion and the achievement of sufficient market scale. In particular, services aimed at residential consumers rather than business markets will require mass markets in order to achieve price levels which are attractive.

The development of services is contingent on the creation of a market place which allows new applications to be created and expanded. Information infrastructures nowadays provide *the* market place for new services; and the breadth of economic exchange and growth in this market place depends upon how wide a range of technologies and players are allowed to create these infrastructures. New multimedia applications require at a minimum that existing market entry restrictions in the broadcasting and telecommunication service sectors be eliminated and a competitive market be created which allows all potential market participants to supply services. Only in this way will the broad demand for and diffusion of new applications be encouraged, and the necessary economic incentives be provided for investing in advanced network infrastructures.

Integrating existing data, voice and video networks, as well as allowing new market entrants, could optimise development of—and would maximise the economic return on—a range of application investments. However, in order to ensure competitive markets develop with appropriate legal safeguards in place, policy makers need to alleviate the tendency of investors to use proprietary systems of access and operation, and prevent the bundling of access and operating systems with service applications. This can otherwise tend to occur because of the high investment costs with broadband networks and the costs associated with developing new network-based applications.

The role of governments in many economic sectors is increasingly confined to identifying and strengthening framework conditions for private sector activities rather than any direct involvement in the development of products and services. Most OECD countries thus agree that the private sector should lead the way in financing the development and diffusion of information infrastructure applications. Some governments, however, also suggest that they have a role in defining a broad investment perspective along with the private sector for applications which create as yet unknown frontiers of social change and development. This role can be fulfilled through stimulating and building consensus over the use of and demand for information and communications applications.

However, the uncertainty of demand for new applications would tend to imply that governments should avoid trying to influence or stimulate particular private sector application areas. The question of extending universal service coverage is pertinent in this regard since this would, if the concept is expanded to cover certain service applications, help market development in those exclusive areas. Care should be taken therefore not to expand the existing concept of universal service at the present embryonic stage of infrastructure and service development.

Governments can play a similarly indirect role in a number of pre-competitive R&D areas where initially high costs may deter long term private investment. But again, this role can be achieved without subsidising or trying to determine the commercial success of particular applications. Government grants for pilot projects should, therefore, be based on general criteria rather than favouring specific private sector application areas or individual firms.

The level of prices and pricing structures plays the most fundamental role in the successful development and diffusion of applications. By reducing the costs and uncertainty for the private sector in developing open systems and integrating existing networks, and by ensuring open standards in applications technologies, governments can help the realisation of economies of scale and thus help lower unit costs to be achieved. By pursuing these goals within a competitive framework, they can ensure that downward pressures are kept on pricing structures.

In any case, existing experience indicates that applications which are presently viewed as promising may have a long gestation period before their full impact is realised. Slow growth and the insufficient development of services in some areas results to a large extent from high prices, which have in turn occurred from an absence of competitive markets. Even within a competitive market framework, it is important to be realistic as to the rate of diffusion of new technologies and services. Many of the existing technologies and services require a significant period before they can attain high penetration rates.

The development of information infrastructures is thus likely to be evolutionary as a result of factors on both the supply side and the demand side. From the supply side, new technologies need refinement, standards need to be finalised, and prices for new technologies need to fall before investment becomes profitable. New applications also take time to be developed and tested. On the demand side, users need to be persuaded of the economic value of new applications, residential users need to be convinced of the utility of new services and be willing to pay for them. As a result, governments should be wary of trying to "force-feed" the development of information infrastructures and applications.

An important area where governments can have a direct influence in applications development is through their role as large potential users of information infrastructures. The administrative functions of government can benefit to a large extent from networked applications, including local and national administration, taxation, policing and justice. Governments also have responsibility for the provision of a wide range of services to the public, ranging from healthcare, education, traffic management, and security. All these areas can benefit to some extent from networked applications both in the context of improving the efficiency and cost of service delivery but also in terms of creating economies of scale and reducing the unit costs of production. Governments can thus play an important role in the stimulation, diffusion and development of applications by accelerating their own use of information infrastructures.

The development and use by governments of information infrastructure applications provides them with a challenge. Their use of a range of potential applications will likely in the longer term help reduce costs of service provision and improve their quality. In the short term, however, it is likely that the required expenditures will increase as a result of development and investment costs as well as the costs of transition from one form of service provision to another. In the face of the present emphasis on cutting government spending, budgetary allocations for education and health establishments and government departments may need to be reviewed in order to provide necessary investment and operating expenses.

Questions which need to be addressed include:

• What measures should governments take, if any, to encourage the growth of mass markets for networked applications of integrated voice, data and audio-visual services? (Should the role of governments be restricted to removing market barriers to private sector investment, or is a more active role required in stimulating demand to encourage growth in particular sectors?)

• What is the necessary role of governments in ensuring open technology and network standards? (Do governments need to encourage the private sector to develop networks which allow high bit-rate two-way communications and the development of highly interactive service applications by a wide range of service providers and users?)

• In what ways can governments reorganise their own activities to support private sector development of new applications areas?

(How can governments make their own provision of services more efficient through the use of information infrastructures? In what ways can governments support private sector R&D to stimulate the development of information infrastructures?)

Session 3: Regulatory Frameworks for Information Infrastructures

Regulatory restrictions on telecommunications operators offering broadcast services, as well as on broadcasting entities offering communications services, limit potential investments in information infrastructures and the development of networked applications of integrated voice, data and audio-visual services. In order to speed up investment in advanced information infrastructures increased competition in networks and services is required. However, the evolving vertical integration of the industry which would result from the removal of existing regulatory barriers also needs to be carefully regulated if it is not to result in market closure to new entrants.

The different structural characteristics of the existing sectors means that a fundamental review of existing national policy frameworks and regulatory safeguards is required if the process of integration is to be smooth and open. The surest way to ensure that the abolition of existing regulatory restrictions results in increased competition rather than reinforced monopolies is through implementation of an extensive framework for inter-connection of and equal access to distribution networks for services. Safeguards on the design and pricing of access termination point technologies will also be important.

The need to extend and refine existing definitions of universal service has been suggested in the context of national information infrastructures which integrate different existing networks. The feasibility of doing so, the services which could be included in any new definition of universal service, the costs involved and their allocation are all important issues which need examination. In particular, the composition of any set of services established as basic to universal access will determine the level of network technology and investments which service providers will be expected to make. This in turn will set limits on the number and type of viable service providers which any given market can sustain. Minimum universal service requirements may restrict market access by creating a fixed set of costs which may be necessary for market entry and thus set a minimum level of returns required for profitability, as well as the economies of scope and scale required to achieve these returns.

Conversely, establishing a basic set of services as open to universal access also gives investors an idea of the minimum market size of investments and their returns. This may encourage investments in networks and services which may not otherwise occur. In countries with a relatively low per capita income, however, such investments may have to be made by governments in order to be viable. Governments should be cautious before making decisions on the extension of universal service and in particular in determining who will bear the appropriate costs. While it is important to avoid excluding segments of society from access to information infrastructures. it may also be appropriate to allow for greater maturity in the development of applications and network diffusion before finalising decisions on extending universal service mandates.

Security, privacy and intellectual property protection are also indispensable for realising positive economic goals and social values from the development of information infrastructures. Without these basic legal elements, growth of the infrastructure may be hampered or the infrastructure may not be used to its full potential. Confidentiality, integrity and availability of the entire infrastructure, protection of private information, and payment for use of proprietary information are all required to assure confident use of the infrastructure. Equally important, though, is that the goals of security, privacy and intellectual property protection be achieved in balance, so that solutions to one do not vitiate the other.

The issue of remuneration for use of works on the infrastructure must also be appropriately addressed, both through legal and technological measures, to encourage creative efforts to develop content for the infrastructure. Questions and concerns about the effects of information infrastructure on privacy and personal autonomy may have important economic effects on the use of the infrastructure and are closely linked to cultural characteristics. Do we import the privacy status quo of the three-dimensional world, such as it is, into the information infrastructure? Alternatively, given the nature of the information infrastructure, is greater protection of personal data and privacy required? Or, due to the properties of the infrastructure, must it be accepted that there will be a lower level of protection of personal data and privacy? All of these questions are vital to the infrastructure and have yet to be addressed.

Questions which need to be addressed include:

• What regulatory and policy reforms are needed to facilitate the growth of national information infrastructures and new network applications of voice, data and audio-visual services? (What are the difficulties governments face in ensuring that vertical integration of telecommunications and broadcasting regulatory frameworks does not lead to market closure?)

• What if any set of services need to be universal to guarantee participation in the information society, and/or to encourage network and service development?

• What are the basic legal provisions for privacy, intellectual property rights and security needed to ensure that users and providers of applications can use, and are encouraged to use information infrastructures? (What are the appropriate principles for balancing the goals of individual use, commercial use and public order considerations with regard to encryption policy? What are the best solutions to ensure remuneration for use of content? What is the appropriate balance for protection of personal data and privacy in the information infrastructure, both on national and global levels?)

Session 4: From Global Information Infrastructures to Global Information Society

In recent years much emphasis has been placed on the globalisation of OECD economies and the shift towards a global information society. The development of information infrastructures and the increasing liberalisation of international communication markets provides scope for greater integration of economies, increased economic activity and trade and greater sharing of knowledge and information through global infrastructures. The development of international information infrastructures and new networked applications of voice, data and audio-visual services is essential for the growth of international services.

Information infrastructures are undermining existing international institutional infrastructures while at the same time providing the foundation for future international markets for the exchange of goods and services. Unlike other infrastructures, information infrastructures bundle together transport, access and a universal market—available instantly and capable of quickly arbitraging away price differentials and balancing supply and demand. It is clear that rules need to be established which both support and balance the commercial and financial forces which are being unleashed by these infrastructures.

For information infrastructures to develop at an international level requires even more definitely than at a national level that a coherent set of principles be put in place. Yet existing international institutions address telecommunications issues from different sets of economic principles in a largely uncoordinated manner. The relationship amongst the different institutions needs to be defined more clearly and forcefully at a high level—as much as the workings of individual institutions themselves—if issues such as open and equal access and competitive interconnection are to be established and effectively maintained. Current negotiations to liberalise basic telecommunications and infrastructures and services must be encouraged to reach rapid conclusions and consideration may need to be given eventually to extend the scope and discussions to cover information infrastructures widely defined.

It is also important that OECD countries ensure that the developing economies are not excluded from the developing global information infrastructures and participation in a global information society. Many of the considerations concerning the social and economic impacts of information infrastructures, and the question of access to universal service, expressed in previous sessions are faced in a more acute way by developing countries. OECD countries need to consider how the development of international information infrastructures can occur in a way which does not exclude the majority of humankind, but in a way which is also economical.

Since infrastructures are, by nature, international, it would also be inefficient and perhaps counterproductive for each nation to devise individual solutions to legal questions concerning security, privacy and intellectual property rights. There is an urgent need for international debate and resolution of the necessary rules that will underpin the information highway. For example, a consensus is emerging that it may be useful and timely, both on a national and an international level, to begin a multilateral dialogue to identify principles for encryption policy.

Questions which need to be addressed include:

• What are the implications of the issues raised in the previous three sessions for international or global information infrastructure development? (Are there areas of infrastructure and applications development which need to be given priority at the international compared to the national level?)

• What international guidelines may be necessary in order to avoid frictions and encourage applications for international services development between countries arising from government activities in this area?

• How can existing international organisations best work together in promoting and regulating the development of international or global information infrastructures?

Part IV: National Policies for Information Infrastructures: An Overview [DSTI/ICCP(95)10]

The ICCP's Special Session will examine the economic impacts and policy issues raised by the development of information infrastructures (II) and international, or global information infrastructures (GII). This paper aims to provide an outline of positions adopted by or proposed for governments on the issue of information infrastructures.

Reports from the following OECD countries have been examined: Australia, Canada, Denmark, France, Germany, Japan, the Netherlands, Norway, Sweden, the United Kingdom and the United States. The programme of the EU is also expected to provide an integrated vision to the European Union countries. G-7 countries have started to examine the possibilities of undertaking co-ordinated

actions to stimulate applications and the creation of global information infrastructures. The sources used are mentioned in appendix A.

It should be noted that the decision-making process in many
countries is still on-going. As information infrastructures develop,
governments and their advisors are likely to integrate new insights
in their policies, and additional reports are being prepared to
address specific aspects of information infrastructures. In addition,
in some countries national reports have been prepared by Ministries, whereas in others the reports have been prepared by Commissions or advisory bodies which means that the different
recommendations made in the reports have not yet been adopted
as policy in many cases. For the purpose of this paper, however, the
existing recommendations have been used. As a consequence the
paper must be viewed as a provisional overview of national initiatives, policies and reflections of the country in question.

Without exception, governments have a positive attitude towards
the developments in information and communication technology.
The general conviction is that they will result in economic and
social benefits: information infrastructures are expected to stimulate economic growth, increase productivity, create jobs, increase
the quality of services, and improve the quality of life. The opportunities provided by the new technologies enable governments to
react positively to economic and social challenges. Besides the
similarities, however, there are also differences. First, programmes
adopt different priorities for the development of information
infrastructures. Some focus mainly on services and applications
while others primarily discuss networks and infrastructures. Second, the programmes take the country's specific economic, cultural and social situation as a starting point.

In the sections that follow, the policies proposed to or adopted by
different governments are outlined in relation to the issues to be
discussed at the Special Session.

Session 1: The Economic and Social Impacts of Information
Infrastructures

All programmes stress the economic benefits of information infrastructures. Its development is expected to stimulate economic

growth, create high-skilled jobs, and increase productivity, both in the private and public sector.

Economic growth

In Japan it has been estimated that by building a nation-wide fibre optic network for broadband (fibre-to-the-home), the multimedia market plus regular telecom marketwill attain a level of approximately 123 trillion yen (US\$ 1230 billion) in 2010, the year in which the construction of the network is proposed for completion (MPT pp. 13–14). The United States estimate that the National Information Infrastructure will create as much as US\$ 300 billion annually in new sales across a range of industries (US p. 13). The other programmes forecast economic growth, however, without giving estimates of its magnitude.

The content industry is envisioned to be one of the most dynamic sectors to develop. Services like video-on-demand and interactive games are expected to boost the entertainment and audio-visual industry. Publishers and information providers will be able to develop new products and services based on broadband networks. New technologies provide new opportunities for sector-specific services like education, training, healthcare and other services.

Building new networks and expanding existing ones is also seen as a major stimulus for the economy. In the United States expenditures between US\$ 50 and US\$ 100 billion are expected to upgrade telecommunication facilities for the National Information Infrastructure, while in Japan it is estimated that it is necessary to spend an annual average of about 1 trillion yen (US\$ 10 billion) to build an information infrastructure before the year 2010 (Japan p. 46). In France, to build a fibre network to every household by the year 2015 is estimated to cost between FFr 150 billion and FFr 200 billion (between US\$ 30 billion and US\$ 40 billion) (France p. 102).

To access the information and communication services, customer premises equipment like PCs and interactive terminal equipment will be needed. In 1993, OECD total hardware expenditure for information technology was US\$ 132 billion (IT Outlook 1994, p. 22). Although no estimates have been made by the different countries for expenditures in this area, it is most likely the market for customer premises equipment will grow on a steady basis as the information society develops. Indications of these developments were already present in 1994: in this year the world-wide personal computer market grew 20 per cent, driven by a vibrant home market and competitive pricing.

Information and communications technologies have been impacting on user industries for some time. These technologies provide possibilities to rationalise production and service delivery and increase productivity, both in the public and private sector. Estimates made in the United States indicate an increase of productivity by 20 to 40 per cent by the year 2007 (US p. 13).

One sector mentioned in national programmes in particular for reducing costs while increasing the quality of service is in health care. Costs in this sector have been increasing constantly and are expected to continue to increase in the future. Information infrastructures are viewed as providing the possibility to alter this trend. For instance, by using Electronic Data Interchange (EDI) to manage information flows between clinics, practitioners and insurance companies, dramatic cost reductions are foreseen. Potential cost reduction is also expected from Telemedicine and Personal Health Information Systems (US, p. 14, 15).

The OECD public telecommunication service sector generated revenues of US$ 395 billion in 1992 amounting to some 2 per cent of GDP. Investment by public operators has averaged around 3 per cent of gross fixed capital investment for OECD countries, amounting to some US$ 102 billion in 1992 (Communications Outlook 1995). The development of information infrastructures will stimulate this market and is expected to increase the share of these industries, according to some estimates, to between 10–15 per cent of GDP.

Employment
Significant increases in economic activity are expected from the development of information infrastructures and related applications in all countries and it is expected that there will also be a positive effect on employment. Japan, for instance, expects employment in the multimedia sector to outnumber that in its automobile industry and generate 2 430 000 jobs by the year 2010 (MPT pp. 13–14). The United States expects as many as 300 000 jobs in the

next 10–15 years to be created in the Personal Communications Services Industry (US p. 13). Estimates made in France envision the number of employees in the information services sector to double by the year 2015 up to 600 000 (France p. 57). Other national programmes also predict job creation as a result of the development of information infrastructures, especially in new content industries, although estimates are not provided.

National reports do not specify to what extent estimates of job creation constitute a net increase in jobs taking into account any negative impacts information infrastructures may have on employment. It is important for governments to be aware of the potential of information infrastructures to reduce as well as create employment and ensure that appropriate polices are in place, especially retraining, to compensate for this impact.

The geographical impact
Traditional production of goods and delivery of services has been tied to geographic areas because of the need for skilled labour, access to certain information, and customer markets. For this reason most economic activity is centred in and around urban areas. Information infrastructures provide development opportunities in rural areas while at the same time providing opportunities to reduce or reverse over-concentration in urban areas. Norway and Sweden, for instance, with their sparse population and considerable distances, envision new opportunities for rural areas by exploiting information technologies (Norway, Sweden p. 24). Japan also mentions new opportunities for its regions which might take some pressure off the Greater Tokyo Metropolitan Area (MPT p. 8).

Social and cultural implications
As discussed earlier, information infrastructures are considered to provide potential benefits to the economy. But the promises of information infrastructures go beyond this, since they are also viewed as providing opportunities to address social challenges. For instance, information infrastructures may enable a certain level of service to be maintained in rural and sparsely populated areas through using remote delivery of services such as distance educa-

tion or telemedicine (US p. 14, MPT Japan p. 8, Norway). People with special needs, such as the elderly and the disabled, will have more possibilities to participate in society (MPT Japan p. 7, Denmark p. 97, Germany p. 4, Norway). Information infrastructures provide a tool to reduce environmental damage by reducing the use of paper (MPT p. 12), reduce traffic by using teleworking (Bangemann p. 25, Germany p. 18, Norway), and increase efficiency of traffic flows through the use of traffic information systems (MPT p. 10, Denmark p. 77, Bangemann p.27).

In general, the widespread use of information infrastructures is expected to have a significant social impact by transforming the way we live, work and play. For instance, as a consequence of the development of flexible firms the working environment is expected to change. This affects skills required from employees, the content of jobs or the geographic location from where work is done. Constant change requires constant updating of knowledge and skills (life-long learning). Present working time arrangements can be transformed into more flexible ones using information infrastructures.

Specific attention is given in national reports and policy papers to the potential threat of a two-tier society of "haves" and "havenots": those familiar with the use of information infrastructures and who therefore are able to participate in and benefit from the information society, and those not familiar with the technology or unable to obtain access to it (Denmark p. 16, 29, Bangemann p. 6, Germany p. 10, US p. 8). To avoid this threat, countries want to ensure that information infrastructures are available to all by expanding the concept of universal service. Education and training is another fundamental element in preparing people for the information society.

Education

For a number of reasons the implementation of information infrastructures in education is considered to be important. First of all, by using information infrastructures new and better forms of education and training are possible. These infrastructures enable institutions to support a more diverse range of curricula activity and reduce their dependency on local teaching resources. Teachers and students can have access to a greatly expanded range of educational material on the network. Information infrastructures allow for distance education or remote learning regardless of location or time, reducing restrictions on access to education services (Bangemann p. 25, Netherlands p. 19, Australia interim report p. 23, US p.17, Denmark pp. 59–60, Canada p. 9, Germany p. 4, Norway, Sweden pp. 10–11, UK p. 8).

By using information infrastructures in education and training, school children, students and employees become familiar with the technology. For the individual this is important given the need to work and live in a society that is more and more based on information technology: for enterprises it is important to have human resources capable of using and/or developing new information services in order to stay competitive nationally and internationally (MPT p. 53, US p. 16, Sweden p. 10, Canada p. 31, Bangemann p. 6). Most OECD countries have started or will start building networks linking schools, integrating computer-based education material as well as starting pilot projects for various specific educational and training applications. References in national reports to the protection of culture and language applies particularly to education. Several countries emphases the necessity of developing applications based on the national identity i.e. culture and language (Sweden p. 11, Denmark p.29).

Demand
The promises of information infrastructures are significant. However, much of their impact will depend on the development of demand. In the past, various new technologies have developed mass-markets in a relatively short time, whereas others have taken decades or have not really taken off. In general, preconditions for the successful introduction of new technologies are related to user-friendliness of both hardware and software, their prices, the extent to which these technologies meet customer's needs, and the existence of substitutes. Given the scope and complexity of the issues involved in information infrastructures there are a number of analysts who believe that it will take at least one generation before the information society can be considered mature. The transformation towards an information society must as a result be consid-

ered evolutionary rather then revolutionary. This may imply that estimates concerning economic growth might at this stage be rather optimistic.

Session 2: Market Development and New Applications

The physical infrastructure
Information infrastructures are largely based on broadband communication technologies. Unlike existing networks which are restricted as to the datastreams they can carry, broadband networks can carry integrated data, video, text and voice traffic and therefore have the capability to carry multimedia services and allow interactivity. There is still insufficient consensus as to whether information infrastructures require fibre to the home, fibre to the curb, or whether other network architectures are appropriate. Rapid technological developments in transmission technologies (compression techniques) suggest that a sufficiently high data rate may be obtained to satisfy many requirements without immediately investing in fibre-to-the-home. This, together with the existing costs of investing in fibre and uncertainty about residential demand, is a major reason why private investors are cautious and often choose to upgrade existing networks rather then investing in fibre-to-the-home on a mass scale.

Most OECD countries discuss the appropriate technologies for the delivery of applications over information infrastructures only in terms of trends and developments, and leave the decision on specifics in the hands of industry. For example, the United Kingdom's report stresses the fact that: "The government considers efficient infrastructure is best developed by competing providers, rather than by promoting a single all purpose switched two-way infrastructure.. . A competitive environment tends to reduce the gap between the development and the deployment of new technologies, products and services, thereby rapidly increasing the products and services available to customers. It is worth noting that there is a good deal of debate—and disagreement—as to how highly developed communications networks will need to be, and how fast new, interactive services will be taken up. A key advantage of competition in infrastructure and services is that market pressures promote innovation, investment, and experimentation." (UK pp. 4–5).

On the other hand, proposals have been made for active support and stimulation by governments in the extension of broadband networks. The most far-reaching proposals have been made in Japan and France, where it has been recommended to invest in fibre-to-the-home to be completed, respectively, by 2010 and by 2015 (MPT p. 27, France p. 108). Both countries are stimulating the development of cable television networks (MPT News, October 31, 1994). The European Commission has proposed a series of guidelines as well as a multi-year action plan for the development of ISDN as a trans-European network. In addition, the concept of a European Integrated Broadband Communications infrastructure is being promoted.

Many governments also see a need to establish general frameworks or visions for the development of applications. Following the recommendations of the Bangemann Group, the Commission is setting up a European Broadband Steering Committee involving all relevant actors to develop a common vision and to monitor and facilitate the realisation of overall concepts through, in particular, demonstrations, and choice and definition of standards (EU p. 8, Bangemann p. 21). In the United States, the National Telecommunications and Information Administration has been holding hearings around the country to get the views of interested parties on the National Information Infrastructure initiative, and has established the Information Infrastructure Task Force and Advisory Committee to obtain and co-ordinate the views of government agencies and the private sector. Australia established a Broadband Services Expert Group and the Communications Futures Project to define the impact of developments in information and communication infrastructures and applications for Australian business and society. Governments promote the use of information infrastructures and raise awareness of the possible benefits (Bangemann p. 26, Denmark p. 80, Norway, UK p. 16). Governments also have constant dialogue with, among others, the private sector to exchange visions and positions (Canada p. 13, Germany p. 14, UK p. 10, US p. 7).

Applications

In regard to the development of information and communication applications governments, in general, see their role as facilitating and stimulating the development and use of applications by putting the appropriate regulatory frameworks in place which are based on a competitive market.

There is a range of multimedia products and applications being developed for different markets. It is generally agreed that public assistance needs to be minimised and that the private sector already has the experience to exploit various applications in order to improve the goods or services delivered, increase productivity, reduce the 'time to market', and enhance flexibility and competitiveness.

The residential market, already an important consumer of information, communication services, and entertainment services, may become one of the principal driving forces in the development of information infrastructure markets. This would provide the necessary critical mass for new information and communication services (Bangemann p. 9, MPT p. 29). Entertainment applications such as video-on-demand, and interactive games are considered to be the most promising areas (Australia interim report p. 27, Denmark pp. 69–75, 94, Bangemann p. 10). Other applications for this market are, for example, teleshopping and teleworking. Teleworking is an application governments show special interest in, mainly to reduce commuting traffic.

The public sector, as a large potential user of information and communication services, can stimulate the development of information infrastructures through providing the critical mass for new service applications. By becoming leading-edge users of information infrastructure applications, governments would be able to set an example and show the benefits of these technologies and applications to society as a whole. For instance, the use of information infrastructures is viewed as enabling an improvement of public services, reduce costs and improve flexibility. But the potential benefits go beyond economic-driven objectives as they can contribute to a more transparent, responsive public administration with services better accessible for the public (Canada p. 9, US p. 17, Sweden 14, Denmark pp. 33–44, Germany p. 18, Norway, UK p. 17,

MPT p. 10, Netherlands p. 20, Australia interim report pp. 21–23, Bangemann p. 5).

Testbeds

In various cases governments are participating in pilot projects and testbeds to demonstrate the potential of information infrastructures and stimulate their development by working closely together with all the actors involved. For some years now the European Union has supported the development and deployment of networks and applications, including telematic services for small and medium-sized enterprises, telematic applications for transport in Europe, trans-European public administration networks, and urban information highways (EU p. 12). In order to stimulate the development of information infrastructures most countries have pilot projects, in some cases assisted through government funding. The G-7 countries have launched a number of joint projects on a global level to be initially undertaken by the G-7 partners, but which will become open to all countries. The 11 pilot projects include a global inventory of information regarding major national and international projects and studies relevant to the promotion and development of the global information society; facilitating the establishment of international links between the various high speed networks and testbeds supporting advanced applications; cross-cultural education and training; electronic libraries; electronic museums and galleries; healthcare applications; and government online (Chair's conclusions issued by the G-7 Ministers, 27 February 1995).

Research and development

Research and development has contributed to the development of information infrastructures. At the same time information infrastructures have enabled scientists to improve and expand their research, often interacting with colleagues all over the world, sharing data and information regardless of their geographical location. All OECD countries are aware of the importance of research and development in general, and information infrastructures-related R&D in particular. Governments are supporting this by increasing or reallocating existing funding to information technology-based areas (Denmark p. 57, Canada p. 11, Bangemann

p. 30, EU p. 10, Germany pp. 14–15, MPT p. 47, Norway, US p. 23, UK p. 10).

Standardisation
To maximise the potential provided by information infrastructures, interoperability of networks must be attained on a national and an international level. Standardisation is essential to achieve interconnection and interoperability. Being aware that setting standards can provide a competitive advantage, governments want to co-operate more closely with industry and standardisation agencies (US p. 9, Sweden p. 19, MPT pp. 54–55, Canada p. 24, Australia interim report p. 54, Denmark p. 83, Norway).

Financing
In general, OECD countries consider financing information infrastructures to be primarily the responsibility of the private sector. By introducing or further expanding competition private investment will be stimulated, ensuring cost-effectiveness, lower prices as well as improved and widened services (UK p. 1, US pp. 7–8, Netherlands pp. 8, 12–13, Sweden p. 18, Australia interim report p. 10, Canada p. 13, EU p. 10). Governments also stimulate private investment by providing tax incentives, and loan guarantees (US p. 8, MPT p. 46, EU p. 10, Germany p. 11).

Commercially non-attractive projects, for instance in rural areas or specific facilities for the disabled and the elderly, might have difficulty in obtaining private investment funds. In these cases OECD countries consider additional public funding or provide grants for non-profit institutions (Canada p. 13, Australia interim report pp. 57–58, US p. 23).

Pricing
As experience has shown, competition is important in reducing prices. However, existing telecommunication tariff structures for access and use of information infrastructures, especially in monopoly markets, hinder rather than stimulate the development of a dynamic markets. Even in many markets that have recently liberalised prices may be insufficiently low to stimulate new applications. The national reports studied do not analyse the issue of tariffication.

Session 3: Regulatory Frameworks for Information Infrastructures

Although many of the developments described are already taking place, the real take-off of information infrastructures and the information society has yet to come. Governments are now in a position to facilitate and accelerate these developments, as well as anticipate and counter any undesirable side-effects. To guide their strategies and objectives, most countries have put forward a set of principles. The 5 main principles which several OECD countries agree with are:

i) Open access

In order to realise the economic and social objectives set by governments, full access to networks and the information transmitted over these networks is a necessity for service providers and users alike. Specific regulatory and technical conditions to enable interconnection of networks and interoperability of services at the national and international level is essential (EU p. 4, MPT p. 52, USA p. 9, Sweden p. 18, Canada p. 13, Denmark p. 25, Norway).

ii) Encourage private investment

The private sector must play the leading role in developing the information infrastructures. Government's role is to encourage private investment by creating a suitable environment: competition and tax incentives are part of this policy (Australia interim report p. 55, 57, Bangemann p. 8, EU p. 3, Canada pp. 13–14, Germany p. 19, MPT pp. 46, 50, USA pp. 7–8, Sweden p. 7, UK p. 15). In some cases governments consider additional funding to ensure all its citizens are being served (Canada p. 13, Netherlands p. 24, Denmark p. 24).

iii) Promote competition

It has increasingly become accepted by OECD countries that opening-up markets to competition in telecommunication equipment, services and networks stimulates the development of information infrastructures by reducing prices and tariffs, stimulating private investment, and improving and stimulating new services

(UK pp. 1, 4, Sweden p. 18, US p. 8, EU p. 3, Bangemann pp. 8, 12, Canada pp. 13–14, Netherlands pp. 12–15, Australia interim report p. 10, MPT pp. 47, 50 , Denmark pp. 86–87, Germany p. 11).

For this reason, countries with partly liberalised telecommunication markets are expanding competition in areas up to now reserved to monopolies. The United States, for example, is reforming communication legislation to allow competition in cable television and local telephony markets (US p. 8). Japan will review its current regulatory framework, which already allows competition in all fields of the telecommunication industry, to further promote private sector activities (MPT p. 49). Canada will apply pro-competitive policies, to the greatest extent possible in all aspects of the information highway (Canada p. 13). Australia also promotes competition wherever appropriate (Australia interim report p. 10).

Apart from the United Kingdom, Sweden and Finland—who have already liberalised telecommunication markets—European Union members will adopt a regulatory framework which allows for competition in telecommunication services and infrastructures as from 1 January 1998. Some countries have an additional transition period. The Netherlands has decided to partly open its telecommunications market earlier by allowing a second fixed link operator to enter the market as from the end of 1995 (Netherlands pp. 12–13).

iv) Ensure universal service
All countries believe that participation in the information society must be ensured through the availability of information infrastructures to all at affordable prices. To achieve this the current concept of universal service must be expanded (US p. 8, Australia interim report p. 10, Canada p. 13, MPT p. 51, Norway, Sweden p. 18, EU p. 5, Denmark p. 24, Germany p. 10, UK p. 18, France p. 117). However, national reports do not go into detail as to the scope of an expanded universal service concept or the type of financing mechanism envisaged.

v) Effective regulatory framework
Governments must provide an effective legal and regulatory framework which stimulates the development of information infrastruc-

tures. Regulation and legislation must be effective in the sense that they provide an environment in which information infrastructures can fully develop. Important issues in this respect are the convergence of telecommunication and broadcasting, the security of information systems, the protection of personal data and the privacy of individuals, and intellectual property rights (Australia interim report p. 10, Canada p. 13, UK pp. 11, 20, Norway, Sweden pp. 13–14, Germany p. ii, Netherlands pp. 11, 15, MPT pp. 49, 53, US p. 9, France p. 48)

As a result of technological developments, historical distinctions between the characteristics of the telecommunication, broadcasting and computing industries are gradually disappearing. This enables cable television companies to provide telephony services and public telecommunication operators to provide services like interactive television and video-on-demand. Separate regulation of telecommunication and broadcasting, however, hinders the convergence of these sectors, and through this new economic activities. In order to enable the growth of an integrated services market many OECD countries are in the process of reviewing their legal and regulatory framework (MPT p. 51, Netherlands p. 15, Denmark p. 71, US p. 8, Australia interim report p. 51, Germany p. 12, Norway, Sweden p. 14). Although many OECD countries underscore the importance of safeguarding their culture and language, existing regulations in the field of entertainment, notably in broadcasting, will probably be adjusted to meet the requirements of the new information services.

With the widespread use of information infrastructures in modern societies, protection of privacy and personal data as well as the security of information systems must be assured in order to maintain public confidence. Another challenge concerns defining intellectual property rights which provide the right balance between protecting right holders of content, on the one hand, and the free circulation of information and knowledge, on the other. Realising the development of information infrastructures depends on solutions acceptable to all actors involved, and OECD countries consider these issues to be of high priority and address them both on a national level and an international level (UK pp. 20, 21, Canada p. 14, US pp. 9–10, Australia interim report pp. 73–79, MPT p. 53,

Denmark pp. 45–46, Germany p.10, Norway, Sweden p. 13, Netherlands p. 11, France pp. 100–101).

Timetable
Many countries have published a time schedule for the completion of various proposed policy initiatives. The scope of these initiatives, however, varies. For instance, the proposals made in France have suggested a goal to finish the building of the network infrastructure for the year 2015, the Japanese report recommends completion of the network by the year 2010 (France p. 108, MPT p. 35). The Australian Expert Group recommends broadband links be provided to all schools, libraries, medical and community centres by the year 2001 (Australia final report p. 60). In the United States the aim is for all classrooms, libraries, hospitals and clinics to be connected to the national information infrastructure by the year 2000 (Administration White Paper on Communications Act Reforms p. 5). The Danish government wants networks and information services such as electronic mail and EDI operational in both the public and private sector before the year 2000. Various concrete actions, mainly in the public domain, are scheduled in the next few years (Denmark pp. 28–29). Sweden has also published several actions in the public domain to be finished within the next few years (Sweden p. 11, 13, 15,). The Netherlands has published a timetable concerning adjusting and reviewing its legal and regulatory framework in the period 1994–1998 (Netherlands pp. 13–17).

Session 4: From Global Information Infrastructures to Global Information Society

International competition
It is recognised by all countries that their national economies will benefit if the potential of information infrastructures is exploited, and that they will lose their competitiveness if they lag behind. The United States points out that information infrastructures will help U.S. businesses remain competitive (US p. 5). The Bangemann report states in this context that the first countries to enter the information society will reap the greatest rewards and will set the

agenda for the countries who must follow. The report also stresses that countries which temporise, or favour halfhearted solutions are likely to face disastrous declines in investment and a squeeze on jobs (Bangemann report p.5). A similar statement is made by Australia where it is argued that the development of broadband services and networks needs to be encouraged to maintain that country's international competitiveness (Australia interim report p. 5). Canada also states that to succeed in a global economy based on information, the national communications networks must be knitted into a seamless and powerful information infrastructure serving all Canadians. If Canada does not match the efforts of its competitors in accelerating infrastructure development, opportunities for network, product and service development—and the resulting economic growth and new jobs—will be seized by firms in other countries (Canada p. 5).

But countries also stress the international benefits of information infrastructures. One of the main characteristics of the information society is globalisation. Flows of goods, services and information provide opportunities for cultures to meet and learn from each other (MPT.p 3). New information technologies give more opportunities for expression of the multiplicity of cultures and languages (EU p. 11). Culture in itself can be exported, contributing to economic growth and job creation (Australia interim report p. 43, Canada p. 20).

When it comes to importing these cultural products, however, there are some countries that regard this as a threat. Countries have emphasised the need to protect their culture and language (Canada pp. 11–12, Denmark p. 73, Sweden pp. 7, 25).

Building on national strength
Most countries have identified their national strengths and based their action plans on them. The existing national telecommunication infrastructure is considered to be a valuable asset on which the future information society can be built. Other pillars mentioned include: medico-technical industries (Denmark), publishing sector (The Netherlands, The United Kingdom), IT industry (Canada, US), financial sector (Denmark, the Netherlands), electronics sector (US).

Some countries view that their strength can also lie in their policy structure: both Sweden and the United Kingdom consider their regulatory and policy framework which put privatisation and liberalisation in place, as a competitive advantage. Other national strengths include a highly-skilled and highly-educated labour force (Australia, the Netherlands), and the widespread use and knowledge of information technology (Denmark).

Appendix A

Australia: Networking Australia's Future (July 1994, Broadband Services Expert Group, Interim report); Networking Australia's Future (December 1994, Broadband Services Expert Group, Final report)

Canada: The Canadian information highway; building Canada's information and communications infrastructure (April 1994)

Denmark: Info-society 2000 (November 1994)

European Union: Europe and the Global Information Society: Recommendations to the European Council (Bangemann Group, 26 May 1994); Europe's way to the information society. An action plan (European Commission, 19 July 1994); Green Paper on the liberalisation of telecommunications infrastructures and cable television networks part II

France: Les autoroute de l'information (Gérard Théry, 1994)

Germany: Multimedia: Chance und Herausforderung (Multimedia: opportunities and challenges) (March 1995, Bundesministerium für Bildung, Wissenschaft, Forshung und Technologie)

Japan: Reforms toward the intellectual creative society of the 21st century: Programme for the establishment of high-performance info-communications infrastructures (31 May 1994, Telecommunications Council, Ministry of Post and Telecommunications); Programme for advanced information infrastructure (May 1994, Ministry of International Trade and Industry)

The Netherlands: Actieprogramma Elektronische Snelwegen—van metafoor naar actie (Action programme Electronic highways—from metaphor to action) (December 1994)

Norway: Norwegian information infrastructure (6 March 1995); Innspill til norsk bidrag til informasjons-infrastruktur (Proposal for a national Information Network) (25 January 1995)

Sweden: Information technology: wings to human ability (August 1994)

United Kingdom: Creating the superhighways of the future: developing broadband communications in the UK (November 1994)

United States: The national information infrastructure: agenda for action (15 September 1993); National information infrastructure: progress report September 1993–1994; Global Information Infrastructure: agenda for cooperation (February 1995)

G-7: G-7 ministerial conference on the information society: theme paper (Brussels, 23 January 1995); Chair's conclusions issued by the G-7 ministers (27 February 1995)

Chair's Conclusions from the G-7 Ministerial Conference on the Information Society

Following the remit of G-7 leaders at their Naples Summit in July 1994, Ministers from G-7 countries and Members of the European Commission met in Brussels on 25 and 26 February 1995 in the G-7 Ministerial Conference on the Information Society.

Progress in information technologies and communication is changing the way we live: how we work and do business, how we educate our children, study and do research, train ourselves, and how we are entertained. The information society is not only affecting the way people interact but it is also requiring the traditional organisational structures to be more flexible, more participatory and more decentralised.

A new revolution is carrying mankind forward into the Information Age. The smooth and effective transition towards the information society is one of the most important tasks that should be undertaken in the last decade of the 20th century. The outcome of this Conference shows that G-7 partners are committed to playing a leading role in the development of the Global Information Society.

Our action must contribute to the integration of all countries into a global effort. Countries in transition and developing countries must be provided with the chance to fully participate in this process as it will open opportunities for them to leapfrog stages of technology development and to stimulate social and economic development.

The rewards for all can be enticing. To succeed, governments must facilitate private initiatives and investments and ensure an appropriate framework aiming at stimulating private investment and usage for the benefit of all citizens. They should also create a favourable international environment by cooperating within the relevant international organisations such as WTO, ITU, WIPO, ISO and OECD.

Our Vision Can Only be Realised by Means of Collaboration

G-7 partners are resolved to collaborate on the basis of the following eight core principles in order to realise their common vision of the Global Information Society:

- promoting dynamic competition
- encouraging private investment
- defining an adaptable regulatory framework
- providing open access to networks

while

- ensuring universal provision of and access to services
- promoting equality of opportunity to the citizen
- promoting diversity of content; including cultural and linguistic
- diversity
- developed countries

These principles will apply to the Global Information Society Infrastructure by means of:

- promotion of interconnectivity and interoperability
- developing global markets for networks, services and applications
- ensuring privacy and data security
- protecting intellectual property rights
- cooperating in R&D and in the development of new applications
- monitoring of the social and societal implications of the information society

An Information Society Devoted to the People

Policies aimed at a rapid and successful transition to the information society must ensure the highest possible levels of participation and avoid the emergence of two classes of citizens. Universal service is an essential pillar in the development of such a policy strategy.

The creation of jobs and improvement of the quality of work are of paramount importance. The policy process must be backed up by collaborative research at an international level to investigate the impact of information and communication technologies and services on employment.

The information society should serve the cultural enrichment of all citizens through diversity of content reflecting the cultural and linguistic diversity of our peoples. The private sector should therefore develop and build information networks with abundant capacity to accommodate a wealth of information, both locally produced and that developed in other regions and nations.

The knowledge-based economy demands greater openness and creativity in schools and universities, and the acquisition of new skills and adaptability through life-long training. An open approach to education that combines local and national cultures and promotes mutual understanding between our citizens is required. Access must therefore be tackled at its roots by providing citizens with the tools to learn in an information society. Advanced multimedia information services can meet such requirements whilst complementing and enriching the traditional education and training systems.

The information society is a new, complex and abstract concept and as such it requires considerable effort in promoting public awareness and understanding.

G-7 partners are determined to ensure that the information society addresses the needs of citizens. They committed themselves to:

• Promote Universal Service to Ensure Opportunities for all to Participate: By establishing universal service frameworks that are adaptable, they will ensure that all citizens will have access to new information services and thus benefit from new opportunities. They will evaluate the impact of information services and technologies on society using existing organisational resources. Strategies to prevent marginalization and to avoid isolation will be developed.

• Study the Impact of the Information Society on Jobs: They will encourage the OECD to complete its work on the effects of information technology on employment. In addition, the OECD is invited to launch a complementary study on the employment impact of information series. Academia, government and the private sector should expand their efforts to assess the impact of the information society on the economy, trade and the workplace. Research on employment effects will provide valuable input for policy decisions.

• Serve Cultural Enrichment for all Citizens through Diversity of Content: Citizens should be provided with access to all content, including a strong present for indigenous cultural products and services. Diversity of content, including cultural and linguistic diversity, should be promoted.

• Encourage Private Sector Development of Information Networks and Provision of New Information-Related Services: They will pursue worldwide cooperation in encouraging the development of a Global Information Infrastructure to stimulate the creation of an abundant capacity to accommodate and to enable a diverse mix of content for all citizens.

• Pursue Adequate Education and Training: They will exchange information on new ways of educating, training and retaining. Information technology training should be integrated into the regular school system. The development of vocational training on information technologies will facilitate the adjustment of workers to structural and organization changes throughout their lives.

• Improve the Understanding of Effects on the Quality of Life: They will encourage projects and joint actions, in particular to demonstrate the possibility of flexible and better quality of work, improvements in healthcare, educative leisure, urban development and greater participation of the disable in society.

• Foster Public Support by Raising Awareness and Understanding: They agree to exchange experiences on the best means to raise pubic awareness and sensitivity towards the Global Information Society.

• Encourage the Dialogue on Worldwide Cooperation: They call on industrialised countries to work towards the participation of developing counties in the Global Information Society.

Current Regulations Need to Evolve

The regulatory framework should put the user first and meet a variety of complementary societal objectives. It must be designed to allow choice, high quality services and affordable prices. It will therefore have to be based on an environment that encourages dynamic competition, ensures the separation of operating and regulatory functions as well as promotes interconnectivity and interoperability. Such an environment will maximise consumer choice by stimulating the creation and flow of information and other content supplied by a wide range of information and other content providers.

Open access to networks for service and information suppliers and the mutual enrichment of the citizen through the promotion of diversity, including cultural and linguistic diversity, as well as the free expression of ideas, are essential for the creation of the Global Information Society.

Competition rules need to be interpreted and applied in the light of the convergence of new technologies and services, market liberalisation and encouragement of new entrant, and growing global competition. Competition authorities should not prohibit the emergence of global players. Productive forms of cooperation to promote economic efficiency and consumer welfare should be allowed while shielding against risk of anti-competitive behavior, in particular risks of abuse of market dominance.

G-7 partners are therefore committed to:

• Ensure Citizens' Access Through Universal Service in the Respective Market: This will require consultation on both the scope and the means of providing universal service, especially with regard to its financing, whilst ensuring that the development of networks and the provision of services can be carried out without undue burden on any actors.

• Open up Markets to Allow the Development of Global Systems: This is to be accomplished by pursuing liberalization of services, infrastructure, equipment procurement and investment, within an appropriate framework. Special emphasis should be given to the negotiations in the WTO, notably on such sectors as basic telecommunications, which are important to see concluded successfully by April 1996.

• Pursue the Interconnectivity of Networks and the Interoperability of Services: This is to be achieved through the promotion of a consensual standardisation process which is market-led and which encourages open interfaces. Cooperation amongst all actors should be built on private sector-led dialogue aimed at identifying critical interfaces. This should be backed up by swift tests and trails to identify appropriate standards corresponding to the critical interfaces. Accelerating the standardisation process conducted by international bodies will contribute to developing timely and market-responsive standards. Mutual recognition of test results should be pursued. This process will be backed up by developing global testbeds.

• Provide Open Access to Networks for Service and Information Suppliers: It is agreed that open access to the Global Information Infrastructure and the people that it serves is essential in order to encourage firms to provide services, create new jobs and provide mutual enrichment to the citizen through the promotion of diversity, including cultural and linguistic diversity, as well as free expression of ideas. This should take place in all countries within a framework which will prevent abuse by dominant actors.

• Implement Fair and Effective Licensing and Frequency Allocation: For fair and effective allocation of scarce resources, transparency needs to be assured by means of promoting objective selection and awarding criteria. Further cooperation, notably under the auspices of the ITU, should be pursued in the field of frequency band harmonization, particulary for international mobile and personal phoneservices. International dialogue on the development and the implementation of global mobile and personal systems is encouraged.

Allow for Productive Forms of Cooperation While Shielding against Anticompetitive Behaviour

This will require that competition and regulatory authorities meet at regular intervals in international fora such as the OECD and other relevant bodies to exchange information and views about the evolving regulatory process and the application of competition rules. Cooperation on the enforcement of competition rules should be encouraged whilst paying particular attention to the confidentiality of commercial data. Work towards a multilateral framework is welcomed. A first step in this process would be for competition and regulatory authorities to provide an accurate description of their regulatory framework.

Protecting privacy and personal data alongside the safeguarding of plurality of opinion play an essential role in maintaining citizens' confidence in the information society and thereby encourage user participation and strengthen competition and market access.

Only if security of information is effectively guaranteed will individuals or organizations take full advantage of information infrastructure. Citizens and society should be protected against criminal abuse of the developing networks.

Providing high levels of legal and technical protection of creative content will be one of the essential conditions to ensure the necessary climate for the investment needed for the development of the Information Society. Thus, there is a need for internationally recognized protection for the creators and providers of materials that will be disseminated over the Global Information Infrastructure.

G-7 partners will increase efforts to find creative, technological and policy solutions to:

• Protect Privacy and Personal Data: The protection of personal data requires that national as well as regional data protection provisions are defined and properly enforced and that international cooperation and dialogue are encouraged.

• Increase Information Security: Authorities should work collectively to increase the reliability and security of national and international networks. This will be achieved by developing security principles that are commensurate with the risk and magnitude of harm.

- Protect Creativity and Content Provision: Measures will be developed through national, bilateral, regional and international efforts, including in the World Intellectual Property Organization, which will ensure that the framework for intellectual property and technical protection guarantees that the right holders enjoy the technical and legal means to control the use of their property over the Global Information Infrastructure.

Interactive Applications Will Change the Ways We Live Together

Information and communication technologies will present new opportunities and challenges in the way we access and disseminate information and content. Interactive multimedia services and applications are the most visible components of the information society. Their emergence and eventual penetration at all levels of society means rethinking and restructuring the traditional communications methods. This will create a change in environment and the ways we live together. Sharing experiences on emerging applications would provide us with an understanding of their impact and benefits. Public authorities have an important catalytic role to play in the promotion of research, applications and generic services. They can also further initiatives in the development of applications in areas of common public interest. International cooperation on joint projects provides an opportunity to demonstrate the benefits and uses of the information society.

G-7 partners recognize the impact interactive applications will have on society and are committed to:

- Share Experiences on Emerging Applications: An inventory of major applications could provide knowledge of new and emerging employment sectors. Information on impediments to the realisation and dissemination of new applications will be exchanged.

- Act as a Catalyst for the Protection of Research, Applications and Generic Services: They will increase cooperation efforts in selected joint projects of common interest, especially on basic technology, including interconnectivity, interoperability and human interface for universal series. Comparable opportunities for participation in projects will be offered.

• Promote Joint Projects to Demonstrate Our Commitments: They use the opportunity of this ministerial Conference to identify eleven selected joint party projects (ANNEX). Participation of other partners is encouraged. The projects selected aim at demonstrating the potential of the Information Society, at contributing to solve various important issues for realising the information society and at stimulating growth, in particular in relation to job creation, while involving all actors concerned at all levels any in any country.

They call on all interested parties to join as soon as possible so that twice cooperation and projects can be effectively initiated by the time of the Halifax Summit.

Draft Executive Summary—G-7 Pilot Projects

G-7 members along with the European Commission decided to take the opportunity offered by the Ministerial Conference being held in Brussels on February 25–26 to identify a number of selected projects where international cooperation could be an asset. these projects would aim at demonstrating the potential of the Information Society and stimulate its deployment. The projects will be initially undertaken by the partners but are meant to be open. The participation of other partners, including international organisations, is encouraged.

Further refinement and investigative studies will be undertaken in order to define in further depth the project contents and their implementation framework.

The work undertaken in G-7 Pilot Projects thus far was based on joint deliberations and consensus on Theme Areas identified to be of common international interest for the Information Society. These selected themes were then rendered into more concrete project proposals through formal and informal discussions and meetings. Further refinement of the proposals and studies of implementation scenarios are still required for all the projects considered.

It is expected that the consequences of the joint action in this area will provide a concrete contribution to the requirements of the global information society and will demonstrate its potential for the well-being of all citizens.

Objectives of the Action

The key objectives for the launching of Pilot Projects for the Information Society are to:

• support the goal of international consensus on common principles governing the need of access to networks and applications and their interoperability

• establish the groundwork for productive forms of cooperation amongst G-7 partners in order to create a critical mass to address this global issue

• create an opportunity for information exchange leading towards the further development of the information society

• identify and select project of an exemplary nature having tangible and clearly understandable social, economic and cultural benefits which will demonstrate to the public the potential of the information society

• identify obstacles related to the implementation of practical applications serving the creation of a global information society

• help to create markets for new products and services, where appropriate

Principles

The main principles guiding the selection and implementation of the theme projects are the following:

• have clear added-value for the development of the Information Society by: increasing the effectiveness of information exchange; launching common actions; and initiating co-operation at a global level

• give meaning and content to the concept of Information Society for the citizen taking into account their cultural and linguistic diversity

• stimulate cooperation amongst different players: industry, academia, administrations, public authorities, etc.

• avoid the creation of new bureaucracy or institutions

- have as a general rule any expense covered by existing programs
- have included open access as an integral part of its design
- are open to non-G-7 countries as well as public and private organizations, including international organisations and standardisation bodies.

The Selected Theme Area Projects

The following are a description of the proposed themes selected forinitial implementation. Other theme areas of common economic and social concern, such as applications for seniors and people with disabilities, are being pursued and opportunities for other cooperative projects studied:

- Global Inventory: to create and provide an electronically accessible multimedia inventory of information regarding major national and international projects and studies relevant to the promotion and to the development of the global information society. An assessment of social, economic and cultural factors impacting on its development will also be undertaken;

- Global Interoperability for Broadband Networks: to facilitate the establishment of international links between the various high speed networks and testbeds supporting advanced applications;

- Cross-Cultural Training and Education: to provide innovative approaches to language learning in particular for students and for SME's.

- Electronic Libraries: to constitute from existing digitization programs a large distributed virtual collection of knowledge of mankind, available to a large public, via networks. This includes a clear perspective toward the establishment of the global electronic library network which interconnects local electronic libraries.

- Electronic Museums and Galleries: to accelerate the multimedia digitisation of collections and to ensure their accessibility to the public and as a learning resource for schools and universities.

- Environment and Natural Resources Management: to increase the electronic linkage and integration of distributed databases of information relevant to the environment.

• Global Emergency Management: to encourage the development of a global management information network to enhance the management of emergency response situations, risk and knowledge.

• Global Healthcare Applications: to demonstrate the potential of telematics technologies in the field of telemedicine in the fight against major health scourges; to promote joint approaches to issues such as the use of data cards, standards and other enabling mechanisms.

• Government On-Line: to exchange experience and best practice on the use of on-line information technology by administrations on the establishment of procedures for conducting electronic administrative business between governments, companies and citizens.

• Global Marketplace for SME's: to contribute to the development of an environment for open and non-discriminatory exchange of information and to demonstrate, particularly through EDI, the interoperability of electronic and information co-operation and trading service on a global scale, for the benefits of SME's.

• Maritime Information Systems: to integrate and enhance environmental protection and industrial competitiveness for all maritime activities by means of information and communication technologies including applications in the area of safety and the environment, intelligent manufacturing and logistics networks.

Contributors

Walter S. Baer (baer@rand.org) is Senior Policy Analyst at the RAND Corporation in Santa Monica, California, where he directs studies of information infrastructure and the public policy and commercial implications of new communications, information and educational technologies.

Antonio J. Botelho (abotelho@dctc.puc-rio.br), is Special Assistant to the Technical-Scientific Centre Dean's Office, Pontifical Catholic University of Rio de Janeiro. He is also conducting research on the historical roots of Brazilian postwar aeronautics technological ideology sponsored by a National Science Foundation Minority Postdoctoral Fellowship.

Jason Dedrick (jdedrick@uci.edu) is a Senior Research Fellow at the Center for Research on Information Technology and Organizations <http://www.crito.uci.edu> at the University of California, Irvine. His research interests include economic development, industrial policy, technology diffusion, and the globalization of the computer industry.

William B. Garrison, Jr. (WBG@csis.org) is Director of the International Communications Studies Program of the Center for Strategic and International Studies in Washington, DC. He also serves as a Director of the Telecommunications Consulting Group. He is the author of a series of case studies and several journal articles on telecommunications restructuring in the United States and other countries.

Andrew Graham (Andrew.Graham@balliol.oxford.ac.uk) is Fellow and Tutor in Economics at Balliol College, Oxford University. He was Economic Adviser to the Prime Minister (1966–1969 and 1974–1976) and from 1988 to 1994 was the chief economic adviser to the Rt. Hon. John Smith, QC, MP, Leader of the Labour Party. He is currently running an ESRC research project on public policy toward the Information Superhighway focusing on the implications for access and citizenship.

G. Harindranath (g.harindranath@rhbnc.ac.uk) is a Lecturer in Management Information Systems in the School of Management at Royal Holloway College, University of London. His research interests include information infrastructure policy issues, international outsourcing, and technology and development.

Milda K. Hedblom (hedblom@augsburg.edu) is a professor, lawyer and consultant. She is a Senior Associate and Director of the Telecommunications and Information Society Policy Forum at the HHH Institute of Public Affairs, University of Minnesota. She is also Professor and Chair of the Department of Politics at Augsburg College, Minneapolis, Minnesota, and telecommunications consultant for Dain International Services.

Kuk-Hwan Jeong (jkh@nca.or.kr) is Vice President in charge of the Information Society Research Division of Korea's National Computerization Agency. His chapter was written when he was visiting the University of California at Irvine in 1995–1996.

Brian Kahin (Kahin@harvard.edu) is Adjunct Lecturer in Public Policy and Director of the Information Infrastructure Project in the Science, Technology, and Public Policy Program at the John. F. Kennedy School of Government, Harvard University <http://ksgwww.harvard.edu/iip>. He is also General Counsel for the Annapolis-based Interactive Multimedia Association.

Wolfgang Kleinwächter (stieler@rz.uni-leipzig.de), Director of the NETCOM Institute of the Media City Leipzig, is Acting Chairman of the IRISI Management Committee. He is also President of the Legal Section of the International Association of Mass Communication Research (IAMCR), and was Visiting Professor at the School of International Services (SIS) at the American University in Washington, DC.

John Leslie King (king@ics.uci.edu) is Professor of Information and Computer Science and Management at the University of California at Irvine <http://www.crito.uci.edu>. His research concerns the relationships between technical and institutional change, and most recently, the problem of designing complex information systems that must function in highly institutionalized sectors and settings.

Kenneth L. Kraemer (kkraemer@uci.edu) is a Professor in the Graduate School of Management and the Department of Information and Computer Science and Director of the Center for Research on Information Technology and Organizations <http://www.crito.uci.edu>, at the University of California at Irvine. His research interests include the management of information systems, the organizational implications of computing, the business value of information technology, and the globalization of the computer industry.

Herbert Kubicek (Kubicek@informatik.uni-bremen.de) is Professor of Applied Computer Science and Director of the Telecommunications Research Group at the University of Bremen, Germany <http://infosoc.informatik.uni-bremen.de>. He is a member of the Bundestag Commission of Inquiry on "The Future of the Media in Economy and Society, Germany and the Information Society."

Lee McKnight (mcknight@rpcp.mit.edu) is a Lecturer in the Technology and Policy Program, Principal Research Associate at the Center for Technology, Policy, and Industrial Development, and Associate Director of the Research Program on Communications Policy at the Massachusetts Institute of Technology <http://rpcp.mit.edu/People/mcknight.html>. He is co-author of *The Gordian Knot*, and co-editor of *Internet Economics*, both from MIT Press.

Ben A. Petrazzini (bpetrazz@usthk.ust.hk) is Assistant Professor in Telecommunications and Networking Policy in the Department of Information and Systems Management and the School of Business and Management at the Hong Kong University of Science and Technology < http://www.bi.ust.hk/~bpetrazz/>. His work concentrates on the telecommunications and information sector of developing countries.

Marc Raboy (raboym@ere.umontreal.ca) is a Professor in the Department of Communications at the University of Montreal. He is the author or editor of several books on mass media and communication policy, including *Public Broadcasting for the Twenty-First Century* (Luton, UK: John Libbey Media/University of Luton Press, 1996).

Thomas Spacek (spacek@bellcore.com) is Executive Director of National Information Infrastructure and Internet Initiatives at Bellcore. His responsibilities include economic, business, market, policy, applications, and technology issues for making the National and Global Information Infrastructure (NII/GII) a reality. He has been instrumental in formulating policy for the U.S. NII and framing critical NII/GII issues internationally.

Annemarie Munk Riis (arris/INT@cbs.dk) acquired her industrial policy experience working for the European Commission and the Danish Ministry for Business and Industry. She is currently writing her doctoral dissertation on "The Political Economy of Universal Service: The Cases of Denmark, France and the U.S." at the Copenhagen Business School's Institute for International Economics as part of a joint telecommunications project with the Berkeley Roundtable on the International Economy.

Eduardo Talero (Etalero@worldbank.org) is Principal Informatics Specialist in the Telecommunications and Informatics Division of the World Bank. He supervises technical support of the Bank's worldwide informatics project portfolio and formulates the Bank's informatics lending strategy.

Thierry Vedel (Vedel@msh-paris.fr) is a Senior Research Fellow with the National Center for Scientific Research and is based at the National Foundation for Political Science in Paris. His current work deals with public policies in the area of new communication technologies and the impact of new media on political communication. He also teaches at the Institut d'Etudes Politiques in Paris and at the Institut Français de Presse (Université de Paris 2).

Shalini Venturelli (Sventur@american.edu) is Assistant Professor of International Communication Policy and Law in the School of International Service at the American University in Washington, DC. She is also Chair of the Communication and Human Rights

Committee of the International Association for Mass Communication Research.

Joel West (joelwest@uci.edu) is a doctoral student at the Graduate School of Management, University of California at Irvine <http://students.gsm.uci.edu/~joelwest>. Previously he was president of a start-up software development company and a computer magazine columnist. His research interests include new product development and diffusion of technology, emphasizing the Japanese information technology industries.

Ernest J. Wilson III (ewilson@bss1.umd.edu) is Director of the Center for International Development and Conflict Management at the University of Maryland, and Senior Advisor to the Global Information Infrastructure Commission. He has worked on information and telecommunications issues at the White House, USIA, the Council on Foreign Relations, the World Bank and other organizations.

Poh Kam Wong (fbawpk@leonis.nus.sg) is director of the Center for Management of Technology <http://www.fba.nus.sg/cmt/> and deputy director of the Graduate School of Business at the National University of Singapore. He earned his B.S., M.S. and Ph.D. degrees at the Massachusetts Institute of Technology. His current research interests include East Asian science and technology policy, industrial development strategy, and information infrastructure policy in particular.

Index

DATE DUE